Origins of Legislative Sovereignty and the Legislative State

Volume Seven
(Book I)

By A. London Fell

Origins of Legislative Sovereignty and the Legislative State

*Forthcoming

Origins of Legislative Sovereignty and the Legislative State

Volume Seven

World Perspectives and Emergent Systems for the New Order in the New Age

Book I: Western Hemisphere (Current News History)

A. London Fell

Westport, Connecticut
London

Library of Congress Cataloging-in-Publication Data

Fell, A. London.
  Origins of legislative sovereignty and the legislative state / A. London Fell.
    p. cm.
  Includes bibliographical references and index.
  ISBN 0-899-46140-9 (v. 1)
  ISBN 0-899-46141-7 (v. 2)
  ISBN 0-275-93973-1 (v. 3)
  ISBN 0-275-93974-X (v. 4)
  ISBN 0-275-93975-8 (v. 5.1)
  ISBN 0-275-95689-X (v. 5.2)
  ISBN 0-275-96753-0 (v. 5.3)
  ISBN 0-275-93976-6 (v. 6.1)
  ISBN 0-275-98509-1 (v. 6.2)
    ISBN 978-0-275-93977-9 (v. 7.1)
  v. 1. Corasius and the Renaissance systematization of Roman law — v. 2. Classical,
  Medieval, and Renaissance foundations of Corasius' systematic methodology —
  v. 4. Medieval or Renaissance origins? — v. 5. Modern origins, developments, and
  perspectives against the background of "Machiavellism." bk. 1. Pre-modern
  "Machiavellism." bk. 2. Modern major "Isms" (17th–18th centuries). bk. 3. Modern
  major "Isms" (19th–20th centuries).
    1. Legislation—History. 2. Law—History and criticism. 3. Political science—
  History. 4. Coras, Jean de, 1513–1572. I. Title.
  K284.F44   1983
  340'.09 19   81022332

British Library Cataloguing in Publication Data is available.

Library of Congress Catalog Card Number: 81022332
ISBN: 978-0-275-93977-9

First published in 2008

Praeger Publishers, 88 Post Road West, Westport, CT 06881
An imprint of Greenwood Publishing Group, Inc.
www.praeger.com

Printed in the United States of America

To My Family and Friends

Preface

This is Book I (*Western Hemisphere*) of Volume Seven (*World Perspectives and Emergent Systems for the New Order in the New Age*) in the series entitled *Origins of Legislative Sovereignty and the Legislative State*. This book on the Western Hemisphere comprising North and South America will be followed by another book on the Eastern Hemisphere comprising a larger expanse from Western Europe to Eastern Asia, to be rounded out with global or worldwide considerations. Consistent again with the main title of the series, contexts of legislative sovereignty and the legislative state will be featured, as emphasized also in the titles of the main parts of both books.

The three main parts of this first book deal in turn with "United States Government and Society," "United States Foreign Policy," and "Latin American Governments and Societies," followed by an Annex on "Canada and North American Blocs," with an Epilogue on "U.S. and Other 'Union' Models." The lengthy first chapter in Part One continues the focus on U.S. presidents from the Founders to Reagan in our previous two books on American historical traditions and themes, moving ahead with coverage here from Reagan and Bush Sr. to Clinton and Bush Jr. Ensuing chapters take up further dimensions in contemporary U.S. affairs, including foreign policy as a bridge to other regions of the world in this and the next book.

The subtitle for this and the next book has turned out to be more appropriate than could have been envisioned (before the catchphrase "new world order" was popularized around 1991) when it was scheduled in 1989–1990 for placement in the series subtitle opposite the main title page of Volume IV published in 1991, just as the Cold War was ending and the Communist blocs were collapsing. As in the case herein of Latin America, the fading out of the old order of Cold War dictatorships was giving rise in the 1990s to an emergent new order of more democratic (and free trade) tendencies, often patterned around U.S. models, albeit often imperfectly or incompletely so, within the contexts of their own cultures and traditions. The nascent new order for the new decade of the 1990s and then for the new century and new millennium is still an ongoing "work in progress." In a different sense, the United States itself was experiencing an emerging new order in its domestic and foreign affairs in the 1990s and beyond—first with the call for a "new world order" under President Bush Sr. around 1991, then with the impetus toward a more global economy under President Clinton, and more recently through the crusade against international terrorism under President Bush Jr.

As indicated in the titles of the present Book I on the Western Hemisphere and in its sequel Book II on the Eastern Hemisphere, the main subjects and sources revolve around "current news history," as also reemphasized in the titles of the several main parts within. What this means in terms of newspapers, news magazines, and other public venues will be introduced in Chapter One. Issues and viewpoints uppermost in the "public mind" as expressed in the public press through news reports and accounts are often best epitomized in their titles and other headings, of which abundant use will be made below in what amounts to a new genre. In their own unique way, news headings can serve as potent documentary evidence in themselves.

In order to be more "user friendly," hopefully, the running heads at the tops of pages in the main text and in the corresponding notes collected together at the back of the book indicate the chapter numbers for the reader's easier cross-referencing back and forth between text and notes. Within each note at the end of each paragraph, the sequence of abbreviated citations of sources follows the same sequence of the individual news headings quoted in our main text, whether they are separated by semicolons or periods. In a different matter, such combination of words as legislative-executive, legislative/executive, or even legislative executive, can, in a few cases, vary according to nuances of usage.

Contents

PART THREE: *LATIN AMERICAN GOVERNMENTS
AND SOCIETIES IN LEGISLATIVE AND OTHER CONTEXTS OF
SOVEREIGNTY AND STATE: CURRENT NEWS HISTORY*

Origins of
Legislative Sovereignty
and the
Legislative State

Volume Seven
(Book I)

Chapter I

Introduction

In order to apprehend the scope of the present book, one should bear in mind its relation to the books before and after it. The preceding book dealt with modern America from Lincoln to Reagan, while the present book's first two parts continue that story from Bush Sr. and Clinton to Bush Jr. The third part of the present book, together with the concluding annex, deal with Latin America and Canada, respectively. The present book focusing on the Western Hemisphere is to be followed by the next book on the Eastern Hemisphere. The weight given in the present book to United States affairs during the two recent decades is due in large part to the country's dominant place in the Western Hemisphere (comprising North, Central, and South America); its paradigmatic influences (pro or con) have been felt throughout the hemisphere. When taken in its totality, this seventh volume will be seen to focus primarily on "world perspectives" in the two hemispheres, in which the United States has played a crucial, often controversial, role. Yet the global picture itself will be most key.

1. WORLD PERSPECTIVES

When around 1989 the subtitle of this volume was prepared for listing opposite the main title page in Volume IV (published in 1991), the catchphrase "New World Order" had not yet been popularized by the first Bush Administration to characterize the Cold War's aftermath following the collapse of the Soviet empire. What this author had had in mind by the subtitle "World Perspectives and Emergent Systems for the New Order in the New Age" was different from that ensuing phrase; and it remains to be treated in wider contexts of globalism and global affairs (in which the United States has remained the world's only "super-power"). Nevertheless, this volume's subtitle remains even more apt at present writing in 2007 than it was nearly two decades ago.

If one considers the fuller sweep of the present series, centering on European and American historical issues of sovereignty and state, it is entirely appropriate to turn near the end to the broader "perspectives" of *contemporary* or *current* world affairs for the light they shed on *legislative* sovereignty and the *legislative* state as the key *modern* components featured throughout the series. To what extent can it be said, based on the most fundamental levels of current public thinking, that sovereignty and state are still today viewed primarily in legislative contexts?

The accumulated extensive evidence presented below on recent Western Hemispheric affairs over nearly two decades leaves little doubt as to the ever-continuing central importance of legislative sovereignty and the legislative state. Among current countries, the United States has perhaps best demonstrated and exemplified the ageold concept of legislative self-determination begun by late-16th-century European thinkers, albeit in ways hugely different. At virtually every level—federal, state, and local—this U.S. orientation will be seen to occur, even to the point of federal agencies becoming increasingly like "mini-legislatures," along with the president as "legislator-in-chief." For Latin America in the 1990s and up to present day, "the rule of law" has been making significant strides forward, and to that extent legislative features of sovereignty and state have been expanding, albeit unevenly, across nations, regions, and blocs.

What still remains to be considered, once both Western and Eastern Hemispheres have been explored, is the role of truly "world" organizations and affairs in the light of advancing trends during this same period and into the future. On what ultimate supra-national levels can or could a "new world order" (a phrase no longer popular but still suggestive here) embody principles of legislative sovereignty and state—that is, outside the more traditional bounds of nation-states featured throughout much of this series? Answers to that question must await the outcome of future events and developments. Yet in limited ways it will be reasonable to project ahead on this matter in our next studies, on the basis of the accumulated materials showing the legal–legislative frameworks of many world organizations and trends during the contemporary era from the 1990s to the present.

2. WESTERN HEMISPHERE

The weight given in this first of two books on "world perspectives" to North and South America in relation to the second book to follow on the world's remaining land mass may seem somewhat unusual until one appreciates the geographic division of the world into the Western and Eastern Hemispheres. After all, the huge continuous land mass stretching from France on its Atlantic coast to China on its Pacific coast—or between the island nations of England and Japan—seems to dwarf in size the territories of the Americas. Moreover, what is commonly called Western civilization extends in area east from Europe to the far Mediterranean and west to the Americas. Still, the long-standing division of Western and Eastern Hemispheres, notwithstanding the preponderance of land mass occupied by the latter over the former, gives justification in various ways to the present organization in two books, starting here with the Western Hemisphere.

Within the Western Hemisphere the position of the United States today stands out for special attention in view of its dominant role there and its influence or example throughout the world. On one level, the prominent place given to United States domestic affairs in the large first part of this book points up the many diverse ways in which U.S. models *par excellence* of legislative sovereignty, and state can serve as paradigms for understanding those topics in the affairs of other countries, which exhibit them in their own ways. More specifically, for instance, the U.S. systems of federalism or federation could provide useful standpoints for newly organizing other areas such as in Latin America where emergent systems are often still unsettled or even unsettling. On another level, as glimpsed in Part Two below on dimensions of U.S. foreign policy, the legislative parameters of sovereignty and state are widely apparent in their own governmental ways, while reflecting the wider far-reaching U.S. role in world affairs.

In Latin America—where the U.S. Congressional model rather than the European Parliamentary model is dominant—the U.S. paradigm and influence is particularly striking at various levels. With the breakup of the Cold War and of old-style dictatorships in the early 1990s, the formations of diverse democratic institutions was under way in many Latin American countries, often with U.S. help and example. That process has been continuing with ups and downs.

In Canada—with the Parliamentary model of in-house Prime Minister rather than a separate executive branch—the legislative features of sovereignty and state in a long-enduring stable democracy are widely evident. The system of provinces, like that of states, affords ample issues, such as Quebec separatism, through which to view key themes of present interest.

Of broader hemispheric (and global) import are the developing blocs or groupings of nations in North, Central, and South America along economic, political, and legal lines. One such grouping is the well-known NAFTA for North American Free Trade (including in this case Mexico with Canada and the U.S.). Other kinds of economic blocs are found among Latin American countries and regions. The legal–legislative dimensions of sovereignty and state can often be viewed in those arrangements. Less known is the current Central American grouping of a number of countries into a single supra-national or regional Congress, to which they send representatives to do the legislative and other business of that body. In decades and centuries to come, could Latin American countries become more integrated, at first on the model of the European economic, political, and parliamentary union—or eventually like the American federal system of quasi-independent states under a common central government? Where would sovereign self-determination then lie in legal–legislative terms? Even broader questions could be raised for the Western Hemisphere as a whole on into the more distant future. Regionalization and globalization will likely remain growing trends with far-reaching import for issues of sovereignty and state into the far distant future. The basic themes and premises of this book, volume, and series will continue, one way or another, to occupy a place on center stage in future developments—as they have done in historical discussions over many centuries past. The importance of those issues themselves will continue amid the changing dynamics of "emergent systems for the new order in the new age."

3. CURRENT NEWS HISTORY

The subject of "current news history," as encapsulated in this volume through headlines and other devices represents a new genre. The more recognizable category of "current history," as used in a contemporary journal by that name, has been here transformed through focus on the daily "news" over a period of nearly two decades. Almost exclusive attention is given to apt quotations from apt titles and subtitles taken from suitable newspapers and news magazines, going back from present day in 2007 to around 1989–1990 or sometimes earlier—a period coinciding with the emergence of the post–Cold-War world. By concentrating in this fashion upon the stories, issues, and trends uppermost in the public press, we hope to capture the most basic expressions of the importance attached to sovereignty, state, legislation, and the like, along the lines articulated by historical spokesmen as reported in this series.

The methods of selecting and collecting news accounts and their headings had to be carefully controlled so as to be representative and manageable. As it is, only a typically small portion of the vast materials kept and filed over many years could be used when it came down to the actual writing of sections in this volume. Even then, only leading American news sources could be assembled and sorted into the myriad bulky files needed for this enterprise. A far vaster collection of foreign press reports, not to mention a far wider selection just of American news sources, would have been prohibitive and onerous, without improving the results intended here. The aim has not been to assemble diverse interpretative viewpoints from a huge range of different types of news sources, but rather a more simple straightforward presentation of daily, weekly, and monthly narrative accounts of events as they unfolded—accounts then to be woven together into our own presentation of key issues and topics. To use news reports themselves as evidence in the complicated fabrics woven here around them has required constant quotations rather than summaries. Our discussions are closely tied to the titles, subtitles, and other main rubrics in articles of the public press so as to be in sync with them as primary evidence supporting our premises. To use journalistic news accounts as basic texts for building our own picture of points of view uppermost in current history may seem unusual in relation to the non-journalistic sources employed in our previous books; but the method works just as well in order to achieve comparable results and proofs. News headings and other lead-ins to news reports in the public press are often valuable telltale distillations of the key points about the events and reports themselves. Such evidence can speak well for itself as proof positive of that which we seek to demonstrate about themes uppermost in the public mind as expressed through the public press and epitomized through news titles, subtitles, and other headings.

In a most poignant sign of what we are saying, a recent news report (to be featured further in our next book) has well articulated a key point in its main title: "Serbia Asserts Its Sovereignty Over Kosovo In Legislation." Reinforcing this idea of legislative sovereignty is that of the self-determination of the corresponding legislative state in the subheading: "Those working on Independence for Kosovo fear conflict." This struggle for sovereignty between the province of Kosovo in the former Yugoslavia (United Slavic Countries) long dominated by Serbia was highlighted in the fall of 2006 (NYT, Oct. 2, 2006, A8).

As pointed out in the beginning of Chapter II to follow, the presentations of quotes there and in Chapter III are typically arranged into many different series of segments (each in quotes) separated by semicolons. In each segment of quoted material from a separate news source, the main title of the news article appears first whereas the subtitles and other headings follow in parentheses, so as to indicate to the reader which is which. From Chapter IV on throughout the book, each segment of separate quotations is more often separated from the other by a period, rather than by a semicolon, while weaving the segments together into a series of complete sentences. The series of individual segments are thus more narratively presented by combining news headings and subheadings into a series of single sentences without the use of parentheses to set off the subheadings. By following the order of citations in the Notes corresponding to each paragraph in our main text, the reader can gather which sources are being used in which cases in the "mainstream" and other American presses. The Key to Abbreviations at the beginning of the Notes should be useful.

PART ONE

United States Government and Society in Legislative and Other Contexts of Sovereignty and State: Current News History

Chapter II

The U.S. Presidency

Having studied in our two previous books U.S. Presidents from Founders Jefferson and Adams to contemporaries Ly. Johnson and Reagan, we begin the present book on American government in "current news history" with a chapter on U.S. Presidents from Reagan and Bush Sr. to Clinton and Bush Jr. Ensuing chapters will deal in turn with the U.S. Congress, the U.S. Supreme Court and other courts, federal departments and agencies, state and local governments, and various sectors of U.S. life and society. The continuing main themes and perspectives of this series will again be uppermost.

In this and succeeding chapters, the focus on "current news history" covers a number of recent years and myriad representative news accounts. These accounts have been selected primarily for their factual information or broader usefulness, while keeping in mind they often convey political bias—something the present writer has tried hard to avoid for himself through nonpartisan or bipartisan presentations, showing different sides of issues wherever possible or relevant. Aside from rare brief items quoted below from news articles, the main titles of such accounts will typically be given first followed by further descriptive subheadings or other short quotations in parentheses, with semicolons placed between each article's information when arranged in a series in Chapters II–III, superceded, by periods from Chapter IV on. News sources will be listed in corresponding sequences in footnotes at the end of each paragraph.

1. PRESIDENT REAGAN'S SECOND TERM: IRAN–CONTRA

In 1987, President Ronald Reagan's next-to-last year in office, public perception of his presidency was changing, as reflected in various kinds of news stories. One article was entitled "A Change in the Weather: As Reagan's era recedes, compassion and Government activism regain favor." It began with the following observation: "It happened with surreal swiftness. One moment, the pageant of Reaganism was proceeding, with brilliant fireworks over the harbor. The next moment, the Iranian scandal burst up through the floorboards. . . . The Reagan Administration, that phenomenon that had defined so much of the '80s, that had given the decade its agenda and style, seemed to collapse in a bizarre shambles." Moreover: "If the U.S. were a parliamentary democracy, the Reagan Government might have fallen." Even so: "The nation is beginning to look beyond Reagan now," for "Americans had a suspicion that Reaganism had gone too far in trying to rescind the compassionate [activist] functions of Government."[1]

Under the cloud of the Iran–contra scandal, the American "Presidency [was] under a microscope," according to another news story at the same point in time in 1987. The subtitle—"Series of troubled administrations tied to persons, not system"—was echoed in the article's references to the need for "above all the standards of integrity and respect for the law. On this score, both the Nixon and Reagan presidencies are seen to have fallen short."[2]

However, said another news heading, "US introspection baffles Europeans." "Europeans are baffled and worried by the fall of former presidential candidate Gary Hart and the congressional probe of the Iran–contra scandal. . . . And why, they ask, must a President's actions be subject to prolonged legislative probing? European executives enjoy power with few restraints." These concerns go back to the times of Watergate and the Vietnam War.[3]

In any case, a few months later: "White House exuberant over [Oliver] North's success" in his Congressional testimony in the Iran–contra scandal. "Reagan moves to capitalize on apparent turn in public opinion," read the subcaption to this lead news story. "Despite his assertions that his actions were approved by his superiors and his assumption that President Reagan approved the diversion to Nicaraguan contras of funds from the sale of arms to Iran, Colonel North's testimony failed to provide the 'smoking gun' necessary to prove that the President was involved."[4]

Even so, three editorials from this period of 1987 zeroed in on the rule of law and the perceived infraction thereof. According to one heading, "Reagan Ignites a Constitutional Crisis." In this way, "If the puppets are subject to the law and violate it, the puppet master cannot escape accountability. . . . But when the President's status . . . is transformed from a political stance into a shield against the rule of law, a constitutional crisis is at hand." Another editorial—"The Laws Unfaithfully Executed"—declared: "The Iran–contra [Congressional] committees charge Ronald Reagan with the second worst offense for a President. They contend that he did not fulfill his constitutional oath 'to take care that the laws be faithfully executed'. . . . There were laws forbidding weapons deals with terrorist nations. . . . Laws forbade military help for the contras. . . . [which Reagan violated]." In another—"Above the Law in the White House"—Reagan's position was again doubted: "President Reagan argues that a law passed by Congress (and which he signed) cannot prevent him from dealing in hostage ransom and military aid."[5]

Finally, a front-page headline similarly reported on "Reagan's view of law called into question." The story began: "President Reagan's new line of defense on the Iran–contra affair is generating lively debate among legal experts about who is responsible for American foreign policy." "Many constitutional scholars are nonplussed by Mr. Reagan's assertion that he has not violated a law of Congress—the Boland amendment—because the law does not apply to him. Others say they think the law is ambiguous and open to differing interpretations." As if to echo this controversy, an editorial in the same issue took up the provocative question "Citizens or Congress: Who should elect the president?" The telling caption reads: "The Founding Fathers did not expect the rank and file of voters to know enough about individual candidates to be able to select wisely the one most qualified to be president." The model of the British parliamentary system is cited as an alternative. Another news story from this time pointed out: "Today, the principal threat to the system the Constitution created is the growth of power in the executive branch."[6]

The role of legislation in issues of sovereignty and state became uppermost in the 1987 Iran–contra affair. The U.S. Constitution in Article II sets forth the primary roles of the President to execute Congress' laws and the laws of the land, while being Commander-in-Chief and ultimately responsible for foreign policy. If the three federal branches are separate and co-equal, how far does the role of

Congress in declaring war or enacting laws extend to a check on the executive branch?

2. PRESIDENT BUSH SR.'S TERM

Starting Out

When the first Bush presidency began, in the aftermath of the largely popular Reagan Administration, it was unclear how successful George Bush Sr. would be after emerging from the shadows of the Vice Presidency following his election in November 1988. What kind of leadership would Bush provide in domestic and foreign affairs, especially in relation to Reagan's strong style? Would Bush continue his predecessor's Republican tendencies to deemphasize the federal government's role in domestic programs and to turn back the Democratic legacies of "New Deal" and "Great Society"? Would Bush continue Reagan's emphasis upon foreign policies that engaged America in the spread of democracy particularly in Communist countries? Or would Bush set a more Wilsonian agenda by encouraging strong self-government both at home and abroad?

Some of the news highlights of Bush Sr.'s first year in office in 1989 conveyed an ambiguous, vacillating, yet positive approach to noted foreign dictatorships. On China, the following disparate headlines, subheadings, and captions were mixed: "Bush and China: *Un-Realpolitik*" ("Why Ally With Deng Against a Democracy Movement That Loves the West?"); "Bush Gambles on China Trip: Playing the Expertise Card"; "Bush Is Right on China" ("Democrats' cheap shots undermine courageous realpolitik"); and "Bush and the New Moralism About China" ("Shunning Beijing would gain us little"). On the Soviet Union it was "Easier Said Than Done" ("Bush and Gorbachev set ambitious goals at Malta, but they left little time for the hard bargaining still to come"). On Panama, "Bush Aides Admit A U.S. Role In Coup, And Bad Handling" ("Troops Blocked 2 Routes at Request of Rebels, White House Says").[7]

Perhaps most interesting of all, on control of foreign policy, there was "A Balance of Bush, The Congress and the Contras" ("In the competition for power, the President makes a tactical retreat"). As there reported, "Ever since Congress . . . passed the War Powers Act of 1973 and other measures intended to strip the Presidency of its imperial trappings, it has continued to mount a close watch over executive actions." Regarding aid to the Nicaraguan contras, "Mr. Bush was determined not to repeat the experience of the Reagan years, which were marred by Congressional denials of funds for military aid to the contra rebels."[8]

On domestic affairs, as well as foreign policy, Bush Sr. still had, by the end of his first year in office, "A Second Chance for Vision." "America," the editorial began, "had a fair idea of what it was getting in George Bush: a competent, cautious steward with a slim agenda and no taste for what he called 'the vision thing.' He would make changes at the margins of the Reagan Revolution without disturbing the core. . . . The end of the cold war does more than challenge old assumptions. It inspires high hopes that America will shift resources from receding foreign threats to neglected domestic needs." A few months earlier, Bush was dubbed "Mr. Consensus" ("Cautious and personable, George Bush is a President who listens, leans heavily on advisers—and usually comes down in the middle").[9]

As for Bush's domestic legislative initiatives of 1989, two examples must suffice: "Bush Clean Air Plan Called Energy Policy in the Making" ("Cleaner fuels would replace dirtier ones on a grand scale") and "Bush Offers Housing Plan to Aid Poor, Homeless and New Buyers." The fate of Reagan privatization policies was not yet apparent.[10]

Gaining Momentum

Among the first President Bush's catchwords that became a label for his presidency was "the Big Mo," or momentum, in addition to others such as "the vision thing" and "read my lips" on "no new taxes," the latter having been a campaign pledge. Some instances of these and other perspectives in the news will be useful, as well as much wider considerations, first on domestic and then on foreign issues, during the year 1990.

The domestic record for the first President Bush was as yet unclear in the first half of 1990. Would he become "Lyndon Baines Bush?" ("He sounds like Great Society II, until you look at his budget"). Bush seemed to be taking decisive charge—or was he actually vacillating?—in relation to Congress and the legislative arena. For instance, in chronological sequence in early 1990: "President Opens Legislative Drive" ("Capital Gains Tax Cut Urged and Farm Policy Outlined in Talk on '90 Agenda"); "Fight Over Tax Cut Heats Up as Bush and [Senator] Moynihan Dig In"); "Tougher Enforcing of Child Labor Laws is Vowed"); "U.S. [Bush Administration] Plans to Shift Responsibility For Many Road Projects to States") ("Higher Local Fuel Taxes and Tolls Are Expected"); "Child Labor Law Vio-

lations Sought [by Bush Labor Department] in Nationwide Raids";
"Child Labor Violations Widespread" (as testified by Bush Labor
Secretary); "As Bush Hails Progress by Blacks, Veto Is Seen on
Rights Bill" sent to him by Congress; "President Signs Law for
Study of Hate Crime" ("Gay Rights Leaders Go to First Official
Event"); "Caution Prevails as the President Meets Lawmakers on
the Budget"; and "Regulators See Mistake By Bush Son," concern-
ing a Savings and Loan Association.[11]

The domestic record became somewhat clearer and the performance more decisive for Bush as the second half of 1990 progressed.
Illustrative news reports were as follows: "The Lip-Reading Slo-
gan Aside, Mr. Bush Deserves Some Applause" ("Acting Presidential, he had the courage to change his mind on taxes" and "Perhaps
he can now spearhead a bipartisan attack on the deficit"); "Eating
His Words" ("Cornered by the deficit, Bush proclaims his own brand
of 'thinking anew' and signs on to the T-word. But who will be pay-
ing what?"); "President Defends His Son's Integrity In Savings In-
quiry" ("A Vow Not to Interfere" and "Political Pressures Grow—
Senate Backs a Life Term in Major Fraud Cases"); "Bush Now
'Concedes A Need For Tax Revenue Increases' [by Congress] To
Reduce Deficit In Budget. . . . Break With Pledge" ("President Also
Calls for Cuts in Military and Civilian Programs"); "Republicans
Fear Kiss of Death As Bush Moves His Lips on Taxes"; "President's
Ban of Assault Guns May Be Eluded"; "Sununu [Bush's Chief of
Staff] Resumes Talks on Rights Bill" ("Seeking to address Bush's
opposition to job quotas"); "Bush Leaves G.O.P. Rift in Congress,
Begins a Campaign Swing in South"; "Bush Shifts Stand On Tax
Rise Again; Congress Baffled" ("Dizzying Tax Course Endangers
His Image" and "Big Battles Seen Likely in House and Senate Over
Capital Gains"); " 'Let Congress Clear It Up' " ("Bush's pratfalls
last week underscored the evanescence of presidential power");
"Bush League: The President Stumbles, Congress Bumbles. Boooo!"
("Between their flips and their flops on the budget, the President
and Congress looked like a bunch of stumblebums. The public wasn't
laughing"); "Bush. No Mo Big Mo" ("The President is the big loser
in the budget fiasco"); "President Proposes New Civil Rights Legislation" ("Attempts to Reach Compromise Are Abandoned; Congress Challenged to Act Quickly"); "Vowing to Veto Rights Bill,
President Offers Alternative" ("The President tries to extricate
himself from a dilemma"); "White House and Congress on Verge of
Tax Deal"; "President Vetoes Bill On Job Rights" and "Showdown
Is Set" ("Bush Cites a Quota Plan" and "Close Votes Seen On Override"); "Substantial Power on Spending Is Shifted From Congress

to Bush" ("Procedure Intended to Guarantee Cuts Are Made"); "Bush Signs Major Revision of Anti-Pollution Law"; "U.S. Plans A Shift On Road Spending" in "ambitious five-year plan" in proposed legislation by Bush Administration ("Federal road aid would grow, but it would cost states more"); "Administration Backs Revamping Of Banking and Securities System"—"To Revise Banking Law"; "U.S. [Justice Dept. under Bush] Drops Bias Suit Against Md."; "Federal Reserve Acts To Increase Lending By Banks" ("Move Seems to Be Response to White House Pressure for Help on Economy"); "Miscalculations Put a Tight Lid On '92 Budget" ("Administration officials said today that spending limits set in the new budget law were slightly lower than the amount needed to continue the services at existing levels . . ."); "Bush, the Veto President" ("Echoes of the odious King George"); "Bush Backs Move For Limiting Terms Of U.S. [Congressional] Lawmakers" ("An Amendment Is Sought" for "President's Plans. . . . Lawmakers Are Wary"); "Race and College Aid: Recent Supreme Court Rulings Open Way For U.S. Move Against Favoring Minorities," with import for Congressional legislation; "Bush Signs an [Executive] Order Raising Officials' Pay"; "Ruling [announced by Education Dept. under Bush] Highlights a Rift Among Blacks" on preferential treatment in scholarship aid; "White House Retreats on Ruling That Curbs Minority Scholarships" ("An effort to get the President out of a political bind"); "Struggle at White House" ("Mishandling of Scholarships for Minorities Reflects Search for a Civil Rights Agenda"); and "Still No End to Turmoil at Legal Services," which a President provides for in the budget and for which Congress appropriates the money.[12]

A similar kind of selective chronological news highlights for President Bush in foreign affairs during 1990 yields some telltale items in relation to legal–legislative matters and speaks for itself. These include, more briefly, the following: "Bush Hails a Thaw in China; Congress Is Skeptical" ("Lawmakers Fail to Find Any End to Oppression and Favor Sanctions"); "Bush, Citing Security Law, Voids Sale, of Aviation Concern to China"; "Ban Erased On Visiting Radicals"—"under a law signed by President Bush"; "Bush Urges Congress to Act On Aid to New Democracies" ("Nicaragua and Panama 'need our help to heal deep wounds' "); while Ex-President "Reagan Testifies He Did Not Order Any Illegal Acts" in the Iran–contra affair, saying "He Did Not Know Extent of Aides' Involvement"); "Bush Is Now Reported Willing to Accept Big Cuts in the '91 Military Budget" ("A Seismic Shift In Official Opinion"); Pres. Bush "Making the Best of a Bad Trade Law"; "Bush Gains Time As Moscow Delays Law On Emigration" ("Conflict With Congress Over

Soviet Trade Pact Seems to Be Averted for Now"); "Who Has the Power to Make War?" (at issue is the pre–Iraq War debate between President and Congress); "Bush to Guard Secrecy, Kills Espionage Agencies' Budget" ("By withholding his signature, Mr. Bush pocket-vetoed the legislation: it could not have become law unless it had been signed within 10 working days after it reached his desk."); and "Bush Offers Loans to Soviets to Ease Shortages of Food" ("A Law is waived to get supplies for the winter" and "U.S. Moves to Help Cold War Rival Much As It Aided World War II Foes").[13]

Overall, press outlook on the Bush presidency in 1990 was mixed and evolving. Asked one editorial, "Why Not Prudence Plus Leadership?" "Good or Just Lucky?" asked another ("The President Seems to Be on a Roll, Though It May Simply Be the Times"). Or again: "Bush's Unrealpolitik" ("He conducts foreign policy as if having a policy were a mistake"); "The Conflict Within George Bush" ("It's fun trying to figure out who's ahead, George Bush or his conscience"); "Please, Not Another Failed Presidency" ("Bush is looking a lot like Carter"); and "Bush: From Sizzle to Fizzle" ("The line 'read my lips' was not an endearing joke to people who have to pay the penalty for reading his lips").[14]

Seeking Legislative Leadership

On into 1991 the press' pronouncements on Bush overall were guardedly improving. Named "Man of the Year" by *Time* in January, he appeared in the lead story's title as "A Tale of Two Bushes" ("One finds a vision on the global stage; the other still displays none at home"). Stated therein was "A Case of Doing Nothing"—"A conscious strategy for defending the [domestic] status quo." By the end of 1991, many headlines would turn downward on the economy, as in "Bush's Time to Act" ("Passive Approach on the Recession Collides With Harsh Political Reality"); and "Blame Bush for the Recession." Some news reports of 1991 on the domestic agenda were "Longing for the intensity that the U.S. brought to the Gulf War," while bemoaning "Bush's No-Risk Policy" ("Why he won't propose a bold domestic agenda").[15]

Nevertheless, the year 1991 found President Bush Sr. seeking an expanded role as legislative leader. On a wide array of domestic issues and programs, the following illustrative news accounts tell a compelling chronological story. They suggest a mounting attention to domestic legislative regulatory matters. In the first half of 1991: "Bush to Propose Financial 'Super-Regulator' " for five agencies ("A third plank in the White House Plan to change regulation" in banking); "With New Law, Budget Makers Face New Limits"; "Administration Presents Plan for Sweeping Overhaul of Banking Industry" ("Ownership Rules, Set in 1930s, Would Be Eased" in "time of financial stress"); "Bush's Energy Plan Emphasizes . . . Fewer Limits on Opening Nuclear Plants"; "Unshackling the Troubled Banks . . . is sure to face a fierce fight in Congress"; "Banking Reforms Call for a Shrinking U.S. Role in Rescues"; "U.S. Rules [set by "Bush Administration"] Would Force Businesses to Make Alteration for the Disabled"; "Bush Proposes an Alternative Rights Bill" in "quarrel over business interests and quotas"; "U.S. In Showdown With California On Nursing Homes" ("Dispute On Regulations"); "U.S. [Bush Administration] Proposes Rules on Disabled in the Workplace"; " '88 Law on Medical Labs Goes Unenforced by U.S."; "Bush's Education Vision" ("President Must Prove His New Proposals Can Meet Test of Feasibility and Fairness"); The "Bush . . . plan to provoke radical change in America's troubled schools . . . [lacks] the money . . . [to] make a difference"; "In Bush Presidency, The Regulators Ride Again"; "Sununu: A Case Study On Flaunting the Rules" ("Presidential aides often forget that they are public figures, too" [and not above the law]); "U.S. Mandates Test for Lead In the Water"; "Focusing on Welfare" ("Bush Plays Private Acts of Decency Against the Government as a Helper" and "Assailing the Great Society, Bush seeks a good society"); "Bush Scolds Congress at Princeton" ("A renewed attack on lawmakers, but milder"); "Bush Aides Push State Gun Cases Into U.S. Courts" ("Aim Is Stiffer Sentences" and "Plan Welcomed by Local Law Agencies but U.S. Judges Face Growing Back Log"); "Bush Enters Malpractice Debate With Plan [that he "will send to Congress"] to Limit Court Awards" ("States That Do Not Comply Will Be Penalized"); "Battle Is Looming On College Aid To Poor Students" ("Bush's Plan [he "will submit . . . to Congress"] to Help Only the Neediest Draws Fire From a Range of Lawmakers"); "Debate on Plan to Limit Lawsuits" [was "sent to Congress"]; "Bush's Plan on Banking Still Faces Obstacles" ("The savings and loan fallout makes it harder to change banking laws"); and "The President's Legislation: A Status Report" (on energy, education, crime, transportation, banking, and civil rights).[16]

Continuing on in the same fashion in the second half of 1991 were the following cases in point: "Bush Plan for Bank System Meets Attacks in Congress"; "Bush Rejects Senate Agreement On Rights Measure"; "President Is Sent Measure To Widen Jobless Benefits"; "Administration Proposes ["rules" subject to "Congressional review"] Opening Vast Protected Areas to Builders"; "Rush to Sign Jobless Measure But Block Money," on budgetary grounds; "Ad-

ministration Issues Rules to Limit Medicaid Payments to States";
"Bush Wants A Rise In Banks' Lending" ("Presses Regulators to
Ease Up in Effort to Aid Economy"); "Bush Eases Rules In Effort
to Spur Lending By Banks"; "Bush Sets Rules to Curb U.S. Lawyers' Litigation"; "President's Plan to Name Successors [in emer-
gency] Skirted Law"; "Bush Vetoes Abortion Bill; Attempt to Over-
ride Fails"; "Bush To Order End Of Rules Allowing Race-Based
Hiring" (". . . Using Executive Move to Offset Legislative Compromise"); "With Bush's Stand Uncertain, Lawsuit Is Threatened Over
New Rights Law"; "Top U.S. Aides Back Away From New Wetlands Rule" ("New Proposal to Honor 1988 Campaign Pledge by
Bush"); "Reaffirming Commitment, Bush Signs Civil Rights Bill"
("The image of a wavering President spreads fear in his party");
"President Threatens to Veto Anti-Crime Bill as Too Soft" [on de-
fendants]; "At Heart of Debate on [V.P.] Quayle Council: Who Controls Federal Regulations?"; and "U.S. [Bush Administration] Alters Rules on People With H.I.V."[17]

On the foreign front in 1991, a few salient topics can be raised.
"By moving decisively to blunt Iraq's aggression, Bush begins to
shape a brave new world order." "Riding the victory train" ("How
the President plans to convert his Gulf War success into a long-term
political triumph"); "Administration Advances Strategy for a Solo
Superpower's Global Military Role"; "For Bush, a Familiar Pattern
Resumes: Agenda Focuses Overseas, Not at Home" ("Domestic
Policy Defined Largely by Opposing Democratic Initiatives"); "Europeans Call Bush Plan Dawn of a New Era"; "Bush Rewrites the
Nuclear Rules"; "Can 'America First' Bring Jobs Back?" The Bush
Administration's handling of foreign affairs throughout this period,
as in the "Gulf War," must await further attention in our later stud-
ies on that region.[18]

Battling the Regulatory State

During his last full year in office, 1992, President Bush Sr. proceeded
ever more strongly to do battle with the regulatory state across a
broad front in ways ever more evocative of the doctrinaire approach
of the "Reagan revolution." The role of the federal government came
under increasing scrutiny. Critics who disagreed with Bush's domestic policies and actions in this regard often pronounced his
Administration's record weak or poor, due to his inaction on the
nation's needs at home in contrast to his bold initiatives abroad.

A sampling of news reports as 1992 progressed tell the story. They
begin in January with how "The "Veep [Dan Quayle] takes on Bush's

regulations" even though "Federal Regulation [Is] Growing Despite Quayle Panel's Role," in consequence of laws already passed by Congress on such topics as the environment. What followed was a long succession of anti-regulatory reports and measures: "In Move to Spur Economy, Bush Is Urged to Order 90-Day Ban on New Federal Rules"; "New Rules Are Said to Be Stalling Communications"; "Bush to Ease Regulation Of Gene-Altered Goods"; "White House Sees a Mission to Cut Business Rules" ("Deregulation's political appeal is unproved"); "Bush Extending Regulation Freeze as [a great] Success Over Red Tape"; "The Environmental Pollution President" ("Bush is quietly gutting the Clean Air Act"); "Bush to Relax Air Pollution Regulation"; "Environmental Laws Are Eased By Bush As Election Nears" ("Pattern of Easing Rules On Environment Is Seen"); "No More Blank Checks for Regulations"; "Frustrating Spate of New [Federal] Rules [despite Bush] for Clinics" ("More red tape for many doctors and dentists"); "President Bush Vetoes Bill That Would Regulate Cable TV Rates"; and "Quayle . . . Seeks to Relax Wetland Protections." Even so, there were other reports of new rules under the Bush Administration, as when "U.S. Discloses Tougher Rules To Revamp Treasury Market" and, at the end of his term, "Environment Gets Flurry of Final Acts."[19]

All in all, in 1992, the domestic verdict was somber. "Wanted: An Economic Policy," reported one cover story, for "President Bush is set to unveil new plans for the economy. But America needs a more far-reaching strategy." Yet "President's Message Expected to Lay Out Plans for a 'New Domestic Order.' " Bush's January State of the Union message included a section on "Revamping of Government," calling for "a 90-day moratorium on any new Federal regulations and "a top-to-bottom review of all regulations, old and new, to stop the ones that will hurt growth and speed up those that will help growth." So his intention, at least, was more evenly balanced than might otherwise be suggested. However, the "Bottom Line: A Hands-Off Government" ("Budget as Bush Campaign Manifesto"). Said others: "Missing from Politics: The Blueprint For the Future"; "Deep Freeze the Regulatory Freeze" ("President Bush's delay of rule-writing won't help growth and may weaken health and safety laws"); and "Consumer Groups Attack Regulation Freeze."[20]

On a wider domestic front in 1992, the following criticisms were made: "Bush Is Vague on Health Plan"; "Bush Links Rivals' Plan to Socialism"; and "Social Programs Grew But Largely Because of Bush's Neglect"; "Bush Domestic Policy Agenda Seen As the Weakest in a Generation." As for Bush and Congress: "Rising Feud Produced a Legislative Deadlock" ("A Relationship Rarely So Sour, or

Unproductive"); "Divided Government: Messy but Not Fatal"; and "Divided Government Is the Best Revenge" ("Bush's campaign against Congress is risky"). The contentious debate continued over "What should the federal role be in our society?"[21]

All the above domestic matters under Bush's watch in 1992 were offset by his more widely recognized achievements on the world stage for the "new world order," yet not without criticism there too. "Bush's Roles on the World Stage had Triumph, but Troubles Too." On "Bush's Mission," "Some See Old Compass in a World Remade." Others saw "Boldness Without Vision" and "no larger framework for American foreign policy." Legislative and judicial disputes could arise, as when "Bush Vetoes Conditions [in Congressional legislation] of Trade Status of China"; and "Judge Sees Plan by White House to Defy Orders and Purge Data" ("Some Want to Study Tapes for Iran–Contra Clues").[22]

3. PRESIDENT CLINTON'S FIRST TERM

"Reinventing Government"

After the election, even before he took office in January 1993, "Aides Say Clinton Will Act Swiftly to Void Bush Policies," while "Looking to Set Right Agenda" and "Revamping Office For a New Politics" ("A Bold Image Is Sought"). There was much talk of a "Mandate For Change" ("What Clinton Will Do"), with wife Hillary "poised to reinvent the role of President's spouse" as "bully pulpit"—all marking "The End of Reaganism." There were comparisons drawn with F.D.R.—"The White House's New New Dealers" ("Mustering a Mandate to Break the Gridlock").[23]

By the time of the Inauguration, it was already being hailed in one national weekly as "The Age of Clinton." Reported another headline, "Ready or Not, Clinton Is Rattling the Country," with a caption on "Activist government is here again. Amid shouting over homosexuality came word: 'The President is going to speak out now on health care, his economic plan and national service.'" This would be, according to one essayist, "The Second Coming of Neo-Liberalism."[24]

A bold broad set of plans and agendas were soon introduced in early 1993. "Clinton Plan To Remake The Economy Seeks To Tax Energy And Big Incomes," while "A Split Congress Sits Back, Waiting to See if Clinton's Plan Sells" following a major speech by Clinton to Congress. Moreover, "Clinton Seeking $31 Billion in Stimulus," while "Also Set to Push a Revamping of Welfare." Clearly, "The President's Fine Print Asks Fundamental Change." Fittingly, in late

February, "Clinton, in Hyde Park Visit, Urges A Renewal of Roosevelt's Legacy." Attesting further to this new era were other articles of 1993. They included: "New Clinton. New Era" ("Delay health reform. It would be disruptive"); "How to Hawk the New Deal" ("Clinton Talks Right While Walking Left"); "Hillary Clinton's Potent Brain Trust On Health Reform"; "House Democrats Unite to Approve Clinton's Budget"; "Clinton's Plan Gets Moving" ("With unaccustomed unity, House Democrats give the President big victories on budget and economy"); and "Breaking Through" ("Clinton pushes his economic plan through the House and gains a chance to reshape the Supreme Court").[25]

Despite such reports of Clinton's early 1993 successes in steering his agenda and plans through Congress, other reports were more critical. Said one editorial by liberal Anthony Lewis, on "The Clinton Challenge": "The Administration lacks not brains but backbone." Differed another editorial by liberal Arthur Schlesinger, Jr., in "A Clinton Report Card, So Far," in April: "He's carrying his programs to the country well." Said Republican ex-President Reagan in a February editorial, "There They Go Again" ("Mr. President, where is that 'new Democrat'?"). Meanwhile, on foreign policy, a March editorial by Republican ex-President Nixon, cautioned about "Clinton's Greatest Challenge," which Nixon said was that "The West must wake up. Russia is the key to global security." Soon thereafter in April, "President Urges America To Back Help For Moscow" ("Clinton Says Bolstering Russia Will Aid U.S. Economy and Preserve World Peace"), although "Poll Shows Support Weak." Clinton himself had already called in a February editorial for "National Service—Now" ("Federal seed money, but local management"). As is often the case, foreign policy and initiatives by the White House were often tied to Congressional as well as public support.[26]

On the key topic of health care reform, as Clinton's first year in office progressed, there was special attention in the news. Clearly this was perceived to be a bold new plan, one getting a mixed reception, though at first mostly favorable. It was called "Radical Surgery" ("Steered by a reformer who ponders every option, Clinton's health-care plan stresses freedom of choice"). At the heart of "Health Planners' Radical Idea: Same Coverage for All." Anticipation was high: "Are You Ready?" ("The Clinton health-care plan will soon be unveiled," "Almost every doctor in the U.S. would work under price caps"). "Clinton's Health Plan" was headlined in one cover story as "the most sweeping reform since the New Deal." As "Clinton Asks Backing For Sweeping Change In The Health System," in a national address, he "Seeks to Write a New Chapter in the American Story."

However, "As Health Plan Comes Together, Big Price Tag Comes Into Focus." With such news reports as "Clinton Facing Reality Of Health-Care Reform" ("A plan that won applause in the campaign brings risks in office"), it was not long before "Clinton Delivers Revamped Health Plan" to Congress ("Lawmakers say a more modest law is likely"). Even so, with big government controls, "Insurers Fear They'd Be the Big Losers in a World of Managed Health Care." Meanwhile, "Officials Predict Deluge of Suits On Health Plan."[27]

"The Core of Clintonism" was beginning to emerge in 1993 as "an ideology demanding a vast expansion of government powers." One verdict on "Overturning The Reagan Era" was that "It's painful, messy and modest, but Clinton's budget signals a new course for America." Yet other reports pointed to "The Incredible Shrinking President," asking "Is Clinton up to the job?" at a time when his "approval ratings dip to record lows." As "Skeptics and Lobbyists Besiege Student Loan Plan," was it "A blueprint for efficiency or bureaucracy?" Another verdict was that "Clinton's Economic Strategy Ended Up Looking Like Bush's" ("A theory of growth that has never worked is now the sacred text"). Meantime, the "Clinton Myth of Nonideological Politics Stumbles" because "In reassuring centrists, the President angers liberals." Said another news report: "Presidents keep duplicating efforts to eliminate duplication in Federal agencies. Really? They're at it again."[28]

The Administration's much publicized efforts in 1993 to "reinvent government" were spearheaded mainly by Vice President Al Gore. According to "Gorezilla Zaps the System," "Al Gore seeks to 'reinvent government,' but beware the bureaucracy's seasoned heel draggers," while Gore is "forging a role as reformer, legislative arm twister and adviser in chief." Similarly, "Gore's Views on Better Government May Be Easier to Utter Than Deliver," with "New steps taking a whole library of failed blueprints for efficiency." On "Federal Cutbacks Proposed by Gore for Next 5 Years," "Clinton Vows Strong Backing" for "Merging Some Agencies," while "After all the managerial jargon the final word is 'cut.'" Other viewpoints were sometimes less hospitable to "Al Gore's Misguided Mission," preferring to say "Let's disinvent government." Even so, "Gore's Efficiency Plan Draws Nods in Congress (for Now)."[29]

Seizing the Legislative Initiative as Legislator-in-Chief

From the very outset of the Clinton Administration, it quickly became clear that the main dynamic was the new President's efforts to seize the legislative initiative in relation to Congress, as the foregoing more general news appraisals have already at times suggested. Even before being sworn in, "Clinton Discusses Legislative Plan With Top Democrats of Congress" "in Hopes for a Quick Start." "Clinton and Top Legislators Pledge Amity on Economy," while "Avoiding Gridlock by Wooing Both Sides of Aisle." There seemed to be echoes of the "New Deal" legislation made during F.D.R.'s "first hundred days" as "Clinton Plans to Spread the Wealth In Increased Public Works Spending." In two of his first announcements as President-elect on his legislative intents, Clinton invoked a liberal agenda that was sure to incite conservatives' ire: lifting the ban on gays in the military in "His First Move on Policy," while being "Ready to Act on 2 Abortion Regulations."[30]

In early 1993, immediately after Inauguration Day, there occurred a wide array of Executive legislative initiatives that reversed many Reagan–Bush policies. For instance, "Clinton Orders Reversal Of Abortion Restrictions Left By Reagan And Bush" in a "Big Policy Change" as "Thousands Protest." Again, the "President Promise[d] to Lift Military Gay Ban." Through "Clinton's Departure," "The Reagan–Bush Era Is Left Behind In a Flurry of Executive Moves" ("Government as part of the solution again").[31]

The gay ban issue quickly heated up in early 1993 as "Lawmakers Revolt On Lifting Gay Ban In Military Service," to the point that "Fierce Opposition in Congress Is Threatening to Sidetrack Domestic Legislation" proposed by "Clinton [who] faces the threat of a major defeat early in his Presidency." Not surprisingly, then, "Clinton Accepts Delay In Lifting Military Gay Ban," as "President Tells Pentagon to Draft Order for Him to Sign in 6 Months." Although "Clinton [had been] Sticking To Plan Letting Gays in Military," he was "Given Options for Changing Military Gay Ban" as some in Congress sought "to compromise with the Pentagon" during the summer of 1993. Finally, at that point, "Accord Is Reached On Military Rules For Gay Service" through "Compromise By Clinton."[32]

As the year 1993 developed, the Presidential–Congressional dynamics on legislative issues and programs intensified across a broad spectrum of activity. Early on, it was reported that "Congress Hears the Public and Moves Behind Clinton . . . But Plan for Economy Still Faces A Long Road." The "Administration [is] Completing Plan To Ease Rules on Bank Lending." A "Sweeping Reversal Of U.S. [Federal] Land Policy Is Sought By Clinton." To the question of "Who Will Regulate the Regulators?" it was answered in one editorial "A White House council—but one that works openly." There was "Protest and Praise Over Clinton's Orders" as "Hundreds of abortion foes are arrested at clinics." Meanwhile, "Looking for Allies to Pass Economic Plan, Clinton Courts Congress Nonstop." Also, "Clinton Would End Ban On Aid To Poor Seeking Abortions," on which "Congress To Get Request." After a few months into the first term, "White House [Is] Forced to Be Single-Minded in Congress" so as not "To Push More Than One Issue at a Time." When "Clinton Sends Congress Spending Package," it is called "A Proposal With Hopes For Passage."[33]

Again on health care, the legislative process was arduous. It also became "A White House Fight" in that "On Health Care, It Is Hillary Clinton versus President's Economic Advisers." As "[Bill] Clinton And Allies Twist Arms In Bid For Budget Votes" in Congress, the "First Lady Sets Aggressive Tone For Debate on Health Care."[34]

On the budget and taxes, "By shedding bad habits and letting Congress have its say, Clinton ends his losing streak." There was "The Primordial Ooze of a Budget Bill" in its journey from President through Congress before passage into law. "Despite all his compromises, Clinton still must push hard to get his budget passed."[35]

On other fronts in later 1993, "Clinton Seeks More Powers To Stem Illegal Immigration," while in addition "White House Moves on Easing Food-Pesticide Law" and "White House Asks Revision Of Rules To Save Wetlands." In strategic move, "Clinton's Advisers Study New Moves To Spur Economy" through "Options [That] Bypass Congress." However, "Making Deals, Not Waves, Is Strategy for [passage of] Health Plan." Now Hillary was winning personal "Raves on the Hill," "if not the health plan" itself. The drama went on as "{Bill] Clinton wows the crowds with his vision for reform, but can he persuade Congress to help him deliver his dream?" Meantime, "Clinton Seeks to Regulate Medical Specialties," while at the same time "President Moves to Lessen Grip of White House on Regulations." In addition, "Clinton Vows to Fight Congress On His Power to Use the Military." In September through November President Clinton first delays "turning it [his health-care plan] into law," yet "finally presents" it to Congress, facing "an uphill fight." Toward the end of the year, "Clinton Signs Law Protecting Religious Practices." He also "Plans Change in the Law Banning Military Aid to Pakistan." He "Proposes Tough New Rules On Bias By Banks." He sought "To Require States To Finance Abortions Of Poor."[36]

But where in the midst of all the above kinds of domestic legislative preoccupations in 1993 was foreign policy? Said one news article, "There's Nothing Like Foreign Policy for Producing Ennui." Or, "Like It or Not, We Must Lead" ("Where is Clinton's leadership and vision on foreign policy?"). All in all, it might seem that the domestic vs. foreign emphases by Bush and Clinton were thus far somewhat reversed. Certainly their policies and priorities on domestic issues of the legislative state were often hugely different, although each, in different ways, was dealing with precisely *that*, i.e., the legislative state. Even so, the Clinton Presidency was just beginning and its longer track record had yet to be established. Perhaps its first year of intense legislative activity, especially in getting far-reaching proposals through Congress, bears remote comparison with F.D.R.'s first presidential year.[37]

Facing New Hurdles

Already in 1994, the Clinton presidency increasingly faced a series of new obstacles, beginning with its general image. As for "The Porcelain Presidency," "These two [past] years may be Clinton's best." After the Republican Congressional victories in the November midterm elections, Clinton faced new roadblocks to the passage of his programs, as new House Speaker "Gingrich Moves Quickly To Put Stamp on House" and "White House [Is] In Struggle To Take Back the Agenda." Clinton was urged to "Get Off the Floor . . . And act like a President." Now came the talk of "Reinventing Bill Clinton." More grimly, "A Crippled President Strives Not to Become a Lame Duck." Notwithstanding, Clinton pressed ahead. Changing his course in "The 12-Minute Makeover," "Clinton tries gamely to recast himself as a tax cutter and department dropper. But is it too late?" More optimistic was "How Clinton Can Be F.D.R."—"All he needs is to stick to his guns (and win)." Al Gore and Hillary Clinton were also coming to help in the rescue: "Gore, the Soldier of Streamlining, Returns to Lead Clinton's Charge" and "Belying rumors of self-doubt, the First Lady reappears, unapologetic and as feisty as ever." Emboldened and taking a page from the resurgent Republicans in Congress, as he "Sounds Opening Themes of '96 Campaign," "[Bill] Clinton Outlines a Plan for Less Government and Tax Cuts for the Middle Class" ("Clinton's Budget Plan: Shifting Into Reverse").[38]

The Clinton Administration's further wide legislative activities continued on in 1994 but were somewhat less pronounced and more tentative in the wake of its bold beginnings in the previous year and in the rising Republican Congressional tide later that year. Some samplings of press stories are indicative as 1994 progressed: "Clinton Puzzles How to Delay Welfare Reform Yet Seem to Pursue It"; "Clinton Plans Revision To Ease Toxic Cleanup Criteria"; "U.S. [Clinton Administration] Imposes New Alcohol Test Rules"; "U.S.

Seeking [Legislation] to Ease Restrictions on Export of High-Tech Products"; "Clinton Seeks Ban on Export of Most Hazardous Waste"; "Clinton's Air Traffic Plan Touching Off Dispute in Congress"; "Clinton to Unveil Jobs Bill That Focuses on Retraining"; "Clinton Offers Plan on Merchant Ships"; "U.S. Moves on Two Fronts To Reshape Logging Rules"; "Clinton Administration Is Criticized as Too Ambitious With Vaccine Distribution Plan"; "U.S. Proposes Healthier Food At All Schools" ("New Rules Would Cut Fat and Cholesterol"); "The Clinton Welfare Bill: A Long and Stormy Journey to Congress"; "Clinton Offers Delayed Proposal to Redo Welfare" ("Little hoopla for a plan and little Congressional action expected this year"); "Clinton's Plan: DOA?" ("As critics take aim, the President ducks and weaves to defend his health-care reforms"); "Clinton Asks Senate Leader to Insist on Coverage for All"; "Going Flat Out" ("The Clintons launch a last big road show for health reform but show limits of their resources to cut a deal"); "Clinton's Veto Power" ("Wave that pen again"); "More Clinton Proposals Face Danger in Congress" in "Obstacles for Trade Accord and Superfund"; "Clinton Is Urged to Abandon Fight Over Health Bill"; "National Health Program, President's Greatest Goal, Declared Dead In Congress" (due in particular to rising Republican opposition); "Hillary Clinton Says Administration Was Misunderstood on Health Care"; "Clinton Assails G.O.P. for Effort to 'Kill It or Just Talk It to Death' " ("After months of watching Congress shoot huge holes in his legislative agenda, President Clinton fought back today"); "G.O.P. to Lead Senate [after November elections] In Big Blow to Clinton"; "Reagan Revolution Redux" ("Now the G.O.P. must make good on its [Gingrich's] 'contract with America' "); "Alone in the Middle" ("The President is likely to find the new Congress a sharply divided body resistant to dealmaking"); "Pollsters Say Health Care Helped Sweep Away Democrats"; "Clinton Aide Criticizes G.O.P. Plans for Tax Cuts"; and "President Outlines Cutbacks to Pay for Tax Relief Plans" (but they "Face Many Obstacles" in Congress). From these perspectives, the Clinton legislative agenda was already reaching, perhaps, the point of diminishing returns, even though the legislative process was still uppermost, yet comparisons might be drawn with F.D.R.'s post–first-year record and the many Congressional reversals he faced.[39]

As for foreign affairs in 1994, there was also a fading-out of the "honeymoon" phase of Clinton's first term. It was called "Clinton's Obstacle Course" as "The President's swing through Europe will test his ability to define America's role in a complex postwar world." Or again, "Dropping the ball?" ("While Clinton focuses on domestic affairs, U.S. world leadership suffers from lack of attention and too frequent back-and-forth policy switches"). At this point came ex-President Nixon's "Last Testament," in which he gave "His Parting Advice to Bill Clinton: America Must Lead." Yet when later on "Taking His Show On The Road," "Clinton's new success in juggling foreign problems is more than just good luck." Moreover, back in May, well prior to the November election setbacks, "Clinton Defends [His] Foreign Policy Record."[40]

Predictably, much of the Administration's policy matters in conducting foreign affairs revolved in 1994, as in other years, around legal–legislative issues especially in relation to Congress. Toward year's end, "Clinton Asks G.O.P. to Back Free [Worldwide] Trade" ("Will electoral setback [in the November elections] damage ambitious program?"). Over previous months, Clinton experienced easier going in asserting his powers in foreign policy especially in relation to Congress. For example: "Clinton to Reinstate Power to Move Fast On Japan Sanctions"; "Some Lawmakers Say Clinton Can Order Haiti Invasion"; "Clinton Frees Russia From Curbs on Trade" ("A move by Clinton to create good will as he prepares to meet with Yeltsin") and "Clinton Lifts Ban on Contacts with Sinn Fein" ("U.S. says the I.R.A. political wing seems committed to peace").[41]

Meantime, Clinton's personal legal troubles began to mount in 1994, including in relation to Congress. On the subject of the Whitewater investigation into his and Hillary's Arkansas years: "Clinton Asks [Attorney General] Reno To Name A Counsel On His Land Deals" as "President Bows to Pressure as He Tries to Avert Potential Inquiry by Congress"; "[Democratic Senator] Moynihan Urges Prosecutor To Study Clinton Land Deal"; "President Rebuts New Accusations Over Whitewater" ("Republican Lawmaker Accuses Administration of an Effort to Silence Investigators"); "Hillary Clinton Tackles Questions on Whitewater and Commodities Investments"; and "Bringing Another Presidency [Nixon's] and Inquiry to Mind." On the Savings and Loan legal case, "10 Clinton Aides Called In Inquiry On Arkansas S. & L." ("Reach of Investigation Is Furthest Since the Iran–Contra Case"). On another legal front, "Suit Accuses President Of Advances," as "Woman Bases Case On Civil Rights Law" with "Sex Harassment Suit Based on 1860's Law."[42]

Reasserting the Legislative Initiative

Starting to gear up for his next presidential campaign, Clinton seemed to bounce back in 1995 not long after the Republican victories in the mid-term Congressional elections in late 1994. Any talk of "Requiem for the Clinton Presidency" was premature. First Lady Hillary Clinton and Vice President Al Gore were reemerging in more commanding fashion. "Shifting Debate to the Political Climate, [President] Clinton Condemns 'Promoters of Paranoia.' " There was "A New Path for the New Democrat: Clinton Is Going It Alone." Toward year's end, strongly reassertive toward Congress in the unusually intense budget battle, "Clinton Gives Rallying Cry to the Troops On the Hill."[43]

As the year 1995 began, and "King Newt [Gingrich] and His Court Explore Virtual America," the undaunted "Clinton Goes To Heartland To Push Plan For Education," while his "Welfare Meeting Ends In Agreement On Common Goals." In his late-January State of the Union speech before Congress, "Clinton, With Bow to G.O.P., Reaffirms His Themes of '92 And Asks New Cooperation." Therein he also said, concerning illegal immigration, "we are a nation of immigrants but also a nation of laws." The Republican response by Gov. Whitman added that "success is not measured by the number of laws passed but in results." Shortly thereafter, invoking "Emergency Power," "Clinton Offers $20 Billion To Mexico For Peso Rescue; Action Sidesteps Congress" ("Risky Course for Clinton"—"Losing Support on Loan Guarantee Issue, President Chooses to Seize the Initiative"). Not surprisingly, "Clinton Budget Falls Short Of Republican Demands," and in the process "The President laterals a hot potato to Congress."[44]

Again on the counteroffensive legislatively, "Clinton Taking Hard Line on G.O.P. Revision of Crime Bill" ("Promises To Veto Measure On Police Funding"). Similarly: "Clinton To Fight Measure Revising Rules On Lawsuits" ("Landmark Legislation"); "Rejoining the Welfare Debate, Clinton Attacks G.O.P. Plans" in bills for overhaul; "Defending Hiring Preferences, Clinton Details Plan to Review Them"; "Clinton Newly Assertive, Lays Out Priorities for Legislation"; "Clinton Seeks Broad Powers In Battle Against Terrorism" after Oklahoma attack; "Clinton Bans Traffic in Front of the White House"; "Clinton Endorses Anti-Terrorism Measure," saying "Nothing can justify turning this bill into a political football"; "Clinton vs. Congress: The Race Is Set"; "With First Veto, Clinton Rejects Budget Cut Bill" ("New Offensive Opens Against the G.O.P."); "Clinton Offers His Plan For Balancing Budget" ("President makes an effort to regain ground lost to the G.O.P."); "Administration Proposes Federal Regulation of Health Insurance"; "Clinton Threatens a Veto of Bill Curbing Regulatory Powers"; "New Affirmative Action Guidelines Issued" by Clinton Administration; "Environment Gets a Push From Clinton" "against a wide array of [G.O.P.] Congressional proposals that would weaken several major environmental laws"; "Much School Prayer Legal, Clinton Says" ("The President acts to outflank calls for a constitutional amendment"); "Clinton to Toughen Rules on Lobbying the White House"; "President Issues Executive Order To Buttress Toxic Emission Rules" ("Using a Presidential power to show Presidential style"); "Clinton Announces Restrictions on Tobacco Products" ("A governmental shift from simply limiting advertising to controlling products"); "Clinton Prods Senate on the Welfare Overhaul"; "G.O.P.'s Plan to Cut Medicare Faces a Veto, Clinton Promises"; "President Voices Optimism On Hopes For Welfare Bill"; "White House Considers Toughening Its Anti-Emissions Program"; "President Warns Congress to Drop Some Budget Cuts" ("Gingrich tells Clinton to 'think twice' about vetoing the budget bill"); "Mr. Clinton Wields the Veto" on certain budget bills; "President Vetoes Stopgap Budget" as "Shutdown Looms"; "As Long Promised, President Vetoes the G.O.P. Budget"; "With No Budget, Clinton and Republicans Pass the Blame"; "2 More Spending Bills Vetoed But Clinton Offers to Negotiate"; "Welfare Bill Cleared by Congress and Now Awaits Clinton's Veto"; and "Clinton Vetoes Military Authorization Bill." Clearly, the preceding series of high-stakes multiple dramas over a surge of Presidential vetoes against Congressional legislative measures came to a great climax as 1995 drew to a close, against the more general background, during the course of that year, of resurgent legislative initiatives by the President.[45]

There was also a corresponding reaffirmation of presidential powers and initiatives in foreign affairs including in relation to Congressional lawmakers during 1995. For instance, "The Clinton Administration Reversed U.S. Policy on Cuban Refugees" by "Acting in secret" as "a small group made a major change." Several months later, "Clinton Signs Order Easing Travel, Aid and Money Transfers Between U.S. and Cuba." Another case was Bosnia: "With Congress Or Without It, Clinton To Aid U.N. in Bosnia"; "Clinton Defies Congress in Aid For Europeans' Bosnia Force" ("Dole and Gingrich protest on a power-of-the-purse issue"); "White House Seeks to Halt Bosnia Bill" ("Fears Senate Action Would Disrupt Allies [Efforts] to Curb Serbs"); "Clinton's Policy on Bosnia Draws Criticism in Congress" ("Lawmakers say the American position seems unclear"); and "Clinton Lays Out His Case For U.S. Troops In Balkans" ("Republican Leaders . . . Sit Out Clinton's Pitch to Skeptical Public").[46]

Building Bridges to Congress

A basic story of 1996 was how President Clinton, building momentum in his re-election campaign, was also building bridges to Congress and the public. In his January State of the Union speech, with Speaker Gingrich seated behind him, "Clinton Offers Challenge To Nation, Declaring 'Era Of Big Government Is Over' " in an "Appeal to Voters" as he "Revives Theme of '92 and Tries to Preempt G.O.P. Message" while "Talking Like a Front-Runner." On "What Clinton Is Doing Right," a reporter shortly thereafter said "He seizes the middle ground from frustrated Republicans and suddenly looks Presidential." Others were soon reporting on "The Making of the Rhetorical Presidency" ("Clinton's speeches begin to portray a man full of confidence") and "A President Who Can Absorb Body Blows." More to the point, "Despite His Reversals, Clinton Kept His Focus on Middle Ground" and, "Seizing the Crime Issue as His Own, Clinton Blurs Old Party Lines." Just as "Clinton's Welfare Shift Ends Tortuous Journey as a New Democrat" ("Election Politics Stall Proposal"), so too "Clinton Began His Term Like a Social Crusader, [and] Ends It Like a Politician" ("while taking most of the Republican issues away from them"). Likewise, the "President's Pragmatism Yields Strong Economy" ("But Can Clinton Take the Credit?").[47]

Building his bridges to Congress became ever more a Clinton project after his November 1996 victory, with Speaker Gingrich and the Republicans somewhat humbled by the Democrats' better-than-expected showing. It was called "A Mandate to Get Along" between Clinton and Gingrich. Similarly, "Historic Election Prods Clinton and Congress to Build a Bridge Across the Partisan Divide" ("Big question in Congress: Will it be cooperation or confrontation?"). In "The Balance Of Power . . . Republicans hold the House, but Speaker Gingrich will need to find common ground with Gephardt's Democrats." For his part, "Clinton Promises to Create a 'Coalition of the Center.' "[48]

During this election year, the Executive–Congressional legislative process moved ahead along various lines. In March, for example, "Clinton Meets With G.O.P. To Discuss Legislative Aims" in his "First Encounter with [Republican Presidential nominee Senator] Dole Since Primaries." The veto power was still being exercised. On abortion, "Use of Women in Vetoing Abortion Bill Highlights Clinton Strategy to Win in Fall" and "Saying Women Shouldn't Be Pawns, Clinton Vetoes Bill Barring Late Term Abortion." Clinton obviously had his critics, while seeming to take issues away from Republicans—"Clinton, in Emotional Terms, Explains His ["Much

Attacked"] Abortion Veto." More generally on "The Line-Item Veto Versus the Constitution," "Add the line-item veto to the president's powers and a strong-willed president might well become unassailable." Other legislative matters proved contentious, as when "Dole–Clinton Legislative Fight [on Health Bill] Previews Campaign to Come" and "Clinton Challenges Congress to Pass Terrorism Bill He'd Approve." Saying "Whatever needs to be done, we will do it," "Clinton Sets Tougher Rules for Air Security" after a major crash. In the end, once again, with his sweeping reelection victory despite the Republicans managing to keep control of Congress, the "President's Success Lay in Ability to Co-opt Republican Issues."[49]

4. PRESIDENT CLINTON'S SECOND TERM

Gearing Up and Gearing Down

President Clinton's second term began in early 1997 with renewed energy including in relation to Congress. In January, "Clinton, Sworn In For 2d Term, Assails 'Bickering And Extreme Partisanship' " and "Sees a Time of Healing for New Government and New Century," while taking "Presidential Refuge In Political Center." "Asserting his power, President Clinton reanimates his office" in "The Second Start." In his early February State of the Union Message to Congress, the "President, Citing Education As Top Priority Of 2d Term, Asks For A 'Call to Action,' " saying "That Much Can Be Done Despite Shrinking Budget." When "Clinton Presents '98 Budget," he "Seeks Tax Cuts and Vows End to Deficits." Some major decisions lay ahead: "American Airline Pilots Strike But Clinton Orders Them Back"; "Gore Promises Labor Leaders Tough Rules on Contractors"; and "President Orders Federal Agencies to Hire Off Welfare Rolls." The veto power reached new levels: "President Makes First Use of New Veto" as "3 Narrow Items in Money Bills Are Killed"; "Clinton's Great and Timid Step" as "The line item veto controls Congress"; and "Clinton Again Exercises the Line Item Veto" as he "Vetoes 38 Military Items, Drawing Many Lawmakers' Ire." On the I.R.S.: "White House Says It Supports A Bill To Overhaul I.R.S."; "Clinton will trigger fire storm if he vetoes an IRS reform bill. But he has no choice" ("Rubin [Treasury Secretary] vs. Capitol Hill"); "Reversing Course on I.R.S., Clinton Takes the Wind Out of Republican Sails" ("From Political Fight To Bipartisanship"). In their "Conspiracy Of Celebration," "Congress and Clinton finally balanced the budget. But in their haste to hand out goodies, they missed a chance to defuse some time bombs."[50]

Yet near year's end in December 1997 there were also signs of a slowing down in Presidential activity. "A Mellow Clinton at Ease in His Role" was looking ahead into his "Second Term: From his Big Battles to Comfort and Command," while "Looking at the End of a Political Life." "Increasingly, the Clinton Presidency Is Defined by the Many Parts of Its Sum." In "Clinton's Drip, Drip, Drip Presidency," the "President avoids big congressional battles—and redefines how Oval Office sets policy."[51]

On foreign policy there were also varied signs and stories of winding up as well as a winding down during the first year of Clinton's second term. "Is Clinton Ready to Lead the Hemisphere?" "Clinton Plays to History, With Renewed Panache" ("At first, Clinton confined himself to domestic matters. That has changed"). "Clinton Retreats On Trade Power" and is "Bruised"—"A Handicap for Clinton But U.S. Still Dominates," while "Tone of 'Protectionism' Is Sensed by a G.O.P. Leader in House." Overall, "Clinton Rushes to Craft Global Legacy" ("From the Mideast to Asia, he aims to dispel idea that his policies are shortsighted, weak"). Meanwhile, "Gore Walks a Political Tightrope at Kyoto Talks" ("Trying to balance the demands of environmentalists and industrialists"). Also, "Remember Al Gore—Environmental Leader?" ("His mistake has been to let the Beltway environmental groups set the agenda, and then play the compromise game").[52]

Part and parcel of the perceived signs of a winding down of the Clinton Presidency in the first year of its second term was the rising tide of legal troubles faced by the Clintons due to investigations, court cases, and Congressional activities. These difficulties had already been growing in 1996 but had not been sufficient to derail the re-election campaign. There was the Whitewater case (with perceived echoes of Watergate), the F.B.I. files, missing billing records, the travel office (or Travelgate), and other matters stemming from Clinton's Arkansas years as Governor. These matters took on new intensity and urgency in 1997, along with the increasing alleged sexual matters. A brief sampling of these developments in news stories must suffice, with some legal–legislative ramifications: "Harassment Case Against Clinton Now at Highest Level"; "The President Is Not Above the Law"; "Clinton's next trial" ("Why illegal documents will bedevil the Democrats"); "Clinton Teeters On Legal Edge Of Finance Law"; "Fund-Raiser Helped Members of Congress"; "Gore Says He Did Nothing Illegal In Soliciting From White House"; "The Law According to Gore"; "Anything Goes— It's the Law" ("The Clintons lead the way in hiding behind legalities"); "Whitewater Counsel Says He Has Evidence Of Obstructed

Justice"; "White House Vows to Appeal Order to Open Notes"; "The Limits of Presidential Immunity"; "Reno, In Letter To Congress, Rejects Most Allegations That Clinton Violated Law"; "Clinton Says Fund-Raising Was Within 'Letter of Law' "; "Money in politics is a problem, but persecuting Al Gore is no solution" ("In 100 years of this law's existence [Pendleton Act of 1883], no one has been tried for the 'crime' of which Gore is accused"); "Clinton And His Enemies" ("A winning equanimity in the face of attack").[53]

Facing a Legal Avalanche

The Clinton presidency was increasingly faced in 1998 with an avalanche of legal–constitutional troubles that threatened to derail it. The avalanche had been building up in 1996–1997 and now came thundering down on Bill Clinton personally and on his office.

In January there were "Subpoenas Sent As Clinton Denies Reports Of An Affair With Aide At White House." "Accusations Presenting Many Issues at the Law," read another headline on Clinton's alleged affair with ex-intern Monica Lewinsky when she worked at the White House. "When Reckless Laws Team Up," read another, a "Harassment suit plus independent counsel equals runaway train." Reacting immediately, "White House Starts Effort To Contain Its Problems" as "Clinton Prepares to Speak of Policy, not Predicament," with "No signs of an allusion to scandal." In the meantime, "Job Approval Rate Holds Despite Scandal, Poll Says." Still struggling to focus on his legislative agenda, as the "Ripple Becomes Media Tidal Wave," "Clinton, With Crisis Swirling Puts Focus On Social Security In Upbeat State of Union Talk," in which "He Proposes Billions in Spending for Variety of Social Programs." Yet it was quickly becoming "Starr At War," while "As the Clintons strike back, the prosecutor struggles to build his case." Then it became "The Clinton Rally" in which "The president . . . was flying high— and Kenneth Starr's investigation was struggling." It was also called "The Age of Entrapment" in terms of "An Alderman, the President, and law enforcement excess." At any rate, it was during this same period in January–February 1998 that Clinton scored a solid achievement in Congress when announcing in early January that he would "Seek a Balanced Budget for 1999, Two Years Earlier Than Expected." He finally submitted "First Balanced Budget Plan in Nearly 30 Years."[54]

In March, after "Executive Privileges Invoked In Clinton Aides' Testimony," the "White House's All-Out Attack on Starr Is Paying Off With His Help," for "Starr's errors have given the White House some ammunition" and "may have gone too far," despite "Echoes of Watergate." The pace of events was quickening still further. Paula "Jones Lawyers Issue Files Alleging Clinton Pattern Of Harassment Of Women," while Clinton gave "Testimony for Deposition in Jones Lawsuit." A few days later, "White House Attacks Credibility Of Aide Who Accused Clinton." Then "President's Team Demands Dismissal of Jones Lawsuit," while "Clinton Asserts [Executive] Privilege to Bar Query to Aides." Negative editorials on Clinton abounded even in liberal news publications—as in one by evangelist Billy Graham on "The Moral Weight of Leadership" ("Those with the greatest standing in society need the highest integrity") and another by conservative columnist William Safire on "U.S. Versus Clinton" ("A President against the law," whose "power-abusive attempt to carve out a personal privilege that places him above the law" may result in impeachment). Nevertheless, other reporters were wondering "Why is he so darn popular?"—"Now he seems unsinkable. What happened?" Or, "Outrageous Fortune"—"The slings and arrows of sex and politics have not denied Clinton high ratings. Is it a new kind of Teflon, or do foes just lack the right weapon?" Then, in early April, "Paula Jones' Case Is Dismissed" as "Judge Says Even If Tale Is True, Incident Was Not Harassment" ("The ruling puts in question a separate criminal inquiry by Kenneth W. Starr"). Whereupon "White House Pushes Starr To End His Investigation," although Starr says he "Won't Be Swayed From the Criminal Inquiry," perhaps instead "pursuing the charges of perjury."[55]

Seeing the End of the "Imperial Presidency"?

The rest of 1998 was increasingly tumultuous. According to an August report on "Breakdown on the Road to History," "Bill Clinton thought 1998 would be the year to cement his place in the big book of Presidents. But Starr is doing most of the writing." A week earlier, a portentous assessment in an editorial by Arthur Schlesinger, Jr., author of *The Imperial Presidency* in the wake of the Nixon era, exclaimed "So Much for the Imperial Presidency."[56]

The legal imbroglio from April on in 1998 was already fast developing as "Clinton Aides Step Up Attack on Starr Inquiry" ("Anticipating a report to Congress, the Administration mounts an offense as a defense"). Yet Congress was not yet sure of itself, as reported in " 'You Must Play by the Rules' " ("With the Paula Jones case dismissed and Congress skittish, Kenneth Starr becomes the final arbiter of Clinton's fate"). Meanwhile, the "White House Bid To Cite

'Privilege' Fails, Lawyers Say" ("Prosecutor Wants Clinton Aides To Testify About Lewinsky"). But then "Judge Rejects Bid To Cite 'Privilege' In Clinton Inquiry" and "Says Secret Service Can Be Forced to Testify About the President." Whereupon the "President Decides to Abandon His Claim of Executive Privilege. But He Still Presses for Attorney–Client Privilege." Next, the Supreme "Court Rebuffs Starr's Plea On Privilege" and his "Request To Speed Review." Again, "Justices Deal Starr a Defeat, Holding That the Attorney–Client Privilege Survives Death." Shortly thereafter, "In Slap At Starr, A Judge Dismisses Hubble Tax Case, Citing Prosecutor's Tactics." Then Federal Appeals Court "Judge Turn Down Justice Dept. In Bid to Block Agents' Testimony." When "Clinton Agrees To Testify For Lewinsky Grand Jury," "Starr Retracts Subpoena." In early August Congressional "Lawmakers Call For Explanation In Lewinsky Case." An August editorial by a former Democratic Congresswoman from the Nixon era, now less than friendly to Starr, focused on "Not Why We Wrote The [original Independent Counsel] Act."[57]

The above legal entanglements between President, Court, and Congress would now become ever more complex and threatening as 1998 went on. "Starr May Have Breached Ethics Rules, Judge Says." Also, "Former Special Counsels See Need To Alter Law [Ethics in Government Act of 1978] That Created Them." Despite these adverse signs for himself, "Starr to Confront President After Four Years of Gathering Evidence." The following day, "Clinton Admits Lewinsky Liaison To Jury" and "Tells Nation 'It Was Wrong,' But Private." Early September showed some signs of "Support for Clinton As [He] Apologizes to Senators and Aides." But "Starr Report Is Said To Claim Perjury And Abuse Of Power By President in Lewinsky Case." Upon issuing and sending his 445-page report to Congress on September 9, "Starr Finds A Case For Impeachment In Perjury, Obstruction, [and] Tampering," while "Clinton Staff Derides 'Lurid' Account of Lewinsky Case." But "What's an Impeachable Offense? Past Is Fuzzy," asked one headline, with the caption " 'High crimes and misdemeanors' define an exact definition for the 1990's." After the Starr report went to Congress, the "White House, In Rebuttal to Starr, Assails Report As 'Smear Campaign.' " Even so, the "Impeachment Report Is Not the Final Word in Starr's Sweeping Inquiry" ("No criminal charges have been filed, at least not yet"), with "Sharp Divisions on Judiciary Panel" and "Censure ... Getting Closer Look." Two news magazines with featured comments on the Starr report addressed the unsettling questions it raised for Congress and the public: "A rocky road to impeachment" ("Congress has one eye on the evidence, the other on the polls") and "High Crimes? Or Just A Sex-Cover-Up?" ("Starr shows all the ways Clinton tried to keep Monica quiet. It's not Watergate").[58]

Following Clinton's grand jury testimony later on in September 1998, "Poll Finds Clinton In Strong Rebound Since Video Airing," while even before then "Most in Poll Say President Should Remain In Office." But the legal saga was not winding down. By mid-November "It's Impeachment or Nothing, Scholars Warn Lawmakers at Hearing" before House panel. By that point, "Starr to Accuse President of Obstructing His Inquiries." Then "Clinton Responds to [Congressman] Hyde's Queries" but "Yields No Ground" to Hyde's Judiciary Committee. In mid-December, as the climax neared, "Facing Impeachment Vote, Clinton Denies Perjury and Says He Will Not Resign." As "Judgment Day" approached (while "The president awaits his punishment"), the question was "Will They Really Do It?" But then on December 17–18 there was a pause—"Impeachment Vote In House Delayed As Clinton Launches Iraq Air Strike, Citing Military Need To Move Swiftly." But then "House to Debate Impeachment Today As U.S. Continues Air Assault on Iraq."[59]

On the legislative front in 1998, it was reported that "Clinton Perfects the Art of Go-It-Alone Governing: Feeling stymied by G.O.P. on the Hill, president pushes agenda through executive orders, vetoes, and publicity." Some examples might include: "White House Adds Broad Protection In Medicare Rules" ("Strengthening 1997 Law"); "Clinton To Punish Insurers Who Deny Health Coverage" ("Those Evading a '96 Law to Be Forbidden to Cover Millions of Federal Employees"); "Clinton Plans $25 Million Initiative on Infectious Diseases"); "U.S. Bolsters Housing Aid For the Elderly"; or even "Clinton Turns His Aura Into Campaign Gold" ("Despite Starr probe, president gets smiles, cheers, and checks from party faithful"). At the same time, there were setbacks for Clinton's presidential powers, as when Supreme Court "Justices . . . Bar Veto Of Line Items In Bills" ("Spending At Issue," "Clinton Calls Ruling on His Power a 'Defeat' for all Americans") and "House Rejects Expanded Trade Power for President." Still alive was the Presidential–Congressional tug-of-war as when "Clinton and G.O.P. Press Rival Plans on Health Care." Presidential preemption in foreign affairs was exhibited when "U.S. Cruise Missiles Strike Sudan And Afghan Targets Tied To Terrorist Network" in late August shortly after Starr's questioning of Clinton and Clinton's ensuing public admissions, not unlike the later U.S. bombing of Iraq in December as the House moved toward impeachment.[60]

Mounting a Legislative Counteroffensive

Following the House's vote in early October to hold an impeachment inquiry and its vote in late December to impeach Clinton, the Senate in mid-January 1999 began hearing the House's case against Clinton and in late January began debate on the issue after Clinton's defense team concluded. It was a prolonged period of high drama and uncertainty for all sides. In mid-February however, Clinton was finally acquitted of the two charges of perjury and obstruction of justice, yet he was strongly rebuked by both sides of the aisle. These matters will be included in our next chapter on the U.S. Congress. What follows here is a look at the legislative counteroffensive mounted by the Clinton Administration in 1999 and into 2000, an effort no less striking than the well-known transparent bombings overseas cited directly above but less well perceived by reporters and historians as part of a highly significant domestic effort and pattern by the self-described "comeback kid."[61]

In January 1999 it was "Clinton on trial" as "A placid president and a tense Congress prepare for their historic—and unprecedented—day in court." It was now "In the dock of history" "As Clinton talks policy, [and] the Senate agrees on the shape of his trial." In connection with his State of the Union address before Congress in later January, "Unbounded, Clinton Presses Social Security Plan" according to which the Federal Government would invest for the first time in the stock market to strengthen Social Security. In his address, "Clinton Outlines His Vision for Nation's Transition to the 21st Century." In "The last campaign . . . Everything Clinton did during his amazing week [in late January] served one purpose: to save his skin." It was asked "Does he want a deal or a fight?" ("A resurgent Clinton jabs his agenda at the G.O.P. and seems to leave little room for compromise"). In the meantime, "Gore Seeks to Protect Trade From World's Fiscal Crisis."[62]

As the Clinton crisis was nearing its culminating point, "Starr Is Sure He Has Constitutional Authority to Indict Clinton in Office. . . ." More to the legal–legislative point originally was "The law that bit Clinton," an article in which the observer commented on "a 1994 law that allowed harassment lawyers to rummage around in the sexual histories of accused men and grill them. . . . But without this law, President Clinton could not have been questioned under oath about Monica Lewinsky in the Paula Jones case. No Lewinsky, no need to lie about Lewinsky, no impeachment."[63]

To be sure, there were many ensuing reports of a fallen presidency. "Thanks to Clinton, 'We've had the minimalization of the presidency,' [Democratic Senator] Moynihan says," in mid-February 1999. "The Presidency Is Still There, Not Quite the Same," read another account. In March there were reported "Telltale signs of twilight in Clinton's presidency." In foreign policy (April), "How a President, Distracted by Scandal, Entered Balkan War" ("Diplomacy Stumbles Amid Ultimatums, Miscalculations"). Such reports were not quite so negative as another story a half-year earlier on "American Caligula" ("Clinton's problem . . . is a fundamental lack of respect for his country").[64]

Yet signs of a resurgent legislative counteroffensive were emerging. The following self-evident news accounts, in chronological sequence, were illustrative during the course of 1999: "Clinton to Unveil Spending Plan Marked by Conservatism" ("Budget Includes New Domestic Programs and More Money Interests"); "Temptations [for Clinton] of a big U.S. budget surplus"; "Clinton Orders Job Relief In Aftermath of [Oklahoma] Tornadoes"; "Clinton Urges Film Industry to Limit Violence on Screen"; "White House Will Propose Public School Choice Plan"; "Gores and Clintons, Relaxed and Intent, Turn to Initiatives on Mental Illness"; "Clinton To Unveil Plan To Allocate Budget [Surpluses] Windfall" ("Social Security, Medicare and Other Programs to Benefit—Political Fight Likely"); "Clinton Outlines Plan For Surplus" that "May Allow G.O.P. Tax Cuts and New Spending"; "Clinton Restricts Imports of Brazilian Steel—and Australian Lamb"; "U.S. [Clinton Administration] Issuing New Rules to Gain Contracts" ("A Federal bar to corporate lawbreakers"); "Clinton Plan to Seek Out Those Eligible for Food Stamps"; "Clinton Urges G.O.P. in Congress to Shrink Tax Cut Plan to Aid Medicare"; "At News Conference, Clinton Takes On All Comers and Denies He Is 'Winding Down' " (". . . a chance to show command of the issues"); "White House Used Auditors Against a Bill . . . On G.O.P. Finance Plan"; "Clinton Refuses Subpoena for Material on Clemency" ("Says Congress Lacks Authority Over the Matter"); "In a Reversal, White House Will End Data-Encryption Export Curbs"; "Clinton Urges Stronger Law Setting Rights For Patients"; "President Urges Government To Reach Uninsured Children"; "Clinton Orders Government to Try to Hire More Disabled"; "U.S. [Clinton Administration] to Release Rules On Use of Donor Organs"; "Clinton Renews His Appeal on Gun Control" ("But Prospects for Passage Fade as Congress Remains Deadlocked"); "Clinton Is Going on the Offensive to Offer the Elderly a Drug Plan"; "Clinton's Rules on Medical Privacy Fuel Debate Over Patients' Rights"; "[G.O.P. Congressional] Lawmakers chafe at Clinton's use of executive orders"; "Clinton Signs Final Budget Bill and Turns to

New Year" ("Thoughts on fiscal battles to come over how to spend projected surpluses"); "U.S. Seeks to Restore Limits on Cable Sex Programming"; "Clinton Calls Brady [anti-gun] Law a Success and Backs More Limits"; "A Clinton Order Seeks to Reduce Medical Errors"; "U.S. Uses Threat of Lawsuit as a Lever for Deal on Guns," thereby angering the gun industry at Clinton Administration for usurping or circumventing powers of Congress' regulatory domain; "Clinton Tells Gays He Will Seek to Change Way 'Don't Tell' Policy Is Used"; "Stricter Pollution Controls [by Clinton Administration] Set for Cars and Light Trucks" ("New rules hold vehicles to the same emission standards"); "Clinton Allays Criticism of New Pollution Rules"; "Online pharmacies draw federal scrutiny" ("The Clinton Administration proposes rules to prevent internet drug-sale fraud"); and "Clinton Plans New Vouchers For Working-Class Housing" "in the federal budget that he will send to Congress."[65]

By the fall of 1999, the "White House Inquiry Still Stews As Starr Prepares to Step Down." "Starr, Defending His Inquiry, Urges Clinton to 'Get Himself Right With the Law.' " Yet as the probe waned, public attention was being drawn in 1999 to various other long-range features of the Clinton presidency as it was entering its final phases. These features included: "Clinton's imprint on the judiciary"; "How Clinton reinvented the center" ("His move to the political middle helps unite Democrats, co-opt GOP issues, and is shaping run for White House"); "Clinton's Twin Aims: Win the War [in former Yugoslavia] and Keep the U.S. Electorate Content"; "A Just and Necessary War" (title of an editorial by Clinton); and "The Clinton presidency's feminine mystique" ("Clinton's style has resounded with many women").[66]

Rounding Out a Massive Legislative Record

In 2000, rounding out the massive cumulative legislative record of the Clinton Administration, was another strong major series of disparate initiatives and measures that cast further doubt on the view that the "imperial presidency" had ended. Some of the highlights were as follows, again in chronological sequence: "President's Decree Protects Thousands of Miles in West"; "Clinton Seeks New Spending to Enforce Laws on Guns"; "A Government Edict [by Clinton Administration] On Care for Disabled" ("Using a Supreme Court decision to get more humane care for the disabled"); "Clinton To Order Steps To Reduce Medical Mistakes" ("A Mandate for Hospitals"); "Time Sensitive Clinton Presses Agenda" ("President Urges Republicans [in Congress] to Back His Last Group of Initiatives");

"White House Steps Up Effort for Support of China Trade Bill"; "Power Array Pushes the China Trade Bill" spearheaded by V.P. Gore in Congress; "President Views Success of China Trade Bill as His Foreign Policy Legacy" ("National security has become the rallying cry"); "Clinton to Order Medicare to Pay New Costs"; "Clinton's campaign to end-run Congress" ("He's making policy changes by executive order" [and circumventing Congress' authority?]); "Blocked by Congress, Clinton Wields Pen" ("The White House continues to make policy by decree"); "President's Veto Sets Up a Battle on Marriage Tax"; "President Vetoes Effort to Repeal Taxes on Estates" ("Republicans Vow A Fight"); "Clinton Plans to Issue Rules Expanding Patients' Rights" ("The president tries to get around an impasse in Congress"); "Clinton Orders A New Auction of the Airwaves"; "Clinton Seeks to Regulate Common Gas to Clean Air" ("He May Encounter Opposition in Congress"); "Clinton to Issue New Rules On Medical Data Privacy" ("First Federal Standards for Confidentiality"); and, in a judicial matter, again showing his circumventions of Congress, "Clinton Names A Black Judge" and "Skirts Congress."[67]

On other, more general fronts in 2000 and again suggesting a Clinton rebound despite some additional personal setbacks, news reports like the following appeared, often with further relevance for his legislative agenda and his legacy: "Time Again for Clinton's Reinvention" especially in relation to his January State of the Union message to Congress; "Clinton's wage gap plan may boost Gore"; "Clinton Claims Bragging Rights to Nation's Prosperity" when putting forth "Grand Ideas" and "Keeping an Eye on Legacy," all in his State of the Union address; "In Glow of [that] Speech, Clinton Basks in Public Warmth"; "How historians size up Clinton: 'Not too bad' " ("President gets high marks for booming economy, low for personal control"); "A Teary Look Back: As the Clinton presidency enters its last months, nostalgia is setting in"; and "The Antitrust Administration" ("Clinton's antitrust team leaves a legacy of vigorous enforcement").[68]

At the same time, criticisms of the Clinton White House continued, albeit less pronounced, in 2000. On rules and laws in relation to national security, for instance, it was asked "Could the U.S. Be Exporting Trouble?" ("Looser rules on supercomputer sales may put nuclear capability in the hands of rogue nations"). More pointedly, "Bush Leads G.O.P. Criticism of Gore Over Russian Arms" and how "a secret pact flaunted the law and threatened security." Yet the "Arms Deal Tied to Gore Is Called Within Law" by Clinton Administration. As for Clinton's personal legal troubles, there were still calls for "Bringing Justice to Clinton" even though "Holding presidents accountable takes legal finesse." In April, "President Says He Won't Seek a Pardon if He's Indicted." In May, "Arkansas Panel Recommends That Clinton Be Disbarred." In September, "Whitewater Inquiry Ends" as "A Lack Of Evidence Is Cited In Case Involving Clintons," while "White House Sees Major Victory." At end, in November, it was said that "Gilded era yields a diminished presidency." Thus the pros and cons of the Clinton era were still being debated, although the above legislative accounts speak volumes by themselves.[69]

5. PRESIDENT BUSH JR.'S FIRST TERM

Winning the Y2K Election (Or, an "Accidental President" Without Congress' Support?)

For many weeks after the presidential election in November of "year two thousand" ("Y2K"), it was not clear who won—George Bush Jr. or Albert Gore. At the end, in electoral votes, it came down to who won the state of Florida, which went through prolonged turmoil in figuring out the results. Although Bush was eventually declared the winner there, the outcome was much disputed by the Gore team in hopes of a reversal, which failed to occur. The Florida courts became involved as did the Florida legislature. Looking back in June, one news report, entitled "Florida Revisited: How Vague Laws, Faulty Planning and Human Error Led to a Fiasco," concluded as follows: "A confounding array of vague laws, arbitrary local decisions and erratic leadership by Florida Secretary of State Katherine Harris's office resulted in turmoil across the state." A week later, the same publication reported on "The [Florida] System's Broken, But This Is No Way to Fix It" ("Legislation toward statewide purges of voter rolls risks a repeat of the Florida foul-up"). Calls for nationwide reforms in states' voting systems continued to grow in order to ensure the legitimacy of election outcomes. Criticisms of the U.S. Supreme Court for having taken up the case, and for letting stand the Florida Court's ruling on Bush's behalf as the declared winner, continued to be heard. In the following December, "Ending Impasse, [U.S.] Senate Leaders Agree to Overhaul Nation's Voting Systems." In October 2002, almost two years after the Y2K election, "Congress Passes Bill To Clean Up Election System" ("Federal Role Expanded" as "U.S. Offers States Money and New Standards"). Two weeks after that, "Bush Signs Legislation Intended to End Voting Disputes."[70]

Thus a case could be made for the deciding role of legislative issues in the disputed Y2K election and its aftermath. Clearly, the role of legislation and legislatures was paramount. Further light will be shed on this topic in sections further below on the U.S. Supreme Court and on the state of Florida. Already by March of 2000 it had been reported that "Rights Panel Chief Warns Florida on Elections"—she was "Waiting to see how legislators change voting system" that had led to the Y2K fiasco.[71]

During the many weeks of confusion and uncertainty over the results of the Y2K election, one could wonder if the eventual winner could lead effectively, considering the unusual narrowness and difficulties of a declared victory. A week or so after the election, "Bush Sues To Halt Hand Recount In Florida." Shortly before that, "Gore Campaign Vows Court Fight Over Vote With Florida's Outcome Still In The Air." By January, however, "Results Official, at Last: Bush Defeats Gore." By inauguration time later in January, Bush was coming into his own: "Despite his narrow win, Bush presses his agenda. . . . Some things look the same, but the son has a clearer idea of what he wants to do." By the end of January, "Bush Transition Is Largely a Success. All Agree" ("Analysts Find a Few Missteps but Note a Deft Touch in Dealing With Congress"). Although "Court Battle for Presidency Rages On in Legal Circles," attention was being brought to "Mr. Bush's Smooth Start."[72]

The question arose as to whether George Bush Jr. was—due to the circumstances of his election and a divided Congress—an "accidental President" without public mandate or Congressional support for Executive legislative initiatives or agendas. The answer to that question depended in part on one's particular perspective. It also depended on the perspectives to follow on Bush's first term as a whole, leading to the further question of whether he in fact became an "Imperial President" acting as a kind of "super-legislator with a strong public mandate and a decisive Congressional majority.

Reversing Clinton's Initiatives and Policies

In mid-January of 2001, before he was inaugurated, it was said "Bush Hopes to Review and Reverse Recent Clinton Initiatives." The changes to come would be partly a matter of Bush's style as "C.E.O., U.S.A.": "The first president with a business degree actually does have a plan—sell, delegate, and get out of the way." Or was this approach a neo-Reagan downsizing and deregulation but with less involvement by the President? "Under a New Administration, Rules About to Be Published Might Now Perish." Straight off, "Bush Reverses Clinton Policy on Federal Aid for Abortion Counselling Overseas." Now it was "Bush Rules! It's Good To Be President" ("Executive orders require only the stroke of a pen. Some of Clinton's are less inviolate than others"). In March the "Senate Votes to Repeal Clinton Workplace Injury Rules." Then the "House Joins Senate in Repealing Rules on Workplace Injuries." It was significant as well as symptomatic when "Work-safety rules fall in post-Clinton era," for "With G.O.P. in control, Congress is undoing a major labor–union victory." Meanwhile, "Bush Is Facing Battle in Congress Over Plans to Reduce or Limit Spending on Many Programs." In May "Bush Will Modify Limits By Clinton on Forest Roads." It was "The Feeling Of a Coup" with "Mr. Bush's radical moves and policy reversals." As for "Clinton's 'Last-Minute' Rules"—"Upon closer examination, last January's presidential decisions were years in the making."[73]

Quickly taking charge in January 2001, the new President Bush was pressing ahead with his new agenda. "The inauguration over, Bush pushes his agenda—and reaches out for allies." In "Romancing the Lawmakers," "Bush plans to round up support among the Democrats." It was called "No Mandate, but Plenty of Ambition" ("From Bush's long-range agenda, you'd think he'd won by a landslide"). Already by late February, for a variety of reasons, attention was drawn to "The Incredible Shrinking Ex-President," Clinton.[73a]

As for his general approach as "Another kind of leader," "Will Bush's CEO-style management work in Washington?" Comments were directed to "Bush's first tests using the bully pulpit." His "Presidency Takes Shape With No Fuss, No Sweat." Yet in the "Corporate Look for the White House," "Bush, a self-styled on-time president, delegates easily and often." He was "Trying to Run a Country Like a Corporation." Meantime, it was "The V.P. as Prime Minister," for "Cheney will wield unusual power in running the country." He was called "Dick Cheney, Energy Czar." Thus, "Quietly but Firmly, Cheney Is Emerging as a Washington Power Broker."[74]

Dealing with Congress

During his first year in office in 2001, President Bush dealt with Congress on many different specific legislative fronts. In late January in one of his first major moves, "Bush Introduces Proposal To Improve Education." In early February, "Bush Tax Plan Sent to Congress, and Jostling Starts." In later February, "Bush, Spelling Out Agenda To Congress, Makes Tax Cut Centerpiece Of The Budget." As expected, "First Bush Budget Proposes To Raise Aid For Education." Then the "Senate Takes On Bush's Education Bill as Some Conservatives Grumble." By early May, "G.O.P. Lawmakers and White House Agree on Tax Cut." By early June, the "President's Signature Turns Broad Tax Cut, and a Campaign Promise, Into Law." Whereupon in July, "Bush, After Gaining Tax Cut, Is Taking Aim at Tax Code." Here, then, was a prime example of the contemporary presidency out in front of Congress in spearheading the legislative process.[75]

Despite the close election and a divided Congress (with the Senate at 50/50), President Bush advanced his legislative program in the weeks and months after taking office, submitting a series of plans and measures to Congress in an orderly fashion somewhat in the manner of a British Prime Minister. True, much of his efforts were aimed at reversing Clinton's measures and deregulating many sectors of society. Yet Bush was no Reagan-like crusader against government itself, for he contributed in many ways to the further buildup of government. Some of his approaches in mid-2001 were as follows: "Bush Asks Congress to Grant Him a 'Fast Track' in Trade Talks"; "Bush, Pushing Energy Plan, Offers Scores Of Proposals To Find New Power Sources" ("Excessive Regulation Is Blamed for Energy Woes"); "Administration Clarifies New U.S. Rules Guarding Privacy of Patients"; and "Bush Says He Will Veto Any Bill Broadening His Stem Cell Policy."[76]

Entering the Post–9/11 World

The Bush Administration's focus changed after the terrorist attack on New York's World Trade Center on September 11, 2001. As reported on the front page of one New York newspaper in later October, Congress passed, and the President signed into law, sweeping anti-terrorist legislation. In late November, the same newspaper showed extensively how "Bush's New Rules to Fight Terror Transform the Legal Landscape"—together with such captions as "Bill With Long Name And Longer Reach," "Swift Secret Justice And No Appeals," and "Swept Up in a Dragnet, Hundreds Still in Custody and Ask Why?" In that same publication, Republican Senator Arlen Specter, in an editorial "Questioning the President's Authority" believed that "Congress should have its say on military tribunals." Two days later "Groups Gird For Long Legal Fight On New Bush Anti-Terror Powers," while, for his part, "President Defends Military Tribunals In Terrorist Cases," saying that "Foe 'Has Declared War.' " In early December, it was asked on "War-Powers: Is

Bush Making History?" Issues were being raised by some on "War and the Constitution" with regard to secret detentions, military tribunals, faith in the courts, and the rule of law. At that point, "Bush Claims Executive Privilege in Response to House Inquiry." Critics claimed that "Big Brother Is Watching" as "The Bush administration seeks to give the FBI and Justice broader surveillance powers."[77]

Thus in very short order in the last months of 2001, the Bush Administration had largely transformed its main focus and agenda in domestic as well as foreign affairs with regard to its anti-terrorist measures. At root it was a transformation in law and legislation in new variations on our central themes of sovereignty and state in legislative perspectives. In early December, a news issue presented a series of articles on "The Powerful Bush Presidency" that indicated the broad growing sweep of presidential power quickly being amassed. In the first article, on "The Powerful Presidency," it was said that "Bush's White House claims authority rivaling FDR's." In "Justice for All?" "Critics say [Attorney General] Ashcroft's aggressive methods to fight terrorism go too far." In "The Dragnet's Downside," "Former FBI officials say long-term investigations are needed to quell terrorists." In "A New Anxiety," "Immigrants who felt welcome here feel a chill in the air since Sept. 11." In "A Role Reversal," "Criticism of the U.S. war in Afghanistan is coming from the right, not the left."[78]

On into 2003 the same themes prevailed. "Taking Command in Crisis, Bush Wields New Powers." As for "America as Reflected in Its Leader," after 9/11, Americans "now see the president as they want him to be." In his late-January speech to Congress, "Focusing on Terrorism, Bush Declares a Secure U.S. the Top Priority."[79]

Affirming Wartime Powers and Sovereignty

As President Bush's buildup of anti-terrorist efforts were underway, he naturally sought financial and other support from Congressional lawmakers. In February 2002, "President Submits $2 Trillion Budget That Raises Deficit" and that "Seeks Military Buildup, Tax Cuts and Otherwise Austerity." The following August, with the "Administration Seeking to Build Support in Congress on Iraq Issue," "France and Britain Press for Working With U.N." In September, "President To Seek Congress's Assent Over Iraq Action" and "Will Meet With [British Prime Minister] Blair and Talk to U.N." The question was "How Far Can Bush Go Without Congress?" although "Aides say he needs no further approval to attack Iraq. . . ."

In the meantime, "Bush Tells Congress to Move Quickly on Terrorism Insurance." In October, "Bush Strikes Deal For House Backing On Action In Iraq" through "A Bipartisan Agreement." Shortly thereafter, "Bush Will Use Congress Vote To Press U.N." for "a Tough Ruling to Make Iraq Disarm." In November, "After G.O.P. Triumph [in Congressional elections], Bush Sets Security Department and Tax Cuts as Priorities." Not just in his efforts to take Iraq to task over its alleged involvement in the 9/11 terrorist attacks in the U.S., Bush was projecting U.S. authority in other foreign affairs. For instance, "Bush Says [Palestinian leader] Arafat Must Go If U.S. Is to Back New [Palestinian] State."[80]

Press coverage of President Bush's copings with Iraq and with Congress in relation to Iraq during the year 2003 again offers an instructive chronicle of events and positions with import for legislative perspectives on issues of sovereignty and state. In April, Bush was referred to as "The Power of One" inasmuch as "However you feel about the war, George W. Bush is the real thing: a leader." Examples to come in 2003 of Bush's leadership and initiatives on Iraq included the following: "On Order From Bush, U.S. Troops in Iraq Begin Disarming Iranian Opposition Groups"; "President Urging Wider U.S. Powers In Terrorism Law," saying that " 'Unreasonable Obstacles' Hinder Pursuit of Suspects"; "White House Orders Overhaul of Iraq and Afghan Missions"; and "Bush Seeks $87 Billion and U.N. Aid for War Effort" ("Iraq Is Labeled Central Front for Terror"). At the same time, many questions and criticisms of Bush's handling of Iraq were being raised. On Iraqi weapons, "Bush May Have Exaggerated, but Did He Lie?" Or, "America Must Let Iraq Rebuild Itself." At any rate, in mid-2003 the Supreme "Court Affirms Bush's Power to Detain Citizen as Enemy" ("A victory for expansion of the president's authority"). In Iraq, meanwhile, as a possible legislative sign of sectarian extremism to come, "Back From Exile in Iran, [Iraqi] Cleric Urges Laws Based on Islam."[81]

Throughout 2004, controversy heated up over the Bush Administration's handling of U.S. involvement in Iraq. In January, "Bush Disputes Ex-Official's Claim That War With Iraq Was Early Administration Goal," even before 9/11." By March, "Bush Allows [National Security Adviser] Rice To Testify On 9/11 In a Public Session," with "Private Interview Set for President and Cheney" ("Behind the [Executive] Privilege That in the End Bowed to Politics"). Becoming ever bolder, "For Bush, Realpolitik Is No Longer a Dirty Word." In an April news conference, "Bush Asserts 'We Must Not Waver' on Terror or Iraq," saying "He'll send more troops if needed."

The full transcript of that news conference contains various uses of the word "sovereignty." At that point, the "White House Eyes A Powerful Post For Intelligence" ("Proposal for New Director Could Pre-empt Report by 9/11 Commission"). A fundamental issue being raised by some in the press was over "The Imperial Presidency And the Constraints of the Law." Another issue was over "Politics and the Patriot Act," which was much supported by Bush in that it enhanced Executive authority in the war against terror. In April, "Bush and Cheney Tell 9/11 Panel of '01 Warnings . . . Overseas."[82]

Administration viewpoints on issues of sovereignty and state in connection with law and legislation were appearing in the press in 2004 as plans for a new Iraqi government were being discussed. In April, "Bush Aide Warns Senate [That] Sovereignty for Any New Government In Iraq May Be Limited" in a "Possible Clash With U.N." Closely identifying this idea of sovereignty with legislative power, the same article's subheading points out that "Interim Leaders Could Not Pass New Laws, Bush Aide Tells Congress." Reaffirming his commitments to Iraq in a May statement at the Pentagon, Bush pledged "to transfer sovereignty to an Iraqi government as quickly as possible. . . . We will honor rule of law." Also, in a May speech at the U.S. Army War College in Pennsylvania, Bush looked toward the goal of a "self-governed Iraq"—including a "stable democracy," "free representative government," "a sovereign Iraqi government," and a "sovereign nation." A June news article pointed out that "The New Government Faces Bargaining Over Its Power," with a question over "How full will Iraq's promised 'full sovereignty' be?" Similarly that month, " 'Sovereignty' at issue in final push for Iraq transition plan" ("Members of U.N. Security Council are pressing the US to ensure that caretaker Iraqi government has full control").[83]

At the end of June 2004, "U.S. Transfers Power To Iraq 2 Days Early," although "Extent of Government's Control Unclear as It Formally Steps In." At the same time, U.S. Supreme Court "Justices Affirm Legal Rights of Those Deemed 'Enemy Combatants' " ("In Classic Checks and Balance, Court Shows Bush It Also Has Wartime Powers"), with an editorial on "Reaffirming the Rule of Law." That editorial seemed to recast the one a month earlier by a liberal columnist on Bush as "A President Beyond the Law" ("How Guantánamo's prisoners are tied to the crimes in Iraq"). Yet in July a commentator observed that, in its ruling in one case that previous term, "The Supreme Court revisits the issue of executive secrecy, inflating the White House's power."[84]

Pursuing the Domestic Agenda with Congressional Lawmakers
(Or, the "Imperial President" as "Super-Legislator"?)

During this period in 2002–2004 of heightened presidential wartime powers and Congressional Republican mid-term victories, the Bush Administration vigorously pursued (as "super-legislator?") its extensive domestic legislative program with Congressional lawmakers. For 2002, the following headings, prior to the November mid-term elections, represent illustrative indicators arranged in chronological sequence: "White House Is Backing Foes of Finance Bill" ("Party Is Pressed to Fight While Shielding Bush"); "Bush's Plan on Welfare Law Increases Work Requirement" ("Bipartisan support is seen for revisions of a landmark 1996 law"); "Bush Offers New Drug Plan Similar to One Court Barred"; "Bush Renews Push to Partly Privatize Social Security"; "Bush Promotes His Education Agenda and a Senate Candidate" ("Adding talk of Afghanistan to that of domestic goals"); "Bush Seeking New Rules to Help Investors . . ."; "He Picks His Fights Carefully" ("Bush lets legislators do their thing, but some GOP critics say that can be dangerous"); "Bush Plan to Avert Work Injuries Seeks Voluntary Steps by Industry" ("A promise of federal enforcement against industries with high accident rates"); "Bush Makes Fervent Bid to Get Senate to Ban Cloning Research"; "White House Proposes New View of Education Law to Encourage Single-Sex Schools"; "White House and Senate in Trade Accord" ("Broader Power for Bush, Help for Displaced American Workers"); "Senate Approves Bill Giving Wider Trade Authority to Bush"; "Bush to Seek Unlikely Allies In Bid to Alter Clean Air Act" ("An effort to include blacks, labor and environmentalists"); "Administration Proposes Easing of Rules on Air Pollution to Help Power Plants Modernize"; "Bush Plan Would End A Monopoly For Amtrak"; "Lawmakers' Reviews Mixed On Bush Plan for Amtrak"; "Bush Facing Test in House As Economic Agenda Stalls"; "Senate Backs Tough Measures to Punish Corporate Misdeeds" ("Legislation Would Go Beyond Bush's Proposals"); "Bush on Wall Street, Takes a Tough Stance Against Corporate Wrongdoing"; "Bush Rolls Back Rules on Privacy of Medical Data" ("Reverses Clinton Limits"); "Bush, Citing Threat of More Vast Fires, Wants to Ease Law on Logging in the West" ("Plan Would Build on a Move Supported by Congress to Thin Western Forests"); and "Bush Seeks More Rules to Protect 401(k) Plans."[85]

The mid-term Congressional elections in November 2002 resulted in such headlines as "Victorious Republicans Preparing A Drive For Bush Agenda And Judgeship Nominees." Also, "Senate Republicans Prepare to Regain Leadership Roles," and "Republicans Have Edge But Passing Bush's Plans May Require Compromise."[86]

In the immediate aftermath of the 2002 mid-term elections, "Bush's Way Is Clear to Press His Agenda for the Economy" ("Tax Cuts, Lower Spending and Lesser Role for the Fed Are Expected to Be Central"). Likewise, "Shift of Political Power to Bush's White House Reshapes the Landscape" ("Influence Over Congress Grows but So Do Risks"). "With the Republicans Forced to Regroup, an Ambitious Legislative Agenda Hits a Snag" ("A sudden change of leaders in the Senate creates problems"). And "White House Identifies Regulations That May Change."[87]

In a continuation of this same story in 2003, the following developments are illustrative: "Bush Signs Bill to Extend Unemployment Benefits" ("A day-old Congress sends help to many Americans"); "Bush Enters Fray Over Malpractice" ("States Can Limit Emergency Access In Medicaid Cases," "A Reversal In U.S. Policy"); "How Bush Gets His Way On the Environment" ("With the nation distracted by terrorism and the economy, the President has quietly maneuvered to challenge limits on drilling, mining, logging and power generation"); "So, Now Bigger Is Better?" ("Despite his campaign rhetoric, George W. Bush is expanding the federal government"); "The Radical Presidency of George W. Bush"; "Bush Prepares Health Plan Aimed at Small Businesses"; "The Reagan Revolution Redux" ("Embracing big tax cuts and deficits, Bush moves away from compassionate conservatism"); "White House Unveils Plan For Medicare Drug Benefits" ("An Incentive to Join Private Insurance Plans"); "Bush Proposes Major Changes In Health Plans" ("Critics See Less Security and Fewer Benefits"); "Fight Is Likely in Senate as Bush Sends Tax Cut Plan to Congress"; "Bush's bold agenda, soaring stakes" (". . . prescription drug plan is latest move for an administration bent on shaping history"); "White House Proposes New Rules for Overtime" ("Altering the Tests to Qualify for Extra Pay"); "The End of Taxes as We Know Them" ("Bush's fiscal revolution has just begun, and the economy will never be the same"); "Bush Issues Racial Profiling Ban But Exempts Security Inquiries"; "Senate Democrats, With Republican Help, Block Administration's New Overtime Rules" ("Surprising resistance to a plan businesses had lobbied for"); "Bush Signs Ban of Procedure for Abortion" ("The president promises to promote a 'culture of life' "); and "No Escaping the Red Ink As Bush Pens '04 Agenda" ("The deficit limits the president's election-year proposals").[88]

Bush's preceding presidential patterns in pursuing his bold domestic agenda with Congressional lawmakers became ever more pronounced during the presidential election year of 2004, closing with his decisive victory and mandate. Illustrations are again as follows: "Bush's education law transforms schools" ("Two years on, the 'No Child Left Behind' law draws continued criticism—and shifts focus to worst-off schools"); "Bush Seats Judge After Long Fight, Bypassing Senate" ("President Acts with Congress in Recess"); "White House Minimized the Risks of Mercury in Proposed Rules, Scientists Say"; "Out of the Spotlight, Bush Overhauls Nation's Regulations, Often Suiting Industry"; "Rewriting the Rules: Bush's Business-Friendly Revisions"; "Bush Celebrates Victory" (". . . President Cites 'A Duty to Serve All Americans,' " "Mandate Seen for 2nd Term with Gains in Congress"); "Confident Bush Outlines Ambitious Plan for 2nd Term" ("Focus on Social Security and Tax Code"); "President Feels Emboldened, Not Accidental, After Victory"; "Don't Expect Timidity" ("Bush is certain to make his reelection a mandate"); "President George W. Bush: American Revolutionary" ("Eagles rather than doves reside in the Oval Office Christmas tree. . . ", "Don't Call It A Dynasty . . . But that's what the Bush family is."); and "Administration Overhauls Rules for National Forests."[89]

6. PRESIDENT BUSH JR.'S SECOND TERM: FIRST PHASE

By the time of George Bush Jr.'s reelection and reinauguration as President, it had become clear that he could no longer be called an "accidental President" having neither public mandate nor Congress' support for his Executive initiatives and programs. More apt was the description voiced by some that he had become, with his wartime powers and Congressional majorities, a neo-"Imperial President" acting as a kind of "super-legislator." The first year of Bush's second term seemed to justify that assessment. Thereafter, however, would the "second honeymoon" be over and a "lame duck" status weaken his presidency?

At the outset of his second term in 2005, President Bush was ever more in command of his office. "Bush, At 2nd Inaugural, Says Spread of Liberty Is The 'Calling' of Our Time" ("A Presidency Altered by 9/11 and Words Shaped by That History"). His was called "A Crisis Presidency" as "Bush reprises a successful first-term tactic." As "Bush's second term establishes another political dynasty," the term "Family Business" was being used by some. So, too, once again, was the term "Imperial Presidency." Bush's agenda with Congress was pressed from this position of re-election strength. For instance, in his State of the Union address to Congress, "Bush Describes an Overhaul of Social Security as Essential." Later on, "Bush Asks House and Senate to Send Him an Energy Bill." He was also called "The Uncompromising Mr. Bush" as "Defeats only stiffen the president's resolve to advance his own agenda." Court victories on his legislative front were forthcoming, as when "U.S. Court Backs Bush's Revisions In Clean Air Act," so that "Factory owners enjoy greater flexibility in controlling emissions."[90]

Yet warning signs as well as storm clouds lay on the horizon in 2005. On stem cells, for example, "Bush's Ban Could Be Reversed," became "As states push ahead with new research that the public seems to want, Congress is poised to expand the uses of federal funding beyond what the President's order allows." "Mandate," one essayist in May felt, is no longer such an apt term, for "All of a sudden Bush's [re-election] victory looks less like a major realignment." Moreover, "For This President, Power Is There for the Taking," for "Bush has tried to restore authority to the executive branch. Will his success last beyond his tenure?" In June it was asked, "Overdrawn on Political Capital?" inasmuch as "Recent defeats for Bush bring whispers of 'lame duck' from opponents." Also at that point "Bush's Support On Major Issues Tumbles In Poll" as "Congress Also Suffers," even though "The Public Still Gives Its Approval to President's War on Terrorism." Then in September, four years after the 9/11 terrorist attack came "A Hard New Test for the President: Opportunity and Risk in a Major Disaster" when hurricane Katrina devastated the Gulf Coast. But "Can Bush do large-scale relief?," for this was "Not the New Deal." Even so, "Bush Pledges Federal Role in Rebuilding Gulf Coast" and "Offers Programs for Housing and Work." By October "A New Frontier" was reached in that, "Like Jimmy Carter in the 1970s, Bush adjusts to being president in an age of limits." Meanwhile, it was reported that "Bush Education Law Shows Mixed Results in First Test."[91]

Also problematical in October was "Cheney Aide Charged with Lying in [C.I.A.] Leak Case," with "Rove's Fate Unresolved—[a] Political Crisis for the White House." Now there was "In Indictment's Wake, a Focus on Cheney's Powerful Role." At many points the Cheney affair centered around legal–legislative issues, as when "Cheney Defends Eavesdropping Without Warrants," whereas "Spy Briefing Failed to Meet Legal Test, Lawmakers Say." At the same time, "Defending Spy Program, Administration Cites Law" ("A surveillance statute allows exceptions, a letter to Congress says"). Accordingly, "'01 Resolution Is Central to '05 Controversy" ("What was authorized in an authorization for the use of force?"). At that point one editorial criticized "Mr. Cheney's Imperial Presidency."[92]

Debate continued in 2005 on "War Powers in the Age of Terror," for "In this struggle, Congress can't give a president a free pass." In December, "More Humble, but Still Firm: Bush Claims New Set of Powers." By the end of the year, it was called "The Year We Questioned Authority," with the result that "For President Bush and other political figures, it was the end of the free pass."[93]

Chapter III

The U.S. Congress

Among the many issues to be confronted in this broad yet focused look at the U.S. Congress and its central place in the legislative arena is the concomitance and counterpoise provided by the U.S. presidency in legislative matters. To what extent, for instance, have recent U.S. Presidents become more active or dominant in the legislative process in ways analogous to British Prime Ministers as leaders in Parliament? With the enormous growth of legislation and legislative activity at the U.S. federal level, to what extent has the constitutional separation of powers become increasingly blurred in the making of legislation?

Answers to such questions can lead to other queries on matters of sovereignty and state. True, the changing balances of powers at the U.S. federal level is a shifting dynamic equilibrium, with changing imbalances often occurring from one period to another. Yet continuing patterns can also often be observed amid the changing liberal/conservative trends in political parties and political philosophies. For example, the conservative and liberal presidencies of Reagan and Clinton, respectively, displayed some common patterns of active or even dominant leadership in the legislative process ordinarily associated with Congress itself. Then there is the whole question of Congress' rising flood of legislation stretching from Reagan's administration to that of Bush Jr. The ever expanding role of Congress in the growth of the legislative state and legislative sovereignty at the federal level is a theme of great import. Congress' legislative role in foreign as well as domestic policy-making is of crucial concern.

As in the previous chapter on the U.S. presidency, beginning with Reagan and the Iran–Contra affair, so too in this chapter on the U.S. Congress, foreign as well as domestic affairs will be considered, although the present Part I is primarily concerned with U.S. domestic matters, while an ensuing subsection will focus on U.S. foreign issues. Here as elsewhere, the massive news materials compiled over many years will be reduced and condensed for purposes of this volume.

1. CONGRESS DURING REAGAN'S SECOND TERM

The "Reagan revolution" against big government in the early 1980s during President Reagan's first term was made possible by his broad leadership over the legislative process and agenda in Congress, as was seen in our previous book. Yet the Iran–contra affair during Reagan's second term found "Congress Awash With [Its Own Independent] Ideas to Expand the Welfare State." Elaborating upon that suggestive title, a 1987 news article pointed out the following: "Now Mr. Reagan's political power and popularity have been eroded, most notably by the Iran–contra affair, and with Democrats controlling both houses of Congress, the White House is on the defensive. . . . The new surge of interest cannot be explained entirely as a reaction to Federal budget cuts or . . . [to] Mr. Reagan's conservative ideals. Mr. Reagan himself, in his State of the Union Message in 1986, set off a new wave of interest in catastrophic health insurance and welfare revision [etc.]." The corresponding subtitle was also indicative: "Democrats Sense the Time for Social Spending Has Finally Arrived."[1]

Another sign in 1987 of Congress trying to exercise greater legislative muscle occurred when "Congress tries to plug the trade drain." The question was: "Mood favors legislation, but will President sign the bill if it passes?" "Attempts," however, "to legislate changes in international trade are highly controversial."[2]

Of further interest in 1987 on Congressional legislative powers in relation to the Reagan White House and the Iran–Contra affair was the issue of the War Powers Resolution. A news article later that year reported that a "Former secretary of state calls War Powers act 'unenforceable' " ("Gulf resurrects issue, but constitutional test is unlikely, Rogers says"). In that interview, William Rogers, Secretary of State under President Nixon, called the Resolution "neither constitutional nor enforceable," although it "highlights the need for consultation with Congress on foreign military action." The resolution, or act, had survived a presidential veto by Nixon in 1973. "The resolution," as reported, "requires a president to consult Congress within two days of committing troops to action" and harmful dangers. Congress had passed the resolution in frustration over the course of the Vietnam War. A month before this interview, the Senate had voted down an attempt "to apply it to the US forces deployed in the Gulf."[3]

2. CONGRESS DURING BUSH SR.'S TERM

"Is Government Dead?"

Toward the end of President Bush Sr.'s first full year in office in 1989, a news magazine's cover story posed the question "Is Government Dead?," with a subtitle answering in the negative—"Unwilling to lead, politicians are letting America slip into paralysis." Portraying a weeping George Washington on its front cover, the article contrasted the "can-do" government during the Reagan era with "The Can't Do Government" of the first year of the new Bush era. "Paralyzed by special interests and shortsightedness, Washington no longer seems capable of responding to its growing challenges." The growing question of "whether the Government—from Congress to the White House . . . —can govern at all . . . " fell hardest here on Congress and "Special-Interest Politics. Congress last week seemed to be moving toward approval of the Administration's plan to cut the tax on capital gains . . . as well as repeal of the . . . catastrophic health-care program for the elderly that was passed last year with the wholehearted approval of the Reagan White House."[4]

A variety of other news reports at the same point in time pointed to rising shortcomings in Congress' responsiveness to national needs. An editorial on "Civil Rights Laws, Dead and Alive," criticized the lack of much needed "Congressional correction" of some faulty recent Supreme Court decisions. "Congress must impress on the Court that the battle for equal rights is not yet won and that the laws needed for the struggle are, as Congress has long intended, to be construed generously." In medical matters attention was drawn to "Congress in Retreat: How Medicare Changes Fell on Hard Times in a Hurry," with particular consideration of the catastrophic-care debate; the "House Acts to Kill '86 Medicare Plan of Extra Benefits," despite "Wide Protests by Elderly on Surtax"; and "Loss of Program That Helps Pay Cost of Long Illness."[5]

Retreat by Congress in later 1989 on many Reagan-era initiatives and programs was driven in large part by budgetary constrictions and the Gramm–Rudman law on balanced budgets. At first, "After Skirting Budget Law, Congress Considers Change," but the warning went up "Don't Mess With Gramm–Rudman" ("Simply changing the law will not automatically reduce the deficit"). Eventually, the "New Budget Falls Within Deficit Limit" ("No new taxes, and few new programs"). A casualty of budgetary cuts came when Congressional "Lawmakers Agree to Trim Star Wars' Spending" in "A reversal of momentum for a cherished Reagan program." In late November, "Congress Ends Session With Much Work Undone."[6]

On two highly visible matters in later 1989, Congressional lawmakers clearly had the upper hand over the Executive branch. In one case, an "Amendment Protecting Flag Is Defeated" as "The Senate delivers a sharp rebuff to Bush." In another, "Bush Agrees to Notify Congress on Covert Actions."[7]

"Congress: It Doesn't Work. Let's Fix It."

A lengthy cover story in a news magazine issue of April 1990 bore the provocative title "Congress: It Doesn't Work. Let's fix it." The concluding section—"If U.S. lawmakers want to be serious about reform, this agenda might be a good place to start"—discussed in turn the following areas needing reform: excessive numbers of committees and subcommittees, the budget process, the Gramm–Rudman law on the deficit, PAC donations, campaign spending, guaranteed incumbency, and the party system. Earlier that year appeared a newspaper editorial on "The Cloud Over Congress." It began: "Fundamental is the need for Congress, scandal scarred, to restore its own integrity." Its chief concerns were with political action committees, spending limits, alternative financing, and "sewer money." Among other such accounts were: "Put Sanity Back Into Our Elections" (questioning "how serious Congress is about passing campaign-finance legislation"); "Incumbent Campaign Loopholes in Law That Pay Off With Re-election"; "An Office That Has the Capital's Ear" ("Congress's investigative arm, at the zenith of its powers"; "Studying how government works, and doesn't"); "Who Robbed the Thrifts? Congress" ("Democrats drove the getaway car"); and "Campaign Surgery" ("Bill in Congress to Tighten Spending May Be an Attempt to Impress Voters").[8]

The tortuous legislative paths and impasses of 1990 in Congress over the national budget can serve as a case in point about Congress "not working." In May it was reported that "Warily Congress and White House Gird for Budget Joust" in which "Democrats will let Bush make the first move on taxes." But then "Democrats [were] Irate Over Bush Silence" due to "President Insisting Congress Has Main Responsibility on U.S. Fiscal Matters." Part of the problem was that "Budget-Deficit Law Is Facing Change" inasmuch as "Meeting the Gramm–Rudman limit would be devastating." Would it be "The Death of Gramm–Rudman?" ("Widely Regarded as Failure, Budget Law Is Itself Targeted"). Also, "Faltering Hopes for Accord on Deficit Are Dimmed Further by Gulf Crisis" as "Fiscal and military worries compound a basic resistance." Over the months the impasse continued. "Bush Rejects Delays in Deadline For Automatic Cuts in Spending," while "Legislators Accept PAC Money While Urging Finance Changes" ("Groups Complain Legislators Want It Both Ways"). By September "Doubts [Were] Voiced on Congress' Ability to Act on Big Domestic Policy Bills." As a consequence, "Swift and Wide Impact Is Expected If Negotiations on U.S. Budget Fail."[9]

In the final Congressional budget battles during the fall of 1990, "Arm Twisting in Capital Is Just Short of Physical," while "Lobbying Is Fierce as House Debates Budget Accord." With crisis looming over Congressional foot-dragging and temporizing, "President Vetoes Stopgap Budget. Shutdown Begins" as "Effort To Overhaul Fails" and "Bush Vows Flexibility but Lets U.S. Closures Go Ahead—New Bargaining." A low point was thus reached in early October when "House Sustains Veto as Budget Stalemate Continues," with the result that "There was little forgiveness or understanding for America's leaders yesterday among the thousands of tourists who either did not know the government had shut down or came to the Mall area anyway because they could not believe something as abstract as the budget deficit could matter to National Park Service rangers or Smithsonian museum guards" (with blame for this "Debacle" of "Political Gridlock" to go all around). Although quickly thereafter a "New Budget Deal Is Forced And Approved By The House In Move To Break Deadlock," it left "Bush Uncommitted," while "Debate Brings Delay and Disruption." Swift on the heels of these reports came the news that "Impasse On Budget Is Ended—Stopgap[!] Spending Measure Averts [Further] Federal Shutdown," as "Helter-Skelter Day Reflects Miscalculation at the Top," with result that "After Budget Trauma, Still More Trauma."

When "New Budget Ideas Offered as Tug-of-War Goes On," "Bush Spurns Proposal by House Democrats on Taxing Rich."[10] In "The Budget Battle: Another Impasse, as Deficit Mounts," for "Behind the Dealing on Deficit Reduction, Deals That Could Swell the Deficit" ("Congressional Budget Negotiators Take Care of Some Constituents" and "While Congress Trims the Budget, It Enlarges Programs and Debt").[11]

By late October in 1990, although in general "Not a Class Act," "After one last round of political wrangling, Congress clears the way for a budget deal by playing the politics of resentment." As "101st Congress Wraps Up Work Belatedly and a Little Battered," "Fight Over Deficit Clouds Its Accomplishments." Having wider import, "The Budget Battle Reflects the Strains in the System." It had been a "Dose of Reality," for "After a decade of budget delusion, Congress and the White House take a significant step toward controlling the deficit." But what was the verdict on Congress itself and on the outlook for its future handling of such matters?[12]

Other problems with Congress' public image and role in domestic affairs mounted in 1990. Chief among them was the Savings and Loan "scandal" involving some members of Congress. Brought to the public's attention, the matter was investigated by Congress itself. It was reported that "Favoritism Is Found in Some S. & L. Cases," as "Congressional Investigators Report Regulatory Lapses." However, "Four Senators Deny Doing Favors For Keating in Exchange for Cash" ("After a year, a chance to reply to accusations"). As "5 Senators in S. & L. Case Plan to Challenge Ethics Panel's Legal Authority," "Beyond the broad challenge, each Senator plans a different strategy." They were defending themselves against charges of accepting campaign contributions from Keating and others in return for favorable treatment on the failing S. & L. banks, that is, for "Protecting Banks In Severe Slump." Then a senior S. & L. "Regulator Singles Out [Senator] DeConcini For 'Impropriety' on Failed S. & L.," "Drawing a line between intervention and influence." By mid-December, the "Keating Five Are in the Dock, But Congress Is Being Judged" ("Not the Civics-Text View of Washington at Work"). It was billed as "Congressional Shame, Public Cynicism." As expected, "S. & L. Regulators' Slowness [Is] Tied to Need to Win Votes of Senators." Not surprisingly, "Bank Law Changes Face Hurdles in Congress." The drive was on for Congressional "Term Limits—A Symptom, Not a Cure" ("They're catching on just the same"). Among others, V.P. Dan "Quayle Leads Drive to Limit Congress Terms."[13]

In foreign affairs, Congress' handling of the China situation was further illustrative of Congress' problems. "Bush Is Set Back By House Override Of Veto On China," in "Repudiation of U.S. Overtures in Wake of Beijing Crackdown" on dissenting students. Shortly thereafter, "Senate Votes Sanctions Against China." At first it was said that "On China, Congress Is Almost Assertive." But then a "China Breach" was reported as "Congress sets the tone for an election year with a bruising—and losing—challenge to the President's foreign policy. So much for bipartisanship." But these doings of early 1990 came well before the government shutdown and S. & L. mess of later 1990.[14]

"U.S. Laws Delayed by Complex Rules and Partisanship"

The preceding subheading taken from a news article's title in early 1991 encapsulates the growing perception during that year that the Congressional legislative process was not functioning as it should if Congress was to be a fully operative co-equal branch of the U.S. Federal government, albeit the White House was partly to blame in this respect. Among the many diverse problems cited in that article are the massive complex details and mandates that Congress typically writes into its laws, which often become a wilderness maze not easy for others to sort through, make sense of, and carry out. Examples are given by that article in such areas as nursing homes, laboratories, homelessness, air pollutants, chewing tobacco, and education. White House people were among those complaining of such problems.[15]

A variety of other similar problems with how Congress was not functioning properly in the legislative arena were also on the rise as 1991 went on. "A Catfish That Oinks . . . and other tales of how Congress wastes money on pork-barrel projects" was one criticism. Another news article posed a question and a solution in "Do They Have the Nerve?" and "An idea for breaking the legislative logjam and establishing accountability." Another public concern was over "Perk City"—"Wonder why Congress is so arrogant about bounced checks [in members' personal accounts there]? Perhaps because its members are so used to the freebie life." It was "An Institution Under Duress" in that "Congress' Committees Stumble, and Change." Indeed, " 'Now Is the Time for Change' on Capitol Hill," for "Reform-Minded Members of Congress See Opportunity in Current Public Disgust With [that] Institution." On the torpid pace of legislative processes, "Bush's 100-Day Challenge Haunts Hill" as

"Democrats Remember Taunt as Bills Lumber Slowly Through Congress." (Pres. Bush had taunted Congress when suggesting that since U.S.–led forces won the Gulf War in 100 hours, Congress could pass the needed legislation in 100 days, albeit it was already 249 days and with no such legislation yet in sight at the time of his address to Congress on the subject at war's end.)[16]

At the same time in 1991, there were counterbalancing viewpoints. "It Isn't Graceful, but the Laws Get on the Books," with regard to a wide range of subjects: the Gulf War, unemployment benefits, trade with China, abortion counseling, the military pay raises, civil rights, crime, transportation, campaign finance, banking overhaul, and energy. "After Senate Backs Bush and Blocks Anti-Crime Bill, Congress Goes Home," at which point "Both sides say Congress had a productive year." Because of the "gag rule"—which allowed the Bush and Reagan administrations to make recess appointments during Congressional adjournments—some reports decried "Bypassing Congress" and "Making Law Backward," thereby circumventing the making of legislation by majority rule and the peoples' will. True, "Lawmakers' Constituents Complain About Economy and Congress Itself." But another report found "Regulatory Overhaul Advancing" as "Momentum is building rapidly in Congress . . . to repudiate and rewrite many laws and economic regulations that were pillars of the New Deal of the 1930's." Concerning "Legislation and Crises, Illusions and Realities," "Pragmatism still manages to find a way in the Capital."[17]

Congressional efforts in 1991 to cope with banking reform and banking scandal present an interesting legislative story. In January, "Bush Speech to Urge Bank Law Changes." It was soon reported that "Bank Losses Worst in 50 Years, But No Danger to System Is Seen," albeit "Big Rise Is Expected in Average Size of Failures." It was urged that "Congress Must Take Fresh Look at Nation's Complex Banking Problems." There was "A New Plan to Overhaul Supervision of Banks." But was all this "Reform, Or A Crackdown On Banking?," while "A bill in Congress would put a choke chain on regulators and impose harsh constraints on ailing banks." More banking bills followed. But by September, "Bank Reform Takes a Hit" as "A Congress Confronted With Scandals Is Distracted From the Main Issue." Congressional scandals involving Senators Cranston, D'Amato, Hatfield, and others including the so-called "Keating Five," swirled around accusations of favorable treatments of failing Savings and Loan banks. Yet "As Bank Legislation Evolves, the Bankers Worry," for "The industry wants an overhaul, but not at all costs." In October, reports of abuses rose on the "Private Bank for Congress," leading to public recriminations. It was also cautioned that "New bank laws won't help without real enforcement." Another article lamented "Bank Reform Deformed!" In November, "House Turns Down Banking Overhaul," partly in acquiescence to Bush and big bankers. In the end, "Banking Regulators Issue Not-Too-Tough Rules." A "Cacophony of Lobbying Overwhelms Bank Bill." Following a mid-November report that "Congress Will Try Again To Revamp Banking Laws," "House Defeats Plan to Revamp Banking Laws." The Congressional banking scandal likewise came to a rather unsatisfactory close "As Keating Case . . . Comes to a Close, Confusion Over Ethics Rules Remains."[18]

Congressional legislative action was also bogged down in 1991 over campaign finance reform. As in the cases of banking reform and banking scandals, the competing complex proposals before Congress threatened to bring the legislative process to an impasse. In March "House and Senate Leaders Are Split On Overhaul of Campaign Financing." In May "Senate Approves Bill to Limit Campaign Spending," but there were "Dim prospects for agreement with the House and President." In November "House Approves Overhaul of Campaign Spending." But there real reform seemed to rest in limbo, again involving legislators' own self-interest.[19]

On other fronts in 1991 the picture was mixed. On the one hand, there was a "Quota Quagmire" ("While racial tensions are rising in the country, Washington politicians are bogged down in a rancorous dispute over a new civil rights bill") and "Rescuing Health Care: A Herculean Task for Congress in 90's." On the other, there was, for example, the "Senate's Rule for Its Anti-Crime Bill: The Tougher the Provision, the Better" ("Sweeping aside qualms about a broad expansion of Federal power"). Back in early April, the Congressional agendas on banking overhaul, campaign finance, civil rights, gun control, and fast track for trade deals were "Seeking more to pay for domestic programs," as "Democrat's Budget Plan Assures Conflict With Bush." Soon thereafter, "House Rejects Bush Budget Plan and Adopts Own." But by year's end much steam had gone out of this drive. Part of the reason was Bush's use or threat of the veto power, to which Congress often stood up with varying success, but there was much more involved as well.[20]

"Fine Line for Congress: Politics vs. Legislation"

On into 1992, the last full year of President Bush Sr.'s term, the above subheading's quotation, taken from a September news article, continued to grow. As lamented in that piece, it had become "a session noted more for scandal [including the Thomas–Hill battles] than lawmaking," with the Democratic-controlled Congress still needing to deal with the Republican president's campaign agenda for re-election, "while demonstrating to [complaining] voters that they can enact important legislation." Innumerable other such news articles throughout that year reflected Congress' decline in public estimation and its perceived lack of legislative competence. According to "Feeding Time at the Capitol Hill Piranha Tank," "What began as an embarrassment about overdrawn checks [within Congress] has turned into an orgy of tarring and feathering." Another article, on "Congress *Is* the Problem," suggested "how Bush can tame the bloated monster." Already by April, "Election-Year Gridlock Fouls Washington Mood," for "Just one major law has been passed. There's blame and venom to spare." Or, again, "The Gridlock [102nd] Congress . . . Will be Remembered as Much For Its Embarrassments as Its Legislation." A tongue-in-cheek suggestion in one opinion piece was "Let's Restore Genuine Democracy by Choosing Congress by Lottery."[21]

Many members of Congress in 1992 voiced their own deep discontent with Congress' seeming paralysis as a legislative body. "It's Not Just The Voters Who Want To Change Congress—So Do Members" ("[Republican Sen.] Domenici's Lament: Initiatives and courage get snared in the tangled web of committees"). As explained in "Why Washington Doesn't Work," "Republican Senator Warren Rudman is quitting because even though politicians know what to do about the nation's problems, they are afraid to lead." Another piece put it more starkly, "Rudman, Irked by the Senate, Is Retiring," saying that "Government . . . is 'not functioning.' " It was not merely a discontented few within Congress. "Citing Rise in Frustration, Dozens of Lawmakers Are Quitting." As the trend gained momentum, "Mr. Smith Leaves Washington," as some quitting "disillusioned" Congressmen tell "how to change a stalemated system." As expressed in an opinion piece by Representative Dan Gallo in a Congressional journal, "Why Washington Doesn't Work" "is the lack of leadership, not corruption."[22]

Naturally, there were various counterbalancing assessments that year. For instance, "Minority Candidates See Congress as Useful Tool . . . [,] Contradicting the anti-government spirit of 1992." After the November elections, with Democrat Bill Clinton as President-elect, "Congress Is Hoping to Enter a New Era," albeit "With Democrats in power, inaction will be hard to excuse." That rosier outlook by some in early January 1993 remained to be seen amid the continuing, deeply entrenched anti-government voices of 1992. That

Fall's election season had also been stirred by the optimistic/pessimistic vision of federal lawmaking advanced by the alien/independent presidential candidacy of Ross Perot. For example, "Perot Vision: Consensus by Computer," whereby " 'Electric Town Hall' Would Link Officials and Public by TV." As reported, however, "Lawmaking By Citizens Faces Hurdles."[23]

Congress' banking scandal in 1992 illustrated the public's ire over Congress' failings more broadly. "It's Bank Panic, Congressional Style, As House Faces Up to Bad Checks." On "Checks and Balances And the Angry Voters," it was "Foley in a Harsher Light," for although "Once Welcome, the Speaker's Quiet Style Is Criticized Amid the House Bank Affair." In March "Congressional Officials Disclose 21 Names in House Bank Affair." Nevertheless, "Check Abuse Prosecutions Would Face Difficulties," for "If laws were broken, sloppy records could thwart action." As reports mounted of foot-dragging and resistance by members, "Blowing the lid on [Check] Kiters Inc." intensified, while "Voters will settle accounts for the House this fall." In April, matters became worse when "Committee Names All Who Overdrew At the House Bank," as "New List Puts Total at 325."[24]

In the legislative process of passing a new bill on taxes in 1992, there were Congressional logjams, in addition to presidential initiatives and obstructions. In January, with "Little on its Agenda, Congress Plays Wait-and-See as New Session Starts." Soon enough in March, "Tax Bills and Capital Gains Cut Turn Into Capitol Games" in "Cat and Mouse With Bush's Request." After the "Tax Bill, Senate Version, Is Voted by Finance Unit," "Bush vows a veto." Later in March the "Tax Bill Is Passed by Democrats [and Congress as a whole] and Vetoed by Bush," all this seen to reflect campaign-year's political struggles. As political partisanship intensified over tax legislation in Congress, attention was turned by some to broader reform issues such as "How to Simplify the Crazy Tax Code."[25]

In the pervading legislative context of the top economic issue perennially before Congress, namely the process of enacting a budget bill into law, 1992 proved of particular significance. In May "Support Grows for Balanced-Budget Amendment" by "Trying to stop Government borrowing by outlawing it." By that point, it was becoming clear that Pres. Bush was for such an amendment while presidential contender Clinton was against it. In June "Balanced-Budget Amendment Fails to Gain House Approval . . . [and] Plan Dies for Year." But the matter was far from over. In July "House Votes to Break 1990 Budget Act." Then Democratic Senator "Byrd Says Senate Will Defeat Measure for Balanced Budget." As explained by the *State Legislatures* journal that year: "For much of the 1980's, the federal budget process was dominated by the Gramm–Rudman–Hollings law, which prescribed fixed deficit targets to be met each year.... The Budget Enforcement Act of 1990 that repealed Gramm–Rudman–Hollings includes changes that may be as radical as the original Gramm–Rudman–Hollings Act of 1985 ... [so as] to ensure enforcement of the five-year agreement...."[26]

The legislative and counter-legislative "tug of war" between Congress and the White House in 1992 thus became entangled that election year with strong partisanship. The often invoked veto power at times also begged the question of which federal branch had ultimate legislative sovereignty, as when in September "Senate Votes to Override President's Veto of the Family Leave Bill," as "A campaign battle spills into the halls of Congress." Not surprisingly, in early January of 1993, "Bush Vetoes Not Forgotten As 103d Congress Convenes," while "Democrats begin by concentrating on things they agree about." The regulatory dimension of legislative power (or the legislative dimension of regulatory power) became a similar kind of partisan battleground in 1992. In July, for instance, "House Votes to Eliminate Money for Regulatory Council Headed by [V.P.] Quayle," followed ten days later by a critical look at "Congress as Regulator."[27]

With the rise in the 20th century of federal agencies increasingly exerting legislative-like powers, it was natural that those agencies within the Executive branch would at times vie with Congressional legislative authority, while the White House itself would seek some control or oversight over Congress' regulatory-legislative jurisdictions. Congress, in turn, would greatly wish to assert its own authority in relation to the Administration. These struggles over the veto and regulatory powers seemed also to shape up in 1992 and other years as competing efforts by the two branches to be "first among equals." Notwithstanding the rise of the U.S. presidency as the oft-called "super-legislator," Congress could often act as if in accord with its dominate lengthy place at the beginning of the U.S. Constitution, written at a time when the presidency was but a pale shadow of its later so-called "imperial" position.

The issue in this subsection on Congressional "politics vs. legislation" especially in struggles with the White House was also apparent during 1992 in foreign affairs. According to one news account, "Bill to Aid Former Soviet Lands Is Stuck in Capitol Hill Quagmire" because "Domestic Issues and Elections Block Momentum." Likewise, in the year before, when there was "New Pressure for Tough Trade Laws," "Congress and the President disagree over regulatory legislation." Small wonder, then, that in later 1992, toward the end of Bush's presidency but before the elections, another account of the "Congressional Record, After Two Years and 36 Vetoes" pinpointed a key problem: "Between Gulf War and Political Sniping, [There Were] Legislative Casualties," in that the "102nd Congress Often Was Thwarted By Senate Filibusters and Bush Vetoes."[28]

3. CONGRESS DURING CLINTON'S FIRST TERM

"Moving toward Gridlock II"?

A mid-January caption in 1993, "Moving toward Gridlock II," seemed to presage for Congress, at the outset of President Clinton's first term, the same kind of troubles experienced during Bush Sr.'s Administration. That scenario was reinforced at the end of January in "Break the Billion Dollar Congress," according to which "PAC payoffs are the biggest hurdle to health reform." By early April it was a "Truly Modern Filibuster: Choreographed Gridlock," for "The deliberative body deliberately doesn't move." At that point, "G.O.P. Filibuster Stalls Passage Of Clinton's $16 Billion Jobs Bill." It was called "Republicans Redux," because, "Filibustering in Senate, G.O.P. Strives To Make Itself a Power to Deal With," so that "Forget the Issues, the real fight is about building up party power." In later April "G.O.P. Senators Prevail, Sinking Clinton's Economic Stimulus Bill," as "Democrats Limit Plan to $4 Billion in Jobless Aid."[29]

But meanwhile in 1993, the legislative logjam in Congress seemed to be breaking up in matters relating to the national budget—that annual all-important and top-priority economic issue in the Congressional legislative process. In later March "Senate Approves First Step in President's Budget Plan." In April "A Line-Item Veto Is Passed, But It Has Key Restrictions" in "A modest victory for a President whose programs face struggles." In May "Clinton's Tax Package Passes Big Test, Clearing House Ways and Means Panel." Then "Clinton Puts Down Democratic [House] Revolt On Economic Plan." In late May "House Narrowly Approves the President's Budget Plan" in "A Victory Most Precious" although "Senate Is Hurdle." In mid-June "Senators On Finance Panel Reach Accord On A Budget With Gas Tax And Key Cuts" in "A Compromise Plan." A day later, "Democrats on the Senate Finance Committee . . . started muscling the first big chunk of President Clinton's budget toward a Senate vote and enactment into law," while "Democratic unanimity leaves Republicans on the sidelines." Soon thereafter, "Invective

Flies as Senators Debate Clinton's Package" and "G.O.P. Alternative Beaten." But then "Budget Survives Senate Struggle; New Fight Ahead," as "Vice President's Vote Breaks Tie." In July the "Undoing Of Budget Starts In Capital" as "House–Senate Conferees, in Rare Spotlight, Face Task of Shaping Single Bill." Then "Budget Haggling Begins In Earnest" when "Lawmakers Must Reconcile More Liberal House Bill With Senate Frugality." In August "Conference Ends in Compromise and Optimism" when "Negotiators Reach Accord On Five-Year Budget Plan." Then "House Passes Budget Plan, Backing Clinton[,] . . . After Hectic Maneuvering," with "Suspense in Senate." The final passage of the budget into law (or resolution) marked the end of a strenuous and prolonged Congressional "dance of legislation," to use the old phrase, even with Democrats now in firm control. Yet a crucial point here is that the national budget remains an enduring *legislative* focal point in Congressional economic matters.[30]

By the end of 1993 it was being reported that the Congressional legislative logjams were loosening up in other areas as well. For instance, thanks to "The Gridlock Breakers" "Passage of the Brady bill caps a solid session for the 103rd Congress." This particular ending eventually came after much wrangling just a month earlier in a reported "Sour End to Strong Year" as "Congress Makes Progress Against Gridlock, But Gun Issue Shows the Job Isn't Complete."[31]

Although Congress gave other legislative victories to President Clinton in 1993, as when in November "House Backs Free Trade Pact In Major Victory For Clinton," it gave him much resistance on other subjects, such as his health care proposals. Yet allusions were made in the press to: "Healthy Discontent" ("In Congress, health-care reformists are engaging in finger pointing as liberals and conservatives push alternatives to Clinton's plan"), "Here Comes Doctor No" (in a "major assault to refashion President Clinton's health-reform plan"), and " 'Alliance' to Bury Health Care" ("Republicans warn of Government intrusion").[32]

Congress itself as an institution continued to take heat throughout 1993 more generally. In the "Chaos Theory in Congress," "Hasty votes pay off." Offsetting (or compounding) this situation was "Congress Facing Long List Of Tough Issues This Term," while "Some lawmakers face an 'overload of legislation.' " Said others, "Free the Economy From Congress," adding "We need jobs, not political fear and myopia." "The Senate Power Grab," in its improper questioning of Supreme Court nominee Ruth Ginsburg, was another situation. And "The Trouble with Rosty" (powerful Democratic Congressman Rostenkowski) and "His post-office scandal could disrupt Clinton's legislative ambitions." Under growing constituent criticism for its members' spendthrift ways, "Congress Is Pressed to Join In Nation's Belt-Tightening."[33]

"Congress Is Following Its Own Trail Toward Consensus on Health Care"

Among the many plans and proposals that went through the legislative machinery of Congress during 1994, the most conspicuous undoubtedly concerned health-care reform, which was becoming a *cause célèbre* not least because of White House pressure to pass it into law. A "Long Legislative Route For Clinton Health Plan," when "Tracing the steps to a final vote on a health care bill," was anticipated in February. A "Gold Rush Fever Grips Capital As Health Care Struggle Begins," for "Everyone Sees a Stake, and It's Usually Money." It quickly became "A Bloody Clash of Egos" when "Pride and prejudices emerge as five congressional committees vie to craft historic health-care legislation." By early May, it was becoming ever clearer that "Congress Is Following Its Own Trail Toward Consensus on Health Care." At that point "House Ways and Means Panel Tests Its Mettle Against Health Care Dragon," while chairman Democrat Rep. "Rostenkowski wants a major bill as a legacy," so "With its leader under a cloud, a committee hurries to break a logjam."[34]

There was then in mid-May 1994 "A loud display of partisanship in two major Congressional [House and Senate] committees" as "Health Care Hearings Open in Squabbles." Although in mid-June "Health Legislation Gains in Senate With Progress in Two Committees," a week later "Strain Shows In Committees On Health Bill" as "Democrats Struggle To Make Progress." The "House G.O.P. Is Thwarting a Health Bill," while "Democrats Unite against [Republican Rep.] Gingrich strategy." As the intricate and uncertain ups and downs continued, "On Health Congress Moves to Take Bold Action Subtly . . . to give time a chance"; and "Health Coalition Strongly Opposes Compromise Plan." In late June, it was reported that "Health Care Makes Progress on Rocky Path." A few days later "2 Senate Leaders [Democrat Moynihan and Republican Dole] Propose Health Plans." Then "Dole Begins Gathering Backing for G.O.P. Health Plan." Meanwhile, "Health Legislation Forcing Hard White House Choices" over its promises vs. pragmatism.[35]

As the drama unfolded, mid-July 1994 "Health Care Plans Are Setting Congress on Collision Course With Destiny." Strikingly,

"Health Debate Recasts Lawmaking Process" in that "Health negotiations resemble a game of hot potato." In early August "Clinton Tries to Pressure Republicans on Health Care Bill" at the same time that "Senate G.O.P. Heats Up Attack on the Health Bill." Then "Debate Begins in Senate On [Dem. Sen.] Mitchell Health Bill." Whereupon, "Clinton Says Mitchell Bill Is His Minimum." Not to be outdone, "Lobbyists Are the Loudest In the Health Care Debate."[36]

The situation quickly unraveled in later August 1994. "Health Care Bill's Prospects Dim With the Hardening of Stances" as "A Crucial Compromise Plan Seems to Be Stalled" due to "New Obstacles in Legislative Path." Even "Clinton's Allies On Health Concede That Broad Plan Is All But Dead, This Year" with "Voters . . . Anger Over Partisan Politics." Then, "With Hopes for a Health Care Overhaul Faded, a Search for Minor Repairs." In the end, the "Grand Plan to Overhaul Health Care Becomes Victim of Time" ("Did the Democrats Misread the Signs?", "From a Promise To Deep Secrecy," "Planning Falters As Crises Appear," "An Issue Is Lost in the Labyrinth" of committees, and "The Mitchell Plan Runs Into a Snag").[37]

The obituaries for health-care reform kept coming in September 1994. "Better Off Dead?" ("Lawmakers act as if modest reform is still alive, but it may do more harm than good.") Or again, "Any Additional Delay for Health Bill Means Death for Proposal This Year."[38]

The final nails on the health-care coffin in later 1994 were driven in by the sweeping Republican Congressional victories in the November elections and by the rise of ultra-conservative Representative Newt Gingrich. "Gingrich, Now a Giant, Aims at Great Society" and with "A big agenda: 'We simply need to erase the slate and start over.' " Victory meant for "Gingrich: 'Cooperation [with White House, Congressional Democrats, etc.], Yes. Compromise, No.' " The "Election Has Altered Regulatory Landscape[, leaving] . . . President Less Able to Advance Goals [and] . . . New curbs on the Administration's ability to govern by executive acts [vis-à-vis a hostile] . . . Congress." Interestingly in December 1994, in the face of all these circumstances, "While Congress Remains Silent, Health Care Transforms Itself" ("A New Breed of H.M.O.'s," "Seeking to Control the Market").[39]

If Congress was intended by the Founders to be an untidy (though not corrupt) place for vigorously exercised checks and balances, which could lead at times to extremes of confrontation or stalemate, Congress continued to receive its share of unforgiving public criticism during 1994 prior to the Republican Congressional victories in the November elections. There were reports in June of "Gloom

Under The Dome." ("Despite Rostenkowski's alleged sins, Congress is trying to clean itself up. But is it getting any more effective?" A huge majority in polls said no.) It was called the "See-Nothing Congress" ("Whitewater cover-up rolls on"). Also, "Striving for Legislative Accomplishment, Congress Lands in a Struggle Against Itself" ("For the Democrats, even moves forward incite suspicion"). More starkly, in October, "Lawmakers Claw Their Way Toward a Bitter Conclusion to the Session" ("The session can't come to an End soon enough for most of those involved"). Still lamented was "The High Price of Gridlock" ("Lawmakers head home to voters who appear primed to punish Democrats for the mess in Washington"). Similarly in October, "Rancor and Disappointment Mark the 103d Congress" ("Republicans and Democrats disagree even on their accomplishments"). Already back in April, "Many in Congress Are Deciding They Want Out, to the Democrats' Dismay." There were calls for "Self-Limiting Terms in Congress" because too many members had been there too long. On war powers, other kinds of criticisms were that "An acquiescent Congress has made it easy to blame an imperial presidency." After the November Congressional elections came shifts in public sentiment. "Americans Like Republican 'Contract [with America],' Poll Shows." Whereas in March both House and Senate turned down various cost-cutting and deficit-controlling budgetary proposals, now in December "Republicans Plan Sweeping Barriers To New U.S. Rules" ("House Proposal Would Impose a Ceiling on Overall Costs of Federal Regulations").[40]

"G.O.P.–Led Congress Convenes and Begins Trying to Reduce the Role of Government"

Early January of 1995 marked the beginning of the "first hundred days" of the new G.O.P.–led Congress' sweeping Reagan-like "revolution" in government through legislative means and aims. "Voters Expect Upheaval In Political Landscape," with "G.O.P. Set to Lead Congress to Right." As part of efforts to reform Congress itself as "Part of G.O.P.'s 'Contract With America,'" "House Set to Make Members Subject to the [Civil] Rights Laws" that they have imposed on Executive branch agencies, with "Bipartisan support for a Republican plan." The new House Speaker's broad new agenda was called "The Newt [Gingrich] Deal," a pun on F.D.R.'s sweeping "New Deal." As "Republicans . . . Take Reins," "G.O.P.–Led Congress Convenes and Begins Trying to Reduce the Role of Government." In the Senate, "Republicans try to take control of the agenda" as Senator "Dole Offers Foreign Policy Initiative." At the state level in New York, Governor Pataki's State of the State address to the state legislature called it "A New Era." The Clinton "Administration and G.O.P. [Are] Promising to Compromise." Yet Gingrich was now dubbed "King of the Hill" with his "plans to pull off his revolution." As "Master Of The House," "In a flurry of festivity and legislative reform, Newt Gingrich ascends and Washington becomes a town with two bosses." Clearly, "Republicans Want to Renew Vision Of Reagan (Then Redo His Math)," while "The list for cuts is long." Although "Fast Out of the Starting Gate, . . . the Route Ahead Is Long." One TV commentator compared Gingrich's rise in Congress to the role of a British Prime Minister in Parliament, without a direct national election but with the backing of a duly elected legislative majority. Another TV commentator said that legislative power had now shifted back from the White House and President to Capitol Hill and House Speaker.[41]

Already in January 1995 the Gingrich Congress' legislative assaults on big federal programs spanned a broad spectrum of subjects. "A Hostile House Sets Its Sights On Funds For Arts" as "Federal Role Reassessed." "Welfare Overhaul Chorus Begins on a Cautious Note" as "Lawmakers are ready to give states a bigger role but not the dictator's chair." As another basic part of Gingrich's "Contract with America," "House Passes Amendment to Balance Federal Budget." As a "Proposal Beyond Politics," "Balanced Budget Amendment Is Seeking Fundamental Changes for the Government." In a counterthrust, "Senate Democrats Threaten Balanced Budget Measure" and Seek Specifics for Erasing Deficit by 2002." But "In Attack on Gingrich, Democrats Use His Tactics and Reap Chaos." Even so, it became "Hard Going for the Easy Part" in that "The popular balanced-budget bill was to be a sure winner, but attacks from all over may bring it down."[42]

In February 1995 "G.O.P. Contract Gains, But Obstacles Remain" as "Signs of a dispute over the balanced-budget amendment are growing." The list of targets for the new G.O.P.'s assault on federal bureaucracies, regulations, and spending was growing. "Backed by Business, G.O.P. Takes Steps to Overhaul Environmental Regulations." "House Backs Line-Item Veto for President; Move Would Shift Budgetary Balance of Power." "House Debating Measure That Would Cut New Police." "Senate Democrats Fail to Shield Social Security From Deficit-Cutters." "Conservatives Forge New Strategy To Challenge Affirmative Action." "Republicans Advance [Legislative] Proposal to Reshape the Welfare System" and "Seek to Cut Aid to Teen-Age Mothers and Aliens." "House Votes Bill To Cut U.N. Funds For Peacekeeping." "Congressional Republicans Take

Aim at an Extensive List of Environmental Statutes." House "G.O.P. [Is] Targeting Social Programs For Budget Cuts," "But Democrats Fight Back as Clinton Attacks Proposal on School Lunch Funds." "House Votes to Freeze Regulations as Democrats Fail to Gain Health and Safety Exemptions." "Democrats in Congress Seem Stuck in Denial Stage of Grief." As for the "Congressional Chain-Saw Massacre," "If Newt Gingrich gets his way, the laws protecting air, water and wildlife may be endangered." "House Considers Bill to Impose Extensive Review Process on New Rules for Health and Safety." "Critics Say G.O.P. Cuts Put Unfair Burden on the Needy," as "The Contract with America is moving from the abstract to the concrete." Naturally there was interest in "The Local Forces [in Georgia] That Helped Shape Gingrich as a Foe of Regulations."[43]

The continuation in March–April of the new Republican-led Congressional "revolution" against big inefficient government, especially in the House after decades of Democratic domination, finally brought out numerous press reports on the legislative record of its "first hundred days," in allusions to the legislative record of the "first hundred days" of F.D.R.'s "New Deal." The "House Approves A New Standard For Regulations" but "Opponents Say the Measure Would Alter a Generation of Environmental Laws." "House Clears More Limits On Environmental Rules," with "Mandated Compensation for Landowners" ("An idea some say would make saving natural resources prohibitively costly"). "House Approves Deep Cuts in Regulations" in "A bill that could have a major impact on the environment." "Getting All Unbalanced" when "The G.O.P. juggernaut slows down as the budget amendment goes down to defeat in the Senate." "Republicans tap $100 Billion from Budget to Pay for Tax Cuts." "Debate in House on Welfare Bill Splits Republican Bloc." "House Backs Bill Undoing Decades of Welfare Policy," with "Control for the States." "Senate Reaches Accord on Plan to Change Rule-Making System," a "Measure [that] Would Give Congress Power to Veto Regulations Issued by U.S. Agencies." "House Turns Back Measures To Limit Terms in Congress," in "First Defeat For Contract." For "The Rebels With Cold Feet," "As unpopular points in the contract come due, Republicans find it harder and harder to stick together." "House Votes to Cut Taxes By $189 Billion Over 5 Years As Part Of G.O.P. 'Contract,'" but "G.O.P. Gets Mixed Reviews From Public Wary on Taxes." Yet what about "Beyond the First 100 Days"? Had it been "100 Days of Attitude"?[44]

On April 7, 1995, the "Speaker, Celebrating 100 Days, Pledges to 'Remake Government'" ("An unusual broadcast from someone who is not the President"), while, "At Capitol Rally, G.O.P. Lawmakers

Applaud Themselves and Their Work" (in "Ticking off the items in the Contract with America"). At the same time, President "Clinton Defines The Limits Of Compromise With G.O.P.; Gingrich Urges 'Dialogue'" amid President's "Threat Of Vetoes." "G.O.P. Blitz of First 100 Days Now Brings Pivotal Second 100" as "House Republicans Move On to an Uncertain Fate." Was it, "After 100 Days, a 'Legacy of Unfairness,' or a 'Bolder Direction'?" One editorial called it "The 100-Day Hurricane." It seemed at times that these "first hundred days" had legislatively undone much of what F.D.R.'s "first hundred days" had legislatively created in a new federal system designed to put the nation back on its feet. But the debate over the "Contract" would continue, as the outcome hung in the balance.[45]

"After Republicans' First Hundred Days of Activity, Congress Is Ready for More"

The preceding news heading in later April 1995 suggested even bigger things to come. Was the British system of Prime Minister in Parliament becoming more in vogue through the Speaker in the American Congress, thereby tipping the balance away from the Executive to the Legislative branch? It was now being reported that "Speaker Gingrich Thinks Big About Leadership," while, "As a Model, Gingrich Takes Presidents, not [his own] Predecessors."[46]

But storm clouds were gathering on the horizon, particularly in the national budgetary process. Now it was "Crunch Time: Wrestling With Tight Budgets and Tax Anger." In May, for instance, "Budgetary Matters Intrude On Call for Medicare Unity" "As G.O.P. Asks Bipartisanship, [But] Gets Questions," with "A rocky reception for Mr. Gingrich and [Senate G.O.P. leader] Dole, courtesy of the White House." The various G.O.P. House-led reform efforts were sometimes meeting with G.O.P. Senate resistance as well, although both bodies were taking heat over their shared reform efforts. It was labeled "The Most Unkindest Cut" when "Medicare, farm subsidies, pensions and more are in the balance: Welcome to the second 100 days." That was the fallout after "House Committee Issues 7-Year Plan To Erase Deficit" (while "Senate Is Outdone"), according to which "Medicare and Medicaid Are Main Targets of G.O.P.'s Program," even though "Administration Rejects Plan As Based on False Promises." To be expected, "Budget Cuts Provoke Interest Groups' Fury," as "Veterans, Farmers and Elderly Mobilize." At this point, "[Democrat Sen.] Moynihan Joins Welfare Fray With Bill of His Own" and "Attacks Effort to End Entitlement Feature." In addition, "Senate Dismisses Clinton's Fiscal Plan," while "Democrats

Are Silent as G.O.P. Seeks to Embarrass White House." As a special news magazine report on "The Budget Revolution" announced on its front cover, "This Time It's Serious: The chopping has begun. For the first time in decades, Congress is committed to balancing the budget. It will mean slashing as much as $1.4 trillion and cutting programs that affect virtually every American citizen. But surprise of surprises: people want it that way. The tough choices are on the table, and it's about time." After the House approved a balanced budget plan, so, too, did the Senate in late May, followed at the end of June by both G.O.P.–led Houses in a jointly approved version.[47]

But the fallout and fireworks were just beginning. One full-page newspaper ad in July bore the provocative title "Is Newt Gingrich Above the Law?" Another news story's headline pinpointed the British model—"The Speaker Speaks, the Tax-Prime Minister." Still another announced, "Here Comes the Pork" as "The Republicans who promised to make historic budget cuts are cutting some sweet deals as well." Then in August came "A virtual declaration of war against the legislative branch" on other issues: " 'This Congress Is on the Wrong Track,' Clinton Declares." At this point the British model was again pointed out: "House Party—With Political Discipline It Works Like Parliament." Speaker Gingrich was starting to be weakened by growing ethical charges, soon to be formally investigated. An outcry against "The G.O.P. Legislative Blackmail" was also heard in November.[48]

Then came the government shutdown due to deadlock over passage of the national budget. In mid-November of 1995, "Federal Workers Go Home as Both Sides in Budget Impasse Stiffen" as "Congress and the President struggle over principles and public opinion." In December it was "Back to the Bench" in that, "As the budget battle intensifies, Gingrich lowers his profile." Reports were coming in on "Newt's Cash Machine," for his "GOPAC was just the start. Newt Gingrich is master of the Beltway money game." Notwithstanding mounting criticisms and accusations against Gingrich, *Time* magazine named him "Man of the Year" in January 1996. Its story on "Newt's World" dealt with "How one man changed the way Washington sees reality." Speaker Gingrich himself was a primary leader of the government shutdown. "For Congress at Midpoint: To the Left or the Right, Gridlock [Is] Everywhere." The public's ire and the upcoming November elections were weakening the G.O.P. hardline agenda already by January 1995. Finally, at the end of March, "Republican Lawmakers and White House Reach a Compromise," with "Debt and Line-Item Veto Bills Approved." A day later, "Gingrich Gets Mild Rebuke From Panel In Ethics Case." In late April, there were "New Ethics Complaints Filed Against Gingrich." A couple of days later, "Congress And White House Finally Agree On Budget, 7 Months Into Fiscal Year." Or again, "Congress Votes to Approve '96 Spending Bills After Long, Bitter Dispute." The above sequences of Newt's troubles and Congress' acquiescence can be duly noted. Then, too, Bill Clinton may have been mindful of possible impending legal troubles of his own. For in June it was "Whitewater on the rise" ("The president and his [re-election] campaign must contend with a newly invigorated investigation").[49]

The legislative activities of the 104th Congress were now in transition. According to one report, "Political Issues Push Congress To Set Aside Its Legislation." According to another, "With [November] Elections Drawing Near, Legislative Logjam Breaks and Congress Buckles Down." Whatever the case in final results, legislative action was forthcoming, along with further partisan struggles. In July "After Record Delay, Pressure Builds for Budget Reform," as "A pending election makes those facing blame seek solutions." At the same time, "Senate Approves Sweeping Change In Welfare Policy," while "President Welcomes Bill but Still Sees Room for Improvements." By mid-August there was "A blizzard of bills from Congress," but "Will welfare reform worsen life for the poor?" As the November election drew closer, a key question was "Can the Democrats recapture the Hill?" Headlines in September for the Republicans in Congress were not promising as "Gingrich Faces 4 New Charges From House Ethics Panel" and "Gingrich Ethics Inquiry" was setting off "Alarm Bells" for the G.O.P.[50]

Final verdicts and outcomes were mixed. If by September 1996 the "104th Congress Falls Short of Revolution," the "G.O.P. Legislators Win Frugality Fight Though Goals Are Unmet," for, "Military aside, few programs are left untouched by spending cuts." An October assessment of "Clinton and Congress" was that it was "A Partnership That Sprang From Self-Interest" ("The 103rd Congress—Early Rejoicing, And Then the Fall"; "The 104th Congress—Wounded President Regains His Strength"; "The 105th Congress—Ahead: Revolution Or Incrementalism?"). The Gingrich Congress' perceived excesses included "The color of money" ("In the fight for control of Congress, interest groups are betting millions.") and "How Congress Curtailed the Courts' Jurisdiction." Yet those excesses were perhaps offset by "A Radical Change" such as "Enshrining a balanced budget." As for Gingrich himself, after his November reelection and that of the President, "Gingrich Sees Improved Relations Between Congress and Clinton." Similarly, newly elected "House Freshman Label Themselves as Pragmatic" ("An incoming class seems comfortable with compromise"). In December, a House ethics subcommittee "Panel Concludes Gingrich Violated Ethics Rules but Severe Penalty for Him Is Unlikely" (after "An admission to false statements and to bringing discredit on the House"). Finally, in early January, the House "G.O.P. Narrowly Re-Elects Gingrich As House Speaker, Despite Ethics Accusations." Looking back upon the Founders, Gingrich had earlier depicted them as intending that "Congress Shall Be Nothing if Not Contentious." He certainly had acted accordingly and with a mixed record during his rise to leadership in the 104th Congress. The story was not yet over.[51]

4. CONGRESS DURING CLINTON'S SECOND TERM

"105th Congress Convenes Facing a Full Plate of Reforms"

With the "105th Congress Convenes Facing a Full Plate of Reforms" in early January 1997, questions over the re-elected Speaker Gingrich and his role continued and even intensified. In mid-January, a House "Panel, Citing Pattern Of Ethics Flaws, Seeks A Gingrich Reprimand." A few days later, the full "House, In A 395–28 Vote, Reprimands Gingrich," with stiff financial penalties for breaking the rules and adding to costs of the investigation. By mid-February, with both sides now somewhat more conciliatory, "Clinton and Republican Leaders Agree on Five Goals," including on matters relating to the budget. Because of the booming economy, the "Federal Budget May Shrink Even Without Amendment," but a "[Balanced] Budget Amendment Heads for Defeat in Senate." In addition, the "House Rejects Term Limits, Bringing Drive to Dead Stop." In early March "Republicans Stew Over Losing Streak On Major Reforms." As part of his and Congress' problems, "Former Allies Torment Gingrich." It was still "Newt In The Crosshairs" ("G.O.P. snipers have taken aim at the Speaker, but no one has figured out how to govern with a Big Agenda and a tiny majority."). In April Gingrich was called by some of his ardent foes a latter-day "Robespierre of the right" and "Genghis Newt." Meanwhile, "Few in Congress Support Any of 57 Measures to Overhaul Campaign Financing Laws."[52]

In counterdistinction to the new Congress' reform efforts—which were off to a slow mixed start, being still partly stymied by the prolonged Gingrich imbroglio—the long-standing impasses over the national budget was opening up. At the beginning of May 1997, "After Years Of Wrangling, Accord Is Reached On Plan To Balance Budget By 2002," as "Both G.O.P. and Clinton Claim Victory in Deal Built on New Deal." A major factor was that "Economic Boom Busts the US Deficit." In The "Washington Windfall," "A booming economy helps Congress and Clinton Glide to a historic budget-balancing deal." Critics explained "How prosperity gave us a lousy budget deal" ("showered with $225 billion in newfound revenue, politicians got too comfortable."). In later June "House and Senate Pass Legislation to Balance Budget." In late July "House And The G.O.P. Announce Deal To Balance Budget And To Cut Taxes," and "Passage Is Likely."[53]

But by now, in mid-1997, "Forget the Fracases: GOP Rules on Hill," as "Republicans, with White House help, set agenda on budget, taxes, other key issues." There was now a "New Period of Pragmatism in Congress." As was also now said, "The Revolution Is Dead. Long Live the Revolution," for "Gingrich put down some rebels. But rebellion is now part of the House landscape." Confrontation was again in the air, as in, for instance, "The GOP's judicial freeze" through "A fight to see who rules over the law." In their "Empty-Bench Syndrome," "Congressional Republicans are determined to put Clinton's judicial nominees on hold."[54]

By the spring and summer of 1998 Congressional confrontation was further on the rise once again. "Fractious House Republicans Slow the Pace of Lawmaking," along with "Expectations that Gingrich will depart to run for president and to GOP uncertainties." After reports that "Gingrich . . . Seeks Softer Image," it was soon "No more Mr. Nice Speaker" ("Why is Gingrich back on the attack?"). Much of the answer to that question could be summed up as the "[Clinton] Scandal's Price: GOP Chops Up Bill's Agenda." Meantime, "House Republicans Battle Over Beliefs and What They Mean to Budget," and "House Republicans Resume Drive to Cut Government and Taxes." True, "In Slap at G.O.P. Leadership, House Stops Move to Deny Food Stamps to Immigrants" and "Budget Feud Reveals Chasm Dividing GOP." Yet House "Panel Approves Deep Cuts in Programs Championed by Clinton." Also, "Gingrich Questions Clinton's Policy on Iran Arms Inspection," and "Congress Confronts [Attorney General] Reno" on certain issues. In addition, "Assault on the Tax Code Begins" ("With IRS reform under way, Republican lawmakers turn their attention to simplifying or abolishing the US tax code."). Indeed, the "House Votes to Dump Tax Code by 2003." On balance, then, the Republican-led House was still alive with prospects for reform legislation and political advancement.[55]

"Chaos in Congress" or "A Do-Something Congress"?

Then, in the fall of 1998, came the House's impeachment actions against the President in the Monica Lewinsky sex scandal and other matters. The major headlines told the story in a nutshell. At the start, "Report Sent By [Special Counsel Kenneth] Starr To House; Impeachment Process Weighed; Clinton Seeks Party Support." In the high-stakes "Impeachment Politics," it was "Clinton vs. Gingrich: A weak president faces a foe who can overplay his hand." In "The Fast Track To Impeachment" "The public wants the scandal to end, but Gingrich cannot afford to cut a deal just yet. He's got to placate the faithful and settle some scores." The Gingrich vs. Clinton divide was growing deeper. Events were heating up and moving faster. In early October of 1998 the "House, In A Partisan 258–176 Vote, Approves A Broad, Open-Ended Impeachment Inquiry." It was now called "Chaos in Congress."[56]

In the meantime, the increasingly rancorous partisan divides in Congress did not augur well for its ability to attend to the hard business of legislating. Once again, in early October of 1998, such squabbling served to show "Why Congress Budget Train Is Seldom on Time [or on track]." For "If spending bills aren't passed," very soon, "a government shutdown is possible." Fortunately, in mid-October, "Lawmakers Work on Final Details of an Agreement on the Budget." At that point, "Budget Accord Is Reached; Both Sides Claim A Victory As Shutdown Is Averted." Soon thereafter, "By Wide Margin, House Passes $500 Billion Budget Bill." Quickly, then, the "Spending Bill, Laden With Pork, Is Signed Into Law." As for "Why There's So Much Left in Congress' 'In' Box," "With thousands of bills, even issues with bipartisan support don't get resolved": "It would take 100 Congresses to debate all the bills introduced every year. Not to mention small resolutions." Finally, there was "As Congress Session Ends, a Question of Legacy" (and "A reprimand, a coup attempt, and an impeachment inquiry"). And "As Election Nears, Expectations Shift for Both Parties."[57]

Following the mid-term Congressional elections in early November 1998 came the swift downfall of Speaker Gingrich in the new incoming 106th Congress. "Facing Revolt, Gingrich Won't Run For Speaker And Will Quit Congress" ("Only Four Years After Triumph, a Fall of Surprising Suddenness"). The "Man of a Thousand Ideas Falls Prey to His Flaws." In the "Fall Of The House of Newt," "An election shock ignites a Republican revolt. Gingrich is only the first victim in the growing fight for the party's future." In the final analysis, according to one TV commentator, Speaker Gingrich failed in his last two years to control the legislative agenda in contradistinction to his control over it during his first two years, due largely to his flaws, Clinton's rebound, and the impatient public's perception that the Republicans rather than the Democrats bore the main responsibility for the recent government shutdown. For a time, Congress' control of the legislative agenda was reminiscent of its later-19th-century role in relation to the Executive branch.[58]

In the immediate aftermath of Gingrich's fall in November 1998 and with the hoped-for end to the recent political fighting, one newspaper's editorial now called it "A Do-Something Congress" ("The political benefits from bipartisan teamwork should subdue partisan squabbling"), in contrast to the above-cited editorial the month before in October, "Chaos in Congress."[59]

"Governing by Investigation?" ("Impeachment mire raises the question of how effectively Congress governs")

However, a month afterward in December 1998 it was back to a renewed uncertainty over "Governing by investigation?," as "Impeachment mire raises the question of how effectively Congress governs." ("The impeachment inquiry harms not only the president's prestige but Congress' too.") The resumption of the impeachment hearings progressed slowly and haltingly in the immediate wake of the midterm elections. "More Lawmakers Seeking Impeachment Escape Hatch" as "Hearings rev up this week, but Clinton may have upper hand in election aftermath." In "The Lone Starr Hearings," "Ken Starr took his case to Congress and lost: he became the target, and few people paid attention." In later November the House "Impeachment Panel Starts Work On 3 Articles Against President" on "Counts of Perjury, Obstruction, [and] Abuse of Power."[60]

But events then moved swiftly ahead. In mid-December, a House "Panel, On Party Lines, Votes Impeachment; Clinton Voices Remorse, Invites Censure." A week later the full "House To Debate Impeachment . . . As U.S. Continues Air Assault On Iraq," with "Bitter Clash on Timing" as "Grave Issues Roil Capital." The next day, "With Partisan Raucous, A Bitter House Debates The President's Impeachment." A day later, "Clinton Impeached . . . [And] Faces A Senate Trial," while developing a "Strategy for Governing And Facing the Senate." The exploding partisan political fighting was building upon a complexity of longer-developing trends, including "Over 24 years, the rise of single-issue politics" (or, "How the Sunshine Harmed Congress").[61]

In early January of 1999, "A Full Impeachment Trial . . . [Is] Likely As Compromise Fades." A day after that report the "Clinton Trial Opens, but Process Talks Go On" ("For Senate, a Stirring Time Of Worry and Wonderment"). Then the "Senate, In Unanimity, Sets Rules For Trial" ("Preserving the dignity of the institution and giving a sense of credibility"). In mid-January "Senators, as Jurors, Hear Arguments by the House." A week later, "Senators Are Heard From, but the Legal Terms Still Do the Talking." A day after that, the "Lewinsky Issue Throws Trial Into Turmoil Along Party Lines." Then in early February the "Senate Decides Not To Call Lewinsky As A Live Witness; Votes To Show Tape Instead," while "Marathoner-Lawmakers Now Sprint for the Finish Line." At this juncture, "Damaged By Trial, Senators Standing Sinks In New Poll" ("Republicans Are Blamed . . . [and] Many Conservatives Fear Losses in 2000 Election—Clinton Is Still Popular").[62]

On February 8, 1999, a key Republican prosecutor in the Senate trial, Representative Henry "Hyde, In Closing, Demands Senate 'Cleanse Office' " ("But Clinton's Defense Urges That 'Voices' of Nation Be Heard"). Then, "As Senate Goes Into Lockdown, Quiet Fills Capitol," while, "Out of Earshot, the Senate Deliberates Clinton's Fate." At this point, "Clinton Vows Strong Drive to Win A House Majority, Advisers Say," and "Republicans Respond Angrily to Reports of Clinton's Vow." Finally, on February 12, "Clinton Acquitted Decisively: No Majority For Ethics Charge," while "President Says He Is Sorry And Seeks Reconciliation."[63]

In the immediate aftermath, one thing was clear: "The Fallout of the Trial Is Far From Certain" ("A divergence on whether Clinton can rehabilitate his Presidency"). Whatever the eventual verdict on the Clinton presidency, "Congress has just demonstrated that an impeachment based on partisanship cannot succeed under a process that, like the Presidency itself, is founded on so steadfast a rock." Yet whether or not it came down to a "Self-Inflicted Wound" due to "The House managers' excess" is not a question that can be resolved here.[64]

"Putting Trial in the Past, Senators Work on Policy"

Indicative of the stability of U.S. government immediately following the national trauma of President Clinton's impeachment and trial was the government's quick return within days to regular routine operations in both the Congress and the White House. In an illustrative story dated February 14, 1999, just two days after Clinton's Senate acquittal, "Putting Trial in the Past, Senators Work on

Policy" (" . . . Senators of both parties [have now] turned to issues like Social Security, taxes and foreign policy. . ."). Was there not a remote parallel here to the national government's immediate resumption of its normal business just a few days after President Kennedy's assassination? Much different was the aftermath of the impeachment and trial of President Andrew Johnson, who, unlike President Clinton, remained extremely unpopular and weakened. Yet in one of history's more curious unnoticed reincarnations, Johnson's brief forlorn return as Senator shortly before his death to the very body that had tried him bears an inverted indirect parallel to Clinton's wife Hillary becoming a highly successful Senator even before his presidency ended. Such broader comparisons aside, the future of the 106th Congress' ongoing performance, particularly in the wide arena of legislation, remained an open question.[65]

For Congress, in any case, returning to business as usual largely meant returning to politics as usual, leaving questions ahead for its record on its main activity under the Constitution, legislation. Already, on February 19, 1999, just days after the presidential trial's end, an article on "Pawing through the detritus of impeachment" declared that "The trial left an atmosphere of unusual bipartisan harmony among Senators, so maybe concrete achievements are possible." A week or so later, it was "A Curse on the House" as "The Republicans in Congress . . . remain spellbound by the G.O.P.'s right-wing base. This is the end of Reaganism, the real legacy of Newt Gingrich—and Speaker Dennis Hastert's everyday nightmare." By mid-March it was "New Speaker, New Style, Old Problem (but Worse)." By September, "Anti-Federalism Measures Have Bipartisan Support," in that "Hoping to shift political power back to the states, a broad bipartisan coalition in the Senate and House of Representatives is preparing legislation that would make it harder for Congress and the executive branch to adopt laws and rules that pre-empt the states on a wide range of issues, like drugs, the environment, health and worker safety." In January of 2000—with the upcoming November elections for the next president and Congress, and with Clinton still in office—it was (no) "Surprise! Politics tops agenda in Congress" ("Legislators return to capital, but there'll be no big bills, lots of campaign oratory"). The following June it was called "A Pretend Congress." Then in October the "Gridlock Congress turns to bully pulpit" ("From Hollywood to tires, the 106th may be known for hearings more than its laws"). That month it was also dubbed "The Un-Congress" because of its lack of real legislative work. In early November, just prior to the elections, it was labeled "An Ineffectual Congress." Finally, in December, "With Minimal Fanfare, Congress Calls It Quits" in "A quiet conclusion to two years of high-intensity partisanship."[66]

For the budget, it was a familiar yet less rancorous legislative process in the 106th Congress in later 1999 and 2000 than in some previous sessions—an accomplishment in itself. In March of 1999, "Congress Passes G.O.P.'s Budget, Voting Largely Along Party Lines." In May it became "Congressional Budget Chaos" due in large part to partisan posturing. In July "Senate Approves Big Cut In Taxes, Courting A Veto" because it "Threatens U.S. Surplus, Clinton Says." In August "Congress Passes a Tax Bill Along Largely Party Lines." Then in October "Clinton and G.O.P. Take Step Toward a Budget Accord." A few days later, "Standoff on Budget Yields An Unexpected Dividend" when, "Without Tax Cuts or Spending Increases, Debt Is Trimmed Almost by Default." By November there came a "Budget lesson: Restraint slips away in an era of surplus." A few days later, "Senate Approves Budget Package, Ending Deadlock" but with "Spending Limits Broken." By later November, with budget agreement reached, "Underlying Tensions Kept Congress Divided to the End," with "Few Compromises and Fierce Politicking in Session Characterized by Standoff." As the next budget cycle for the following fiscal year (October 1 to September 30) began in Congress in the new year (typically after the president's State of the Union Message to Congress usually in later January along with his budget proposals), it was announced in later January 2000 that the "Federal Surplus Soars In Forecast By Budget Office" ("Under Any Formula, Numbers Add Up To a Fiscal Outlook Brighter Than Expected"). In the fall of 2000, the new surpluses led to struggles with the White House over excess spending, amid reports that "Binges Are Part of the Budget Fare" ("Ignoring mandates, Congress's spending exceeds its plans by billions every year"). In mid-December "Congress Adopts Contentious Spending Bill, Ending Its Work," as "Congress and Clinton reach agreement on issues large and small."[67]

In foreign affairs, major contentions between Congress and Clinton arose in 1999–2000. In April 1999 "In 2 Votes, House Challenges President Over Kosovo" and "Insists on Final Say on Troops on Ground." A key issue was whether in such situations "Only Congress Can Declare War." On another front, in October 1999 "The Senate Votes Down Nuclear Test Ban Treaty" in "A blow for the President watched around the world" in move that "Evokes Versailles Pact Defeat." Whereupon "Clinton Says 'New Isolationism' Imperils U.S. Security," and he "Attacks G.O.P. for Rejection of Test Ban." One article opined that "Eight months after impeachment, the defeat of the test ban proves that the air in Washington is still radioactive. And its likely to get worse."[68]

Meanwhile, in 2000, Congress turned to campaign finance reform, led by Senator John McCain and others, in an often uphill struggle. In the words of one March news account, "McCain [who lost to Bush in the 2000 Republican primaries] Returns to an Uneasy Senate," where "Reform is Popular, but not necessarily Campaign Finance Reform." According to another account, "He's popular every place but Congress," where ". . . McCain's colleagues hate him." A special news investigation in May reported that "Lavished with campaign cash, lawmakers are 'reforming' bankruptcy—punishing the downtrodden to catch a few cheats." Then in June the "Senate Approves Step To Overhaul Campaign Finance" in a "Surprise McCain Victory" ("Tax-Exempt Groups Are Target").[69]

5. CONGRESS DURING BUSH JR.'S FIRST TERM

"Drawing the Battle Lines on Capitol Hill"

In the aftermath of the disputed Y2K election of early November 2000, while "Drawing the Battle Lines on Capitol Hill," "Democratic leaders hope to use the presidential election uproar as leverage this session" of Congress in 2001 and beyond.[70]

Straight off, at that same point in January, with the newly elected 107th Congress then beginning, came Senator "McCain's Campaign Finance Bandwagon" once again, by which "The senator is ready for a legislative showdown with his former rival, Bush" Jr., the new president. In March the "Senate Opens Debate on Campaign Finance" in "A narrow victory for McCain on an early test vote." At that point, "Senators Defeat Effort To Derail A Soft-Money Ban" as "The Senate handed a decisive victory today to the supporters of an overhaul of the campaign finance law, comfortably defeating a rival proposal that would have limited but not prohibited the unregulated large donations to the political parties that escalated to nearly $500 million in the last election." In "The Senate's Moment for Change," "McCain's Crusade Is Just One Reason for Immanent Success," for "Some lawmakers see a system that could harm them." In early April in "A McCain Victory, Campaign Finance Bill Passes In Senate, 59–41; House Foes Vow Fight." In June "House Republicans Seek New Way to Block a Campaign Bill." In July "House Critics Call McCain A Bully on Campaign Bill." For "McCain's House of Pain," it was asked "Will his campaign-finance bill survive the gauntlet?" Then in mid-July the "House Shelves Campaign Finance Bill After a Fierce Rules Fight" and "A Cloudy Future," while Republican Speaker "Hastert Has 'No Plan' to Bring Finance Bill Back to the Floor" (and, meanwhile, "Republicans Report Record In Donations And Cite Bush").[71]

Adding to the complicated and fractious post-election political situation in Congress—particularly in the Senate with its members evenly divided between the two parties—was the stunning news in May 2001 that a "G.O.P. Senator [Jeffords] Plans Shift, Giving Democrats Control In Setback For White House," leaving "Republicans Grim" in "a historic shift." With their new majority leader-to-be, Senator Daschle, "Democrats, Primed for Power, Are Eager to Put Their Priorities on Agenda." The G.O.P. had been "Bushwacked!" as "The Senate's flip makes it a whole new ball game." The sudden reversal of power was reportedly the first time in American Congressional history that the Senate leadership changed hands without an election resulting in change of party not only for majority leader but also for key committees such as Foreign Relations and Judiciary, where the chairmen set the agendas. Clearly, it now became "A Different Agenda," for "Once in control, Senate Democrats will be moving their issues to the top of the list." In June "The Democrats say they plan to focus on avoiding gridlock with bipartisan deals" where "The key is Compromise." Yet a month or two later, with the party shift in agendas well under way, "Congress Shows a Stubborn Streak," while "Bush lacks the ability to force action on Capitol Hill." In the meantime, there were, "On Hill, signs of a GOP schism with Bush." In December the "G.O.P. Pushes to Make [the new Democratic Majority leader Tom] Daschle Appear a National Villain." At that point, "Both Parties Deflect Blame For Stalemate On Economy."[72]

Shortly before the historic shift of power on Capitol Hill in May–June of 2001, the "Senate Passes Budget Plan With A $12 Trillion Tax Cut" and the "G.O.P. Declares Victory After 65–35 Vote." Soon thereafter, "Congress Adopts Budget Proposal With Big Tax Cut." Momentum had clearly been building. Said "Congress on tax cuts: No stopping us now." Then in later May a "Dogged Fight by Senate Democrats Delays Tax Cut Bill." It was during that period that "G.O.P. Senator Weighs Switch That Would End 50–50 Split." Finally, a week later, "Congress Passes Tax Cut, With . . . Big Margin for Deepest Trims in 20 Years." Even so, in the fall "Lawmakers' Votes on Economic Legislation Will Test Talk of Bipartisanship." When a "Divided House Approves Economic Recovery Plan," it was "Reviving a partisan fight over who gains from tax breaks."[73]

From a different angle, an article on "Speak in Code" suggested that "Instead of cutting taxes, Congress ought to ax some of the increasingly complex rules." Likewise, it was said "Congress, Audit Thyself!," so that "Rather than beat up the IRS, Congress can simplify the tax code." A call in one editorial to "Stop Conference Roulette" and to "Expose secrecy in legislating" bore relevance for those trying to overcome the excessively complex, voluminous, and obscure legislation often produced (or even deviously written) by Congress.[74]

"Congress in Search of Its Soul"

A useful epithet for characterizing the overall role of Congress during three years of 2002–2005 is that it was a "Congress in Search of Its Soul." That was the title of an editorial in February 2002 on a decisive moment for the House of Representatives on whether to approve campaign finance reform. A related searching question at that same time was "Can the Senate Police Itself?" ("The [Senator] Toricelli case raises some old questions"). That January there had been "A New Rallying Cry for Reform" by Congress on campaign financing. A chief catalyst was when "Enron Woes Revive Debate on Campaigns," leading to "A re-energized push for a bill to revamp political contributions," especially soft money. In February it quickly became "Campaign Armageddon" at a decisive moment for Congress. In "A Big Win for Reform" a few days later, House "Sponsors Thwart Moves to Scuttle Ban on Soft Money." The next day, "House Backs Broad Change In Financing Of Campaigns; Fast Senate Action Sought." Then, in "An Extraordinary Victory" in later March, and with a Senate 60 to 40 vote, "Campaign Finance Bill Wins Final Approval In Congress And Bush Says He'll Sign It." The new reform legislation was well timed in view of the upcoming November elections of 2002 for Congress. "Twenty-eight years after the last campaign-finance reforms," in the wake of Watergate and the 1972 presidential elections, would the "new rules . . . be tough enough to clean up the game?"[75]

"By Acquiring Full Control of the Congress, Republicans Gained New Responsibility" after the elections of November 2002. Various telling reports then appeared in November through January. "Its Eyes Fixed on Terrorism, Congress Puts Off Many Bills," while an "Array of Domestic Issues Await New Session." There were "Signature laws that may not have signature" ("Hard part for campaign finance, school, and corporate reform is implementation"). "Frist's ascension further shifts power to White House" ("Tennessee Republican Senator's rise to majority leader [replacing Democrat Daschle] will bolster Bush's agenda, but carry risks"). Then came the flurry of reports in January 2003 on the makeup of the new 108th Congress. "In a New Republican Era, [Tom] DeLay Is Drawing the Agenda for Congress as in-coming majority leader of the House" ("Building a power base one lawmaker at a time"). "A struggle over money and staff paralyzes the Senate, where precedent, and compromise, rule" ("Fighting for Power in the New Senate").[76]

Reports became mixed in 2003–2004 with various swings of the pendulum in the balances of power and with Congress still struggling to sort out its role. In February 2003 it became "Congress and the President. One Party, but Divided." In May "Congress watches its power ebb" ("A wartime president now fights terrorism perpetually, prompting Congress to cede power in some areas"). In August "Congress begins to say 'no' to White House" ("House and Senate assert independence on issues ranging from media to surveillance"), while "In Congress all roads lead to a conference room" ("A split House and Senate increasingly send disputed bills to a joint committee. The saga of the energy bill."). Another prime example occurred shortly before, in June 2003, when "House–Senate Conference Committee Could Take Weeks to Work on Medicare [Overhaul Bills]" ("G.O.P., in a Turning Point, Claims Medicare Leadership"). In September there was a "Big agenda—and a more vocal Congress" ("From prescription drugs to Iraq and tax cuts, new rifts open in Washington"). In October "Rewriting Top Legislation Is an Invitation-Only Party" ("Republican reins are tight on conference committee work"). By the following May of 2004, "Feeling Left Out on Major Bills, Democrats Turn to Stalling Others." Later that month complaints were voiced over "Congressional Inaction" because "The House, most of the time, is not in session." After the Congressional elections the following November, coupled with Bush's re-election, came the "G.O.P.'s bolder reign on Hill" ("Republicans are quickly showing a postelection confidence while Democrats struggle to regroup. But dangers lurk for both parties.").[77]

On the budget and tax cuts the Republicans in Congress were increasingly able during this period to implement the Bush proposals. In April 2002 "House Passes Bill to Make Bush's Tax Cut Permanent" ("Despite long odds, a bill will be useful in the '02 races"). A year later in April–May 2003—after news on "The Senate Rebels" and "How will Bush handle the budget revolt in Congress?"—a "$318 Billion Deal Is Set In Congress For Cutting Taxes" (as V.P. "Cheney Brokers Accord"), whereupon "Bush Signs Tax Cut Bill, Dismissing All Criticism." Over a year after that, in September 2004, even before the Republican gains in the November elections, "Congress Approves A Bill To Extend Bush's Tax Cuts."[78]

Congress was ever mindful of its legislative–constitutional powers of the purse and of the declaration of war through its role in the Iraq war during the years 2000–2004 and beyond. In September 2002 "Congress Nears Resolution On Backing Force in Iraq." In October "Lawmakers Begin Push To Give Bush Authority On Iraq," although "United Voice on Iraq Eludes Majority Leader," Democrat Tom Daschle. A week later, "Congress, Granting Broad Mandate, Authorizes Bush to Use Force Against Iraq" ("G.O.P. Backing Is Solid—Democrats' Votes Are Sharply Split"). The next day, "Bush Will Use Big Victory In Congress To Press U.N." Nearly a year later, in September 2003, "Congress's List Is a Lengthy One, With Iraq at the Top," while "Domestic Issues Include Drug and Energy Bills." That October "Lawmakers Back Request By Bush On Funds For Iraq" in "An $87 Billion Package—Afghan Money Is Included." Then, in April of 2004, "Bush Aide Warns Senate [That] Sovereignty for Any New Government in Iraq May Be Limited" ("Possible Clash With U.N.," "Interim Leaders Could Not Pass New Laws, Bush Aides Tell Congress"). In May "Congress toughens [its] war oversight role," as "Scale of the prison scandal, plus concern about irrelevance, force lawmakers to tighten monitoring." A series of steps on 9/11 soon followed: "9/11 Panel Is Said To Sharply Fault Role Of Congress" ("Sees Oversight Failures"); "9/11 Proposals Lead The Agenda Facing Congress" ("Action on Panel's Report"); "Lawmakers Offer Bipartisan Bill on 9/11 Panel Proposals"; and "Accord Reached in Congress On Intelligence Overhaul" ("Measure, Backed by 9/11 Panel and Bush, Calls for New Post"). After the president in later December signed into law the intelligence bill worked out by the House and Senate, the "9/11 Panel Members [Were] to Lobby for a Restructured Congress."[79]

6. CONGRESS DURING BUSH JR.'S SECOND TERM: FIRST PHASE

Congress during the first phase of President Bush Jr.'s second term was still struggling to "find itself" in the midst of a re-energized powerful presidency, but was becoming more assertive on its role in various issues facing it in 2005 and early 2006. What would happen after that initial phase, given the historical precedents for a presidential slowdown in the later parts of a president's second term, was still to be seen.

To one news writer's mind in later January of 2005 there was no doubt as to Congress' true role, for "To Founders, balance of power should lie with Congress." In reality, the news accounts on the state of affairs in Congress were mixed. Queried one report, "Who's minding Congress?" ("Corporate titans may now be toeing the line, but what about the congressional titans?"). Urged another, "Bring Democracy to Congress," for "our national government is dysfunctional" owing in particular to the surreptitious manner in which congressional business is often conducted. Now it was "Lawmakers Under the Microscope" as "Members of Congress face scrutiny as the Abramoff investigation heats up." It was said that " 'Purple power' pulls new laws through House" ("Many Democrats, fearful for their seats, vote with the GOP—and the old bifurcation fades."). From another angle, "Let's legislate consensus-building." In later December 2005 a "Messy Congressional Finale" occurred when "Rebels in the G.O.P., Seeing Bush's Polls, Halted Easy Majority Rule." At the same time, the "Battle for Congress Looms as Parties Set Stage for Another Politically Turbulent Year."[80]

Soon enough, in January, came renewed problems for House Majority Leader, Republican Tom DeLay, a strong backer (as "The Hammer") of Bush's agenda. DeLay was forced to resign that post due to involvement in an election-year lobbying scandal. "Caught in an Ethical Snare[,] DeLay focus on fundraising powered GOP gains but led to legal problems." His departure was significant for the G.O.P., for back in October it was noted that "DeLay's Power Transcends the 'Majority Leader' Title" ("The Hammer's vast sphere of influence stretches beyond Capitol Hill and K-Street"). Even more troublesome at that point was news that a "Lobbyist Accepts Plea Deal And Becomes Star Witness In A Wider Corruption Case," causing "Tremors Across Capital" ("Abramoff Accord," "Bribery Investigation Is Expected to Reach Into Congress"). Where all this would end remained to be seen.[81]

At issue in the Senate in 2005 was the confirmation process for the president's judicial nominees. They were generally opposed for being too conservative by Democrats, who employed the filibuster in order to thwart Republican domination. In May "Fight On Judges And Filibusters Opens In Senate," with "Bitter Partisan Division" and with "Minority Power at Issue in Democrats' Bid to Stop Bush Appointments." Not surprisingly, the "Senate's Business Slows as Filibuster Fight Intensifies." The issue was "More Than Judgeships," for "The fight over filibuster is at the heart of our democracy." At the same time, the "Filibuster Fight Is Bruising the Image of Capitol Hill." As "The Senate Nears the Point of No Return," "A singular institution could be transformed by the filibuster fight." Then, in later May of 2005, a "Bipartisan Group In Senate Averts Judge Showdown," enabling "3 Blocked Nominees to Get Votes" although "Filibuster Rule Stands" ("A Modest Victory for the President, but Challenging Tests Still Lie Ahead"). Further struggles did indeed lie ahead. In early July, "Out of Practice, Senate Crams For Battle Over Court Nominee."[82]

Also again at issue in the Senate during this period was the war in Iraq. In November 2005, "Senate G.O.P. Pushes for Plan On Ending War" ("Lawmakers to Revisit Detainee Rights Issue"). Increasingly, "On War, Senate Flexes Muscle" ("From torture to Iraq strategy, it asserts more authority in dealing with the White House"). Related or not, the next day "In Loss For G.O.P., House Rejects Spending Plan" as "22 Republicans Vote No," and the "Decision Highlights Party Troubles and a Divide Over Fiscal Policy." Increasingly clear in February 2006 was the "Senate target: Bush's war powers" ("In coming days the Senate will ask tough questions about the Patriot Act and NASA wiretaps"). In March "Congress eyes own window on Iraq war" ("Lawmakers create blue-ribbon panel to give it independent reviews of progress in Iraq").[83]

On a related issue there was at first in 2005 "Little Progress in Bid to Extend Patriot Act" as "Civil liberties advocates call for open deliberations on the F.B.I.'s powers." When in July "House to Take Up Patriot Act Extension," "Bush Presses for Renewal, but Democrats Seek Restrictions" ("Democrats invoke civil liberties and Republicans stress national security"). A week later, the "Senate Makes Permanent Nearly All Provisions of Patriot Act, With a Few Restrictions" in a "Compromise that civil rights advocates say they can live with." In November "Senate Approves Limiting Rights Of U.S. Detainees," while "Ending Legal Challenges," in a "New Law [That] Would Nullify Supreme Court Ruling on Guantánimo." The next month there was a "Compromise Reached on Renewing Patriot Act." However, a week later, "Senators Thwart Bush Bid To Renew Law On Terrorism," as "Account of Secret Eavesdropping Enters Debate on Patriot Act" in "A fight about the balance between national security and personal privacy." In January the "Basis For Spying In U.S. Is Doubted," as a "Study by [Bipartisan] Arm of Congress Questions Legality." Finally, in March 2006, the "Senate Passes Legislation To Renew Patriot Act."[84]

Now that President Bush's second term was entering its second year—with his "political capital" largely spent following the first year after his re-election—would the Republican-led Congress now take on a more independent role in relation to him? In this connection, was a news article written just before Bush's triumphal second inauguration in January 2005 prophetic? Entitled "To the Founders, Congress was king," it took special note of the almost kingly ceremonies and celebrations soon to occur in the nation's capital, all far removed from the less exalted presidency envisioned by the Founders. For they thought that Congress would or should be the main focal point of the new tripartite federal system. "The nation's Founders expected Congress, not the president, to be where the action was. The president was supposed to be, well, more like an 'errand boy' for Congress. . . . [They] envisioned a supreme legislative branch as the heart and soul of America's central government." Although the balance of powers increasingly tipped during the 20th century in favor of presidents, especially during wartime, the news article seemed to favor for 2005 and beyond a more assertive role for Congress, including in the Mideast wars.[85]

Chapter IV

The U.S. Supreme Court and Federal Courts

1. THE COURTS UNDER REAGAN AND BUSH SR.

200th Anniversary of the Constitution

During the 1987 commemoration of the 200th anniversary of the creation of the U.S. Constitution, a number of news articles dealt with the healthy tensions intended by the Framers in their separation of Federal legislative, executive, and judicial powers. One piece was aptly titled "Governing: 200 Years Of Tension." According to another on "Separate powers strengthen constitutional system," the Founders' "concept of separation of powers is still vibrant today—and a continued protection to the populace from potential governmental abuse or oppression . . . [as well as being a key to many recent] battles between the president and Congress. . . . And it is at the center of an ongoing debate over judicial authority—and whether the jurisdiction of the courts should be broadened or limited [the former position being generally supported by liberals, the latter by conservatives. At bottom is the issue of] . . . judicial authority to overrule legislative and executive decisions [—a] . . . tug of war . . .

[now lying behind] the controversy over nomination[s] . . . to the U.S. Supreme Court . . ."[1]

Indicative of that issue was, at the same point in 1987, the news that the "Supreme Court broadens scope of civil rights laws" in "Two rulings [that] extend protection to Arabs, Jews, other minorities." As reported elsewhere, "Justices Hold Ethnic Groups Entitled to Relief Under 1866 Race Law." Also at that point in time it was reported that "High Court Voids Curbs On Teaching Evolution Theory," rendering "Louisiana Law Nullified," as "Justices Say Legislators' Aim Was to Promote Religion, Not Academic Choice."[2]

Such perspectives are ingrained in the Court's central role in relation, for example, to the "Constitutional cornerstone: the First Amendment" (" 'Congress shall make no law respecting an establishment of religion, or . . . abridging the freedom of speech . . .' "). As attested then in an article on "Time to change the Constitution?," concerning "The struggle over war powers": "Attempts to read the Constitution as if it were not a legal distribution of authority misconstrues its meaning."[3]

Interfaces with the Legislative Branch

During the period from 1989 to 1991, the Supreme Court issued many further rulings that interfaced directly with acts of Congress in important ways. Illustrative for present purposes were the following accounts. "New Limit Is Placed on Scope of 1866 Rights Law [in Reconstruction-era Civil Rights Act of 1866]." "Justices Narrow a Law on Free Legal Service." "[Federal] Law [in Victims of Crime Act of 1984] That Created Crime Victims' Fund Is Upheld." "Patriotism and Politics Mix in Reaction to Flag Ruling," as regards Court's overturning of the Flag Protection Act of 1989. "Justices Bolster Race Preferences At Federal Level" ("Court Affirms Power of Congress to Aid Minority Broadcasting" and "Promotion of Minority Broadcasts"), thereby upholding two federal Affirmative Action programs. "High Court Narrows Shield Libel Law," leaving "For courts and newsrooms, a ruling that may prove unsettling." "Court Considers Whether Voting Rights Act Covers Judgeship Races." "Justices Uphold U.S. Rule Curbing Abortion Advice," with "Clinic Aid At Issue," while "plaintiff had argued that the [Federal] regulations were not authorized by Congress and that they violated the free speech rights of clinic employees . . . [and] patients. . . ." "High Court Rules Aliens Can Sue Over Procedures in Amnesty Law" in the 1986 immigration law. "Court Ruling to Lift Curbs on Formerly Desegregated Schools." "Justices Weaken Impact of U.S.

Child Welfare Act" of 1980. "Court Avoids Decision On Time Limits of Laws" in "An effort to restrict scope of the Civil Rights Act" of 1991. "Court Upholds Widened Use of U.S. Extortion Law." "Supreme Court Eases States' Obligation Over Toxic Waste" in "A Victory for New York," as "Justices Say Congress Cannot Order Legislatures in States to Solve Disposal-Site Problems."[4]

Similar interfaces between Federal Courts and Congress as the Legislative branch can be illustrated for the same period as follows. "New Law [passed by Congress] Erects Barriers to the Federal Docket," while "Thousands of civil lawsuits will be diverted to state courts." "U.S. Judge Strikes Down New [Federal] Flag Law," as "The ruling brings new calls for a constitutional amendment." "Court Backs F.C.C. In [Its] Licensing Rules" "consistent with the authority granted the agency under the Communications Act of 1934" ("Applicants Need Not Specify Method of Meeting Public Service Requirement"). "Phone Companies Are Permitted To Provide Information Services," "But Judge Stays His Ruling to Allow for Appeals," that is, "for the newspaper industry to appeal the decision and then, if necessary, to carry the fight to Congress." "Government Branches Endangered" when "Impeachment Ruling Reopens Separation of Powers Debate" in "A court challenge to the affairs of the Senate"—a situation in which, by injecting himself into "the debate about how Congress may conduct impeachment proceedings, a Federal district judge here [in D.C.] has sought to throw into turmoil some fundamental notions about the constitutional relationship between Congress and the courts."[5]

The combined effect of the preceding examples of the Courts' interfaces with the Legislative branch of the Federal government is to show some of the many disparate ways in which the Judicial branch has not only worked out its constitutional role of interpreting and adjudicating the laws made by Congress. It has also become in ways an integral part of the Legislative branch and the legislative process. It is far from being the seemingly lesser, albeit coequal, branch, even though relegated by the Framers to a few short passages in the Constitution's third article, following the lengthy first two articles on the Legislative and Judicial branches respectively. The Judicial branch has, in recent history, become a mighty power in America. The impact of the Federal Judiciary's rulings and decisions upon the Legislature's laws and rules has continued to mount during conservative as well as liberal eras in its history.[6]

The collision course set for the Supreme Court nominee Clarence Thomas in his hearings before the U.S. Senate in mid- to later 1991 involved, in its final showdown, a high-stakes public TV spectacle never before witnessed in similar confirmation processes. Accused before the Senate of sexual harassment toward a black liberal female colleague earlier in their careers together, Judge Thomas, a conservative nominated by President Bush, launched an aggressive counter-offensive that eventually helped to win him confirmation. But the resulting firestorm left little doubt about the Supreme Court's central importance as a potential battleground in its interfaces with Congress. Heightening the drama were the unusually bitter divisions in Senate and public over political, racial, philosophical, and other viewpoints (including on abortion and on natural law or rights). In one telltale turning point, "Vote On Thomas Is Put Off As Senate Backing Erodes Over Harassment Charge," while "Judge Denies Allegations as Senate Encounters Storm of Outrage." Thomas' narrow Senate confirmation in mid-October ended a "Bitter Battle," according to one front-page headline.[7]

Interfaces with the Executive Branch

It is true that the Framers of the U.S. Constitution intended the three Federal branches to be not merely strictly separate bodies but also interrelating powers operating in a fluid state of dynamic tension through a system of checks and balances. Yet the question of where balance ends and encroachment begins has at times been a different matter in U.S. constitutional history. The two preceding chapters have found instances of encroachments by the Legislative and Executive branches into each other's spheres and roles as well as into those of the Judicial branch. The preceding subsection in this chapter has found examples of the Judicial branch's encroachments on the Legislative branch during the Reagan and Bush Sr. eras. Here we may note others in the Judiciary's relation to the Legislature. Sometimes a mild encroachment can become a strong infringement, or even a serious usurpation (as in some cases above of Presidents as "super-legislators"?).

For the Reagan–Bush Sr. years, the case of Iran–Contra again provides useful perspectives. In 1990, after Reagan had left office, the cases of John Poindexter and Oliver North, former White House Aides, gave insights into the Federal Judiciary's arguable partial encroachments upon Executive privilege in handling certain kinds of laws enacted by Congress, especially concerning foreign policy, which traditionally has laid with the Executive. Some representative headlines and captions revolve, first, around Reagan's Iran–Contra testimony: "Reagan Declines To Release Diaries To A

Former Aide" ("Cites Executive Privilege," but "[Federal] Judge Orders Ex-President to Give Taped Testimony in Iran–Contra Case"); "Reagan Court Filing Clarifies Claim of Executive Privilege"; "Iran–Contra Judge Is Urged to Bar Public at Questioning of Reagan"; "Active or Passive Iran–Contra Role? Point-Blank Questioning for Reagan" ("Reagan's reputation and Poindexter's freedom may be at stake"); "Press and Public Barred From Reagan Deposition" ("Ex-President's taped testimony to be edited to delete secrets"); "Reagan Testifies in the Poindexter [former national security adviser] Case"; and "Judge in Iran–Contra Trial: Forceful Wielder of the Law" ("Role in Rights Legislation"). Subsequently, "Poindexter Is Found Guilty Of All 5 Criminal Charges For Iran–Contra Cover-Up" ("Ex-Security Chief Misled Congress to Protect Reagan, Jury Finds," as "The highest White House aide to be convicted since Watergate"). However, a few months later, "Appellate Court Overturns Part of Conviction of [Oliver] North" ("A ruling in favor of North casts doubt on all Iran–Contra cases").[8]

Other bold Judiciary interfaces with the Executive branch in 1990–1992 impacted the Bush Administration. "Supreme Court to Decide on Minority Ownership Rules," as "Justices Rebuff President Bush" in reopening a touchy issue involving affirmative action and F.C.C. rules, raising the question "What are the limits on Government programs?" "High Court Decides Budget Office Exceeded Power in Banking Rules," as "Bush is dealt a major setback in efforts at deregulation." "High Court to Rule Quickly on Flag Burning Law," with "The flag as symbol: A campaign issue in the remaking?" As they prepare to try court cases, "Lawyers Expect Ambiguities in New [Civil] Rights Law [signed by President Bush in later 1991] to Bring Years of Lawsuits." "Appeals Court Overturns Bush's [Executive] Order on Haitians" fleeing their homeland, that they be stopped at sea and returned. Soon thereafter, "High Court Will Take Up Bush's Policy on Haitians," while "The U.S. says that judges cannot unmake foreign policy." On another matter, "[Federal] Court Orders U.S. [Drug Enforcement Administration] to Rethink [Its] Ban on Marijuana in Therapy."[9]

Other directions in the Judiciary's interfaces with the Executive centered around nominees to the Supreme Court, which was in a state of flux after "Brennan, Key Liberal, Quits Supreme Court; Battle For Seat Likely" ("Abortion [Is] At Issue," and "With His First Vacancy to Fill, President Is 'Not Afraid of a Fight' "). Much later a leading liberal newspaper carried an editorial on "Doubting Thomas" by a leading liberal columnist sharply critical of President Bush's nomination of conservative anti-abortion Judge Clarence

Thomas. That editorial bemoaned "A worship of the Presidency," arguing that "The most disturbing trend in the contemporary Supreme Court is its exaltation of Presidential power . . . in the executive [branch], at the expense of Congress and individual rights. . . . Thomas will almost certainly intensify that trend" if confirmed. At issue in another like-minded editorial in that newspaper was not the potential for Judicial infringement upon Executive authority—for Thomas being in conflict with Bush—but for Thomas becoming in "cahoots" with him e.g. on abortion law, involving "Low Roads to the High Court" through "Executive Extremism."[10]

Judicial Activism

Verdicts by the press on judicial activism at the Supreme Court and Federal courts were mixed during the term of President Bush Sr. and often depended on one's own political leanings. An op-ed essay by rejected High Court nominee Robert Bork, a staunch conservative, declared "At Last, an End to Supreme Court Activism," inasmuch as "[Judge] Souter's reluctance on the issues is just what we need." From another perspective, however, it was said that "Conservatively Speaking, It's An Activist Supreme Court" ("Now, an Abortion Reversal"). Judicial activism could and did take many other forms aside from rulings on abortion. According to liberal columnist Anthony Lewis, it was "Court Against Congress" in connection with "Judicial activism on habeas corpus." As pointed out in "The Supreme Court: Taking the Side of the States," "The high court will rule on a number of issues this session, and its decisions are likely to be in favor of states' rights." In the minds of many, this latter tendency had already been confirmed in the Court's rulings, as expressed in an editorial on "Federalism, Despoiled." Queried one news magazine essayist back in 1979, "Have the Judges Done Too Much?"—to which many news writers in the period under discussion could say resoundingly, "yes."[11]

As already signaled above, abortion became a hot-button issue for judicial activists, especially through conservative judges in the early 1990s. In mid-1992, "High Court Affirms Right to Abortion, but Allows Most of Pennsylvania's Limits," as "Long Battles Over Abortion Are Seen." Meanwhile, "Clinics [Are] Eager to Learn Impact of Abortion Ruling," while "Each side expects a flurry of activity at the state level." In that same newspaper issue was an article about how "Selection of Conservative Judges Insures a President's Legacy," adding to "Concern About Bush's Choices for the Court." According to a piece on "Gagging the Clinics," "The

Justices did not disturb the constitutional right to an abortion but made it illegal to disclose the procedure in federally funded centers," so that " 'Government . . . may validly choose to fund childbirth over abortion,' " quoting conservative Chief Justice Rehnquist. The states' situation was made clearer still in late 1992 when "High Court Spurns Guam Bid To Revive Curbs On Abortion," "Refuses To Hear Appeal," and "Reaffirms June Ruling That States Cannot Nullify Roe v. Wade Principles." Was all this also a case of judicial lawmaking? Earlier, in mid-1990, "High Court Says States May Require Girl to Notify Parents Before Having Abortion," a ruling on Minnesota's abortion law.[12]

On issues of Court jurisdiction in states' affairs concerning taxation, the following news articles were illustrative during 1989–1992. "Justices [Are] to Study Power of Judiciary in Taxation," with the question "How far can the courts go in a state's domain?" "[Supreme] Court Says Judge[s] May Order Taxes To Alleviate Bias," as "Ruling in Missouri Case Affirms a Broad View of Judiciary's Role" by "Expanding the scope of Federal judges' authority on tax increases." "Oh, Those Imperial Judges" was an editorial on the preceding Court decision in the Missouri case. "Judges Affirm Law in California Restricting Property Tax Increases," involving "Proposition 13: perhaps unfair, but not unconstitutional."[13]

The High Court exhibited a further active role in rulings tending to give states more leeway in line with notions of "federalism," along widely divergent paths. For instance, "Justices Curtail Federal Reviews of Pleas by State Prison Inmates," especially in death penalty cases. Or, "States May Ban Nude Dancing To Protect 'Order,' Justices Rule," backing "Limits to Free Expression." Also, "Court's Ruling On [Limiting] Terms Gives Boost to Backers" in "California Case [that] Points Way for Other States." On more local issues, "Justices Rule Localities May Impose Pesticide Rules Stiffer Than U.S. Law," as "A 'regulatory partnership' on pest control is recognized." In addition, "Ban Is Left Intact On Subway Begging" when "U.S. Supreme Court Refuses to Hear New York Case." However, when "Justices . . . Back Protesters' Right To Burn The Flag," "Laws Are Affected in 40 States." On a different front, the Justices reinforced their conservative leanings as they "Uphold Punitive Damages In Awards By Jury" and decline to set "Limits on Discretion in Verdicts" in "A modern ruling rooted in the earliest days of the legal system."[14]

Another dimension of judicial activism during this period lay in some Court rulings on issues of foreign affairs. Concerning Haiti, "U.S. Starts Return Of Haiti Refugees After Justices Act," as "Court Lifts Injunction" and "Thousands who fled Haiti's turmoil can be forced home." Concerning Mexico, more extremely: "[Supreme]

Court Says U.S. May Kidnap Foreigners" when "The Court rules a doctor's abduction [for trial in U.S.] did not violate a treaty," while "Mexico Reacts In Anger" because "Mexico sees an insult to its sovereignty"; "U.S. Tries to Quiet Storm Abroad Over High Court's Right-to-Kidnap Ruling"; and "To Mexico, High Court Sounds Like a Bully." On Panama, "Opening Its Case, U.S. [through Federal prosecutors] Calls Noriega 'Small Man,'" when "For first time in the U.S., a foreign head of state stands trial"; and "U.S. Jury Convicts Noriega Of Drug Trafficking Role As The Leader Of Panama," which "Verdict Is First Against Foreign Head of State in Nation's History." On Iran–Contra, "[Federal] Judge In Iran–Contra Trial Drops Case Against [Oliver] North After Prosecutor Gives Up," with "Inquiry Continuing," yet "Walsh Says the Immunity Granted by Congress Is a Huge Obstacle."[15]

Political Ideology

Press reaction was swift when in July 1990 "Souter, New Hampshire [Judge], [Is] Named By Bush For High Court; No 'Litmus Test,' President Says." Typical was one news essay's query, "Right Turn Ahead?: A Liberal Justice's [William Brennan's] resignation [after long career going back to Warren Court] brings an end to an age of judicial [liberal] activism. Now Bush may try to accelerate the Supreme Court's conservative trend." Some months after Souter was confirmed and took his seat there appeared another illustrative news essay on "Right Face!: In the final stretch of the term, a conservative majority solidifies its hold on the Supreme Court and prepares an assault on the Warren legacy."[16]

Yet "Another Blow to Liberals" occurred in June 1991 when Thurgood "Marshall Retires From High Court," as "Only Black Justice, After 24-Year Tenure, Leaves in Frustration," according to a leading liberal newspaper. "An Energized Conservatism At High Court" is how another such newspaper characterized this event, together with "Marshall's Exit Seen Aiding Abortion Foes," leaving "Rights Activists Likely to Turn to Congress." The last-mentioned issue also carried a cartoon depicting "The Rehnquist Ascendancy" in a heavily rightward-leaning Supreme Court structure, along with captions on "Marshall's Vision—and the End of Court-Led Reform" and "The Radical Agenda of a Triumphant Chief Justice." When the Court term began in fall 1991, "Consequential Cases Are Likely to Test the Supreme Court's New Majority," for "The Court is poised for an attack on many of its liberal precedents."[17]

In nominating another black judge, Clarence Thomas, to replace Marshall, President Bush was choosing someone who was as far right as Marshall was far left. Therein lay grounds for the unusually hard-fought confirmation contest in mid- to later 1991. Political ideology came increasingly to the fore, as suggested previously, along with more personal allegations of Thomas' past sexual harassment that transfixed and divided Americans as the drama played out on national TV. As reported in "Marching to a Different Drummer," "By choosing Clarence Thomas, who says integration is an impossible dream, Bush sparks a debate over the goals of the civil rights movement." Indeed, Thomas' ultra-conservatism fueled the ire of liberals intent on stopping him by bringing charges, through his ex-colleague Anita Hill, of sexual harassment. Now it even became "Fear of Flirting" even though "It's dangerous to politicize sexual harassment." To be sure, "High Court's Aloofness [Is] Pierced by Thomas Fight." Indeed, "Americans [Are] Riveted By Lesson in Civics," for "Sexual harassment has become topic No. 1 around the country." In mid-October it came down to "Tonight!" and "The [Senate's] Vote's Too Close to Call," as announced by one conservative newspaper, while "Bush pressures Dems as drama builds to 6 p.m." In the end, Thomas was confirmed by the Senate.[18]

Political ideology had played a part in other ways, too. On the "Supreme & P.C. Court," "Conservatives have their own brand of political correctness." In the Thomas hearings, there was much discussion of "Judges, Democracy and Natural Law." In "Sizing Up the Talk of 'Natural Law': Many Ideologues Discover a Precept," and "Jefferson, Madison and Lincoln were adherents." Even so, " 'Natural Law' . . . [Is] An Elusive Tradition." Not altogether clear was the relationship between "Law and Natural Law," as well as between "Clarence Thomas, God, and the Court in the 21st Century," that is, between " 'Natural Law' and the Nominee."[19]

By mid- to later 1992, it was—according to Op-Ed column by Robert Bork, a previously unsuccessful conservative nominee for the High Court—"Again, a Struggle for the Soul of the Court" in terms of "Constitutional principles vs. liberal activism." In early October, "High Court Begins Session Today, Testing an Energizing Centrist Coalition." At the same time "[Federal] Judge [Is] to Rule on Regulations Barring Abortion Advice in Subsidized Clinics" after "A last-minute hearing on a major issue in abortion politics."[20]

Judicial Lawmaking

The elements of judicial activism and political ideology, whether liberal or conservative, can lead to forms of judicial lawmaking. During 1991–1992, there appeared various warnings in the press against this proclivity. They included: "When Courts Write Laws," a column by conservative George Will; "Beware the Judicial Override," for "Thomas may limit Congress on affirmative action"; and "The Runaway Supreme Court," so called because "The Court's distaste for civil rights laws has been evident at least since its decisions three years ago misinterpreting the job discrimination statute."[21]

Judicial lawmaking can take many different forms, perhaps most conspicuously exhibited in legislative-like rulings or rules (decisions) overturning or abrogating federal, state, or local laws. The following reports are illustrative. "Supreme Court Overturns Law That Bars Criminals From Profiting on Stories," as "A unanimous court says that New York's 'Son of Sam' law infringes free speech." "Part of Child Pornography Law Is Overturned." "Judge Overrules Decency Statute for Arts Grants" ("At issue: Can artists take U.S. funds and still speak their minds?"). "High Court Voids Law Singling Out Crimes of Hatred." "U.S. Court Suspends Capital Law Aiding Minority Businesses." "In Retreat, Supreme Court Limits Scope of '65 Voting Rights Act." "Top Court Could Overturn Roe [v. Wade] Without Saying So," so that "An abortion law may survive as a shell of a case with no force." "High Court's Ruling Limits Law on Grand Jury Secrecy."[22]

Other manifestations of, or attempts at, judicial lawmaking included the following. "Appeals Court Ruling by Thomas Limits F.C.C. Affirmative Action," in that "The newest Justice would restrict requirements." "Rehnquist Opposes Bill That Seeks Shift in Gun Trials to U.S. Courts." "[Supreme] Court Invites Congress to Act on Mail-Order Tax," since "The states say they are deprived of $3 billion a year." "U.S. Panel Seeks New Rules on Using DNA Evidence in Courts," for "The Panel wants the Government to oversee crime laboratories," while "Judges Are Asked to Bar 'Genetic Fingerprinting' Until Basis in Science Is Stronger."[23]

2. THE COURTS UNDER CLINTON

"Super-Legislative" Powers?

During the Clinton presidential era, questions arose as to whether the Supreme Court was acquiring "super-legislative" powers in relation to federal, state, and local affairs. In a 1995 lecture, Supreme Court Justice Scalia underscored the common law tradition of "Judicial lawmaking" that has gripped the American mind. Said one news piece, "Sure Justices Legislate. They Have To," explaining that "Making laws is our job, not judges', legislators say. Trouble is, they often don't finish it. In some big cases, the Supreme Court just did." In mid-2000, "The High Court Rules; the Law of the Land Changes." Also in mid-2000, "Justices Sidestep Constitutionality in Rulings in Federal Arson and False Claims Cases" ("Accepting a new case that continues to test the limits of federal authority"), while "Court to Hear Clean Air Test of Congressional Authority." In early 2000, "[High] Court may rewrite rules of arrest," as "Justices weigh striking down Miranda decision that launched 1,000 cop shows." Also in early 2000, conservative Senator Hatch said on TV that the Supreme Court should not be "super-legislators in black robes," referring to such cases as Roe v. Wade, which legalized abortion.[24]

Many other people over the years have likewise criticized the practice of "legislating from the bench." Yet still others have said that, while they should not become legislative substitutes for Congress, the Justices have often made rulings in key cases brought before them in lawsuits where Congress was loath to act, as in the regulation of tobacco and asbestos. Even so, still others respond, "They Interpret the Law, They Don't Reshape It," adding that "The Rehnquist Court is a far cry from Warren's and Reagan's judicial activism."[25]

During the Clinton years came numerous face-offs between the Court and Congress. In 1994, "High Court Considers Limits of Congress' Power" in "Arguments on speaking fees and a ban on guns near schools." In 1995, "Justices Rule That Congress Overstepped in Legislating Reversal of a Court Decision"; and "The High Court Loses Restraint" when "deciding that Congress lacks the power to outlaw gun possession within 100 feet of a school" and thereby "needlessly question[ing] . . . previously settled law." In 1996, "New Laws Curb Federal Court Powers." In 1997, "[Chief Justice] Rehnquist Criticizes Congress On Raises." In 1998, "Senate Inaction on Judicial Posts Is Imperiling the Courts, Rehnquist Says in a Report"; and "Counting the people: Court to settle dispute," as "Justices to hear arguments today on controversial census method that could alter makeup of Congress." In 2000, "Was it law or poetry? The Supreme Court once again says no to Congress."[26]

Court politics again played a part. In mid-1993, early in his presidency, when "Unmaking the G.O.P. Court Legacy," "Clinton regains ground in a war for the soul of the Federal Judiciary." At the same point that year, "The High Court Counterrevolution [Comes] in Fits and Starts." It was then, in mid-1993, that Clinton's "High Court Nominee [Ruth Ginsburg] Defends Judges' Use of Broad Powers" and "says [that] disputes over 'judicial activism' arise when the courts are forced to resolve issues that lawmakers are too timid to handle."

As reported in another piece, "Ginsburg Affirms Right Of . . . Abortion," while having a "Sense of Judicial Limits As Safeguard of Equality," and also "warning about judges who try to impose their beliefs on society."[27]

Other judicial activity from 1993 to 2000 can be brought to bear on the question of the extent to which it exhibited "super-legislative" powers or tendencies. In 1993: "Test of a 'Hate Crime' Law Reaches Center Stage"; "Court Voids Ban on Animal Sacrifices" in a "hybrid church"; and "Court Ruling lets Trade Agreement Move to Congress," in relation to the Administrative Procedures Act. In 1994, "Justices Limit '91 Rights Law To New Cases." In 1995: "[High] Court Rejects States' Right To Set Limits For Congress"; "Focus [Is] on Federal Power" as "Close Vote on Term Limits Shows Extent of Court's Division Over 'First Principles' "; and "Justices . . . Reject Districts Drawn With Race The 'Predominant Factor,' " with "New Voting Rules" "Gutting the Voting Rights Act." In 1996: "[Federal] Panel of 3 Judges Turns Back Federal Law Intended to Regulate Decency on Internet," involving a "Free Speech Case" for "A Complex Medium That Will Be Hard to Regulate"; and "9 Legislative Districts Ruled Unconstitutional by [a Federal court panel of] Judges." In 1999: "Pivotal Rulings Ahead: Supreme Court to Begin Review of Americans With Disabilities Act," while "The Justices' decisions will help chart a wide-reaching act"); "Defining who's called disabled" is key as "The Supreme Court considers cases that hinge on the law's vagueness"; and "In Test of New U.S. Law, Death Sentence Is Upheld," as "Justices take the first step in interpreting an expanded law." In 2000: "U.S. Judge Says Microsoft Violated Antitrust Laws With Predatory Behavior"; "Justices . . . Void Women's Right to Sue Attackers in Federal Court" ("In Latest of Their Rulings on Federalism, Justices Again Curb Congress' Power"); "Justices Reaffirm Miranda Rule, . . . A Part of 'Culture' "; "Justices Consider Scope of the Disabilities Act" ("May Congress enforce the equal protection guarantee?"); and "Court Overrules Law Restricting Cable Sex Shows," as relates to "Free Speech Protection."[28]

Clearly the cumulative weight and effect of rulings like the foregoing by the Supreme Court and Federal courts amounts to an expansive legislative-like power that often pushes against traditional boundary lines of Congressional lawmaking powers. The same tendencies also apply in what has amounted to judicial abrogation of Congress' laws or the Courts' prior rules. As in the cases of Miranda and Roe v. Wade, so many long-accepted rulings by the Courts have in themselves become settled laws of the land.

"Super-Executive" Powers?

If in its relationships to Congress the Supreme Court, as well as Federal courts, exhibited some "super-legislative" proclivities during the Clinton presidency, the question arises as to whether judicial powers in relation to the White House, culminating in Clinton's struggles with the Courts in the later 1990s, exhibited "super-executive" tendencies. If Executive orders and decisions, like judicial rulings, are sometimes "super-legislative" in relation to the Legislature, then the Judiciary can as well pose "super-executive" quandaries for the White House. A broader question arises as to the increasing extent of overlappings or infringements between the three Federal branches, with contemporary import for the separation of powers in a pervading legislative medium of sovereignty and state.[29]

In the beginning years of the Clinton presidency, the Supreme Court and Federal courts were agreeable enough for the White House as Clinton sought to bring them more into line with his liberal views after the twelve years of their more conservative directions under Bush and Reagan. In early 1993, two months after his inauguration, "Clinton Pledge on Diversity May Reshape U.S. Courts," with "More Than 100 Vacancies," while "Congress Is Likely to Add More Seats, Creating Chance for New Judicial Landscape." As "Blackmun Plans To Leave Court" in 1994, leaving "Liberal Legacy," his "Departure Is Unlikely To Alter Ideological Makeup of Bench." When Clinton nominated Breyer to replace him, "A Nominee Deemed Politic, Not Political," "Bipartisan Support [Is] Seen as Clinton Sidesteps Risky Senate Fight."[30]

In 1994–1997, after the first year or so of the Clinton presidency, the Judicial branch tended to chart an increasingly independent and confrontational course including in relation to the Executive branch and its federal departments and agencies. In 1994, for instance, "U.S. [Justice Department] Ordered to Tell How It Decides to Seek Executions," as "A [Federal] judge asks if race plays a role in requests for the death penalty"; and "Justices, in Ruling on Free Speech, Put Limits on Government" agencies and their ability "to punish employees for what they say." In 1995: "[Federal] Judge Overturns Pentagon Policy on Homosexuals"; "[Federal] Court Says U.S. [E.P.A.] Can't Require Ethanol as a Gasoline Additive"; "Justices Cast Doubts On U.S. Programs That Give Preferences Based On Race"; "Farewell to Old Order In the Supreme Court" as "The Right Goes Activist and the Center Is a Void"; and "The Soul Of A New Majority" appeared when, "In most of the Supreme Court's rulings this year, the combination was five right, four left." In 1996: "Justices to Decide Legality of Drug Property Seizures" although "Government's [Justice Dept., etc.] Dual Strategy Is In Question"; "Disorder in the courts? Left and right both gripe about Clinton's taste in judges"; "Federal Judges Condemn Plans for a Line-Item Veto" by the President, with "Independence of the Judiciary Emphasized"; "Rehnquist Joins Fray on Rulings, Defending Judicial Independence"; and "One Angry Man" ("Even on a conservative court, [Justice] Antonin Scalia manages to seem embattled)." In 1997: "[Federal] Judge Voids Law Giving President Line-Item Veto," and his "Ruling Says Congress Cannot Delegate Its Authority to Repeal Spending Acts"; "High Court Grants Prompt Hearing on Line-Item Veto"; and "Curb on U.S. [Justice Dept.] Role in Redistricting" emerges as "Court Eases Policy Requiring Greater Minority Representation."[31]

If many court rulings during this period were aimed at the Executive branch not just under Clinton but also under his liberal predecessors L.B.J. and F.D.R., the focal point became, more and more, Clinton himself as various scandals began to unfold starting in 1997. For example, as that year further developed, "Supreme Court . . . Rejects Clinton Request To Put Off Suit On Sexual Harassment" by Paula Jones, in "Mounting Diversions From Clinton Agenda"; "Clintons Lose In Top Court Over Fight For Notes"; and "[Federal] Judge Rules Government [White House and Justice Dept.] Covered Up Lies on Panel." At the same time in 1997 came news articles on such topics as "The New Look of Liberalism on the Court," as seen through Justice Ruth Ginsburg (aside from conservatives Rehnquist, Thomas, and Scalia); and "Federal Judge Overturns Murder Verdict, Fueling Feud on Judicial Power."[32]

In 1998, it was "So Much for the Imperial Presidency" in the face of special prosecutor Kenneth Starr's investigation. As for "How Court Shaped Clinton Inquiry," "President's travails are rooted in high court rulings that open White House to more scrutiny." Also, "Supreme Court Takes a Skeptical Look at Line-Item Vetoes" in "A debate over how laws are made and unmade."[33]

Things reached a climax in 1999–2000 as the Court became ever more assertive of its authority in diverse areas. "The Judicial Branch Has Obligations, Too" in that "The High Court could overturn a Senate verdict." "Are Courts Getting Too Creative?" "Clinton Is Found To Be In Contempt On Jones Lawsuit," while "Judge Says He [Clinton] Testified Falsely on Lewinsky Sex Relationship." "Justices Decide Who's In Charge." "The Supreme Power" was emerging as "The Court rewrites the Constitution." "Justices May Review Nondelegation Doctrine" in "Rulings about the balance of power between Congress and the President." "With rulings, [high] court declares itself supreme," for "From Miranda to FDA decisions, court calls itself ultimate decisionmaker." It was " 'Judicial Supremacy' " at the High Court as "Close votes and key decisions end a session with a mixed message for the law books." In other matters, "[Federal] Judge Orders U.S. To Turn Over Data In Secrets Inquiry"; and "Nuclear Scientist Set Free After Plea In Secrets Case" as "Judge Attacks U.S. Conduct" ("Sharp criticism of the government's conduct from a federal judge"). In the end, it came down to "The War Over the Supreme Court: How Bush or Gore Could Tip the Balance."[34]

The Regulatory State

The preceding two subsections on the Judiciary's "super-legislature" and "super-executive" proclivities under Clinton have shown its full involvement with the other two branches in the continuing buildup of the regulatory legislative state. The Courts' rulings have become interwoven with the laws and orders (or rules) of the Legislative and Executive branches respectively in the complex fabric of the regulatory legislative state. In addition to the Supreme Court, Federal courts have regulated the interworkings of American life and society. The Federal courts' intricate extended rulings on A.T.&T. cases during this period have well illustrated a likeness to regulatory agencies in the Executive branch that have often functioned as co-partner with the Legislative branch in the wider legislative process. In other words, the Judicial branch might be seen as another co-equal partner in the wider contemporary lawmaking process. Meanwhile, the increasing volume of new U.S. laws has given rise to a flood of new litigation and expanded rulings by the Courts at all levels of the American system.

Momentous new legislative-like rulings came to light at the end of the Supreme Court's term in mid-1997. "In 9 Extraordinary Months, the High Court Developed a Vast Panorama of Landmarks" hailed by the press as "Benchmarks of Justice." The Court's final rulings issued at that point were called "Two Days That Shaped the Law." The Court's important role in the broader lawmaking process was there aptly suggested. Three years later, in mid-2000, on the subject of "Reining in regulators," it was asked, "Will the Supreme Court clip Washington's wings?" That question was accompanied with an observation: "For many years, through administrations Republican as well as Democratic, the regulatory power of the federal government has seemed to be growing." The question of what the Supreme Court might do about this situation, short of clipping its own regulatory wings, was there left an open one.[35]

The ensuing two subsections provide illustrations of how much the regulatory state during the Clinton years was built upon rulings by the Judicial branch no less than upon the laws of the Legislative branch and the orders or rules of the Executive branch. Issues of federal *vs.* states' rights and public *vs.* private matters came before the Courts with particular significance during this period. Judicial rulings on them added greatly to the multi-layered fabric of the regulatory state.

Rulings on Federalism *viz* States' Rights

On some of the Judiciary's most striking cases or issues involving federalism (i.e., decentralized government) and states' rights in general were, from 1994 to 2000 during Clinton's presidency, the following reports: "Federalism Gone Wild" ("Unloading a U.S. burden on state courts"); "Justices Step In as Federalism's Referee" ("Reassertion of Limits on Washington Power"); "Rehnquist-Led Court Shifts Power to States" ("But emerging 'judicial federalism' divides justices"); "States' Powers Among Hard Issues on Supreme Court's New Agenda"; "High Court Faces Moment of Truth in Federalism Cases" ("Making a foray along the border that separates Federal and state power"); "Justices Seem Ready to Tilt More Toward States in Federalism" ("Little evidence that the High Court will retreat on the idea of state sovereignty"); "Federalism Awaits '00" ("With the High Court Narrowly Divided, Power to Appoint Looms Over an Issue"); "When the State Trumps the Feds" ("The Supreme Court limits age discrimination suits"); "Battles on Federalism" ("High Court Ruling Limits Congress," "Finding the U.S. overreached in the Violence Against Women Act"); "How Long Should the Arm of the Federal Law Be?" ("The Supreme Court ponders the scope of its authority as a new term opens"); and "Federalism Debate at Heart of Environmental Case Before Justices."[36]

On a further wide range of issues and cases during Clinton's first term, the Judiciary dealt with federalism and states' rights. These include, from 1993 to 1996, as follows. "Justices Say States May Make Union-Only Pacts in Public Works Projects." "Court Questions Districts Drawn To Aid Minorities." "Term Limits [Are] Under Judicial Fire." "High Court Rules Against Local Curbs on Shipping Trash." "Justices Give States Control of Water Quantity, Too." "Justices [Are] to Decide if States Can Limit Terms in Congress." "Justices Void Order Requiring Florida Redistricting," as "A limit is placed on judges' remedies under the Voting Rights Act." "Baby Ruling Sets the Stage For New Fight," as "State Adoption Law Faces Test in Courts.." "Supreme Court [Is] to Rule on Anti-Gay Rights Law in Colorado." "A Gun Ban Is Shot Down" in "A historic Supreme Court decision [that] opens the door to redefining the power of the Federal Government." "Justices Allow Unsigned Political Fliers" in "High Court Ruling [that] Casts Doubt on Election Laws of Many States." "Judges Apply Federal Law To State Political Conventions." "Court Overturns Ban In New York On Aided Suicide" and "Shift Is Historic." "Court Voids [N.Y. State] Aiding The Police In Wage Disputes," for "Judge Finds State's Power to Decide on New York Labor Pacts Unconstitutional." "Elections Will Tip the Judicial Balance" inasmuch as "Clinton judges would likely increase federal power, while Dole appointees would bolster state power."[37]

Further examples along these lines of federalism and states' rights during Clinton's second term, from 1997 to 2000, are as follows. "Court Limits U.S. Say Over Voting Districts" in a "Serious setback for voting-rights law." "Justices Limit Brady Gun Law As Intrusion On States' Rights" ("U.S. Power Curbed," "States Can't Be Forced Into Making Checks On Backgrounds") in "A new chapter in a debate over the essential nature of shared authority." "Federal Anti-Bias Law Protects States' Disabled Inmates, [Supreme] Court Says." In "A showdown over scope of federal powers," the "U.S. Supreme Court, with a track record of siding with states, faces key case in federalism fight tomorrow" over back pay—and, "If the federal government . . . can subject the states to private suits, it is a severe encroachment." "2 Cases Test Immunity Of States From Lawsuits," as "Supreme Court Weighs Federalism Issues" in "A debate [that] focuses on balancing the rights of states and private property." "Age Bias Case in Supreme Court Opens a New Round on Federalism." "States' Rights Adherents on Top Court Appear to Be Given Pause." "Justices Weigh States' Rights vs. Treaty Rules" involving "A question of whether state, U.S., or international rules apply." "Justices [Are] to Decide Foreign Policy Question in Massachusetts Boycott of Myanmar," while "At issue is whether state and local governments can set foreign policy." "U.S. V. States: What's the proper balance?" in "Court's bid to recalibrate balance of power." "Justices Uphold Ban on States' Sales of Drivers' License Information," giving "A rare federal victory in a continuing battle over states' rights." "Supreme Court Will Revisit States' Rights in Bias Case" in connection with "Cases that challenge Congressional authority and primary voting rules." "Justices Say States Can't Set Own Tanker-Safety Rules." "Justices Weigh Issues of States' Making Foreign Policy," where "The question is not what to do about

Burma, but about Massachusetts." "Wetlands and federal power" are key in a "Case before the Supreme Court [that] will shape how much say Uncle Sam has in local conservation"—while "The Corps' rationale would justify federal regulation . . . of virtually all human activity." There could be "A Judicial Threat to Clean Water." "Hearing a Final Clinton Federalism Case," "Justices Consider Suit Against Alabama Over English-Only Matter."[38]

Further illustrations along these same lines from 1997 to 2000 are indicated below.[39]

Rulings on Public *vs.* Private Matters

The Supreme Court's (often legislative-like) rulings on public *vs.* private matters steadily mounted during President Clinton's second term. These rulings spanned a wide spectrum of subjects, often involving First Amendment rights for individuals in such areas as civil rights, religious freedom, marriage, abortion, and so forth. The conservative tendencies of the Court, as led by conservative Chief Justice Rehnquist, were sometimes balanced by the more liberal Justices during Clinton's liberal presidency, but at other times that was not the case.

Prior to Clinton's second term, there had been such notable decisions as when, in 1994, "High Court . . . Limits Public Power on Private Property," while "Shifting the burden of proof in restricting property use to local governments." Federal Courts, too, had ruled, as when in 1996 "Court Upholds Clinton Policy On Gay Troops" concerning "Don't Ask, Don't Tell." Also in 1996, "For First Time, U.S. Court to Weigh Claim of Rights Abuses in Foreign Land," as "The Argentine junta's pursuit of a victim has let him seek redress."[40]

Impacting the laws of the land in 1997, the Supreme Court's many, far-reaching rulings and hearings on public *vs.* private matters included the following, as seen from different angles. "High Court Hears 2 Cases Involving Assisted Suicide," concerning which "Justices, in an Unusually Personal Session, Reveal Their Reluctance to Intercede." "Is There A Right To Die?," "The Supreme Court weighs an issue that may prove to be as contentious—and ethically murky—as abortion rights." "[Supreme] Court Tests Limits Of Religious Liberty" ("Can Congress pass laws to protect practices?"). "High Court Questions Reach of Law on Religious Liberty." "[Supreme] Court Eases Curb On Providing Aid In Church Schools," and "Public Districts Allowed to Send Teachers Into Parochial Schools," thereby "Shrinking the space separating church and state." "High Court Voids A Law Expanding Religious Rights" and "Puts Limit On Congress" in "6 to 3 Decision [that] Is Warning to Branches of Government on Power of Justices." "[High] Court Lowers Wall Dividing Church and State," "Reversing a past decision, [as] justices allow public school teachers to teach in some religious-school classrooms." "High Court Clips Protections for Religious Freedom in U.S." through "Ruling [that] extends from spiritual healing Yarmulke to workplace." "[High] Court, 9–6, Upholds State Laws Prohibiting Assisted Suicide; Protects Speech On Internet." "High Court Is Criticized for Striking Down Federal Law Shielding Religious Practices." "[High] Court's Moral Stamp"—"Decision to throw out Internet porn law won't deter cybercrime cops." "High Court Agrees to Decide Just What Congress Meant When It Said 'Carrying Arms,' " after "A simple phrase has spawned years of litigation."[41]

Similar patterns of the Judiciary continued in 1998–2000. "Justices Question Iowa Law Allowing the Police to Search Cars in Traffic Violations." "High Court Curbs Claim On Privacy In a Home." "Cases Give Court Chances To Define Church And State" in "New Term's Opportunity." "After 23 years, the Supreme Court Turns Again to the Limits on Campaign Contributions." "The Supreme Court on Privacy" looks at Congress' Driver's Privacy Protection Act. "Justice Stevens Blocks New Laws On Late Abortions in 2 States." "Vermont High Court Backs [Legal] Rights of Same Sex Couples," as "A ruling casts a broad net over partnerships." "[Vermont] Ruling will stir [other] states on same-sex marriages." "Justices Uphold Ceiling Of $1,000 On Political Gifts" as "1970's Ruling Passes Test." "Justices Appear Set to Reject Law Banning Late Abortion" in "A case [that] appears to hinge on a statute's vagueness, not its underlying intent." "[High] Court Rules That Governments Can't Outlaw Type Of Abortion." "Foes Of Abortion Start New Effort After Court Loss" in strategy "to Rewrite the Statutes So They Will Pass Muster With Supreme Court." "Federal Judge Rules That Law Governing Kosher Food Is Unconstitutional" due to "First Amendment Breach." "[High] Court weighs states' rights vs. civil rights" in a case that "could overturn a major part of a landmark disabilities law."[42]

3. THE COURTS UNDER BUSH JR.

The Final Legal Ruling on a Disputed Presidential Election

An historic five-week saga gripped the nation from early November to mid-December in 2000. The disputed presidential election culminated in the Supreme Court's final legal ruling that decided the winner to be George Bush Jr. instead of Al Gore. Along the way lay complex constitutional issues filled with uncertainty, confusion, and drama. The main final disputed battleground in the State of Florida centered, in recounts etc., on its legislature and high court. The U.S. Congress could have had the ultimate deciding role, but it was the U.S. Supreme Court—to which Bush appealed while Gore concentrated on Florida—that decided to halt the ongoing Florida recount, thereby giving the victory to Bush. Of present interest are press perceptions of the Supreme Court's politicized "super-legislative" role as the ultimate arbiter in its final ruling.

The Supreme Court's potential role in the disputed Y2K election unfolded slowly at first, with the Florida state court being a more immediate factor. A headline in mid-November asked, "Will judges decide the 2000 election?" In late November, "Meanwhile, Congress Is Waiting in the Wings," for "Although precedents are murky, preparations are being made if it has to decide the outcome." Meantime, there was much discussion about "The Rules of Law in Florida"; and also about "Florida's Legislative Tripwire." But by December 1 it was called "The Supreme Court's Moment." A day later, the "U.S. Supreme Court Presses 2 Sides on Vote Case" as "Justices Ask Whether Florida Court Ruling Is a Federal Issue," while ". . . in Florida, Justices Refuse Bid for Recount." Concerning "The Legal Challenges," especially Gore's challenge on the final Florida certification, "The law is an ass, Dickens wrote. Not really. A close look at the statutes and rulings shows a method to the madness." Even so, some uncertainty persisted, as in "Now for a truly scary scenario: What happens if Congress gets to decide it all?"[43]

As "Bush takes his case to the U.S. Supreme Court"—which agreed to hear both sides on whether Florida recount should continue—and "Gore vows to fight on in Florida," events were moving rapidly. "Gore Loses Florida Recount Case; Puts Last Hope In [Florida] State High Court." In Florida: "With Court Set To Hear Appeal, Legislators Move On Electors"; "Florida High Court Hears Gore's Appeal on Vote"; and "Florida Court Backs Recount," with "Bush Appealing To U.S. Justices." But then, on December 9, "U.S. Supreme Court, Split 5–4, Halts [Stays] New Count[,] . . . Favoring Bush." Then, "Bush v. Gore Is Now in Hands of Supreme Court" ("Collision With Politics Risks Court's Legal Credibility"); and "Justices' Questions Underline Divide On Whether [Florida] Hand Recount Can Be Fair."[44]

Finally, on December 12, "By Single Vote, Justices End Recount, Blocking Gore After 5-Week Struggle," as "The Court Rules for Mr. Bush." The "Supreme Court . . . ruling determines [that] Florida recounts are unconstitutional" (while "Clinton's 'Cinderellas' ["ex-

ecutive branch agency heads"] face regulatory midnight"). Even
more bluntly worded was "Court Overturns Recounts, Giving Bush
the Presidency."[45]

Many responses to the U.S. Supreme Court's final decision are
particularly germane here. A day after the ruling, it was asked in
one news story, "Who Makes the Laws?: That's the real issue in
Bush *v.* Gore," adding that "The problem with American governance
today is what has become normal in the name of judicial interpretation." Another newspaper story was on "How the justices laid down
the law." Increasingly apparent were the amorphous overlappings
between federal and state bodies—as well as between the Supreme
Court's judicial role and the legislative capacities of Congress and
the Florida legislature. One sign was an eleventh-hour cover story
on "Chaos: Will the U.S. Supreme Court overturn the Florida decision? Will the Florida Legislature trump the State Court? Will the
election end up in Congress?" In the end, "Fairly or not, court takes
on political hue," whereas "The split nature of the tribunal—and
the nation—will mean increased scrutiny over whether it acted properly." In any case, "Our System Leaves the Loser Standing," for
"Even in a soured election, be glad there was a legal arbiter," the
Supreme Court.[46]

On many different levels in these matters, there was abundant
evidence of legislative sovereignty and the legislative state. Just as
in previous chapters where the Executive and Legislative branches
were found deeply engaged in their own forms of lawmaking, so also
was the Judicial branch in the disputed Y2K election. A controlling
judicial framework was argumentation over whether the Florida
court and U.S. Supreme Court were endeavoring to make new law
rather than to interpret already existing federal and state laws.
Democrats supporting Gore said the Republican-dominated U.S.
Supreme Court was legislating from the bench, whereas Republicans for Bush said the Democrat-dominated Florida Supreme Court
was doing so. The U.S. Supreme Court took up the Florida court
case, in which Gore was deeply involved, after Bush appealed to it.
If the Florida recount issues had remained in the Florida state legislature, the probability of Congress' ultimate involvement would
have been enhanced. Nevertheless, at all levels and branches in the
massive complex legal disputes, the chief framework was legislative—that is, in argumentation over how to interpret and apply existing state and federal laws. This fact was on public display in the
extended presentations and cross-examinations on both sides at the
U.S. Supreme Court's hearings, prior to its final decision, on Bush

v. Gore on December 11, 2000. There, Justice Kennedy was one of those concerned that the Florida Supreme Court was improperly making and rewriting laws after the election. Justice O'Connor was one of those who believed that a court does not have to give deference to a legislature in such cases. Justice Ginsburg was one of those who pointed to the all-powerful legislature.[47]

The Politicizing of Judicial Power?

At the start of Bush Jr.'s presidency, a question was posed as to whether "For Justice to Be Blind, Must Justices Be Mute?" Or, one can ask, must judges be non-partisan and without political bias or political ideology in order to be fair, or is that an unreasonable standard of expectation? In any case, there loomed in 2001 and beyond "A Battle for the Courts." A key High Court decision in June 2002— which "Upholds System That Pays Religious Schools' Tuition"— "Moves Issue to the Front Line of Political Debate" as "The Battleground Shifts."[48]

Questions of judicial political ideology were coming to the forefront in 2001–2005. Examples included: "Tilting the Scales Rightward" ("How ideology has taken over the federal bench"); "Blocking Judicial Ideologies"; "The Supreme Court's Confident Activism" ("From deciding the presidential election to campaign finance, the justices waded right in"); "Judging by Ideology" ("The political beliefs of judicial appointees cannot be ignored"); "Taking Over the Courts" ("Judicial activism is a worry for Republicans, too"); "It's the Law, Not the Judge" ("But these days, the bench is the hot seat as the judiciary is personalized"); and "So What's the 'Right' Pick?" ("Conservatism comes in many shades. The shade Bush chooses will be crucial").[49]

With the death in later 2005 of Chief Justice Rehnquist came "Complications For Both Sides In the Battle For the Court." Similarly depicted was "How the high court's first vacancy in 11 years is setting off a passionate struggle to tip the balance." The latter story came two months earlier in connection with Justice O'Connor's impending resignation. Subsequently, as the first (successful) nominee to face confirmation hearings, Judge Roberts declared that he had no ideological or political "platform." But would he, one article asked, continue "The Rehnquist Legacy" of trying "to turn back the Warren Court?" As for the second (successful) nominee, "A True Conservative," to undergo confirmation hearings, Judge "Alito's nomination . . . presents leaching moment for the right." Even so,

"Alito's Life Suggests a Conservatism by Temperament, Not Party Ideology." Then, "As Hearings Begin, Alito Says Judges Should Not Bring an Agenda to Court," although "Partisan Tenor of Alito Hearing Reflects a Quick Change in Washington" following the Roberts hearings, as "Focus of Confirmation Hearings Quickly Turn to Limits of Executive Branch's Power." Alito's adult life up to this point was depicted as "Against the Liberal Tide." In the end, both Roberts and Alito were confirmed, with Roberts becoming Chief Justice. By July of 2006, "Roberts Is at Court's Helm, But He Isn't Yet in Control," as "Term Ends, Showing a Conservative Turn, Though Not Always a Decisive One."[50]

A Decisive Role in the War on Terrorists

In the aftermath of the attacks on the United States in New York and Washington on September 11, 2001, the U.S. Supreme Court and Federal courts played a controversial, decisive, even activist, role in the war on terrorists. In the course of 2002: "Terror could tilt court on states rights"; "Courts roll back secrecy in war on terror" ("Series of rulings hits Justice Department for undermining rights of 9/11 detainees"); "A New Court for Terrorism" ("Our judicial system can't handle this war"); "In Tense Times, a [Federal] Court Insists on Open Doors"; and "The Difficult Balance Between Liberty and Security" ("Keeping a sense of proportion on the Supreme Court").[51]

Such reports continued in 2003 and beyond. They included: "Using the Gavel to Strike at Terror" ("Victims' Families Turn to Lawsuits for Justice and Answers"); "U.S. [Federal] Courts Reject Detention Policy In 2 Terror Cases" ("Appellate Judges Rebuff Bush on Citizen and Afghan Captives"); "Citing Free Speech, Judge Voids Part of Antiterror Act"; and "Law In A New Sort Of War" (" 'Enemy combatants' line up to plead for legal rights before the nation's highest court").[52]

In April of 2004, the "Supreme Court Hears Cases of Citizens Detained by U.S.," while "The administration yields no ground on indefinite detention." At that hearing, there was "Examining [or] questions about judicial authority." In the fuller lengthy transcripts of that hearing obtained by this writer, in addition to newspaper excerpts, there was much said about sovereignty and legislation, as in, for instance, references to the "territorial sovereign jurisdiction of the United States." Two months later in June 2004, the "Supreme Court Affirms Legal Rights of Those Deemed 'Enemy Combatants,' " as "In Classic Check and Balance, Court Shows Bush It Also Has Wartime Powers," thereby "Reaffirming the Rule of Law" and setting "New limits for a wartime president" in "The Court v. Bush." An editorial two months later on the court cases fought by detainee lawyers against the Executive branch—in the wake of the Supreme Court's ruling, with its many gaps along with those in Congress' laws on the subject—dealt with "Making Law at Guantanamo" (where many detainees were held).[53]

Developments continued. In July 2005 a Federal judicial "Ruling Lets U.S. Restart Trials At Guantánamo" in a "Victory For White House," as "Court Says Administration Did Not Violate Global Law or Constitution." A year later, in June 2006, "Justices . . . Reject President's Plan To Try Terror Detainees," a "Ruling . . . Likely To Force Negotiations Over Presidential Power," in "A setback for the contention that 9/11 justified expansive White House actions . . ." ("Military Panels Found to Lack Authority—New Law Possible"). Finally, in early 2007, "After Bush Administration . . . placed the National Security Agency eavesdropping under court supervision," "Senators Demand Details on New Rules"—"Will court approvals be case by case or be issued as broader orders?"[54]

The Question of an "Imperial" Judiciary Usurping Congress' Legislative Power

The issue posed in this subheading came quickly to the fore in 2001 at the start of the new Bush Administration when "Justices Give the States Immunity From Suit by Disabled Workers." The Court's ruling on the "Limits of [Americans with] Disabilities Act" prompted one editorial on how "The Court Usurps Congressional Power." Then, when Supreme "Court strikes down race-based challenge to districting," "The decision may affect lawmakers trying to draw voting districts this year." Moreover, "Supreme Court Limits Scope Of a Main Civil Rights Law." One news piece highlighted the key issue as being "The High Court's Target: Congress." At the same time, "Juries, Their Powers Under Siege, Find Their Role Is Being Eroded." In relation to Congress' Disabilities Act and other matters, an editorial on "The Supreme Court's Balance of Powers" opined that "Our elected leaders must reclaim their proper authority." Reinforcing the above picture was a book reissued at that time with the interesting title *The Ruling Class: The Supreme Court*, by William Rehnquist. On a different front, a Federal "Judge Blocks New Forest Protection Rules." Also, a Federal "Court Lessens

Federal Power To Shut Down Meat Plants." More to Congress' liking was when "Justices Uphold Curbs on Coordinated Political Spending" in "A ruling that delights Congressional advocates of a ban on soft money."[55]

Similar patterns continued in 2002. "Justices Unanimously Curb Scope of the Disabilities Act," with "Plaintiffs suing under the . . . act find[ing] it increasingly hard to prevail." A Federal "Court Rules Detention Law Unconstitutional." " 'Virtual' Child Pornography Ban Overturned." According to "One Nation Under Judges"—concerning the Supreme Court's ruling against the Pledge of Allegiance's "one nation under God"—". . . the role of the courts in American government is large and growing." Also in evidence was "The Imperial Presidency vs. the Imperial Judiciary." A book with a liberal agenda, reviewed that year under the caption "Bench Press," bore the provocative title *Courting Disaster: The Supreme Court and the Unmaking of American Law*. Reviewed under the caption "Decisive Influence" was another book with an indicative title, *First Among Equals: The Supreme Court in American Life*.[56]

In mid-2003 "Justices, 6–3, Legalize Gay Sexual Conduct In Sweeping Reversal Of Court's '86 Ruling," citing "Privacy Right," as "Texas Sodomy Law Held Unconstitutional," prompting "Scathing Dissent" and leaving "Conservatives Furious Over Court's Direction." Conservative outrage was exemplified by radio talk-show host Rush Limbaugh when he accused the Court of becoming "a politburo"—"an unelected super-sized city council" that improperly takes sides in cultural issues and ignores, as Justice Kennedy recognized, the states' "sovereign" rights of self-determination. Another conservative commentator, Robert Novak, likewise responded on a TV talk show that "the Supreme Court acts as a super-legislature." Affirmative action was another perceived area of excessive legislative-like activism by the Supreme Court. Overall, "In a Momentous Term, Justices Remake the Law, and the Court," for although "Unchanged for Nine Years, Court Still Proves Capable of Surprise." As one columnist put it, "In Changing the Law, the Justices Turned to Its History." According to a feature story, "As speculation builds about new faces on the Supreme Court, a close look at the Chief Justice's legacy shows the many ways the court has diluted[!] Washington's power." One might ask if one of the ways the Court had "diluted" federal power was by blurring the distinctions between the Judicial branch as interpreter of laws and the Legislative branch as maker of laws, that is, by becoming more like a lawmaking body. Meanwhile, the Judicial branch was at times becoming resistant to outside checks on its judicial powers. "Federal judges rebel over limits to sentencing power," as "Congress' move to tighten guidelines to better control 'maverick' judges draws broad criticism from bench."[57]

In 2004, "Chief Justice Attacks a Law As Infringing On Judges." "Detention Cases Before Supreme Court Will Test Limits of Presidential Power." "Federal Judge In San Francisco Strikes Down Federal Law Banning Form of Abortion." "U.S. [Federal] Court Blocks [E.P.A.] Rules For Snowmobile Emissions." "Federal Law on Sentencing Is Unjust, [Federal] Judge Rules." "[Federal] Judge Strikes Down Section of Patriot Act Allowing Secret Subpoenas of Internet Data."[58]

In 2005, "Rehnquist Resumes His Call for Judicial Independence." In "Sentencing and Sensibility," "Congress should let judges do their jobs." "Supreme Court Transforms Use of Sentence Guidelines" as "Discretion in Federal Cases Is Given Back to Judges," while "White House Fought New Curbs On Interrogations, Officials Say." "Judge for Themselves," about "Why a Supreme Court ruling on sentences puts more power back on the bench." "Juvenile death penalty abolished." In "Chopping Off the Weakest Branch," "Attacks on judicial independence echo the events of 1801." Rather than "One Role, Two Hats," "The Supreme Court's leader should have fewer powers."[59]

In the nomination and confirmation process for the new Justice Roberts in 2005, some pertinent statements were aired on radio and TV. Senator Corzine inquired about Roberts' views on "Congress' right to make law. . . ." Senator Schumer was concerned that Roberts ". . . can overturn precedent and make law." President Bush said Roberts "will not legislate from the bench" but strictly apply the Constitution. Roberts himself said "Roe v. Wade is the settled law of the land [on abortion]." He said, in press reports, "I Believe That No One Is Above the Law Under Our System." News reports centered on such topics as: "Roberts Parries Queries on Race And End of Life"; "The Court v. Congress" (Senator "Specter's Questioning Reflects Recent Battle As Justices Move to Curb Lawmakers' Powers"); and "Nomination for Supreme Court Stirs Debate on Influences of Federalist Society."[60]

Similar sentiments were voiced soon thereafter in the fall of 2005 when President Bush nominated Judge Harriet Miers to fill another vacancy on the Supreme Court, a nominee who eventually bowed out. Bush said she would not be one "to supplement the legislative process." One news report on "A Volley of Complaints" declared that "The confirmation game now focuses on the court's attitude toward Congress." Likewise in late 2006 prior to the mid-term Congressional elections, both Pres. Bush and Senate Republican majority leader Frist warned against Democrats appointing "activist judges who legislate from the bench."[61]

Legacy of the Rehnquist Court

With further regard to the Rehnquist Court's legacy on issues of federalism, there appeared a variety of news accounts. For instance, "Rehnquist legacy takes shape" as "High court, usually measured, ends term by trumpeting its long-term intention of reassigning power to the states." Also, "For a Supreme Court Graybeard, States' Rights Can Do No Wrong," as "Justice Rehnquist's 30-year battle for federalism [in terms of decentralization in federal, state, and local powers] pays off." And, "Justices Say U.S. May Prohibit The Use of Medical Marijuana," while "Federal Law Prevails in 11 States with Legalization," in "A split in a coalition that often restricts federal power."[62]

Along different lines in mid-2006, "Congress and the Courts Are Trying to Rein In Executive Power" because "After Sept. 11, the president expanded his authority." It may have been an attempted end run by the White House around the High Court when a day earlier "Administration Prods Congress to Curb Detainee Rights." In an illustrative case earlier in 2006, "Justices Reject U.S. Bid To Block Assisted Suicide" and "Say . . . Attorney General Was Wrong in Oregon Case," which involved complicated issues of each state's sovereign rights in matters of statutory interpretation in relation to questions of federalism.[63]

In the end, a significant legacy of the more conservative Rehnquist Court, not unlike that of the more liberal Warren Court earlier on, was its strong practice of judicial review. The principle of judicial review, which goes back to Chief Justice John Marshall in the early 19th century, has enabled the Supreme Court to strike down, as unconstitutional, laws of Congress and the states, as well as rulings by lower courts. As it became applied and developed, this principle was employed to justify, at different times and in different ways, a legislative-like authority, in the Supreme Court's rulings, to make and unmake laws of other bodies. If "To the Founders, Congress was king," in that the "balance of power should lie with Congress," some Founders like Jefferson were unwilling to let the Court's appointed members overrule the laws of Congress' elected members. Yet the Founders' uses of classical themes of great lawgivers in relation to the Supreme Court (where they adorn the chamber's upper inside walls) helped to set the stage for these later developments.[64]

Chapter V

U.S. Federal Departments, Agencies, and Commissions

Chief among the myriad separate bureaucracies in the contemporary U.S. Federal government are over a dozen Cabinet Departments within the Executive branch, along with many dozens of more independent agencies and commissions, as well as corporations, that have been created by Congressional statutes or, in some cases, Executive orders. These bureaucracies have long been growing to huge proportions under both Democratic and Republican Administrations, whether with centralizing or decentralizing agendas respectively. So massive have these contemporary Federal bureaucracies become in their individual regulatory capacities as veritable mini-legislatures through their promulgation of quasi-legislative rules, that they have added enormously to, and become a part of, the wide legislative activities of the Federal government. They have done so on their own and in conjunction with the Chief Executive, Congress, or, indirectly, the Supreme Court through their disparate kinds of rule-making and rulings. What follows is a limited selective look at illustrations of these and related activities, inclusive of those, as in Congress itself, that are more broadly contextual.

1. DEPARTMENTS AS MINI-LEGISLATURES

Justice: Under Bush Sr. and Clinton I

Having its beginnings in the Judiciary Act of 1789 as a one-man part-time Office of Attorney General to enforce U.S. laws, to ensure the administration of justice, and to advise presidents, the enlarged modern Department of Justice was established as an integral part of the Executive branch by act of Congress in 1870 shortly after the Civil War, owing to the increased litigation of the United States. Since then, the Department has grown ever larger, with vast control over enforcement of U.S. laws and related matters. In view of the growing legislative-like activities of the Office of the President in the Executive branch—expanding out from "executing" the laws to include the issuance of rules, regulations, and orders—it is natural that the Justice Department itself has in like manner become expanded, as have many other departments and agencies within the Executive branch. In a telltale sign of this transformation, one TV commentator in December 2001 referred to the role of the Justice and Defense Departments as being to "promulgate regulations" dealing with military trials and other matters after the war in Afghanistan and the terrorist attacks on the U.S. originating there that September.[1]

Among the few news clippings saved on the Justice Department during Bush Sr.'s presidency are two suggestively titled accounts from 1991–1992—"Caesars at the Justice Department" and "U.S. Weighs New Limits on Asylum" ("Reagan-era proposals to restrict entry may be revived")—on different activist aspects of the Department. During this same period, the Justice Department was embroiled in controversy for not taking sufficient measures in law enforcement, as when its "Handling of B.C.C.I. Case Arouses Deep Suspicions" ("When Watchdogs Nod"). Then, a half year later, "New Attorney General [Barr] Shifts Department's Focus" to "The top priority: stronger law enforcement." Not long thereafter: "U.S. Claims Teledyne Faked Tests On Parts for Missiles and Aircraft"; "House Bank Inquiry Is Widened As Justice Dept. Issues Subpoenas" in "A possible high-stakes battle between two branches"; "Justice Dept. Role Cited In Deception On Iraq Loan Data," as "Officials Say C.I.A. Was Asked to Conceal Findings From Court"; and "Justice Dept. Criminal Unit Is Investigating F.B.I. Chief" in "Ethics Review [that] Comes as Bureau's Help Is Asked In Iraq Loan Inquiry."[2]

At first, the Justice Department was off to a rocky start in early 1993 at the outset of President Clinton's first term when his new "Attorney General-Designate Baird [Is] Fined for Undocumented Workers" in her home. The case exposed how "Laws [Are] Often Disregarded for Household Workers" who are illegal aliens. At the same time, in aggressive actions against one of its most crucial divisions, "Justice Dept. Says F.B.I. Director Abused Position for Small Gains." Clearly, "Clinton urgently needs a new Attorney General to handle the monumental task of revamping the government's most troubled department" euphemistically characterized as "Law and Disorder."[3]

By July 1993 it was Janet "Reno: The Real Thing," as "Clinton's popular, straight-talking Attorney General wants to revolutionize law enforcement, but will the White House let her?" Already in March she had been off to a fast start as new "Attorney General Seeks Resignations From Prosecutors" in wider "Fast Changeover By Reno." Then, in January 1994, "Special Counsel in Clinton [Land] Deals Depends on Congress, Reno Says," as "New Law on Prosecutors Is Called Key to Action." Two weeks later, "[Special] Counsel [Fiske Is] Granted A Broad Mandate In Clinton Inquiry." By May, "Justice Dept. Is Preparing to Argue Clinton Has Immunity From Lawsuit." Meanwhile, "Aides Improve Justice Department Management But Some Worry About Close Ties to White House." Conversely, as time went on "In the Loneliest Spot," "Clinton loyalists think she's [Reno's] not on the team. No wonder Republicans want Reno to keep her job."[4]

Broadly aggressive and activist in typical fashion during 1995–1996 were the following cases: "Justice Dept. Scrutinizes McDonnell Douglas"; "U.S. Sues to Block Microsoft In Its Bid to Acquire Intel"; "U.S. [Justice Dept.] Joins Effort to Transfer Retarded Into Group Homes"; "U.S. Convenes Grand Jury To Look at Tobacco Industry"; "U.S. Sues Mine Companies Over Pollution"; and "Justice Dept. Vows Scrutiny Of Bell Deals" in "A Goal of Competition In Local Phone Markets." In a sign of counterreaction to its possible overreach, "Judge Rebukes Justice Dept. For Review of Compuserve"; and "A Good Idea Gone Wrong," inasmuch as "The independent counsel system, designed to protect the law, instead now encourages abuse of the legal process."[5]

More directly illustrative of the regulatory legislative-like activity by the Justice Department in 1995–1996 were the following items: "Justice Dept. Forces Changes In Law School Accreditation"; "Reno Tightens Rules on Use of Lethal Force by Federal Agents"; and "Justice Dept. to Call for Veto of Affirmative Action Ban."[6]

Justice: Under Clinton II

During President Clinton's second term, the Justice Department under Janet Reno was increasingly active and assertive in the public eye as the chief law-enforcement agency, while often seeming to go beyond the Department's usual bounds in the recent past, whether as a result of its own initiatives or of outside circumstances. Many of the lesser cases were intensive in-depth involvements in narrow areas of public interest, as when: "U.S. Sues to Block Merger Plan of 2 Long Island Hospitals"; "U.S. Suing Louisiana On Prison Ills"; "Reno's Handling[s] of Reports of Chinese Spy Are Criticized" in "A question of . . . Dept. oversight at the Los Angeles labs"; "Justice Department to Monitor New Jersey Police Over Racial Profiling" in "Rebuke For [Gov.] Whitman"; "Justice Dept. Sues to Alter Conditions At a Prison"; and "U.S. Charges John Gotti Jr. With Extortion . . . In Alleged Mafia Scheme." Beyond these limited minor examples were three major wide-ranging cases in point that greatly captured the public's attention.[7]

The first of these major cases dealt with "Reno's New Focus: It's Clinton—after months of criticism for not naming an independent counsel, Janet Reno turns her gaze his way." With "Spending At Issue," "Reno Announces An Initial Inquiry Into Clinton Ads." Not long thereafter, "Justice Dept. Questions President In '96 Campaign Finance Inquiry." One editorial in a liberal newspaper countered that "Ms. Reno Undermines Justice." Much later, "Justice Aide Seeks an Outside Prosecutor to Look at Gore's '96 Fund-Raising" ("For Reno, too, another time of testing"). On another matter, "Clinton Criticizes Officials' Actions Against Scientist" in "Los Alamos Case" in "a rebuke of the Justice Department," although "Reno Says Apology to the Accused Isn't Needed."[8]

In the second case in point, "Tobacco Industry [Is] Accused of Fraud by U.S.," with "Government Seeking Billions Spent on Health Care for Smoking-Related Ills." Nonetheless, the tobacco "Industry calls it a 'political stunt.' " As one tobacco law analyst said, "This is potentially their biggest legal challenge. . . . It could force changes in the . . . industry itself."[9]

The third case in point of high visibility for Reno's Justice Department during this period from 1997 through 2000 concerned the fate of a little Cuban refugee boy, Elián Gonzalez, whose Florida relatives defied Reno and the court judges who wanted him returned to his father in Cuba. At first, "U.S. Set To Order A Speedy Return Of Boy To Father" as "Reno Moves On Custody." Then, as "Boy's Relatives Defy U.S. And a Judge Delays Action," "Block by Block,

a Wall Rises in Little Havana" in Miami. It was called "Reno's Showdown" as "The attorney general makes a risky personal move to
end the standoff over Elián Gonzalez. But did she lose her nerve at
the crucial moment?" Yet "Cuban Boy Stays In U.S. For Now, A
Court Decides." Then, "U.S. Gathers Officers, Preparing To Take
Cuban From Miami Kin," although "Legal Fight Over Boy Could
Last For Months." When, in the end, "Cuban Boy Seized By U.S.
Agents And Reunited With His Father," who took him back to Cuba,
there was "Outrage In Miami" as "Police Fire Tear Gas as Hundreds of Angry Protesters Take to the Streets in Miami." Much debated then was "Elián and the Law" ("Examining the critics' arguments"). On "The law and a little boy," it boiled down to "An
administration's muddled reasons for removing Elián."[10]

In line with its above activism under Reno more generally, but
more directly impacting the legislative arena, was the Justice
Department's central involvement in the heated controversy over
the independent counsel statute. In "Rethinking a Law," "Time and
Targets Alter Capitol Views on the Independent Counsel Statute."
Also in December 1997, "Reno Rejects A Prosecutor On Clinton And
Gore Calls," while "Bitter G.O.P. Vows To Fight" as "Her Ruling
Suggests No Wrongdoing Is Found In Fund-Raising." A year later,
with Reno again at center of controversy, "A verdict clearing Espy
is the latest sign that the independent counsel statute is likely to
perish." In February 1999, "Independent Counsel Statute Seen in
Danger As Hearings Near"—"A law likely to be a casualty of impeachment." For it was being called "A Too-Independent Counsel."
At that point in February 1999, "Senate Is Urged to Delay Decision
on the Counsel Law," while "Reno and Starr [Are] Said to Agree on
Framework for an Inquiry," and "Focus is on Independent Counsel's
Tactics," with "An agreement that is thrown into question by a judicial order." In March the "Justice Dept. [Is] to Urge End to Counsel Law." Two weeks later, "Reno to Urge Senate to Abandon Statute on Independent Counsels." Soon afterwards, "Starr to Ask
Congress to End Law That Gave Him His Job." Finally, in June
1999 "Attorney General [I]s Taking Control As Independent Counsel Law Dies."[11]

The Justice Department's tough regulatory quasi-legislative
stance toward Microsoft, in late 1997 and beyond, in "US vs.
Microsoft," signalled possibly "A New Cold War For 21st Century .
. .," as "Antitrust dispute indicates that sides see regulation of the
rapidly changing software industry in completely different ways."
"Will Reno Brake Windows?: Justice's challenge to Microsoft's
strong-arm browser tactics hint at a larger showdown on the hori-

zon." With battle lines drawn, "Microsoft Terms U.S. Challenge 'Perverse.'" Reportedly, "Justice Suit Barely Slows 'Unstoppable' Microsoft." Soon enough, however, "Microsoft Case May Be Prelude to a Wider Antitrust Battle" involving "Tough issues of smokestack-era law in the computer age." Advancing to new level, "U.S. and States File Suits Claiming Microsoft Blocks Competition Over Internet." Was it "Antitrust Excess?" Then, "Headed For Battle," "A historic antitrust case looms as last-minute talks between Microsoft and the feds fall apart." However, in July 1998, "Government is dealt blow in Microsoft case." Seizing the legislative initiative a year later in August 1999, "Justice Dept. [Is] Proposing Bill To Foil Computer Encryption." Seeking further regulatory action in 2000, "U.S. And 17 States Ask Judge To Cut Microsoft In 2 Parts," with "Serious Curbs Also Sought." Finally, in June 2000, "Microsoft Breakup Is Ordered For Antitrust Law Violations," although "[Bill] Gates Calls Ruling [by a Federal Judge] Unjustified."[12]

Two among miscellaneous other matters, both in 1998, are: "Justice Dept. Belatedly Finds New Defense of Line Item Veto" in 1998; and "Reno Lifts Barrier To Oregon's Law On Aided Suicide."[13]

Justice: Under Bush Jr.

The dramatic shift in strong judicial activism from that exhibited by Attorney General Janet Reno during Clinton's Democratic administration to that displayed by John Ashcroft in Bush Jr.'s Republican administration was bridged over in part by their unusually forceful uses, in different ways, of their newly asserted regulatory and other powers that moved well beyond the more traditional and less visible roles in chief law enforcement. Both figures became highly controversial in their own ways as they pursued their agendas, often political as well as personal, in the administration of justice.

At first, Ashcroft faced a challenging testing time. In January 2001 he was called "The Wrong Choice for Justice" in that "Ashcroft will ignite the most furious nomination fight since Bork and Tower." Some doubted that he would duly grasp that "An attorney general is sworn to uphold all the laws, even those he cannot abide." At pointed Senate hearings, however, "Ashcroft Promises to Enforce All Laws," even "Laws He Dislikes." Yet despite Democrats' perception of him as an extremist, "Senate Confirms Ashcroft As Attorney General, 58–42, Closing A Five-Week Battle."[14]

Initial developments in 2001 during Ashcroft's conservative regime as Attorney General were somewhat predictable and uneventful. On the criminal front, for instance, "U.S. Executes a Second Killer in a Week," while "Rules Could Increase Capital Prosecutions"; and "Eyes Are on Justice Dept. In Rhode Island Death Penalty Case" in connection with "The administration's principles over capital punishment and states' rights." On the corporate front, "U.S. Abandoning Its Efforts to Break Apart Microsoft" after "A Huge 4-Year Crusade"; and "U.S. vs. Microsoft: Going Back to Square One."[15]

Then came the terrorist attack on the World Trade Center on September 11, 2001, which led to tough, even radical, new regulatory and other measures by Ashcroft's Justice Department. That November: "Ashcroft Plan Would Recast Justice Dept. In a War Mode"; "Justice Dept. Announces Tougher Immigration Rules," although "Critics Say Measures Will Affect Those Who Aren't Terrorists"; "U.S. Makes It Easier to Detain Foreigners" in "The New Regulation," while "Critics of sweeping legal changes build to a political force"; and "Justice Dept. and Senate Clash Over Bush Actions." In December: "Ashcroft Weighs Easing F.B.I. Limits For Surveillance" ("Rules Existed Since 70's"); "Senate Bill Would Stiffen Some Controls Over Visas," while "Attacks in U.S. Inspire Europe to Tighten Laws"; and in "Rough Justice," "The Attorney General has powerful new tools to fight terrorism. Has he gone too far?" On into 2002: "U.S. Begins Crackdown On Muslims Who Defy Orders to Leave Country"; "Ruling Clears Way to Use State Police in Immigration Duty After Sept. 11"; "Justice Dept. Balks at Effort to Study Antiterror Powers" in "Curt Responses to Congressional Inquiries"; "Washington Bends the Rules," for "Ashcroft's Justice Department needs to be reined in"; "Justice Department Moves to Use Its Expanded Powers to Spy on Possible Terrorists"; "A Second Tier of Justice" in "A parallel legal system—without constitutional protections—is in the works for terror suspects"; and "Unequal Justice—Why America's Military Courts Are Stacked To Convict." In 2003: "The Justice Department is seeking wider powers to investigate suspect terrorists—A Further Erosion of Civil Liberties?"; "Congress Gets A Report" as "Justice Dept. Lists Use Of New Power To Fight Terror"; "Ashcroft Seeks More Power To Pursue Terror Suspects"; "U.S. [Justice Dept.] Will Tighten Rules On Holding Terror Suspects"; "U.S. [Justice Dept.] Will Defy [A] Court's Order In Terror Case"; "Report [by Justice Dept.] on U.S. Antiterrorism Law [Patriot Act] Alleges Violations [within Justice Dept.] of Civil Rights" in report to Congress "likely to raise new concern among lawmakers about . . . Justice Department" in its tough handling of "terrorism investigations under the 2001 law"; "Administration Plans Defense of Terror Law, With Ashcroft to Lead Effort" while "Presenting antiterrorist legislation as a necessary tool," contrary to some critics who seek repeal of parts of Patriot Act; and "Has Ashcroft Gone Too Far? Even Republican stalwarts are beginning to criticize his approach against terrorism." Not surprisingly, Ashcroft was replaced subsequent to Bush's reelection in late 2004. In later 2004, his successor, Alberto Gonzales, called it "a Department of Justice guided by the rule of law."[16]

Across a broad range of other key issues during President Bush Jr.'s first term and beyond, the Justice Dept. projected an activist energetic agenda in legislative-related or legislative-like ways. "U.S. [Justice Dept.] Seeks [in a federal court] to Limit Environmental Law's Reach Over Coastal Waters." "It's the Law, But Nobody Wants to Enforce It—Why does the U.S. government [Justice Dept.] ignore the killings of Americans in Israel?" "Ashcroft to Defend Ban on Some Abortion Protests, Angering His Longtime Allies." "Justice Dept. Bars Event By Gay Staff" ("Prohibition Is a First By a Federal Agency"). "Defending '03 Law, Justice Dept. Seeks Abortion Records." "Move by U.S. on Suicide Law Draws Suit in Oregon." "Justice Dept. Weighs Lifting An Anti-Bias Order on Hotels." "In Shift, Justice Dept. Pushes to Widen Rights to Own Guns" and "is criticized for throwing 'red meat' to the gun lobby." "Under Ashcroft, Judicial Power Flows Back to Washington"—"The attorney general asserts federal control on the death penalty and other social issues." "Justice Department Tracking Staff's Contact With Congress" ("Lawmakers see an effort to discourage whistle-blowers"). "Attorney General's *Edict* [emphasis added] Exceeded [His] Authority in Oregon, Panel Says," as a Federal court "Ruling Upholds Law Authorizing Assisted Suicide."[17]

Defense and Homeland Security

During the presidency of George Bush Sr., the Defense Department, or Pentagon, was a core component of his vision of an expanded "new world order," following the demise of the Soviet Union, under the leadership of the United States. One critic called it "The Pentagon's Superpower Fantasy" inasmuch as "No nation can dominate the world anymore." Conversely, "Pentagon [Is] Seeking 140,000 Reduction In Reserve Forces," albeit the "Move Is Criticized In Congress." In mid-March of 1992, "Pentagon Charts Military Options For Bombing Iraq" as "Officials Suggest President Is Likely to Use Force Unless Baghdad Yields on Arms." The rest is history.[18]

In the first year, 1993, of Clinton's first presidential term, "Months After Order on Gay Ban, Military Is Still Resisting Clinton," while "Little Is Done on Drafting a Policy, Officials Say." "Pentagon Plans To Allow Combat Flights By Women; Seeks To Drop Warship Ban." "Pentagon [Is] Seeking to Cut Military But Equip It for 2 Regional Wars," as "Clinton's Strategy Endorses Bush's Basic Doctrine" for "post–cold-war" world. "Pentagon Fights Wider Ocean-Dumping Ban." "Pentagon Spells Out Rules For Ousting Homosexuals; Rights Groups Vow A Fight." In 1995, on "Why the Pentagon Gets a Free Ride," "As the budget knife cuts deep, defense is spared because of a dubious two-wars-at-once doctrine." The next year, "Congress Exceeds Pentagon's Dreams In Spending Plan," as "Military is exempted from doing more with less."[19]

In 1997 during the first year of Clinton's second term, "Pentagon To Trim Thousands Of Jobs Held By Civilians," with "Military Shifts Planned," although "Congress May Balk." Then, in 1999, the following news stories appeared. "Pentagon Seeks Command For Emergencies in the U.S." and "Clinton Seems Likely to Approve New Plan." "Pentagon Defied Laws and Misused Funds, Panel Reports," for "Money Was Shifted to Projects That Congress Had Cut Off or Never Approved." "Pentagon Sets Up New Center For Waging Cyberwarfare." Then, in mid-2000, "Congress Continues Work on Bill to Finance Pentagon Programs."[20]

Near the end of President Bush Jr.'s first year in office, 2001, and in the wake of the war in Afghanistan, it was said that the Defense and Justice Departments were chiefly concerned to "promulgate regulations" on military trials and other such matters. Fittingly that year, "[Sec. Of Defense] Rumsfeld's Office Reverses China Ban" as "A Memorandum Is Rescinded After the White House Objects." An "Apostle of American Might," Rumsfeld was "Arguing again for a costly remodeling of the American armed forces." His was "a radical new plan for the Pentagon." Washington was "Making Way for Pentagon Reform."[21]

Subsequently, from 2002 to 2006, the following sequence of reports appeared. "President [Is] to Ask That Congress Increase Military Spending," the "Most Since Reagan Era." "Pentagon Seeks Exemption From Environmental Laws" as "It Cites Training and Weapons Testing Curbs." As "Rumsfeld Sets Up Showdown Over Weapon," he "Announces Plans to Ask Lawmakers to Cancel Crusader Artillery." "Bush Will Formalize a Pentagon Policy of Hitting First" against Iraq, etc., in "A significant move away from the military doctrine [i.e., containment] of the cold war era." Increasingly in "A War Over Environmental Rules," "The Pentagon seeks relief

from laws that protect habitats on its military training grounds."
Then, "Congress Agrees to Bar Pentagon From Terror Watch of
Americans." "Pentagon Ban on Pictures Of Dead Troops Is Broken"
when "Flag-Draped Coffins Are Put on the Internet." "Delays on 9/
11 Bill Are Laid to Pentagon" through its "Lobbying against a loss
of budget powers over spy agencies." "Pentagon Is Asking Congress to Loosen Environmental Laws" inasmuch as "Having troops
in Iraq may now sway lawmakers to accede to a wish." Not surprisingly, "The Pentagon's Secret War On Terror" involved an "aggressive new plan of attack." "Pentagon Revises Its Rules on Prosecution of Terrorists" "Under legislation . . . [by which] the government
is poised to restart tribunals the Supreme Court halted . . . "[22]

In the aftermath of the 9/11 terror attacks on the United States,
various new measures for homeland security received wide public
and press attention. At first, for instance, "The debate over a national ID card heats up, raising privacy concerns." Then, "The [new]
homeland security chief's [Tom Ridge's] plans to shake up agencies
are meeting resistance." And so forth.[23]

In this environment in early 2002, "The Bush administration
opened the door . . . to creating a cabinet-level department of Homeland Security as lawmakers increase their demands to make Tom
Ridge, the domestic security chief, more accountable to Congress."
"At issue is Congress's power to oversee an agency." In mid-2002,
"Congress Gets [Bush] Administration's Bill Setting Up Security
Dept.," inclusive of C.I.A. and F.B.I., "a bill that would reorganize
much of official Washington." However, "Congress doesn't rubber-
stamp homeland defense" because "Some 88 committees oversee
security agencies. Lawmakers have their own ideas on terror. . . ."
Also at issue were "Freedom Vs. Security" and "Guantanamo Jus-
tice. . . ." Soon enough, "Congressional Panels Recast Homeland
Security Dept.," with "Congress Putting Its Stamp on Domestic
Security Dept." After "House Approves Homeland Security Bill"
in later 2002, so, too, did the Senate. After "Senate Votes, 90–9, To
Set Up A Homeland Security Dept. Geared To Fight Terrorism,"
the "U.S. Bureaucracy Faces Its Biggest Overhaul in Half a Cen-
tury." Several days later, "Bush Signs Bill Creating Department
For Security" with Ridge as its head. In "New Rules for a New
Department," "Bush gets the flexibility he wants to manage homeland security, but employees are wary." At that same point—as
"Administration Begins to Rewrite the Decades-Old Restrictions
on Spying" in Executive quasi-legislative fashion—"The military's
expanded role in domestic security reopens a debate." By early 2003,
Ridge "quietly shaped his new department and became part of Bush's

inner circle." At that time, "U.S. [Homeland Security] Plans to Toughen Rules For Cargo Shipping Industry." Similarly in 2004, "U.S. Takes Steps to Tighten Mexican Border" regulations, etc. In 2005 "Patriot Act, Part II: The political tug of war intensifies" for Homeland Security etc. as "Bush calls for strengthening the antiterror law, while critics worry about greater potential for civil-rights abuses."[24]

Energy

During President Clinton's first term, in 1994, "The Energy Department, the nation's keeper of nuclear arms and enigmas, is seeking [in "less restrictive" outlook] to revamp or dismantle the legal machinery that has amassed at least 32 million pages of secrets, [in] a stack that would rise three miles high." Toward the end of Clinton's second term, in 1999, "Energy Dept. Will Cut Standards for Its Workers' Exposure to a Metal Tied to Lung Disease." In 2000 a "Report Faults Energy Dept. as Failing to Gain Lab Staff's Support for Tighter Security," in connection with the lost or missing disks at Los Alamos' nuclear weapons laboratories, thereby raising the question of a regulatory agency's bureaucracy being too big for its director (sometimes dubbed the "energy czar") to control.[25]

At the start of President Bush Jr.'s first term, in 2001, the Energy Dept. continued its independent appetite for "promulgating" rules and regulations. "The Energy Department issued a rule today that will increase the efficiency of new residential air-conditioners and heat pumps," thereby "Expecting a reduction in energy bills and pollution from power plants." Even so, "Energy Chief Sketches Plans To Curb Rules Limiting Supply" in response to the energy crisis in California and elsewhere. "Clinton Energy-Saving Rules Are Getting a Second Look" as Bush "administration adds to its review of Clinton-issued rules." "Bush Relaxes Clinton Rule On Central Air-Conditioners," "Weighing higher consumer prices against improved energy efficiency." However, "3 States Plan a Court Fight On Air-Conditioner Efficiency," "Battling the Bush team to keep a Clinton rule." An example of a presidential order to the Energy Dept. occurred in late 2001 when "President Bush ordered the Energy Department . . . to increase the United States' emergency supply of oil . . . to its capacity over the next few years. . . . "[26]

In 2002–2003, the Energy Dept. came increasingly to exercise an independent, often quasi-legislative, authority, with mixed results and prospects. For instance, "the Department of Energy showed that several recommendations . . . were written into the White

House's national energy report and into an executive order signed by President Bush." The deeper dimension, when that "Executive Order Followed Energy Industry Recommendations," was that Bush was criticized by environmental and other groups for outrightly favoring the trade group's proposals submitted to the Energy Dept. and then to Bush, whose language in Executive order adopted even much of their language. In mid-2003 a wide northeast power blackout was blamed by some on energy deregulation. Others put the blame on a "Set of Rules Too Complex To Be Followed Properly, Or Not Complex Enough. . . . [E]ither the rules for power transactions on the electrical grid were broken, or they were inadequate, even though they are hundreds of pages of detailed specifications covering seemingly every emergency." With the "Energy Dept. Taking Over National Blackout Inquiry," there was "New urgency for energy legislation that was ignored after 9/11."[27]

Quickly enough, the "Blackout has led to calls for more regulation and for Congress to pass long-delayed energy bill" "now plodding through the legislative process." However, the "Energy Bill Draws a Deeply Split Utilities Lobby." Meantime, "A former critic learns to love the Department of Energy" as "Blackout Puts Fresh Focus on Ex-Senator," Spencer Abraham, the Secretary of Energy. In late August, "U.S. [Energy Dept. Sec.] Orders Use of Cable Under [Long Island] Sound" in a "Federal Ruling." In addition, "Energy Dept. Seeks Power [from Congress] To Redefine Nuclear Waste." In Congressional hearings, "Hundreds of [Past] Rule Violations [Are] Tied to Possible Blackouts." In October "Congress Moves Toward Mandatory Rules [and Standards] for Electricity," notwithstanding a forthcoming report by the Energy Dept. on the August 14 blackout. In November, "Even With Bush's Support, Wide-Ranging Legislation May Have Been Sunk by Excess."[28]

Adding to the vast overlapping jurisdictional complexities of Federal energy regulations—with typical Washington interconnections to Department, President, and Congress—was the Federal Energy Regulatory Commission. Illustrations abounded in 2001–2003. "Federal Agency Orders Power Generators to Justify Prices" when "Addressing concerns of price-gouging in California." "Critics Say U.S. Energy Agency Is Weak in Oversight of Utilities" as that "Federal Agency Faces Pressure to Act in California Energy Crisis." That agency's "Board Orders Limited Price Caps for California Power." Yet "Plan on California Energy Has No Shortage of Critics" in that "U.S. Regulators' Effort Satisfies Very Few." Then that "Federal Government [Agency] Widens Regulation of Western Power" in ten more states. As reported shortly before, a "Senate Committee Votes to Repeal a [66-year-old] Law Limiting Utilities" and to transfer some of the authority under that law to the Federal Energy Regulatory Commission."[29]

Commerce, Interior, Transportation, Labor, Housing

The huge organizational size of other Federal departments like Energy goes far in explaining their autonomous scope as regulatory quasi-legislative bodies unto themselves while also serving in that capacity as a legislative vehicle for the president. The Commerce Department was aptly characterized as follows in 1995 during Clinton's first term, with Ron Brown as its Secretary, when it and he came under Congressional investigation: "A sprawling agency is a focus of debate on big government" as "G.O.P. Puts Heat on the Commerce Dept." Shortly thereafter, "G.O.P. Finds It's Not Easy To Make Cuts In an Agency" and to "Shrink . . . Bureaucracy." A year following his untimely death, Brown was described as "The Joyful Power Broker," as "Washington mourns Ron Brown, the Secretary of Commerce who conquered barriers and the world." The Department of the Interior in 2001 early in Bush Jr.'s first term was rhetorically reported to issue "The New Law of the Land" as "Interior's [Sec.] Norton says to ranchers and environmentalists: Can't we just get along?" A half year later, "Bush White House Reverses Clinton Decision on Mining"—"Removing Veto Power [!] From Interior Dept." and "removing unduly burdensome . . . mining regulations" in "A move welcomed by the mining industry and criticized by environmentalists." In 2002 the "Interior Dept. Ruling on Methane Could Undermine [!] Bush Proposal" "for a vast expansion of methane gas production in the West. . . ." The Department of Transportation during Clinton's second term ". . . Proposes to Tighten Rules On Safety of Commuter Planes" and "Says the New Steps Would Save Scores of Lives." Also, "U.S. To Ease Rules To Make Air Bags Less Dangerous" in a "Trade-Off In Protection." Later, during Bush Jr.'s first term, the "Senate Deletes Higher Mileage Standard in Energy Bill" and "rejected a measure . . . to stiffen fuel-efficiency for cars and trucks," favoring the auto industry over environmentalists and sending the matter back to the Transportation Dept. for it to revamp gasoline-use standards in place since 1985. Two months later the Senate encouraged further initiative in regulatory power when "4 Lawmakers Urge Transportation Dept. To Allow Pilots to Carry Guns."[30]

On a different front during Clinton's first term, "Labor Dept. Agency Proposes [Directly to Congress a] Ban On All Smoking in the Workplace": "With a bill to ban smoking in virtually all buildings in the country except private ones temporarily stalled in Congress, the Labor Department seems prepared to do by regulation what the Congress has not done by law[!]." In Clinton's second term, "After Long Delay, U.S. Plans To Issue Ergonomic Rules" in "Effort To Limit Injuries": "Opponents in the House of Representatives tried this year to delay the rules for further review, but the Senate has not acted, so the Labor Department is free to issue the rules[!] The White House has decided to act now, as Congress has left town." However, early in Bush Jr.'s first term, "Senate G.O.P. Moves to Nullify Clinton Rules on Worker Injuries": "Using an unusual legislative weapon, Senate Republicans plan . . . to try to repeal a far-reaching set of [Labor Dept.] rules on workplace injuries that have been fiercely opposed by business groups." Three years later, the "Senate Blocks New Rules [by Labor Dept.] On Pay for Overtime Work." Thus, acting as a quasi-independent legislative-like department, either on its own or for the president, Labor, like other departments, has often typically entered the lawmaking arena along with Congress, there engaging as a partner in the sometimes contentious "dance of legislation." A critic declared with pointed phraseology in 2003 that effort was needed to "prohibit the Labor Department from promulgating rules. . . ."[31]

At other times, a department has itself asked Congress directly for more powers, as in 1993 when "HUD's [Housing] Chief Seeks Wide New Powers"—"Cisneros Asks Congress's Aid in Dealing With Property Acquired by Default." In 1996, it was called "A HUD Strikeout" insofar as "Strict rules could evict families from public housing." In 2004, acting as Federal monitors, "HUD Orders ["and . . . demanding"] Nassau County To Repay Money for Grants" after "numerous violations were discovered."[32]

Agriculture, Health, Treasury

The regulatory powers of the Federal Departments and the legislative powers of Congress have long had complex interrelationships, as in the case of the Agriculture Dept. under Presidents Clinton and Bush Jr. For instance, the Dept. under Clinton was criticized by Republicans in Congress such as Senator Dole for issuing too many rules and regulations on the meat industry, which they wanted reduced rather than increased, whereas the Agriculture Secretary defended his Department's "rule-making process" in addressing the need to modernize safety rules so as to protect against E-coli bacteria, etc. In 2001 "Federal and Congressional investigators are examining possible lapses and misconduct in meat safety regulations in New York and New Jersey. . . . The department's investigators and the Senate Agriculture Committee are also looking into whether proper safeguards were taken during a lengthy [N.Y.C.] refrigeration failure. . . ." In 2002 "Members of Congress today introduced legislation that would restore the Agriculture Department's authority to set and enforce standards for Salmonella in meat and poultry. . . ." In 2003 "The Agriculture Department will argue in Federal District Court that [a Nebraska slaughterhouse] . . . should be . . . shut down [over] . . . E-coli. . . . Consumer advocates and members of Congress have warned [against] . . . the government's inability to enforce health safety rules in the meat and poultry industry. . . . They argue that the Agriculture Department will need new explicit powers from Congress before the department can enforce rules strict enough. . . . 'This is an extraordinary case. . . .' "[33]

On different matters, during the Clinton Administration, after years of neglect, "the Department of Agriculture will . . . announce a sweeping set of proposed regulations that will cover all organically grown food. . . ." Similarly, "The Department of Agriculture announced today . . . the first standards that the federal government has ever imposed for the labelling and processing of organic foods. . . . [They] were ordered by Congress and then took the department more than a decade to produce. . . ."[34]

During the Bush Administration, on the one hand, the Agriculture Dept. "Gives More Discretion To Forest Managers on Logging" with "Less Stringent Rules on Environmental Reviews"; while, on the other, it "Imposes Stricter Rules for Genetically Modified Crops." The first of these two preceding cases may exemplify Bush's deemphasis on the environment, but the second reflects election-driven politics. According to "Mr. Deregulation's Regulations: Shift of Politics, Mad Cows and Dietary Pills to Die For" (2003), there is "a simple White House maxim these days: with an election approaching, even a president who came to office assailing government regulation cannot do too much to protect consumers."[35]

As for presidential promulgation of rules and regulations in quasilegislative fashion through the Department of Health and Human Services, in tandem with as well as in lieu of Congress, "President Clinton [2000] . . . will issue sweeping new rules to protect the privacy of medical records by requiring doctors and hospitals to get consent from patients before disclosing health information. . . . [These] new rules, completing four years of work, . . . [are] the first comprehensive federal standards for transactions now regulated by a jumble of state laws" after "Congress directed the administration to adopt privacy standards under a 1996 law passed with bipartisan support."[36]

The interrelationships between the Treasury Department, Congress, and the White House were at a turning point in 1991 during Bush Sr.'s presidency when the "Free-Wheeling Treasuries Market Is at Turning Point With Congress" following the announcement by the Solomon Brothers brokerage house "that it had cheated in several recent Treasury auctions." Two days later, "House Panel Assails Treasury Regulation" as "Solomon Describes Lax Unit" and "Tells House Panel Bond Trading Desk Ignored Many Rules," while "Lawmakers warn that tighter rules for bond dealers are likely." A week later, "Treasury, Responding to Solomon Scandal, Issues New Rules," "Deflecting complaints in Congress and favoritism charges."[37]

Whereas the above tightening of certain Treasury regulations took place under the Republican Bush Sr., a deregulation of other Treasury rules occurred under the Democrat Clinton in an apparent reversal of usual stances by the two political parties. In 1995 "The Clinton Administration plans to call . . . for legislation that would allow commercial banks, Securities firms and insurance companies to merge, forming giant financial service companies. . . . [Republican] Treasury Secretary . . . Rubin will urge Congress to repeal the Depression-era Glass–Steagall Act. . . ." Even the liberal *New York Times* called it "Mr. Rubin's Sensible Bank Reform," which would "wipe away rules . . . that are unsuited for modern financial markets."[38]

Two further role (rule) reversals by the Treasury Department on other fronts occurred during Bush Jr.'s first term. "Moving to carry out a crucial part of the antiterrorism legislation signed into law . . . by President Bush, the Treasury Department imposed new regulations today on a wide variety of financial institutions and other businesses in an effort to cut off the flow of money to terrorist groups." In Congressional testimonies, the Treasury Secretary and Comptroller General "Urged" "New Rules . . . to Avert Looming Pension Crisis."[39]

2. AGENCIES AND COMMISSIONS AS MINI-LEGISLATURES

E.P.A.: Under Bush Sr. and Clinton

Like numerous other Federal agencies under the aegis of the Executive branch, in which the President appoints their heads, the Environmental Protection Agency has been an independent establishment ever since its creation in 1970. Not an official full-fledged

Cabinet Department, it has recently acquired a kind of Cabinet-like status while still remaining an independent establishment. Its increasingly complex administrative bureaucracy along with its far-flung authorities and responsibilities have made its quasi-legislative regulatory power and jurisdiction often seem to be that of a mini-government alongside other independent Executive establishments. As with other such agencies, party politics and interest groups have sent the E.P.A. through changing cycles of regulation and deregulation. Under Bush Sr. and Bush Jr. the tendency was toward deregulation, whereas under Clinton greater regulation gained the upper hand. In both cases, the legislative-like nature of the regulatory process was often exhibited in a variety of striking ways. Amid varying interfaces with the White House, Congress, and the states, the E.P.A. has remained unto itself in its dealings not just as law-enforcer but as a kind of rule-making lawmaker.

Under President Bush Sr., the following news stories were somewhat typical on the E.P.A. as regulatory rule-maker. "U.S. [E.P.A.] Sets Rules to Curb Landfill Pollution." "E.P.A., in a Reversal, Lifts a Ban on Farm Chemicals." "E.P.A. [Is] Urged to Ease Rules on Cleanup of Toxic Waste": "In response to President Bush's call to review Federal regulations, a top official of the Environmental Protection Agency has proposed changes in laws for cleaning up toxic waste sites that would reduce the Government's enforcement of standards and eliminate some environmental safeguards." "Tighten the Rules On Seafood Safety." "President Overrules EPA on Clean Air, Approving Major Concession to Industry," and he "Curbs Clean Air Provision . . . On Public Notice Rule For Emission Increases." "Industries Gaining Broad Flexibility On Air Pollution" through "Relaxation Of A 1990 Law" [the Clean Air Act], as "Panel Led by [V.P.] Quayle [Is] Victorious Over Environmental Agency—Lawsuits Predicted." "Administration's Regulation Slayer [Assistant to Quayle] Has Achieved a Perilous Prominence."[40]

During Clinton's first term, "E.P.A. Seeks Emissions Agreement for Northeast," with "States, auto makers and environmentalists in a 3-cornered battle." "E.P.A. Settles Suit and Agrees to Move Against 36 Pesticides." "E.P.A. to Allow Flexibility in Auto Emission Testing" as "Some States Balked At More Strict Rules." "E.P.A. Wants to Rewrite Law on Nuclear Cleanups to Focus on Riskiest Sites." "House Bill Would Block New E.P.A. Pollution Rules" so that "Oil Emission Order Wouldn't Be Enforced." "G.O.P. House Leaders Succeed In Advancing Limits on E.P.A." and "its ability to enforce pollution laws." "Threat to Cut E.P.A. Budget Reflects a New Political Shift." "Demoralized, E.P.A. Works To Set Goals" and "Standards." "E.P.A. Bill, Modified, Still Faces Veto Threat." "Brief Clause in Spending Bill Would End E.P.A. Veto Over Wetlands Development" and "Power to Protect Wetlands." "Court Backs E.P.A. Authority On Disclosure of Toxic Agents."[41]

During Clinton's second term, "EPA Chief Browner wore down everyone, right up to the President, in her battle to toughen rules" on clean air. "Northwestern States Pressure the E.P.A. to Act Against Smog." "E.P.A. Presses Sweeping Plan to Publicize Data on Pollution in Five Industries . . . in a campaign to control emissions by using public pressure." "E.P.A. Acts to Require Big Cut In Air Emissions by 22 States" in its "proposed rules." "E.P.A. Steps Into Auto Pollution Dispute" as "Auto makers hope to block the spread of strict emission rules." "Environmental Agency Under Fire on Safety Rules" when "Facing thousands of decisions and not a few critics." "U.S. Orders Cleaner Air In 22 States." "E.P.A. to Give States Edict [!] On Clean Air for U.S. Parks," "But Deadline on Enforcing Rules Is in 2004." "Agency Will Ask Congress To Drop Gasoline Additive . . . Found to Pollute the Water." "E.P.A. Orders [!] 392 Plants in 12 States to Cut Emissions in Half." "Appeals Court Upholds E.P.A. Rules to Reduce Smog in the Northeast." "E.P.A. to Issue Tougher Rules on Diesel Fuel." "E.P.A. Institutes Water Regulations Before Bill Blocking Them Becomes Law" in Congress. "E.P.A. Says [New York City's] Lead-Paint Law May Increase Risks to Children." In "Probing authority of EPA to be nation's clean air cop," the "Supreme Court probes sharper limits on regulators in a possibly far-reaching case," while "Critics say that Congress has granted too much discretion to executive branch agencies." Finally, in mid-2000, a prominent conservative talk-show host declared that the E.P.A.'s imposing of pollution standards without approval by Congress (or the voting public) was a prime example of an extra-constitutional usurpation of Congress' authority by an Executive branch agency under Clinton–Gore![42]

E.P.A.: Under Bush Jr.

In 2001 during the first year of the new presidency of George Bush Jr., the E.P.A. under Christine Whitman made and unmade, accepted and rejected, a wide variety of rules and regulations, often in particular relation to those issued by the preceding Clinton Administration. At times just as mixed in her policies relating to those of the Bush White House as to those under Clinton, Whitman tended to typify an agency head preoccupied with the massive day-to-day complexities and dynamics of an independent regulatory bureaucracy in the Executive branch through its own extensive direct relations with Congress, the Courts, and the states. The patterns set in that expansive first year were largely continued during ensuing years. The ongoing operation of the E.P.A. as a kind of mini-legislature in its extensive rule-making, in addition to its law-enforcing, has long been apparent albeit unnoted.

The following news reports, again arranged in roughly chronological sequence, were illustrative of the E.P.A. in 2001 during Bush's first year in office. "Whitman Promises Latitude To States On Pollution Rules." "Critics [Sierra Club] Try to Turn Whitman Against Her [!] Emission Plan." "Supreme Court Upholds E.P.A.'s Authority on Air Rules," "Rejecting an industry effort to consider cost before setting rules," and reaffirms "the bedrock principles of the Clean Air Act." "Whitman Backs Clinton Rules Designed to Cut Diesel Pollution." "Moves on Environment Disappoint Industry" as "Bush's Early Acts Anger Oil and Mining." "Despite Appearances, Whitman Says She and Bush Agree on Environment," even though her "E.P.A. Supports Protections Clinton Issued for Wetlands." "Bush [Administration] Endorses Rule on Lead Emissions Proposed by Clinton." "[Appeals] Court Backs Most E.P.A. Action On Polluters in Central States." "E.P.A. Delays Further Rules On Clinton Era." "Whitman To Issue Order [!] To Dredge Hudson For PCB's." Whitman said that she and agency made that decision on dredging the Hudson and that she later so informed the White House. "For the EPA, Change Is in the Air" as "Bush plans to shift the enforcement role to states, but critics are crying foul." "Hostile Environment": "In an administration dominated by oilmen and deregulators, . . . Whitman is shading things as green as she can." "E.P.A. Faults Ohio Agency Headed by a Bush Nominee." "E.P.A. to Adopt Clinton Arsenic Standard" after outcry when "Bush Administration Had Suspended Enactment [!] of Stricter Level." "Whitman Says PCB Dredging Will Proceed . . . [and] Rejects G.E. Plan To Scale Back [Hudson River] Cleanup."[43]

Early in 2002, "Top E.P.A. Official Quits, Criticizing Bush's Policies" and "A White House described as 'determined to weaken the rules.'" Soon thereafter, "White House Rejected a Strict E.P.A. Alternative to the President's Clear Skies Plan," thereby "Sparing the utility industry the costs and burdens of more controls." Subsequently, "Whitman . . . caught by surprise . . . when the E.P.A. issued a letter supporting a ban on snowmobiles in Yellowstone National Park," as "A stance that conflicts with Bush policy creates a stir." ". . . Whitman Holds Her Ground" "on diesel-powered buses and trucks" in a "big exception to the Bush administration's pro-industry attitude on environmental matters. . . ." "E.P.A. Says It Will Change Rules Governing Industrial Pollution" as "Bush Prepares Major Easing Of . . . Rules" in "Move Demanded by Officials in Northeast States." "Whitman Dispels Talk That She Wants to Quit."[44]

Coming increasingly to the fore in early 2003 were Congress' complaints that the E.P.A.'s new pollution rules were overturning or violating Congress' limits on air pollution in the Clean Air Act and earlier legislation. Then, "7 States to Sue E.P.A. Over Standards on Air Pollution," "Seeking federal regulation of carbon dioxide." "Vowing to Enforce the Clean Air Act, Whitman [Is] Also Trying to Change It," reflecting "split personality on pollution rules" in relation to "the Bush administration's proposal to revamp the Clean Air Act, legislation that the agency's top officials support." "Critics Say E.P.A. Won't Analyze Clean Air Proposals Conflicting With President's Policies." "E.P.A. Drafts New Rules for Emissions From Power Plants." Fittingly worded in legislative fashion, the E.P.A. "enacts [!] rule," according to one radio source, while on different occasion Whitman herself referred to "when we enact [!] the new rules . . ." on diesel-fuel emissions![45]

Following Bush's 2004 re-election and Whitman's departure from the E.P.A., the same kinds of regulatory and rule-making issues continued. In 2004, "Tougher Emission Rules Set for Big Diesel Vehicles"; "An Industry Gets Its Way" when "The EPA's revised rule on hazardous waste favors a big GOP donor," whereby "an administration [is] determined to roll back what it considers to be regulatory overkill"; and "U.S. [Federal Appeals] Court Blocks Rules For Snowmobile Emissions," as "The E.P.A. is told to explain its rationale for new standards." In 2006, "Union Leaders Say E.P.A. Bends to Political Pressure"; and, especially controversial, "E.P.A. Whistle-Blower Says U.S. Hid 9/11 [Toxic] Dust Danger" under Whitman.[46]

F.D.A.: Under Bush Sr. and Clinton

As one of the numerous large agencies within the Department of Health and Human Services, the Food and Drug Administration has often had as much reach and notoriety as the E.P.A. It has also exhibited patterns of lesser or greater actual regulatory control and oversight in its legislative-like or quasi-legislative capacities during the successive presidential administrations of Bush Sr., Clinton, and Bush Jr.

In the final year of Bush Sr.'s term, 1992, "Report Says F.D.A. Is Lax On Over-the-Counter Drugs." Also, "F.D.A. Faulted on Inspection of Medical Devices," while one Republican Congressional investigator said that "the most well-intentioned statutes and regulations cannot work if there are miscommunications, bureaucratic fumblings or simple inertia . . .," such that even the Republican White House pressured the F.D.A. to speed up its internal efficiency and operation. In addition, "Cornucopia of New Foods Is Seen As Policy on Engineering Is Eased" as, according to V.P. Quayle at "a briefing of industry executives," "part of the Bush Administration's 'regulatory relief plan.' "[47]

During the first two years of Clinton's first term, 1993–1994, prior to the new Republican control of the House after the mid-term elections of 1994, a pattern of greater regulatory growth was evident, as a few examples illustrate. "F.D.A. Seeks Rules On Drugs' Testers." "F.D.A. Seeks Tighter Rules On Safety of Blood Supply" as it "issued new guidelines." "U.S. Agency [F.D.A.] Suggests Regulating Cigarettes as an Addictive Drug." "F.D.A. Imposing Stricter Rules on Food Labels." "F.D.A. Seeks to Stiffen Rule on Medical Devices."[48]

After Republicans took decisive control of the House of Representatives after the late-1994 elections, led by Newt Gingrich as assertive Speaker, the regulatory tide turned and retreated somewhat. In early 1995, "F.D.A. Becomes Target of Empowered Groups." "Congress [Is] Moving To Revamp Rules On Food Safety," while "Reducing Federal Role," although "G.O.P.'s Plan to Have Agencies Justify Regulations [instead of having an independent hand] Faces Tough Battle or a Veto." According to one TV discussion, with reference to "F.D.A. law," Gingrich says that the F.D.A. makes illegal too many things, calling for reforms to reduce and relax its regulations, which critics call overly punitive toward the drug industry.[49]

The F.D.A.'s agendas and struggles continued in 1995–2000 on many more fronts than can be explored here. Tobacco offers an example in the successive stories to follow. In mid-1995 "Tobacco [Is] Held to Be Drug That Must Be Regulated" in a "Political Handoff to Clinton From F.D.A.," although "Congress is not likely to favor anti-smoking regulations." "[F.D.A.] Proposal on Tobacco Gets Some White House Backing" in "A step that may not be so politically hazardous after all." "President To Give F.D.A. A Big Role To Fight Smoking" as "New Restrictions [Are] Due." Then, in mid-1997, "[Federal] Judge Rules F.D.A. [Is] Able To Regulate Tobacco As Drug" and "Industry Is Dealt Stiff Setback. . . ." Yet "F.D.A. [Is] Taking Cautious Path In Its Regulation of Tobacco." "Clinton Officially Rejects Limits on F.D.A. in Tobacco Plan." "Overloaded F.D.A. Is Facing Biggest Challenge, Tobacco," "As it contemplates expanding its vast regulatory repertory to include tobacco." "F.D.A. Lacks Authority to Regulate Nicotine, [Federal] Court Rules," citing "Evidence That Congress Kept Power to Regulate for Itself," although "Government To Appeal." "[Supreme Court] Justices [Are] Skeptical of U.S. Effort For Jurisdiction Over Cigarettes." "How far can FDA go in regulating tobacco?," as "The Supreme Court is hearing . . . its most important public-health case in half a century." In late 1999 it was asked on one TV show whether the F.D.A. has statutory jurisdiction to regulate the tobacco industry, or whether it needed to get that jurisdictional authority through Congressional legislation, around which the Clinton Administration's F.D.A. had tried to do an end run. Then, in early 2000, "High Court Holds F.D.A. Can't Impose Rules On Tobacco" and "Finds That Congress Was Bypassed," while presidential candidates "Bush and Gore See Ruling As Prod for New Controls." Response was swift. "[Congressional] Legislators Planning Response To Justices' Ruling on F.D.A." in reaction to new push by "Antismoking advocates . . . for legislation to overturn . . . Court decision . . .," even though "G.O.P. leadership is balking. . . ." At the same time, "Clinton Urges Giving F.D.A. Oversight of Tobacco" and "Challenged Congress . . . to restore the . . . [F.D.A.'s] ability to regulate tobacco. . . ."[50]

F.D.A.: Under Bush Jr.

The mixed reports on the F.D.A. during Bush Jr.'s presidency have taken a variety of forms. In early 2001 it was called "The Leaderless F.D.A.": "Although we've heard a good deal about the Bush administration's efficiency in making appointments, it is curious that there appears to be no effort to fill the critical position of commissioner of the . . . [F.D.A.]." In 2003 "Bush Announces an Easing of Rules on New Genetic Drugs" as "An important campaign issue is address: rising medicine costs." In 2004 "Bold Moves at the F.D.A. Come as Surprise to Many" as "Drug agency proves less predictable than critics had expected" (with accompanying photo of Bush and F.D.A. head shaking hands). However, later that year, "At the F.D.A., [there are] Strong Ties to the Drug Industry and Less Monitoring." In 2005 "F.D.A. Imposes Tough New Regulations for an Acne Drug." In 2006 "F.D.A. Rules Will Regulate Experts' Ties to Drug Makers" through "Guidelines [That] Focus on Financial Influence" in "A move to appease critics who say some advisory bodies give tainted advice."[51]

Actively engaged on the legislative front with Congressional lawmakers, "F.D.A. Officials Press Legislators to Oppose Bill on Importing Less Expensive Drugs"; and "Fighting Methamphetamine, Lawmakers Reach Accord [with] F.D.A. to Curb Sale of Cold Medicine." In "Why I'm Fighting Federal Drug Laws From City Hall" in "Santa Cruz's battle over medical marijuana," the main focus is the Drug Enforcement Agency (or Administration), which is the leading Federal agency (under the Justice Dept.) in enforcing narcotics and controlled substances legislation. As such, the D.E.A. presents another reminder of the complexity of the vast expansive Federal agencies having intricate regulatory interrelationships, in this case with the F.D.A., albeit setting the latter off in this area as more a rule-making body.[52]

On the judicial front, "[Federal] Judge Voids Rules on Pharmaceutical Tests," inasmuch as "The F.D.A. is said to have overreached on a mandate regarding tests on children"; and "U.S. To Prohibit Supplement Tied To Health Risks": "F.D.A. Ban Is First Under Restrictive '94 Law—Court Battle Is Seen."[53]

F.C.C., F.T.C., F.A.A., F.E.C.

The independent Federal Communications Commission—after the first two years of Clinton's first term when it was augmenting its regulatory reach—was increasingly hampered, like many other agencies, by the deregulatory efforts of Congress following the Republican takeover of the House in the mid-term elections of 1994. However, the regulatory vs. deregulatory debates continued to underline the quasi-legislative character of the F.C.C.'s vast role in rule-making. These and related patterns engaged the F.C.C. during the presidencies of both Clinton and Bush Jr.

Illustrative during the Clinton era of the F.C.C. as rule-maker, rule-unmaker, and rule-reviser in a kind of mini-legislature, were the following press accounts. Asked one news article in 1995, "Has the F.C.C. Become Obsolete?," pointing out that "Technology Moves Fast, Determining the Public Interest Takes Time." Argued another, "Give the F.C.C. Back Its Bite," adding "Deregulation is great—up to a point." Varying news angles in 1996 included the following: "F.C.C. to Set Stricter Local Phone Rules," and it "Intends Strict Oversight To Encourage Rivalry"; "F.C.C. Eases Equal-Time Rule for 3 Networks"; and "After a Year of Law [Telecommunications Act of 1996], Scant Competition," and "With New F.C.C. Plans Due, a Battle on Access" looms, especially since F.C.C.'s critics say its regulations are ineffective in stimulating competition." In 1997–1998: "Sweeping Changes [of "Rules"] in Phone Industry Approved by F.C.C."; "F.C.C. Chief Backs Off on Rules for Free Air Time for

Candidates"; and "F.C.C. to Ease Rules on Stations' Hiring of Women and Minorities" after "a court decision invalidating its affirmative action requirements." In 1999: "U.S. Expands Police Powers To Monitor Cellular Phones," such that "under the rules announced . . . by the [F.C.C.] . . ., they ["Federal and local agencies"] will also be able to determine the general location of a cell phone . . . under surveillance"; and "F.C.C. Begins Rewriting Rules for Industry" pursuant to the Telecommunications Act that "broadly deregulated the industry." In 2000: "F.C.C. Cancels Rules on Religious Broadcasting"; and "F.C.C. Told [by a Federal court] to Repeal Its Order on Replies" through "two long-established rules that had required radio and television stations to . . . free reply time for opponents of political candidates. . . ."[54]

During the presidency of Bush Jr., deregulatory tendencies were much in evidence for the F.C.C. as rule-maker and rule-unmaker, but counterbalancing forces were also at work, often involving dynamics with Congress and Court. In 2001: "Federal Court Rules Agency Erred On Mandates For Minorities"; "New F.C.C. Chief Would Curb Agency Reach"; and "The F.C.C. Loosens Its Media Rules." In 2002: "F.C.C. Rules On Ownership Under Review" as "U.S. Court Orders Study Of TV-Market Limits." In 2003: through "Partisan Vote In F.C.C.," "Regulators Ease Rules Governing Media Ownership," a "Change . . . [That] Allows Big Companies to Expand in Print and Broadcast" and "to Get Bigger"; whereupon "F.C.C. Media Rule Blocked In House," which "passed legislation" in a "Move to Limit Reach of Networks . . . [in] Face-Off With Bush" Administration and its support for the rule; and then "U.S. Court Blocks Plan To Ease Rule On Media Owners" in "Last-Minute Order [That] Deals Blow to Conglomerates and the . . . F.C.C.," with "Market Power at issue." In 2004: "Court Orders F.C.C. to Rethink New Rules on Growth of Media"; and "Internet Grants to Schools Halted As the F.C.C. Tightens the Rules." In 2005: "Powell to Step Down at F.C.C. After Pushing for Deregulation"; and "F.C.C. Eases High-Speed Access Rules" and "Aids Phone Companies."[55]

The Federal Trade Commission is designed primarily as an independent law-enforcement agency to enforce the laws that prohibit business practices harmful to competition and consumers. Yet the F.T.C. is also, like so many other regulatory agencies, a rule-making body having direct impact on the lawmaking process, albeit in more limited ways than the Commerce Department to which it is loosely related. Typical manifestations of the F.T.C.'s law-*enforcement* role occurred when: "F.T.C. to Fight Rite-Aid–Revco Drugstore Merger" because "A link of the 2 biggest chains is called a threat to consumer prices" (1996); "Rite Aid Drops Revco Bid After Regulatory Opposition" (1996); "F.T.C. Rejects Deal To Join Two Giants Of Office Supplies" (1997); "F.T.C. Sues Intel, Saying It Violated Antitrust Laws" (1998); and "The Regulatory Signals Shift" insofar as "F.T.C. Serves as Case Study of Differences Under Bush" over "large corporate mergers" (2001).[56]

Indications of the F.T.C.'s regulatory rule-*making* activity as well as lawmaking influences came when: "Commissioner Gives F.T.C. New Teeth, Broadening Its Antitrust Role," such that "An agency that stumbled during the Reagan era grows more active" (1996); "F.T.C. Issues Guidelines for Mergers" as its "Report Urges Emphasis on Efficiency and Competitiveness" and its "Regulators seek consistency. . ." (1996); "F.T.C. Calls for Laws to Protect Children on Line" (1998); "Federal regulators" in "F.T.C. Guidelines Restrict Ad Claims for Supplements" (1998); "F.T.C. Said to Seek [New] Law on Online Privacy" (2000?); and "FTC backs ["approved"] Net privacy regulations" (2000).[57]

Established as a Federal agency in 1958 and made a component of the Transportation Department pursuant to another Act of Congress in 1967, the Federal Aviation Administration (formerly Agency) is designed to protect public aviation safety. Its vast rule-making involvements to that end have included the following quasi-legislative examples: "U.S. Would Tighten Rule On Takeoffs When Ice Is Threat" (1992); "Agency to Issue New Plane Fuel Tank Rule" through "More requirements stemming from the explosion of T.W.A. Flight 800" (2001); "F.A.A. [Makes] Reviews on Passenger Weight After Crash" (2003); and "[F.A.A.] Flight Rules Were Written For Roomier City Skies" (2004). Meanwhile in 2003, "Congress and Bush Split On Privatization at F.A.A."; and "Capitol Dispute Threatens To Shut Much of F.A.A." as "Law Authorizing Agency Nears Expiration."[58]

Established like other agencies by Act of Congress (1971), the independent Federal Election Commission administers and enforces laws regulating the acquisition and expenditure of funds to ensure compliance in Federal election campaigns. Like so many other Federal law-enforcement agencies, the F.E.C. also has an independent quasi-legislative rule-making role to play both on its own and in relation to Congress and Court. In 2004, for instance, "U.S. [Federal] Judge Orders Election Agency To Tighten [Its] Rules," as "Parties Tussle Over Which Finance Regulations Apply for '04 Race," and "to enact [!] tougher restrictions on how millions of dollars are spent on campaigns. . . ." In 2005, "F.E.C. to Consider . . . how revamped campaign finance laws apply to political activity on the Internet. . . . [Pursuant to a 2002 law,] the F.E.C. . . . issued extensive rules to accommodate the law's provisions. . . . But a federal judge ruled last year that many of the F.E.C. rules were too lax and . . . asked it to address the question of Internet activity."[59]

Thus, in its primary role of law enforcement, such an agency often acts as a crucial rule-making body or even as a kind of mini legislature, in furtherance of that role, even when applying and adapting Congressional legislation.

I.N.S., I.R.S., S.E.C.

Not all Federal agencies are deemed successful in their law-enforcing or rule-making activities, as exemplified by the Immigration and Naturalization Service, once part of the Justice Dept. and now part of Homeland Security under title of Citizenship and Immigration Services. In early 2001 prior to the 9/11 terror attack on the United States, "After Complaints of Abuse, Immigration Service Issues National Standards for Its Jailers" and "for the treatment of its detainees." In early 2002 after the 9/11 terrorist attack, "Congress [Is] Set to Break Up Beleaguered Agency." Soon thereafter, "Bush Endorses Abolition of Immigration Agency." A day later, "House Votes . . . to Abolish the I.N.S." And so on. However, one critic of Congress' move to split up the I.N.S.'s services and enforcement into separate divisions called it "Reform That Leads to Chaos" inasmuch as "Congress has the wrong idea on fixing the I.N.S.," which is deemed the second least popular agency in the Federal government.[60]

The Internal Revenue Service, established by an Act of 1862 to administer and enforce the internal revenue laws and related statutes, is, although part of the Treasury Dept., one of the most freewheeling independent Federal agencies. The I.R.S.'s massive rule-making activities and its "enforcement" intrusions into the private sector have blurred many sprawling lines between Congress' enactments in the mammoth tax code and the I.R.S.'s promulgations of vast rules pertaining to them—all having deep impact on citizens' lives not least because of confusion and abuse that have often resulted therefrom. During the Clinton Administration in 1997–1999, the following news reports were telltale: "Snooping by I.R.S. Employees Has Not Stopped, Report Finds"; "Clinton Presses a Proposal to Simplify the Tax Code, with Changes Large and Small"; "Republican Leaders Beginning a Drive for Sweeping Revisions in the Federal Tax Code"; "Legislation Reining In the I.R.S. Clears House"; "I.R.S. Admits Taxpayers' Rights Are Abused by Improper Tactics"; "Finance Chief In the Senate Unveils Bill Curbing I.R.S."; "Senate Committee Is Told of a Vast Range of Abuses by I.R.S.";

"Staff Says I.R.S. Concealed Improper Audits and Rogue Agent"; and "Senate Votes . . . To Overhaul I.R.S. After Complaints," while "White House to Seek Changes When the Senate and House Meet to Reconcile Bills."[61]

During the Bush Administration in 2001 and 2003, for instance, "Victims' Funds May Violate U.S. Tax Law," with "No Sign I.R.S. Will Bend Rule for Sept. 11 Donors"; and "I.R.S. Tightening Rules for Low-Income Tax Credit" in "A new burden of proof as an agency aims at fraud."[62]

The Securities and Exchange Commission likewise has a vast leg- islative-like role as independent rule-making agency in conjunction with its function as administrator and enforcer of Federal securi- ties laws protecting investors. During the later Clinton years, for instance, "S.E.C. Proposes Stricter Accounting Rules." Early in the Bush era that followed, "S.E.C. Nominee Says Rules Need Review," for "he would undertake a comprehensive review of the agency's rules and regulations with the aim of simplifying and reducing them. 'Our laws are, in the main, nearly 70 years old, and reflect a time . . . light years away from what we now confront daily. . . .' " The pre- ceding statement identifying S.E.C. rules as laws speaks volumes about the agency's rule-making as a form of lawmaking. Further along in the Bush years: "S.E.C. Waves Some Rules to Try to Ease Market Volatility" as it "issued an order . . . waving certain regula- tions . . ."; "S.E.C. Adopts New [Ethics] Rules For [Stock] Analy- sis"; "S.E.C. to Revise Rules on Electing Company Directors"; "S.E.C. Adopts New Rules For Lawyers And Funds"; "[S.E.C.] approved new rules . . . to require mutual funds to adopt new ethics codes . . ."; "S.E.C. Feels Pressure To Weaken Some Rules"; and "S.E.C. to Propose New Rules on How Executive Pay Is Reported" in order "to help investors figure out what top officials really take home." Even so, the S.E.C. has not always been as much in charge as desirable, as when in 2002 "SEC: Too cozy with those it regu- lates?"; or when in 1999 "As Huge Changes Roil the Market, Some Ask: Where Is the SEC?" when "Online, After-Hours Trading Con- fronts the Agency."[63]

3. RULES, REGULATIONS, AND LAWS

Regulatory Sovereignty and the Regulatory State?

So pervasive are the rules and regulations made by the multitudi- nous Federal rule-making bodies—whether on their own or in con- junction with mandates from the White House, Congress, or

Courts—that it would often appear that they are as much a supreme part of legislative sovereignty and the legislative state as the laws themselves, with which they are often so closely identified as to be one and the same thing even when rules are adopted in applying laws. Needless to say, the number and scope of the Federal rule-making bodies and the rules they issue—whether via departments, agencies, commissions, or corporations—are far vaster than the foregoing materials may suggest. One way of looking at this subject is in terms of the great debates over regulation vs. deregulation that have occupied so much attention ever since the Reagan years, as alluded to above.

A case in point began during the Clinton era in 1995. There was an effort led by Republicans in Congress, and opposed by Clinton Democrats, to "Stop the Regulatory Machine" in the agencies themselves through a bill that would limit their excesses but not hamper their self-operating bureaucracies. Then, "Democrats Force the G.O.P. To Pull Anti-Regulation Bill" concerning health, safety, environmental, and other rules. "Vote on Regulatory Powers [Is] Thwarted" by "Senate Democrats, struggling to preserve Federal regulatory powers against a bill that would greatly limit them. . . ." It was "a mortal blow to a bill central to the Republican agenda." Later, in 1996, "[House] G.O.P. Is Revising Plans to Reduce Regulations." Then, "Opponents Nervous as a Democrat Tries Regulatory Overhaul." Meanwhile, the Clinton Administration via the Federal agencies: "Tightens Welfare Rules"; "Tightens Rules on Supercomputers Sales to 13 Foreign Groups"; and "Tighten[s] Rules on Money Transfers." Somewhat later, "[V.P.] Gore Orders Changes In E.P.A. Procedures" in "A Nod to Agriculture on Pesticide Rules" and "A reminder to use discretion in applying an environmental law." A news report of that period reflected the public's impatience with onerous Federal rule-making: "How Many People Does It Take to Write a Rule?"—a question answered with an illustrative "flow chart . . . from Department of Education . . . [on how it] promulgates [!] rules . . ." through a massive complex bureaucratic procedure made even more stark by the fact that "education is just one of 50 topics in the Code of Federal Regulations." More facetiously, in connection with cases investigated by the Senate on campaign finance practices, "Selling Favors Is Allowed. Just Follow the Rules."[64]

A large factor looms behind the pervasiveness and massiveness of Federal rules and regulations—whether acting like, within, as, in place of, or supplemental to law and legislation. The Federal departments, agencies, commissions, and corporations issuing them often do so not on their own bureaucratic initiative but in conjunction with directives from the White House, Congress, or the Courts. Thereby lines often become further blurred between rules and laws, regulations and legislation, lying at the heart of sovereignty and state at the national level.

Examples of pronounced presidential directives on, or involvements in, rules and regulations, usually via specific Federal departments or agencies, were legion under Clinton and Bush Jr. Under Clinton: "Clinton Seen Issuing Work Rules That Stalled Spending Agreement" and "Budget Deal"; "Clinton Announces New Rules For Child Safety Seats in Cars"; "Clinton to Offer Rules on Privacy of Medical Data" "and attacks Congress"; and "No Retreat on Clean Air" as "Clinton administration issued several major rulings . . . to reduce smog-causing chemicals." When running for president in 2004, "[Democrat John] Kerry Says His Economic Plan Calls for Federal Spending Caps and Clinton-Era Rules." Subsequently, on the medical front, ". . . Bush Rolls Back Clinton's Medicaid Rules." Later, "Bush administration . . . unveiled rules for the new Medicare drug benefit. . . . Issuance of the rules is one of the most significant events . . . [after] Bush signed the new Medicare law. . . . The rules . . . will govern . . . [those] involved in the new program." Still later, ". . . Bush administration . . . issue[s] strict standards" in "Medicaid Rules . . . [and is] Tougher About Proof of Citizenship," "follow[ing] a tussle with Congress." Shortly thereafter, "White House [set] to Ease Rule On Medicaid Documents" and to "exempt millions . . . from a new law" in order "to pre-empt a ruling by a federal judge . . . [on grounds] that Congress had intended to exempt [them]. . . ." On the terrorist front, "President Signs New Rules To Prosecute Terror Suspects," that is, "Bush signed legislation . . . that creates new rules for prosecuting . . . suspects. . . ."[65]

Also legion are examples of Congress' vast rule-making activities in close conjunction with, or even one and the same as, its sovereign lawmaking for the United States. "House Passes Tighter Rules On Filing for Bankruptcy": "The bill, which may become the first major piece of legislation to be signed by President Bush, is subject to approval by the Senate." "Congress [Is] Close to Establishing New Rules for Drivers' Licenses" in a "Senate version of the intelligence bill" and "House . . . version. . . ." "Ready to Tackle Fishing Rules": "Congress may overhaul the regulations that determine who can catch what, and how much," through "bill[s] "passed by Senate and pending in House." "Congress Passes Bill to Tighten Lending Rules."[66]

To be added to this mixture are the "rulings" handed down by Federal courts and often seeming to carry a kind of regulatory or even statutory mandate. For instance, "[Court] Ruling May Shift Power to Writers"; and "Setback for Vouchers" as "court rules that Cleveland gives parents too few alternatives to parochial schools."[67]

An Inherent Self-Determining Power by Each Self-Operating and Legally Constituted Federal Regulatory Bureaucracy to Make Quasi-Legislative Rules for Governing Its Own Affairs?

A question of balance between independence and dependence in their powers to make rules and regulations, within their own jurisdictional purviews, has long underlaid the operations of the Federal Executive departments, agencies, commissions, and corporations, which in many cases have been created by Congress. That is to say, to what extent does each of these myriad separate bureaucracies within the Federal government have or exercise a self-determining regulatory power to promulgate, abrogate, or revise its own legislative-like rules covering the areas and concerns that fall within its own governmental domain? Considering the enormous expansion of the regulatory scope and operations of these Federal departments, agencies, commissions, and corporations, these huge self-operating Federal bureaucracies possess, by their very nature and mandate, great leeway and autonomy in their own rule-making functions.

The question posed in the subsection title immediately above can be briefly considered indirectly from different angles through a variety of news reports on instances and contexts of greater or lesser self-acting operations by these bureaucracies. Pointing up regulatory excesses are such reports as the following. "Regulatory Power Is the Dangerous Kind" in connection with grants from the Departments of Energy and Defense. "Regulators as Partners" when "Medicare pays private groups of doctors and hospital executives to assure quality." "N.A.S.D. Fines a Member And Vows Stiff Regulation" as "Big Rise in Enforcement Spending Is Seen." "Law Revises Standards for Scientific Study" and "Agencies to Face Challenges on Health and Environmental Research," as "A law passed quietly is facing loud debate on how rules evolve." "FEMA Shows Leniency In Its Rebuilding Rules For Much of New Orleans" when "A Federal decision opens the door to flood insurance and new mortgages." "Deep Security Flaws Seen at State Dept.," where "Recent Lapses Are Part of Pattern of Vulnerability, Officials Say," as "Investigations find a lax bureaucracy that resists precautions." "Bush Gives State Dept. Priority In Helping Nations to Rebuild," while "Trying to resolve an old Beltway debate: Who's in charge."[68]

In the aftermath of the 9/11 terrorist attack on the United States, there arose "The Mounting Powers of Secrecy" within the Federal government, according to a report in late 2005. In early 2006, "Basis For Spying In U.S. Is Doubled" as "Study by Arm of Congress Questions Legality" of actions taken by the National Security Agency under orders from President Bush. Also, "In Limelight at Wiretap Hearings: 2 Laws but Which Should Rule?" over the N.S.A.—"Does 'necessary and appropriate force' include this surveillance?" In 2003, in "[Tom] Ridge's Rise to Homeland Security," "He quietly shaped his new department and became part of Bush's inner circle," while the new Department transformed within its broad spheres of operation more than two dozen existing independent agencies.

As for the F.B.I. after the 9/11 terrorist attack, "Tighter Oversight at F.B.I. Is Urged After Investigation Lapses" as "Internal documents point to violations of law and F.B.I. policy." "For a Different Game, Make Different Rules," for "The FBI was a mess—then the terror wave began. Can Mueller reform it on the fly?" ("Are They Up To The Task? Federal agencies are being sorely tested by terror. . . ."). In "Changing the Standard," "Despite Civil Liberties Fears, F.B.I. Faces No Legal Obstacles on Domestic Spying"—"An agency's rules arose from concern about free speech." Even before the 9/11 attack, "F.B.I. Setting Standards for Computer Picture File of Criminals." "F.B.I. Tightens Its Rules On Files for White House." In "The FBI's New Global Reach," "Fighting terrorism takes the bureau abroad where law enforcement follows harsher rules."[69]

Corasius' Principle in Contemporary America?

Once again in the present series, we have occasion to refer back to the ideas of Joannes Corasius in the 16th-century background to Jean Bodin, father of modern ideas of legislative sovereignty. It will be remembered from our first two volumes that Corasius, going against many of his late-medieval and early Renaissance predecessors, conceived of the power to make laws as an innate power residing in all or most legally recognized bodies and corporations in conducting their own affairs, regardless of questions over their jurisdictional right to do so. Each state's inherent right to make laws for the regulation of its own affairs within its own domain and territory became for Corasius the most supreme mark of sovereignty, an idea developed by his follower Bodin in its most classic and influential formulation, which found key American expression in writings by Presidents Thomas Jefferson, John Adams, and Woodrow Wilson.

The questions raised in the titles of the two preceding subsections about regulatory sovereignty and the power to make rules on the part of U.S. Federal departments and agencies lead to a further question. To what extent does Corasius' basic principle, as just briefly summarized, offer a parallel, however loosely and indirectly, to the powers and operations of U.S. Federal departments and agencies in promulgating their own rules, while acting within their own mandates as regulatory bodies? Do they act as mini lawmaking bodies whose rules often resemble, or are equivalent to, regular laws and legislation? It has been suggested many times in the present chapter that the vast massive bureaucracies of these Federal bodies are often so self-operating and self-determining, whether as Cabinet departments or more independent agencies, that they can ofttimes be difficult to control or direct on the part of White House or Congress. Their innate rule-making authority and activity have become so extensive as to be largely self-operating and self-determining, albeit within their operational spheres and limits imposed by the three branches of the Federal government. It would thus seem that the power to make rules is indeed inherent within those bodies and is relatively independent of any outside questions about their jurisdictional rights to do so within their own purviews. Yet the fundamental conditions of their operations and functions under law must always be kept in mind.

The distant indirect historical parallels with which we are here dealing are obviously not close or exact, but they do offer some intriguing insights into the workings and character of the multiple U.S. Federal bureaucracies that have grown so huge in the last century that it sould be surprising if they did *not* take on a life of their own. If not legislative sovereignty *per se*, the legislative state, here again, offers another compelling factor. At the same time, because of the parallels above between regulatory sovereignty and legislative sovereignty, the latter does itself take on an added dimension in which regulatory bodies provide microcosms of the sovereign legislative process. It was Corasius himself who declared that the principle of each state's rightful sovereign independent ability to make laws for itself represented an innate power, one that inhered in many lesser legally recognized and legally constituted bodies within the state, such as corporations and guilds, and was not hampered by outside questions over their jurisdictional rights to do so in governing and conducting their own affairs. In the case of U.S. Federal agencies and corporations having statutory authority to promulgate rules and regulations within their own sphere of operation, this principle established long ago by Corasius has found further later expression, however remotely, under much different yet recognizeable circumstances.

Ongoing Struggles for Sovereignty

In the end, however, the struggles for sovereignty involving the U.S. Federal regulatory agencies has continued on unabated. In August 2007 "[Bush] Administration Rules May Limit Child Health Program," presenting "Hurdles to States' Plans to Expand Insurance to Middle Class" under the Children's Health Insurance Program, as "The White House acts on policies Congress has not embraced." A few months earlier, "Bush Steps Up His Attack on the Regulatory System, Endangering Important Health and Safety Protections"; "Public Citizen [News] Fights Efforts to Undermine Government Regulations," such that "Vehicle Safety Makes Small Strides." Early in 2007 "Bush Directive Increases His Regulatory Sway" by "Putting White House appointees in supervisory roles" under "an executive order published . . . in the Federal Register," according to which "each agency must have a regulatory policy office run by a political appointee to supervise the development of rules [etc., thereby strengthening the] White House in shaping rules . . . [so as] to exert its power after the takeover of Congress by the Democrats." These recent ongoing struggles for regulatory-legislative sovereignty harken back to earlier ones pitting a White House Democrat against Congressional Republicans as in 1994 in connection with "legislation that would strictly limit the ability of Federal agencies to write regulations on health, safety, and the environment."[70]

Further complicating this political picture in spring 2007, Republican-dominated Supreme Court "Justices Say E.P.A. Has Power to Act on Harmful Gases," actually mandating that the "Agency Can't Avoid Its Authority—[in a] Rebuke to Administration," thereby raising "Prospects of more legal action if the agency fails to regulate emissions," a "Ruling [that] Undermines Lawsuits Opposing Emissions Controls." In other words, "the high court said that laws passed by Congress to protect the environment require the EPA to swing into action" by virtue of the Clean Air Act.[71]

In any case, "With the Democrats now in control of Congress, the White House faces a new assault on its environmental policies"; the tide had turned on this and so many other fronts when in early 2007 "Jubilant Democrats Assume Control on Capitol Hill"; while several months later "Congress struggles to ramp up oversight" as "Its efforts to challenge powers claimed by the executive branch are faltering on partisan lines." "The Democrats' 100-hour blitz" may have had some indirect influence in the Court's 2007 ruling on the E.P.A.'s environmental oversight responsibilities, even though a year earlier federal appeals court "Judges Overturn Bush Bid To Ease Pollution Rules" in response to "Lawsuit On Clean Air Act" and to call for "Stricter Approach Pushed by Group of States and Environmentalists."[72]

Chapter VI

States of the American Union

For the sake of chronological clarity, it is convenient once again to employ an overall presidential frame of reference when treating the U.S. states in general in the first section of this chapter. Just as in the three previous chapters on Congress, the Courts, and the Departments, a presidential frame of reference is used as an easily recognizable organizing principle or device. In further sections below on individual states, the chronological organizations will center around successions of state leaders or around the issues involved. Throughout, there is not necessarily a causal connection between the leaders in office "during" the periods being discussed, although in some cases there may well be.

1. THE STATES IN GENERAL: STRUGGLES FOR SOVEREIGNTY

In multiple diverse ways have the struggles for sovereignty taken place on the part of the American states in general. There have been struggles for sovereignty, directly or indirectly, between the states and the Federal government, between state legislatures and Congress, between states and Federal agencies, between states and their individual cities, between state authorities and citizen referendums or ballot initiatives, between governors and their state legislatures (paralleling those between Presidents and Congress), and between the states themselves. The dynamics have often included issues of centralization and decentralization, regulation and deregulation. Often involved as well have been legislative issues of sovereignty and state, particularly concerning questions of a legally recognized body's inherent self-determining authority to institute laws or rules for its own affairs—the same general principle evoked in the concluding section of the previous chapter on Federal departments and agencies. When we turn from the states in general to particular states and finally to special cases at chapter's conclusion, the struggles for sovereignty, especially in legislative and related contexts, will be further on display.

During Bush Sr.'s Term

Using the period of George Bush Sr.'s presidency in 1989–1993, taken here as our initial frame of reference, the states in general were in transition between the Reagan and Clinton eras, between Republican policies of decentralization or deregulation and Democratic trends toward centralization and regulation. Yet all along, the legislative buildup kept mounting. By 1989 the part-time "citizen legislator" in the states was "becoming a rare breed" as "Lawmaking in States Evolves Into Full-Time Job" owing to the steadily growing complexities and demands of state lawmaking. No longer relegated to obscure bound volumes in state archives and libraries, "Statutes are now as close as a computer terminal" as "New technology transforms bookshelves into a battleground" over access to and uses of state statutes. For instance, part of the problem of "Governing Long Island" (a "Jurisdictional Jumble") was not just the presence of so "Many [Overlapping Different] Governments" but also the multiplicity of lawmaking bodies without there being a clear delineation of which one was making statutes for which constituency, so that " 'Most people have no idea who does what.' " That case is symptomatic of a more widespread development in other regions.[1]

In 1990, "For States and Cities, 'New Federalism' Meant New Burdens" to help pay for it. Also, "The Supreme Court has killed federalism, the states say," leading "15 States [to] Rally Behind Calls for Constitutional Amendment to Add to Their Power." Meanwhile, "As Battles Over State Legislative Seats Go, So Goes Power in the Congress." On another front, the "Number of Ballot Initiatives Is the Greatest Since 1932." "Ballot Initiatives ... [Are] Limiting Government Role." As for "The State of the States: Broke," for "With expenditures growing and revenues shrinking, Governors and legislatures are scrambling to balance their budgets." The "Legacy of the 80's for States and Cities . . . [Is] Big Bills and Few Options."[2]

As the year 1991 evolved, various state trends came sharper into focus as reflected in diverse salient news reports. The "State of the States" was "Rocky, Almost Everywhere," with "Gloom, caution and, inevitably, new taxes." "Is This the Year the States Finally Get the Hill's Attention?," even though "Washington has been mandating more and more state spending by passing laws requiring states to improve their services to the elderly, children and others in health programs, especially, but also in the environment, drug-fighting and many other fields." "Bush Would Let the States Decide How to Spend $15 Billion in Aid." Yet "Mayors Attack Proposed Shift of Aid" inasmuch as "Cities fear the states will skim off urban funds." More strongly put, "Washington's Plan To Funnel City Aid Through the States [and block grants] Enrages the Mayors," while "The White House . . . wanted to negotiate with the governors and with the National Conference of State Legislatures on what Federal programs should be turned over to the states." As for "More Dictates from the Feds," "Federally imposed mandates on the states offer congressional leaders a way to take credit for popular programs without incurring additional costs." It was "Harsh Times in State Legislatures." "States and Cities Are Pushing Hard For Higher Taxes"—with "Recession and Cutbacks in Federal Aid . . . Cited"— and for " 'a new Federalism,' " in which the debate over national concerns like education, public health insurance and programs for the poor is shifting from the White House and Congress to state and city governments[,] . . . especially in connection with "states [that] enacted laws intended to raise billion[s] in annual revenues." "Cities [are] on Their Own." "The States Are Becoming the New 'Big Government,' " with a "crazy-quilt of contradictory local regulations"; "But They Still Need Washington," for "Without Federal Help, Our Economic Havoc Will Grow Worse." As "State and Local Taxes Rise To Loosen Recession's Grip," "Hard-pressed lawmakers bank on forecasts of a turnaround," while "Some governors say states cannot raise taxes quickly enough to cover the rising costs of programs that are required by Federal law." It became "Legislatures in the Living Room," as "state legislatures are telecasting their proceedings themselves." Meanwhile, "States Win at the Supreme Court," for "In the 1990–91 session the Rehnquist Court consistently upheld state laws and powers, especially those challenged on constitutional grounds." When the Supreme "Court Considers States' Power to Fine [a] U.S. Agency," "In a pollution fight [involving Ohio and the Dept. of Energy], it's the U.S. vs. the States." Seizing the initiative, in a sign of joint action, "9 States in East Plan Pollution Rules," as "Officials join to attack urban pollution."[3]

In 1992 conditions were worsening. It was becoming "The war between the states—for new business. . . ." Also, "New State Laws [Are] Reflecting Tough Times." Yet "Recession [Is] Leaving State Governments More Efficient." As "States Try to Re-regulate Health Care," "Legislatures repudiate Federal faith in free medical market." There was "An Antidote to Federal Mandates" in that " 'The states have the mechanism to take care of their own business.' " Yet "State Legislators [Are] Leaving [Office] in Droves" in "A trend that some say bodes ill for democracy." In efforts at "Putting a Lid on Congress," "14 State Measures on U.S. Term Limits Gain Momentum in a Cry for Change," but ". . . Restrictions on Federal Lawmakers May Violate the Constitution."[4]

During Clinton's First Term

In early 1993, the first year of Bill Clinton's first presidential term, there were "Cheers From States for Clinton's Plan," as his "economic plan is drawing praise from a bipartisan coalition of governors and from experts in state fiscal policy, who say that for the first time in years Washington has stopped trying to shift costly programs to the states." "As U.S. Policy Makers Debate, States Move Ahead on Health Care Overhaul." "Way Ahead of Bill," "Unable to wait any longer for federal reform, states and companies are launching their own programs to cut costs and extend coverage to more of those now uninsured." Regarding "The States as Health Care Labs," however, "Federal standards could rein in experimentation." As "States Head for a Clash Over Company Benefits," will it be "Federal or state control of health plans?" On the same matter, there was "A Warning By Governors . . . to Keep Any Federal Programs From Overtaking Their Own Initiatives" through Clinton's "proposal for a uniform system of health insurance" that "Administrative officials . . . are drafting [in] . . . legislation for the President and Congress." On a different front in 1993, both "States and Government Lag In Meeting Clean Air Law" of 1990, for, "Three years after Congress passed the Clean Air Act, the Federal Government [E.P.A.] and the states are consistently behind on many of the law's demanding timetables. . . ." In the meantime, the "Court's Outlawing of Congress's Veto Casts Shadows on State Legislatures" in a variety of ways.[5]

Many further struggles between states and the Federal government in 1994 involved matters of legislation. "6 or More States [Are] to Flout Federal Law On Paying for Incest or Rape Abortions" in "A clash of wills with Washington. . . ." "States' Eagerness to Change Welfare [law etc.] Rattles Washington." "GOP Governors Push Big New Tax Revolt—At the State Level," as Federal "Mandates Pose Problems." "In Wave of Anticrime Fervor, States Rush to Adopt Laws" as " 'Three strikes, you're out,' becomes a battle cry." "House Passes Bill to Let States Limit Trash Imports" in "Vote [That] Increases Threat to New York's Plan." Yet as conditions improved in later 1994, the "Growing Economy Produces Surplus In State Budgets" and a "Rush To Enact Tax Cuts." Yet amid this "Fervor for Tax Cuts," "Will Clinton be tempted to join in?"[6]

States seemed to be coming back into their own in 1995. "U.S. Cities Are in Their Best Financial Shape in Years. . . ." "New State Laws Enacted for '95 Focus on Crime." "Republicans' Drive to Ease the Burden of Mandates on States and Cities Slowed a Bit" as "The Senate today began debate on legislation that would reshape relations between Federal and local governments by making it harder for Washington to impose rules on cities and states without paying for the costs." But some questioned "What's the Rush on [Cutting] Mandates?," a part of Republican Congressman Gingrich's "Contract with America." In any case, it was "Devolve and Conquer" insofar as "No longer supplicants, Governors are fast becoming the heroes of the new political order." "Democratic Governors Oppose Plan Shifting Welfare to States" through "a bill devised by House Republicans" who were "Trying to change a system that has evolved for 60 years." "G.O.P. [through governors and members of Congress] Seeks Medicaid Overhaul, Giving Vast Authority to States." "G.O.P. Governors Urge Big Changes For Welfare Bill," with "More Flexibility Sought," as "State Leaders Want Senate to Revise the House Measure and Relax Restrictions." The "Drive for Block Grants [from Capitol Hill is] Pitting State Against State." Despite the continuing economic growth in states, "State Budget Deficits Force Legislatures to Back Down on Universal Coverage" and "Ambitious Plans On Health Care." Some argued that "Block Grants Will Worsen Poverty" because "States will dump the burden on local officials." "Term-Limit Groups Appeal To States, Ignoring Congress," while "A Constitutional Convention may be the best hope." "State Lawmakers Prepare To Wield Vast New Powers" as "Republicans Plan to Transfer Authority Over Welfare and Safety to Legislatures."[7]

The states continued, on the whole, to increase their independent roles in relation to the Federal government during 1996. "Many States Fail to Fulfill Mandates on Child Welfare." The "Supreme Court Limits U.S. Power to Subject States to Suits" in "Another

signal that the Justices are reconsidering the issue of states' rights."
For some observers, it was "Lurching Toward States' Rights." For
others, it was "An Accountability Issue," for, "As States Gain Political Power, a Ruling Seems to Free Them of Some Legal Reins."
Still others saw "A No-Win War Between The States" as "Politicians are handing out fatter tax breaks than ever to lure jobs to
their areas. They may be devastating U.S. cities in the process."[8]

At the same time, in 1996, there were mixed reports on welfare
mandates and reform. "States Feel Crunch to Meet Welfare Bill
Requirements" ("Timing, Lack of Funds Present Challenges").
"State Welfare Chiefs Ask For More U.S. Guidance," that is, for
"more Federal guidance on how to carry out the new welfare law,"
since "Just New Authority Isn't Enough, They Say." "Most States
Find the Targets in the New Federal Welfare Law Well Within
Reach." "Actions by States Hold Keys to Welfare Law's Future."
"So Far, States Aren't Rewriting the Book on Welfare Plans." "Loop-
hole in Law Permits States To Put Off Cuts in Food Stamps."
"States' [Own] Authority [Is] Disputed On Use of Welfare Money,"
for "Federal Rules Are Applied to All Spending," that is, "New law's
limits apply to more than Federal dollars, U.S. officials say."[9]

During Clinton's Second Term

Other changes in the states were occurring in 1997 during the first
year of Clinton's second presidential term. "Term Limit Laws Have
Been Transforming Many [State] Legislatures." "Abortion Battle
Shifts To State Legislatures," while "State bans of partial-birth abor-
tions could lead to a challenge of Roe v. Wade." "U.S. Welfare System
Dies As State Programs Emerge," with "Emphasis on Work . . . the
Common Thread in a Patchwork of Decentralization," although,
when "Removing the [Federal] Barriers That Prevented Work"
("Toothless Rules, Then Painful Ones"), "Many States Set Tighter
Rules." "Cities, Once on Fiscal Ropes, Rebound Strongly." "With Their
Budgets in the Black, Governors' Skies Turn Blue." "A new breed
of activist mayors is making City Hall a hothouse for innovation."[10]

In 1998 came further trends toward states' autonomy. "[Supreme
Court] Justices Rule One State's Court Cannot Bind Another's Court
to a Deal." "Ballot Initiatives' Popularity Sparks Debate on Problems," "But Is It Good Government?," while one observer has called
the growing phenomenon "a fourth branch of government in many
cases," such that "California launched a democratic movement that
now flourishes in 24 states." The "Right of States to Extradite Fu-
gitives Is Upheld" by Supreme Court. Yet "The War Between the

States . . . and Washington" was not dead inasmuch as the states were actively "muscling aside Congress and the Clinton Administration" through independent action on social programs, pro or con. "States Take Lead in Health Legislation" as "Laws to Protect Patients Find More Support Outside Washington." "High Court Hears Case on States' Power in Referendum Process." In "Limiting a State's Sphere of Influence," a Federal "Judge Rejects Law on Myanmar as Foreign Policy Infringement," that is, as "Setting Foreign Policy, Locally."[11]

In early 1999 the High "Court Turns Back An Effort To Limit Ballot Initiatives" in states, citing "Free Speech Right." According to a piece on "Federal Power, Undimmed" in "The High Court's restrained ruling on state's rights" in June: "The Court held that a state's sovereign immunity shields it from state–court lawsuits that seek money damages under certain Federal law," while a "previous ruling had already shielded states from such suits in Federal courts." Is "Power to the States . . . Rehnquist's legacy?" As the Court's term ended in June, it was accordingly held by a majority of the Justices (led by Kennedy) that the "sovereign" national government in Congress or Court cannot interfere or overlap with the "sovereignty" of the states individually or collectively. One dissenting Justice (Souter) argued against a "dual sovereignty" through states' rights and pointed instead to the Federal government as "ultimate sovereign," notwithstanding (Kennedy) that the Court has ruled in the recent past that "Congress cannot interfere with state legislatures." The main context here is again the states being sued. Meantime, "State Courts Are Sweeping Away Laws Limiting Injury Lawsuits": "More than a decade after states began enacting laws to cut back big jury awards and curtail injury lawsuits, state courts across the country are overturning one measure after another, contending that Americans have a powerful right to settle their disputes in court."[12]

In other respects during 1999: "An Insurance Fraud Shows the Gaping Holes in the Regulatory Net Cast by the States"; "States unite to fend off 'meddling' from Washington" as "Governors assert more authority as power flows away from a fractious Washington toward state capitals" ("States muscle into power vacuum," "In past few years, 'Congress has done very little' on big social issues"); and "Anti-Federalism Measures Have Bipartisan Support." According to the last report: "Hoping to shift political power back to the states, a broad bipartisan coalition in the Senate and House of Representatives is preparing legislation that would make it harder for Congress and the executive branch to adopt laws and rules that pre-empt the states on a wide range of issues, like drugs, the environment, health and worker safety.... [This] legislation would provide local authorities with broad new power to go to court to challenge Federal laws and regulations that fail to explicitly mention what state statutes and regulations are pre-empted."[13]

The preceding trends and other ones reached a high point during 2000, the last full year of the Clinton presidency. "Citing 1966 Federal Law, States and Cities Are Wrestling Control of Prisons From the Courts." "Term Limits Force Changes In Many State Legislatures." "The states take the lead on gun control," for "While Congress stalls, local officials act." In connection with "Life in limbo: the transplant wars," "States, Congress fight over life-saving organs," while the Senate and House put forth conflicting measures on the subject. As reported in "Court and Congress: Another ruling for states' power," "This week's Supreme Court decision striking down part of the Violence Against Women Act as beyond Congress's power over interstate commerce" challenges "conservative critics [who] often condemn as undemocratic the Supreme Court's power to hold legislative actions unconstitutional." "Referendums From States Are Seeking to Overhaul Health Care System in the U.S." "More states step in as product-safety czars." "States and Cities Flout [Federal] Law On Underground Fuel Tanks." In "Where Congress Fears to Tread," "State lawmakers are taking the initiative in setting employment and workplace policy." With "A Dwindling Faith In Deregulation," "States Seek New Ways to Harness Electricity" while "Approaching Electricity Deregulation More Cautiously." "House and Senate Agree On Drunken-Driving Law" in "Bill [That] Uses U.S. Aid to Make States Comply." It was asked "Are States Above the Law?" after yet another sign of the High Court's infatuation with state sovereign immunity particularly in relation to Congress' legislative power "to enact broad civil rights laws...."[14]

During Bush Jr.'s First Term

State trends carried over from the Clinton era into the first term of President George Bush Jr. starting in early 2001. "New State Laws Tackle Familiar National Issues" as "Topics Include Drug Costs and DNA Tests." Further "Shift of Powers to States and Local Levels Is Seen Under Bush," with "More Say on Federal Social and Public Works Programs." In turn, "Many States [Are] Ceding Regulations to Church Groups."[15]

Already in 2001, another shift seemed under way as "Free Spending in Flush Times Is Coming Back to Haunt States." Indeed, "States

Head Into the Red." "States [Are] Calling For More [Federal] Help With Medicaid." "Tax Codes in Laws of States Could Reduce Federal Rebate" inasmuch as "Laws meant to give taxpayers relief could penalize them."[16]

In 2002, "From Coast to Coast, the States Ring In a Raft of New Statutes" with "A lot of changes, from smoking and drinking to health care and taxes." In "New year [came] new laws," in that "Across the US, local codes deal with moldy homes, date-rape drugs, and kids—or even hamburgers—in cars." "States Seek to Counter U.S. Deregulation" as "Suits and New Laws Represent a Public Break With Washington." "Governors Want Congress to Ease Welfare Work Rule," "Seeking Changes in the '96 Law as Shaky Economy Makes It Harder for Poor to Get Jobs." "They Give, but They Also Take: Voters Muddle States' Finances," as "Legislators Say Citizen Initiatives Don't Add Up." "Study by Governors Calls Bush Welfare Plan Unworkable" in their "study ... presented ... to Congress, which plans to start drafting a new welfare law soon. ..." Yet Congressional "Republicans Rally Behind Welfare Proposals That States Oppose," while "Girding for battle over how many on welfare must work." As "States Worry About Bush Welfare Rules," "A 'big government' argument [is] turned against Republicans." When "Justices . . . Expand States' Immunity," with references to issues of "sovereignty," some observers saw "A Narrow View of Federal Power" and "Discord [among Justices] about what level of government has what authority." Others saw in the "Narrowed Right to Challenge the States" the High Court's "judicial overreach . . . taken to a new level." When "Boom–bust economy . . . launches a quest for stable revenue and revised tax codes," "Strapped states recast fiscal nets." A new "Federal Law on Failing Schools Has States Scrambling to Comply." "Justices [Are] to Revisit Prickly Issue of States' Immunity to Lawsuits Beyond Their Borders." "While Congress Is Sleeping [,] . . . The real political action is at the state level." "For Struggling States, All Solutions Point to Washington."[17]

States were becoming increasingly pressed and even rebellious during the course of 2003. "9 Northeast States File Suit [in Federal Court] Over New Rules on Pollution" put out by the "Bush administration," that is, by the E.P.A., "which published the rules, defended them[,] and said the administration followed proper procedures in issuing them administratively rather than seeking legislation," all avowedly in line with the Clean Air Act. "State G.O.P. Legislators Think the Unthinkable" when "Anti-Tax Fervor Fades as Revenues Fall Short," for "States are in their worst financial

shape since World War II." "States Are Relaxing Education Standards to Avoid Sanctions From Federal Law." "3 Northeast States
Win Verdict Against Utility" in "First Such Ruling on Pollution
From Northeast," as part of a possible "long battle between regions."
"States Plan Suits on Power Plants, a Battle E.P.A. Quit," "But Officials Give Limited Resources to Enforce the Clean Air Act." In
this connection, "Regulation Begins At Home," for "If the Bush administration won't enforce the law, the states will."[18]

On state legislation more generally in 2004, "New state laws run
social gamut" in broad "new regulations for the coming year." "More
state laws to govern life's minutiae," with the result that "There
are so many new laws at so many levels that no one can possibly
keep track of them all." More particularly that year, "States' End
Run Dilutes Effect of Federal Laws For Special Ed Students," insofar as "Some states use a technique that makes it easier to show
success in exams." "14 States Ask U.S. to Revise Some Education
Law Rules" in "Another request from states seeking flexibility in
carrying out the laws." "Parts of Special-Ed Bill Would Shift More
Power to States and School Districts."[19]

During Bush Jr.'s Second Term

During the first half of President Bush Jr.'s second term in 2005–
2006 several news items illustrated the continuity with themes and
topics in the states during his first term. "Federalism Has a Right
to Life, Too," yet "With its Schiavo law, Congress demeans the
states." "States take clean air measures into their own hands," while,
"Although the Bush administration has backed off carbon dioxide
regulations, others are pushing the issue." "States hit back on school
reform law" and "rebel against mandates of school testing" by "either refusing to adopt all of the No Child Left Behind Act or suing
the US to block it."[20]

On other matters, the High "Court widens scope of property seizure," ruling "that local governments can take homes and other property for private development," citing the "public use" clause of the
5th Amendment. That ruling involved a "Case of Eminent Domain,"
"Clarifying the Power to Seize Private Land for Public Use." Subsequently, "States Are Taking Steps to Curb Government's Right
to Seize Private Property." In various other ways, it was "States to
the Rescue." For instance, "State lawmakers take the lead on minimum wage, ID theft," etc.; and "States Take Lead on Ethics Regulations for Lawmakers and Put Limits on Lobbyists," as "National
Democrats' Vow of Reform Is Eclipsed by Statehouses."[21]

2. NEW YORK

Turning first to New York State as one of the most revealing cases of the struggles for sovereignty that have long occurred within each of the individual states, we focus naturally on the arena of legislation. Sovereignty and state are most clearly seen from legislative perspectives in New York as in other states. From the governorships of Mario Cuomo (1991 through 1994, third term) and George Pataki (1995 through 2006, three terms), we will turn to New York City's government during a succession of mayors—David Dinkins, Rudolph Giuliani, and Michael Bloomberg. More so than perhaps a U.S. President in his dealings with Congress, recent New York Governors have resembled British Prime Ministers in closeness of daily dealings with the state legislature in connection with the increasing volumes of laws and rules issued by them (and judges) for regulating the full range of everyday life. Legislative sovereignty and the legislative state (or regulatory sovereignty and the regulatory state) have become increasingly in evidence. Only a limited selection of the vast materials collected by this author over nearly two decades of current news history can be included here as elsewhere.

During Cuomo's Third Term

Notwithstanding his visionary State of the State Address ("Journey Toward the Next Millennium") to the State Legislature in early January 1990, at the start of the last year of his second term, Governor Cuomo was quickly drawn back into his ongoing contentious struggles with that body over the intricate multitude of legislative issues and processes involved in passing budgets and framing laws. Typical types of news reports from 1990 through 1994 on the state budget in the legislative process were as follows. "Senate Votes Death Penalty Despite Cuomo's Veto Stand." "Cuomo and Legislators Agree on Delaying Tax Cut," in "A deal so delicate, no one wants to talk about it." "Cuomo Plans Tougher Rules On Emissions," with "New Controls Expected to Add to Costs of Car." "Cuomo's Hard Line: Don't Let Budget Woes Recur," as "The Governor rejects lawmakers' moves to soften his proposals." "Budget [Is] In Turmoil As Cuomo Rejects Lawmakers' Plan," while "Governor Says He Cannot Be 'Blackmailed'—Delay Is Risk to New York City." "Legislative Leaders Present Their Budget Plan to Cuomo" and "press to end a record fiscal stalemate." "Cuomo Says Legislature's Budget Is Not Balanced and Plans Vetoes." "Appeals Court Rebukes Cuomo on Late Submission of Budget Bills." "Legislators Toss Insults, But

Can't Pass a Budget," while "Pain of Statehouse Impasse Is Being Felt," and "Budget gaps and tax increases may result." "Leaders In Albany Finally Announce A Budget Accord" in "A legislative agreement [that] reflects fiscal health."[22]

As for the framing of laws more generally, it was indicatively reported in 1992 that "With a Budget in Hand, Lawmakers Can Now Turn to the Business of Legislating." An area of particular concern during the same period was election laws. "Once Again, New York's Arcane Election Laws Shape [Presidential Primary] Race." For "Election-Law Revisions: The Time May Be Now" as "A suit involving [Paul] Tsongas throws a spotlight on the state's laws." "Cuomo [Is] Near Showdown On State Election Law," raising the question "Will the Governor take up a popular crusade against the Legislature?" "In One Big Sweep, Albany Backs New Voting Laws and Districts" after "Political expediency moves lawmakers and Cuomo to act."[23]

Included in the more routine "Business of Legislation" were the following. "Cuomo Panel Pressures the Legislature to Adopt Stricter Limits on Tobacco Ads" in order "to make it more difficult for young people to smoke." "Regulation of Grass Roots Transit [Is] Planned" under a bill passed by the State Legislature and soon to be signed by Governor Cuomo. "[N.Y. State Supreme] Court Outlaws Old Practice By Legislators" of "Recalling Albany Bills Ruled Unconstitutional." "Cuomo Seeks Sterner Laws For Juveniles." "Lawmakers Finish Session In Albany At Odds On Issues," leaving "Legislature In Disarray," while "Cuomo, Facing Election Year, Seems to Have Little Left to Show on Crime Plan [etc.]."[24]

In 1990 the New York "State Legislature's 4,000-member staff . . . [is] by far the largest legislative staff in the country." This fact helps to explain the especially voluminous masses of legislation produced each year by that body, with the Governor often acting as a kind of legislator-in-chief. Symptomatic of this vast enterprise were the "Legislative Reports" put out by one longtime State Senator, Roy Goodman. His Fall 1990 report to his constituents featured a detailed outline of his ambitious legislative activities under the heading "Senator Goodman Has Been a Sponsor of Over 850 New Laws in the Last 25 Years." Two years later, in his Fall 1992 report, the same heading cited "Over 900 New Laws." By the time of Goodman's 2001 Legislative Report to constituents, his legislative program had grown to mammoth proportions. Obviously the sum totals of new laws and rules produced in those years, as well as before and since, by the full N.Y. State Legislature and the Governor, in conjunction with the myriad State agencies as well as courts, would leave little doubt on the wide applicability of our term "legislative state."[25]

During Pataki's Three Terms

After his first election as Republican Governor in late 1994, "Pataki Begins His Next Campaign: Transforming the State Government." "Pataki Plans Major Overhaul To Shift Direction in Albany." However, "After 20 Democratic Years," "For Assembly and Senate, Slim Changes" were forecast in that year of the Republican takeover of the House of Representatives midway in Clinton's first term, while "Assembly Speaker [Sheldon Silver] Voices Doubts On Pataki's Pledge to Cut Taxes," whereas "Democrats May Offer Another Plan." But "Pataki Tells His Advisors To Streamline Government" and "to tighten the state's belt." At his inaugural in early January, he is called a "pragmatic conservative." "Pataki Is Proposing Deep Cuts, In Welfare and Work Incentives." A liberal editorial called it "The Shrinking Welfare State."[26]

On a host of separate initiatives during Pataki's first year, 1995, the following stories were representative not only of the Legislature's immense activity but also of the Governor as once again a kind of legislator-in-chief, with lawmaking and rule-making exhibited on a vast scale. Courts, too, became a predictable part of this mix in their virtual promulgation and abrogation of rules and laws respectively. "Pataki and State Leaders Agree On Details Of Plan To Restore Death Penalty." Soon thereafter, "Death Penalty In New York Is Restored After 18 Years" as "Law Takes Effect Sept. 1." "Pataki Will Lift Some Regulations For Health Care," "Calls Them Oppressive," and "Says Rules for Hospitals Went Too Far—[while] Some Proposals Need Legislative Action." "Pataki Proposes to Deny Shelter To Homeless Who Break Rules," "Shifting the Balance to Personal Responsibility." "Pataki [Is] In Accord With Lawmakers On Tax-Cut Plan." "Pataki and State Legislators Say They Have Agreed on a Budget," such that "New York Spending Is Reduced for the First Time Since 1943." Yet "Pataki's Visions for Medicaid and Welfare Run Into Albany's [Legislature's] Hard Knocks." "68 Days Late, Lawmakers Pass $33 Billion New York Budget." "Detailed Rules Regarding Executions Are Released by the State." "Pataki Unveils New Rules To Fight Welfare Fraud." "Pataki Proposes Legislative Plan to Curb Violent Crime by Youths." "Top New York State Judge Issues Rules to Ease Life on Civil Juries." "Judge Strikes Down G.O.P. Rules For New York's Presidential Race."[27]

In 1996 struggles for sovereignty between N.Y. Governor and Legislature came more to the fore after their relative "honeymoon" during Pataki's first year. Several instances must suffice. "In Battles Over Justice, Pataki Claims Sweeping Power for Executive Branch."

"Legislative Leaders Join to Fight Budget Cuts Proposed by Pataki." "Sensing a Shift by Constituents, Legislature Stands Up to Pataki." "Albany Faces A Shortfall: Legislation," as "Budget Impasse Curbs Other Major Initiatives." "Albany Bills Are Links in Tangled Chain" in that "A Budget Is Held Hostage While Other Issues Remain Unresolved." There was a "Cry for Help: '. . . How Do I Vote?'" as "Frenzied Lawmakers Cast Ballots on Bills They Haven't Read."[28]

Although by early 1997 it was "Paralyzed, Again, in Albany," by late 1997 "Leaders in Albany See a Relatively Calm Legislative Session" ahead; and in spring 1998 "Legislature Passes Budget Only Weeks Past Deadline." A key reason for this turnaround was the approaching elections of late 1998, which gave Pataki a second term and a wider platform for his possible wider ambitions. In early 1999, "Pataki, Starting His 2d Term, Sees State as Model for Nation." As the Legislature's session ended in June 1999, there remained much discord and no state budget, yet in August a deal was reached.[29]

By 2001, the legislative state, or regulatory state, was in need of both looser and tighter regulations in certain areas. For one thing, there was need for "Revising Rockefeller-Era Code to Permit More Treatment and Judicial Discretion" and for introducing "Lower Mandatory Terms" as "Pataki Presents His Plan To Ease State Drug Laws." For another, "At Core of Adoption Dispute Is Crazy Quilt of State Laws," while "Critics Link Abuses to Lack of Regulation"; "Experiment in Assisted Living Exposes Confusion on Rules," that is, "Regulatory Confusion"; and with need for "Tighter Rules for Housing of Mentally Ill," "Pataki Moves to Reshape System of Adult Homes." Efforts to reform or repeal the strict Rockefeller drug laws of the 1970s were a saga in themselves, with urging and proposals by both Pataki and Cuomo. By 2004 "Time Eases Tough Drug Laws, but Fight Goes On." In 2005, "Law Easing Drug Sentences Goes Into Full Effect. . . ."[30]

Meanwhile, from the late 1990s through the rest of Pataki's governorship, the N.Y. courts were not only actively entering the legislative arena but assuming further legislative-like authority, often at odds with other branches. "Law Barring Execution After a Guilty Plea Is Struck Down by Judges in New York." "[New York's Highest] Court Backs Law Docking Legislators," yet "No Transfer of Power to Governor [Is] Seen." "Legislator [Assembly Speaker Silver] Can Sue Pataki Over Legality of Vetoes" under a "[N.Y.] High Court Ruling, a Setback for Governor." "Court Voids Law Barring Con Ed Fee." "Court Overturns State Law Allowing Racetrack Slots." "In Tiny Courts of New York, [There Are] Abuses of Law and Power" as "Judges Without Legal Degrees or Oversight Rule in Arcane System Across State."[31]

Struggles for control of the N.Y. state's agenda between Legislature and Governor heated up during Pataki's last term. "Legislating the New York Way . . . [means] Chronic Gridlock." "In Albany, Bills Move When Leaders Cut Deals Behind a Closed Door." In 2003, "In Budget Fight With Legislature, Pataki Threatens to Run State With Emergency Bills." "Legislators Pass Spending Bills as Pataki Whets [*sic*] Veto Ax." "Legislature Overrides Pataki's Veto on Budget." By 2006, when "Pataki Vetoes Legislature Budget's Tax Cuts," in "A period of worsening relations with the Legislature," and "Saying He Can't Be Overridden, Governor Reasserts His Power" through "Supervetoes." Quickly enough, however, "Legislature Overrides Most Budget Vetoes by Pataki," thereby "Setting the stage for a constitutional clash over Albany power." By late 2006, a "Formidable Task Awaits [Governor-elect] Spitzer: Trying to Get Albany to Budge," although "Challenging an entrenched Legislature risks souring the honeymoon." Thus an apt wider suggestiveness can be seen in late 2006 news that "U.S. Rebuts Tax Preparer Who Says [N.Y.] State Is Sovereign."[32]

Fittingly in early January 2007, upon "Moving In With Big Plans to Remake State Government," the new Democratic Governor, Elliot "Spitzer Is Sworn [In] And Begins Push On Ethics Rules," with "Executive Orders Issued." A day later, "Spitzer Requests Sweeping Array of Legislation, Covering Much of [N.Y. State] Government" in "A Drumbeat For Reform" and "In Nod to Realpolitik, Offering Carrots to Both Sides," that is, when he "proposed overhauling almost every corner of the state's operations and policies in his first address to the Legislature. . . ."[33]

During a Succession of N.Y.C. Mayors

A crucial new legislative foundation for New York City's government was established in 1989 after "[U.S.] Justices Void New York City's Government; Demand Voter Equality In All Boroughs," singling out the powerful Board of Estimates for preempting the City Council. "[Charter Revision] Commission Puts Focus On a Stronger Council." Would there be "A 2-House Legislature for New York City?," as "The charter panel wrestles with an idea that U.S. cities shun." Shortly thereafter, "New York City Council [Is] in Line for New Power, but Is It Ready?" "Give City Council Increased Power, New York Is Urged" by Charter Commission. Soon again, "Charter Panel Rejects Estimate Board and Turns to Council." Finally, "Panel, for Now, Finishes Reshaping the Government." This whole sequence of events took just under two months, a stunningly short length of time for such important matters to be conducted.[34]

With its newfound legislative power in relation to the Mayor, the N.Y. City Council became a microcosm of the N.Y. State Legislature in its dealings with the Governor, with the Mayor likewise often acting as a kind of legislator-in-chief in relation to that body (and also at times to the State Legislature). Early in the term of Mayor David Dinkins in May 1990, "Council Struggles to Exercise Its New Powers." In June, "Dinkins and the Council Reach a Tax Agreement." On another matter in October, "Dinkins Links Part of Teachers Raise to Approval of Legislature," "Creating an out card in case things get worse?" In other ways that November, "Dinkins [Is] Hurt by Not Wooing Albany." Yet a few months later, "Dinkins [Is] In A Pact With [State] Legislators On Crime Program" in "A Big Victory For Mayor." At later points, "Dinkins Seeks to Loosen [State] Rules [in N.Y.C.] on Homeless." Perhaps more typical for the Mayor in his struggles to have his plans enacted into law was when in mid-June 1991 "Council Passes Far-Reaching Bill on Civil Rights" for New York City, "to be signed into law by Mayor Dinkins." The Mayor took an increasingly active role as when in mid-1991 "Dinkins Alters Banking Rules on South Africa." At that same point, there was even more general report on "Dinkins Idle Comment: Law Doesn't Apply To Me" and his belief that "his job is so important that his drivers can't always obey the city's strict car-idling law." As for being "Regulated Senseless in New York City," "In the war on lead paint, health is not concern No. 1." The vast numbers of such cases of complaints about overregulation covering so many areas of City life would go far to explain the endless struggles between Mayor, Council, and Albany for reform.[35]

Under the strong-willed two-term N.Y.C. Mayor, Rudolph Giuliani, the mounting struggles for supremacy between his City Hall and the City Council, with its increasing legislative forcefulness, often produced a clash of legislative wills. The illustrations to follow point up the legislative basis of N.Y.C. government as a kind of mini state, or city state, in itself. During Giuliani's first year in office, 1994, came a variety of successive news reports as follows. "Council Chief Opposes Giuliani On Decentralizing of Government." "Council Panel Passes Bill on Privatization Oversight." "Mayor's Veto of Food Vendor Bill [Is] to Stand" as "City Council Backs Away From a Confrontation With Giuliani." "2 Council Committees Pass Bill to Create Policy Agency" and "Would Investigate Police Corruption." "Giuliani Rejects City Council Budget Plan," whereupon

"Vallone [Council's Speaker] Vows to Override Veto, and Legal Showdown Looms." "Mayor [Is] Overridden on Budget." "Mayor [Is] Moving Ahead to Put City Services in Private Hands" through "a Fundamental Shift." "Mayor Vetoes Bill Creating A Panel To Monitor Police" ("Override Called Likely"), and believes "Council Proposal Gives Too Much Power to Independent Agency." During 1995 the plot thickened: "Giuliani Seeks Deepest Cut In City Spending Since 1930s"; and "Council Overrides Giuliani On Veto of Pathmark Plan" as "Queens Project Leads to Rebuke for Mayor." In 1996 "Giuliani Fails on Vote to Override" and "New York City Police Union Retains Its Influence in Albany." In 1997 came "A Move to Shift Balance of Power In New York City" as "City Council Seeks More," and "Vallone Says Charter Revision of 1990 Is Not Enough— Mayor Begs to Differ."[36]

Although in mid-1997, several months prior to Giuliani's re-election victory, there was "An Agreeable City Council" (by which "Mayor's Budget [Was] Endorsed Without Rancor 4 Years in a Row"), the legislative struggles persisted. In 1998: "City Council Sues Giuliani Over Charter Commission"; "Council Votes To Override Shelter Veto," while "Giuliani Renews Threat To Open More Centers"; and "Giuliani Escalates Fight With Council on Homeless" by "Put[ting] Shelters in Opponent's District," i.e., against "a City Council member who had sponsored legislation to regulate such shelters." In 1999 it was called "The Giuliani Way: Sue and Be Sued and Sometimes Win by Losing." In 2000: "Council Democrats Plan To Dare a Giuliani Veto" as "Differences between the mayor and the speaker grow stark"; and "For Giuliani and the City Council, a Battle of the Budget."[37]

During the Giuliani era, N.Y.C. legislative struggles with state legislative authorities were also legion. "Pataki Plans to Seek Repeal of Array of Regulations for City's Shelters," "Changes [that] may face opposition." "Mayor Sues Over State Law On Police Contract Disputes." "In His Budget, Giuliani Steps Up Clash With Pataki." "Giuliani Files Lawsuit Challenging Tax Repeal" and "Claims State Bypassed Mayor and Council."[38]

In relation to Federal authorities, for instance: "Giuliani Widens Attacks on [New Federal] Welfare Law's 'Unfair Tone' " that "Violates 5th Amendment"; "U.S. Judge Strikes Down [N.Y.C.] Ban on [City Employees] Talking to Press"; and "Law Limiting Cigarette Ads Is Overturned [by Federal Judge]" after "Grocers Challenged Ban Imposed by City Council."[39]

Across a wide regulatory front, then, the various contending groups in New York City waged their legislative campaigns. Typical were the following. "Giuliani Proposes Tough Law on 'Dangerous' Dogs, Angering Owners." "Council Close to Renewing New York Rent Regulations." "City's New Waste Agency Flexes Regulatory Muscles" as "Customers [Are] Given Rights to Cancel Contracts." "Ignoring Zoning Laws Helped New York City Succeed in Spite of Itself."[40]

Even though in early 2002, "3 Months Into His Term, [the new Mayor Michael] Bloomberg Has Set a New Tone for City Government," the preceding patterns in the legislative arena carried over into his first term. "For Mayor and Council Speaker [Gifford Miller], Signs of Strain Replace Public Praise." "[Mayor's] Welfare Veto Is Overriden by Council [Legislation]," with "Work Rules Softened; Mayor Plans Challenge." "City Council Weighs a Budget of Its Own" in "A drastic measure that has been used in New York only once, in 1998." "Council, Ignoring Veto Threat, Approves Tough Lead-Paint Bill." "Vetoes Deepen Friction Between Mayor and City Council." "Judge Rules Bloomberg Must Carry Out Equal Benefits Law He Vetoed." "After 77 Years, Cabaret Laws Face Revision," as "New Regulations [Are] Sought For Nightclubs in City," with the "Bloomberg administration . . . poised to rewrite the . . . laws. . . ." "With 2 Deaths, Transit Agency Tightens Rules for Subway Work." The "[State Legislature's recent] Brownfield Law [Is] Criticized as a Good Idea Badly Executed" by mandating "A Cleanup That's Easier Legislated Than Done." "[State] Legislature Deals Setback to Mayor in Declining to Allow More Charter Schools."[41]

Staten Island and Nassau County

In 1997, when "New York City Celebrates A Century of Uneasy Unity," it was pointed out in one news article: "The Mayors of Brooklyn and New York vetoed the idea, only to be overridden by the State Legislature. . . . Clearly, the wedding of the modern New York City from more than 40 local governments a century ago was not easy." In this light, it is interesting to note how the present-day Borough of Staten Island, for instance, sought more recently to secede from the City and to become an autonomous entity legislatively and otherwise. In late 1989, "[Governor] Cuomo Signs Bill on Process for S.I. Secession," with referendum to be held a year later. In early 1990, "Albany Assumes Final Say Over Whether Staten Island Will Secede," and "State leaders . . . [agree] on a bill that would give the Legislature the final say" over the matter, thereby creating obstacles contrary to Cuomo's efforts favoring secession. In later 1990, "Staten Island Votes a Resounding Yes on Taking Step Toward Separation." By 1993, "Staten Island Secession Becomes More Than Fringe Threat." Also, in 1992, "Secession Is Proposed for Queens," but "Can a Breakaway Borough Fare Better Alone?"[42]

At the county level in New York State, Long Island's Nassau County, bordering New York City, offers a useful case on the central importance of creating a new, autonomous legislature having inherent power to make laws for regulating county affairs. Prior to 1993 there had been such reports as in 1991 when "Nassau [Is Seen] Lagging As Suffolk [County] Towns Adopt New Laws" on "Making Accessory Apartments Legal." In 1993, however, a "Legislature Is Proposed For Nassau." Later that year "Nassau Residents Offer Ideas for New Legislature."[43]

During 1994 momentum was growing. "Remaking Legislature Wins Praise" as "Panel Offers Plan For Nassau County." "Plan for Nassau Legislature Is Delivered" as "[Federal] Judge [Is] Given Proposal for 18-Member Body With 2 Minority Seats," the same judge "who a year ago declared Nassau's present form of government unconstitutional," the new Legislature being planned as, in itself, "A New Government for Nassau County." "Nassau Faces A Challenge: Government From Scratch." But then, "Nassau Supervisors Fail to Set Up a Legislature." Amid "Wrestling Over Legislative Districts," "A Government [Is] Struggling to Be Born," as "Nassau Endures a Lesson in Civics and Power Politics," with "Echoes of 1781 as a government is overhauled." Finally, that year, "Nassau Board Approves a Legislative Map" in "A New Look for Nassau Government."[44]

As this story continued, "the fledgling band of lawmakers that took office here Jan. 1 [1996] as the newly created Nassau County Legislature is a hit," following "the Board of Supervisors it replaced. . . ." In 1999 "Nassau Legislators Wrest Financial Control From County Executive" through "Strong measures to prevent another $300 million deficit." In 2000 "Nassau County Legislature Approves Plan Including 15 Percent Property Tax Increase." Also in 2000, "Legislators Will Try An Override" of "the line-item vetoes that [the] County Executive . . . made to their four-year fiscal rescue plan."[45]

In 1997 it was asked in neighboring Suffolk County, "Should East End Secede? Suffolk Pleads for Unity," as "A county executive urges togetherness as rural communities seek to go off on their own" despite the growing "cry for independence." As in the preceding cases of certain N.Y.C. boroughs, however, such cries for independence did not materialize. Showing nevertheless the potent independent powers of the already existing Suffolk County Legislature, in 1998 the "Suffolk Legislature Orders LILCO [Long Island Lighting Company] Takeover on Ballot," while "Foes Cheer Vote as Blow to [Governor] Pataki's Plan," albeit some questioned this as "A rate-relief act or a windfall for stockholders?"[46]

3. NEW JERSEY

During Florio's and Whitman's Terms

Among the most dramatic gubernatorial efforts to engineer a large legislative program through a State Legislature occurred in New Jersey in the early 1990s under Democrat Governor Jim Florio. His initial successes led eventually to his unpopularity and downfall, due especially to the huge new taxes he championed. Highlights during 1990 included the following news accounts. "Florio Proposes Drastic Change In Car Insurance." "Senate Passes Florio's Plan On Insurance" with "Reduction In Premiums for Autos." "Legislators Tangle Over Trenton Budget" as "Republicans and Democrats blame each other for a fiscal squeeze." "Tax Rally in Trenton Assails Florio and Displays Petitions." "Florio and Tax Protesters: Battle Could Be Long One," and, "With legislative elections next year, time seems to favor the Governor." "4 Democratic Legislators Demand Repeal of Part of Florio Tax Plan." "Leaders of New Jersey Tax Rebellion Take Aim at Legislature." "Fearful Democrats [Are] Leaving Florio's Legislative Shadow."[47]

Over the course of 1991 Trenton legislative battles continued to occupy center stage. "After a tax revolt, the Governor turns to less controversial issues," with "Florio Shifting Style to Let Legislators Set the Agenda." "Trenton [Is] Set to Debate Bills on Citizen Lawmaking" after "Angry taxpayers push for popular votes on laws." "Budget Package For New Jersey [Is] Signed Into Law." "Citizen Lawmaking Measure Dies in Trenton." "A Year Later, [Florio's] Gun Law [Banning Assault Weapons Is] Still Ignored." "With Anti-Florio Wave, G.O.P. Takes Legislature." "Florio Vows To Revamp Health Care," "But Acknowledges Legislative Obstacles," saying " 'The election results did not take away my voice.' " "Democrats Seek to Undo Unpopular Tax Package" as "Lame-duck legislators scramble to take action before leaving Trenton." "Trenton Senate Votes to Repeal Most of Tax Package," yet G.O.P. still not satisfied. In the end, this particular "Tax Repeal Effort by New Jersey Democrats Fails."[48]

Much the same legislative issues and patterns continued to dominate in Trenton during 1992–1993, with the final result of Governor Florio being defeated for reelection. "Legislators Break Promise

And Propose Glut of Bills." "Trenton Senate's G.O.P. Files Bill to Cut Sales Tax," such that "Florio's least popular tax increase may be repealed." "New Jersey Legislation Escalates Commuter Tax War." "G.O.P. Vows Budget Fight With Florio" and "Aims to Override Veto And Watch Over Cuts." "G.O.P. in Trenton Rejects Citizen-Lawmaking Plans: In Shift, Initiative Proposals Are Defeated." "Trenton Legislators Vote Repeal Of Florio's Assault Weapons Ban." "Republicans Halt for Breath As They Undo Florio's Efforts." "Florio Signs Bill to Overhaul Health Coverage for Poor." "Defying Florio, Assembly Votes to Get Rid of Ban on Assault-Type Weapons" as "A bid to override a gun-bill veto now goes to the State Senate in Trenton." Leading up to the late 1993 elections, "Poll Shows 1990 New Jersey Tax Rise Winning Favor"; and "Florio Gets Singled Out By Kennedys For Courage [Award]." In the end, Florio lost, as "'90 Tax Rise Overshadows Trenton Races." Just after the election, with Florio once more engaged on the legislative front, "2 Bills May Give Florio His Final Battles." In last-minute developments in early January 1994, "New Jersey Legislators [Are] To Address Florio Vetoes," while "Rejecting a new tax puts Governor in rare position"; and "In Last Session, Republicans Let Two Florio Vetoes Stand."[49]

A further kind of legislative sovereignty and legislative state was evidenced during the governorship of Christine Whitman. Her more conservative Republican policies and programs centering around tax cuts again placed at center stage the legislative process and her as legislator-in-chief. Yet ongoing struggles for legislative leadership were often involved.

In 1994, shortly after Whitman's governorship began, "G.O.P. Leaders Support Whitman's Tax Cut Bills." Yet "After Florio, Localities Fear Impact of State Aid Cuts." In March, "Senate Approves Whitman's Plan for 50% Income Tax Cut." Now "Whitman Budget Means State Layoffs." "Trenton Acts on a Wide Range of Bills." "For Whitman, Applause in the Early Acts." In June "Legislature and Whitman Agree on Budget." In August "Whitman [Is] Latest to Urge Laws On Notices of Sex Offenders" (eventually called "Megan's Law"); and, a few weeks later, "Fast Assembly Passes 7 Bills On Sex Abuse" as "Lawmakers in Trenton Bypass Usual Hearings."[50]

Legislative highlights in the news during the rest of Governor Whitman's first term covered a wide gamut, with her as leader. In 1995: "Legislature Approves Whitman's Income Tax Cut"; "Fight Against Mandates [Is] Gaining on Many Fronts," with Whitman approving a new law repealing many of them; and "Whitman Strongly Endorses Programs for Affirmative Action." In 1996,

"Whitman Lifts a Burden From Local Governments" through "New Law [That] Bans Unfunded State Mandates." In 1997: "Trenton Approves Bill Overhauling Welfare System," as "Measure Offered by Whitman Softens the Harshest Parts of the New Federal Law"; "Whitman Signs Law Barring Parole for Child Molesters"; "New Jersey Assembly Votes To Ban Abortion Procedure," but "Whitman says she will not sign if certain exceptions are not made"; "Whitman and Legislators Plan $16.8 Billion Budget" with "More for Schools and Protection of Children"; "Big Increase In Spending Is Signed ["into law"] By Whitman"; "Whitman and Lawmakers Back Auto Insurance Bill"; "Whitman Offers Proposal On Auto Insurance Reform," with "Calls for Option to Choose Coverage Level," amid complex dealings between Governor and the State Legislature; "Legislators Promise Overhaul of New Jersey Car Insurance" and its high costs; "After 3 Years, 'Megan's Law' Is Set to Start In New Jersey"; and "New Jersey's Senate Overrides Whitman's Veto of Abortion Curb," and "Ban on Types of Late-Term Procedure Is at Issue."[51]

In early 1998, after her re-election, there was, "This Term, a New Dynamic for Whitman and Legislature." That year: "Whitman Takes On Taxes And High Insurance Rates"; "Whitman and New Jersey Senate Reach Car Insurance Compromise"; "Whitman Announces Plan To Improve Transportation," at the same time that "Trenton's Houses Vote at Last to Revise Auto Insurance"; and "Legislators and Whitman Agree on Budget," with higher revenues enabling higher spending. In 1999, Congress' "Anti-Federalism Measures Have Bipartisan Support" in its efforts at "legislation [that] would provide local authorities with broad new power to go to court to challenge Federal laws and regulations that fail to explicitly mention what state statutes and regulations are pre-empted." In 2000: "Whitman May Move Alone To Improve School Buildings" after "Legislative and Legal Fights Stall Work"; "Citing Depression-Era Law, New Jersey Moves to Take Over Camden's Finances," while "Whitman . . . was considering asking for legislation to permit the state to take over the city completely"; "Whitman Proposes New Water and Sewage Management Rules for New Jersey"; and "Stricken Camden Is to Become Ward of the State" through action of the Legislature with Whitman's approval.[52]

During McGreevey's and Corzine's Terms

When, following the departure of Governor Whitman to become E.P.A. director under President Bush Jr. and Republican Donald "DiFrancesco [Was] Sworn In as Acting Governor," the "New Jersey Constitution Requires Him to Retain [His Pres. of] State Senate Post," thereby adding extra weight to the role of governor as legislator-in-chief. His official oath of office—taken in late January of 2001—included a pledge to ". . . maintain the rightful laws of the State. . . ." He was succeeded by Democrat James McGreevey who was sworn in as governor in early 2002.[53]

In early 2002, with the economy sliding, not only Republicans in the State Legislature but also some of his fellow "Democrats Join in Attack On McGreevey Budget Plan." A year later, "Trenton Lawmakers Seek Alternatives to McGreevey's Austere Plan." In mid-2003 "Senate Committee Standoff Delays McGreevey's Budget"; yet finally "Last-Minute Deal Is Reached." That year's other legislative highlights for him included: "Amid Pomp, McGreevey Signs Racial-Profiling Bill"; and "McGreevey Signs Law Easing the Rules for Auto Insurance." In 2004, "After 15 months of debate," the N.J. "Legislature Votes to Raise Taxes for New Jersey's Richest." New Jersey was included, not surprisingly, in a news report that year on "More state laws to govern life's minutiae," according to which report "There are so many new laws at so many levels that no one can possibly keep track of them all."[54]

After Governor McGreevey resigned in August 2004 due to personal scandal, he was succeeded by fellow Democrat and Senate President Richard Codey, who like DiFrancesco now wore two hats, which, despite his interim status as governor, seemed to enhance his role as legislator-in-chief. Hence by mid-2005, "An acting governor tackles some of New Jersey's thorniest issues." After the election of November 2005, Codey was succeeded by New Jersey's U.S. Senator Jon Corzine, whose experience as a Capitol Hill legislator prepared him well for his new-found gubernatorial leadership.[55]

At his inauguration in mid-January, Governor Jon "Corzine Pledges a 'New Era' for New Jersey" and "Offers a Blunt Message on Austerity and Ethics." Two months later, "Corzine Proposes Tax Increase and Cuts in Spending"; and "Legislature Approves Corzine Plan to Revive Road Fund." Then came Governor Corzine's July showdown with the Legislature over the budget, during which "Corzine Orders New Jersey Government Shutdown." Two days later, "Corzine Calls Special Joint Session to Resolve Budget Crisis," as "A post-holiday shutdown of more state services looms." After several further days, however, "Corzine Ends New Jersey Shutdown and Approves Budget" "After Six Days That Shook New Jersey," involving "Budget Brinksmanship and Shifting Alliances." By the following November, "Legislators Come Up With 98 Ways To Chip Away at New Jersey's Taxes." In mid-December, with Legislative "Session Over, Corzine Vows To Keep Up Fight on Benefits" in "A [budgetary] power struggle[!] over how to handle soaring costs, ease taxes and pay down state debt." All in all, the role of governor as legislator-in-chief was being played out in fine fashion, helped along by Corzine's legislative experience at the national level as well as by his executive business expertise at a top investment firm. The theme of struggles over legislative sovereignty in the legislative state was also being exhibited. Finally, on a different note, in early 2007, the N.J. State Legislature—under urging by Governor Corzine to reduce the state's high property taxes—was pressed to help consolidate costly operations for many of the several hundred autonomous N.J. municipal entities, despite their efforts to preserve their "sovereignty" as in the case of one of three Cape May independent entities.[56]

4. CONNECTICUT

When in January 1991 Lowell "Weicker, an Independent, Is Sworn In, Asking Bipartisan Support," a year of acute struggles between Governor and Legislature was being ushered in. At that point, it was "Weicker and the Assembly: New Lines of Power," with an adage that "The governor proposes; the Assembly disposes." Yet "With a Hybrid Regime, Weicker Faces a Budget Crisis." In May the political and legislative struggles for power were intensifying: "Weicker Income Tax Plan Dying As Bipartisan Opposition Grows"; "Legislators 2, Weicker 0 On Taxes and Gambling"; "Weicker Says He'll Veto No-Income-Tax Plan"; "Hartford Legislators Vote Budget, Setting Up Standoff With Weicker." Then in June, "Weicker Vetoes Budget Bill; Special Session Is Expected." In July, as "Weicker Loses Again in His Bid For Income Tax for Connecticut," "Governor Begins Shutdown of Some State Offices," yet "Weicker Has Emerged As a Gloves-Off Idealist." It was billed as a "Connecticut Budget Slugfest: Will Veto Be Vetoed?"[57]

This central drama of legislation (a more apt rubric here than the older "dance of legislation") heightened further in August 1991: "Connecticut Assembly Passes Tax Plan," as the proposal expands levies on a whole array of consumer goods; "Weicker Vetoes Another Budget Over Tax Issue"; "4th Temporary Budget Is Signed by Weicker"; "Budget Is Passed For Connecticut With Income Tax," such that "After Six Months, Legislators Approve Flat 4–5% Rate—Weicker Signs Bill"; and "Tax War, the Sequel, May Play in Connecticut," inasmuch as "What the legislators fought, the voters may protest." Finally, in

December, "Effort To Repeal New Tax On Income Fails In Hartford" as "Bill Dies With Quick Veto" and "Weicker Weathers Override Bid for a Fourth Time, Ending Anti-Tax Battle for '91."[58]

But the legislative and other battles were not over. Following these events, in early 1992, "Weicker Proposes Steep Spending Cuts, Especially on Social Programs"; and "Weicker Budget Proposals Overshadowed by Tax Fight," as "Legislature's Changing of Rates Is Opposed." At that point, Weicker was called "The Gutsiest Governor In America: Elected as an Independent just when the recession was destroying his state's economy, . . . Weicker took the tough road of budget cuts and taxes." By mid-1994, "The Income Tax, and Its Possible Repeal, Is Back as a Campaign Issue in Connecticut."[59]

As Weicker's successor, Republican Governor John Rowland ended up in a much different struggle with the State Legislature in Connecticut. In 1997 "Rowland Says He Violated Ethics Law." In 2004: "Legislators [Are] to Begin Impeachment Inquiry on Rowland"; "Court Upholds [House] Panel's Authority to Subpoena Rowland" and "To Demand Testimony"; and "Gov. Rowland Resigns Under Pressure."[60]

5. CALIFORNIA

Citizen-Legislators and Direct Democracy (or Popular Sovereignty)

In California the notion of citizen-legislators through ballot initiatives, arguably in a kind of direct democracy (or popular sovereignty), was gaining momentum in the 1990s. In 1990: "No Lack of Initiatives" as "California debates a thicket of environmental proposals"; in "The Greening of the Golden State," ". . . California will vote on the most sweeping environmental reforms ever proposed"; "Ballot Becomes a Burden in California" with "A 250-page ballot pamphlet—just to outline the measures"; and "At End of California Ballot, a Pot of Debt," for "If Voters Approve 10 Ballot Measures, State Borrowing Will Shatter Records." In 1992, "Californians [Are] to Vote on Letting Doctors Assist the Terminally Ill in Suicides." In 1994: "Taking on California, Philip Morris Wins a Place for Tobacco Issue on the Ballot" in "All-out attack by a manufacturer on smoking ban"; "A Ballot Proposition Gives Voters the Opportunity to Influence National Immigration Policy"; and "California Immigration [Ballot] Measure Faces Rocky Legal Path." In 1996: "Foes of Affirmative Action Are Gaining in Ballot Effort"; "California Reformers Swipe At Ballot Initiatives"; "Affirmative Action Ballot Too Vague, Judge Says"; "California [Is] to Vote On Legalizing 'Pot' For Medicinal Use"; "Stakes Are High as California Debates Ballot Initiatives to Rein In H.M.O.'s"; "Litigation Valley" occurs "In California, [as] high-tech firms battle securities lawyers over a plaintiff-friendly referendum"; "U.S. Judge Blocks [California] Voters' Initiative On Job Preference"; and "An Orwellian Assault on Democracy" occurs when "In California the people banned affirmative action. But will they have the last word?" In 1997: "Federal Appeals Court Upholds California's Ban [in Proposition 209] on Preferences"; and "California's [Proposition 209] Ban on Preferences Goes Into Effect" albeit with "A subtle tug of war as a law ends public affirmative action." In 1998: in "California's New Boot Camp for Ballot Initiatives: The Oaks Project wants to help people take a leading role in American politics"; and in "Rule by Proposition: A new study finds that America's most populous state seems to have given up on representative government" (a book review). In 1999, "Legal woes beset ballot initiatives" when "Direct-style democracy is dealt a new blow as California court rejects another measure" (on Indian gambling).[61]

As a consequence of these and other related developments during this period, a number of legislative problems were arising in California. "California Tried Democracy and Look What Happened" after "First the voters seized upon ballot initiatives; then the well-financed and lobbies did." "California's Fiscal Crisis Tests Government's Role." "Term Limits, Party Discipline and Power ... [Are] Recipe for Legislative Chaos in California." "California Lawmakers Feel Pinch as Voter Anger Promises Political Curbs." "California's Squabbling Legislature Just Stumbles Along." "The Professional Legislature And Its Discontents: ... Why doesn't California work better?" "... Government Goes on Automatic Pilot" as "Congress blunders down California's road to gridlock." "California Politicians Reel After a Vote Limiting Terms." "California Legislature Challenges Ballot Measure Limiting Terms," with "A word for voters' action: unconstitutional." "Limits on California Terms Are Upheld."[62]

The ballot-initiative trend in California continued in 2000 and beyond: "Ballot Initiative That Would Thwart Gay Marriage Is Embroiling California," creating "Sharp differences over the meaning and intent of Proposition 22." "The Cost of California's Direct Democracy ... [is seen when] Voter initiatives lock the state into budget mandates with no wiggle room." "In California, the Propositions Keep Rolling Along," while "Barely noticed, but on the ballot, is an example of what plagues Sacramento." "Ballot Plan to Ease '3 Strikes' Law Divides Californians and a Victim's Family." "California Revolts, Again" when, "As Gov. Gray Davis . . . faces a recall drive, Arnold Schwartzenegger celebrated the anniversary of Proposition 13" and begins, "In the long experiment with direct democracy, a wild new chapter."[63]

Governor and State Legislature

The foregoing reference in 2003 to "a wild new chapter" opening up in California's long history of ballot initiatives alluded to recall efforts under way against Governor Gray Davis. Further successive reports from 2002–2003 tell the wider story: "Flurry of Legislation Puts California Governor in the Hot Seat," "forcing Gov. Gray Davis to decide whether to sign dozens of bills backed by liberal lobbies but sharply opposed by business interests." "California's Governor Signs," for example, a "Series of Anti-Gun Measures." "California's recall fever harks back to Progressive Era." "At center of recall fray, [is] a maverick court," insofar as "The Ninth Circuit Court of Appeals has often upset status quo with liberal rulings." In "California's Political Earthquake"—caused by "The recall election that cost Democratic Gov. Gray Davis his job" and that gave rise to the new Republican Governor Arnold Schwartzenegger—"The aftershocks are unpredictable, but Schwartzenegger's appeal has incumbents nervous."[64]

Aside from the unusual recall of Governor Davis, a more typical picture of legislator-in-chief emerges for his predecessor and successor, Governor Pete Wilson and Governor Schwartzenegger. In late 1991, Governor Wilson, for instance, in "Cutting the Costs," "offers a sweeping plan to slash payments and change the behavior of the poor." Less than a year later, "Austere Budget Passes in Cash-Starved California." In early 1995 he declared that "California . . . is a sovereign state, and not a colony of the Federal government." In late 2003 "[Gov.] Schwartzenegger Wins Lawmakers' Approval for Fiscal Plan." In early 2005, "Schwartzenegger Proposes Overhaul of Redistricting" in his annual State of the State address," in which he "called on the Democratic-controlled Legislature to enact a fundamental overhaul that would include that most sacred of political cows, the way Congressional and legislative districts are drawn." Later that year, "Schwartzenegger Orders Election on 3 Proposals."[65]

The legislative record of California between 1994 and 2005 included a wide array of high-profile measures that were not without problems and setbacks but that were characteristic of a state often identified nationally by its legislative activism and advances. Some successive examples must suffice. "California Car Rules Set a Model for the East" in "A move to encourage auto makers to compromise on emissions." "3-Strikes Law in California Is Clogging Courts and Jails." "California Lawmakers Target Assault Weapons." "California's 'blockbuster' gun bills" are such that "If key gun-control measures pass in Golden State, ripple effect may be felt across America." "Toughest Law Yet on Assault Guns Is Enacted by California." "Trailblazing California Broadens the Rights of Its H.M.O. Patients" through "a package of bills signed" by the governor. "California Moves to Extend Gay Rights With New Laws." "California Becomes First State With Law to Set Ratio of Nurses per Patient in Hospitals." "California Lawmakers Press Energy Plan" "to Help Support the State's Ailing Utilities." In "The Disaster of Deregulation," "California's experience with blackouts and soaring prices is a caution." "New Regulations in California Will Reduce Diesel Emissions." "Once Braced for a Power Shortage, California Now Finds Itself With a Surplus." "California Lawmakers Vote To Lower Auto Emissions." "California Takes the Lead on Curbing Auto Emissions: A new state law could lead to a redesign of every car sold in America." "California: trendsetter or 'rogue state'?"—"Golden State charts own liberal course on autos, stem cells, and paid family leave" in "Bold California measures [that] buck national consensus" to the extent that "California frequently acts like a *sovereign* nation [emphasis added]." "California pushes broad abortion-rights legislation," and, "With most states hostile to extending rights, the package of bills is remarkable." "California Lawmakers Move to Fight U.S. Pollution Rules" (under President Bush Jr.) in "A closely watched effort to restore stricter rules from the old Clean Air Act." "California Backs Plans For Big Cut In Car Emissions" with "Toughest Rules in Nation—Challenges Expected From Automakers." "California Lawmakers Pass Bill on Same-Sex Marriage" in "A contentious issue [that] lands on the governor's doorstep."[66]

6. FLORIDA

In the early 1990s there were partial echoes at the state level in Florida of New Deal Democrats who in earlier eras spearheaded executive-legislative agendas on social programs at the national level. "Governor [Lawton Chiles] Turns Florida Into His Lab for Change." It was called "Government Reform, Florida Style: With the support of the Legislature, Governor Chiles has put together a 'bureaucracy busting' plan to bring flexibility and innovation to state government." Subsequently, "Florida Blazes Trail to a New Health-Care System" as "The Florida Legislature approved a sweeping overhaul of the state's overburdened health-care system . . ., making Florida the first state in the nation to combine free-market competition and government regulation in a way similar to the Clinton Administration's plans for controlling soaring medical costs." By 1999, however, "An Era Is Fading in Florida For New Deal Democrats" due to various circumstances.[67]

That year, 1999, arose an illustrative issue in the change of policies under Republican Governor Jeb Bush, brother of Governor George Bush of Texas. In his "move to end affirmative action," "Florida's Bush says class rank works better." An editorial on "Affirmative Action in Florida" pointed out that "Governor Bush's executive orders have provided a reasoned basis for the coming decision over affirmative action. . . . [B]ut the State Legislature will have ample opportunity to shape them as the process moves forward." In 2000 came the "First Test After End of Affirmative Action" when "Minority Enrollment Rises In Florida College System."[68]

It will be remembered that in our initial chapters the legislative framework in Florida state government tended to be uppermost in late 2000 during that state's struggles to resolve the disputed Y2K presidential election.

7. TEXAS

In the early 1990s, "Winds of Change Sweep The Lone Star State" as "Maverick [Democratic] Governor Ann Richards shakes up the good ole boys with a package of wide-ranging reforms." At that point in 1991, "Consumer and Environmental Bills Pass in Texas" in "A shift for Texas and a victory for Gov. Richards." Under Richards, "Texas Lawmakers Confront School Financing Issue Anew." In 1992 "Texas Lawmakers Again Reject Plan to Equalize School Financing," having been called into special session by Governor Richards to deal with the problem and her proposals, which were not adopted, thereby putting renewed pressure on the Legislature to confront the issue anew. In 1993 "Legislature in Texas Sends School-Aid Plan to Voters" in "An effort to force rich school districts to aid poor ones."[69]

With the new administration of Governor George Bush Jr. starting in 1995, "Texas Collides With the Clean Air Act" as "States look for flexibility in meeting pollution standards." Even so, as later illustrated, "Texas execution shows Bush's limited role" as governor, inasmuch as "The Lone Star State, wary of executive clout, gives the governor little authority to pardon." Assessing Bush's record as reputed reformer, with "gutsy moves and service to Big Business," one report in 2000 pointed out how "Texas Gives Its Governor Little Power . . ." in appointments, the budget, staffing, and in the Legislature (which only meets every other year), ". . . but Bush Has Tried to Leave His Mark" on tort reform, education, taxes, welfare, and pollution. Shortly after Bush became president in early 2001, "Back in Texas, Bush's Legacy Is Under Fire in Legislature" as "Lawmakers in Texas perceive a different climate under the new governor" and in the battle "over efforts to toughen environmental legislation introduced by President Bush when governor."[70]

Then there is an obscure footnote. "In Small [Texas] Town, [Overton], the Fight Continues for Texas *Sovereignty* [emphasis added]" and "the independence of Texas," all harking back to unfinished 19th-century struggles.[71]

8. SPECIAL CASES ON SOVEREIGNTY AND SELF-DETERMINATION

Hawaii

In 1992, "A Century After Queen's Overthrow, Talk of Sovereignty Shakes Hawaii," and "The islands rumble with ethnic pride and pent-up anger." In 1995 a "Bill Giving Native Hawaiians Sovereignty Is Too Much for Some, Too Little for Others" ("112 years after United States troops helped to overthrow the independent Kingdom of Hawaii and 12 years after Congress apologized for it") as a bill giving "sovereignty to the native Hawaiian people is poised for a vote—and likely approval—in the United States Senate despite opposition. . . ." In 1996 "Native Hawaiians Vote in Referendum [or Plebiscite] on Creating an Ethnic Government"—while looking back at 1959 when "Congress approves legislation making Hawaii the 50th state" and at 1993 when "Congress passed a resolution apologizing for the overthrow of the monarchy." Soon thereafter, "Native Hawaiian Vote Favors Sovereignty."[72]

Puerto Rico

In 1990 the issue of Puerto Rico's future status was reaching a climax, or so it seemed. While some deemed "Statehood For Puerto Rico . . . A cultural and economic disaster," others, including New York Congressman Bill Green, supported "Self-Determination for Puerto Rico." Meanwhile, "Puerto Rico Chief [i.e., Governor] Says

U.S. [President Bush Sr., etc.] Exerts Pressure for Statehood." With "Congress to Consider Puerto Rico Future," "Sharply Different Approaches in House and Senate May Delay Plan for Plebiscite." Later that year, "House Panel Backs Bill on Puerto Rico Vote" "on statehood," authorizing a vote next year and forcing Congress "to decide within six months of the referendum whether to accept its results." Two weeks later, "House Votes Bill For Puerto Rico To Decide Status," so that "For the first time a house of Congress supports self-determination in Puerto Rico."[73]

A period of wrangling ensued among Congressional legislators over self-determining statehood for Puerto Rico. In 1991: "Referendum on Puerto Rico's Future Could Be Delayed Until 1993"; "Constitutionality of a Choice for Puerto Rico's Future Is Challenged" (the three options for Puerto Rico being statehood, enhanced commonwealth status, and independence); "Proposals [Are] Dim on Bill for Puerto Rico Referendum"; "[Senator] Moynihan Tries to Save Puerto Rico Referendum"; and "Senate Panel Derails Bill on Puerto Rico Referendum" as "Prospects fade for a vote on an island's future." In 1993, "Threat of Statehood in Puerto Rico Leads to a Restored Tax Break" as "Lawmakers opt for a gradual change in a tax scale."[74]

Anticipation mounted in Puerto Rico in 1993. "Puerto Rico's Identity [Is] Up for a Vote." "State of Anticipation: The Caribbean island agonizes over whether to seek admission to the Union." "Puerto Rico Debates Statehood or Status Quo as a Vote Nears." In the end, "Puerto Rico Votes to Continue Commonwealth Status," thereby "Remaining Puerto Rico, Politically," and "Rejecting the changes posed by statehood or independence" while "Keep[ing] 41-Year Relationship With U.S."[75]

Events soon repeated themselves. Four years later, in 1997, "Governor of Puerto Rico Presses Statehood Battle: Re-elected, He Renews Call for a Plebiscite." In 1998 "[U.S.] Senate Is Lukewarm, but Some Seek Vote on Puerto Rico," although, "Without the majority leader's support, a bill faces an uncertain future." Later that year, "With a Vote for 'None of the Above,' Puerto Ricans Endorse Island's Status Quo."[76]

District of Columbia

It was reported in 1995 that "The District of Columbia Struggles Under Burden of Self-Government" and "Home Rule." D.C. was dubbed the "District of Calamity" in that "The capital is a city falling apart. How much of the crisis is the mayor's fault?" "Trying to

Fix the Nation's Capital, When Everything Is Broken," was becoming increasingly difficult by 1996. "District of Columbia Is Ordered [by Congress] To Make Deep Cuts In Spending." In 1997 Clinton's "White House Offers New Ties to District" in which "U.S. Would Take Over Tax Collection, Pick Up Other Expenses." At the same time, "Congress Whittles Away Power of Capital's Mayor," Marion Barry. "Under Congress' Thumb," "Washington, D.C., gets federalized." At that point, after one report that "Despair Grows Over Problems of Governing U.S. Capital," another report declared that "After Malaise, a New Mood [Is Emerging] in Nation's Capital" with a new Mayor-elect in later 1998. By 1999 "District of Columbia Is Back On Path to Self-Government."[77]

Relations between D.C. and Congress were still unsettled in some respects during 2000–2004. "Is Taxation Without Representation Still Tyranny? Why residents of the nation's capital should be excused from paying federal taxes." "Congress and District Clash Over a New City Ordinance" as "House Opposes Coverage of Contraceptives." "House Approves D.C.'s Law On Rights of Domestic Partners." "Don't Tread on D.C.," for "Congress unduly intrudes on the capital's affairs," even though "Congress has the constitutional right to impose a school voucher program on the District of Columbia . . . [and] the legal power to relax the district's strict gun control law. . . ." "International Panel Backs Seat for Capital in Congress" and "Says U.S. Violates Washingtonians' Rights."[78]

Indian Territories

In 1990, Indian "Tribal Leaders Sign Treaty On Sovereignty," and their "Mutual Defense Pact Aims to Guard Rights." Nearly a year later, "Sovereign Once Again, Indian Tribes Experiment With Self-Government" while "Trying to break the shackles of dependency." As "Indian Legislators Break New Ground," "A handful of Native Americans are pioneers in mingling the worlds of state and tribal governments." It had been a "Long Road from Federal Domination to Self-Determination." In 1992 "U.S. Would Cede 400,000 Acres to Hopis to End Indian Dispute" in the American West. In another development, the "Issue of Indian Sovereignty [Is] Behind Gambling Case" in Florida in 1993. Three years later in New Mexico, "Indians Take On the U.S. In a 90's Battle for Control." In Montana in 1998, "Backlash Grows as Indians Make a Stand for Sovereignty." Three months later in New Mexico, there was "Mixing [of] Tribal Tradition and US Law" when a "Program gives native Americans access to one of the nation's most powerful professions." "Indian rights and traditions hang in balance" in 1998 when the "Supreme Court hears arguments . . . on an 1837 treaty that allows hunting and fishing methods in Minnesota banned by state law."[79]

In 2000 "U.S. Is Returning 84,000 Acres to [Western] Indians," "the largest return of public land to American Indians in the continental United States in more than 100 years. . . ." That year in Washington State, there was a "Test of Indian Sovereignty And Government Resolve" as "Alcohol Ban Is at Center of Rare Dispute." As reported from New Mexico in 2002, there is "New status for Indian law: It'll be on the bar" as "Newly wealthy tribes enter the economic mainstream and bring their sovereign legal status with them," while "Indian law issues confront lawyers on a daily basis[,] . . . and an astonishing number are ignorant about these laws." According to a 2003 newscast, Indians in California are recognized as a sovereign nation by Federal law, even to the point of restricting U.S. police from entering Indian territory to investigate such matters as theft.[80]

EPILOGUE

Governor as Legislator-in-Chief

A recurrent theme throughout this chapter has been the governor of a state acting as legislator-in-chief, especially in relation to his (or her) state's legislature and to his (or her) independent executive authority. Similarly in cities, such as New York City, the mayor often has a role as legislator-in-chief in relation to his city's council and to his independent executive authority. At the level of borough and county, too, as in the cases of Staten Island and Nassau County, a similar phenomenon can be observed. This common pattern represents a kind of microcosm of the President as legislator-in-chief when steering his legislative agenda through Congress or issuing his executive orders independently. This growing symbiosis between executive and legislative functions and branches has also increasingly paralleled the British and European models of the prime minister acting in and through parliament as its legislator-in-chief when steering his legislative agenda through the governing legislative body. This comparison holds true in a loose sense notwithstanding the U.S. separation of powers in which the President is not a member of Congress, unlike in Britain where the Prime Minister is a member of Parliament. An end result of this U.S. trend has been to expand the legislative component of sovereignty and state into an all-important and all-identifying force.

At the same time, the U.S. states themselves, as microcosms, legislatively, of the Federal government, with vast lawmaking operations of their own, have extensive inherent powers to legislate for their own affairs. We have already seen how the U.S. Federal departments, agencies, commissions, and corporations often possess their own power to make rules and regulations that function as laws within their own spheres of operation. The principle of legislative self-determination within each state or legally recognized body thus affords many diverse perspectives on American government in current news history.

It is useful to note that the 19th-century legal theorist John Austin found a key ultimate location of sovereignty in the United States to be the state legislatures. In his day, however, the U.S. state legislatures were somewhat differently positioned in relation to Congress as the national legislature, where U.S. senators had a direct link to their state's governing bodies, while Congress itself was not overshadowed by what has been called in modern times an "imperial presidency." Austin's intricate mode of "analytical jurisprudence," by which he searched for where sovereignty lay in a given nation or political–legal system, might not give him that same result here today, but his accent on state legislatures as a key ultimate source or location of U.S. legislative sovereignty remains instructive.

Federal Systems of States for Other Continents?

The model of the American federal system of legislative states—in what is sometimes called "federalism" or a decentralized form of government—could become useful for governments on other continents where the basic political–legal structures are still in flux and evolving.

The case of Europe offers perhaps the most fitting opportunity for such considerations. There the traditional nation–states have been gradually forming, over recent decades, a common set of structures—economic, political, and legal—wherewith to unite them into a "European Union." The extent to which the European countries will or can merge their individual identities into a single larger national unity in a "United States of Europe" remains to be seen. But if they were to reconfigure their essential legislative sovereignties into something resembling the American system of legislative states, they could retain their self-determinations within an overarching federal structure having an effective and authoritative central legislative government, however separated or divided into distinct branches or compartments. In this fashion, the age-old nation–states of Europe would not be losing their traditional legislative sovereignties but would largely retain them within a greater super-national (or supra-national) legislative sovereignty. Since Europe is today roughly the same size as the continental United States, with roughly the same size population, an enlarged and unified nation–state of Europe could become manageable.

Looking ahead several decades or even centuries, one can similarly envision an "African Union" or "United States of Africa" in which the present-day nations–states would be grouped together into a system of legislative states having self-determination under a common legislative sovereignty in whatever form of super-national (or supra-national) government. The myriad, often underdeveloped and warring African nations might seem less promising candidates for such a merger than the countries of Europe, until it is remembered that principles of sovereignty can apply even to the smallest inchoate entities, such as the Indian territories of the United States.

If an overarching super-national unity government, having legislative sovereignty in a federal system of individual self-determining states a la the United States, could help to bring greater stability to Africa, what would the prospects be for Asia and in particular the troubled and divided Middle East? Could the distant future ever witness there something comparable to an "African Union," much less a "European Union?" Or would a solution lie at an even higher level of unity and civilization?

In the far-off future, a more "universal" sovereign legislative state could become plausible. The "clashes of civilizations" in current times might then be replaced by some sort of integrated universal or world civilization. Legislative sovereignty and the legislative state could still prevail at world, continental, and national levels but within an expanded "new order" of federalism. Whether or not the United Nations could be transformed for such purposes is another question. So, too, is whether such a framework would be in the best interests of the United States at present, especially given its long-standing problems with actions and policies of the United Nations. Yet the United States should be able to keep its superpower status within a new international legal–political order enabling greater peace and stability. With federal systems of states in nations like Iraq?

A more concrete indication of "world perspectives and emergent systems for the new order in the new age" (the subtitle devised by this author around 1989 for this volume in advance of its appearance in the listing at outset of Volume IV in 1991) must await the completion of the present two books on the Western and Eastern hemispheres. For now, we focus on the central themes of legislative sovereignty and the legislative state on a case by case basis.

Chapter VII

Sectors of American Life and Society

The list of paired topics in this chapter is broad and lengthy, inclusive of most every sector of life and society in the current American scene from the 1990s to present. The aim, once again, cannot be complete coverage of each sector but rather a comprehensive look, within each, at some representative topics and issues. In light of the foregoing chapters on the remarkable extent of the legislative/regulatory frameworks paramount at federal, state, and local levels of American government, it will come as no surprise to see their comparable permeation of everyday life and society, which have already been entering our discussions in chapters above and awaiting separate focus here.

1. BUSINESS AND ECONOMICS

During Bush Sr.'s and Clinton's Terms

In the second half of President Bush Sr.'s Administration, which inherited Reaganomic deregulation and ended in economic recession, the following news accounts on business and economics give glimpses into the myriad changing dimensions of the American legislative/regulatory state. "Regulators Question International Loan Network of Sales Tactics." "Regulators Are Faulted in Problems of Big Insurer" as "Executive life's woes reflect weak oversight in most states, critics say." "The Watchdog Wakes Up" as "Food companies can target the days of anything-goes regulators. A new FDA commissioner is cracking down on deceptive labels." "Bank Rules Gain Urgency After Collapse." "Under Pressure by Congress, Regulators Cut Subsidies on Sales Made in 1988" in "Some S. & L. Deals." "Solomon's Infractions Call Attention To Light Regulation of Bond Trading" in which "all Americans have a stake." "Regulators Add to Ties Abroad," with "S.E.C. in Pact With Europeans to Help Police the Markets." "Regulators Prepare for Biggest Round Ever of Bank S. & L. Failures." "U.S. Is Assailed on Bank Regulation" when "The Government's top auditor criticizes the Bush Administration." "Some [Congressional] Legislators Are Skeptical" when a "[U.S.] Regulator Lowers Estimate Of Costs Of Savings Bailout." "S.E.C. Asks for Sweeping Changes In Rules Covering Mutual Funds" in its "package of regulatory and legislative proposals." "The Oil Industry Likes to Keep Regulations Close to Home," inasmuch as "Federal Environmental Oversight Is Limited" and "Congress will decide whether state oil producers should pay more for cleanup or continue federal exemptions." There were conservatives who saw a "regulatory reign of terror" toward the banking industry during the Bush Administration.[1]

Naturally the picture changed somewhat for regulatory matters in business and economics as the Clinton Administration's first term progressed. "Lending-Bias Rules Create Quandary for Banks," for although "Regulators are more aggressive, . . . they're not always clear." "A Call for Economic Intervention by Government" on the part of "President Clinton's economists" in order "to tweak the economy" cast doubt on recent "free market" approaches. "U.S. Tightens Rules To Help Investors In Municipal Bonds," such that the S.E.C. "issued new rules" whereby "state and local governments and authorities would have to issue annual financial reports. . . ." "Bank Regulators [in a Treasury Dept. Agency Are] Taking Close Look At Lending Rules." In "Saving Money or Saving Lives?," "A Bill to Reduce Mining Regulations Alarms Safety Experts." There was a call by some for "Giving Business A Chance to Test The Wings of Deregulation." With "Business Scaling Back Plans To Defang Federal Regulators," Congressional allies were being forced to alter legislation stalled in Congress in order to help its passage. "Criticizing Regulations, [Republican Sen.] Dole Courts Small-Business

Owners." By later 1996, there was a "Bill to Revise Securities Regulations Ready for Clinton." At that same point, a "Powerful Bull Market Sends Dow To Its First Closing Above 6,000."[2]

These trends continued during Clinton's second presidential term, which saw a booming economy. "Congress [Is] Set to Debate Hedge Fund Oversight" in quandary over "How to regulate something that has no precise legal definition?" "Merger Wave Spurs New Security" through antitrust action and increased attempts at regulation. "Wary Of Global Control," "Industries Press Plan For Credits In Emissions Pact" through "New Legislation [That] Would Offer Companies Incentives for Early Cuts in Pollution." When "Eying The Competition," "Corporate espionage is so pernicious that the U.S. passed a law to curb it. But in today's global economy, dirty tricks are all in a day's work." "Corporations mobilize against the threat of a federal internet privacy-protection law." "Senate Votes to Drop Barriers Between Nation's Financial Industries." "House Debates Financial Overhaul Law Today" in order "to repeal 1933 regulations." "Congress Passes Wide-Ranging Measure Ending Depression-Era Restrictions on Banks" (in Glass–Steagle Act of 1933). "Revised Banking Legislation Raises Concerns About Privacy." "Clinton Signs Legislation Overhauling Banking Laws." "U.S. Takes Aim At Tax Shelters For Companies" as the Treasury Dept. "issued new rules" to discourage abuses. "Congress and Regulators Start Efforts to Crack Down on Deceptive Lending Practices." It became "A monopoly game with new rules" when a "landmark antitrust ruling" "weakens Microsoft, but also shows how hard it is for antitrust law to keep up with technology's pace."[3]

By April of 2000 the stock market was beginning to experience sharp declines, with warning signs for business and for the economy more broadly. Looking back in November, near the end of the Clinton presidency, some news reports credited Alan Greenspan (as head of the Federal Reserve) together with Clinton himself, through their hands-on regulatory policies, for having "built one of the best economies ever." Others in early 2001 were less sure, saying that "Confidence, not the Fed, determines our ups and downs" in "The Mystery of Economic Recessions"; or, on "Economic Delusion, Political Disaster," there was (said John Kenneth Galbraith) "An overblown reliance on tax cuts and the Fed."[4]

During Bush Jr.'s Terms

From the beginning of the new Bush Administration in early 2001, with the stock market steadily falling and the perceived need to change economic course, a centerpiece became "Deregulation: A Movement [Grows But Is] Groping in the Dark." "Business Flexes Its Muscles" as "Congress kills rules to prevent workplace injuries." It was "So Long, Red Tape" as "The business lobby, bolstered by early wins in the new administration, readies a broad agenda." In a "Farewell to the short-lived politics of prosperity," the "Fate of the Federal Budget Surplus Depends on Ideology and Accounting." By the end of 2001 "Economists Make It Official: The Nation Is in a Recession." Shortly before, "Bush Tries to Steady Economy Jolted by [9/11] Attack," while "White House, Congress and the Fed Debate How to Avert Recession."[5]

Over the Bush years in various regulatory matters for business, there were strong actions taken as in the following cases spanning 2002–2007. "U.S. Trust [Corp.] Is Fined $10 Million in Bank Secrecy-Law Case" by "Federal and New York regulators. . . ." "Stiff Overhaul of Mine Safety Rules Passes in Congress." In "How Will Washington Read the Signs?," "The Race Is On for Tougher Regulation of Business." Concerning "Competition vs. Regulation," "The Microsoft [Antitrust] ruling shows how hard it is to reign in a monopoly." "Regulators Penalize Microsoft In Europe." Congressional "Negotiators Agree On Broad Changes In Business Laws," with "Passage Expected Soon" for "Measure [That] Would Make It Easier to Punish Corrupt Auditors and Top Executives." "Bush Aides And Business Meet on Shift In Regulation" since "Many of the executives have urged the rollback of laws passed in the wake of the Enron and Worldcom scandals as well as limits on liability from government and shareholder lawsuits"—"A relaxation sought by those who see the U.S. as uncompetitive."[6]

The biggest and best-known regulatory saga of business boom and bust during the early Bush years, 2001–2002, centered on the company Enron, as reflected in the following sequence of telltale headlines. "Regulators Struggle With a Marketplace Created by Enron," "An energy giant [that] has enjoyed unalloyed lobbying success in Washington." "Enron's reach in Congress" and "deep connections to both parties" has renewed "calls for campaign-finance law" in a "Washington drowning in soft, unregulated money." "Web of Safeguards Failed as Enron Fell: Warnings, Inside and Out, Were Not Heeded." "Unaccountable in Washington," members from oil-producing states in "Congress set the stage for Enron's failure." "Enron collapse fuels debate over US regulators' role." With "Enron on Their Minds," "Policymakers are poised to revisit the sensitive issue of pension regulation." "Enron, Preaching Deregulation, Worked the Statehouse Circuit Hard." "Turn Out the Lights. The

Party's Over," for "After Enron, Deregulation Looks Less Sexy." "Rule Makers Take On Loopholes That Enron Used in Hiding Debt": "Responding to the collapse of Enron Corporation, regulators, legislators, and the chief accounting rule makers proposed changes yesterday in the way companies do business and report their finances. . . ." "Accounting Rules Let Enron Disguise Rapid Rise in Debt By Listing Loans as Trades," whereas "Higher debt levels might have been a warning to creditors and investors." By mid-2002, however, with "Enthusiasm Waning in Congress For Tougher Post-Enron Controls," the prospects of "Legislating to Prevent the Next Enron" were dimming. Yet soon thereafter, "Bush Signs Bill Aimed at Corporate Fraud," "Vowing to end 'the era of low standards and false profits.' "[7]

2. TRANSPORTATION AND COMMUNICATIONS

On transportation, as the 1990s progressed, the following legislative/regulatory headlines represent a rough cross-section for present purposes. "Off Course: Airline deregulation was supposed to bring about increased competition, more passenger convenience and lower fares. But the idea took some strange turns." "Off and Humming" and "Driven by fear of draconian environmental laws, carmakers are finally getting serious about electric cars." "Lead-Foot Habits Prompt Search for New Emission Rules" as "the Government re-addresses the pollution problems of speeders." "New rules require different color fuels [especially for diesel] and ban all mixing." "California Regulators [Are] To Meet on Electric Cars," and, "In a review, the feasibility of zero-emission rules will be determined." Acting on recent crashes, "Government Sets A Safety Review At Every Airline" and "Transportation Secretary Also Orders a Speeding of New Commuter-Plane Rules." "Amtrak Is Ordered [in a "ruling" by a Federal judge] Not to Eject the Homeless From Penn Station." "On a Wing and a Fare: Deregulation [Is] Decoded" and is "Where to Lay the Blame For Crummy Service." "Ending of Federal Speed Limit Wins Congressional Approval," whereby "States would have more authority over transportation policies and rules." "Speed Limit Restrictions May Fall by the Wayside" as "West Awaits the Go-Fast Sign from Clinton." "U.S. [in Transportation Dept. "emergency rules" issued by one of its agencies] Orders Passenger Trains to Slow Down After Some Stations." "Experts Fault U.S. on Safety Rules for Railroads," saying that "Fatal Crashes Were Preventable." With "No Barrier To Mayhem," "U.S. airport security is lax compared with other countries. The FAA is in no hurry to improve it." "Safety Groups Steer Toward Stiffer Laws For Not Buckling Up." "Clinton Signs Wide-Ranging Measure on Airport Security." "TWA 800 [Crash] Probe Leads [National Transportation Safety Board] To Urge New Safety Measures." "U.S. [National Highway Traffic Safety Administration Is] to Issue Rules ["regulations"] on Simpler Use of Car Seats." "Flying Blind: In a startling new book, a federal whistle-blower [calling for increased regulations] reveals how FAA cover-ups and sloppy practices have put air travelers at risk." "Tentative Accord Is Reached On Giant Transportation Bill." As for "The Killer Trucks," "Lax safety rules . . . [and] long hours wreak havoc on the roads."[8]

Some similar transportation themes in 2000–2006 were as follows. "Senate Votes to Revise Law That Limits Payments in Air Crashes" in "An attempt to help the families of Flight 800 victims." "The Costs of Governing Less" included "Exhibit A: cuts in the highway safety [regulatory] agency and the Firestone scandal." "Stricter Rules for Tire Safety Were Scrapped by Reagan," whose "Proposals Followed Earlier Firestone Recall," whereas now "New Congressional hearings may look at regulations drafted two decades ago." A new "Tire recall may pave way to new safety standards" as "House and Senate hold hearings. . . ." Accordingly, "Highway Safety Agency Seeks More Money and Authority." "Congress May Tackle Vehicle Rollovers," such that "Regulators may soon proceed with rating vehicles' stability." "Bill to Toughen Drinking Law Holds Up Transportation Bill." "Airlines and Federal Regulators [Are] at Odds" in "Dispute [That] Focuses on How Many Hours a Pilot May Work Each Day." "Deaths Spur Laws Against Drivers on Cell Phones." As for "The World of Airport Safety" after the 9/11 terror attack, "Security measures vary greatly, but most outperform the United States." For "Ensuring a Safe Flight" and "For air security, federal rules, not federal workers," are key. "Congress Agrees to U.S. Takeover For Air Security," with "a larger federal role than Republicans wanted." In "Shoring Up The Nation's Ports," "A new law should help stop terrorists at the water's edge, but it's an awfully big job." Congressional "Legislators Move to Toughen Federal Rail Oversight" in "regulating rail safety." On "Coffee, Tea or Regulation?," "As Grumbling Grows About Airlines, Some Eyes Turn to Washington" with a look back at "The Good and the Bad Since Deregulation." "Daring Veto, Senate Passes Roads and Transit Measure." There was a "Slight Shift In S.U.V.'s In New Rule On Mileage" in "Bush administration's long-awaited plan to overhaul fuel economy regulations [that] was released yesterday. . . ." By late 2006, "U.S. Eases Rules on Gels and Liquids in Carry-Ons" as "The

Transportation Security Administration announced a new policy on liquids and gels that can fit in a quart-size zip-up plastic bag top."⁹

In communications during the 1990s, there were the following reports. "Keeping the News in Step: Are the Pentagon's Gulf War Rules Here to Stay?" for "Covering the War," with "Second Thoughts On Restrictions." For "Viewer Privacy in the Interactive Age," "Without safeguards, interactivity will mean junk mail at light speed for helpless consumers." A Federal judge's "Ruling Frees Phone Concerns To Offer Cable Programming." In "A Phone–Cable Vehicle for the Data Superhighway," "A Planned Uniting of 2 Monopolies Arouses Concerns Among Regulators." "U.S. Ready To Ease Its Legal Barriers In Communications," "Spurred By Technology." "New Law Regulating Cable TV Gets Skeptical Response From High Court" "In search of constitutional markets for the information age." In "Rules of Road on Information Highway: Law Makes Harassing by Computer a Crime." In decontrol effort, "House Passes Bill Curtailing Rules On Phone And TV." "New Rules to Require More Disclosure by Telemarketers" as "The F.T.C. seeks to distinguish legitimate operators from con artists." "TV Ownership Rules Stall Communications Bill." "Congress Votes To Reshape Communications Industry, Ending A 4-Year Struggle," with "Clinton Set to Sign Bill That Is Expected to Spur Competition." "Protests to Greet Communications Bill" as "Opponents Say Rule on Smut Will Limit Free Speech on Internet." "We're All Connected" as "The long-awaited telecommunications bill sweeps away old boundaries. Get ready for a free-for-all." A year later, people were still "Trying to Resolve Jurisdictional Rules of the Internet." "High Court Rules Cable Must Carry Local TV Stations," "Reject[ing] Argument That Mandating Channels Is Violation of Free Speech," "A U.S. Judge Strikes Down Parts of the Telecommunications Act" so that "Regional Bells May Offer Long-Distance Service." "New Rules on High-Definition TV Roils Toshiba and Hitachi."¹⁰

As the next decade, from 2000 to 2006, developed in communications, the initial trends toward deregulation fostered by the Republican Bush Administration were soon counterbalanced by its efforts at greater regulation following the 9/11 terrorist attack. All the while, the pros and cons of regulatory effectiveness continued to be debated. Concerning "Web Filters For Children," "Parental and local vigilance are better than federal laws." "Congress Will Allow Ban on Internet Taxes to Expire." "Does a 9/11 Law Mean More Snooping or Less?" insofar as "Adapting surveillance rules to the Internet leads to a bitter clash." "Has post–9/11 dragnet gone too far?," for, "As White House pushes to expand domestic terror laws, critics worry limits on civil liberties will become permanent." "Law to Bar Junk E-Mail Allows a Flood Instead." "[Vice President] Cheney Pushed to Widen Eavesdropping Program" through National Security Agency. "Congress weighs rules on Net access," that is, "As the Senate debates Internet regulation . . . , the big issue is equal access to services."[11]

3. SCIENCE AND TECHNOLOGY

With the rapid expansion in science and technology during the 1990s, the regulatory/legislative efforts to keep up with it were often much in the news. "U.S. [Is] Ending Curbs On High-Tech Gear To Cold War Foes" Russia and China. As for "Digital Technology . . . [and] Rotary Laws," "Let competition rule on the infohighway." On "Brave New Embryos," "U.S. rules for studies of early development are sure to stir up a storm." "Security of Personal Data Is Lost in Cyberspace." "To get around U.S. gambling laws, the first online casinos are setting up their card tables offshore" when "Betting on Virtual Vegas." On "Cyber Porn," "A new study shows how pervasive and wild [and unregulated] it really is. Can we protect our kids—and free speech?" "Facing Pressure in Congress, Opponents of Curbs Yield on Pornography Issue" as "Accord [Is] Reached For Limiting Smut On The Internet." When "a showdown at a [Connecticut] power plant exposed the federal government's failure to enforce its own rules" on nuclear safety, and "caught the Nuclear Regulatory Commission at a dangerous game that it has played for years: routinely waiving safety rules to let plants keep costs down and stay online." Meanwhile, "Congress waters down a computer privacy bill," thereby facilitating "Peeking at your P.C." "Ban Cloning? Not a Chance," inasmuch as "The President and Congress can try, but science can't be stopped." "Experts Urge No Hasty Curbs on Cloning," while "Cardinal O'Connor and scientists oppose a ban on research." "Export Laws [Are] Challenged by Sale of Encryption Software Abroad." "When Your Name Isn't Yours," "Regulators want to crack down on cybersquatters. But let's not go too fast." Saying "They're Trying to Change the Rules," Microsoft's Bill "Gates insists on the right to determine what goes into Windows, but he seems open to compromise on other issues."[12]

During 2000 and beyond, a similar story unfolded as science and technology further rapidly developed, with new "high tech" frontiers leading the way and the regulatory/legislative state still trying to keep up. "High tech often wins on the Hill" as, "Microsoft case aside, both parties woo the industry," that is, "Congress finds it can cooperate on one issue: high tech." "Database Legislation Spurs Fierce Lobbying," as "Collectors of information on the Internet square off against its users" with particular input by the National Association of Regulators, which has "members in every Congressional district" and is "one of the capital's most formidable lobbies." "Law Limits Aid to Russian Space Station." "Congress set to launch a NASA overhaul." In "A Law's Fetal Flaw," "Parents can now conceive babies whose cells can cure a sick sibling. But what if the pregnancy goes wrong?" "At 1,200 Pages, the Energy Plan [Bill] Weighs Itself Down." "Senate Blocks Energy Bill; Backers Vow to Try Again," while "11th-Hour Bills Irk Lawmakers Who Were Left in the Dark."[13]

4. CULTURE AND ENTERTAINMENT

During the Gingrich-led Republican takeover of the House of Representatives following the 1994 mid-term elections, right-wing conservatives endeavored to clamp down on the loose standards on sex and violence in culture and entertainment. In "Pulling the Fuse on Culture," "The conservative all-out assault on federal funding is unenlightened, uneconomic and undemocratic," such that "Congress is now full of indignant wannabe reformers who know next to nothing about American culture." There were also attempts at "Censoring Cyberspace." "Artists and Arts Groups [Are] Angered By New Rules for Federal Grants." "House Approves Measure To Kill Arts Endowment." Many other such restrictions arose.[14]

Many forms of entertainment faced regulatory/legislative restrictions during and after this period. In "The Fight for Digital TV's Future," "Fear of Japan got HD TV going. But now, the race is for money and airwaves. The referee? The F.C.C." "F.C.C. [Is] Joining [with "Lawmakers" in] A Move to Curb Violence on TV," that is, "Federal regulators and members of Congress say they hope to clamp down on broadcast violence and require more programming for children by taking advantage of a recent court decision that upheld restrictions on indecent programs on television and radio." "Congress Criticizes Baseball's New Steroid Policy as Misleading," for "It seems that baseball's tougher rules may not be so tough after all." A month later, "Uniform Steroid Rule Is Proposed in House." With further regard to "The Decency Police," "A year after Janet Jackson [who exposed her breast during a Superbowl half-time show on TV], activists and Congress are revving up their drive to clean up the airwaves. Now cable may be next. Has TV gone too far—or have the critics?"[15]

5. EDUCATION AND LIFE STYLES

Educational Standards, Mandates, and Reforms

Among the myriad topics prominent in the public press on education have been those involving educational standards and reform. During the presidency of George Bush Sr. in the early 1990s, "Rutgers President Defends Codes That Prohibit 'Hate Speech.'" Yet at the University of Michigan "President Warns Against Stifling Of Campus Ideas" and "Sees Free Speech Threat" when the "Idea of 'Political Correctness' Gives Rise to Intolerance. . . ." Likewise a few years later, historian Arthur "Schlesinger Sees Free Speech in Peril" and "denounces 'ideologies' from the left." Also under Bush, there was "Testing, Testing, Testing" as "The Administration's proposals for a national exam system have drawn fire from all sides. They probably shouldn't."[16]

Developing further in the mid- and later 1990s during the Clinton era were the many-sided issues over "The Case For Tough[er] Standards" in public schools as "Governors and corporate leaders launch a new drive to demand more from students. History's lesson: Enemies are everywhere." Albert Shanker, President of the American Federation of Teachers, called for "National (not Federal) Standards." "With New Deal Fervor, Clinton Pushes Education Plan" in "An ambitious $51 billion plan for education." One conservative newspaper queried "Whose National Standards?" Then, in "An effort to set the terms of a brewing public debate on education," "Clinton Presses Plan to Test Pupils on Federal Standards." Two years later, "Eager to toughen the standards in public schools, politicians are calling for an end to 'social promotion.' But forcing kids to repeat a grade may hurt more than help," said article on "Held Back."[17]

On other related fronts during the later 1990s, "Clinton [Is] To Urge More U.S. Control On Aid To Schools" and "To Stick to Policy, Not His Trial, in State of the Union Address." "Reinventing federal education policy," "Congressional Republicans have their first shot at changing an ineffective school spending program. Will they take it?" "Conservatives Open Drive Against Affirmative Action" as "Campaign Focuses on College Admissions." "In a Revolution of New Rules for Students, Colleges Are Turning Full Circle," endeavoring to regulate (against bad) student conduct on college campuses" ("In Place of Parents, College Officials"). The "Senate Takes Partisan Turn On Education Legislation," with both sides "Eager to show that education is foremost on their minds," inasmuch as many favored "allowing states to waive certain requirements" and to "loosen restrictions on how $10 billion in Federal money . . . can be spent, so long as schools show improvement." A week later, in both House and Senate, "Education Bill Passes, Providing Gains for G.O.P." On a different matter the year before, another chapter in the long-standing regulatory/legislative question of desegregation opened up as "Public Schools Are Forced to Confront Issues of Preferences" when "Desegregation efforts in many school districts are seen as being in peril."[18]

In the presidential campaign of 2000, it was said that "Under Either Bush or Gore, New Federal Role in Schools" would take place— "Bush emphasizes student testing, while Gore stresses improving schools." "Bush and Gore Stake Varying but Plump Claims to Federal Role in Education" with "A common emphasis, but differences." After the campaign, which Bush won, there was "Coming: bigger US role in schools" as "Legislation is solidifying in Congress to give Washington much more [regulatory] oversight of student academic achievement."[19]

In 2001, during the first year of the new Bush presidency, there was indeed renewed impetus on standards and reforms in education. "Students Find Drug Law Has Big Price: College Aid," as "Critics Say '96 Rule Is Biased Against Poor." "Congress' Virtual School Reform" involves "An education bill that's scarcely worth the trouble." "School Leaders Contend Laws May Cause Lower Standards," while "Warning of a dumbing-down effect to avoid sanctions on federal aid." "Congress Pushes for School Reform." Then, "Congress [House] Reaches Compromise on Education Bill." Finally, at the end of the year, with accord reached, "Education law [becomes] biggest in 35 years," and "The Senate is set to mandate testing in grades three to eight. But states could stall." Early in the next year, "Focusing on Home Front, Bush Signs Education Bill." The year after that, "Thousands of Schools May Run Afoul of New Law" because "States with high standards put schools at greater risk of failure.[20]

In 2004 and beyond, the struggles intensified between federal and state authorities over the new regulatory/legislative mandates on educational standards and reforms. "Some School Districts Challenge Bush's Signature Educational Law." "Bush Education Officials Find New Law a Tough Sell to States." "U.S. Set to Ease Some Provisions of School Law" after "States Object to Rules on Teachers and Tests," leading "to an effort to find more flexibility in No Child Left Behind" law. Notwithstanding, "Teachers' Union and School Districts in 3 States Sue Over No Child Left Behind Law." A call then arose, regarding "Every State Left Behind," that "Washington must take over standards and testing." As for its effectiveness, in 2005, "Bush Education Law Shows Mixed Results in First Test" as "Math Scores Rise, but Reading Declines"; and in 2006 "Schools Cut Back Subjects To Push Reading and Math" as, "Responding to No Child Left Behind Law, Thousands Narrow the Curriculum." In early 2007, there was a "Federal–Local Clash in War Over Teaching Reading" in connection with the "federal reading program" set up by the Bush Education Department through Congressional "Reading First Legislation" aimed at "turn[ing] the nation's poor children into skilled readers by the third grade," although for many reasons "Some school districts pass up millions in government aid" and consequent mandated federal standards.[21]

Private Rights vs. Public Policy, Safety, and Access

One of the most central and pervasive issues in life styles in the growth of the new technology age, during the 1990s and the post–9/11 terrorist world of 2001 and beyond, was that of private rights vs. public policy, safety, and access. It involved widespread regulatory/legislative parameters and implications.

In the early 1990s, "Somebody's Watching You" insofar as "business, government, and even the folks next door are tracking your secrets" and, "Using computers, high-tech gadgets and mountains of data, an army of snoops is assaulting our privacy." "Clipper Chip Sparks Debate Over Privacy vs. Public Safety" as "Encryption Device Widens Debate Over Rights of U.S. to Eavesdrop" ("Chipping Away at Privacy?"). "What Happened to Privacy?" when, "In cyberspace, all data are for sale." "Federal Caller-ID Rule Sparks Privacy Debate." With regard to "Public Rights In Private Domains," "A ruling allowing leaflets makes malls more like Main Street." On a different note, "Unmarried Couples [Are] Challenging State Law Barring Their Adoption Plans" due to the way "Unwed couples fall through the legal loopholes."[22]

In the later 1990s and shortly thereafter, the growing "Invasion of Privacy" hindered "Our right to be left alone, bit by bit, in Little Brotherly steps." "What Privacy Rights?"—"Medical records, phone calls, E-mail—nothing is sacred." "In cyberspace, there is no real wall between public and private," leading to "The Eroded Self." "The Identity Thieves Are Out There—And Someone Could Be Spying On You," causing "Internet Insecurity." "In codes of privacy new cracks appear," for, "As lawyers debate confidentiality code today, the ethos is under siege in US life."[23]

In the aftermath of the 9/11 terrorist attack on the United States in late 2001, regulatory/legislative efforts were under way to protect public safety and security, with mixed implications and impacts on privacy rights. As for "National ID Cards: One Size Fits All," that is, "Where some see a boon to law enforcement and airport security, others see a threat to privacy and civil liberties." On "Access Denied," "A fine line falls between national security and the public's right to know." Concerning "Security vs. Privacy," "Financial transactions are now subject to government security." With "Security Act to pervade daily lives," "The Homeland Security Act that President Bush is poised to sign is sweeping in scope and will have big consequences, intended and unintended, on everything from civil liberties of Americans to due process for immigrants." However, former Vice President "Gore Says Bush's War on Terrorism Is Ineffective" and involves "A 'systematic invasion of privacy.' " In any case, a "Study [entitled "Security and Privacy"] Seeks Technology Safeguards." There were now "New Tools (and Qualms) for Domestic Spying in Federal Campaign Against Terrorism." "Have we pulled the curtain on privacy?"—"Perhaps there's a higher vantage point that discloses a path to safety and security without trampling freedom." Intent on "Keeping the Lid on Personal Information," "State legislatures are working on ways to protect consumers against identity theft." In mid-2005, "House Votes for a Permanent Patriot Act" as "Lawmakers beat back challenges to the scope of antiterrorism law." A year later, in "The Death of Privacy," "Phone calls are just the tip of the iceberg." Even so, there were "Differing Views on Eavesdropping," with "Americans . . . divided on an antiterrorism program, a new poll finds." Meantime, on a different matter, the Supreme "Court widens scope of property seizure" and "rules . . . that local governments can take homes and other property for private development."[24]

6. SEXUALITY AND ETHNICITY

Sexual Harassment and Bias

A major topic of wide public interest in America during the 1990s and beyond in matters of sexuality (the earlier long history of which in America was studded with a rich firmament of regulatory/legislative acts)[25] has been that of sexual harassment. This topic—which in a number of unfortunate cases has involved lawmakers themselves firsthand—has spanned a wide spectrum of cases. In 1992–1993, for instance, there were the following. "Schools Are Newest Arenas For Sexual Harassment Issues," as when, among many such cases in different states, "in the California legislature, a bill was introduced last month to make sexual harassment by students grounds for suspension or expulsion." Interest was also drawn, by comparison, to a spate of laws and codes of conduct issued by European countries against sexual harassment in the workplace—"Harassment or Flirting: Europe Tries to Decide" ("The culture accepts familiarity. But should the law?"). "A U.S. Senator (Brock Adams) cries foul to sexual-misconduct charges." "Ex-Aides Allege Sexual Advances by Senator Packwood." "Accusations Against Senator [Bob Packwood] May Pose Test for Congress." "Accusations Against Hawaii Senator [Daniel Inouye] Meet a Silence in His Seat of Power." "Senate Ethics Panel at a Crossroads" as "Packwood Case Poses Tough New Test for Disciplinary Process." "[Supreme] Court Sets a 2-Year Limit On Sexual Harassment Suits" in "Ruling [That] Says Time Is Factor in Such Cases." "Top Investigator at Government Health Agency [Is] Accused of Sex Harassment." "Senate Backs Tough Action On Packwood" and "Votes To Subpoena Packwood Diaries," even though "A right to privacy is invoked against the power of Congress."[26]

Such accounts continued on in 1995–1998. "Students Use Anti-Bias Law to Attack Sexual Harassment by Classmates," while "School officials see they could face legal penalties." "Packwood Complaints Have a Nervous Senate Hearing Echoes of Anita Hill." "Packwood Says He Is Quitting As Ethics Panel Gives Evidence." As "issued" by the Department of Education, "New Guidelines on Sexual Harassment Tell Schools When a Kiss Is Just a Peck." "Sexual Harassment: The Paula Jones case shows how confused the law is. Here's what's legal and what's not," while President "Clinton's fate rests on laws that tie even lawyers into knots" (in "Sex And The Law"). "The Court Weighs Differences In Sexual Harassment Law." In "A Matter of Definition," Anita Hill's OP-ED asked "Have we forgotten the foundation of sexual harassment law?" "[Supreme] Court Spells Out Rules For Finding Sex Harassment" and "Makes Suits Easier to Win While Giving Employers a Defense," as "Decision Heartens Jones Team." In "The New Rules Of Sexual Harassment," "The Supreme Court defines what harassment is and who can be held responsible."[27]

There were parallel news reports on sexual bias. In 1991, a "Rash of Sex-Bias Suits [Is] Expected From New Law" (passed in 1991—subsequent to the Civil Rights Act of 1984 and with more restrictive provisions—shortly after the Thomas–Hill hearings in 1991), as "Women get new incentives to pursue bias cases." A few months later, "High Court Opens Path for Students to Sue in Sex-Bias Cases" and "Rejects [Bush] Administration's Position on Scope of

1972 Law." As its "Ruling Reshapes Gender Outlook," the "US Supreme Court forces colleges to rewrite policies giving parity to women's sports." Over two years later, "The new women's issue . . . [is] bankruptcy law" after a Congressional "bill would give creditors more leverage to pressure financially troubled families. A growing number of these are headed by women." In 2000, the "Case of Princess Accused of Pushing Maid Down Stairs Reveals a Failing of a New Law."[28]

Sex Crime

In 1990s sex crime, "Tougher Laws Mean More Cases Are Called Rape." "[N.J. Supreme] Court Says Sexual Assault Can Occur Without Force" in a "Ruling [That] Upholds Trenton's Tough Rape Law." "Judge in Florida Voids Statutory Rape Law." "Lawsuit By Priest Charges Sex Abuse," which "Case Is First Use of Rackets Law to Make Sex Charges and Against the Church." More generally, in 1995, "Yes, Statutory Rape Is Still a Rather Big Deal." That year, a "Sexual Assault Trial Puts a Chicago Congressman's Career on the Brink." Also, "Megan's Law [named after a young N.J. girl killed by rapist] Won't Reduce Sex Crimes" because "The key is longer sentences without parole." In a related way the next year, "House Approves Bill to Require Notification on Sex Offenders" in "Legislation . . . Modeled After New Jersey Statute." Then "Clinton Signs Bill on Warning of Sex Offenders." More broadly, "Clinton Backs Plan to Track Sex Offenders Nationwide." "States Are Rushing to Curb Sex Crimes," and "California leads way with crackdown on statutory rape, [with] use of 'chemical castration.' " However, "In United States, Canada, New Laws Fail to Curb Demand for Child Sex." A better model would be a "Longer Arm of the Law" as in the way "Australia goes after its nationals who abuse children abroad." "Justices Sound Sympathetic but Troubled on Law to Confine Sex Offenders." "High Court Refuses to Hear Challenges to 'Megan's Laws.' " By 1998, "Sex-Crime Laws Draw More Flak" as a "California case highlights tension between children's safety and offenders' privacy." It was asked, "Do 'Megan's Laws' make a difference?" in that "Pariah status may not deter sex offenders." A "Trial Is Testing Louisiana's Sodomy Law" in "The Latest Chapter in a State-by-State Legal Campaign." A Federal "Court Upholds Law Barring Pornography Of Children." There was another "Wave of Laws Aimed at People With H.I.V.," and their "Protection of Public in Tough Measures Is Shift in Focus," albeit "Criminalization Laws [Are] Troubling to Officials."[29]

Such reports continued on past 2000. "In 16 States Sex Offenders Serve More Than Their Time Under New Laws," for "Completing a sentence does not necessarily mean release," but "Can predictions of criminal behavior justify keeping people in custody?" In sexual abuse cases, such as those facing the Catholic Church, "U.S. Laws Post Risk Of Steep Penalties," financial and otherwise. "Laws on Sex Offender Lists to Get Further Look." "[Supreme] Court Appears Ready to Reverse a Sodomy Law." In various ways by 2003, there was "A seismic shift in sex-case law." A year later, "Is the rape-shield law working?," inasmuch as "Personal details about Kobe Bryant's accuser are slipping into the press and courtroom—a serious setback, some say, for rape-case reform. But others argue that Kobe Bryant's lawyers are simply giving him the best defense possible."[30]

The New Puritans?

In the early 1990s, another outlook on certain foregoing matters was voiced through qualms over "Pornography and the New Puritans," with particular regard to "the pornography victims' compensation bill now under consideration by the Senate Judiciary Committee—that same bunch of wise men who dispatched such clearheaded, objective jurisprudence in the Clarence Thomas hearings. . . . The bill would encourage victims of sexual crimes to bring suit against publishers and distributors of material that is 'obscene or constitutes child pornography'—*if*" it caused a sex crime or offense. Accordingly, when "Pornography Foes Push for Right to Sue," "What some call protection, others call censorship."[31]

There were, indeed, "Passions over Pornography" as "A bitter debate divides feminism and some of its liberal backers. At issue: free speech vs. the civil rights of abused women." "Despite Ban Threat, Cybersex Stays Hot." Even so, "On-Line Service Blocks Access To Topics Called Pornographic," while "Complaint by Germany Has Worldwide Impact." At the same point in time, in "Rewriting 'The Scarlet Letter,'" "Hawthorne's Heroine Goes Hollywood" in a "new Disney version."[32]

In the later 1990s, a Federal "Judge Blocks Law Intended To Regulate On-Line Smut." Also, Federal "Judges Visit Cyberspace Sites In Suit Over An Indecency Law," with regard to "Protections for children and issues of free speech." In a ruling, "High Court Splits On Indecency Law Covering Cable TV," permitting certain commercial channels to ban indecent programming but "Community-Access Channels Are Freed of Restrictions for Protecting Children," for "Technology is said to make an indecency law unnecessary." That same 1996 "ruling on Internet speech may be symbolic but have little practical effect" even though "Opponents of Indecency Rules On Internet Win Another Case." That year, "Yesterday's Morality Police Teach Lessons for Today," and "Books on Film Censorship Offer Cultural Context." In 1997 there was a "Spirited Debate in High Court On Decency Rules for Internet," but "Does a law to shield children stifle speech?" As for "Adultery, the 19th-Century Sin," it was still a cases of "When the private becomes public." According to Robert Bork's 1997 OP-ED piece, "And Now, The Sin Police," "The morally superior want to ban liquor and legislate virtue." Similarly the next year, in "Cover That Keyhole," another observer wrote that "Bill Clinton may behave badly, but the really worrisome guy is Ken Starr." On "Wield a new moral yardstick," "Some see 'sexual McCarthyism' in exposing politicians' infidelities; others see call for higher standards of conduct."[33]

A New Tolerance?

When asking whether there was, in other respects, "A New Tolerance?" in sexuality during the 1990s and beyond into post–2000, a number of select topics enter one's response, such as abortion, gay rights in general, gays in the military, contraception, and so forth. There will then follow other topics on this subject in matters of ethnicity.[34]

Turning first to abortion, the ensuing items from 1991 to 2005 center around various legislative dynamics. "1871 Law [Is] at Issue in Abortion Dispute" in which "Abortion foes say women's rights are not involved." "House Acts To Ban Abortion Method, Making [Its] Use [a] Crime," in "Bill . . . Focused on Infrequent Procedure That Opponents Graphically Attacked." "House Votes to Override Clinton's Veto of Abortion Bill," and "The tide has turned at last, abortion opponents say." "Protests at Abortion Clinics Have Fallen, and New Law Is Credited." "Senate Fails to Override Veto of Ban on Type of Abortion" known as "partial-birth." "O'Connor Calls on President To Sign Bill on Abortions," with "Banning of Late-Term Procedure . . . at Issue." "House, by Broad Margin, Backs Ban on a Type of Late Abortion," yet Senator "Lott Says Senate Lacks Votes to Override a Veto." "Appeals Court Upholds Ban On a Type of Late Abortion." "Senate Votes to Ban a Controversial Abortion Procedure." "Senate Revisits Ban of Abortion Procedure; Passage Expected and Bush Gives Support." "Abortion Might Outgrow Its Need for Roe v. Wade." Nonetheless, the Supreme Court's long-standing decision permitting abortion in Roe v. Wade continued to be called "the law of the land."[35]

Gay rights during this period are also apropos. In 1993, "Gay Marchers Throng Capital in Appeal for Rights" in "A Celebration Mixed With Demands" as "March Takes Gay America To Milestone." Soon enough, "Gay Rights Laws Can't Be Banned, High Court Rules," declaring "Colorado Law Void" and "Discriminatory"—"For some, . . . 'the most important victory ever.' " "President Would Sign Legislation Striking at Homosexual Marriages." "High Court Boosts Gay Rights In Key 'Culture War' Decision." In House subcommittee, there was a "Bitter Debate, Then a Vote for Rejecting Same-Sex Marriage." In "The new civil rights battle," "The Supreme Court hands gays a win in the struggle between tolerance and tradition." "Anti-Discrimination Proposal Delays [U.S.] Senate Vote on Bill Opposing Same-Sex Marriage," while "Foes of Gay Marriage Are Foiled in California Senate." "Bill Against Same-Sex Marriage Is Passed" in U.S. Senate. "Clinton Signs Bill Denying Gay Couples U.S. Benefits." "Laws Aside, Some Members of Clergy Are Quietly Blessing Gay 'Marriage.' " "Do Homosexuals Need More Legal Protections?"—"Murder of a gay student in Wyoming . . . raises doubts on hate-crime laws." "Gay Couples Are Divided by '96 Immigration Law" because "Under 1996 Act, Personal Commitments Are Not Recognized." "The problem with laws protecting women and gays" is that "Good Causes Make Bad Laws." "House Backs Adding Gays to Hate Crime Law." "Social change has yet to bring legal equality for gays," who enjoy "More Respect, but too Few Rights." There was a "Big boost for privacy rights" when, "In a ruling on a Texas law, the Supreme Court strengthened both gay rights and abortion rights." Concerning "Gay Marriage and the Law," "What would it mean if rights end at the state line?" "What Marriage Means to Gay Couples: All That Law Allows Others." In mid-2004 "U.S. Senators Block Initiative To Ban Same-Sex Unions" when "Amendment, Endorsed by Bush, Fails After Days of Debate." Some state legislatures were approving same-sex civil unions, such as in New Jersey in early 2007, whereas only Massachusetts by that time had approved regular marriage for same-sex couples.[36]

As for gays in the military in the late 1990s, "War Is Hell. So Is Regulating Sex," leaving the conundrum of "How to reconcile a warrior culture with modern standards of sexual behavior." "Let's Be Honest About Sex in the Military" and realize that "The rules should be sharpened." Not long thereafter, "Pentagon to Tighten Army's Fraternizing Ban."[37]

Other matters of regulatory/legislative interest on sex and sexuality in the mid-1990s included contraception and other practices. "Fears, Suits and Regulations Stall Contraceptive Advances."

"High-Tech Pregnancies [Are] Testing Limits of Science, Law and Parental Hope." In a "New Law," "Congress Approves Ban on Genital Ritual" in the United States in reaction to "A rite of passage prevalent among African immigrants."[38]

On the same question just posed for sexuality on "A New Tolerance," a similar "yes and no" response applies to matters of ethnicity. Here various changing viewpoints could be noted before and after the 2001 terrorist attack with regard to immigration etc., in addition to other wider considerations. Already by 1992, a "Study Points to Increase In Tolerance of Ethnicity." A year earlier it was asked "Whose America?," inasmuch as "A growing emphasis on the nation's 'multicultural' heritage exalts racial and ethnic pride at the expense of social cohesion." It was called "The Fraying Of America" because "When a nation's diversity breaks into factions, demagogues rush in, false issues cloud debate, and everybody has a grievance." Showing the need in 1995 for "Making the Law Colorblind," "Crack will put you away, cocaine won't. Why?" "Nation's Campuses Confront An Expanding Racial Divide." "Will Clinton's race-relations initiative go beyond rhetoric?" when "Talking the talk, But. . . ." In 1999 came "The Final Showdown on Interracial Marriage" over the question of "Will Alabama revoke Dixie's last miscegenation law?" That year, "Racial Profiling Tops N.A.A.C.P. Agenda," with one black spokesman declaring "We've seen open season on black people." Much later, in 2006, "More Muslims Are Coming to U.S. After a Decline in Wake of 9/11."[39]

Affirmative Action and Desegregation

When "Defining The Issue" in the early 1990s, it was asked "To what extent should the law try to correct historic inequalities in employment?" As a result of "A New Push for Blind Justice," "Preferences for minorities and women are under attack in the courts, in Congress and on the ballot." Said one OP-ED piece, "Affirmative Action Must Go." A "Broad Group Visits President [Clinton] On Affirmative Action's Future," whereupon "He Says He Fears Issue Will Splinter the Nation." "Programs Based On Sex And Race Are Challenged" by Congressional Committees and Court." In "Fixing Affirmative Action," "American political leaders have now to erase the new injustice without regenerating the old." "Waning of Affirmative Action Leaves Many With a Sense of Uncertainty." "Affirmative Action Overhaul Before '96 Grows Less Likely" as Congressional "G.O.P. [Is] Putting Off A Ban" and "President . . . Is Expected to Set Forth Only Minor Revisions." In California[,] Board [of Regents] Ends Preferences In College System" in "A Victory For Governor [Pete Wilson]." Yet "Clinton Gives Fervent Support To Affirmative Action's Goals."[40]

Then in the later 1990s—with regard to a "Bad Law on Affirmative Action" as issued by the Supreme Court in 1978 in its Bakke decision approving preferences for sake of diverse student body in higher education—a "U.S. Court of Appeals declared that the Bakke decision is no longer good law." This was yet another instance of the Court's rulings being taken as the law of the land and as equivalent to or on a par with legislation. (Affirmative Action itself began under President Johnson's 1965 Executive Order.) To be expected, that "bombshell court ruling" received wide press attention amid wider national trends. Presidential candidate U.S. Senator Robert "Dole Sees Failure Of Three Decades In Anti-Bias Fight," "Backing California Initiative" and calling "Laws He Once Backed Misguided." In an OP-ED article of 1997 House Speaker Gingrich and California regent Connelly said "Face the Failure of Racial Preferences" because "Bankrupt social policies will not educate our children." On the same day, "Defending Affirmative Action, Clinton Urges Debate on Race" and "Calls Diversity Essential and Issues Warning on Resegregation" while urging a new set of racial initiatives. Yet two years later in "The post-affirmative age," "Colleges, under siege from the courts, are in vanguard of trying to achieve diversity without using racial preferences."[41]

Beyond 2000 on "Race and the Uses of Law," Ronald Dworkin's OP-ED article declared that "Affirmative Action is for the future, not the past." Not long afterward, "U. Of Georgia Cannot Use Race In Admission Policy, Court Rules," "Finding that adding nonwhites does not assure diversity." By early 2007, "Colleges Regroup on Diversity Efforts After Voters Ban Race Preferences."[42]

On legal segregation and desegregation, much of the changing policies and controversies in the 1990s and beyond revolved around legal regulation and deregulation. After many "Years on the Road to Integration," there were "New Views on an Old Goal." In one newspaper's book review on David Armor's *Forced Justice: School Desegregation and the Law*, concerning "The Case Against Busing," it was reported that "Court-ordered school desegregation hasn't worked, . . . so let's try something else." According to another such review of a book, concerning "Color-Blind in the Marketplace," "A conservative blames regulation for the troubles of black Americans." Then, "After Era of Experimenting on School Busing, Desegregation Debate Resurfaces" as "Recent court rulings give preference to neighborhood schools." Now it was "Back to Segregation" because, "After four decades of struggle, America has now given up on school integration," while "frustrated blacks dust off the concept of 'separate but equal.' " By 2000, "School Is Out on Desegregation in the Classroom," and "The few programs to create racially balanced schools are in legal and political jeopardy."[43]

Welfare and Immigration

Welfare reform went through a striking and complicated legislative/ regulatory process in the later 1990s, as some highlights will illustrate. A "Senate Panel Approves a Vast Overhaul of Welfare," while "Supporters and opponents agree the occasion is momentous." The "White House Seeks Areas of Welfare Accord With G.O.P." when, "With some changes, the President [Clinton] might accept the Dole legislation." Then the "Senate Approves Welfare Plan That Would End Aid Guarantee" for the poor after "A Run Of 60 Years," "Offer[ing] States Wide Latitude." This event was called "The Big One: Washington's Political Earthquake," a "Seismic Shift In the Parties [That] Reflects View on Business," after "The Social Engineers Let Welfare Go Unfixed." Yet with "Welfare Overhaul, Stymied in the Capitol, Proceeding at the State Level Nonetheless," the state legislatures, in particular, "Move Ahead on the Limits Envisioned in Congress." Was this really "The end of welfare as we know it? So far, reform has been less than revolutionary." Then "Clinton Says He Will Sign Welfare Bill to End U.S. Aid Guarantee," giving to "States Broad Power," as he "pre-empts [1996 Republican Presidential candidate] Dole . . . and moves further from the left." Then the "Senate Passes Welfare Measure, Sending It for Clinton's Signature." And "Clinton Signs Bill to Cut Welfare and Change State Role," so that "With Welfare Overhaul Now Law, States Grapple With Consequences." Over a year later, "Tougher Welfare Limits Bring Startling Results, But Deepen Frustration" "as Welfare Rules Change." Several months later, "Rigid Enforcement of Welfare Rules Is at the Heart of Welfare Cuts," with "Trouble Making the System Work." Yet soon it was said that "Move from welfare to work goes well as deadlines hit." "Who Should Still Be On Welfare?: Thanks to tough new rules, welfare roles have dropped almost 50% in the past six years. Now what should we do about the rest?"[44]

Immigration reform was another area, like welfare reform to which it was partly related, that passed through a complicated legislative/regulatory process from 1994 to the Immigration Act of 1996 and its long aftermath. A crucial dramatic issue was illegal immigration. A "Congressional Commission Calls for Crackdown on Illegal Aliens." Putting out "The Unwelcome Mat," "As the [California] Proposition 187 debate roars, the U.S. begins an intensive effort to seal off a 2000-mile border." An "Anti-Alien Movement [Is] Spreading in Wake of California Measure." "Congress Is Planning to Adopt the Most Stringent Curbs on Immigration in 71 Years" because "The public's anger over illegal aliens is pushing lawmakers." The "Senate Votes to Toughen Stance on Illegal Aliens" even though "Critics say such a law might cut off emergency services to the needy." Furthermore, "Congressional Bills Threaten Aid for Immigrant Students." Meantime, "Debate Over Immigration Bill [on legals and illegals] Yields Deep Political Divisions and Unusual Alliances." The "Bill to Limit Immigration Faces a Setback in Senate"—with "Division into 2 Measures . . . Likely"—through "A parliamentary move in a campaign year [that] may prevent a cut in legal aliens." Then the "House Approves Ending Schooling of Aliens" in a "Bill [That] Would Let States Expel Some Children." "Uncle Sam, bar the door," for, "As Americans grow wary of new immigrants, Congress moves to crack down on illegal aliens." Then "Senate Votes Bill To Reduce Influx Of Illegal Aliens," but "Measure Faces Reconciliation With a House Version, and Perhaps a Clinton Veto." Complicating matters further, "Strictness on Legal Immigrants Jeopardizes Bill on Illegal Aliens" through "Legislation [That] Would Severely Restrict Public Aid." As "Immigration Overhaul Moves Toward Vote," "Critics say the bill could put thousands of children onto the streets." "Some Immigrants Begin to Lose Food Stamps Under New Law," with "New York . . . Among States Taking Early Action." "House Votes 2 Bills to Curb Illegal Immigrants."[45]

Three weeks after "President Clinton signed a bill changing immigration rules," the U.S. "Government [Justice Dept.] Is Quickly Using Power of New Immigration Law" of 1996. Several months later, "Immigration Rules Enrage Russian Envoys in Seattle" over "Russian sailors . . . at the center of a diplomatic dispute." The new immigration "Law May Endanger Legitimate Refugees," and "Bipartisan panel urges Congress to change rules for asylum seekers." Soon thereafter, "Immigration Law's Fine Print Emerges, Setting Off a Debate About Welfare Provisions" as "A new income level sets up a roadblock for the unification of poor families." Also, the "New Rules at U.S. Borders Are Provoking Much Criticism." In "An immigration roundup," "Tough new laws are booting out the bad and the not-so-bad." The "Change in Laws Sets Off Big Wave of Deportations" after "Nearly 300,000 Are Expelled in 2 Years, a Record." A year later, in 1999, "As More Are Deported, a '96 Law

Faces Scrutiny." Then in 2000, "Correcting A Mistake," "The House softens the '96 immigration law." In early 2001, "Change in Law [at the end of the Clinton Administration] Stirs Hopes of Immigrants."[46]

After the 9/11 terrorist attack of 2001, there was a call for "Safer Borders," for "Securing our transport network against terrorists." "Vast requirements draw new scrutiny as authorities seek to keep terrorists out," while "Tightening the rules on legal immigration." "Immigrants Feel the Pinch of Post–9/11 Laws" when "The authorities 'look at us like we're terrorists.'" Congressional "Lawmakers Attack Immigrants' Use of Antitorture Law to Block Deportation." Questions were raised by some about "The Rule of Law and the War on Terror." In 2004, "Bush Would Give Illegal Workers Broad New Rights" in "Plan [That] Effectively Offers Amnesty—Fight Is Seen in Congress." In that "Well-Timed Reform," "Bush reaches out to Hispanics with an election-year plan to ease immigration law." In 2006, "Bill To Broaden Immigration Law Gains In Senate" and "Would Legalize Millions." Over a week later, "Senate Deal Set For Immigration, But Then Falters" due to "Conservative Opposition." "Where the G.O.P. Veered Off Course" was when "Tough immigration legislation prompted Latino voters to side with the Democrats." A "Bipartisan Group [Is] Drafting Bill For a Simpler Path to Citizenship," whereby "Financing for a 700-mile fence along the Mexican border could be cut off." Meanwhile, an "Arizona County Uses New Law to Look for Illegal Immigrants" and "invokes a state measure to enforce the border."[47]

7. CRIME AND PUNISHMENT

The politics of legislation at federal and state levels on crime and punishment was particularly intensive in the 1990s and 2000, well before the more volatile developments after the terrorist attacks of 9/11 in 2001. The changing tides of controversies and questions over crime and punishment, such as on gun control and the death penalty, pointed up once again the centrality of legislative/ regulatory topics. In 1994, "While California's tough three-strikes [and you're out] law falters, prevention programs are keeping kids in line," while seemingly "Going Soft on Crime." In 1995, "Does the Brady [gun-control] Law work? It snags some felons, but it's undermined by loopholes and illegal dealers" in "A Small-Bore Success." By other accounts, "Handgun Law Deters Felons, Studies Show" as "45,000 Are Denied Purchases in Year." "Brady putting up a fight, the states are giving in to new legislation as citizens clamor for the right to bear arms" in a "License to Conceal." "Thousands Seek Permits To Carry Concealed Arms" as "New Virginia Law Reflects Fears of Crime." "Assault Gun Ban Faces New and Capable Nemesis" as "House Freshman Pushes for Repeal." On another matter, "House Panel Adopts a Broad Measure to Fight Terrorism," under which "U.S. agent could pursue street criminals under a committee's plan." Several months later, however, "Bill On Terrorism, Once A Certainty, Derails In House" in "A New Distrust Of F.B.I." after "Waco and Idaho Hearings Help Destroy Consensus Formed After Oklahoma Blast." In any case, "Homicide Rate Drops Significantly in Nation's Big Cities," although murders could rebound as the number of teen-agers increases." With "More in U.S. . . . in Prisons," "Will there be more prisoners than students in America?"[48]

At the start of 1996 concerning "Law and Order," "Crime rates are down across the U.S.—some dramatically. Is this a blip or a trend?" But then the "House Kills Sweeping Provisions In Counterterrorism Legislation." In "Echo of Gunshots Past as House Votes" "to end a gun ban . . . , relatives of victims watch and wonder." "Congress Sets Stage For Swift Executions" in "A battle . . . between the Supreme Court and Capitol Hill on oversight powers of federal courts." "Clinton Signs Measure on Terrorism and Death Penalty Appeals." "Antiterrorism Bill Creates New Tools To Blot Out Crime," but "Will the death penalty deter future bombers?" Through "The law that grief built," "Oklahoma families help politicians get tough on murderers." "Successes Reported for Curfews, but Doubts Persist." "Long Arm Of U.S. Law Gets Longer" on "terrorist crimes that did not occur on American soil." "President Calls for Bipartisan Support to Pass Stronger Measures to Combat Terrorism." When "Listening in On Terrorism," "Current wiretap laws shackle investigations." "Secure, and Dangerous"—"Legislation could put people under suspicion for their political views." "Clinton Blasts G.O.P. Critics Of Terror Bill." "Clinton Suggests An Array Of Steps To Foil Terrorism" as he "challenged Congress . . . to finance a catch-all collection of . . . measures. . . ." Meanwhile, "A Large Drop in Violent Crime Is Reported." "After a Decade, Juvenile Crime Begins to Drop." Indeed, "Crime Rate May Be Down, but the Problem Stays Hot With Politicians, and Voters." "Criminal and Welfare Rules Raise New Issues of Fairness." The "Supreme Court Weighs Rights of States in Enforcing Brady Gun Control Law."[49]

In 1997–1998, "Congress wants to crack down on juvenile offenders. But is throwing teens into adult courts—and adult prisons—the best way?" As "US Seeks to Halt Flow of Illegal Gun Imports" and "Gun-Control debate intensifies," "Clinton prepares to order a 90-day suspension of imports of semi-automatic weapons." "Report

Links Crimes to States With Weak [Laws on] Gun Controls." "A New Law Requiring Locks On Handguns Takes Effect." "Clinton Calls For Closing Big Loopholes In Gun Law." However, "New Laws Won't Stop Hate." "Hate Laws Don't Matter, Except When They Do." "Punishment Alone Fails to Contain Juvenile Crime."[50]

In 1999, with the dynamics of the legislative process intensifying on gun control, "Now gun-makers are in the cross-hairs" in "A legal assault on firearm manufacturers." A Senate "Bill Would Subject Guns To Federal Safety Controls." "In Renewed Battle Over Weapons Control, Both Sides Use Attack to Advance Agendas," with one side saying "Gun laws won't prevent random violence." "Senators Reject Plan to Regulate Gun-Show Sales but Back Voluntary System." "Reversing Stance, [Senate] Republicans Urge A Gun-Sale Curb" "At Shows" in "Measure [That] Requires Background Checking, but Democrats Are Critical." "Senate Passes Bill Requiring Safety-Devices for Handguns." "Senate Votes Gun Curbs Hours After School Shooting" in Georgia. "Small-Print Provisions of [Senate] Gun Bill Please Federal Officials Most" because "Bill would make it easier to prosecute straw buyers of guns." "Clinton Faults House G.O.P. Gun Measures" and "Accuses N.R.A. of Wearing Down Limits Backed by Senate." House "G.O.P. weighs perils of a weakened gun-control bill," but "some want a law with less punch than Senate version." House "G.O.P. [Decides] to Separate Gun-Control Measures From Juvenile Crime Bill." "House Vote Deals A Stinging Defeat To Gun Control" as a "Weaker Measure Passes." "Gun-Control Bill Is Rejected in House in Bipartisan Vote." Vice President "Gore Calls on Republicans To Pass a Gun Control Bill," casting "Republicans as Election-Year Issue." "Timid anti-gun groups are part of the problem" through "Laws That Can't Stop a Bullet." "Behind drop in US murder rate . . . [is] a decline in gun crime," in that "Gun-control efforts and crackdown on firearm crimes . . . may be abating violence." Meantime, in "A Nationwide Backlash," "State and local governments are taking aim at the gun industry, either by enacting legislation or by filing lawsuits." "Drawing a bead on kids"—"Why a law designed to target teen violence isn't working." "Can laws really trigger gun control?"—"City and federal suits face hurdles in forcing safety code on gunmakers."[51]

Then, in 2000, "Gun-control movement makes strides in states, courts." Yet "Mentally Ill Slip Through a Hole in a Landmark Gun Control Law." And "Number in Prison Grows Despite Crime Reduction," as "Stricter Parole and Sentencing Laws [Are] Cited." "In most states, parole is a thing of the past" as "Several cases in California—and the spread of laws elsewhere—underscore the fall of parole nationwide."[52]

8. HEALTH-CARE AND MEDICINE

Legislative regulatory "tugs of war" by Congress, the White House, Federal agencies, states, political parties, and interest groups were a dominant factor in the ongoing surging struggles from 1991 to 2006 to reform and overhaul the American health-care industry. The same held true for its intricate multifaceted operations more generally.

By the second half of President Bush Sr.'s term in the early 1990s, there was growing recognition of "The crazy quilt of health insurance" as "A Sick System." "Washington Tries to Sort Out Health Insurance Proposals." An uncertain mixture of regulations set by government, the health industry, and the marketplace was moving slowly along. For instance, "F.D.A. [Set] to Review Regulations Backlog"; and "Health Industry Is Moving To Form Service Networks" in "Market-Driven Alliances," inasmuch as "Without Washington Legislation, Professionals Are Merging So They Can Compete." But by the very end of Bush's term, partly because of pressure built up over issues in his unsuccessful campaign for reelection against Clinton, "Under Political Steam, Health-Care Issue Gains Wider Support in Congress," even though, "Talk aside, a far-reaching health plan remains on the back burner."[53]

Against this background, the emerging Clinton Administration sought greater Federal legislative-regulatory controls in health-care reform and other medical matters, as led in part by First Lady Hillary Clinton. The Clinton agenda was stymied by the Republican takeover of the House and by the Clinton scandals, yet the long-range Federal legislative regulatory thrust left its mark in these as in other areas.

Under Clinton: Toward Greater Federal Legislative-Regulatory Controls

By the outset of Clinton's presidency in early 1993, "The Ideological War Over Health Care" was heating up, as "Conservatives Ignore History" and "Liberals reverse their traditional role." On the one hand, some said "Health Care Is Healing Itself" and "Price controls won't work"; and, "Wanting Help on Health Care, Many Worry About Government as a Helper," "fear[ing] they will get an insensitive bureaucracy instead of help," with "Opinions on health care deeply divided . . . [through] fire and passion." On the other hand, "U.S. [F.D.A.] Moves to Regulate Tissue Transplant Industry," "Seeking rules to insure safe[ty] and effective[ness]"; "Revolution in Health Care Industry Means Big Business for Specialist Lawyers"; and, "Entangled by Law, Boy Stays In Hospital That Failed Him."[54]

The struggle between the two political sides in the health-care debate heated up in 1995 and 1996 following the House Republican victories led by Newt Gingrich in the late-1994 mid-term elections. From then on, the legislative framework of health-care reform was controlling. That year, "G.O.P. Announces Its Plan For Overhauling Medicare," with some seeing "In the House Medicare Legislation . . . A Throwback to Budget Gimmickry" and "in some legislative fine print . . . the 'lookback sequester.' " The "A.M.A. [Is] Backing Republicans In Plan to Overhaul Medicare." With Republicans more in favor of the states, and Clinton the Federal government, in shaping health-care reform, "House Acts to Let States Bar Many Medicaid Abortions." "Angry Opposition Attacks the Process," with "Democrats Say[ing] Republicans Are Pushing Medicare Plan Too Fast." "Medicare Overhaul Bill Is Sent to House Floor" in "An escalating [legislative] fight for the political high ground on the budget." The "House Votes To Curb Costs Of Medicare By $270 Billion; President Promises A Veto," while "Senate Approval Will Set Stage for Clash on U.S. Spending," and, "For Elderly, Bill Promises Entry Into a Market of Shifting Forces." "House, Over Strong Democratic Opposition, Approves Bill to Broaden Health Insurance." "President Finds Benefits in His Defeat on Overhauling Health Care" and "Is Seeking Some Limited Goals," having made "Bold Move to Assure Universal Coverage" (with "everyone . . . required to join a health-care plan, and business . . . to provide coverage for all workers"), whereas "Republicans Try[ed] To Limit Federal Role." "U.S. [F.T.C. and Justice Department] Issues Guidelines to Help Doctors Form Health Networks" in "A policy move that appears to please doctors as well as H.M.O.'s." "Laws Won't Let H.M.O.'s Tell Doctors What to Say," while "16 States Give Patients Right to Be Informed," as "H.M.O. gag rules become a state and Federal issue." "U.S. [Dept. of Health and Human Services] Bans Limits On H.M.O. Advice In Medicare Plan," saying "Gags Violate Law," with "Congress Expected to Take Up Similar Rules That Apply to Private Insurance." "U.S. [Federal Health Care Financing Administration] Limits H.M.O.'s In Linking Bonuses To Cost Controls" in "New Rules [That] Apply to Medicare and Medicaid but Will Set a Nationwide Example."[55]

On various other fronts in 1996, "Ready to Test New Cigarette, Maker Fears Tough Rules" by Food and Drug Administration. "Quirk in Medicare Law Yields Bigger Bills for Outpatient Care," with "Officials Say[ing] Burden on the Elderly Is Increasing." "New pesticide standards [through bill passed by the House] will benefit children" by "Serving up a safer food supply." "Clinton Approves A Series Of Curbs On Cigarette Ads," with "F.D.A. to Treat Tobacco as Addictive Drug in Effort to Stop Minors' Smoking," although "Long Legal Fight Seen Likely." "Under New Law, Nursing Homes Might Reject Legal Immigrants." "Doctors Are Focus Of Plan To Fight New Drug Laws" as "Officials Deal With Narcotics' Medical Use."[56]

From 1997 to 2000, despite many setbacks, efforts for reform and regulation of health care continued on all sides during President Clinton's second term through further legislative struggles with Congress, the states, and interest groups. During the first half of Clinton's second term, "Congress Weighs More Regulation On Managed Care" as "H.M.O.'s and Employers Fight Federal Rules Establishing Treatment Standards." "New Health Insurance Rules Spell Out Rights of Workers." "Confused By Law, Nursing Homes Ban Legal Immigrants" in "Fear Over Lost Benefits" as "Struggle to Interpret New Rule Prompts Some Providers to Refuse All Noncitizens." "Battle Lines Are Being Formed In Congress' Medicare Fight," while "Big cuts will shape the future of the Federal health plan for the elderly." In "A magic Medicare moment," "The Senate, whatever its motives, has forced the issue." "U.S. [Clinton Administration] Alters Medicaid Rules, But New York [and Republican Governor Pataki] Isn't Notified." "Clinton [Is] to Call for Health Plan Regulation" through "A 'Bill of Rights' for Consumers [That] Portends a Bitter Fight in Congress." "Clinton Plans New Health Care Fight" "On Eve of [Mid-Term] Election Year, [through] a Proposal to Overhaul H.M.O. Rules." "Flouting Laws, Hospitals Overwork Novice Doctors." "Business Coalition [Is] to Fight Legislation Protecting Patients' Rights." "States Push to Legislate Managed Health Care." "Legislating a Patient's Rights" was becoming ever thornier. "Presidential Panel Sees No Need for a Law on Patients' Rights." "House Republicans Unveil Bill to Define Patients' Rights." "2 Patients' Rights Bills Take Divergent Roads," with "Democrats and Republicans . . . Far Apart." Needing "Patience for a bill of rights," "States [in legislatures] begin to move on HMO reforms while Congress argues." "Senators Reject Bill To Regulate Care By H.M.O.'s," with "Patient Rights At Issue," as "Health Care Measure Is Victim of Intense Lobbying Effort and Clinton Sex Scandal."[57]

During the second half of Clinton's second presidential term, in "The People Vs. H.M.O.'s," "most Americans can't sue their health insurer. Reform [urged on Congress by Clinton in a Patient's "Bill of Rights"] is about to change that." "Help for the Uninsured May Rest in Tax Code," which "Is the Focus of New Health Care Bills" in Congress. In "The deal that got away," "The president pulls the plug on a proposal to fix Medicare." "Clinton Plans to Cut Medicare Over the Long Term While Expanding It to Cover Drugs" "for all beneficiaries." "Clinton Details His Proposal for Overhauling Medicare," while "Senate Agrees on Framework To Weigh Patient's Rights Bill," as "Democrats appear to have engineered another victory." "Who Will Swallow Medicare's Bitter Pills?" in "The next political battle [that] suddenly swings into sight: covering ever more costly prescription drugs." "Health Care Bill Passed By House Intensifies Furor" over "G.O.P. Tax Break Measure," which, "Denounced by Democrats, . . . [is] Melded to Legislation They Want on Patient Rights." "House Passes Bill To Expand Rights On Medical Care," with "Suits Allowed in Insurance Denials," as "Lawmakers rebuff Republican leaders on managed care." "Is universal health care still in the works?" as, "Step by step, Clinton has enacted many elements of his failed plan for federally funded health care." "Health care reform may be coming but in little pieces" as "GOP in Congress shows signs of making a deal with President Clinton on some budget health proposals." "Political Battle Lines Are Clearly Drawn in Fight Over Medicare Drug Coverage," "a major issue in this year's [presidential] election," thereby "Revisiting an age-old debate: government vs. the marketplace." "U.S. [Clinton Administration] Plans Tighter Rules On Medical Files' Privacy" as part of a "Patients' Bill of Rights," in "Regulations [That] Go Beyond Those of Last Year." "Whose Pill Is Sweetest?: In the [presidential] debate over reforming Medicare, Bush says HMOs should take charge, Gore says Washington." In the presidential election-year debate over health policy, some saw the trend as being "Toward Universal Coverage."[58]

On still other legislative-regulatory fronts in health-care and medicine during this period, "Senate Votes Ban on Late Abortion, but Veto Is Likely Again." Because of "outbreaks of disease in the U.S." due to "increases in . . . imported fruits and vegetables," the "President Wants to Tighten Rules on Imported Produce." "Clinton Again Vetoes Measure to Ban a Method of Abortion." "Marijuana Advocates Sue To Stop Federal Sanctions," against which "Californians Claim Free Speech Violations." "States And Cities Impose New Laws On Young Smokers." "Senate Panel Sends Smoking Bill to Floor for Tough Test." "Marlboro Man to Congress: Drop dead,"

"But an antismoking law is likely anyway." "Give Doctors Tougher Rules," urged one OP-ED piece, for "Most medical mistakes could be averted." Through "A Lockbox for Medical Records," "Patients' information will be better protected under new privacy rules." In "Hippocrates vs. Big Brother," "We can't trust the Government with our medical privacy."[59]

Under Bush Jr.: Toward Less Federal Legislative-Regulatory Controls

In line with his tendencies toward deregulation, decentralization, privatization, and federalism (or states' responsibilities) in many other areas of his public policies, President George Bush Jr.'s Administration has tended toward less Federal legislative-regulatory controls in health-care and medicine. Naturally legislation has still provided a central matrix of the new Bush programs and agendas in these matters in dealings with Congress and the states, in addition to the legislative-like Executive rulings by the Administration's departments and agencies, including by the President himself. Yet the regulatory machinery behind legislation on health-care and medicine has tended, on the whole, toward deemphasis on the centralizing role of the Federal government, in favor of more decentralizing approaches. Legislation has obviously been a main medium through which the Bush Administration has necessarily continued to work in order to achieve its objectives, in addition to those of Congress and the states themselves, on health-care and medicine, as in so many other areas. To be sure, there were some partial exceptions, as in the Federal government's intrusions and restrictions at the expense of privacy following the 9/11 terrorist attacks on America, in contrast with its deemphasis on regulatory safeguards to protect patients' privacy in their medical records.

On health-care reform, the legislative path ahead for the new Bush Administration could often be difficult or uncertain. Shortly after he took office in early 2001, "States Ask Bush to Revoke Clinton's Medicaid Rules" because "Health care regulations issued last month [in the final hours of the Clinton Administration] are flawed, officials say." Even so, several months later, a "Bill Establishing Patients' Rights Passes In Senate," a "Measure Setting Standards for Health Insurance . . . [In] Victory for Democratic Leaders." Moreover, two years later, there was "A major Medicare expansion" in "a long-needed overhaul" as "Congress takes up prescription-drug benefits in what may be the biggest enlargement of social services in years." Truer to form, in the presidential race of 2004, "Bush

Describes [Democrat challenger] Kerry's Health Care Proposal as a 'Government Takeover' " urged by "a big-spending liberal." Similarly, "Bush Says Kerry Is Pushing Nationalized Health Care." By 2006, the Bush Administration was coming under heavy attack by Democratic critics and others for failing to address the health-care problem. One editorial faulted the Federal government for doing "such a miserable job of providing health insurance for . . . Americans who lack it," while calling for "Mandatory Health Insurance" and supporting the plans recently worked out by the Massachusetts governor and legislature. Yet by then "Health Care, Vexing to Clinton, Is Now at Top of Bush's Agenda." Then in early 2007, with Democratic mid-term victories in House and Senate, a "Congressional Power Shift Revives Health Care Debate" as "House Democrats try to rush through legislation requiring the government to negotiate lower drug prices for Medicare beneficiaries and overturning President Bush's restrictions on embryonic stem cell research."[60]

"Medical privacy rules give patients and marketers access to health data," it was reported in early 2001. Yet ensuing months told a different story. The "Medical Industry Lobbies To Rein In New Privacy Rules," which are "Intended To Aid Patients," because "Standards Imposed by Clinton Are Called Too Costly" yet are soon to take effect in the new Bush Administration. Then "Health Secretary Delays Medical Records Protections," "Rethinking privacy rules issued as Clinton left office." As for "The Privacy President?," "Bush and the courts lead, Congress to follow." "House Republicans Urge Bush to Ease Health Care Rules," saying that "New federal privacy requirements are . . . unworkable."[61]

The extent to which the new government vigilance after the late-2001 terrorist attacks may have contributed to the shift away from the above developments and toward "A new policy on records" in 2003 when "Health System Warily Prepares for New Privacy Rules." Notwithstanding, as matters became more relaxed again by 2006, "Critics say lax enforcement puts patients' files at risk" due to "An Ailing Medical Privacy Law."[62]

Despite these and other deregulatory legislative directions on medical matters in the Bush Administration's approaches to the Federal government, the basic need for an underlying regulatory legislative framework in the American nation-state remained crucial in one way or another in a variety of other such areas. "Child safety efforts [are] hampered by weak laws" as "Parents face uphill battle to get manufacturers to take responsibility for defective products." "A call for federal oversight of fertility clinics" is made by "Medical ethicists [who] see need for regulation of clinics that create and store embryos." "Bioterror Drugs Stall Over Rules and Logistics." "Meeting Minimum Rules Set By Congress, Clinic Falters on Mammography," while "Senator Says It's Time To Upgrade Standards"—the same "senator who wrote the original law regulating breast-cancer screening." "Opponents of Circumcision Use the Legal System and Legislatures to Combat It." The Supreme "Court considers reach of US disability law," while "In certain circumstances, Congress has the power to mandate what the states must do. Is this one of those cases?" "House Passes Bill Tightening Parental Rule for Abortions; Backers See Hope." "Stem-cell research surges ahead of lawmakers" when "Researchers announce a significant breakthrough as US House is about to consider reversing a stem-cell ban." "C.D.C. [Federal Center for Disease Control] Proposes New Rules in Effort to Prevent Disease Outbreak," that is, "through this proposed rule making." "Diabetics at Work Confronted by a Maze of Laws and Requirements."[63]

Striking in the preceding paragraph, as in so many other cases in this book, are the cross-identifications between legislation and regulations, laws and rules, made by the three Federal branches (not to mention by the states). All this reinforces, once again, the all-encompassing unceasing ebbing and flowing of the legislative-regulatory core of the contemporary American national state.

9. THE ENVIRONMENT

The same kind of policy shifts on health-care and medicine occurred also on environmental and related concerns during the Clinton and Bush Administrations. During Clinton's first term, newly assertive regulatory-legislative approaches were on the rise along with counter-measures against them. "The Regulatory Thickets Of Environmental Racism" involved the effects of "regulations on pollution . . . [upon] minority neighborhoods." "Tougher Car Emission Rules [Are] Requested by Eastern States." "Builders Fight Environmental Laws In an Effort to Reclaim Polluted Land." "Proposed Changes Simplify Rules on Pollution Control" so as "to Reduce Costs for Businesses." "Environmental Groups . . . Urge Opposition to Regulatory Changes" through "a reversal of environmental legislation," led by "the Republicans who now control Congress" in the House. "State Lawmakers Urge House to Reject Changes to Clean Water Act." "Crossing Party Lines on Pollution Bill Clouds Future of Environmental Issues" as "Many Republicans oppose easing clean-water rules." "House Votes Sweeping Changes in Clean Water Act." "Future of Endangered Species Act [Is] in Doubt as Law Is Debated" concerning a "Senate bill would weaken enforcement on private lands." "G.O.P.'s Plan for Environment Is Facing a Big Test in Congress" in "Votes Planned on Curbing Regulatory Powers." "House Coalition Sets G.O.P. Back On Environment" as "The White House Gains." "Critics Fault Federal Enforcement of Laws Regulating Animal Trade." Again at odds with the Clinton Administration, "Congress [Is] Likely to Repeat Many Environmental Disputes as New Budget Takes Shape." "Clinton Signs a Bill on Water Contamination" in "far-reaching" legislation to "help states upgrade municipal water systems." "[Clinton] Administration [E.P.A.] Issues Proposal for Tightening of Air Standards." "Stricter Rules On Pollution Would Have Broad Effects" through "The Clinton Administration's [E.P.A.'s] new proposal to tighten national air quality standards."[64]

During President Clinton's second term, "States [Are] Neglecting Pollution Rules, White House [E.P.A.] Says," with "Sanctions Threatened." "Deadline Nears for States to Develop Antismog Plan" as "Coalition Tries to Avoid New Federal Rules." "House Rejects Bill to Soften Provisions In Species Act." "More G.O.P. Environmental Wars" were raging against "environmental laws." "Nation Holds Its Breath Over Clean-Air Rules" in advance of "White House decision . . . on how tough to make standards." At this point, "Environmentalists Are Putting Pressure on [Vice President] Gore for not doing even more" on "toughening air pollution standards and negotiating deep cuts in worldwide emissions of worldwide gasses." "Clinton Sharply Tightens Air Pollution Regulations [through the E.P.A.] Despite Concern Over Costs." Meanwhile, activist "Courts [Are] Expanding Effort To Battle Water Pollution" in "New Enforcement Tactic" with "Environmental Groups Suing by Employing Little Used Provision in 1972 Law." "A big rise in environmental spending is seen" as "Politicians of All Persuasions Rally Round Rival Bills to Protect Lands." In California "Tough Rules Are Approved For New Paint." A "Landmark bill [on preservation] shows Congress' greener side" through "bipartisan support." In a dilemma over "How to preserve a court victory without throwing out government rules," while "Challenging as Inadequate the Federal Guidance Offered on Environmental Standards," an "Attack on Clean Air Act Falters in High Court." In "Need to balance official authority over air and water," "Two Supreme Court cases challenge federal controls."[65]

Over the course of the Bush presidency in environmental and related areas, there were, first off in 2001, such reports as "Montana Republicans Seek to Ease Environmental Laws" as "A state's business-oriented plan gains momentum with Bush in office." "U.S. Offers Further Delay to Forest Rules" inasmuch as "Clinton Policy Is

Said To Need More Study." "Efforts to Save Wetlands Are Inadequate, Study Says," "Contending that a federal rule meant well but has failed." In a "Free-For-All In A Forest," "Clinton made last-minute nomination, but Bush has delayed full protection. Result: everyone's jumping into the fight over the rules." "Bush Administration Rolls Back Clinton Rules for Wetlands," "Easing the way for developers and miners." "Bush Offers Plan for Voluntary Measures to Limit Gas Emissions." "Bush opts for incentive-based CO_2 cuts." A liberal editorial decried the "Undermining [of] Environmental Law" by "the Bush Administration [which] has spent . . . two years rolling back . . . Clinton's environmental legacy." "Enforcement of Environmental Laws Has Slipped, Democrats Say." "On Environmental Rules, Bush Sees a Balance, Critics a Threat." "Absent a federal effort, the states tend to the 'greenhouse,' " such that "The Warming Is Global but the Legislation in the U.S. Is All Local." "Most States Expect Pollution To Rise if Regulations Change and the Bush Administration's changes to the Clean Air Act were to take effect." But then in early 2004, "Smog regulations just got tougher" in new standards announced by the E.P.A. Less than two weeks later, "U.S. [Federal] Court Blocks Rules For Snowmobile Emissions," as "The E.P.A. is told to explain its rationale for new standards." A year later, "Rebuffing Bush, 132 Mayors Embrace Kyoto Rules" on global warming. In "Cleaning Up the Air," "Some States Adopt California's regulations that automakers call too burdensome." In late 2006, "EPA controversies head to Congress" as "Its staffers go to hill over global warming."[66]

10. GOVERNMENT AND LAW

Finally, many questions have arisen in recent years over the role of American government—especially at the Federal level through laws, regulations, and programs—in solving problems at times of crisis and more generally. Starting here in 1999—"In wake of the Colorado shootings, can tougher gun control or other laws help?," that is, what is "The role of Washington in curbing youth violence?" "Is poverty fixable?: In some places, maybe not. The president's trip to Appalachia highlights years of failed efforts." "Anti-Federalism Measures Have Bipartisan Support" in "Senate and House . . . [which are] preparing legislation that would make it harder for Congress and the executive branch to adopt laws and rules that pre-empt the states on a wide range of issues, like drugs, the environment, health and worker safety." As for "Lean Budget, Bloated Government," "In Washington . . . no program ever dies."[67]

In 2000, as to "What the Microsoft Case Is Really About," "The government is defining and shaping the contours of the new economy." "Bush, in a Broad Attack on Gore, Paints Him as the Candidate of Big Government." "Bush Criticizes Gore's Health Care Programs as Efforts to Create Bigger Federal Role" (with echoes of the earlier Clinton–Gore efforts at "reinventing government"?).[68]

In 2001 and beyond, the role of government was questioned on different fronts as the Bush presidency endeavored to implement its policies in conjunction with Congress. In the beginning, "Bush, for all his sunny national cheerleading, is also the anti-Reagan. Ronald Reagan railed against government in theory but loved it in fact." A year after the 9/11 terrorist attack, in questions over "A Proper Balance," some believed that "The Patriot Act allows government snooping, but at what cost to privacy?" "U.S. [Bush Administration] Issues Rule Over Right-of-Way Disputes on Federal Lands in the West," as "Conservationists again attack a Bush policy." On "The Incredible Shrinking Government, Bush Style," "Whether the impetus is managerial or ideological, the impact may be great." Others asserted that, in fact, "Government Is Getting Bigger," "But Does That Make It Better?" In mid-2004, "9/11 Report Calls for a Sweeping Overhaul of [Government] Intelligence" and "Cites Many Lapses and Inaction at Agencies." A year later, on a different issue, Supreme Court "Justices Uphold [Government] Taking Property For Development" in "Case of Eminent Domain," "Clarifying the Power to Seize Private Land for 'Public Use.' " In the aftermath of the 2005 hurricane that devastated New Orleans, "Breakdown Marked Path From Hurricane to Anarchy" after "Federal Authorities Were Hesitant to Aid Beleaguered State and Local Officials," with "Little Unity in Government." "Despair And Lawlessness Grip New Orleans As Thousands Remain Stranded In Squalor," while "[Government] Response Is Assailed." In late 2005, "Bush Issues Order to Ease Access to Government Information." In Congress there was "An 11th-hour drive to amend Patriot Act," but "some say privacy needs protecting." In 2006 "U.S. [Federal] Judge Finds [that Government] Wiretapping Program Violates Law." In 2007 "House Tightens Disclosure Rules For [Its] Pet Projects" in an "Anti-Corruption Effort."[69]

As for the American legal system and practices of litigation, the mid- to later 1990s saw many efforts at reform especially in and through Congressional legislation. A sign of rising tides of lawsuits came in 1993 when "Armed With New Laws, Middle-Aged and Older Workers Fight Discrimination," leading to ever "More Age Discrimination Cases." Then in 1995 came some decisive actions. "House

Passes Big Change in Legal System," with "Lawsuits Discouraged," in "Measure [That] Would Force Losers in Certain Cases to Pay Their Opponents' Costs." A few days later, "House Passes New Standards Limiting Awards in Civil Suits" by "Overhauling the Legal System: The First Round." According to ensuing news reports that year: "While Washington debates rules about litigation, down in Alabama, the lawsuits grow thick and wild" "Where the Torts Blossom"; "Misguided Legal Reform" was occurring; then "Senate . . . Approves Narrow Punitive Damages Curb" ("On to a conference committee, and an uncertain fate"); "The Law Is a Mess," "But a radical law professor in Chicago is ready to clear it up" (in his book *Simple Rules for a Complex World*); "Push for Limits on Lawsuits Seems to Have Lost Its Way"; and "Lessons of [O.J.] Simpson Case Are Reshaping the Law" ("Fighting a public perception of a system gone awry"). In 1996: "Suing is a state sport. Now there's a backlash" from those "Fed Up with Lawyers"; "House G.O.P. Drops Bid to Curb Civil Suits" and "Quits Tort Reform Plan"; "Backers of Limits on Lawsuits Win a Victory in the Senate" ("The stage is set for a confrontation with political overtones"); and "The campaign to cancel Congress's litigation reforms" would lead to "Lawsuits Unlimited." In 1997–1999: "Limits on Lawsuits and Damage Claims Could Bring Years of Legal Fights" ("A 'bitter pill' for cigarette makers may be more sour for the opposition"); "Laws capping jury awards are the latest battleground for state legislatures, courts," prompting, "In states, a clash of titans over jury awards"; "Asbestos Cases [Are] In for Overhaul By Lawmakers" as "[Supreme Court] Justices Ask Congress to Alter Legal System"; and "Lawyers Contend With State and Federal Efforts to Restrict Their Rising Power" in "a time of challenges from courts and lawmakers."[70]

In 2000–2002 other issues came to the fore. Some groups were "Bringing Lawsuits to Do What Congress Won't," because "For more than three decades gun-control advocates have pressed lawmakers for stiffer measures but the gun lobby ensured that they got nowhere in Congress." "After Sept. 11, [there has been a] Sprawling Legal Fight Over Limits of Civil Liberties." "Litigation cannot bring solace to the victims of Sept. 11," with some people "Facing the Limits of Law, and Lawsuits."[71]

ADDENDA

On gun control and related matters during George Bush Jr.'s presidency, especially after the 9/11 terrorist strikes, there was a curious "internal" legislative conflict or prevarication in its inclinations to ease Clinton-era restrictions on firearms yet also to strengthen them and others in response to the new terrorist threats. In 2001, for instance: "Gun Control Advocates Signal a Retreat" as "supporters look to the states for legislation"; "Bush loosens restrictions on guns" and "rolls back some controls, drawing criticism that it is too pro-NRA [National Rifle Association]"; "Gun Foes Use Terror Issue In a Push for Stricter Laws"; and "More in US carry guns; restrictions lose support" "in post-attack US." In 2002, "Wired for controversy," "Critics say it's time to loosen up a surveillance law"; and "Sniper Suspect Obtained a Rifle Despite Restraining Order and Gun Laws" in "A case that backers of gun control say points to weaknesses in the law." In 2003, "Senate Kills Effort to Extend Life of Broad Terrorist Law." In 2004, "Some gun dealers say the now-expired law against assault weapons sales made no difference"—"A Ban That Didn't Stop Much." In 2005, "Many Say End of the Assault Gun Ban Changed Little." Similarly, in 2003–2004: there were other reports on conflicts over rights vs. security in connection with the post–9/11 Patriot Act: "A fierce fight has emerged over the secrecy and scope of the Patriot Act in the war on terrorism" ("Civil Rights?"); "U.S. Uses Terror Law to Pursue Range of Criminals," yet "Bush Steps Anger Critics of Expanded Powers"; on "How to Protect America, and Your Rights," "Both sides are playing politics with the Patriot Act"; and "House Passes Tightening of Laws on Immigration" ("Drivers' Licenses and Asylum Are Focus").[72]

In a different vein, there were diverse accounts, as in 1997 to 2006, of conflicting viewpoints on religious rights and roles in terms of religious legislation. "Enabled by a new law, churches step into the gap left by the failure of traditional welfare" ("Feeding the Flock"). "Will a new federal law give religious freedom even more protection than it has now? Or will it erode other basic liberties?" ("Law on Bended Knee"). "On the docket . . . [is] religious freedom vs. drug laws" as "The Supreme Court takes up a case involving a New Mexico sect that could be important for other minority religions." "From Day Care Centers to Use of Land, Rules Don't Apply to Faith Groups" when "Religion Trumps Regulation As Legal Exemptions Grow" ("Secular Laws Cede To Religious Exemptions").[73]

The wrenching seesaw public debate in spring 2007 over the Senate's immigration bill, supported by the Bush White House, was dominated by concern over illegals now or to come in the United States who could add to the threats of terrorism. At first in May "Senators [Are] in Bipartisan Deal On Broad Immigration Bill" that "Offers Legal Status to Millions," albeit "Prospect Uncertain in the House." "Immigration and trade bills reflect a willingness to face a changed reality" "in Washington, but Can It Last." Then "Critics in Senate Vow to Alter Bill on Immigration; Calls in Both Parties for Changes" arise as "Lawmakers . . . See Flaws in Measure" that is "backed by Bush but caught in political crosscurrents." "In Congress, a long road ahead [is foreseen] for immigration bill." On the one hand, "Immigration Bill Provision Gain Wide Support in Poll" as "Majority Favors Path to Legal Status for Illegal Aliens." On the other, "Fury Grows Over Immigration Bill," which "riles many" in a "Backlash." Meantime, "Overhaul of Immigration Law Could Reshape New York." In June "President's Push On Immigration Tests G.O.P. Base" as Conservative Anger Rises." "Immigration Bill Stalls in Senate in a Setback for Bush," with "Republicans . . . Key in Blocking Effort to End Debate on Measure" and to send it for a full vote up or down. Democratic Senator "Kennedy's Plea Was Last Gasp for Long-Sought Immigration Measure in Senate" in "An issue that crossed party lines, to leaders' consternation," thus contributing to "failure of . . . bill." "The Grass Roots Roared, and an Immigration Plan Fell" after "A single hot-button word was repeated often and viscerally. Amnesty." Meanwhile, "States, localities push own reform plans" on immigration, "proposing and passing laws at a record pace, irked by federal inaction." Even so, in late June "Immigrant Bill Dies in Senate, Defeat for Bush," with "Both Parties . . . Split on Broad Overhaul." "Immigration Bill Falls Amid Calls To Enforce Laws." An article from this same period on legal integration in education asked questions that could be applied to the crucial immigration issue: "If the Law Changes, Will Society Follow?" or "Can a Law Change A Society?"[74]

The close interconnection between rules and laws, regulations and legislation, in the halls of Congress and the public at large was typified in 2007 when "Senators urge more stringent rules for toy safety," in light of recent dangerous defects, with calls for "revamping of the Consumer Product Safety Commission, includng giving it the power to ban lead in all childrens' toys." "The Need for Regulation" of "All the Nation's Imports" "And Especially Our Children's Toys," as urged in a lengthy "Bush Administration" proposal, will need Congressional legislative approval and funding, with a new regulatory "government Agency" in charge.[75]

PART TWO

United States Foreign Policy in Legislative and Other Contexts of Sovereignty and State: Current News History

Chapter VIII

U.S. Foreign Policy Under Clinton

Having looked extensively at United States government in current perspective, we now turn briefly to United States foreign policy not only as an integral part of that subject but also as a bridge to our ensuing examination of other countries and regions in the Western hemisphere, to be followed by a second book on the Eastern hemisphere. Along the way here, U.S. military affairs will also find a place. The available materials on U.S. foreign policy are perhaps at times less closely tied to "legislative and other contexts of sovereignty and state" than was the case in Part I on U.S. government. Yet among the many direct connections made here between U.S. foreign policy and legislative factors of sovereignty and state are those related to the first and second Gulf Wars and their repercussions. Other more generalized slants on U.S. foreign policy represented here will also prove useful for fitting the United States into the broad main subject of this volume—"World Perspectives and Emergent Systems for the New Order in the New Age"—starting with the Western hemisphere comprising North and South America.

1. GENERAL BACKDROP

In the early 1990s during the presidency of George Bush Sr., the Cold War was ending. The Soviet Union was collapsing, and the Gulf War against Iraq in the Middle East was reaching a decisive climax. In both cases, the outcome marked a victory for the United States yet also a crucial turning point leading in new uncertain directions for U.S. foreign policy and world affairs in general. Also in both cases, the Executive–Legislative powers and processes in U.S. government were crucial in charting the courses ahead for the American ship of state. The central roles of President and Congress in specific legislative contexts of sovereignty and state in the conduct and conclusion of the Cold War and Gulf War during the early 1990s will also find a place when we turn to regions of the Eastern hemisphere in the next book.

In later 1991 and early 1992, there was a real transition underway in U.S. foreign policy. Said one source, "Opinion Builds for Smaller U.S. Role Abroad," with "Attention Shifting to Domestic Problems as Epoch Begun at Pearl Harbor Draws to a Close." However, said another, "Fearing that growing domestic problems may give rise to a new wave of U.S. isolationism, Secretary of State James A. Baker III says the United States cannot afford to become disengaged from world affairs now that it is the last remaining superpower." There were "Tough Questions for U.S. as Companies Seek Ideas Overseas," such as "Will the United States lose its edge in world markets if it ignores the globalization of technology?" But when "Rethinking Foreign Affairs: Are They Still a U.S. Affair?" Or was it "Toward a Policy That's No Longer Foreign?" as "The real global revolution is just beginning." It was reported that "U.S. Strategy Plan Is Aimed at Thwarting Emergence of Rival Superpower" in "A rejection of collective internationalism." Others said "The Pentagon still yearns to police the globe." Yet "Senior U.S. Officials Assail Lone-Superpower Policy." According to ex-President Richard Nixon, "We Are Ignoring Our World Role," and he strongly criticized President Bush for "not doing more to help stabilize Russia in the wake of the Soviet Empire's collapse." "Nixon Scoffs at Level of Support For Russian Democracy by Bush."[1]

As 1992 progressed, the beginnings of a new outlook were emerging. One news article called attention to the " 'Balance of Restraint' in an Unsettled World" and "How the Globalist Reality Can Replace America's Multipolar Strategy." A "Committee [of "foreign policy experts"] Defines U.S. Goal In World" and "Sees a Post–Cold-War Malaise That Can Be Corrected by International Focus." As that "Carnegie panel lays out a new agenda and shows how to finance it," it is "Redefining National Security." Speaking of "Our Country's New Role in the World," the authority McGeorge Bundy noted that "When the Cold War ended, our global responsibilities—and restraints—are changing." Said another, "Forget About the American Century . . ." ". . . And start thinking about America." Or again, there should be "A New Foreign Policy for a New Era."[2]

Then, in the last days of the Bush presidency, "U.S. And Russia Agree On Atomic-Arms Pact Slashing Arsenals And The Risk Of Attack" as "Bush, backed by [President-Elect] Clinton, rushes to meet a deadline." Shortly thereafter, "Bush and Yeltsin Sign Pact Making Deep Nuclear Arms Cuts," while "Clinton says he plans to keep U.S. policy on Somalia and Russia," thereby "Downsizing the superpowers' atomic arsenals to fit a changed world" in "A Last Treaty of its Kind As Bipolar Order Fades."[3]

2. FIRST TERM

Post-War Isolationism or Involvement?

The directions in foreign policy taken during President Clinton's first term unfolded gradually in the midst of a new world situation and a new dynamic at home in relation to Congress and party politics. In 1993, "As Ethnic Wars Multiply, U.S. Struggles to Meet the Challenge" and "Strives for a Policy," for "In Baring Old Hatreds, the Cold War's End Imperils the Peace." The Balkan countries were only one of the many such areas where a resurgent nationalistic drive for independence and sovereignty was in evidence, as the United States sought to maintain its dominant superpower status. For some observers, it was the "Pox Americana, Not Pax Americana" inasmuch as "We can't keep new great powers from arising." To others, "U.S. Power, Less Than Super" meant that "America has no real answer to a resurgent Russian nationalism." Still others were "In Search of the Clinton Doctrine." According to "President Clinton's national security adviser, . . . the Administration's foreign policy vision . . . aimed to replace the cold-war policy to contain the Soviet threat with a policy to enlarge the family of democratic market economies," leaving "U.S. Vision of Foreign Policy Reversed." Secretary of State Warren "Christopher Presses Policy Of Engagement With Asia" in line with "Clinton's decision to renew China's preferred trade status."[4]

Needless to say, the roles of Congress were and would be many in the implementation of the Administration's foreign policy. This involvement became more pronounced, even at times confrontational, after the Republican mid-term election victories of 1994 in the House of Representatives, now led by Speaker Gingrich. Shortly after those elections, Secretary of State Christopher reassured leaders of South Korea and other countries that, in the words of one report, "U.S. Promises To Maintain Foreign Policy" and "G.O.P. Gains Won't Bring Change." However, a few months later, an OP-ED piece by the Secretaries of State and Defense, entitled "Foreign Policy, Hamstrung" ("Clinton should veto this 'national security' bill"), stated: "This week Congress is to consider legislation that would undermine this and every future President's ability to safeguard America's security and to command our armed forces. The measure is deeply flawed. . . . The bill would return the United States to a crash-schedule deployment of a national defense [a la Reagan], designed to protect the U.S. from missile attacks. . . . [T]he bill unilaterally and prematurely designates certain European states for NATO membership. . . . [T]he bill would effectively abrogate our treaty obligation to pay our share of the cost of U.N. peacekeeping operations that we have supported in the Security Council." An editorial on "Global Mandate" ("The public isn't isolationist") declared that, in the wake of the Gulf War, "Mr. Gingrich and [Senator] Mr. Dole . . . want to appeal to Republican isolationists [concerning the U.N. etc., yet also] to Republican internationalists with Wall Street portfolios."[5]

At that point in early 1995, "Foreign Aid . . . [Is] Under Siege in the Budget Wars" inside Congress and between it and the White House. There was a general effort to "Redefine 'Foreign' Aid in Post–Cold-War Era." "Call It Aid or a Bribe, It's the Price of Peace." "Do Fickle Markets Now Make Policy?" ("Mexico is the Vietnam of the economic domino theory"). The "Disunity in Foreign Policy" "between the Republican Congress and Democratic Administration," according to one editorial, is heightened by "Misbegotten Republican legislation that would seriously damage United States interests." Countered Senator Dole's OP-ED response, "Who's an isolationist?"—"Hint: Giving out 'development' aid is not the test." An OP-ED by Arthur Schlesinger Jr. averred that "New Isolationists Weaken America."[6]

The tug-of-war over foreign policy continued in the Legislative-Executive arena. In the Senate Foreign Relations Committee, "Awaiting Clinton's Call, [Senator] Helms Keeps Foreign Policy on Hold" on a wide range of key measures, such that "In his campaign for State Dept. reforms, the Senator takes more hostages." "[N.Y. City Mayor] Giuliani, at U.N. Opening Ceremony [addressed by House Speaker Gingrich], Assails New Isolationist Mood in Congress" as he "again sets himself apart from G.O.P. conservative wing." As the

1996 election-year presidential contenders Clinton and Dole squared off, there was an emerging "Foreign Policy Campaign." Clearly, "Clinton's Foreign Policy . . . [Faces a] Tough Election-Year Test," where "leadership is one thing, but success would help."[7]

Emerging Viewpoints and Challenges

To some observers in 1996, there were now clear signs of "The Third American Empire" in "The new client states stretch[ing] from the Balkans to the Persian Gulf" ("Collect them all!"). Some spoke of "Yankees, come here" insofar as, "Despite limits and setbacks," "U.S. clout overseas is steadily rising." More specifically, "Clinton's Visit to Tokyo Is a Time to Think Big," for "The US and Japan should be able to work out enough differences to focus on their common global agenda." Clinton was becoming a "Foreign Policy Wonk" in his "strategy for '96." Even " 'Green' Issues Become Force In Driving US Foreign Policy": "For decades, the United States has defused national security threats in terms of nuclear arsenals, arms balances, and hostile alliances. . . . [S]ince the end of the cold war, policymakers have become increasingly attentive to 'natural' occurrences, such as poverty and overpopulation, . . . that can implicate US interests abroad," including "[t]he growing importance of environmental concerns in foreign policy. . . ." Meanwhile, "In Post–Cold-War Washington, Development Is a Hot Business" as "Foreign Lending Agencies Attract Deal Makers."[8]

At the same time, "US Diplomacy Enters Era of Uncertainty" around the world. The rise of terrorist threats was a case in point as "Clinton Signs Bill Against Investing In Iran and Libya" in an "Anti-Terrorism Measure," while "Germany and France Condemn Law Since Their Companies Could Face Sanctions." Once again, "Iraq Tests the Limits." In "Clinton's World Vision," "Haiti and Israel aren't 'peripheral,' " contrary to Republican critics who argue that the Clinton Administration "has focused on peripheral national security issues and does not understand the importance of consistency or the need to honor commitments." In the Middle East, as elsewhere, "Clinton's Choice . . . [Is] Chaos or Diplomacy." In humanitarian crises in Africa and Bosnia, with massive miseries and genocides suffered by civilians and refugees caught in conflicts, there was a question to the United States on "How and When to Intervene for Humanity," for if governments would acknowledge the "requirements" and "sanctions" laid down by the Geneva Conventions in such matters and "enforce these laws, as they are obliged to do, there would be less unpredictability about their humanitarian response."[9]

On the one hand, the "World Waits for Clinton's 'Clarity of Purpose' " in "US foreign policy . . . [, which] should [aim at] protection of the national interest and the spread of freedom." On the other, "Increasingly, US Finds Itself Whistling Alone" as "A great backlash is brewing as America's allies become uncomfortable blindly supporting a number of US policies."[10]

3. SECOND TERM

Executive-Legislative Entanglements

At the start of President Clinton's second term, Secretary of State Madeleine Albright set forth a "Blueprint for a Bipartisan Foreign Policy," with "The first tests: the foreign policy budget and chemical arms." Yet reality became a little different during these four years. "When Foreign Aid Makes a Difference," critical Congressional "Republicans are right to complain about waste. But the system can be fixed." Later on, "Clinton battles Congress over cuts in US foreign aid." "Albright complained . . . that Congressional unwillingness to pay what the United States owes to the United Nations has hamstrung the Administration's ability to influence the organization."[11]

Nuclear testing was a key issue. "Senate G.O.P. [Is] to Allow Vote On Pact to Ban Nuclear Tests," for "The Republicans think they can kill a Clinton treaty" "banning nuclear testing," "one of President Clinton's top foreign policy goals." In "New era of doubt over arms deals," "Woes of test-ban treaty may signal end of bipartisan accord on arms control" due to "a raging [Senate–White House] battle over whether . . . [to] ratify a treaty. . . ." "After the Senate's disappointing defeat of the treaty," some still urged "Don't Give Up on the Test Ban" because "There is support from both parties for nuclear nonproliferation." In an "Ailing Foreign Policy," the "Lack of Strategy to Pass Nuclear Treaty Could Hurt Clinton's Authority Abroad" in "A new era of closer scrutiny on national security." Several months later, the conservative Republican "Right's Anti-ABM Weapon . . . [Is] A Senate Clause on Russia"; "Moscow is told how it can beat a new missile shield" as "Russians Get Briefing on U.S. Defense Plan."[12]

As the Congressional–Presidential struggles over U.N. funding and related matters developed in 2000, "Mr. Helms [appearing] at the U.N." struck a much-criticized recalcitrant pose, warning that "the United States would withdraw if the U.N. 'sought to impose its presumed authority on the American people without their consent,' " thereby resulting in their "loss of sovereignty," while "the entire exercise proved to be a revealing discourse on the nature of international law and order in the post–cold-war world." A few days later, Secretary of State Albright addressed the U.N. Security Council and strongly declared that "Only the president . . . can speak for the American people" in such matters, not the chairman of the Senate Foreign Relations Committee. "Senate Fight Snags Aid Bill For Kosovo And Colombia." "Fight over foreign agenda stalls US initiatives overseas" as "Clinton–Congress bickering . . . may ultimately hurt America's image abroad." Over a month later, "One Senator [Judd Gregg] Blocks Spending on Peacekeepers." But then, the same "G.O.P. Senator Frees Millions for U.N. Missions in Sierra Leone."[13]

On a separate matter in 2000, "Senate Approves $1 Billion To Aid Colombia Military" for "Financing War On Drugs," while "House Passes Another Version—Critics Say U.S. Faces Open-Ended Conflict." As "Congress moves to aid Colombia's war on drugs," was it stepping "Into The Quagmire"? Then a "$11.2 Billion Spending Bill Is Readily Passed by Senate" in "A bigger commitment to fight drugs in Colombia." Also, the "House Votes $1.3 Billion to Help Colombia Fight Drug War," and it "Includes Peacekeeping Funds for Kosovo and for U.S. Flood and Fire Victims."[14]

Internationalism with Wilsonian Echoes

Internationalism clearly had its ups and downs in U.S. foreign policy during the Clinton Administration's second term, as with regard above to the United Nations and nuclear arms control. So, too, did coalition-building and use of sanctions. Yet the trend was definitely toward involvement rather than isolationism. To the extent there was a diminishing of internationalism in those and other respects later on in Clinton's second term, especially as its domestic crises intensified, it was a diminishment from higher levels reached earlier in that term despite setbacks.

As for "Why US Sticks With Foreign Policy by Coalition," "This year's [1998's] crises with Yugoslavia and Iraq put multinational alliances to the test." Through "Addiction to Sanctions," "At this rate, the whole world will face U.S. penalties." "Iraq Is Smuggling Oil To The Turks Under Gaze of U.S.," with "U.N. [Embargo] Sanctions Ignored," inasmuch as "Washington Looks Away Since Trade Aids Ally and Kurds Who Keep Iraqis at Bay." Around the world, "U.S. [Is] Backing Off Use of Sanctions, Seeing Poor Effect Abroad." "Unrest in the Balkans is again forcing the United States to further define its role in post–Soviet world security," leaving "America unsettled over global role." Even so, in "Clinton's Positive Thinking: The NATO Alliance Is Alive and Kicking." Addressing the question "Is the West too quick to sanction?," one news report called attention to "The blanket of US sanctions around the world. . . . President Clinton has issued more than half the 125 sanctions ever imposed by the U.S."[15]

There were perceived Wilsonian echoes. Clinton's uses of the United Nations and his difficulties with the recalcitrant Senate and its Foreign Relations Committee Chairman Helms offers a remote partial parallel to Wilson's embrace of the League of Nations as thwarted by the Senate and Helms' distant predecessor, Lodge. So also does Clinton's efforts at international alliances and coalition-building. Then, too, there was the principle of each nations' self-determination as envisioned in Wilson's "Fourteen Points" and in different ways by the Clinton White House.

Various news accounts were suggestive. "Woodrow Wilson Lives" in regard to the question of "Self-determination for Kosovo?," an historic part of Serbia's territory under siege by Serbia in a struggle over "sovereignty" and policies of the United Nations, N.A.T.O., and the United States. Some oblique comparisons between Clinton and Wilson on use of force and war by one democracy against another were made in 1999 (notwithstanding "the Clinton Doctrine of peace and security through a crusade for democracy" alone) in connection with Wilsonian democratic idealism abroad that could be combined with military might: as when "Woodrow Wilson proclaimed a war [to make the world safe] for democracy" and thereby shattered "The Myth of Democratic Pacifism."[16]

Contrariwise, it was said by 1999 that "Foreign policy lacks coherence. So does the world these days"—"So Much for Grand Theories." "As U.S. Relations With U.N. Languish at Low Point, Is Clinton or Congress to Blame?" "Clinton Urges U.N. to Intervene More," "Focusing only briefly on the $1.6 billion the U.S. owes." Yet in "Clinton's Positive Thinking: The NATO Alliance Is Alive and Kicking."[17]

4. THE MILITARY

During President Clinton's second term, there were "New Rules in New Kind of War," insofar as "Strikes against Ossama Bin Laden's terrorist network may represent a model for post–cold-war military action," including in the type of weapons used and in the rules of engagement. Moreover, there were "Lessons of a remote-control war," for "Despite pinpoint-bombing campaign, NATO's

Kosovo victory came at heavy price." "Clinton Describes Terrorism Threat for the Next Century," although his "Military proposals face an uncertain future in Congress" as he "Focus[es] on Germ Warfare" and "Studies Naming Military Chief for Continental U.S., a Plan Rights Groups Oppose."[18]

Meanwhile, "Pentagon [Is] Ready to Shrink Arsenal of Nuclear Bombs" and "Would Save Billions on Arms It Plans to Scrap." "Faced with vacancies, the Pentagon eyes lower standards," "Dumbing down the military." As for "Why US debates cutting warheads," "Some lawmakers urge unilateral US nuclear cuts to induce Russians to winnow its inventory." "By Wide Margin, Senate Approves Missile Defense System" as "Rogue Threat Forces Opposition to Yield." "House Joins Senate in Voting for System to Defend Against Missiles."[19]

The role of Congressional lawmakers was striking in a hot-button issue of theft of military secrets by former cold-war foreign powers. A "bipartisan" "House Report Finds China Stole American Nuclear Secrets" and used them "to Upgrade [Its] Arsenal." Then the same House "Panel Spells Out Spying Charges Against China; Clinton Backs Tighter Security" and "Assures Public of Counterespionage Measures." Albeit "The cold war is over, the spy game isn't," for "US arrest of a Russian diplomat for spying shows how intense espionage remains between old rivals." In later 2000, "Congress Stiffens Law on Disclosing Secrets" through "A bill [that] would make almost all unauthorized disclosures felonies."[20]

At home and abroad, several slants on sexuality involving military laws, rules, and standards enter the picture on Clinton's first term. "Clinton Aides Study Indirect End To Military Ban on Homosexuals." On "Gays in the Military," "An executive order would be overturned" so "Let Congress Decide," argued one commentator back in 1993 who was seeking to "Cancel Reagan's Ban." With "Clinton in Crossfire," "Compromise on the Military's Gay Ban Comes Under Attack From Both Sides." "Military Policy on Homosexuals . . . [Is in] Legal Limbo for White House and Troops." On other matters in 1996: "President Finds a Way to Fight Mandate to Oust H.I.V. Troops"; and "Supreme Court Rules That State-Supported Military Colleges Cannot Bar Women."[21]

Then, during Clinton's second term, "Flinn [Air Force 1st Lt.] Illustrates Gap in Military, Civilian Law," in that "Adultery is treated more harshly, and unevenly, by services." "2 Star General [Longhouser] Is Retiring After Admitting Adultery." "Military Rules on Morality Are Defended" by "Defense Secretary [Who] Denies Services Are Conducting a 'Witch Hunt.' " "Drawing 'A Line'

[Secretary of Defense] Cohen [Is] To Forgive General's [Ralston's] Affair." In comparison, "For Military in Other Nations, Pragmatism Overrules Principle"—"Over There, Different Rules on Sex." In late 2000, "Rules on Gays In the Military Lose Support Of President," who "Admits 'Don't Ask,' Policy Has Been Failure"—for which he "Criticizes The Pentagon," saying that "'93 Policy on Gays in the Military Was Not Properly Enforced by Its Leaders."[22]

Chapter IX

U.S. Foreign Policy Under Bush Jr.

1. FIRST TERM

In the first year of President Bush Jr.'s first term—prior to the 9/11 terrorist attack on the United States and the U.S. counter-attacks on Afghanistan and Iraq—his foreign policies and involvements were noticeably more restrained and even withdrawn in comparison with those of his presidential predecessor. As "Bush's Security Blanket," "Condoleezza Rice [national security adviser] must steer a leader whose foreign-policy outlook is in progress." "On the World Stage, Bush Shuns the Spotlight" and, "In marked contrast from Clinton, . . . prefers the shadows." As for "Who's Making Foreign Policy?," "[Secretary of State Colin] Powell's Steadfast Moderation" "holds the center against conservative viewpoints." Bush's "Major Address on Missiles Buoys Republicans, but Fails to Win Over Bush's Opponents" when, "In Strategy Overhaul, President Seeks Missile Shield," calling '72 Treaty "Outdated," as he offers "A new plan [that] may find critics in Congress and among allies" and that has "few details."[1]

In 2004, "Looking Back at Powell's Claims" in early 2003, one sees, according to one writer, "A Flawed Argument for War" against Iraq, while Powell had "demanded 'solid' intelligence after being shown a smoking gun." According to former national security adviser to President Carter, Zbigniew Brzezinski, Bush chose "The Wrong Way to Sell Democracy to the Arab World." Meanwhile, it was reported, "U.S. Officials Fashion Legal Basis to Keep Force in Iraq," through arguments that give "American commanders the authority needed to maintain control after sovereignty is handed back" to Iraqis in mid-2004, so that, officials say, "Iraqis could hardly claim that Iraq's sovereignty was compromised by having its troops under American command when nations like Britain and Poland had placed military contingencies here under an American general." On "Bush, Kerry and Iraq's sovereignty" a few months before the 2004 presidential election, "This week's milestone—the transfer of power in Iraq to an interim government—is a vital factor in the US election."[2]

That same year saw the waning of America's somewhat softer handling of the Iraq War's repercussions in the Arab world under Secretary of State Powell, which was soon to be replaced with a harder approach under his successor, Rice, in the Bush second term. Several diverse story lines are broadly suggestive: "Strange Bedfellows: 'Imperial America' Retreats From Iraq" ("The world's superpower has never been comfortable as a colonial administrator"); "Talking Our Way to Peace" ("The United States must reassert itself in the Middle East")—an OP-ED piece by James Baker, Secretary of State in the previous Bush Administration; "U.S. Slows Bid to Advance Democracy in Arab World" ("With damaged image, Americans approach a meeting cautiously"); "An Obsession the World Doesn't Share" ("On other continents, America doesn't even get credit for what's going right"); "A Victory for Hard-Liners" ("U.S. foreign policy is likely to take on a sharper edge with Powell's departure"); and "Conflicts Within the Agency [State Department] Pose a Risk for Rice." That year also saw the Administration's stance on interrogating foreign detainees to be steadfast yet precarious with regard to the rules of war and of law: "In fog of terror war, some rules [are] set" ("Congress ended its session trying to specify how to treat terror detainees—and opted to give Bush leeway in interrogations"); and "The Rule of Law and the Rules of War" ("The Geneva treaties apply to Iraq"), an OP-ED article by Alberto Gonzales, counsel to the President and future Attorney General.[3]

2. SECOND TERM

The President Resurgent

In January 2005, following his decisive re-election victory, "Bush, At 2nd Inaugural, Says Spread Of Liberty Is The 'Calling Of Our Time,'" while he also emphasized "the rule of law." There, calling "Freedom 'best hope for peace,'" "Bush . . . linked US security to the spread of freedom." A week later, "Bush Portrays Iraq Vote [by its citizens for a new elected government] As Step In a Global March to Freedom." Likewise, "Bush Presses Russia on Democratic Reforms." In some respects, with "The rise of [Secretary of State] Rice and a new 'realism,'" "The Bush administration's response [is] a more cooperative approach to the world."[4]

The Bush presidency's resurgence soon ran into difficulties in foreign affairs. As for "The Realities of Exporting Democracy," by the end of 2005 and early 2006, "Bush's goal of 'ending tyranny in our world' has run into roadblocks." On into 2006 concern mounted over "A Faltering Coalition" on Iraq, with implications for attempts to deal decisively with Iran's nuclear program. Yet "Behind Bush's hard line on Iran," "more vehement than other nations," "the administration may see the US as the only one prepared to take action." With "Crises Around the Globe," "From North Korea's missiles to Afghanistan's crumbling security, Bush has his hands full." It was "The End of Cowboy Diplomacy" due to "What North Korea, Iraq and Iran teach us about the limits of going it alone." "Bush's Unintended Internationalism" was having its limitations. In "Rethinking the War on Terror," "Courts, Congress and allies press the White House to rework strategy."[5]

Meanwhile, Congress was dealing legislatively with the issue of detainees, with some advantages for the president. In September 2006 "House Passes Detainee Bill As It Clears Senate Hurdle," with "New rules . . . set to become law even as a senator calls them 'un-American.'" Then the "Senate Approves Broad New Rules to Try Terrorism Detainees" in "Bill [That] Strips Terror Suspects of Habeas Corpus and Guides Questioning." In fact, "Detainee Bill Shifts Power To President," and "Creates Legal Basis For Policy on Detainees." Put another way, "A new bill lets Bush define who is an enemy combatant . . . ," "Letting the President Say." In other areas, "Terror Laws Cut Resettlements of Refugees" in "A web of post–Sept. 11 laws [that] snares Cubans, Vietnamese, Laotians, and Burmese."[6]

Congress Resurgent

The tide was turning when in early November 2006 the mid-term Congressional elections brought Democrats to power, with assertive Representative Nancy Pelosi soon sworn in as new Democratic Speaker of the House. The turnover or turnaround increased problems and risks for President Bush's foreign policies especially in the Middle East and Iraq in particular. The situation seemed to be a repeat in reverse of the 1994 mid-term Congressional elections that brought Republican Speaker Gingrich to power as an assertive threat to President Clinton's domestic as well as foreign policies and programs.[7]

Already in November–December of 2006, prior to the incoming Democrats' swearing-in, Congressional Democrats were flexing their new political muscles. "With New Legislation, Democrats Aim to Save Inquiry Into Waste and Fraud in Iraq" through "Investigations . . . expected to reach beyond the military." Seeking "to put their new political power to use in shaping the debate over Iraq," "Democrats, Engaging Bush, Vow Early Action Over Iraq," "Say[ing] They'll Demand Troop Reduction Plan and Bolster Oversight on Other Issues." As "Democrats Push For Troop Cuts Within Months" through "A Phased Redeployment," "White House Says It Is Open to 'Fresh Ideas' but No Timetable." "Democrats Plan to Take Control of Iraq War Spending" while "Trying to Exert Powers of Congress to Alter the War's Mismanagement," albeit "Emergency Bills [Are] Faulted." Among "The Prescient Few, Headed for Power," "Some Democrat lawmakers who opposed Bush's war plan will chair key committees." It was "Culture Shock on Capitol Hill" when "Democratic leaders announce a new 5-day workweek for the House of Representatives." To this Congressional counterthrust by newly resurgent Democrats, "Bush [is] firm on push for democracy."[8]

A sign of the balance of power beginning to shift to Congress on foreign affairs and Iraq was the widespread good reception given in December 2006 to the Baker–Hamilton report on Iraq issued by a bipartisan commission set up by Congress many months before. This "Panel Urges Basic Shift in U.S. Policy in Iraq" in a "Rebuke for Bush—Situation Is 'Grave.' " Yet "Bush Distances Himself From 2 Key Ideas of Iraq Panel" and "Doesn't Embrace Pullback Plan or Talks With Iran and Syria," resulting in "Dueling Worldviews" in that "Baker's Emphasis on Negotiations Clashes With the Mind of Bush." "Bush Aides Seek Alternatives to Iraq Study Group's Proposals, Calling Them Impractical." Contrariwise, "The Iraq Study

Group repudiates Bush's policies for the war and the region." One newspaper took a different tack toward the "Surrender Monkeys" on the "Iraq panel [that] urges U.S. to give up" ("Iraq 'Appease': Squeeze Out W."). On the one hand, said some, "Chaos Overran Iraq Plan in '06, Bush Team Says." On the other hand, said others, there was "Missing: a functional Iraqi State" even though "The weak Iraqi government, riven by factious, is still crucial for stabilizing the nation."[9]

Executive–Legislative Showdowns

In January 2006, with Inauguration Day fast approaching, "Bush [Is] Facing a Deep Divide with Democrats Over Talk Of Increasing Troops in Iraq." "House Democrats' Security Bill Draws Doubt, Even Inside Party." In House and Senate, "Democrats Plan Symbolic Votes Against Bush's Iraq Troop Plan." Once the new Democrat-led Congress convened, the Iraq debates quickly entered into its wide new agenda set forth in "A session of tricky issues and contentious hearings," yet "After the 100-Hour Show Comes the Slog."[10]

The Executive-Legislative showdown heightened when in mid-January 2006, contrary to the Baker–Hamilton proposals, "Bush [Will Be] Adding 20,000 U.S. Troops; [and] Sets Goal Of Securing Baghdad," while he "Says Iraqi Government Could Fall if America Steps Back Now," even though Congressional "Democrats Plan to Fight Expansion Of Troops." "Bush's Plan for Iraq Runs Into Opposition in Congress" with "Devastating Criticism by Both Parties" after "A 2-Month White House Debate On Iraq . . . [Is] Capped by 'the Big Push.' " Although "Gulf Allies Support Goals Of New U.S. Strategy in Iraq," "Senators Denounce Bush Policy Limiting Refuge for Iraqis." As for "How Congress may block 'surge,' " "The House has power to trim war funds, but it's a risky move." In "A backing down on wartime powers," "The White House yields to court oversight of its disputed domestic surveillance program."[11]

Then, in later January 2007, "Bush Iraq Plan Is Condemned By Senate Panel" (Foreign Relations Committee), although its "Resolution Won't Deter Troop Reinforcement." Congressional "Democrats Try to Increase Leverage Over Iraq Policy" and say that "Congress might consider legislation revising the authorization it gave President Bush in 2002 to use military force in Iraq." On the subject of "Congress, the Constitution and War" in regard to "The Limits of Presidential Power," "The president does not have a blank check in wartime." It was noted how intensely among themselves the Committee's "senators wrestled over the resolution on Iraq," "denouncing President Bush's plan to build up US troops in Iraq" and "Feel[ing] Weight Of Iraq Vote." Even so, "Antiwar protesters target Congress," "seeking more than resolutions" by "rally[ing] Congress to oppose troop 'surge.' "[12]

The Political "Slugfest" Intensifies Over Who Has What Power—and Blame (Toward a Constitutional Crisis?)

What was fast becoming a political "slugfest" intensified in February 2007 over who had what powers—and blame—in such a situation. "Between Congress and the president, [there is] a power seesaw." In the complicated "Blame (Name Goes Hex) for Iraq," "The Pentagon strikes back. Congress hones in. And Bush attacks Iran.," as "The finger-pointing grows more intense, with an eye on the history books." Led by the new Speaker, Pelosi, "A Divided House Denounces Plan for More Troops" in "Largely Partisan" "Nonbinding Iraq Measure [That] Is Rare Rebuke for a Wartime President"— "A Symbolic Vote [That] Is a Sign Of Bitter Debates to Come." A day later, the Democratic-led "Senate Rejects Renewed Effort To Debate Iraq" as "Democrats Say They Will Fight On," that is, Senate "rejected an effort to force debate on a resolution opposing President Bush's troop buildup in Iraq."[13]

At this point, on a wider global stage, it was "Back To Reality" for the Administration as "Iraq and Iran are forcing Condoleezza Rice to rethink U.S. foreign policy and deal with the world as it is" in her "hopes to bring peace to the Middle East." Contrariwise, Russian leader "Putin Says U.S. Policies Are Undermining Global Stability" as he gives "Tough Talk About Iraq and NATO Expansion."[14]

It was then in March appropriately asked: "In Wartime, Who Has The Power?" The article's answer was direct. "The Constitution is relatively clear. The president is the Commander in Chief, and he has the power to deploy troops and to direct military strategy. Congress has the power to declare war and can use its control over the purse to end a war. But it has no say over how the war is actually prosecuted, [and that is] a problem for Congress as it debates the course of the Iraq war."[15]

In response, we may add here that in earlier post–World-War I & II wars such as in Korea, Vietnam, and Iraq, there were no formal declarations of war but rather resolutions by Congress to authorize the use of force. Hence the constitutional interfaces between Congress and the President can be unclear and contentious. A president, for instance, can veto Congress' bill to defund a war, but Congress can override. Congress can vote up or down on a president's appropriation request. But what oversight power does Congress have to introduce legislation either for stopping President Bush's troop "surge" in Iraq in spring 2007 (after having passed a resolution in 2002 that authorized "use of force" in Iraq), or for preventing his possible use of force against Iran? Congressional ability to use "oversight" or "advise and consent" provisions is not constitutionally clear-cut.

On into March 2007, the "New Push in Congress to Withdraw Is Response to Spending Request" by White House, as "Democrats Rally Behind A Pullout From Iraq In '08," yet "White House Spurns Idea." Quickly enough, "Congress Gears Up for Debate On Getting U.S. Out of Iraq." "In Congress, Iraq Is A Political Quagmire," for "Behind the war debate, [there is] a struggle for strategic advantage." In narrow vote margin, the "Senate Rejects Democrats' Call To Pull Troops" in "A 2008 Deadline On Iraq," while "House Panel Backs a Similar Measure" in "a spending bill that includes an exit date." On "How Congress might rein in war," since "It has often fallen short of its aims when taking on presidents," "The importance of the stakes in wartime virtually ensures continual struggle between the executive and legislative branches," such that "The confrontation between Congress and the White House over Iraq is developing into perhaps the most heated confrontation since Vietnam over one of the most basic aspects of the US Constitution—its allocation of the power to make war."[16]

In later March 2007, the "House . . . Votes To Set Deadline of Late '08 for Iraq Pullout, but Bush Vows Veto," yet "Democrats Concede They Lack Votes to Override Promised Bush Veto." A few days later, the "Senate Supports Pullout Date in Iraq War Bill" "Seen as Rebuke of Policy—a Veto Is Expected." Whereupon "Bush Rules Out Push by Congress for an Iraq Pullout Date," while "Fighting a new Democratic majority on foreign aid and domestic issues." Then, "Defying Bush, Senate Passes Iraq Spending Measure Calling for Pullout of U.S. Troops," while "Trying to paint the president as ignoring public opinion." True, "Congress puts its marker on Iraq war, but how big?" Meantime, "Congress Expands Scope of Inquiries Into Justice Department Practices and Politics," and "The recent ouster of eight U.S. attorneys is just one area of contention."[17]

By early April 2007, as the wrangling continued to mount, prospects for a constitutional crises loomed ever larger. As "Bush Blames [Congressional] Democrats For Impasse Over [Their] Iraq Bills" on funding for troops, with strings attached on timetables for withdrawal, "Both Sides' Remarks Grow More Heated," while "Pelosi, Warmly Greeted in Syria, Is Criticized by White House" because "Bush says the speaker's trip sends mixed signals." Some observers felt that Speaker Pelosi was overstepping the boundaries between the White House and Congress by conducting her own would-be foreign diplomacy rather than a more acceptable fact-finding mission. At any rate, the "Tussle Over Iraq Spending Bill Reminds Many of a Bitter 1995" battle between Speaker Gingrich and President Clinton, only the stakes this time were rising higher and deadlier. On her Syria trip, in close relation to the impasse over Iraq, "One side sees 'bad behavior.' The other side sees 'tantrum.'" It was fast becoming a "tug of war between White House and Congress over funding for Iraq war." As tensions rose and "Bush Criticizes Democrats For Delay in Iraq Spending Bill," "Will the president budge on Iraq? A showdown looms." "Where's Congress in This Power Play?," for "The unchecked presidential privilege we are seeing now would shock the Founders." "Congress Girds Up For Return To Oversight" in "Probes [that] include alleged contracting abuses in Iraq. . . ." On another front as well, it was "Bush v. Congress: The Looming Battle Over Executive Privilege."[18]

The constitutional face-off continued in 2007. In late April "Senate Passes Bill Seeking Iraq Exit; Veto Is Expected," leaving "Bush Displeased" and "Democrats Divided on How to Respond to the White House." Similarly, "House Approves War Spending Measure That Requires U.S. to Start Pullout From Iraq." Then in early May "Bush Vetoes $124 Billion Bill Tying Iraq Funds to Exit Schedule, Calling It 'Date for Failure,'" yet "Democrats Lack Votes to Override But Vow to Press for War's End." As "[Senator Hillary] Clinton Proposes Vote to Reverse [2002 Resolution] Authorizing Bush to Wage War; Talks on Financing Intensify" as "Presidential politics . . . play a role in the war debate." In later May "Congress Passes War Funds Bill, Ending Impasse." But in late June "Lawmakers [Are] to Investigate Bush on Laws and Intent" in order to counter his "use of bill-signing statements as ways to circumvent Congressional intent," this being "one front in the battle between the White House and some in Congress over the power of the executive branch," with a particular dispute arising over failure to carry out "requirements that the Pentagon include justifications for the Iraq war spending in its annual budget request." A week later "Bush Moves Toward Showdown With Congress on Executive Privilege." A few days later "Bush and Congress [are] locked in power dispute" beacuse "White House won't release documents on domestic surveillance" concerning the war on terror. In mid-July "A Firm Bush Tells Congress Not to Dictate Policy on War," whereupon "House Responds by Voting to Withdraw Combat Troops From Iraq by April 1 [2008]." "Bush fights to control Iraq strategy" as "A Rising Chorus in Congress to cut short the 'surge' has mobilized the administration." As of this writing, what next?[19]

3. RULES AND LAWS OF WAR ON TERRORISM?

"In a War on Terror," observed one news commentator in 2004, "Not All the Rules of War Apply"—"Kill bin Laden? The restraints aren't clear. He's not a ruler." That year it was reported that through a 2003 Pentagon memo "Bush Administration Lawyers Decided That Laws Against Torture Did Not Bind the President" due to "the President's 'Inherent'[!] Authority in a Military Campaign." Also, "U.S. Rules on Prisoners Seen as a Back and Forth of Mixed Messages for G.I.'s." "After the Terror Attacks [of 9/11], [there was] a Secret and Speedy Revising of Military Law."[20]

Late the next year, 2005, "In a controversial article, Charles Krauthammer says that at times, coercion is morally necessary," that is, according to one reviewer, "He Says Yes to Legalized Torture." An editorial on "Torture and the Constitution" criticized the Bush Administration because "Not only have some officials denied that CIA interrogation techniques, which are known to include waterboarding, constitute torture, but administration lawyers argue that the practice doesn't necessarily violate the lesser international legal standard of 'cruel, inhuman and degrading treatment' " as set forth in the "Convention Against Torture and Other Cruel, Inhuman and Degrading Treatment," which the Senate ratified in 1994. Whereupon a set of "New Army Rules [On Interrogation Methods] May Snarl Talks With [Senator] McCain on Detainee Issue" in connection with "legislation proposed by [him] . . . to bar cruel and inhumane treatment of detainees in American custody. . . ." Unfortunately, over a year later in early 2007, the C.I.A., "Wrestling with competing opinions on harsh methods for questioning," is "Still Awaiting Rules On Interrogating Suspects" after "A delay that angers lawmakers who recall the urgency of last year's legislation." Several weeks later, "Bush Allies in Congress Block Bill That Would Require Intelligence Disclosures" by the White House of "the locations of secret prisons run by the Central Intelligence Agency and . . . the amount spent annually by American intelligence agencies."[21]

One may wonder how to reconcile a U.S. rationale for war in Iraq to establish "the rule of law" there with U.S. problems in ascertaining or adhering to the rules and laws of war when fighting terror in Iraq and elsewhere in the Middle East. Even at home, there were various related issues and difficulties. In one odder occurrence in 2005—involving "For Army Recruiters, a Day of Rules and Little

Else"—the Army responded to "reports of widespread cheating to enlist unqualified applicants" and "suspended recruiting nationwide . . . to retrain its ranks in ethics, but officials said they would not lift the monthly quotas that some recruiters see as a catalyst for abuse."[22]

What about the justification or rationale (*casus belli*) for waging the Iraq war in the first place? A variety of unfolding accounts reflected much early opinion in the mainstream press. "[Secretary of State] Powell Defends Information He Used to Justify Iraq War," while "[British Prime Minister] Blair Denies Britain Distorted Reports on Iraq Weapons." "Behind the changing rationales for war," "Even as questions stir around the prewar case for ousting Hussein, current challenges in Iraq could test the US public's support for Bush." On "Bush And Case For War" in connection with "The Uranium Fiction," "C.I.A. Chief Takes Blame for Error in Bush Speech on Iraq Uranium From Africa." "When Frontier Justice Becomes Foreign Policy," "The administration has quit arguing the rights and wrongs of killing enemies." In "A Shift In Tactics," "U.S. Commander In Iraq Says Yearlong Tours Are Option To Combat 'Guerrilla' War." The "March to War [Was] Based on Skewed Intelligence Data on Iraq's Nuclear Plans." "U.S. Report Finds [That] Iraqis Eliminated Illicit Arms In 90's," so that "Weapons Capability Had Eroded Before War, Inspector Says," while "Democrats see the administration's case for war undermined" but "Bush Goes on [Counter]Attack." In any case, the "Strategy to Secure Iraq Did Not Foresee a 2nd War on Insurgency."[23]

What about the 9/11 attack in 2001 as justification for launching the war against Iraq? In mid-2004, the "[9/11] Panel Finds No Qaeda–Iraq Tie; Describes A Wider Plot For 9/11" and "Challenges Bush" in "A Chilling Chronology [That] Rewrites the History of the Attacks." The "9/11 Report Calls for a Sweeping Overhaul of Intelligence." In late 2005, "9/11 Panel Issues Poor Grades for Handling of Terror."[24]

Justification for "A War Without Borders" outside Iraq was becoming more self-evident for many as terrorism spread to other Middle Eastern countries, as when in later 2005 it was asked "Are the bombings in Jordan just the start of al-Zarqawi's spreading his terror beyond Iraq?" In 2004, "10 Bombs Shatter Trains in Madrid, Killing 192"; "Video Claims Al Qaeda Set Blasts in Spain; Officials Arrest 3 Moroccans and 2 Indians"; and, although "President's Foreign Policy Faces Greater Scrutiny After Madrid Attack," "Bush's Campaign Emphasizes Role Of Leader In War" in "New Criticism Of Kerry" in 2004 presidential race. Back in 2003, "Bush Says U.S. Will Not Tolerate Building of Nuclear Arms by Iran." Such situations in the background to justification for a wider war on terrorism could be multiplied many times over. Yet, said one editorial in 2004, "Preventive War . . . [Is] A Failed Doctrine." In time, Congressional legislation, as in the Patriot Act steered by the Administration, conferred a kind of justification of its own for a wider war on terrorism. It was reported, for instance, that "Congress Nears Deal to Renew Antiterror Law" when in later 2005 "Congressional negotiators reached a final agreement . . . on legislation that will extend and keep largely intact the sweeping antiterrorism powers granted to the federal government under the law known as the Patriot Act."[25]

Looking Ahead: The Case of Islamic Turkey

From Clinton's emphasis on "globalism" to Bush's concentration on the war against "terrorism," there has been a seismic shift in U.S. foreign policies, yet one that has accorded a continuing key place to legislative matters in conjunction with issues of sovereignty and state (as reflected in the mainstream press). Perhaps the time will soon come when these two "isms" can be better considered in conjunction with each other. By bringing disaffected peoples, groups, and regions into a more positive global network, peace and security could be better achieved internationally in an emerging "new world order."

It can be hoped that an expanding economic globalization will play a positive role in the Middle East. The rising economic levels of various less fortunate groups could better enable them to share in the responsible political–governmental mainstream of their countries. Disaffected Islamic fundamentalist groups and their allies could thereby become less prone to terrorist sympathies and the destruction of civilized society in which they had an economic stake through responsible political processes and involvements.

Recent developments in Turkey have presented possible opportunities as well as risks. In spring 2007, "Presidential Pick in Turkey Is Sign Of a Rising Islamic Middle Class" as "Turkey's ruling [Parliamentary] party . . . chose a presidential candidate [Abdullah Gul] with an Islamic background. [It was] . . . a move that will extend the reach of the party—and the emerging class of devout Muslims represented—into the heart of Turkey's secular establishment for the first time." But then, in early May, the "Turkish [Highest] Court Blocks Election of Candidate With Islamic Ties"—despite Mr. Gul's backing by the Prime Minister as well as his having kept Islam out of foreign policy during his tenure as foreign minister. Yet a public referendum and early national elections were being planned with the Prime Minister's urging. "The battle for Turkey's soul" went on unabated. "Turkish Islamists Hope to Ride Competence to Victory." But then, "Turkish [Islamic] Presidential Candidate Withdraws, as Voting Stalls Again." Still, in view of the intense struggles for sovereignty within parliament and between parliament and the highest court, could a constitutional crisis in Turkey be averted? Then in August "Turkish Official with Islamic Ties Wins Presidential Election; Pledges Secular State.[26]

This saga's continuation in 2007 and beyond will be looked at in our next book. There, too, will be considered such related promising stories elsewhere as "Religiosity, Not Radicalism, Is New Wave in Indonesia," where by mid-2007 "Militant Islam Garners Little Support."[27]

PART THREE

Latin American Governments and Societies in Legislative and Other Contexts of Sovereignty and State: Current News History

Chapter X

United Mexican States in Government and Society

Turning next to Central and South America in the Western Hemisphere, we begin with Mexico and then proceed southward through various countries of Central America and the Caribbean, then similarly down through South America, ending with overviews of Latin America as a whole and in part. Along the way, U.S. foreign policies and involvements will at times be germane. Again, the guiding hands of leaders as paradigm-builders will become salient together with the legislative groundwork and framework. The same range of press sources as above will be employed below.[1]

As a federal democratic republic, the United Mexican States (officially Estados Unitos Mexicanos) is comprised of 31 states and one federal district, Mexico City. State governors are directly elected for 6-year terms. The chief federal executive, or president, is directly elected by majority vote for a 6-year term and takes office December 1 of the election year. The national bicameral legislature is a Congress consisting of a Chamber of Deputies with 500 members elected for 3-year terms and a Senate with members elected for 6-year terms, with each of the 31 states having 2 members along with 2 for the federal district. Although the federal judiciary is independent of President and

Congress, it tends generally not to oppose the President. The states have their own judiciaries. Clearly, then, the U.S. model has been highly influential, as is perhaps appropriate to Mexico's neighboring geographic and historical status. However, the two political systems bear remarkable differences in actual fact. Depending on one's categories, Mexico is part of both North and Central America.

1. THE SALINAS ERA

"Salinas is modernizing Mexico's economy, but . . . not . . . the . . . political [and legal] system"

The main headline to the above subheading in the U.S. press in 1990, two years into his 6-year term, asked if Mexican President Carlos Salinas is "In a Hurry or Running Scared?" Basically, the Salinas government was resisting, or slow on, political reform of a heavy-handed (corrupt?) System run by the ruling party. To be sure, there were exceptions, as when in 1989 "Mexican Papers Want To Keep Tie With State," whereas "Salinas is trying to reduce the Government's financial influence over Mexico's newspapers," and "newspaper publishers are resisting." More typical was when in mid-1991 Salinas "Says [Mid-Term 1991] Vote Vindicates Change" and "Scornfully Asks for Evidence of Any Fraud—[and] Lauds Market Reform." It was hardly surprising, shortly before, that "Ruling Party Leads in Elections." "Mexican Opposition [Is] Back on Defensive." Afterwards, "Mexican Rulers Yield on State Elections" as the "Governing party protects other results from taint of fraud"; and "Ruling Party Defuses Vote Protest."[2]

In November of 1991 "Mexican President Outlines Program for Changes" and "pledges social reforms in annual speech." Weeks later, "Mexico [Is] Ending Church Restraints After 70 Years of Official Hostility."[3]

Events unfolded perhaps differently than expected. "Protests Bring Ouster of Third Mexican [State] Governor." "Ruling Party [Is] Challenged in 2 Mexican States." "Mexico's Ruling Party Loses a [State] Vote, Faces Fight in 2nd" in mid-1992—that is, "For only the second time since Mexico's governing party was founded in 1929, an opposition candidate emerged victorious . . . in elections." Then, "In Mexico, Crisis Shakes Opposition" as "Traditionalists Back Away in Split Over Party Identity and Role in System." Would there be "A Real Political Pluralism in Mexico?"[4]

In later 1992, "Mexico's Leader Cautiously Backs Some Big Changes." In spring 1993, "Mexico's Leader Shakes Up Party" and "Replaces Chief and Other Two From Cabinet." A half year later,

"Mexico Passes Electoral Changes, But Foils a Presidential Bid." In "Leveling Mexico's Electoral Field," "Salinas Delivers on His Modest Promises of Voting Reform" by "Legitimizing power without risking its loss." "Why Mexico Has Only One Big Hat in the Ring" for president in late 1993 hinged on "How the Ruling Party Keeps It That Way" through election rules and presidential supremacy in appointments, budgets, and taxes.[5]

Looking ahead to mid-1994 election for president, "Mexican President Backs A Successor" (Colosio) who is "Named Ruling Party Candidate." "A Torch Passes, but Not Very Far." As for "Mexico's 2 Faces: Is Political Change Top Priority?" In early 1994, "Mexican Government Is Moving To Open Up Presidential Elections." Yet "Reforms in Mexico [Are] Put in Doubt By Opposition of Leftist Leader," creating "Hurdles on the road to free elections." A few days later, "Mexican Presidential Candidate [Is] Shot at Tijuana Rally." As "The Other Victim," "Stability Is Threatened in the Slaying Of Long-Governing Party's Candidate" (Colosio), as "Mexican Leaders Begin Search for New Candidate." "Nervous and Skeptical, Mexicans See Dark Plots" with "wounds [to] a nation's psyche." "For Mexicans, Democracy Exacts A Scary Price" in that "A bullet adds to the pain of a nation's decades-long struggle toward freedom." A few days later, in the midst of "An unusually high level of criticism in a Mexican election," "Mexican Party Names New Nominee [Zedillo] for Slain Candidate" as "A Tragedy's Stand-In" and ex-cabinet official, who is much criticized after "President picks" him.[6]

Now came "The choice: a clean election or worse turnout." In early May 1994, a "Mexican [Cardenas] Seriously Challenges Long-Ruling Party." "Mexico Invites U.N. to Attend Election to Observe the Observers." Then "Rightist's [Cevallos's] Rise Poses New Threat to Mexican Party's Rule." "Mexicans Bring Fear to the Ballot Box" because "With good reason, Mexicans got in the habit of bowing to the one party that controlled everything. Old habits die hard." Now it was "Mexico on the Edge" through "Broken promises, political unrest, violence." Unfairly, "Mexican TV Picks Its Political Shots," and "Ruling party enjoys extensive coverage." Soon enough, "What happened to the man who was supposed to upset the Mexican elite?," leaving for the "Mexican Challenger: Bold Words, Pale Presence." Even so, "Torn From Within and Without, Mexico's Ruling Party Is Struggling On." Then in mid-August of 1994, "As Mexican elections near, Salinas demands an end to fraud," for "In Last-Minute Rites, Salinas Weds Democracy." But "Will political reforms bring Mexicans their first, clean election?" Moreover, "Are the many parties in Mexico an impediment to democracy?" due to "Mexican Voters' Multiple Choices: Nine Parties." As "Mexico Strives to End Voting

Fraud," "The governing party's credibility is on the line." On August 21 "Mexicans Cast Votes in Large Numbers" "in Election Focused on Democratic Gains." A day later, "Ruling Party's Candidate [Zedillo] Wins Presidency In Mexico, But Opposition Makes Gains" as "Victor Has Wide Margin but Falls Short of a Majority of Votes." "Zedillo Calls For Dialogue With Parties." But "Shadows Blur Mexico Right's Gains." In "The People's Choice (Honest!)," "By electing Zedillo President, the voters hope for peace and stability—and bigger pay checks."[7]

But political setbacks and difficulties continued into the fall of 1994. A "governing party legislator ordered the killing of a powerful Government official . . . to prevent him from pushing forward sweeping political reforms." And "Despite Gains, Press Freedom in Mexico Is Still Limited," with "No outright press censorship, but many less obvious restrictions." "Can the new President break his own party's corrupt stranglehold?" Clearly, then, Mexico's political and legal systems—to whatever extent above that the latter was reasonably evident or determining—had much further to go in the direction of democratic reforms. So, too, did anything resembling real legislative sovereignty or the legislative state, considering the heavy-handed pervasive power of the ruling party.[8]

"A Mexican Conflict Over States' Rights Heats Up"

Throughout the presidential election year of 1994, a particular thorn in the national ruling party's side was the grave threat to the federal government posed by state rebels chiefly in Chiapas in southern Mexico on the border with Guatemala. In opposition to the more rightist governing party headed by President Salinas, leftist "Rebels [Are] Determined 'to Build Socialism' in Mexico." Right away, in early January, "Mexican Copters Pursue Rebels; Toll Is Put at 95." There was, in "Mexico—A Tale Of Two States," for "One represses, the other doesn't," while at root "Supporters of economic liberalization argue that free trade promotes democracy. But often it does not" as "recent experiences in southern Mexico show. . . ." "Mexico Says Peasant Groups and Church Back Rebels." In "Zapatista's Revenge," "A bloody uprising in one of the country's poorest states serves as an embarrassing reminder that Mexico has not quite joined the First World's industrial club." Then "Mexico Orders Cease Fire and Offers Rebels Amnesty." "Spurred by Peasant Uprising, Pact Vows Election Limits" after "Mexican Parties Agree To Reforms." However, "Mexican Rebel Leader Sees No Quick Settlement" because "The guerrillas in Chiapas say they will insist on broad electoral changes." In March "Mexico, Pledging Big Changes, Reaches an Accord With Rebels" in "Tentative Pact [That] Includes New Rights for Indians." Yet over a week later in the same area, "Mexican Conflict Heats Up, With Peasants Seizing Land." Two months later, "A Mexican Conflict Over States' Rights Heats Up" "between the federal Government and Baja California State."[9]

In June "Mexican [Chiapas] Rebels Gather to Rule on Government's Peace Offer." Shortly thereafter, "Rebels in Mexico Spurn Peace Plan From Government" as "Tensions Rise In South" after "Insurgents Cite Fears of Fraud In Voting Set for August—Pledge to Honor Truce." "For Mexico's Oppressed Indians, [There Are] Smothered Hopes and Promises Not Kept." In early August with elections coming soon, "For Ruling Party of Mexico, South Is No Longer So Solid." In "Convention Of Dissent For Mexicans," "Foes of Government Gather in Chiapas" as "Mexico's rebels take their fight to the political arena." A week after the presidential elections in later August, "Mexican Chief [Salinas] Sees No Rebel Solution" in Chiapas. A month later, "Rebels Say Mexican Army Is Breaking Terms of Truce."[10]

"Law Protects Mexico's Workers But . . . Enforcement . . . Lax"

Behind that press headline from mid-1993 lay much of the rebels' discontent in 1994 as just outlined. For in addition to issues of "states' rights" were those pertaining to law, legislation, and enforcement in an emerging modern Mexico still struggling to become more truly and fully democratic. At bottom in that headline's article lay the unrest caused, for some in different parts of Mexico, by the recent rise of free trade as regards Mexico and the United States. In "A Partner's Hurdles" as "Mexico Faces Free Trade," the innuendo was clear: "Labor Rights Exist, At Least on Paper," with "Blacklist Charged At Border Plants" and "Officials Accused Of Intimidation." "Inflation Is Curbed, But Workers Pay," and "Safety Is Slighted: The Wage Is All."[11]

A day later appeared the companion news report also emphasizing in part lax legal–legislative enforcement. "Mexico's Vast Pollution Is Cloud Over Trade Pact" as "Laws Are Flaunted, Reforms Touted." A number of other issues were stressed: "The Boom Is Clear, So's the Blight"; "Paltry Resources (And No Paychecks)"; and "Some Pray the Pact Will Bring Converts."[12]

The free trade movement supported by the Bush Administration in the early 1990s through the U.S.–Mexico Free Trade Agreement

(FTA) meant, said its proponents in 1991, "Yes: If Mexico Prospers, So Will the U.S." "Without a Deal, Salinas' Brave Political and Social Reforms Will Collapse." But in order "To Cut a Deal: Both Sides Can Win If They Compromise."[13]

In late 1991, "Bush Tells Mexico He Wants a Free Trade Pact Soon." In later 1993 the "Trade Pact Is a Clear Political Victory for the Mexican President," with "Joy in the south, conciliatory words up north." But by early 1994, as reported above, the situation had changed. Then, in further pushes for free trade made between the presidential election and the inauguration, the "Mexican Government Panel Instills the Unfamiliar Idea of Competition," although "Trade Pacts and free markets mean reprogramming."[14]

"Sovereignty Hinders U.S.–Mexican Drug Alliance"

To that preceding news heading from 1990 can be added the caption "Washington says 'hot pursuit' but some in Mexico hear invasion." "Efforts by Mexico and the United States to halt drug trafficking across the border are being hampered by strong disagreements over how to go about it, Mexican and American officials say." For law enforcement officials on both sides of the border, there has been a growing concern about increasing militarization of the area.[15]

In the weeks prior to the 1994 presidential election, the situation had become more tenuous still. "Mexico's Drug Fight [Is] Lagging, With Graft Given as a Cause." "In Mexico, U.S. Hones Art of Laissez-Faire Diplomacy." According to the latter article, there was again in the U.S. Congress concern over the need for Mexico's reform of its election system to ensure free elections if it were to engage in free trade with the United States, notwithstanding the Clinton Administration's advocacy of free trade in relation to the North American Free Trade Agreement (NAFTA).[16]

2. THE ZEDILLO ERA

"New Leader . . . Gives Pledge of Democracy"

With the election and inauguration of President Ernesto Zedillo, along with the successful continuance of his Institutional Revolutionary Party (PRI), the "New Leader In Mexico Gives Pledge of Democracy." Within days, however, a familiar kind of dark cloud appeared when "The investigation of a politician's murder shakes Mexico as a new President takes over." At the same time, "Do Term Limits Work? Ask Mexico," with its "Congress of Sheep" and "No

Accountability." Even so, the future seemed promising as "Mexico's New Leader Proposes Overhaul of the Judicial System." Looking back, it was "A Year to Forget: 1994 Leaves Mexico Reeling." After "An uprising on Jan. 1 and turmoil ever since." Then, in January of 1995, "Mexican Parties Sign Accord On Shift to Full Democracy" in "a Pact on Reforms."[17]

Familiar types of threats to democracy surfaced at the outset of the new presidential term. One such threat was the separatist rebels in Chiapas and elsewhere. "Peasants Block Roads in Troubled South Mexican State," Chiapas. "Rebels in Mexico's South Vanish Before a Show of Force." "Mexico's economic crisis seems to be giving the rebels new hope." Then "Another State in Mexico Challenges the Government," Tabasco. "In Mexico, Ruling Party Faces Revolt By Members" in Tabasco and elsewhere. At first, "In Mexico's Peace Talks, A Slow if Hopeful Start" was reported. But then "Mexico Leader Sends Force To Arrest Rebels in South" whereby "Mask is stripped off the guerrilla leader as troops head to Chiapas state." "Behind Mexico's Harder Line On Rebels, [there is] a Political Shift." "Mexico Rejects Rebel's Demand for Troop Withdrawal," leaving impression of "Mexican Zigzag: Growing Image of Inept Zedillo" because of his "Shifting Actions Toward Rebels."[18]

As for economics, "With Peso's Devaluation, Political Problems Loom," said a report a few weeks after inauguration day. A week later, "Mexico's Leader Gives The Nation An Austerity [Recovery] Plan," but "Some Analysts Call Measures Too Weak to Stabilize Peso and Reassure Investors." "Political Setbacks, Economic Miscalculations, and Bad Luck Led to Crash," factors behind "How a Miracle Went Wrong." By early January of 1995 it was called "a Mexican meltdown." "Peso Plummets Anew on Fears [U.S.] Congress Won't Assist Mexico," "Clinton Renews Push but Aid Plan Is Still Stalled." Then, "With Aid, Economy In Mexico Perks Up," but is "Rescue . . . Durable Or Brief?" "Don't Panic: Here Comes Bailout Bill: Faced with a recalcitrant Congress, Clinton puts together his own package of Mexican loans and hopes the cure will stick." In later February, the U.S. Peso "Rescue Package Tightens Restrictions on Mexico's Economic Policies" as "A once-booming nation now stares at austerity," with "U.S. Given Policy Rein."[19]

Other obstacles to democratic reforms and policies pledged by Zedillo also became evident early on, presenting further difficulties for the Mexican government's efforts at legal–legislative empowerment. At the end of February 1995, alongside news that "Mexico Plans Tough Steps as Economy Reels," there were reports that "Mexico Party [Is] Aide Arrested For '94 Killing of Candidate

[Colosio]." "Ex-Leader's [Salinas'] Brother [Is] Held In Mexican Assassination," an "Arrest [That] Shatters Immunity Tradition." In "The Spreading Scandal," "The arrest of an ex-President's brother demolishes the rules of Mexican politics." A week later, "Mexican Corruption Investigation Widens" after "Officials say a Mexican prosecutor amassed money from drug bribes." With the drug trafficking problem growing, tough new measures were needed in "Drug Crackdown Planned [by U.S.] Along the Mexican Border."[20]

Although for a short time the Salinas scandal buoyed public support for Zedillo, the familiar combination of problems—rebels, the peso, corruption, assassinations, and drugs—gained the upper hand. The "Governing Party in Mexico Suffers Landslide Defeat in [mid-February] State Election" in Jalisco." After "100 days of economic crisis and political turmoil," including Salinas' virtual exile, "Mexico's New Leader Finds Job Full of Painful Surprises."[21]

"Mexico Lives by Virtual Law"

By late March of 1995, "Zedillo's Challenge" became his policies whereby "Mexico Lives by Virtual Law," insofar as "The rule of law is not yet a full reality in Mexico, its President says"—meaning that "there is a rule of law, but ... if you don't obey it, nothing's going to happen," even though the president talks tough on violators while "Security police [stand] outside a Government-run pawnshop in Mexico City." The malleability of law appeared in one form when "Rebels in Mexico [Chiapas] Welcome A Law to Advance Talks" through "the promulgation of a new law that offers a framework for negotiations and a temporary amnesty for insurgents." In October "Rebels' Impact [Is] Felt in Mexican [Chiapas State] Vote." A week later the fragility of the rule of law was evidenced when "Mexican [Chiapas] Rebel Leader's Arrest Raises Questions on Peace Talks." Earlier, "Spasm of Violence Is Stalking a Poor Mexican State," Guerrero. Thereafter, "Mexican Report Accuses State [Guerrero] Aides in Killing of 17 Peasants" in "A case that tests Mexico's commitment to human rights."[22]

On through 1995 and early 1996, news accounts of the drug trade further showed the difficulties for the enforcement of laws and rules against drugs. "The Trail of Cocaine Shipment in Mexico Points to Official Corruption." "Mexico Plans Bigger Role For Military Against Drugs." "Mexico's President talks tough about drug traffic," saying " 'I Want Justice.' " "Mexico Reports Troops Capture Powerful Narcotics Trafficker." "To Help Keep Stability in Mexico,

U.S. Soft-Pedals War on Drugs," while, "Despite Gains, Dark Figures Lurk." "Mexican Connection Grows As Cocaine Supplier to U.S." "Drug Traffickers [Are] Smuggling Tons of Cash From U.S. Through Mexico" as "Drug barons fill planes with cash to evade money-laundering rules."[23]

During this period, economic woes continued to complicate matters. "The Mexicans Rise Up Against 'Fiscal' Terrorism." "Mexico Judge In Union Case Is Shot Dead." "Anti-Poverty Program [Is] Under Fire in Mexico," with the question "Who Gains Most, the Poor or the Party?" "Defiant Workers in Mexico Protest Government Policies" in "May Day Demonstration in Capital's Center." "Mexican State [Guerrero] Governor Tied to a Massacre of Peasants Quits."[24]

"Mexico's Political Crisis" was deepening. "The Mexican Collapse" was also having repercussions in the United States. Some positive reports offered a ray of hope, such as "After Bitter Legislative Battle, Mexico Revises Social Security" and the health-care system, allowing for improvements. Yet "Mexico's 'Accidental' Leader Spurns Strongman's Role, Bringing On a Crisis" due to "A Leadership Style That Unsettles Many" in "A Wobbling System [That] Raises U.S. Stakes." "Mexico Is Shown Paper Trail of Illicit Campaign Spending" and "election corruption." "An Audit Agency For Mexico Is Proposed" as "Zedillo Calls for Unit to Fight Corruption." Yet in "Mexico Adrift," "Facing Crisis Upon Crisis, Zedillo Appears [To Be] A Helpless Helmsman, Greatly Off Course." Later, "Mexican [Main Opposition] Party Pulls Out of Talks on Political Reform" in a setback for Zedillo. Still unresolved, "'94 Assassination Haunts a Country" as "Slain Mexican [Presidential] Candidate's Father Demands Justice."[25]

"Can Mexico Be a Stable Democracy?"—"Zedillo Lectures the Mexicans: Obey the Law"

That question was asked in the spring of 1996, answered in part by the need to avoid the "danger . . . that US buoyancy over Mexico's economic recovery will give Zedillo an ill-founded sense of security; he will again postpone political reforms needed for stability." More problematic perhaps than economic recovery were drugs as "Mexicans Tire of Police Graft as Drug Lords Raise Stakes," with lawlessness and corruption growing. On into 1997 came press reports of drugs, corruption, or worse: "Senior Mexican Drug Prosecutor Is Killed by Gunman in Tijuana"; "Drug Ties Taint 2 Mexican Governors, as In-formers' Revelations Widen"; "Ex-Secretary to Patriarch of Mexican Party Tells of Politicians' Links to Drug Barons"; and "Drug Connection Links Mexican Military [Leaders] to Abductions."[26]

On political fraud during this period, there were also the following developments. "Election Fraud Charges [Are] Filed Against Mexico's Ruling Party." "Mexico's Elite Caught in Scandal's Harsh Glare" after "Millions changed hands . . . without paperwork." "In Blow to Mexican Government, Suspect in Slaying [of Colosio, the leading presidential candidate in the 1994 elections,] Is Cleared." "A Fugitive Lawman Speaks: How Mexico Mixes Narcotics and Politics." "Mexico's Cycle of Failure" shows that "A corrupt system can't be reformed from the inside."[27]

At the same time, there were some reports of attempted progress and reform. "Zedillo Lectures the Mexicans: Obey the Law" in his "Call for a new Mexican culture to replace 'submissive disobedience.'" "Mexico Is Near To Granting Expatriates Voting Rights." "Aimed At Election Fraud" was a "Major-Party Deal In Mexico To Bring Political Reforms," presenting "Opportunities for Opposition [That] May Spell End of 7 Decades of Rule by Same Party." "Rank-and-File Mount a Revolt in Mexico's Ruling Party" when, "After years at the top, the party's technocrats come under siege." In "Mexican Justice," "Zedillo has promised to enforce the laws of Mexico fully and impartially, even with top officials of his . . . Party," even though reality has often fallen short of that ideal. "Mexico Cracks Down on Long Tradition of Dirty Politics" as "A clandestine video portrays a leftist candidate for mayor as a violent radical." "After seven decades, Mexican politics are being reshaped," with "Mexicans Venting Outrage at Ruling Party." In "Mexico's Cultural Revolution . . . From Centrism to Competition," "Analysts hail 1997 as the year of democratization and deregulation." True, in later 1996, "Ending Dialogue, Ruling Mexican Party Dilutes Reforms"; and, it was asked, "Is Mexico's Press Free, or Just Taking Liberties?" Yet then, "In Vote Today [July 1997], Mexicans Put Election Reforms to the Test." The next day, "Opposition Figure Declares Victory in Mexican Race" for mayor of Mexico City in a "Major election setback for Mexico's long-governing party." Even so, "Mexico's New Press Boldness Stops at Leader's Desk."[28]

Helping Mexico's efforts at political and social reform in later 1996 and early 1997 was an improving Mexican economy, sharing in the rising American and global economy. "Mexico's Economy Strengthens" "after worse slump in 60 years, but most Mexicans [are] left out." "The Critics Were Wrong," "The [U.S. 1995] Mexican bailout worked." "Mexico's Progress toward Prosperity" was under way.

There was "Solid Recovery From the Peso's Devaluation" as "Latin Markets Again Run With the Bulls." Mexico was also flexing its economic/legislative muscles independently of the United States as when "Canada and Mexico Join to Oppose U.S. Law on Cuba," for "Mexico may adopt a law similar to a Canadian ban on paying U.S. fines" in order "to penalize foreign companies that trade with Cuba."[29]

Meantime, the rebel problem still often seemed intractable, however, further testing Mexican democratization. "Mexico Sends Troops to Hunt New Rebel Group in the South." "Shadowy Rebels Pose New Problems for Mexico." "Rebels Strike in 4 Mexican States, Leaving 13 Dead." "Mexican Leader Vows to Fight New Guerrilla Violence," while "Along with rebels, economic policies are also criticized." "New 'Bad' Guerrillas Threaten A Shaky Mexican [Economic] Recovery." "Mexico Confronts Rebels With Limited Crackdown." "Mexican Rebels Vow a Long Hard Battle."[30]

"Governing Party Loses Control of Congress," and "President Will Now Face Checks and Balances From Legislature"

Those headlines in July 1997, following elections, spoke volumes on the changing political environment in Mexico. This was "A Taste of Democracy in Mexico." "Mexicans Say *Sí* to Real Democracy." Also, "A newly elected [leftist mayor] reformer vows to clean up Mexico City." In August "Mexico's Opposition Parties Plan Control of Congress," involving "Four parties with one aim: congressional independence." In September "Mexican President Pledges to Work With Congress." "Mexico Main Party averts a Legislative Crisis" as "Mexico's transition seems to be going less smoothly than many predicted." "In Mexico's House, Speaker's Stature Signals a New Day," for "At Mexico's apex, two voices replace one—not with harmony, but with mutual respect," as House Speaker gives "first-ever response to a presidential state-of-the-union address." In November "Mexico's Legislators Finally Get Taste of Real Budget Authority." On "The Budget and Mexico: A Vote for Stability," for "It was a very civilized process where democratic values prevailed," such that "In Mexico's Congress, Zedillo passes a major test of his leadership."[31]

But would the new ideal and reality of Congressional–Presidential democratization be able to solve long-standing problems in the country at large? In December 1997 and January 1998: "Violence grows, and a Government seems paralyzed" after "Mexico's Massacre" in Chiapas; and, concerning "Laws of the Jungle," "In the wake of a massacre, Mexico is struggling to avoid slipping even further into chaos." "Mexican Troops [Are] Summoned to Arrest a Police Unit in Chiapas." "Mexico [Is] Stung as Army Swarms Over Chiapas" in February. "Mexico Sees Both Carrot and Stick Fail in Chiapas." In June "Mexico Squeezes Rebels, Provoking New Grief."[32]

During this period, could democratization in government and law-enforcement help with the continuing drug problem? "In U.S.– Mexico Drug War, Two Systems Collide" as "An extradition case highlights the vast differences in law systems." "A Toll of 'Disappearances' Is Linked To the War Against Drugs in Mexico." Yet "U.S. Praises the Mexicans For Effort in the Drug War." "U.S. Officials Say Mexican Military Aids Drug Traffic." "Foiled Drug Pursuit of a Mexican Bares a System Rife With Graft" through bribes of judges and other means. In late 1998 "U.S.–Aided Effort by Mexico Army Against Drugs Fizzles." In early 2000 "A Mexican State Finds Drugs a Power That Corrupts Absolutely."[33]

"Crime," more generally, "Takes Bite Out Of Mexican Rights," evidenced when "Nineteen policemen were arrested . . . for alleged killings of youths in Mexico City." "Rape and Murder Stalk Women in Northern Mexico." "Mexico Can't Fathom Its Rising Crime."[34]

In the midst of all these setbacks and situations came some rays of hope and progress, albeit reform does not necessarily equate with solutions. In early 1998, "The President says reforms are taking hold, and asks the U.S. for support," expressing "A New Optimism on Ending Graft in Mexico City." In early 2000 "Mexico's Chief Justice Strives to Oil a Creaking System." In mid-1998 "Mexico [Is] Ready to Scrap Its Tough Labor Laws" because "Measures meant to protect workers inhibit the creation of new jobs, reformers say."[35]

"For First Time, Mexican [Presidential] Election Is a Real Race"

The real test of the newfound democracy and reform in Mexican government was the upcoming presidential election in mid-2000. An initial favorable sign for democratic elections in Mexico, looking ahead to the upcoming presidential election, occurred in early 1999 when "Leftist Opposition Party in Mexico Wins Two Governors' Races." Naturally "The Governing Party of Mexico, at 70, Works Hard to Cling to Power." Yet in "An attempt to break 60 years of authoritarian tradition," "Zedillo Urges Primary Voting to Pick Nominees" for president "through a series of state primaries that would culminate in an American-style party convention." "For the Mexico Governing Party, Both Changes and Doubts" surface amid "Signs that presidential influence lives on" albeit "Flirting With

Democratic Ways." Yet "Long-ruling party tries switch from hand-picked nomination by leader to first national primary," thereby "Letting light into Mexico politics."[36]

By mid-1999 "Mexico's Presidential Hopefuls Are All New Breed," and "Gone are the Ivy-League–Schooled experts fluent in English." Even so, "PRI [Ruling Party] in Mexico Shows It Can Win," "But 2 State Votes Indicate Potential of a United Opposition," for "Opposition parties lose a race when they split, but win when they don't." At one point along the way, "Mexico's Senate Blocks Election Reforms," whereupon "Finance limits and expatriate voting die as the 2000 Mexican election nears." Also, the "Open Vote Policy Puts Zedillo in Quandary" on whether to "keep the pledge or call the shots?," that is, pledge "Not to Choose Heir" as "Old Rival Surges."[37]

By May of 2000, "For First Time Mexican [Presidential] Election Is a Real Race," with opposition candidate Vicente Fox gaining ground against the ruling party's candidate to succeed President Zedillo. To no surprise, there were still setbacks such as when two months earlier "Mexico's Ruling Party [Is] Accused of Diverting Public Money." Yet it was still, in early July on the eve of the election, "A Presidential vote to watch," with the big question asked "Will Vicente Fox defeat the party that has run Mexico for more than 70 years?" It could finally be said that "No Matter Who Wins, Today's Vote in Mexico Will Be Fateful."[38]

3. THE VICENTE FOX ERA AND BEYOND

"Mexicans . . . Define Democracy" (And Their Congress)

With the presidential election victory of Vicente Fox of the National Action Party (PAW) at the beginning of July 2000, "Mexicans Get a Chance to Define Democracy." His victory pointed up a new "accountability" and "the rule of law." "Mexico, Voting In New Leader, Begins A Political Sea Change," through "Coalition Politics," as Fox "Promises to Modernize Economy and Reform the Bureaucracy," after "The Zedillo Rules Opened the Door," in order to win "The greater war: putting a nation's ideals into practice." Notwithstanding this sea change in Mexican politics, "Zedillo Says He Takes Pride In Improvements for Mexico" through "A selective recounting of triumphs, not unresolvable problems."[39]

Beset with challenges and obstacles, the road ahead for Vicente Fox would not be easy, but his commitment to progress and reform was encouraging. Between election and inauguration, he was off to a determined start. There was a "Familiar Foe for Mexico's New

Leader: Corruption." "Victor In Mexico Plans To Overhaul Law Enforcement" in "A Fight On Corruption." "Despite Mexico's Vote for Fox, Old Party Still Runs Congress." In "The New Face of Mexico's Politics" "We All Won" in "A Modern Bastille Day" with "A President for the Middle Class" with a "Corporate Style," but "Don't Count Your Chickens" before they hatch. "Fox Follows Up On Pledge Of Diverse Mexican Cabinet." "People power grows in Mexico" inasmuch as, "Free from one-party domination, Mexico is on a second honeymoon with democracy. Will it last?" When "Taking On the Corporate Goliaths," "Can Mexico's New Leader Really Work Miracles?" "A Farmer Learns About Mexico's Lack of the Rule of Law" when "Protests over disappearing forests plunge farmers into the justice system." In "A test for the idea that the law knows no borders," "Spain Asks Mexico to Send Suspect for Trial." There were now "High hopes for Chiapas elections," for, "Following a tumultuous decade," upcoming "vote could promote democratic reform in the state." Facing "Bitter opposition from the old establishment," "New Mexican President Vows to Share Power" and "promises reforms at his inauguration" at the start of December 2000.[40]

Throughout 2001 and into 2002, Fox's government faced mounting challenges and stepped up its activities, with various outcomes for law, order, and justice. "Mexico's New President Faces Pesky States' Rights Revolt" in Yucatán, "one of the last strongholds of the former ruling party." "Mexican [Chiapas] Rebels Set Off on Protest Caravan to the Capital," "put[ting] pressure on Mexico's new leader to act." "Zapatista [Rebel] Leaders Take Their Case to Mexico's Congress" in "A milestone for the Indian rebels of Chiapas." "A Death in Mexico Symbolizes the Slow Pace of the Police Reforms That Fox Promised," while "Mexico's leader admits he cannot undo 70 years of abuses in 10 months." It was a "Tough Road for Mexico's Top Lawman" "Under Fire Over Rights Cases," amid "Charges of shielding the military instead of ending abuses." In the "Unbalanced Scales of Justice," Mexico's "petty criminals get harsh sentences while petty offenders go unpunished." Leaving "Nowhere to Run, Nowhere to Hide," "Mexico has stepped up efforts to catch U.S. criminals hiding within its borders." As "Mexico Looks South of the Border," "The government plans to get a grip on illegal immigration from Guatemala and Belize." As "Mexico protests US truck rules," "Fox threatened to retaliate against the US if it enacts proposed truck standards." "Fox Urges [U.S.] Congress to Grant Rights to Mexican Immigrants in U.S." "Mexico Opens Investigation Into Money From Union," as "The government sees a possible link to the former ruling party."[41]

In early 2002 it was reported that the Mexican "Congress Shifts Mexico's Balance of Power," while "Lawmakers get more respect, but many lack experience." "When he took office . . . Fox promised to break a 71-year-old tradition of imposing the president's will on the Congress. 'The president proposes, the Congress disposes,' he declared. [He] . . . may not have realized the change he was setting in motion. In the democratic transition of Mexico, Congress has been remade from an institution that rubber stamps presidential initiatives to the one that holds the cards."[42]

"The Revolution That Fizzled"?

In mid-2005, a year before his six-year term was over, it was said, fairly or not, that "Mexico's President Fox burned out early, and some say warning signs were ignored" in "The Revolution That Fizzled." What were some of these "warning signs" in 2003–2006? The following may offer clues. In 2005 "Politics and law clash in Mexico City" as "The Mayor, under criminal investigation, returned to work" "After a tumultuous week in which . . . [his] political opponents tried to jail him, and more than a million supporters took to the streets to decry what they call a political witch hunt." In 2003 "Mexico Votes and Outlook Seems Bleak for Its Leader" because the "President May Lose Control of Congress" "In the first national elections since the country's transition to multiparty rule," with "a sobering setback" expected for Fox. A few months later, "With Fox Mired in Broken Promises, Eyes Turn to a Popular Mayor" of Mexico City as "A Fresh Mexican Standard-Bearer Emerges." In 2004 "Hundreds of Thousands in Mexico March Against Crime." In 2006 "Mexico prefers to export its poor, not uplift them," while "At this week's summit, reforms under Fox should be the issue, not US actions."[42a]

On the other side of the ledger in 2004–2005, for instance, "Fox bids to reform Mexican justice" in "A proposal sent to Congress [that] would make trials public and presume a defendant's innocence," "one of the most ambitious reform packages since the changes that brought Mr. Fox to office." "Strong Antitrust Laws [Are] Sought in Mexico" because "Under present law, the government has no power to break up a monopoly." "A New Law in Tijuana Regulates the Oldest Profession." Meanwhile, "Mexico gives boost to universal jurisdiction" with "Spain's extradition of an Argentine accused of war crimes . . . [in] a first 'third country' prosecution."[43]

The mid-2006 presidential election had some difficulties that could have threatened the new beginnings in Mexican democratic electoral reform. "In Race for the Presidency, A Populist Candidate [the former Mexico City mayor cited above] Tilts At Mexico's Privileged Elite." "Conservative [Felipe Calderón] Wins in Mexico in Final Tally; [but] Opponent Rejects Vote Count" and issues "A call for a recount and a new phase in a tough political fight." It took two months for Mexico's "highest electoral court" to reach its decision. "Election Ruling In Mexico Goes to Conservative from Fox's Party [Calderón]," but "His [Leftist] Rival Vows to Continue Protests" and "Remains Defiant." "Clearly," said one observer, "something is wrong with Mexico's electoral, judicial and political institutions."[44]

After an unpromising electoral start in July 2006, and then the rocky inauguration period, the presidential path ahead seemed difficult. "Amid Fights and Catcalls, Mexico's President Is Sworn In," with "Calderón Spirited In For Inauguration Lasting 4 Minutes." "Mexico Besieged New Leader Faces Tough Challenges," for his "swearing-in . . . amid demonstrations by foes and supporters is only the beginning." A week after inauguration, "Mexico's Leader Swiftly Embraces Policies of His Leftist Opponent." A week after that, it was reported that "Mexico's Surge in Violence" had continued to mount "In the past year, [with] drug killings . . . nearly doubled and lawlessness and corruption reign[ing]."[45]

But then in early 2007 things started to turn around. "Moving beyond a close election and forging a reputation for effectiveness," "Mexico's President Rides Popularity Wave." "Mexico's New President Sends Thousands of Federal Officers to Fight Drug Cartels." By May, as "Escalating drug war grips Mexico," "President Calderón's popularity has soared as he takes on the increasingly brutal drug cartels." Albeit controversial, it was a decisive new day when "Mexico City Legalizes Abortion Early in Term" through "A landmark decision seen as a 'triumph' and a 'tragic duty.' "[46]

Chapter XI

Other Central American Mainland Nations in Government and Society

1. GUATEMALA

On Mexico's southern border, Guatemala today has an elected president and a National Legislature under a recognized constitution and legal system. It has come a long way since the early 1990s, as has its region more generally, in terms of peace, stability, and democracy. It has joined with El Salvador, Honduras, Nicaragua, Panama, and the Dominican Republic in the Central American Parliament or Congress. The country's wrenching earlier struggles presented a far less promising picture.

"Democracy Faces an Uphill Struggle"

Starting in 1990, one encounters such dismal press reports as "Political Violence [Is] on the Rise Again[!] in Guatemala, Tarnishing Civilian Rule." Yet there was new hope when "Court Bars Ex-Dictator From Guatemala Race" for president; and "Guatemala Ballot Marks Watershed" and "Should Pave Way for a Smooth Succession of Civilian Leadership." In early January of 1991 "Right-Wing President [Jorge Serrano] Elected President." In mid-1992 "Guatemala Rivals [Rightist Government and Leftist Guerrillas] In Rights Accord" "Move Toward Ending One of Oldest and Most Violent Wars in Latin America." Yet two months later "Rights Abuses in Guatemala Continue." Then in 1993 "Guatemalan [Pres. Serrano], Supported by Army, Disbands Congress and the Court" amid "fears [of] 'a breakdown in law and order.' " "Guatemala's Power Grab Brings Street Protests" as "the U.S. condemns 'this oppression.' " A week later, "Guatemalan Who Grabbed Power Is Out" as "The military . . . moves to restore democracy." It was a "Counter-Coup: A Military About-Face." The "Army Names Vice President as Leader." Two days later, "Guatemalans Seek to Select New President" and "The court set[s] a 24-hour deadline for Congress to choose a President." A day later, "In Startling Shift, Guatemala [Congress] Makes Rights Aide President," Mr. de León Carpio. In view of "The Palace Coup That Failed," "Democracy faces an uphill struggle in Guatemala."[1]

The story continued with twists and turns. A couple of months later in 1993 "Guatemala Chief, Fighting Corruption, Demands Congress Quit" in "a risky gamble." In spring 1994 "Foreigners [Are] Attacked in Guatemala." In early 1995 "U.S., Protesting Rights Abuses, Ends Military Aid to Guatemala." In May "Guatemalan Ex-Dictator [Is] on Rebound" and "seeks a term as an elected President of Guatemala." In November "Guatemalans see an end to 35-years of civil war" in the first round of voting for president as well as vice president and members of Congress. In the final round of voting for president in early 1996, "Guatemala Election Becomes Vote on Former Dictator," while "Some see . . . the stalking horse for a strongman." Then "Guatemalan Who Pledges to 'Avoid Excesses' Is Narrowly Elected as President," a conservative businessman who promised "A role for the military that it will not 'expand beyond.' " "Guatemala's New President [Mr. Arzú] Shakes Up Army and Police." By March of 1996, "In a U.N. Success Story, Guatemalan Abuses Fall." Difficulties, though abated, continued in 1996. "The man implicated in two murders was on the C.I.A.'s payroll," becoming "For the U.S., a Bad Bedfellow in Guatemala." After thirty-five years of civil war, it was "Guatemala's Uneasy Time: No War but No Peace Pact."[2]

"A Peace Plan and Corruption Cleanup"

Then, in September 1996 "Guatemala and [Rebel] Guerrillas Sign Accord to End 35-Year Combat." "War-Weary Guatemala Gets a Peace Plan And Corruption Cleanup in One Big Week." "Guatemala

Nears the End Of an Era of Bloodshed" because "President Alvano Arzú has pushed for peace and asserted control over the army," "A Milestone Amnesty [Has Occurred] in Guatemala."³

Despite the achievement, many were less sanguine. "In Guatemala, All Is Forgotten" inasmuch as "Guerrillas and generals shake hands—and suppress the truth," leaving "10,000 dead, 40,000 disappeared, and no one will pay." In "Guatemala's 'Adios' to War," "The US and international community still face many challenges." "Rebuilding Guatemala After Negotiating Peace" would not be easy. With "Final Peace Near, Guatemala Braces for Complications" after "40 Years of Conflict," with "Words of skepticism and of Apocalypse," while "Amnesty Law [!] Leads To Feeling of Cynicism." When at the end of December 1996 "Guatemalans Formally End 36-Year Civil War, Central America's Longest and Deadliest," yet, "After 100,000 dead, the peace ceremony is more solemn than celebratory."⁴

The sober rebuilding of a nation on sturdier foundations was under way in the later 1990s and early 2000s. "Guatemala Foes Now Train for Peace," with "Guerrillas and soldiers await[ing] civilian life." "Guatemalan Rights Group [Is] Tracing Abuses in War," owing to "Dissatisfaction with a Guatemalan amnesty law seen as a whitewash." "After War, Guatemala Sees First Fruits of Peace," while "educating Indian rebels is seen as crucial to preventing another civil war." Healing a painful past was not easy when, for instance, "Report Accuses Guatemala, With U.S. Aid, of Genocide." The "Pain of War for Guatemala Isn't Over" in that "Many Are Still Trying to Trace or Find Bodies of the Missing," with "For some . . . no reconciliation." Even so, in later 1999 "A Guatemala At Peace Casts Ballots For President." Then again, there were still reports in 2000 of "Guatemala's lynch-mob justice"; and in 2001 of "War's legacy: Many in Guatemala Still Fear Army" as "The military seeks a new role." And in 2003 "Guatemalan Voters Reject a Former Dictator." An apparent sign of an entrenched legal–legislative system came in 2001 when "Guatemala's new law overrides church objections" through "Reproductive health policy [that] assures funds for contraception and education."⁵

2. EL SALVADOR

The path forward in the 1990s from a long civil war to peaceful national rebuilding was markedly smoother in El Salvador, to the south of Guatemala, with evidences along the way of an established guiding legislature. At first, though, in 1990 there were

"Threats and Party Backlash for El Salvador Chief" after he "moves toward the center without bringing the hard-liners." Several months later, in early 1991, "As Salvadoran Vote Approaches, Terrorist Attacks Arouse Concern." Toward the end of March the "Governing Salvadoran Party Wins Legislative Vote." Soon thereafter, "Salvadorans and Rebels Open Talks to End Their Civil War." A few weeks later, "Salvadoran Assembly [Is] to Take Up Charter Changes." A few days later, "Salvadoran Legislature Passes Reforms in Time." "Patching Up Diverse Factions After Decade of Civil War Is a Formidable Task" facing Salvadorans in "A 'Crisis Of Peace.' " With "Salvadorans Moving To End War," "Leftist Leader Gets High Assembly Post." In September "Both Sides in the Salvadoran Talks Express Optimism on Peace Plan." "Salvador Chief and Rebels Reach a Broad Agreement," though some problems still remained. At the start of January 1992, "Accord [Is] Reached to End Salvador War." "At the Battlefront, Rebels Are Joyful." "The Salvadorans Make Peace in a 'Negotiated Revolution.' " "Salvadorans Sign Treaty to End the War" and "Vow to End Hatred and to Drop Arms" after "12 years of conflict and 75,000 people dead."[6]

Already in 1992 the tasks ahead were challenging but promising for rebuilding as "Salvador Warily Prepares for Peace" after "The war has officially ended, but the political struggle could be just as intense." "Two cheers for Peace: A treaty may end the bloody 12-year war, but prosperity will prove more elusive." "Dispute Over Land Becomes Obstacle To Salvador Peace" after "Ex-Rebels Demand Government Grant Title to a Huge Area Before They Will Disarm," insisting it be "legally turned over to them." Then, "With Formal End to War . . . , Ex-Rebels in Salvador Demobilize." "Civil War Enemies Begin to Work Together to Solve El Salvador's Problems." "El Salvador . . . [Is] A Country Transformed," it being "One place where a peace process has been successful."[7]

Further tasks remained during this period and afterwards. "El Salvador Struggles to Impose Justice" against "death squads [that] may have reemerged as criminal bands." "New Police Force Takes Up Duties in El Salvador." "Salvadoran Moves to Purge Military of Rights Abusers" when, "After a halt, the tortuous journey to peace is resumed." Salvador "Government, Under Fire, Says Order Has Been Issued" and the "Purge Enforced." "El Salvador Finally Removes Military Chiefs." Yet a few years later, "4 Salvadorans Say They Killed U.S. Nuns on Orders of Military." At one point, "As the Elections Near," there are "Frightening reminders of the era of death squads." "El Salvador Bars Voting" "in Area That Favored Guerrillas," so that "Voters Must Travel to Province Center." "Rightist Party Retains Power in Salvador Election." "Newly Elected Rightist Pledges to 'Govern for All Salvadorans' "; while "Pledging to Fulfill Treaty." "A Chastened Latin Left Puts Its Hopes in Ballots."[8]

3. NICARAGUA

Situated between El Salvador and Honduras to the north and Costa Rica to the south, Nicaragua has today an elected president with a six-year term, an elected National Parliament or Assembly, and a legal system with lower courts and Supreme Court, in addition to, since 2004, its delegates to the supranational Central American Parliament. Nicaragua's one-term presidents from 1990 to today (2007)—Chamorro, Alemán, Bolaños, and Ortega (also president in 1985–1990)—have been beset especially in the 1990s with political and economic problems as they steered their country from its extremely turbulent past to its relatively more stable present. Along the way, the national legislative body has had a significant role as well.

In early 1990 with the election of President Chamorro, "Washington [Is] Set to End Embargo and Aid Chamorro Government" after "Opposition Routs Sandinistas" and their outgoing President Ortega pledged cooperation. "Stunned Sandinistas Seek To Define Their New Role" as "A revolutionary front [that now] faces future as a conventional party." "After the Revolution," "The Sandinistas may be down, but they're still not out of power." "Sandinistas Warn They Want Control of Military" ("First, conciliatory remarks; now, what amount to threats"). That September, Nicaragua "Reveals Law Cementing Sandinistas' Grip on Army"—a law drafted shortly before the presidential election while the Sandinistas were still in power and now published on the "official Government register" in an "entirely legal" manner, according to a longtime Sandinista spokesman.[9]

By January 1991 "Nicaragua Sinks Further as Chamorro's Magic Fades." That spring "Chamorro Pleads With [U.S.] Congress For Increase in Aid," saying "Help us build democracy." "Disenchanted With Chamorro, Some Contras Are Taking Up Arms Again" after the heyday of the rebel contra army in the 1980s backed by the Reagan Administration. In June "Nicaragua Talks on Property Seizures Begin" as people "sign petitions that they be allowed to keep land given to them in the waning days of Sandinista rule." A week later it was reported that "Nicaraguan Assembly . . . [Is] No Longer Chamorro's Rubber Stamp" as evidenced in the struggle over keeping property given out by the Sandinista Government. In September Chamorro "vetoed legislation intended to roll back the property give-away arranged by the Sandinista Front before it handed over power...." In December "Legislators Decide to Let Sandinistas Keep Disputed Land," upholding Chamorro's veto of a rollback of the land give-aways.[10]

In mid-1992 the "Newest Strom in Nicaragua . . . [Is] Anti-Gay Law," "After the National Assembly, as part of a reform of the penal code, strengthened the existing law against engaging in homosexuality in a 'scandalous' manner," with Chamorro aides doubting she would veto the legislation as demanded by gay rights groups.[11]

Facing growing general turmoil in spring 1993, "Embattled Nicaraguan [Chamorro] Seeks 'National Accord.'" It was called "A Country Held Hostage" by "Former contras and ex-Sandinistas [who] are both at war with the Chamorro government." Then, "Chamorro and Foes [Are] Settling Disputes, Smoothing Way for Talks with Sandinistas." In early 1994 "Nicaraguan Lawmakers Meet in Effort to Break Deadlock" and "to revise the national labor code." In mid-1995, the "President and Legislature [Are] Dueling in Nicaragua" in "crisis over family dynamics."[12]

In the fall of 1996, "Nicaragua's Bitter [Presidential] Election Fight Ends with Victor [Alemán] Asking for Reconciliation." "Rightist Defeats Sandinista in Nicaragua," supporting "a freer market and U.S. ties." There still loomed "A Turf Fight Over Just Who Owns Land," while "President-elect vows to pursue property seized by the Sandinistas." "With Big Broom, New President Prods Nicaragua" in early 1997. "A Tug-of-War in Nicaragua [Arises] Over Seized Land"— with some people crying foul over lack of "equal[ity] before the law"— as "A policy sets off a post-revolutionary rift over former rebels' real estate,." In September 2000 there remained "Among Unpaid Wages of a Revolution: Competing Claims on Land in Nicaragua."[13]

Events swirled on. In 2004, under President Bolaños, "Nicaragua, 25 Years After the Revolution, Is Still Struggling" after "Conservatives have failed the people, as the Sandinistas did." In 2006 "Nicaraguan Legislature Passes Total Ban on Abortion." "Mayhem and Money, Violence and Corruption, Hobble Nicaraguan Democracy." After the presidential election in fall 2006, it became "Ortega's Encore" as the "anti–U.S. cold warrior . . . made his way back to power in Nicaragua." "Ortega's effort to recast himself from rebel to uniter has helped to propel him to victory." Shortly thereafter, "Nicaragua Eliminates Last Exception to Strict Anti-Abortion Law" when outgoing President Bolaños signed it into law, thereby dashing hopes of women's groups that he "would stop one of the most restrictive abortion laws in Latin America from taking effect"—with the new measure being passed in the Assembly by conservatives taking advantage of the recent election.[14]

4. PANAMA

"U.S. Troops Install a New Government"

After the United States invasion of Panama in December 1989 and the ouster of its strongman ruler, Manuel Noriega, "U.S. Troops Install a New Government in Panama," shortly thereafter capturing Noriega. A few days before the invasion, the National Assembly made Noriega head of the Government with "extraordinary and indefinite powers" overriding the president of the Republic, in which since 1983 he had been commander of the National Guard and the Panama Defense. The U.S. "Congress Generally Supports Attack, but Many Fear Consequences," such as N.Y. Rep. Charles Rangel who said "I don't see the legal authority to use the military." "U.S. [Is] Denounced by Nations Touchy About Intervention" ("From leftist Nicaragua to rightist Chile, condemnation").[15]

Soon enough in the U.S. Congress, "Legislators Express Concern On the Operation's Future," and "The House Speaker hopes the troops will be withdrawn soon," while at the United Nations the "U.S. [Is] Finding Scant Support for Action in Panama." "A history of struggle over covert operations" in Panama involved "White House, Noriega And Battle in Congress," as reported earlier that October. One critical newspaper editorial declared: "Panama for the Panamanians." The same issue's OP-ED piece criticized "Imperialism Bush-Style." The previous day's editorial page, however, told "Why the Invasion Was Justified." So press opinions were still in considerable flux as events rapidly unfolded.[16]

It was not long before "U.S., Panama Report Some Success in Restoring Order," even though "This Mop-Up Could Take Us Years." "Panama Replaces Its Army With a New Security Force," leaving "Third World Likely to Seek Condemnation of U.S." "Noriega Seeks Asylum From Vatican Officials as People Applaud His Surrender." "In the Battered [Panamanian] Capital, People Are Celebrating," and "Resistance to U.S. Soldiers Comes Virtually to an End." "As Word Spreads in Panama, Thousands Turn Out to Cheer."[17]

The post-invasion civilian government led by President Guillermo Endara was off to a mixed start. In January 1990 "Endara moves to revive the economy and end corruption"—" 'Criminal Is Gone,' but Joy Is Fleeting in Land He Ruled," after "Noriega Arraigned in

Miami on U.S. Drug Charge." Some "Scholars Say Arrest of Noriega Has Little Jurisdiction in Law," and "The closest parallel may lie in ancient Rome." In early February "Panama Is Resisting U.S. Pressure To Alter 'Inadequate' Bank Laws." In June "U.S. Has Jurisdiction Over Noriega, Judge Rules." At any rate, "After Noriega, Change Comes Slowly and Panama's President Is Frustrated." In December it was reported that in "Year Since U.S. Invasion, Panama's Problems Mount: While Unemployment, Crime Rise, Morale of Police Plummets," as "U.S. Army Guarantees Endara Stays in Power." "Rebels Are Posing Threat In Panama," and "The police force is suspicious of the U.S.–backed Government."[18]

"Dependence and Sovereignty Pull At Panama's Equilibrium"

By February 1991 it was being reported that "Dependence and Sovereignty Pull at Panama's Equilibrium" and "Split Panamanians." Subheadings in that account were indicative of the wide range of issues involved: "After Noriega, Panama Adapts," "Local Sovereignty Vs. Relying on U.S.," "Ghosts of Past Haunt Endara," "Rebel Uprising Reveals Weakness," "New Security Force Full of Old Guard," "Trouble Blamed on Infighting," "Economic Forecast Fails to Ignite Hope," and "People Reassess U.S. Mission." Other forces were also at work. In June "Political Alliance Ruling Panama Breaks Up." In September, "More Than an Ex-Dictator's Future [Is] At Stake as Trial of Noriega Begins," for he "may not be the only one with secrets." In November 1992, with "Constitutional Change Losing in Panama Vote," "Foes also see a rejection of U.S.–chaperoned Government." "Opponents of Panamanian Chief Say He Must Shift Course or Quit."[19]

"Democracy [Is] at Work, Under Shadow of Dictators." In September 1994 "Panama's New Leader [Pérez Is] Sworn In" after a national election; and he soon "Seeks to Prod the Economy," with "Labor Law and State Industries to Change." In December 1995 "Panama Changes Tune to 'Yankee Don't Go Home' " inasmuch as "Panama doesn't relish the idea of fending for itself." For the United States, a familiar problem in Panama arose in 1996 when "Drug Scandal Taints Panama's President, Who Is Pledged to Combat Trafficking." On a different front in 1997, with import for democracy and self-determination, "Panama Indians Battle Modern 'Invader' Over Mining Rights" as "Tribes united to fight Canadian company seeking to mine on their proposed reserve."[20]

The U.S. handover to Panama of the Canal and bases became a subject of mounting intense anticipation in 1996–1999, together with related concerns. In 1996 "Panama [Is] Charting a Course to Run Its Canal," with "An eddy of competing interests as a waterway's takeover nears." In 1997 "Panama's Balancing Act . . . [Is Over] Security vs. Land Rights." In related fashion, "Yankee go home—unless we say stay: The impending handover of U.S. military bases to Panama triggers a flood of second thoughts." For "Handoff in Panama: Hong Kong Was Just a Rehearsal." "When US Hands Over Bases to Panama, It May Leave Environmental Mess Behind." "Panama Leader [Pérez] Accused of Cronyism Over Appointees to Rule the Canal," whereas "Panamanians want the jewel of the national patrimony in good hands." "As Panama Canal Transfer Nears, [There Is] More Jockeying to Fill a Power Vacuum." "The U.S. prepares to cede Panama the precious waterway, but the canal is already up to its locks in charges of neglect and political favoritism" through "The Canal Chronies [*sic*]." "In Panama Accord, G.I.'s Would Stay" in "Drug-Fighting Role Seen [For U.S. Troops] After Canal Is Turned Over in '99." Then in 1998 "U.S. Accord With Panama on Troops Hits a Snag." Several months later, in September 1998, "Leader's Loss In Panama Clouds Future Of The Canal" after voters rejected a proposal that would have allowed Pérez to seek a second consecutive presidential term. Shortly thereafter, it was lamented that "Ruling Party In Panama Is Profiting From Canal." For its part, the "U.S. Balks at Cleanup of Hazardous Canal Zone Sites."[21]

"A new President will lead her country into complete sovereignty"

On the eve of the presidential voting in May 1999, "Final Return Of the Canal Colors Vote in Panama." As it turned out, "The Widow Of Ex-Leader [a former strongman General] Wins Race In Panama," having been owner of a coffee business. At her September swearing-in, "In Panama's New Dawn, Woman Takes Over," becoming "A new President [who] will lead her country into complete sovereignty"—that is, becoming "The first Panamanian President to lead a completely sovereign country once the United States withdraws its remaining troops and hands over the Panama Canal on Dec. 31" (leaving "our sovereignty fully rescued," as she put it).[22]

The Canal transfer and troop departure was not without difficulty on both sides in 1999 and beyond. "Giving Up The Ship?: The looming handover of the Panama Canal has fired some serious separation anxiety in the U.S." In "Panama's farewell to (American) arms," "A Pentagon pullout hobbles the drug war." "Panama Trouble: Who Hands Canal Over?" ("Albright declines, Gore wasn't asked, but Carter agrees to do the honors.""). "Carter, Proclaiming 'It's Yours,' Celebrates New Era for Panama" after, historically, "A great power gave property to a tiny nation with no capacity to seize it."[23]

As scheduled on December 31, 1999, on the very eve of the new century and new millennium, "To Cheers, Panama Takes Over the Canal." "Panama Canal Sees the Last of the Stars and Stripes," while, according to "One Panamanian's vow: 'We will run it as well or better than the Americans.'"[24]

Panamanian democracy has been evolving in the early 21st century. Although Panama has been an "historic haven for political exiles," one authority stated in 2000 that "As democracy's roots grow deeper . . . Panama will no longer want to take in the scoundrels." Yet in 2001 "Panama Is Putting Journalists on Trial," and, "With Dozens of Cases Pending, Concern About Press Laws Rises." In 2004 "Son of Late Dictator Is Elected The Next President of Panama." And the story has continued.[25]

Chapter XII

Caribbean Nations in Government and Society

1. CUBA

"Castro's socialist dream has turned into a nightmare"

As is well known, Fidel Castro has long been the dictator of Cuba, belying his title of "elected" president of the Council of State, for nearly a half century since 1959. Starting our account here in early 1990, we are struck by the periodic hopes for his fall that were soon dashed. A news report that year pointed out that the "Rising Hopes for Castro's Fall Have Cubans in Miami Abuzz," while " 'Next Christmas in Havana,' the bumper stickers proclaim," constituting "For many exiles, an outbreak of 'wishful thinking–cum madness.' " Such false hopes would continue to be repeated, soon again to be dashed. At that time, it was "Fidel's Race Against Time," for "With communism fading in the East Bloc, Castro faces his toughest challenge as he clings to his Leninist vision of a socialist state," although "Cuba is not the only Soviet client [state] looking at cutbacks in military and economic aid." A year later, "As Castro Grays, So Does Revolution," while, "Despite Castro's Hard-Line Rhetoric, Change Is Coming to Communist Cuba." Even so, "Castro's Failing Socialism Still

Draws Strength From the Myth of the Yankee Imperial Threat"
("In Havana: Castro and the Paranoia of Revolutionary Resistance."). As part of Cuba's momentary hopeful sign, "Castro Reopens The Gate To Exodus." In addition, President "Bush In Over-
ture To Cuban Leader" "Foresees Better Ties if Castro Frees
Prisoners and Holds Democratic Elections."[1]

The tide soon turned. In later 1991 "Havana Closes Communist
[Ruling Party] Congress to Outsiders," journalists and delegations,
due to Cuba's "severe economic and political crisis." At the same
time, "Castro Meets Dissent With an Iron Hand." "Castro [Is] Cracking Down As the Hardships Grow." "Castro Steels a Suffering Nation for Confrontation" as "Loss of Soviet aid plunges Cuba into
economic crisis," while "The Havana leadership shuns any reform."
In early 1993 " 'Down With Fidel' Is Heard in Cuba, but There Is
No Sign Yet of His Fall," and he "Remains Larger Than Life." In
spring 1994 "Economy [Is] Fading Fast, but Not Castro." "Cuba
Police Fight Protesters Over Growing Effort to Flee."[2]

Clearly, with "Cuba Alone," "Castro's socialist dream has turned
into a nightmare. Isolated, hungry, and broke, the country hopes
that a touch of capitalism will save it." Thus it was that in the mid-
1990s "Cuba's Economy, Cast Adrift, Grasps at Capitalist Solutions"
because as "Communism Ebbs, . . . So Does Trade." "A new generation of upwardly mobile Marxists still talks *Das Kapital* but dabbles
in capitalism." "Cuba Opts to Legalize Dollar," with "Marxists Preparing For Historic Shift As Economy Crumbles." "Cuba [Is] to
Allow All Farmers to Sell Some Food on the Open Market." "Cubans Get A Taste of Capitalism" as "Farms Sell Surplus On Open
Market" and "The law of supply and demand goes to work in Cuba."
"Cuba Takes Another Step in Opening Up Its Economic System."
"Castro's Cuba is desperate and open for business," and "Fidel defends his compromises," "facing up to socialism's failures." Meanwhile, however, "With Communism declining, the military takes over
many businesses" and "Party Jobs."[3]

"[Castro's] sovereign equality of states"
(in defiance of U.S. embargo laws and rules)

In defiance of the hurtful U.S. embargo and other restrictions,
Castro urged in 1995 that "the sovereign equality of states" be re-
spected so that Cuba should not have to democratize in order to get
U.S.–led sanctions lifted. He was not alone. Three years earlier,
"U.N. Votes to Call for U.S. to End Embargo on Cuba" in "A Re-

buke to Washington" after "Many Allies Signal Their Anger at New Law That Extends Reach of Restrictions." Some American press spokesmen, too, felt that "The U.S. embargo hurts democracy and helps Castro," with "Hard Line, Hard Luck, for Cuba."[4]

As Castro reversed policy to force the issue, so too did Washington. In summer 1994, "U.S. Halts Hundreds of Cubans At Sea in Abrupt Policy Change." "President Considers a Cuban Blockade." "U.S. Struggles With Rising Refugee Tide." "As Castro sets refugees adrift toward Florida, Clinton decides to undo a decades-old policy and interdict fleeing Cubans at sea." With growing crisis, Florida was "Waiting Anxiously For Rules On Cuba" refugees from Clinton Administration. "U.S. Rejects Castro's Proposal for Talks," "demanding reforms by Cuba." Still, "Castro Hopes His Flood Of Refugees Will Force The U.S. To Make A Deal." Then, in "A Dubious Pact," "Castro Got Little Back for Agreeing to Try to Stop Outflow of Refugees."[5]

Over a half year later, "Clinton Opposes Move To Toughen Embargo On Cuba," saying "Proposal by Republicans Violates World Trade Accords," and the proposed "Legislation Is Criticized." "U.S. Will Return Refugees to Cuba In Policy Switch," while "Cuban-Americans charge the Administration with betrayal." "A Year After Boat Exodus, Threat to Castro Dissipates." "Bill to Tighten Economic Embargo on Cuba Is Passed With Strong Support in the House," yet "Clinton threatens to veto a bill that seeks to cut foreign investment in Cuba."[6]

Subsequently, "U.N. Urges U.S. to End Ban on Cuba." "Latin Nations, With Trade and Tourism, Are Now Ignoring U.S. Efforts to Isolate Cuba" in "A hemispheric shift [that] further challenges U.S. policy."[7]

The U.S.–Cuban struggle over legislative–regulatory sanctions continued on during the Clinton Administration. In early 1996 "Clinton Seeks Wider Sanctions As Cuba Curbs Air Travel": "Denouncing the downing of two private American planes by Cuba as 'a flagrant violation of international law,' President Clinton today . . . pledged to reach agreement with Congress on a pending bill to tighten economic sanctions." Two days later, "President Agrees [With Congress] To Tough New Set Of Havana Curbs" "Blocking Investment" through "Measures [That] Could Hasten Downfall of Castro's Ailing System," although, an Administration official said, "our allies will [not] be pleased with this legislation." Some House critics called it "A Bad Bill On Cuba." Said one account, "Curbs [Are] Expected to Have Little Effect." "As U.S.–Cuba relations hit new low, Castro tells why his air force shot down civilians" after (as he said with a "bristling sense of nationalism," showing "This Cold Warrior Is Back") "Cuban airspace had been violated" as part of dissident efforts to bring down his regime. Unrepentant, "Cuba Moves to Silence a Growing Voice of Journalism." "Cuba Stifles New Dissenters." In mid-1996, "Punishing Cuba's Partners," "U.S. companies are mum—U.S. allies are not—over a [U.S.] law aimed at foreign firms trading with Castro." "Cuba takes a stiff belt" as "Washington wants to hurt Castro by punishing foreign firms on the island. But will they go?" Further on in 1996, "U.N. Renews Call for End to Cuba Ban." Near year's end, "Cuban Refugees in Detention Find They Are in Legal Limbo." In early 1997 "One Key Element In Anti-Cuba Law [Is] Postponed Again," with Clinton set "to waive indefinitely part of a law that punishes foreign companies using American property confiscated in Cuba nearly 40 years ago." Then "Cuba Measure Strikes Back At the U.S.," or, more specifically, "The Cuban Government has approved a law" that "Seeks to Counter [U.S.] Helms–Burton Law." Also, "Cuba Gives Long Prison Terms to Six Who Tried to Flee." One U.S. press commentator argued that "U.S. policy only makes repression worse." Meantime, by the end of 1997, "Car, Bean Nations, Ignoring U.S., Warm to Cuba." In early 1999, "Clinton eases the Cuban embargo, but not much is changing" in "The same old ballgame."[8]

"Castro's Flickering Revolution"

That premature hopefulness back in late 1996 was belied by the ongoing staying-power of Castro's regime, still in place eleven years later as of this writing. But it did point up the often desperate straits that Castro found himself increasingly in as the years went on before and after 2000, forcing his hand on reforms. A similar anticipation was evident in early 1997 when, "Setting the Stage for Transition in Cuba," "Canada's policy of engagement with Cuba could advance American interests—if the US cooperates." Many months later, however, "Cuba's Communists Peer Ahead, Then Opt to March in Place" as "Castro admires China's changes, but they're not for Cuba." Even amid hopeful signs within Cuba there was reluctance to embrace such phenomena as capitalism, much less democracy. In 1998 "Cuba applies the law of supply and demand, and the foreign press pays the price." "Four Decades of Revolution Bring Cuba Full Circle" in a "Welcome to Latin America" and a "Welcome to World Trade." "Cuba Seeks Change, Without Blow to Its System" ("Cuba After Castro: Some See Spain's Evolution as a Model"). In 1999 "In

Cuba's New Dual Economy, the Have-Nots Far Outnumber the Haves." In 2001 there are "In Cuba Clashing Voices Over Ideals and Reality" (pro and con Castro).[9]

A hopeful sign, soon dashed, came in 2002 when former U.S. President "Carter Addresses the Cuban Nation and Urges Reforms," with Castro at his side, and "Asks U.S. to End Sanctions," but "Bush Plans to Tighten Sanctions, Not End Them." "Cuban Dissidents Put Hope in a Petition and Jimmy Carter." But then in 2003 "Cuba Confirms Sentencing Dozens of Pro-Democracy Dissidents." At that point of "Crackdown in Cuba," "Harsh Repression Suggests Castro Felt Worried Enough to Risk Ties Abroad." "U.S. May Punish Cuba for Imprisoning Critics," and "Bush is expected to warn Havana against any new mass migration." As for "The Country Castro Will Leave Behind" ("Goodbye But Not Farewell"), "Does Cuba need a new leader or a new government?" In 2004 it was, "For Many Cubans, an Uneasy Farewell to the Dollar" after "The influx of U.S. currency has fueled a dual economy," with Cuba now "Putting an end to dependency on a symbol of capitalism." In 2005 "Castro [is] tightening grip amid boomlet." In 2006 "Castro's Younger Brother Is Focus of Attention Now," but "What Would His Leadership Bring?" By 2007 there clearly was "In Cuba, a struggle over history's march to democracy," as "recent events there underline the uncertainty that swirls around a post-Castro regime."[10]

A far bigger hope, later disappointed, arose with the Pope's 1998 Cuban visit prearranged with Castro. For one thing, the "Papal Visit Signals Cuba's Eased Stand on Church." "Pope John Paul brings his message of freedom to Fidel Castro's Cuba" in a "Clash of Faiths." "Pope, Arriving in Cuba, Is Welcomed by Castro" and "Urges Havana and the world to open up to each other." "Pope's Call for Clemency Lifts Dissidents' Hopes" after "Dozens of activists have been imprisoned in the last two years." "Pope Is Pressing Castro for Release of Prisoners" in "A papal plea for greater freedom for all Cubans." "Hearing the Pope With Ears of Marx," "Cubans seem to say . . . faith would be easier if human life were too." Even though "Pope . . . Asks Cubans to Seek 'New Paths' Toward Freedom," "Pope Captivates His Marxist Host." "The Pope's Mission Of Hope tries to open Cuba to change; Castro hopes his visit will open the world to Cuba." Yet "Freeing of Dissidents May Not Mean a Freer Cuba." "The Pope giveth, Castro taketh," and "John Paul II attacks communism but deplores the U.S. embargo, too." "After Lift From Pope, Cuban Church Has Letdown" because "Havana is showing little new flexibility."[11]

2. HAITI

With its history of chronic chaos and uncertainty from the 1990s to recent years, interspersed with varying efforts at democracy amid rule by military juntas, Haiti has presented a different political picture than has Cuba under Castro's steadfast rigid dictatorship since 1959. Although Haiti has been primarily a republic with an elected (five-year term) president and legislature (a National Assembly with Senate and House of Representatives), the country has had a rocky and turbulent pathway to the present. Various themes in the news are of interest here albeit in necessarily abbreviated form. The historical progression from the dictatorship of Duvalier (ousted in 1986) to the perennial appearances, disappearances, and reappearances of the pro-democratic Jean-Bertrand Aristide (first elected president in 1990) provides a certain continuity to Haitian current news history; but it falls short of the steadier advancements for democracy found in other Central American countries looked at above besides Cuba. There have been frequent unfulfilled struggles in Haiti (often in conjunction with the United States) to establish democratic government with a legal–legislative system in an actual nation-state where often these elements were in scarce evidence. And yet the struggles are instructive in themselves precisely because of how urgently those elements were needed yet absent at the center of Haiti's perilous precarious picture.

"Haitian Legislators and Aristide Agree on His Return"

Aristide's election as president in late 1990 put an all-too-brief end to Haiti's immediate turmoil. During the months before: "Haitian Bishop Says Military [Government] Makes 'Rubbish' of the Law"; "Haiti's Ruler Quits; Election Is Promised" after "the fifth time in four years that power has changed hands in Port-au-Prince"; "Haitians, Fearing Chaos, Grope for a New Leader"; and "Haitian Voting Is Free of Violence, but Marred by Delays and Fraud Charges." In December "Haitians Overwhelmingly Elect Populist Priest to the Presidency," and "U.S. Vows Enthusiastic Support." "Haiti Leader Faces Task Of Controlling Military," having "called for the arrest of Duvalier thugs." The election was optimistically hailed as "An Avalanche for Democracy." In January 1991 "Haiti's Army Crushes Revolt by Duvalier Loyalists" after "Troops, Storming Palace, Capture Plotters and Free President." In early February, "Haiti Installs Democratic Chief, Its First." As "Haiti's New Leader Takes on the Army," "It is unclear how the six generals will react to being 'retired.'" Another major problem was "Bringing Haiti's Shattered Economy Back From the Brink."[12]

By April 1991 "Honeymoon Sours for Haiti President." In September "Haiti's Parliament Shows Leader Its Backbone." In October "Haitian Troops Mutiny and Arrest President" as the "Military Assumes Power." "U.S. and Latins [Are] Moving to Isolate Haiti." "Haiti's Coup . . . [Is] Test Case for President Bush's New World Order," begging the question of "How far will the U.S. go to defend democracy where there is no oil?" Thus "Haiti's Democracy, Such as It Was, Is Swept Aside by a Chaotic Coup," its president exiled.[13]

Events rapidly unfolded, with a significant spotlight on the legislature. In October 1991 "Haiti Legislature Declares the Presidency Vacant." In the wake of "One Coup Too Many," "Haiti's soldiers fail to reckon with George Bush's determination to preserve—maybe even to restore—democratically elected leaders." But then in early February 1992 "Democracy Push In Haiti [Is] Blunted," leaving "Leaders of Coup Gleeful After U.S. Loosens Its Embargo and Returns Refugees." Going "From Bad to Worse," "As the political standoff drags on, Haiti's people descend deeper into misery[,] and the U.S. gropes for a way to handle the refugee flow." A "Plan for Global Peacekeepers to Soothe Haiti Is Weighed" as "Latin American nations back intervention," albeit "Aristide Condemns U.S. Policy." Then in later February "Haitian Legislature and Aristide Agree on His Return." "Ousted Haitian Leader and Foes [Are] Completing Accord for His Return." A month later in March, however, "Haiti Accord Is Set Back in Parliament." In May "Legislative Bloc Walks Out of Talks" when "Unity Plan [Is] Announced In Haiti."[14]

But events were still moving ahead, as when subsequently in May 1992 "Latin States Back Steps to Restore President In Haiti" through "Tougher Trade Measures" so as "to Isolate the Military by Denying Port Rights." In March 1993 "Haitian Is Offered Clinton's Support On An End To Exile," although "In Pledging to Restore Aristide, U.S. Avoids Strong Steps, Fearing New Violence." After extended complicated negotiations and with threats of new U.S. and U.N. sanctions along with an imposed police force, "Military Chief Signs Accord to End Haitian Crisis." Thus in July 1993 "Haiti's Sides Conclude Agreement."[15]

"Restoring Stability to Haiti"?

With accord reached for Aristide's return, "Restoring Stability to Haiti Is Seen as the Next Big Test." Great challenges obviously lay ahead especially on the economy and the military once Aristide would be back in power. Yet a "Haitian Senator Resists Terms of Pact on Aristide." With Aristide awaiting his return, urging removal of the army and police chiefs, and with the United Nations lifting the embargo as the junta prepares to step down, there were new signs of looming violence. "Public Killing Defines Barriers to Aristide's Return." "Haiti Police Chief Poses Hurdle to Aristide's Return." "Gunmen and Police Brutally Enforce Strike in Haiti." Was it "Haiti: Mission Impossible"? Then "Haiti Justice Minister [Is] Slain As Military Defies the U.S.," casting "A long shadow over a key deadline . . . for democracy." A day later "President [Clinton] Orders Six U.S. Warships For Haiti Patrol" to "Enforce Sanctions." "As U.S. Ships Arrive, Haiti General Refuses to Budge," with "Terror of Duvalier Years . . . Haunting Haiti Again."[16]

"As Aristide Fails to Return, His Foes Celebrate in Haiti," while, "Amid Strife, Haiti Parliament Struggles With Itself." Some said "The U.S. has sided with Haiti's enemies," "Abandoning Democracy." "Aristide Condemns Clinton's Haiti Policy as Racist." Then "Clinton Says Haiti Military Must Go Now." Yet Washington seemed "Hostage to Violence." "U.N. Council Votes Tougher Embargo On Haitian Trade" and "Seeks Aristide's Return."[17]

Supported by the defiant military, a rump group of "Right-Wing Lawmakers in Haiti Swear[s] in a Provisional President" in May 1994, while the Clinton Administration debated on the use of force in an invasion of troops. A few weeks later, "Doubting Sanctions, Aristide [still living in Washington] Urges U.S. Action on Haiti." "Governments Are Joining Haiti Force" to "Keep Order As Aristide Returns," and "Generals call in Noriega's lawyers for consultation." "A Haiti Invasion Wins Hemisphere Support" "if the Sanctions Fail." Soon thereafter, "Haiti Strongman [Is] Reported To Set Retirement Date" in "A sign of strength by Cédras, or a Bluff?"; would he simply serve out the rest of his term to end in a few months? Then, through its "de facto military Government" "Haiti Plans Ballot Likely to Yield a Replacement for Aristide." "Haiti Invasion Led by U.S. Gains Assent In U.N. Vote." "Haitian Military Greets Invasion Vote With Defiance." "Haiti Attacks Critics and Restricts Civil Rights."[18]

"Haiti Is a Land Without a Country"

To that sorry pronouncement in August 1994 was added the caveat that "No government [in Haiti] has provided people with much education or inspired much trust," leaving "Nothing to Build On." Now "Haiti Rulers Hold Relief Fuel, Endangering Lives," inasmuch as

"Medical care and feeding of Haitians depends on fuel." Yet "Embargo Dries Up Haiti Fuel Supply."[19]

Meanwhile, "Legislators In U.S. Differ Over Haiti," "Some Back[ing] Invasion, but Others Are Wary." "Clinton Sees No Need for Votes on Haiti" in "A recurrent battle over who has the power to make war." "President [Clinton] Tells Leaders Of Haiti to Yield Power" in "What Clinton sees as the only possible response to 'terror.'" "Holding Off, Clinton Sends Carter, Nunn and Powell to Talk to Haitian Junta" but "only about the junta's departure." "Talks Give Little Hope To Aristide Supporters."[20]

A turnaround then occurred in mid-September 1994. "Haitian Military Rulers Agree to Leave; Clinton Calls Off Plans For U.S. Invasion," though "Troops to Land" anyway. Strikingly, in accordance with the agreement signed by the junta, the Legislative Assembly will decide by mid-October on amnesty and other matters. The next day "3,000 U.S. Troops Land Without Opposition And Take Over Ports And Airfields In Haiti" and "Junta Cooperates." This was a case of successful "forceful diplomacy."[21]

Problems naturally arose during the rapid subsequent developments in September 1994. Days later, "Haitian Police Crush Rally As American Troops Watch," with "Junta In Control" and "Pro-Aristide Protester . . . Beaten to Death," while Aristide "Demands U.S. Disarm Forces of Military Junta," albeit "Amnesty Law Expected To Clear Junta Very Soon." Then "Clinton Says U.S. Will Deter Abuses by Haiti Police," "But G.I.'s Won't Try to Disarm the Military," and, even though "American Commanders Give Cédras A Warning," "Haitian Military Peruses Fine Print of Accord in Bid to Hold Onto Power." "The Reach of Democracy" was being further tested by "Tying Power to Diplomacy." Shortly, there were "Cheers and Signs of Relief as Beatings Subside" after "U.S. Soldiers Begin Disarming Elite Haitian Military Company." Yet the "Grim Shadow of Economic Reality" was looming large as "Haitians need more, much more than just one man to lead them," while "Demonstrators Show Fear and Joy as They Defy Police in Support of Aristide." "U.S. [Is] to Press Cédras to Disarm His Allies" after "Disorders Follow Clash in Haitian City."[22]

"G.I.'s Take Over the Parliament"

Improvements soon came, due largely at first to American troops' temporary takeovers, with particular regard to the Legislature. "Haitians Rejoice As American M.P.'s Visit Police Posts" with "Thousands Cheer[ing] G.I.'s," "But Haiti's Police Are Jeered as Crowds Celebrate the Passing of Power." "U.S. Troops Will Bar Legislators

From Amnesty Session" ("pro-military lawmakers were elected in voting fraud"). "G.I.'s Take Over the Parliament in Haiti." The "Haiti Parliament Meets, but Delays an Amnesty [Law] Vote" on the military leaders scheduled to leave in mid-October, for "The legislature is bitterly split, and many Aristide foes stay away." A week later, when "The Senate passes amnesty measure already approved by the deputies," "Haitian Bill Doesn't Exempt Military From Prosecution." "Haitians Vote Amnesty but Terms Are Vague."[23]

In the meantime, "As the U.S. expands the occupation, bursts of violence threaten the delicate balance of Clinton's policy," "Walking A Thin Line." "Singing and Dancing, Haitians Defy Military" while praising Aristide, yet "Explosion Rips Pro-Democracy Crowd in Port-au-Prince." A day later "Military-Backed [Junta] 'Attaches' Fire on Pro-Aristide Crowd," while "U.S. troops were stationed away from the protest route, guarding stores." One editorial urged "Don't Manipulate Haiti's Politics." Yet "U.S. Forces [Are] to Widen Role In Curbing Haiti Violence." "To Cheers U.S. Troops Clear Haitian Gunman's Clubhouse" even though, "Beyond the U.S. Raid, Haiti Is Still a Minefield."[24]

Slowly but surely "Haiti's government-in-waiting struggles into the open" as "Aristide Backers Start to Surface" and "Political Figures Who Hid From Junta Are Warily Emerging," while "Haiti's Military Leadership Appears to Be Crumbling," and "Aristide Pledges to Follow Road of Reconciliation and Recovery." "U.S. Scrambles for Recruits to Bring Order to the Streets of Haiti's Two Largest Cities" at the same time as "Clinton Exults in Swift Success of U.S. Military Force in Haiti." Thus "The Iron Fist [of Junta] In Haiti Begins to Lose Its Grip" after it "has terrorized Haiti for three years." Finally, in mid-October, "Haiti's Commander in Chief Resigns" and "Departs to the Rich and Bitter Sarcasm of the People He Ruled." Still, "Business Owners Fear Chaos at the Hands of Mobs When Aristide Returns."[25]

"Behind Shield of American Troops, Aristide Copes With a Stripped Nation"

With their Junta chiefs gone, "Joyous Haitians Decorate the Capital for Aristide," and "The President [Clinton] and Aristide Heap Praise on Each Other," when, on October 15, "Aristide, In A Joyful Return, Urges Reconciliation In Haiti" and "Ecstatic Crowd Greets Elected President as G.I.'s Stand Guard." "Haiti Emerges, Eyes Blinking, In the Sunlight of Democracy," "Now to rebuild the economy and heal old wounds." "With Embargo Lifted, Haitians

Scramble for Trade." "Haitians Seize Men Accused Of Terror Acts," but "Crowds Use Restraint At Aristide's Urging."[26]

Thus "Behind Shield of American Troops, Aristide Copes With a Stripped Nation" and with "A Government [that] barely functions in a country famous for despair," but "Has Aristide turned from priest to politician or populist to puppet?" This continued to be the situation in November 1994. Moving quickly, "Aristide Picks a Prime Minister With Free-Market Ideas." "Sweeping Changes [Are] Seen for Haiti With Nation's Rich Paying More." "Haiti's Capital Throbs With New Life" "with the fear gone." "Aristide's Cabinet Is Sworn and Pledges to Get to Work" as "Haiti looks to building democracy and rebuilding devastated economy." "Aristide Ousts Acting Army Chief" "After just a month . . . [due to] corruption charges." Other difficulties loomed large in November. "U.N. Envoy [Is] Pessimistic About Holding Orderly Election in Haiti." "Legal Vacuum in Haiti Is Testing U.S. Policy." "Fear[ing] Long-Term Operation, U.S. [Is] Pressed to Disarm Opponents of Aristide" in the face of "Foes of the Haitian President [who] still wield power in rural areas." "Aristide [Is] Under Pressure to Set an Election Date"; yet "Haiti Election Is Postponed To Next Year."[27]

But by December–January, 1994–1995, with "Nothing to Build On: Haiti Is Starting at Zero; Aristide Wins Praise." "U.S. [Is] Ready to Declare Haiti 'Success,' " with result that "Transfer of Military Role to U.N. Will Begin Soon." "Getting The Hang Of It," "Despite huge problems, a newly molded Aristide has given his country what it never had before: hope."[28]

On subsequent electoral and related political fronts, was there yet "Democracy in Haiti? Not Yet," at least not in spring 1995. "Haiti Battles to Keep Vote on Schedule." In late June, the "Vote Today [Is] a Turning Point for Haiti," the "First [Election] Since Aristide Returned and the Junta Left." "Testing Fragile Democracy, Haiti Votes," exhibiting "Disarray at Polls but Few Cases of Violence." "As Haitian Tally Proceeds, Signs of Irregularities Mount," for which "Political Rivals Accuse Pro-Aristide Party." "Haiti Leader Hails Election As Major Step," "Valid Despite Flaws." Two weeks later, "Haiti [Is] to Delay Announcement of Results of National Voting." "In Haiti, Democracy Still Flounders."[29]

From early 1995 to 1999, well after Aristide's departure following the mid-1995 elections, problems mounted in Haiti, showing ever greater need for stable government and legal system. In 1995 "Haiti's Fate . . . [Is] Out of Repression, Into a Crime Wave" by "gunmen who terrorize Haiti [and] seem to have found a new trade." "As Haiti's People Call for Justice, Its Penal System Is Slow to Reform."

"Among Haiti's Poor, [There Is] a Land Rush Without Rules." "As confidence in justice ebbs, punishments become direct" as "Haiti Struggles With Both Criminals and Vigilantes." "Aristide Urges U.N. Force to Disarm His Foes," whose "Violence sweeps Haiti on the eve of a U.S. pullout." "U.N. Force Takes Up Duties in Haiti." "Many Haitians [Are] Fearful Despite U.N. Presence," with "Crime and Political Tension on the Rise." "Haiti Parliamentary Leader Is Found Hiding in Queens," arrested on charges of murders for the former junta. In 1998 "Haiti's Paralysis Brings a Boom in U.S.-Bound Drug Trade." In 1999 "Haitian Leader's Foes Raise the Specter of Dictatorship," while President Préval declares aim "to build . . . democracy." Over a half-year later, "Full-Time [Renewed] U.S. Force in Haiti [Is] to Leave an Unstable Nation." Three months later, "Haiti's Paralysis Spreads as U.S. Troops Pack Up [Once Again]." "Civilian Police Force Brings New Problems in Haiti" after "The army is gone, but citizens' fears are not."[30]

"Haiti's nestling democracy struggles to take flight"

After the president's dissolution of parliament in 1999 and the formation of a new government under a new prime minister, a new party won control of the Senate in 2000, and Aristide won the controversial presidential election. But in 2004, after increasing violence stemming from the disputed 2000 election and other controversies, Aristide resigned and left the country. Against that backdrop the press was full of dire pronouncements sprinkled with some more hopeful or indulging viewpoints.

Concerning "Democracy's Collapse in Haiti" in 2000, "The people needed more than infrastructure form the U.S. to succeed." Even so, "Haiti's nestling democracy struggles to take flight." Speaking of "The legacy of U.N. intervention in Haiti," "Parliamentary and local elections have been postponed twice; still waiting for new date." "Few Haitians Turn Out for Runoff Election," "Many say[ing] the process favored the Aristide party." "Aristide's Return . . . [Is] Bad News Perhaps for Him and Haiti." "Give Aristide a Chance" after "Haiti Votes. America must listen—and help the duly elected." Or was it a case of "Haiti's Disappearing Democracy"?[31]

Haitian government and society continued from 2001 to early 2004 to present an unsettled and uncertain picture in spite of seemingly hopeful signs at first. In 2001 "Vowing Peace, Aristide Is Sworn In Again As President" with "Support from Haiti's poor, and suspicion from the opposition." But "Can Aristide Govern in Haiti?" in the face of "Desperate poverty, tainted elections, and now political collapse." "Eight Years After U.S. Invasion, Haitian Squalor Worsens." What is "Aristide of Haiti: Pragmatist or Demagogue?"—in a country "perhaps less violent, . . . [yet] still very poor, caught in a political stalemate." In 2004 "Haiti's Neighbors Are Pressing Aristide for Reforms." "Violence Spreads in Haiti; Toll Is Put at 41." "Haitian Leader's Allies Block Opposition Demonstration." "Haiti's Man of the People Lost His Way" "In a nation that reviles institutions, [leaving] Aristide . . . little to fallback on," although "It's not that easy to navigate between order and chaos," as Russia and Bosnia have also found out, where "Democracy Defies the Urge to Implant It." "Haiti's Embattled Leader Vows to Finish Term" "As Violence Mounts," urging "Opposition to Move Toward Elections." "Weakened Haitian Police Forces [Are] Overwhelmed by Rebel Violence." "In a Capital Under Siege, Loyalists Brace for Battle." "In Haiti, All the Bridges Are Burned," and "It's too late for Aristide to win back our [U.S.] hearts." A key problem was the absence of "the rule of law," the solution being to get people to "work together" "in a legal way."[32]

"A fresh test for U.S. nation-building" in
"A Struggle to Bring Law and Order to Haiti"

"After A Push From the U.S." in March 2004, "Haiti's Leader [Is] Forced Out; Marines [Are] Sent to Keep Order" as "looters take to the streets." The result was "Shattered Democracy in Haiti." "Rebel Says He Is In Charge; Political Chaos Deepens," yet "U.S. Sees No Rebel Role In New Haitian Government." Here was "a fresh test for U.S. nation-building." "Facing New Crisis, Haiti Again Relies on U.S. Military to Keep Order." "An Interim President for Haiti Is Sworn In," while "The power struggle continues in the streets of Port-au-Prince." "Haiti's elusive search for unity" was beset once again with grave difficulties. "A Struggle to Bring Law and Order to Haiti" meant "Building a Justice System and Perhaps Even Prosecuting Aristide," in whose government "The system was used not to protect but to abuse and oppress."[33]

Ensuing reports in 2004 were not promising. "U.S. Begins Transfer of a Shaky Haiti to U.N. Hands." "Five Months After Aristide, Mayhem Rules the Streets." "Storm-Battered Haiti's Endless Political Crises, and Pain, Are Deepening."[34]

Nor were more recent reports in 2006 hopeful. "Kidnappers exploit Haiti's lawlessness" in "Hundreds of Abductions" "amid poverty and political uncertainty." "With gangs rampant in the streets, democracy in Haiti takes a backseat to chaos and insecurity," "Kidnapping an Election" for the presidency in the "poorest country in the western hemisphere." "Mixed Diplomatic Signals From U.S. Helped Tilt Haiti Toward Chaos." In "Haiti's Orphan Democracy," "Aristide's boys were marginal, poor and loyal to the end." Although "Haitians Dance For Joy As Préval Is Declared Winner" in the presidential election, "A hostile gap looms between the victor and a wealthy minority," while "Stumbling Forward in Haiti." Even as recently as February 2007, "U.N. Troops Fight Haiti's Gangs One Battered Street at a Time."[35]

3. DOMINICAN REPUBLIC

Sharing the island of Hispaniola with Haiti, the Dominican Republic reached a decisive turning point in 1978 when for the first time an elected president ceded power to a successor who won a presidential election, all following decades of rule by strongmen and political uncertainty. In 1994 a constitution was formed. In it the presidential duties and powers were set forth (disallowing re-election to a second consecutive term), together with those of the National Legislature (Senate and Chamber of Deputies). Unlike Haiti, the Dominican Republic has had membership since 2004 in the Central American Parliament.

In the 1994 presidential election, one editorial declared that "Mr. Balaguer's Dubious Victory" should be severely scrutinized by the international community due to charges of fraud and irregularities. The political and economic turmoil in neighboring Haiti two months later, intensified by the failure to restore Haiti's ousted elected leader Aristide, prompted calls to "Squeeze the Dominican Republic" and to "Seal the border with Haiti. Don't invade."[36]

Then, in 1996, "Longtime Ruler Overshadows Dominican Republic Election" for president, namely, the aging Balaguer, who had once ruled the country for so long. With "Dominicans to vote for candidates who promise change after decades of strongman rule," a "New Era Opens for Caribbean Country." "Dominican Republic Votes, With New Blood in the Race," exhibiting "After four decades' rule by 2 strongmen, a messy democracy." Yet Balaguer was now "A Dominican Institution Exiting With Aura Intact." "Runoff, Capping Fierce Race," was held; the result was "A New Dominican President." "Dominicans Now Have A New Kind Of Leader." In short order, "Suits Accuse Dominican Ex-President [Balaguer] of Misdeeds." Democracy was slowly on the march.[37]

During ensuing years, there were signs of stability as well as corruption. True, as reported in 1998, "Dominicans Allow Drugs Easy

Caribbean Sailing"; yet, although it was "A Nation Ill-Equipped Against Traffickers," "A Tough New Leader Allows Extradition," with "A Reformer's Future In the Voters' Hands." By 1999 there were "At Last on Hispaniola, Hands Across the Border" between the Dominican Republic and Haiti. In 2000, "In Boom Times, the Have-Nots Influence the Dominican Vote."[38]

The preceding topic of the drug trade is, of course, part of a much larger story in which U.S. efforts at law enforcement against the cartels has had mixed results. In 1996, "With blissful vacationers unaware, tons of cocaine flow through the idyllic [Caribbean] islands, thanks to sharkish drug cartels." Several months later, "9 Caribbean Nations Open Waters to U.S. Drug Pursuit." In 1998 "In the Caribbean, Support Grows for the Death Penalty." At the same time, "With Technology, Island Bookies Skirt U.S. Law." An island with drug-trafficking problems was Granada. In 1994, after "A Decade of Disillusionment in Grenada," "The U.S. invasion teaches lessons in the limits of power." In other ways, as seen in other Central American countries above, the United States has had some effectiveness in law-enforcement against drug-traffickers.[39]

Chapter XIII

South American Nations in Government and Society

1. COLOMBIA

Situated in the northwestern corner of South America, to the east of Panama at the bottom of Central America's isthmus, Colombia has long experienced turbulent struggles in its efforts to become a stable national democracy. Its tripartite central government (president, legislature, and judiciary) as set forth in the 1971 constitution has provided a legal–legislative framework within which the Colombian government has attempted to pursue national stability. But civil wars and drug wars have long torn at the nation's fabric, although present-day conditions and outlooks are decidedly improved.

"Colombia Reimposes Curbs on Marijuana and Cocaine"

A main problem early on and down to recent times continued to be tough talk but weak results on the part of Colombia's leaders in the executive and legislative branches of government. In 1990 "Colombia Swears In President, a Foe of Traffickers"; and "Colombia Presses Drive on Rebels, Smashing Base." In 1991 "Guerrilla Group

Surrenders Arms In Pact With Government"; and "Colombia Disbands Congress to Speed Reforms" because "Officials Writing New Constitution Feared Old Guard Legislators Would Delay Changes." In 1992 "Resurgence in Violence Brings Backlash in Colombia." In 1993 "With Oil Fields as Battleground, Colombia Adopts New Tactics in Rebel War." In 1994 "Colombia Reimposes Curbs on Marijuana and Cocaine"; "Colombia's New Leader Vows To Crack Down on Cali Cartel"; and "Anti-Drug Campaign Hits Resistance in Colombia." In 1995 "Colombia Pledges Crackdown on Drug Trade"; "Colombia Vows Crackdown on Cartels"; "Rocked by Scandal," "Samper's presidency is in peril as an Aide says his boss took campaign contributions from drug lords"; and "One Cartel Dies and the Drugs Go On."[1]

Such problems continued to mount in the later 1990s. In 1996 "Scandal-Ridden Congress Offers President Sympathetic Ear" inasmuch as "Many legislators have also been ethically compromised"; "Colombians wonder whether anything can curb the drug cartels"; "Colombian Legislators Talk of Amnesty, for Themselves"; "Colombian Leader Opens the Way to Resignation"; "Clinton Declares Colombia Has Failed to Curb Drugs"; "Colombia's guerrillas flourish as its president fades"; "Colombia's Legal System Puts Few Rapists in Prison" in "A country that shrugs at sexual abuse of women"; "Rebels Kill 80 in Strongest Attacks in Colombia in Decades"; "Colombia Stays in U.S. Disfavor" because "Proposed antidrug laws may not be enough to end 'decertification' by US"; "Parental Rights Measure [Is] Not So Simple," with "Colombians Divided Over Amendment on Authority Over Children"; "Report Accuses Colombian Army of Links to Killings"; "Tainted by Corruption, Colombian President Is Ceding Power"; and "Oil Companies Buy an Army to Tame Colombia's Rebels." In 1997 "Heroin Is Proving [to be] a Growth Industry in Colombia"; "Colombia's Death-Strewn Democracy" was in crisis; and "Colombia's Senate Passes Bill Giving Jail Leave to Traffickers." In 1998, since " 'Narco-guerrillas' already control half the country—and keep winning," so "Is Colombia lost to rebels?"; As "Colombia's Civil War Tries to Be More Civil" and "As instability threatens region, new leader visits US to ask that Congress do more than just say 'no' to drugs"; and "After three decades of war, guerrillas may get half a country" in "Land for peace in Colombia."[2]

Continuing, in 1999 "The Backyard Balkans" finds that "Colombia President isn't only fighting drug lords, he's also struggling to hold his country together." "Colombia Quake Sets Back Efforts to Negotiate With Rebels." "Executions of 3 Americans in Colombia May Prolong Civil War." "As Colombia Declares an Alert, Rebel

Offensive [by Leftist Guerrillas] Rages On." "Colombia Is Reeling, Hurt by Rebels and Economy." "Rebel Push in Colombia Adds Urgency to Washington Talks." "In Colombia, after 35-years of war, now there's talk of peace" in "A finish to the fight?" Yet "Crisis [occurs] in Colombia [as] . . . Civil Strife Uproots Peasants." "Colombia Extradites Drug Suspect to U.S." as "Washington Hails the First Such Transfer in Nearly a Decade."[3]

"Political Turmoil Adds to Colombian President's Woes"

In 2000 it was asked, "Does Colombia Deserve U.S. Aid," with the rejoinder that "In many ways, the collapse of its government may be the best thing." That year "Insurgencies Leave Colombia Caught in a Web of Drugs and Strife." At the same time, "Political Turmoil Adds to Colombian President's Woes" as "A move to dissolve and replace the legislature backfires." "U.S. Is Stepping Up Aid as Troubles Build for Colombia" while "Public Patience Wanes and Top Aides Quit." "An Aimless War in Colombia Creates a Nation of Victims." "Behind Colombia's Election Hoopla, Rebels Wield Power." "Colombia Holds Elections, For the Most Part Peacefully."[4]

In early 2001 "Colombia, in Risky Move, Plans To Cede Zone [of Territory] to 2nd Rebel Group" "as a path to peace negotiations." Yet six weeks later "Colombia Says It Is Doing Battle Right and Left," with "Now, right-wing militias as enemies of the state." "After Centuries, Colombian Tribes Are Now Imperiled by a Civil War." In "Legalizing Abuses in Colombia," "A new law that has passed Colombia's Congress and awaits the signature of [the] President . . . would give the military dangerous new powers over civilians and lessen the possibility that officers would be held accountable for abusing them." As for "Colombia's Courts: Between a War and a Hard Place." Meanwhile, however, "Colombia's Army Rebuilds and Challenges Rebels." "Colombian Troops Move on Rebel Zone as Talks Fail."[5]

Troubles continued on in 2002 and beyond amid some signs of hoped-for progress. "U.S. [Is] to Give Colombians Data to Help Fight Rebels" as "Washington seeks ways around legal restrictions on aid." "Colombian Rebels Sabotage Peace Hopes" as "Hijacking and Kidnappings Disrupt Progress Made in Peace Talks," for "The government was making offers, but the guerrillas did not reciprocate." "Hard-Liner On the Rebels Wins [Presidential] Election in Colombia" and "promises a military buildup," with "Tough Talk [That] Resonates In a Nation Sick of War." But then "Colombian President-Elect Softens Tone on Rebels," "Hoping to enlist the United

Nations in a peace effort." "After Drug Lord's Release, Colombia Vows to Toughen Laws" and "to get the outlaws under control."[6]

It was one step forward and one backward in 2003–2004 when "800 in Colombia Lay Down Arms, Kindling Peace Hopes"; but "A disappearance throws peace talks into turmoil" as "Colombia Paramilitary Chief Gains Power." Then, "At Colombia's Congress, [Right-Wing Death-Squad] Paramilitary Chiefs Talk Peace." Soon enough, "Rightist Militias Are a Force in Colombia's Congress."[7]

In 2005 "New Colombia Law Grants Concessions to Paramilitaries," yet "Critics see 'impunity and immunity' given for disarmament." "Report Adds to Criticism of Colombian Disarmament Law."[8]

By May 2007 Colombia was the United States' closest ally, and largest recipient of U.S. aid in that region for combating the drug lords. Shortly before, "Colombian [President] Seeks to Persuade [U.S.] Congress to Continue Aid"; yet "Colombia leader faces tough sell." To be sure, troubles persisted on the home front, as when "Cocaine Wars Turn Port [City] into Colombia's Deadliest City," but the concerted efforts to combat the drug trade were a key part of the equation. Further signs of the get-tougher approach came when "Lawmakers In Colombia Urge Firing Of Mediator"; and "Colombia's tenacious top prosecutor" "has been praised for his willingness to uncover the war-torn country's grisly—and politically sensitive—past. But how far will he go?"[9]

2. VENEZUELA

To Colombia's east in northern South America, Venezuela has undergone great political change. Basically, the new 1999 Constitution abolished the preceding bicameral legislature and replaced it with a unicameral legislature (National Assembly) virtually headed by the president (since then Hugo Chávez), to whom it gave the right to legislate by decree in a federal presidential republic. More recently, these developments have reached new heights of consolidated presidential power and of the state's role in the economy.

"Revolution at the Polls"

Prior to the Venezuelan "Revolution at the Polls" in 1999, there were periods of upheaval. In early 1992, "Venezuela Crushes Army Coup Attempt." Several days later, "Venezuela, Wary After Coup Attempt, Censors Press." "Fiery Nationalism Drove Venezuelan Plotters." "A coup fails when civilians prove unwilling to trade their government, however flawed, for a military dictatorship," with "No

Time for Colonels." Soon the "President, Under Fire," "Plans Broad Reform in Venezuela." Weeks later, "Middle Class Protests Cast a Cloud on Democracy in Venezuela." A half year later found "Venezuela Stable, but Fragile, Since Coup Attempt," for "When there is oil, an economy can weather even the worst case of political nerves." But a month later "2D [nd] Day of Violence Wracks Venezuela" when "In Aftermath of Failed Coup, Helicopter Attack Sets Off Battles in Caracas." "Venezuela Still Edgy: Will There Be Coup No. 3?"[10]

In 1993 "Venezuelan Senate Authorizes Trial [in Supreme Court]" as "Senate Chief Becomes Acting President on Vote to Try [President] Pérez for Corruption," leading to his later conviction. Several months later, "Coup Weary, Venezuelans Await a Vote" for new president. "For Venezuela Victor [Caldera]: Will Vows Be Kept?" But then in 1994 the "Failure of High-Flying Banks Shakes Venezuelan Economy." "New Leader Is Squeezing Venezuela."[11]

In 1996 "Venezuelans See Clashes Resuming." "Fed Up With Police, Poor Take the Law Into Their Own Hands" as "Lynch-Mob Justice Grows in Caracas." Then, "With Latin American countries . . . moving away from closed, regulated economies," "Venezuela Gets Big I.M.F. Grant, Backing Market Reforms." "Legally, Now, Venezuelans [Are] to Mine Fragile Lands."[12]

Disruptive patterns continued in 1997, prior to the 1998 election. In "The Venezuela 'Year of Rights,' The Police Kill More Youths." "Venezuelans [Are] Confronting Democracy's Dire State." Then "Venezuelans Elect an Ex-Coup Leader [Hugo Chávez] as Their President," "The first Caracas chief in 40 years to come from the dominant parties." "Blow Your Coup? Some Who Failed Turn to the Ballot Box."[13]

Indeed, "Venezuelan [Chávez] Pulls Off Revolution At the Polls" in late 1998. "Share the (oil) wealth, says Venezuela's big winner," who "demands constitutional reform by powerful means." "Corruption-weary Venezuelans elect a former coup plotter," who is going "From prisoner to president."[14]

A new power shift moved quickly into gear in 1999. In February "New President in Venezuela Prepares to Rewrite the Constitution." "New Chief [Pledges] to Battle Venezuela's 'Cancer' " through "reforms." In July "Venezuelan Leader Pushes for New Charter, but Is It Reformist Tool or a Power Grab?", whereby "The President wants the right to succeed himself, and that upsets his critics." In August "Venezuela Leader Moves a Step Closer to Broad New Powers"; while "Venezuelan Congress Fights Loss of Power" in the midst of "Establishing a new authority and a new Constitution."

"Crisis Deepens In Venezuela As Legislators Spurn Accord." "Rival Assemblies in Venezuela Reach a Shaky Accord," "Averting, for now, a dangerous Caracas showdown." "Venezuela's democracy teeters." Yet "Venezuelans Applaud Leader's Assault on System." "Poor Venezuelans [Are] sold on change." Yet at end of year "Aftermath of Caribbean storm tests Chávez's regime."[15]

"Venezuela's New Conquistador"

By 2000–2002, as "Venezuela's New Conquistador: Chávez Shapes Nation to Leftist Vision," with "U.S. Help . . . Rejected." "Leader Moves To Dominate Civic Groups In Venezuela." "Venezuela's Leader Is Seeking Decree Powers to Speed Change." "Venezuela Military Bristles at Role Ordered by President." With "Revolutionary appeal," "Venezuela's Chávez battles the rich—and the tide of history." "Venezuela's New Oil Law Is Seen as a Risk to Growth," for "Tighter government control could send foreign investors away, analysts say." Setbacks occurred. "Venezuela's Currency Plunges 19% as Controls Are Removed." "2nd Day of Antigovernment Protests Slows Venezuela." "Venezuelan Generals Rebel After Protesters [Are] Killed," while "Some military officers also say Chávez must go."[16]

Crisis ensued, temporarily, followed by recovery. In April 2002 "Venezuelan Leader [Is] Forced Out; Civilian Is Installed." But then "Ousted Venezuela Chief May Be Close to Return" due to "Some support for a deposed leader, but [with] more outrage over a deposed democracy." "In Swift Counterrevolt, Ardent Populists Reinstate Venezuelan Leader." "In Venezuela, Chávez Starts Shuffling Disloyal Officers." "Chávez Shakes Up Cabinet And Promises New Policies." In "Democracy of Another Sort," "Venezuela's Chávez has the opportunity to lead his country past its problems."[17]

Concentration of power was further emerging, again with ups and downs. In October 2002 "Venezuelan Leader Defies Military and Ignores Call for Election." "Venezuelan Marchers Want Police Restored to Civilian Rule." "Venezuelan Court Blocks Order for Nonbinding Vote on President." "Chávez Vows to Regain Control of Oil Industry in Venezuela." "Chávez Rejects Call by U.S. for Early Vote in Venezuela." "Venezuela Strikers [Are] Ordered To Resume Oil Production" whereas "Opponents of the government are trying to force early elections." In early 2003 "Venezuelan High Court Suspends Referendum on President Chávez." "Strike Frays in Venezuela as Foes of Chávez Retreat." "Venezuela's opposition ignores the Constitution," while "Many in the opposition were part of the problem before Chávez." Then "Colombia's Long Civil War Spreads Turmoil to Venezuela." Later on, "Venezuelan Council Rejects Petition to Recall Chávez." In early 2004 "Venezuelan Leader, Battling a Recall, Mocks Bush," saying "Washington is actively supporting ... foes." As for "Venezuela's Fake Democrat," "Does Hugo Chávez represent Latin America's future?" "Venezuela Chief Signs Law Some See as Aimed at His Critics." In early 2005 through "A Government Act Aimed at Foreigners," "Venezuelan Land Reform Looks to Seize Idle Farmland." "Venezuela Will Tighten Rules On Admitting Foreign Preachers."[18]

"Chávez Restyles Venezuela With '21st-Century Socialism' "

In later 2005 Chávez was well along in expanding upon the preceding years' buildup of presidential power through executive quasi- (or pseudo-) legislative decree. "Chávez Restyles Venezuela With 21st-Century Socialism" as "State companies and cooperatives by the thousands are set up." A half-year later in 2006, "Venezuela tightens oil grip" as it "seized the fields of two multinational oil giants." "Seeking United Latin America, Venezuela's Chávez Is a Divider" with "An image of caustic nationalism that many in the region fear," as "the U.S. accuses Venezuela of not cooperating on terrorism." As for "The Postmodern Dictator," however, "Chávez-style politics is not the future of Latin America." Some asked if Chávez, already "a Thorn in the Side of Washington," would become "The Next Castro?"[19]

Venezuelans were further sweeping along, or being swept along by, the Chávez brand of nationalistic socialism. In a later 2006 election, "Venezuelans Give Chávez a Mandate to Tighten His Grip" as he "rules like an autocrat." A month later in January 2007, "Chávez Moves to Nationalize 2 Industries" with "A pledge to take control of companies in the two industries." "Venezuelan Plan Could Cost Millions As Threat of Seizure Shakes Investors" as "Verizon and Others Face Nationalization Idea," while "Foreigners wonder nervously if additional industries will become takeover targets." "Chávez Begins New Term Vowing Socialism" following his re-election and re-inauguration, as he "praises Jesus and quotes Trotsky." "Venezuela Wants Trade Group To Embrace Anti-Imperialism" while "Chávez bluntly defies unity goals of Brazil and Argentina." "Venezuela's Chávez tightens grip," "announcing plans to nationalize power and telecom firms."[20]

Shortly thereafter, in early February 2007, the "Legislature Grants Chávez Broad New Powers to Shape Venezuela." Accordingly, two weeks later, "Chávez Threatens to Jail Violators of Price Controls" amid "Fear that new Venezuelan economic steps could backfire." In May "Chávez Takes Over Foreign-Controlled Oil Projects in Venezuela." In "A Clash of Hope and Fear As Venezuela Seizes Land," "Landowners are trying to sell out as squatters burn and replant their fields." "Venezuela Police Repel Protests Over TV Network's Closing." In June "Chávez Looks at His Critics in the Media and Sees the Enemy."[21]

3. ECUADOR

Below Colombia, on the Pacific coast, lie Ecuador and Peru. In the case of Ecuador in 1996–1997 no sooner had the newly-elected "populist" president unveiled "a plan of neo-liberal economic reform," than he was ousted by the legislature in February 1997 because of his unpopular programs. "In seven months, a landslide victor lost most of his support," and "Ecuadoreans Rally in Drive to Oust President." A day after that report, "Ecuador Congress Votes to Oust President for 'Mental Incapacity.' " Fortunately, "Ecuador's Crisis On Presidency Is Resolved Peacefully," and the Vice President takes over, such that "Nation's First Female Leader Will Serve Until Congress Amends the Constitution." One U.S. editorial decried "Political Madness in Ecuador." Yet "Ecuador's Military Code . . . [seemed less key, inasmuch as] Democracy Is Better," for "The Latin epaulet set may be turning into guardians of democracy." Even so, crises ensued. There were "Horizons in Ecuador, but Paralysis Sets in Early."[22]

In 1999 "Ecuador Chief Issues Decree To Limit Crisis." A week later, "Banks in Ecuador Reopen After Week's Closing, but Taxi Strike Aggravates Tensions" as "Ecuador's austerity program bites, and the people bite back." Then, in early 2000, "Ecuador Army Hands Power to Vice President." "Ecuador's Coup Alerts Region to a Resurgent Military."[23]

Events were becoming repetitive. In 2005 "Ecuador's President Revokes [His Previous] Curbs on [anti-government] Protests," while "An order dissolving the nation's top court remains in effect." A month later, "Ecuador Leader Flees and Vice President Replaces Him." Then again, two years later in 2007, "Ecuador Ever Unstable, Prepares for New Leader's Plans." At that point, "Ecuador backs leftist changes" after "a majority of Ecuadoreans voted . . . to back President . . . plan to elect a constituent assembly that will rewrite the constitution."[24]

4. PERU

"Lawmakers Vote For Charges" and "Leader [Is] Impeached by Congress He Dissolved"

In politically turbulent Peru, the Congressional legislature played a curious role after the election of President Fujimori in 1990. In mid-1991 "Peru Lawmakers Vote For Charges" and "Oppose Ex-Chief's Immunity to Accusations of Ties to Bank Mired in Scandal"— a scandal that "has benefitted" Fujimori in the polls and in his new economic plans for privatizing or reducing state ownership and involvement in the economy. In late 1991 "Peru's Military Is Granted Broad Powers in Rebel War" through "tough emergency decrees," as Fujimori "issued a decree that gives him power to name all military commanders" and "to gain greater control over Peru's army." Several months later in 1992, "Peru Chief Orders New Mass Arrests" and "moves to shore up his broad powers and still the protests." Two days later, however, "Peru Leader [Fujimori] [Is] Impeached by Congress He Dissolved." But "Peru's Basic Problems Won't Be Ordered Away," said one account. By seizing "extra constitutional powers for himself" and "Destroying the law in order to save it," "Peru's anticommunist putsch [by Fujimori against rebels] may backfire." Thus, having assumed emergency, near-dictatorial powers against Congress and the courts, with some backing by the military, Fujimori was soon back in power.[25]

Would it be democracy or dictatorship? In mid-1992 "Peru's Chief, Vowing Democracy, Sets Date for a Revived Congress." Just before that, "Peruvian Guerrillas Test Government With Bombs." Soon another report declared that "Peru's Dictatorship Is Ridiculous but Real." Nevertheless, in early 1993 "Fujimori's public approval ratings have remained steady" as he "Clears a Path With Sharp Elbows." A few months later, "a 'Second Coup' Reveals the Upper Hand." "Army Deploys Tanks in Peru in Challenge to New Congress." Was Fujimori "Dictator? President? Or General Manager of Peru?" But then "Peruvians [Are] Looking More Sourly at Tough Leader." Army involvements in killings were of growing concern, along with military conflicts with Ecuador and guerrillas.[26]

In 1995 "Fujimori Wins 5 More Years At Peru Helm" as "The Man Who Beat Inflation and Terror." A year later "Peru's President Loses Some Luster" as "Stalled Economy Frustrates Voters." In early 1997 "Fujimori confronts a hostage created by a band of [Maoist] rebels he thought he had defeated"; "Tourists and investors may be discouraged," imperiling the economy. A few months later, Fujimori's "Peruvian Troops Rescue [71] Hostages and Kill Rebels as Standoff Ends."[27]

"Economy Grows As a Democracy Is Left to Wither"

That characterization of Fujimori's Peru in April 1997 was coupled with the observation that "After five years, the President and army are strong as ever." Yet "Entrenched Problems in the Emerging Peruvian Market" were looming, due to "corruption and cronyism." "Peru's Stark Poverty Dulls Fujimori's Gleam." "As Peru's Leader Cracks Down, Opposition Grows" in July, with the result that although "A hero months ago, Fujimori is now condemned as an autocrat." "Peru Leader Tries to Defuse Crisis, Denying Military Control."[28]

Looking ahead in early 1999 to possible election to a third term, one press report drew attention to "Fujimori's Burden in Peru: The Magic's Missing." Another pointed to "Peru's Endangered Dissidents" and asked "Why the war on free speech?" There was also the matter of "Peru's backtracking on court—strongman politics?", whereby "Fujimori's withdrawal from human rights court [is] seen as reelection politics."[29]

Sure enough, in late 1999 and early 2000, "Peru's Leader [Is] to Seek 3rd Term, Capping a Long Legal Battle"; "Playing for Keeps . . . [,] Fujimori seeks third term." Soon "Opposition, and International Monitors, [Are] Crying Foul in Peru's Presidential Campaign." On the eve of the April voting for president, "Is Peru's press in peril?"; "Shady Tactics [Are] Said to Cloud Fujimori's Future, No Matter How Peruvians Vote . . . ," for "The president faces his most serious crisis since he shut down the Congress." After Fujimori's preliminary victory, "Charging Fraud, Peruvian Challenger Demands a Runoff." In May "Insurgent in Peru Calls for Election Boycott." Then, with "Fujimori the Victor in Runoff Election," "Protesters Take to the Streets" in "A political battle that has left the country badly paralyzed." In "Peru's Election Turmoil," it was called a question of "Stability vs. Democracy." "U.S. Condemns Peru Election And Fujimori Rule as Invalid." For "The Man Who Would Be Dictator?," "Condemned by the international community, he still has public support at home." But then the "Discredited election stirs unrest in Peru" as "Fujimori wins and democracy loses."[30]

"Congress removes the . . . president" and "Picks a Successor"

The Peruvian Congress was again on the ascendancy for a time. In the fall of 2000, "Rocked by a great scandal, Fujimori calls new elections and vows to clean house. But will he do it?" Then "Peru Congress Ousts Its President, Fujimori Ally." "Peru Opposition Picks Successor for Fujimori's Ally in Congress." "Peru Congress Says Fujimori Is 'Unfit' and Picks a Successor"; that is, "Declaring him 'morally unfit,' Congress removes the President from office." In a "Resignation that leaves a nation's stability in doubt," "Fujimori Quits, and Peru Is Split on Successor." "Peru's New Chief [Is] Sworn In, Vowing to Revive Democracy."[31]

Uncertainties still lay on the immediate horizon. In December 2000, with Fujimori having fled the country, "Investigators pursue the ousted Peruvian president as Congress strips his immunity" in "Time to Settle Accounts." In "The Decline and Fall of Fujimori of Peru: Nation's Lion [Is] Reduced to a Broken Man." But then in February 2001 "Former Leader of Peru Seeks Second Chance After Exile" in "A phoenixlike rise [that] shows the volatility of a nation's political scene." In June "Peruvian Son of the Poor Wins Over an Ex-President," leaving people "Dancing in the streets after an apparently untainted election."[32]

Developments continued on with twists and turns. In 2002 "Congress is debating a major constitutional overhaul, its third in 25 years," in "Peru's never-ending quest for the perfect Constitution." In late 2002 "Peru's Former President [Fujimori] Plots His Return to Power" and "defends his tough approach" in light of 9/11. In 2003 "Peruvian Cabinet [Is] to Resign in Move to Bolster Government." In 2004 "Peru, in Familiar Tactic, Announces Cabinet Reorganization." In 2005 "Peru's Fugitive Ex-Leader [Fujimori] [Is] Trying to Regain Presidency." In 2006 "Nationalism and Populism Propel Front-Runner in Peru": not Fujimori. In June of that year "Ex-President [García] Wins in Peru in Stunning Comeback," "Sixteen years after his presidency ended in economic collapse and heightened guerrilla violence." Unfortunately for Peruvians and their government in 2007, due to drug imports from Mexico and Colombia, "Violent cartel culture now threatens Peru." Looking back at the post-Fujimori hopes in early 2002, one could wonder, for example, about Peru's future prospects when at that point: U.S. President "Bush Vows to Help Peru Fight Rebels and Keep Andes Region Stable," while "Peru Support Of Free Trade Draws Praise In Bush Visit."[33]

5. BRAZIL

"Leaders Take Aim At Big Government"

The vast country of Brazil—extending eastward from Ecuador and Peru across the interior of South America to the Atlantic coast—

has long been a stable democratic nation under a tripartite central government with executive, bicameral legislature, and judiciary. From the 1990s to the present day, the experiences of other nearby countries with coups, juntas, wars, cartels, revolutions, and the like have largely bypassed Brazil despite its periods of serious trouble. A sign of that stability and democracy came in 1990—two years after the promulgation of a new constitution reducing presidential powers—when "Brazilian Leaders Take Aim at Big Government," seeking "to cut civil service jobs and sell state-run businesses." Another sign that year came when "Brazil's Leader [Collor] Makes the Army Toe the Line." Then, "Local Races Help Brazilian Leader when 'Loose Majority' Is Predicted for Collor in Congress—Leftists Dealt a Blow."[34]

Even so, in early 1991 "Brazil Freezes All Wages and Prices" as "Latin America's biggest economy fights an inflation rate of 20 percent." "As Collor Completes First Year, Brazilians Write Off Their Highest Hopes." On certain issues "Brazil's President Backs Army Over Congress." In 1992 "Corruption Charge Taints Brazil Leader." "Despite Scandal, Brazil Exudes Political Health," its "Nascent Democracy Stable, Intolerant of Corruption."[35]

Problems mounted for President Collor in 1992. "Brazilians Demand Collor's Impeachment," with "Demonstrations . . . Largest in Seven Years." "Brazil's President, who made halting corruption his crusade, has become a victim of his own success" as "A Radical Idea Sweeps Latin America: Honest Government." After the Brazilian Supreme Court denied President Collor a delay on impeachment vote in Congress, "House Impeaches Collor; Suspended, He Faces Senate Trial." "Collor Resigns as Senate Trial Begins" and "Successor [Is] Sworn In."[36]

It was then briefly asked in 1993, "Tired of Presidents? Brazilians Will Be Given the Chance to Vote for a King." The response: "Brazilians Vote Down Kings and Keep Presidents." Soon thereafter, however, "Economic Ills Sap Brazilians' Faith in Democracy." "Murder by death squads" was on the rise. "Brazilian Justice and the Culture of Impunity" was stark for "People on Society's Fringe [Who] Seem Fair Game." "New Government Corruption Scandal Leaves Brazil[ians] Stunned," "worried about their democracy."[37]

"Reformist Chief Rides a Bucking Bronco"

In 1995, with "A New President, . . . Brasilia Is Again a Capital of Hope," as he "vows to keep the economy booming." President Cardoso promises "Key Reforms." "In Rio, as Gang Violence and

Kidnappings Rise, So Does the War on Crime." Cardoso having moved rightward politically from his leftward leanings earlier, "Brazil Takes Big Step Toward Ending State Monopoly," as put forth by the Chamber of Deputies (lower house). At the same time, however, "Brazil's Chief Acts to Take Land to Give to the Poor," as he "signed decrees expropriating 250,000 acres from privately held estates, promising that the land will be used to resettle more than 3,000 poor families waiting for places to live and till the soil."[38]

On into 1996 and beyond, the news was mixed for Brazil's president and legislature. On one hand, for instance, "Murders of Brazilian Peasants Raise Calls for Police Reforms." On the other, "Financial Gyrations Fail to Deter Foreign Investors" in "Brazil's Economic Samba." Developments in law and legislation continued to unfold. In 1996 "Brazil Law Gets Women Into the Political Game." "Regulation and High Costs Burden Airlines" as "Opposition Grows in Brazil To High Domestic Air Fares." In 1997 "A constitutional amendment enabling re-election advances in Brazil's Senate" (upper house) as "Brazil's Chief Wins Vote Despite [New] Scandal."[39]

In 1998, "Brazil, Its Forests Besieged, Adds Teeth to Environmental Laws." "Brazil's Reformist Chief [Cardoso] Rides a Bucking Bronco." "Brazil Congress Votes to Scale Down Social Security." "Brazil's Congress Rejects President's Plan for Pension Changes," while "Government is cast into disarray by two top officials' deaths." "President Eases Market Rigors" with "Brazil's Economic Half-Steps." "Brazil's Leader Calls for Reforms, Heartening Investors," as "Brazilians are told they must live within their means," leading later to "Fast Recovery From Brink of Economic Collapse." "Brazil's Austerity Plan Clears Important [Congressional] Hurdle on Pension Cost."[40]

In 1999 "Lawmakers In Brazil Adopt Steps On Austerity"; doing so after "Brazil Devalues Its Currency 8%, Boiling Markets" and jeopardizing Brazil status as "Engine of Latin Nations, Which Buy One-Fifth of Exports by U.S." In the wake of these events, "Legislators In Brazil Are Leaving Ruling Party." In the end, however, "Yes, Investors Panicked. But Brazil Didn't," while "other strengths were already in place." Meantime, "Brazil, High In Shootings, Is Proposing To Ban Guns" with "a new state law prohibiting the sale of firearms . . . already in . . . effect. . . . President . . . Cardoso wants to go even further: his Government has introduced fast-track legislation that would completely ban the possession of arms throughout this nation of 165 million people." More generally, however, "Current legislation is stalled while lawmakers battle," leaving "Brazil's Leader Undercut By His Quarreling Aides." By late 1999, "No

Longer Tolerant of Official Misconduct, Brazilians Now Demand Accountability." Under Cardoso, "Brazil Sets Up New Agency, Civilian Run, Like the F.B.I.," "replacing informal investigation networks left over from military rule...."[41]

The mixed picture continued. By 2000, "Brazil Begins to Take Role on the World Stage" as "A newly assertive partner and rival of the United States." It was "A Developing Nation on the Frontiers of Space." Yet in 2001 "Brazil's scandals [are] hamstringing reform" after "Top leaders [in and out of Congress] are accused of stealing billions, as political fallout spreads widening shadow." Also in 2001 Congress in "Multiracial Brazil [Is] Planning Quotas for Blacks" in the entertainment industry. "Brazil's Effort to Overhaul Its Labor Code Stirs Heated Debate" as elections approach, with President Cardoso calling the current code antiquated and with the Senate preparing to vote on the matter soon.[42]

"Leftist Wins . . . Presidential Race"

In the fall of 2002, "Leftist Wins Brazilian Presidential Race With Largest Margin in Country's History," accompanied by "Talk of a Latin American 'axis of good' between Brazil and Venezuela," "Heralding what many call a triumph of the people." Upon further reflection, "A landslide victory is less of a mandate than it appears," while "Law and Politics [Are] Likely to Curb Power of Brazil's New Leader," da Silva. "Brazil's Election Victor Maps His Way to More Social Equality," yet "Although Mr. da Silva's Workers' Party is now the largest in Congress, it still commands fewer than 20 percent of the seats and he will need broad support to push through any reforms." By year's end, fortunately, "Departing President Leaves a Stable Brazil."[43]

At his January swearing-in, "A Leftist Takes Over in Brazil and Pledges a 'New Path.' " In later January 2003, "Brazil's new leader takes on an unlikely global role" as he "spoke to political and business leaders in Switzerland."[44]

Taking center stage domestically were legislative matters and the legislature process. By April 2003, "Racial Quotas in Brazil Touch Off Fierce Debate" as "Whites Challenge University Admissions" over "a sweeping Racial Equality Statute now before Congress" in order "to improve the lot of the black population." In later 2003 "Party Atop Brazil Government Expels 4 Dissident Lawmakers." In 2004 "Brazil Adopts Strict Gun Controls to Try to Curb Murders" through "legislation [first introduced in 1999] that had to overcome tenacious resistance from the military and a gun lobby generous with campaign donations." In 2005 "Senior Brazil Legislator Quits, Further Weakening President." Shortly thereafter, "Gun-Happy Brazil Is Hotly Debating a Nationwide Ban." Meanwhile, "Loggers, Scorning the Law, Ravage the Amazon Jungle" as "Illegal Cutting Booms Despite Brazil's Ban."[45]

6. BOLIVIA, PARAGUAY, AND URUGUAY

Southward of Brazil like Bolivia, Paraguay, and Uruguay. Bolivia has had a difficult history to current times. In 1992 "Army Unrest Stirs Bolivia, the Land of Coups." The year before, "Bolivians Fear Maoist Rebellion in Peru May Spill Over the Border." In mid-1993 "Bolivian Dictator Seeks Presidency," having "Ruled in 1970's" but now with a "Final Goal: to Win [a] Free Election." In 1998 "Bolivia's Crackdown on [Often Defiant] Coca Growers Becomes Increasingly Deadly" "In a sharp about-turn." In 1999 "Bolivian's Dark Past Starts to Catch Up With Him" as the president's former military dictatorship in the 1970s reenters the picture despite his 1997 win in democratic election. In 2000 "5 More Die in Bolivia Protests After Emergency Is Declared." In 2003 "Bolivia's New Leader Takes Over a Chaotic and Angry Nation." "Two decades of free-market reforms leave many resentful," such that "Bolivia's Poor Proclaim Abiding Distrust of Globalization." "Bolivian Leader Resigns and His Vice-President Steps In." In 2005 "A Rich State in Bolivia Moves Toward More Autonomy." "Bolivian President [Is] to Keep Post After a Crucial Vote in Congress." Three months later, however, "Bolivian Congress Names New President, Setting Stage for Elections." A day earlier, "No. 1 Quits in Bolivia, and Protesters Scorn Nos. 2 and 3." A half-year later, after "A leader makes an early strike against American actions," "U.S. Keeps a Wary Eye on the Next Bolivian President." At that point, "Bolivia's Newly Elected Leader Maps His Socialist Agenda," reflecting "the leftward drift of government in Latin America." In 2006, through "A Mandate for Radical Reform," "The sweeping victory of Bolivia's new president strikes fear into officials and the business elite." "Bolivia's New Leader, Tilting Latin America Further to Left, Vows to End 'Neoliberal Model.' " "Bolivian [President] Nationalizes the Oil and Gas Sector" in "Another government takeover [that] makes investors still edgier." In "Bolivia's Energy Takeover: Populism Rules in the Andes."[46]

Paraguay's developing democracy in the 1990s and beyond held promise. In 1991 "A General Leads Paraguay to Democracy." In 1993 "First Free Election [Is] to Be Held . . . in Paraguay." Then

"Sabotage Disrupts Paraguay's First Free Presidential Election." Even so, "Governing Party Wins Paraguay's Presidential Vote," marking "A clear result in an election marred by fraud." In early 1995 "A Few Potholes [appear] on the Road to Democracy." In 1996 there was "Good News From Paraguay: A Coup d'état Falls Flat," and "The military's failure to seize power in one of the hemisphere's least-progressive countries reflects the commitment to democracy throughout Latin America." In 1998 "Paraguay Court Orders General to Return to Jail." In 1999 "Political Battle Threatens To Destabilize Paraguay," so that despite "Ten years of democracy, . . . no one is celebrating." A few weeks later, "Paraguay's Vice President [Is] Slain In Street Ambush in the Capital." Shortly thereafter, with its new president sworn in, "Paraguay Glides From Desperation to Euphoria." All in all, however, in 2002, "Paraguay is ranked the most corrupt in Latin America by a recent survey," with "corruption still king" there."[47]

In Uruguay in 1994, "Moderate Leftist [Is] Elected in Close . . . Presidential Race." A few months later, "New Chief Tells Free-handed Uruguay It's Time to Take Its Medicine." By 1998 "The Welfare State Is Alive, if Besieged, in Uruguay," with various legislative ramifications. A year later, in mid-1999, "With Kinder Face, the Left Is Blossoming In Uruguay." The "Grief for 19 [Killed in Bus Crash] Bonds Uruguay, Muting an Election's Clamor." In late November "Ruling Party Wins Election For President In Uruguay," "Repelling a strong challenge from the Uruguayan left." In November 2004, "Uruguay's Left Makes History By Winning Presidential Race." In March 2005, "With New Chief, Uruguay Veers Left, in a Latin Pattern," reflecting "A 'pink' tide of South American leaders: socialist, but pragmatists, too." "Leftist Chief Is Installed in Uruguay and Gets Busy on Agenda," as " 'A life with dignity' is promised the poorest Uruguayans." Soon "Uruguay Tackles Old Rights Cases, Charging Ex-President."[48]

7. ARGENTINA

"Argentina Deregulates Its Economy" and "Retreats from Democracy"

Early in conservative President Menem's first elected term, in 1991, "Argentina Stays Tuned to Peronism and Its Politics of Personality," while he "has governed with flamboyance, drama, a bit of the absurd—and a list of serious purposes." In view of Argentina's dictatorial past in its leader Perón, along with its post-war harboring of former Nazis, Argentina was now, in a sense, "A Nation at War With Itself," under its democratic system of Executive, Legislature (bicameral), and Judicial authorities.[49]

When later in 1991 "Argentina Deregulates Its Economy," it "Moves to tame inflation and reignite growth." In 1992 "The Big Push [Is] Toward Privatization." At the same time, "Argentina Retreats From Democracy" because President "Menem has undermined the courts and press." In 1993 "Unrest Shows Argentina the Perils of Privatization." That year "Argentine Files Show Huge Effort to Harbor Nazis." In 1994 "Argentina Is Booming But There Is No Rest For Its Tortured Soul," for "The country fears it is trapped by history, like the athlete who made a comeback, only to fall again." A "New Security Apparatus Resurrects Old Fears." Yet "Argentina Demotes Its Once Powerful Armed Forces," long after "The Falkland War [against England in 1982] diminished the role of Argentina's military leaders." In 1995, "For the First Time, Argentine Army Admits 'Dirty War' Killings" of leftists and dissidents from 1976 to 1983. Economically, nonetheless, "Argentina's Ills Could Help Leader," for in his 1995 re-election bid "The polls favor Menem, who tamed inflation."[50]

In spring of 1995, "Menem Wins 2nd Term as Leader In Argentina by a Large Margin." "Menem's Victory [Is] . . . Seen as Endorsement of Free Market." But in 1996, when "A New Crackdown Pinches Tax-Resistant in Argentina," "A feeling [grows] that the Government in Buenos Aires has gone too far" under Menem, who in his first term "push[ed] . . . a law through Congress that for the first time set prison sentences and stiff fines for tax fraud." It meant "Hard Times for Millions As Argentina Slims Down" after it "regains stability, but drops a safety net." In 1997 "Unrest Erupts In Argentina Over Austerity." The "Rising Outcry in Argentina as Economic Reform Pinches" threatens, for Menem's ruling party, "a possible loss of a majority in Congress." "To Argentines, Judges Are Often Biggest Lawbreakers." In later 1997 "Peronists Lose Congress Elections," leaving the "political landscape . . . suddenly altered." By 1998 "Argentine Economy [Is] Reborn but Still Ailing."[51]

"Money Talks, Sovereignty Walks"

With the election of President de la Rúa in 1999—his predecessor having been barred constitutionally from running again—the "Party of Perón Loses Its Hold on Argentina" due to "Recession, unemployment and [need for] a change." "With the economy sickly, the new leader is proposing a dose of austerity."[52]

Difficulties soon arose for de la Rúa and his party in Congress. In 2000 "Argentine President Is Trying To Keep Coalition Together" in a rising tide of public discontent over his failures after "promising to jump-start a depressed economy and cleanse a political system corroding from corruption and public distrust. . . ." But "Nobody Is Above the Law," while, "From Argentina to Peru, arrests of politicians challenge a culture that condones corruption." In 2001 "Argentina Will Try Former President [Menem] on Arms Charges." Two weeks later "Argentina Austerity Plan Provokes National Strike." Now "Losing Faith in the Free Market," "Argentina once embraced capitalism but now faces a crisis that could have a domino effect." In the fall of 2001, "Argentine Economy Dives, Setting Off Investor Panic," while "Drop in Tax Revenues Brings Fears of Devaluation." The government's imposition in late 2001 of "A limit on cash withdrawals . . . [marks] a system's last gasp?" while "Postponing the Inevitable." Then, "Reeling From Riots, Argentina Declares a State of Siege." A day later, "Argentine Leader, His Nation Frayed, Abruptly Resigns," and "Opposition Party [Is] to Take Over."[53]

Argentine government and society were fast unraveling. In late December 2001 "Interim Presidency [Is] Decided in Argentina but Doubts Linger" in a "New Chapter In an Epic of Frustration." At that point, "Money Talks, Sovereignty Walks," not just because of Argentina giving up control of its national currency, by shackling the peso to the dollar; but also because of its losing governmental control over the economy to chaos. There were "Consequences for the United States in Argentina's collapse," while "Blaming the I.M.F. for imposing rules, not giving help." "Unity Eludes Argentina's Governing Party" owing to "Factional disputes, conflicting ambitions and a presidential election looming." Then, the last day in December, "Argentine [Interim] Leader Quits; So Does Successor" amid "Doubt over whether any government can end the crisis." A day later, at the start of January 2002, "Argentina Drifts, Leaderless, as Economic Collapse Looms." A day after that, "Popular Argentine Senator Steps In to Fill the Void, Becoming 5th President in 2 Weeks."[54]

"Argentine President Unveils Crisis Legislation"

That newest "Argentine Leader [Eduardo Duhalde] Seeks Broad Powers in Economic Crisis" as he "sent Congress a 'public emergency law' that would give him sweeping powers to deal with the economic crisis that has immobilized the country for the last month."

"Old Rules Gone, Argentines Brace for the Unknown." As for "How Argentina Was Ruined," "After 70 years of regimes driven by myths, it's time to focus on reality." In early February 2002, "In New Blow to Peso, Argentine Court Voids Bank Freeze" as "A two-day bank holiday is declared to prevent a run on the banks." "In Argentine Crisis, Military Stays in Step."[55]

Then in April 2002 "Argentine President Unveils Crisis Legislation," and "A plan to convert bank deposits into bonds could buy time for Argentina." The next day brought "2 Blows to Argentine President: Economy Minister Quits and Senate Balks at Crisis Bill." Two days after that, "Argentine Congress Tightens Rules on Bank Withdrawals." "Argentina, Shortchanged," was "a nation that followed the rules [but] fell to pieces." Nearly a year later, "Once Secure, Argentines Now Lack Food and Hope," for "Some 60 percent of all Argentines are living in poverty."[56]

In May 2003, "Argentina's [Next New] Chief Is Sworn In and Comes Out Fighting," taking on "the battle to guide Argentina out of its worst economic crisis." "Argentina Looks to a New Leader," President Kirchner, to cure "Political and Economic Ills [That] Have Shaken Nation's Faith in Itself." Three months later, "Argentine Congress [Is] Likely to Void 'Dirty War' Amnesty," for "A new leader is eager to see those accused of rights abuses face trial." By early 2006, "As Argentina's Debt Dwindles, President's Power Steadily Grows." Then, "For Argentina's Sizzling Economy, [Comes] a Cap on Steak Prices," such that "To control inflation, Buenos Aires has sought voluntary price controls." The legal system was gearing up when in August 2006, "After 30 Years, Argentina's Dictatorship Stands Trial." Early 2007 saw "Argentina's [1970s] Ex-President [Isabel Perón] Charged With Rights Abuses."[57]

8. CHILE

"A Stillborn Democracy?" as "Elected President Replaces Pinochet"

Would it become, "In Chile, a Stillborn Democracy?," inasmuch as "[former President-Dictator] Pinochet still runs the army." That was the question in 1990 when "After 16 Years, General [Is Begrudgingly] Turning Over Power to an Elected President" of Chile, which lies to the west of Argentina along the Pacific coast. As "Elected President [Aylwin] Replaces Pinochet," he "promise[s] on the first day in office: the truth about past repression." A year later, "Response to Chile Human Rights Report [of Past Abuses] Is Violent";

"Chile's Leader and Army Square Off Over the Past"; and "Pinochet Assails Chilean Rights Report." Over a year after that, "Chilean Leader Seeks to Limit Army's Power."[58]

Retrograde steps were bound to occur, especially in connection with the military. In 1996 "Chileans Are Prosecuted For Criticizing Officials," for, "Though Chile has returned to civilian rule, the military chills free speech." In 1997 "Killing Casts Focus on Abuses in Chile's Military" as "Grisly Death Stirs A Storm of Protest." Even so, in late 1997 "Chile's Democracy Dances Around the Ex-Dictator," Pinochet, who, "once a ruthless leader, will retire as Army Chief to be a senator-for-life." That retirement, occurring in early 1998, helped Chile's "return to democracy."[59]

Concerning legal and legislative matters, in 1997 "Chile May Allow Divorce to Snip Those Ties That Bind" in a "Conservative country [that] missed social changes of the '70s; Congress will vote next year." In 1998 "Legislators Try to Block Senate Seat for Pinochet." Notwithstanding, "Elections and open markets are not enough, Latins are told" by "Clinton, in Chile, [Who] Calls for Deepening of Restored Democracy." Then, in fall 1998 "Britain Arrests Pinochet to Face Spanish Charges"; "Arrest Raises New Issues On Tracking Rights Crimes." The Chilean as well as British legal system of justice became involved in complicated issues and proceedings.[60]

"A Chilean Socialist in the Clinton–Blair Mold"

In late 1999 a "Socialist [Lagos] Runs in Chile, Disclaiming Radicalism." In early 2000 that "Chilean Socialist [Is] Narrowly Elected President as Both Sides Offer Reconciliation." He was called "A Chilean Socialist in the Clinton–Blair Mold," being "more Keynesian than Marxist." By later 2001, "Chile's Leader Remains Socialist but Acts Like Pragmatist," while "Facing a weak economy and a powerful military." A week later, "Chilean Government Retains Control of House [Lower Body in Bicameral Legislature] in Elections," reinforcing the socialist president's upper hand in the legislative process. In spring of 2002 "A continent's growth slows, and its social problems grow" in Chile and other nations. At year's end, "After Banning 1,092 Movies, Chile Relaxes Its Censorship." In September 2003, "Chile's Leader Presses Rights Issues Softly but Successfully," albeit "The pursuit of reforms is tempered by political reality"; and "Chile Inches Toward a Law That Would Make Divorce Legal." In March 2006 "Chile's Socialist President Exits Enjoying Wide Respect." His successor was not so fortunate in April 2007 when, "One Year Into Term, Chile's Leader Tries to Reverse

Slide" as he confronted "A corruption scandal and a troubled new transportation system."[61]

During the Lagos presidency, the wheels of justice and the legal system were moving slowly forward in the Pinochet case. In March of 2000, "Freed by Britain, Pinochet Faces New Legal Problems at Home." A few months later, "Pinochet [Is] Ruled No Longer Immune From Prosecution." Soon, "Pinochet's Arrest [Is] Ordered By [Chilean] Judge." Yet by June 2001, "Chile's Effort to Try Pinochet Is Running Out of Steam" as "The 'mentally unfit for trial' argument seems to prevail." In July "Chile Court Bars Trial Of Pinochet" and "Rules He's Too Ill for Charges of Covering Up '73 Killings." Matters were not yet over. In early 2005 "Pinochet [Is] Entangled in Web of Inquiries," with "Signs of progress in three legal cases against" him. Later that year "Pinochet [Is] Held on Charges Linked to Bank Account." In late 2006 there was both "Joy and Violence, at Death of Pinochet"; the "Dictator Who Ruled by Terror in Chile . . . Dies, Evading Trial." Two weeks later, "Chile's Leader [Bachelet] Attacks Amnesty for Pinochet-Era Crimes," yet "A dictator's subordinates may now face justice."[62]

9. LATIN AMERICA IN GENERAL AND IN BLOCS: TOWARD SELF-DETERMINATION ON THE U.S. MODEL?

In conclusion, a multiplicity of diverse trends and themes stand out for Latin America in general during the 1990s. By 1990 "Latin America's Economies Look [Improved] After a Decade's Decline," "Swapping Debt for Hope." In 1991 "Latin Nations Get a Firmer Grip on Their Destiny" as "Preservation of new democracies becomes a prime regional goal." On "Coups and Democracy . . . [There Are Still Cautionary] Lessons From Latin America" insofar as "The armed forces of three Latin Countries are still, at least to some extent, independent power centers." Yet "A New Discipline in Economics Brings Change to Latin America" as "Balanced Budgets and Free Markets Take Hold." In 1992 "As Conflicts [and Wars] Wane, Central America Strives for Long-Term Stability," with "much more optimism and confidence in the future today." "After the Cold War," "Sweeping Political Changes Leave the Latin American Poor Still Poor." In "S. America's Trickle-Down Democracy," "Elected Rulers Find Ways to Impose Programs Over Faction-Ridden Legislatures." In 1993 "Latin America Finds Harmony in Convergence" in "NAFTA and the Hemisphere," while gaining "Cultural Momentum." In 1994 "The New South Americans . . . [Are]

Friends and Partners," with "Generals . . . now taking a back seat to the free traders." "Latin Economic Speedup Leaves Poor in the Dust." "Privatizing In Latin America" leaves "Bridges, airports, power plants and ports in investors' hands." In 1995 "Latin America Resists Populism's Siren Call," for, "Despite reversals, reformist economic policies in the region have remained virtually unchanged." In 1996 "Latin American Nations Rebuke U.S. for the Embargo on Cuba." In 1997 "Central America [Is] Stung by U.S. Law" on immigration. In 1998 "Clinton Urges Latin America to 'Be Patient' on Free Trade." "Central America . . . [Is] A region in need of help" as "Rebuilding Begins," with "Urgent debt solution" in particular need. Meeting in Chile, with focus on social conditions, "Leaders From 34 Countries Give the Free-Trade Zone of the Americas Go-Ahead." In 1999, with "Clinton to Begin Visit to Central America," "Changes are occurring without the clamor and violence of the past." "Latin America's Leftists Say Adios To Revolution," and "Guerrillas who once killed for power now bargain for it with coalition partners." "Latin America's new concerns over 'colonial' interference" shows how much "The idea of a 'right to intervene' has made deep inroads into national sovereignty."[63]

Early in the new century, starting here in 2004, lamentations were expressed over "Latin America's Half-Term Presidents." "For Once, Latin Americans Ask the U.S. to Butt In" because "Democracy, which spread under three [U.S.] presidents, is under stress again." "Latin America Is Growing Impatient With Democracy" due to "Graft and Poverty." "South America, a Rising Force in Agriculture, Is Seeking to Fill the World's Table." In 2005 "Latin Nations Resist Plan For Monitor of Democracy," leaving "the possibility of a diplomatic defeat" for the United States. "Latin States Shun U.S. Plan To Watch Over Democracy" because "Some feared the Bush administration sought a 'democratic police force.' " "Unending Graft Threatens the Democracies of Latin America as Frustrations Grow." There was a "Push to Liberalize the Abortion Laws in Latin America." In 2006 "Latin America tilts to the left, but not toward revolution." In 2007 "Visit by Bush Fires Up Latins' Debate Over Socialism," involving a potent antithesis: "From the president, aid and trade. South of the border, protests against capitalism." "Bush tries new tack with Latin America" in "His five-country tour, which . . . will focus less on trade and more on social issues." "The Pope, Addressing Latin America's Bishops, Denounces Capitalism and Marxism."[64]

Other suggestive topics as appeared in *Current History* in 1998–2003 were: "United States–Latin American Relations: Shunted to the Slow Track"; "The Militarization of the Drug War in Latin America";

"Castro Capitalism Comes to Latin America"; "A Shaken Agenda: Bush and Latin America"; "Osama bin Laden as Transnational Revolutionary Leader"; and "From Counternarcotics to Counterterrorism in Colombia."[65]

The paramount necessity of firmly establishing "the rule of law" in all Latin American countries has long been recognized. During a TV news program in 2007, the "rule of law is [called] the center of everything" in relation to Latin nations, such as Colombia, with respect to the judicial system and the police. Unfortunately, gloomy outlooks have at times been expressed in such books as *The Judiciary and Democratic Decay in Latin America: Declining Confidence in the Rule of Law* (2000).[66]

If the future holds expanding supra-national blocs for Latin America, the paramount importance of legal–legislative frameworks will likely grow at the same levels. Economically, free-trade zones or blocs like NAFTA will need those basic frameworks, perhaps compelling the Latin nations into a common market of the European type. Increased economic integration could bring growing political infrastructures along with legal–legislative ones, as in the European models. The regional Congress or legislature to which a number of Central American nations have been sending representatives is promising, without compromising their own legal–legislative sovereignty over their own affairs. Self-determination both at regional and national levels might thereby be maintained. The "United States" of Latin America, like the "United States of Europe," could emerge on the model, however loosely, of the existing United States in North America. The adjacent proximity of Latin American nations, and their groupings, to the United States, along with their democratic post–Cold-War tendencies in the 1990s and beyond, could make their American-style constitutions (with separate legislative, executive, and judicial branches) adaptable to a new-style federalism and federation. To the extent that the economic framework were to become fully "hemispheric," the political–legal structures in future decades and centuries would be open to many intriguing possibilities.

ANNEX

Canada and North American Blocs

Canada and
North American Blocs

1. "THE . . . DEBATE OVER . . . SOVEREIGNTY"

The long-standing Canadian debate over sovereignty in connection with Quebec and other areas has gone through many twists and turns in the last couple of decades. In 1989 "Quebec Re-elects Liberals Over Separatists" "on a platform of remaining part of Canada." Less than a year later in 1990, "Quebec Crisis Boils Again in Canada," with "The odds . . . very good that the country will break up." At that point it was asked "Is Canada Coming Apart?"—"Maybe not, but the politicians are playing a dangerous game of chicken over the future of the federation." "Canadian Leader [Mulroney] Appeals For Calm On Quebec Dispute" and "Seeks To Avoid Breakup," "But Province's Chief [Bourassa] Is Grim as He Vows Not to Return to Failed Negotiations." In "A potential revival of the idea of a 'two-nation' Canada," "Quebec and Ottawa Forage for a New Relationship." "Quebec Struggles To Find New Role," "to Be More of a Country and Less of a Province." "In Quebec, Yet Another Splintering" centers on "Now, the Indians." "Quebec Premier Asks Army To Remove Indian Barricades." In "The Violent Debate Over Tribal Sovereignty" and "Who Controls the Future?," the deletion of "Violent" and "Tribal" renders this title more widely applicable. By later 1990 "Quebec Once Again Searches Its Soul On Province's Future Role in Canada."[1]

In early 1991 "Quebec Demands Greater Powers if It Is to Remain in Canada." Days later, "Quebec Is Trying Again to Strike Out On Its Own," as "A man who spent years working to keep Canada whole now leads the successionists." "Who's Afraid of Nationhood [for Quebec] Now? Few, It Seems." Meanwhile, "Ontario Recognizes Indian Self-Government." In fall 1991 "Mulroney Proposes New Canadian Framework to Stall Separation." By December there was an "Accord to Give the Eskimos Control of a Fifth of Canada."[2]

In early 1992 "Gloom Prevails at Critical Time in Quebec Dispute," with "Little confidence that Canada can be preserved." "A Sovereign Quebec, He [Separatist Leader Parizeau] Says, Needn't Be Separate." With further fracturing momentum, it was reported that "Canada [Is] Northern Land" after "Northwest Territories Votes to Split Into Two Parts, One as an Eskimo Area." Then, "Lawmakers Provide Plans on Constitutional Change to Keep Canada United." "Quebec Premier Hard-Sells Canadian Federalism." Yet "Canadian Unity Pact Faces Early Opposition." "Canadians Will Choose to Reweave the Constitution or Risk Its Unraveling." Finally, in October, "Canada Rejects Charter Changes as Unity Package Is Turned Down," "Saying no to more autonomy for provinces." "A Canadian Warns: Breaking Up Is Now Much Easier to Do." Others say that, "Back on Track" "After the constitutional referendum, the threat of national disintegration has dissipated."[3]

In 1993 "Mulroney Resigns, Urging a 'Renewal for Canada'"; whereupon "Canadian Tories Name Woman Premier," Kim Campbell, who "Offers 'New Agenda.'" "Canadian Prime Minister Campbell Vows 'Streamlined Government.'" She will "Call General Election" and "Set Vote" for the fall. Meantime, "Premier of Quebec [Is] To Quit" and "Ottawa [Is] to Lose Strong Voice for Keeping the Province Within the Federation." But then "Governing Tories In Canada [Are] Routed By Liberal Party" and "Quebec Bloc Gains." "Quebec Bloc [Is] Set For Ottawa Role," as "Leader of the New Separatist Opposition Says Early Focus Will Be on Economics," due not least to voters' call for jobs as was promised by the new liberal leader, Jean Chrétien.[4]

2. "FEDERALISTS DEFEAT . . . SOCIALISTS" AND A "SOVEREIGN STATE" FOR QUEBEC

The Canadian tide seemed to turn when in early 1995 "Federalists Defeat Quebec Separatists in Canadian By-Elections." Even so, many months later, "Secessionist's [New] Vision for Quebec Pleases Crowds" in October. Soon, nevertheless, "Quebec, By Razor-Thin Margin, Votes 'No' On Leaving Canada" and creating "a

Nation" there. "Quebec's Premier Quits After Vote Loss." Now it was "Canada United, Quebec Divided." "Adieu, Liberal Nationalism." "Quebec Party [Is] Unlikely to Seek a New Sovereignty Vote Soon." By spring 1996 "Quebec Premier Softens His Stance on Independence." "In US, Quebec Premier [Is] to Mute Secession Talk." In fall 1996 "Canada Asks Its Court Whether Quebec Can Legally Walk Away."[5]

Then in 1997, "In Weeks Before Canada Votes, Quebec Again Drives Debate." "As Vote Nears, Canada's Parties Turn Right." "Quebec Secession at Center of Canada's Election." After the election, with "Canada Dividing Itself," "Prime Minister Jean Chrétien stays in power, but no political party can claim a national mandate."[6]

In 1998 "Canadian Court Rules Quebec Cannot Secede on Its Own," "Call[ing] separation difficult, but not impossible." The upcoming "Vote in Quebec May Be Last Fling With Secession." That "election will determine if there will be another referendum on separation," with import for "Quebec's split psyche." The outcome was that "Separatist Premier Keeps Control In Quebec's Provincial Election." Leaving "Quebec Questions," "Election Failed to Give Clear Idea of Where the Province Is Headed," with "The separatist movement . . . still alive, but . . . wounded." Meantime that year, "Canada Pact Gives A Tribe [of Indians] Self-Rule For the First Time"—"a Dangerous Precedent" to critics; "The Inuits' New State" being "Fragile but Full of Optimism."[7]

The debate continued. Was there "Tiptoeing around the secession issue" in "Quebec's Timid Nationalism," as one 1999 editorial charged? Then "Clinton Jolts Canadians With a Plea On Federalism." "Canada's Link to the Queen Grows Livelier." Upon the death of former Prime Minister Pierre Trudeau in 2000, his leadership on behalf of "a United Canada" was vividly recalled; with "Trudeau remembered for redefining Canada." In late 2000 "Quebec's Separatists Lose More Ground" after "High Hopes Founder in the Liberals Wake in Canadian Elections." "After Election Risks, Premier of Canada Reaps Big Rewards," "put[ting] separatism on the sidelines, for now." Although before the 2003 provincial elections the Quebec separatist leader predicted that as a result "Quebec would become a sovereign state" and "would leave Canada and become independent," there was a clear "Quebec Result: Solidly for Canada."[8]

3. LEGISLATIVE MATTERS

A brief sampling of other legislative matters points up the all-pervading scope of the Canadian legislative state in a liberal social system and reputed welfare state with universal health coverage mandated by law. In 1991 "Canadian High Court Narrows Rape

Shield Law" in "A trend toward questioning of sexual pasts." In 1992 "Alberta Chief Fans Language Fight" as "Canada is asked to scrap the laws that enforce bilingualism." "Canada Moves to Strengthen Sexual Assault Law" in order "to remove sex bias in the criminal laws." "Canada Tightens Immigration Law," with "Applicants for Asylum to Be Screened More Closely—Signs of Xenophobia." In 1994 "Mercy Killing in Canada Stirs Calls for Changes in Law." In 1996 "Legislature Acts to Widen Gay Rights In Canada." "Canada Warns U.S. on Law Penalizing Cuba Commerce" ("Legislation and a joint complaint with Mexico to NAFTA"). "Sexuality Exploited Children in Canada: The Law Is Not on Their Side," such that "A change of attitude . . . [and] wording . . . is called for." In 1997 the "Canadian Senate . . . [Has] Substantial Power but Not Much Attendance." In 1999 "Vancouver Is Astir Over Chinese Abuse on Immigration Law." "The role of religion in public life is evolving rapidly, as churches react to cutbacks in the welfare state" as mandated in part through legislation. "Canada [Is] Split As Gun Laws Are Tightened," while, "10 Years Afterward, Attack Stirs Emotion."[9]

In 2001 "Ontario's New Welfare Rule [Stipulates] . . . Be Literate and Drug Free." In 2002 "With a Quebec Law [Comes] . . . Equality for Gay Parents." "Canada [is] poised to ease pot laws." "Canada's Liberals, in Turmoil, Offer New Guidelines on Ethics." In 2003 "Canada Introduces Measure Against Penalties for Marijuana." "Gay Marriage Plan . . . [Is] Sign of Sweeping Social Change in Canada." "Canada's Push to Legalize Gay Marriage Draws Bishops' Ire." "Canadian Legislators Narrowly Reject Move Against Gay Unions." "Canada's Antiterror Laws [Are] Debated in Detention of 19 Suspects." In 2004, as legislators and "Politicians vow to fix the ailing universal coverage system," "Health Care Leads Other Issues in Canadian Vote." "Islamic law tests limits of Canada's Charter of Rights," that is, "Ontario is reviewing an act that allows Muslims to use Islamic law in legal proceedings." "Canada's Supreme Court Clears Way for Same-Sex Marriage Law." In 2005, "In Blow to Canada's Health System, Quebec Law Is Voided." "Gay Marriage Is Extended Nationwide In Canada." In 2006 "Canada's Private Clinics Surge as Public System Falters."[10]

4. NORTH AMERICAN BLOCS AND THEIR "BIGGEST OBSTACLE: SOVEREIGNTY" AND "NATIONS' LAWS"

In 1992 Henry Kissinger called for "A Hemisphere of Free Trade." The "Mega Market" in "The North American Free Trade Agreement [NAFTA] . . . [is] a huge "gamble," said one news report, involving not only the United States and Canada but also

Mexico. Shortly thereafter, "North American Nations Announce Agreement Lowering Trade Barriers" in "A Plan For Growth." A month later, "[U.S.] President and Congress Square Off On North American Trade Accord." By year's end, "Trade Pact [Is] Signed In 3 Capitals." In 1994 "U.S. and 33 Hemisphere Nations Agree to Create Free Trade Zone," the goal being "a treaty for the Americas by 2005." In 1995, showing Washington's attempted influence over such questions, "Clinton in Address to Canadians, Opposes Secession by Quebec." In 1996, with Washington's delay over whether to extend NAFTA inclusion to Chile, there was a "Separate Trade Pact by Canada and Chile"; also, "Latin American and Caribbean countries are forming trade blocs on their own." In 1997 "Clinton [Is] Embarking on a New NAFTA Quest" and "Seeks to Expand the Accord as Well as His Negotiating Power" in "A campaign to convince Congress that America's edge is at stake."[11]

In 2000, in connection with "The Vanishing Border," "Canada feels an economic and cultural threat from its U.S. neighbor," begging the rhetorical question of "How Much Longer for Canada?" Along similar lines in 2001, "Does NAFTA trump countries' laws?," in view of a "NAFTA provision that allows companies to sue governments." In "The Work of a Hemisphere," "On Bush's agenda for Quebec, trade and shared ideals" are key. "Bush's Job at Quebec Talks . . . [Is] to Push Case for Free Trade," while "Hemisphere leaders have waited 6 years for strong signals." "Bush Links Trade With Democracy at Conference in Quebec." As before, the "Biggest Obstacle to Selling Trade Pact: Sovereignty" and "Concern that investors could flout nations' laws"; even so, "Leaders Pledge Broad Cooperation, With Focus on Free Trade," "Spelling out the links between democracy and prosperity in the hemisphere." In 2003 "Canadian [New Leader] Envisions New Role for Nation," including the reduction of "American and European trade barriers." In further signs of emerging "blocs" across national borders, a 2007 story reported on how "Quebec and Vermont Tourists Bond Over Sleepy Border."[12]

In the end, the growing blocs in North America, as in Central and South America, will no doubt continue to expand in the long run; yet the need to protect and strengthen national borders in the war against terrorists will present necessary hurdles for the immediate future. The shape of the emergent "new order" is still uncertain and unfolding; but increasing hemispheric (and global) integration is undoubtedly the longer trend. How questions of sovereignty, state, and legislation will be worked out is even further unsettled; yet they will continue to occupy positions on center stage in political, legal, social, and economic terms. The future role of United States leadership is a subject for further discussion and is full of promise.

Epilogue

U.S. and Other "Union" Models in Future Perspective

The predominance of the United States in the Western Hemisphere in relation to both Latin America to the south and Canada to the north (whether just or not in the eyes of those other regions) raises questions on the role of U.S. and other models as represented in this book on contemporary or current affairs. In terms of Latin America, will the U.S. constitutional paradigm of separate executive, legislative, and judicial branches be influential there beyond their present manifestations as in Mexico, whether directly via the United States or indirectly via Mexico? The same question arises for the influence of the U.S. federal system of states and localities. Likewise, the predominant rule of law and legislation throughout U.S. life and society often still presents even for Mexico a hard act to follow in everyday reality. Many other Latin American nations and regions have experienced far greater struggles than Mexico with corruption, crime, authoritarianism, and the like which have often threatened gains made since the decline of Cold War influences in the early 1990s. To what extent could the U.S. model of a legislative Congress be still further developed among the various Central American nations that have formed their own regional Congress earlier in the current decade? Will the most conspicuous case of "the United Mexican States," as patterned upon "the United States of America," be developed by other Latin nations and regions if supra-national blocs gain momentum in decades and centuries to come? As for Canada, where the European parliamentary system involving non-directly elected prime ministers has taken historical root, will current trends toward free trade and open borders bring, for instance, further inroads of U.S. polities into Canadian constitutional life, including into the formations of government?

Larger questions arise as to the place of U.S. and other "union" models in the emerging hemispheric blocs that could become a central focus in the near or distant future. If the North American bloc of NAFTA for free trade—involving the United States, Canada, and Mexico—can be loosely compared to the European Common Market, would there someday be a comparable "American Union" in a political or even legal–legislative sense? What would then become of legal–legislative systems at the national level, not to mention those of individual states within the United States and other national federal systems? Or would there emerge a "Latin American Union" of individual states patterned after the U.S. model? Where would the principle of legal–legislative self-determination then lie in such Unions of states?

Along such lines a broad wider range of future possibilities opens up. For example, a recent news article has reported that French President "Sarkozy pushes Mediterranean Union," involving "nations as diverse as Libya and Spain." But "Would it be a supra national organization like the EU with its power to set national laws or merely an institutionalized forum for discussion?"[13]

Will the current "European Union" be developed or transformed into a cohesive federal system of individual states? Could there be a viable "African Union," much less a true "Middle Eastern Union"? Or a functioning new-style worldwide "Union of Unions" with new alignments of nations and regions? Such questions lead naturally into our next book on the Eastern Hemisphere, followed by considerations of paradigm-building on a more global or worldwide scale.

Meanwhile, would a system of "states of the Iraqi federal union"— with self-determining individual states under a strong central federal givernment similar to the "states of the American federal union"— be the most adaptable and workable solution to the current Iraqi crisis in government? And not a partition or confederation?

If future latter-day "James Madison" architects strive on a broad worldwide constitutional scale, they should keep in mind his deep researches into history.

Notes to
Chapters II–XIII
and Annex

Key to Abbreviations

BWM	=	*BusinessWeek* Magazine
CBS, CNN, NBC, PBS, etc.	=	TV networks
CH	=	*Current History*
CSM	=	*Christian Science Monitor*
NSL	=	*Newark Star-Ledger*
NWM	=	*Newsweek* Magazine
NYDN	=	*New York Daily News*
NYP	=	*New York Post*
NYT	=	*New York Times*
NYTBR	=	*New York Times Book Review*
NYTM	=	*New York Times Magazine*
PCN	=	*Public Citizen News*
TE	=	*The Economist*
TM	=	*Time* Magazine
USAT	=	*USA Today*
USNWR	=	*U.S. News and World Report*
WP	=	*Washington Post*
WPNWE	=	*Washington Post National Weekly Edition*
WPR	=	*World Press Review*
WSJ	=	*Wall Street Journal*

Notes to Chapter II
The U.S. Presidency

1. TM, March 30, 1987, p. 28–.
2. CSM, March 5, 1987, p. 1–.
3. CSM, May 13, 1987, p. 1–.
4. CSM, July 14, 1987, p. 1–.
5. NYT, May 20, 1987, A31; NYT, Nov. 19, 1987, A30; NYT, May 19, 1987, A34.
6. CSM, May 21, 1987, p. 1–; CSM, May 21, 1987, p. 1–; NYTM, Sept. 13, 1987, p. 41.
7. NYT, Dec. 17, 1989; NYT, Dec. 13, 1989, p. 1–; NYT, Dec. 13, 1989; NYT, Dec. 15, 1989, A43; TM, Dec. 18, 1989, p. 36; NYT, Oct. 6, 1989, p. 1.
8. NYT, April 2, 1989, sect. 4, p. 1–.
9. NYT, Dec. 17, 1989, p. 20; NYT, Aug. 21, 1989, p. 16.
10. NYT, Sept. 24, 1987, p. 22; NYT, Nov. 11, 1989, p. 1.
11. TM, Feb. 12, 1990, p. 23; NYT, Jan. 9, 1990, A16; NYT, Jan. 19, 1990, A1–; NYT, Feb. 8, 1990; NYT, March 7, 1990, A1; NYT, March 15, 1990, A14; NYT, March 16, 1990, A16; NYT, April 5, 1990, A1–; NYT, April 24, 1990, B6; NYT, May 16, 1990, A1–; NYT, May 23, 1990, B1–.
12. NYT, July 3, 1990, A17; TM, July 9, 1990, p. 16–; NYT, July 14, 1990, A1; NYT, July 27, 1990, A1; NYT, July 27, 1990, A1; NYT, Sept. 22, 1990,

A10; NYT, Oct. 11, 1990, D22; NYT, Oct. 11, 1990, A1; NWM, Oct. 22, 1990, p. 84; NWM, Oct. 22, 1990, cover story; NYT, Oct. 21, 1990, sect. 4, p. 19; WP, Oct. 21, 1990, A8; NYT, Oct. 21, 1990, sect. 1, p. 22; NYT, Oct. 23, 1990, A1; NYT, Oct. 23, 1990, A1; NYT, Oct. 30, 1990, A1; NYT, Nov. 16, 1990, A28; NYT, Nov. 23, 1990, A1–; NYT, Nov., 1990, A1–; WP, Dec. 2, 1990, A24; NYT, Dec. 5, 1990, A1; NYT, Dec. 5, 1990, A1; NYT, Dec. 9, 1990, E17; NYT, Dec. 11, 1990, A1; NYT, Dec. 13, 1990, B15; NYT, Dec. 13, 1990, B15; NYT, Dec. 17, 1990; NYT, Dec. 18, 1990, A1–; NYT, Dec. 20, 1990, A1; NYT, Dec. 31, 1990, p. 10.

13. NYT, Jan. 12, 1990, A1–; NYT, Feb. 3, 1990, A1; WP, Feb. 18, 1990, A9; NYT, March 14, 1990, A14; NYT, Feb. 23, 1990, A1; NYT, March 18, 1990, sect. 1, p. 1–; NYT, April 28, 1990, p. 24; NYT, June 6, 1990, A1; TM, Nov. 12, 1990, p. 30; NYT, Dec. 1, 1990, p. 10; NYT, Dec. 13, 1990, A22.

14. NYT, Feb. 11, 1990, sect. 4, p. 24; NYT, Feb. 18, 1990, sect. 1, p. 14; NYT, April 30, 1990, A17; NYT, July 8, 1990, sect. 4, p. 17; NYT, Nov. 5, 1990, A2; USNWR, Nov. 19, 1990.

15. TM, Jan. 7, 1991, pp. 22, 28; NYT, Dec. 18, 1991; NYT, Nov. 12, 1991, A25; NYT, March 20, 1991, B7; NWM, June 24, 1991, p. 20.

16. NYT, Jan. 7, 1991, D8; NYT, Feb. 4, 1991, A14; NYT, Feb. 6, 1991, A1–; NYT, Feb. 9, 1991, A1; TM, Feb. 18, 1991, p. 43; NYT, Feb. 21, 1991, D6; NYT, Feb. 22, 1991, A14; NYT, March 2, 1991, p. 10; NYT, March 7, 1991, A1–; NYT, March 20, 1991, A24; NYT, April 20, 1991, p. 1–; TM, April 29, 1991, p. 52; NYT, April 28, 1991, sect. 4, p. 5; NYT, May 5, 1991, sect. 1, p. 34; NYT, May 8, 1991, p. 1; NYT, May 11, 1991, p. 8; NYT, May 11, 1991, p. 8; NYT, May 17, 1991, A1–; NYT, May 13, 1991, A1; NYT, May 28, 1991, D2; NYT, May 28, 1991, D2; NYT, no data available yet in sequence.

17. NYT, Aug. 1, 1991, D1; NYT, Aug. 2, 1991, A1; NYT, Aug. 7, 1991, A1; NYT, Aug. 17, 1991, A1; NYT, Sept. 11, 1991, A1–; NYT, Sept. 28, 1991, A1; NYT, Oct. 9, 1991, A1; NYT, Oct. 24, 1991, A22; NYT, Nov. 18, 1991, A12; NYT, Nov. 20, 1991, A1–; NYT, Nov. 21, 1991, A1; NYT, Nov. 22, 1991, A8; NYT, Nov. 22, 1991, A1; NYT, Nov. 22, 1991, A1, A20; NYT, Nov. 26, 1991, A1–; NYT, Dec. 16, 1991, B1; NYT, Dec. 17, 1991, A16.

18. TM, Jan. 7, 1991, p. 22; USNWR, March 25, 1991, p. 24; WP, May 19, 1991, A14; WP, June 9, 1991, A4; WP, Sept, 29, 1991, A40; NYT, Sept. 29, 1991, sect. 4, no page no. avail.; TM, Sept. 23, 1991, p. 32.

19. NWM, Jan. 6, 1992, p. 34; NYT, Dec. 24, 1991, A1–; NYT, Jan. 2, 1992, A1–; NYT, Jan. 20, 1992, A12; NYT, Feb. 25, 1992, C5; NYT, March 23, 1992, A3; NYT, April 29, 1992, A22; NYT, April 29, 1992, A25; NYT, May 18, 1992, A12; NYT, May 20, 1992, A18; NYT, Aug. 2, 1992, sect. 3, p. 11; NYT, Aug. 30, 1992, sect. 1, p. 33; NYT, Oct. 4, 1992, A1–; NYT, Nov. 12, 1992, A16; NYT, Jan. 23, 1992, A1–; NYT, Jan. 16, 1990, A1.

20. BWM, Feb. 3, 1992, cover story; NYT, Jan. 27, 1992, A6; NYT, Jan. 29, 1992, A16; NYT, Jan. 30, 1992, A1–, A17; NYT, Feb. 2, 1992, sect. 2, p. 1; NYT, Feb. 2, 1992, sect. 4, p. 13; NYT, Aug. 29, 1992, A10.

21. NYT, Feb. 7, 1992, A15; NYT, Feb. 8, 1992, A9; NYT, Aug. 2, 1992, sect. 1, p. 20; WP, Jan. 17, 1993 [1992?], A28; NYT, Aug. 9, 1992, A1; NYT, Aug. 23, 1992, sect. 4, p. 4; NYT, Aug. 27, 1992, A23; NYT, Sept. 23, 1992, A33.

22. NYT, Jan. 26, 1992, A12; NYT, June 25, 1992, A1–, A25; TM, March 9, 1992, p. 24; NYT, March 3, 1992, A7; NYT, Jan. 15, 1992, A1.

23. NYT, Nov. 6, 1992, A1, A18; TM, Nov. 16, 1992, cover story; WP, Nov. 8, 1992, C1.

24. NWM, Commemorative Issue, Winter/Spring 1992; NYT, Jan. 31, 1993, sect. 1, p. 4; NYTM, Jan. 17, 1993, p. 30.

25. NYT, Feb. 18, 1993, A1–; NYT, Feb. 3, 1993, A1–; NYT, Feb. 19, 1993, A17; NYT, Feb. 20, 1993, A1; NYT, Feb. 19, 1993, A27; WP, Feb. 21, 1993, no page no. avail.; NYT, Feb. 28, 1993, sect. 3, p. 1; NYT, March 19, 1993, A16; NYT, March 21, 1993, sect. 4, no page no. avail.; TM, March 29, 1993, p. 25.

26. NYT, April 12, 1993, A17; NYT, April 11, 1993, sect. 4, p. 13; NYT, Feb. 18, 1993, A23; NYT, March 5, 1993, A29; NYT, April 2, 1993, A1; NYT, Feb. 28, 1993, sect. 4, p. 15.

27. TM or NWM, c. April, 1993, p. 36; NYT, April 13, 1993, A18; TM, May 24, 1993, p. 30–; TM, Sept. 20, 1993, cover story; NYT, Sept. 23, 1993, A1–; NYT, April 19, 1993, A1; NYT, Oct. 28, 1993, A1, A24; NYT, Oct. 1, 1993, A22; NYT, Sept. 27, 1993, A1.

28. WP, May 23, 1993, sect. C, no page no. avail.; TM, Aug. 16, 1993, cover story; TM, June 7, 1993, no page no. avail.; NYT, June 2, 1993, p. 14; NYT, April 1, 1993, sect. 4, p. 1; NYT, June 6, 1993, sect. 1, p. 26; NYT, Aug. 22, 1993, sect. 4, p. 1.

29. TM, Sept. 13, 1993, pp. 25, 29; NYT, Sept. 5, 1993, sect. 1, p. 38; NYT, Sept. 8, 1993, A1, B10; NYT, Sept. 7, 1993, A19; NYT, Sept. 9, 1993, A1.

30. NYT, Nov. 16, 1992, A1–; NYT, Nov. 17, 1992, A18; NYT, Dec. 20, 1992, sect. 1, p. 24; NYT, Nov. 12, 1992, A1; NYT, Jan. 17, 1993, sect. 1, p. 21.

31. NYT, Jan. 23, 1993, A1–; NYT, Jan. 26, 1993, A1–; NYT, Jan. 24, 1993, sect. 1, p. 20.

32. NYT, Jan. 27, 1993, A1, A14; NYT, Jan. 30, 1993, A1; NYT, Jan. 28, 1993, A19; NYT, July 8, 1993, A16; NYT, July 17, 1993, A1.

33. NYT, Feb. 28, 1993, sect. 1, p. 1; NYT, Feb. 24, 1993, A1; NYT, Feb. 24, 1993, A1; NYT, Feb. 3, 1993, A23; NYT, Jan. 24, 1993, sect. 1, p. 21; NYT, March 8, 1993, A1, B8; NYT, March 30, 1993, A1; NYT, month and day not recorded yet in sequence, 1993, A1, A10; NYT, April 9, 1993, A1, A16.

34. NYT, May 2, 1993, sect. 1, p. 20; NYT, May 27, 1993, A1.

35. TM, June 28, 1993; NYT, June 27, 1993, sect. 4, p. 4; TM, Aug. 9, 1993, p. 23.

36. NYT, July 28, 1993, A13; NYT, Aug. 20, 1993, A14; NYT, Aug. 25, 1993, A1; NYT, Sept. 28, 1993, B10; NYT, Sept. 20, 1993, A18–19; TM, Oct. 4, 1993, p. 28; NYT, Sept. 15, 1993, A22; NYT, Oct. 1, 1993, A16; NYT, Oct. 19, 1993, A1; TM, Oct. 25, 1993, p. 36; TM, Nov. 8, 1993, p. 36; NYT, Nov. 17, 1993, A18; NYT, Nov. 27, 1993, A5; NYT, Dec. 9, 1993, A1; NYT, Dec. 25, 1993, A1.

37. NYT, June 13, 1993, sect. 4, p. 3; NYT, June 9, 1993, A21.

38. NWM, July 25, 1994; NYT, Nov. 17, 1994, sect. A; NYT, Nov. 17, 1994, A25; TM, Dec. 12, 1994, p. 42; NYT, Dec. 8, 1994, A1; TM, Dec. 26, 1994, p. 108; NYT, Aug. 12, 1994, A23; NYT, Dec. 19, 1994, A1; TM, Dec. 12, 1994, p. 40; NYT, Dec. 16, 1994, A1, A36.

39. NYT, Jan. 5, 1994, A13; NYT, Jan. 31, 1994, A1; NYT, Feb. 4, 1994, A15; NYT, Feb. 25, 1994, A1; NYT, March 1, 1994, A18; NYT, March 7, 1994, A13; NYT, March 9, 1994, A13; NYT, March 11, 1994, A18; NYT, April 15, 1994, A14; NYT, May 30, 1994, A24; NYT, June 7, 1994, A1; NYT, July 15, 1994, A1; NYT, June 15, 1994, A1; TM, Feb., day not recorded, 1994, p. 20; NYT, July 23, 1994, A1; TM, Aug. 1, 1994, p. 16; NYT, Aug. 24, 1994, A13; NYT, Sept. 11, 1994, sect. 1, p. 22; NYT, Sept. 21, 1994, A1; NYT, Sept. 27, 1994, A1; NYT, Oct. 3, 1994, A14; NYT, Oct. 8, 1994, A1; TM, Nov. 14, 1994, p. 52; NYT, Nov. 16, 1994, A14; NYT, Nov. 16, 1994, A16; NYT, Dec. 20, 1994, A1.

40. TM, Jan. 17, 1994, p. 24; TM, May 2, 1994, p. 50; TM, May 2, 1994, cover story; TM, Oct. 31, 1994, p. 28; NYT, May 4, 1994, A12.

41. NYT, Nov. 11, 1994, A8; NYT, March 2, 1994, A1; NYT, Sept. 9, 1994, A8; NYT, Sept. 21, 1994, A3; NYT, Oct. 4, 1994, A8.

42. NYT, no date recorded yet in sequence, A1; NYT, Jan. 10, 1994, A1; NYT, March 25, 1994, A1; NYT, April 23, 1994, A10; NYT, March 8, 1994, D21; NYT, March 5, 1994, A1; NYT, May 7, 1994, A9.

43. WSJ, Feb. 6, 1995, A16; NYT, April 25, 1995, A19; NYT, June 15, 1995, B12; NYT, Nov. 21, 1995, A16.

44. NYT, Jan. 11, 1995, A1; NYT, Jan. 11, 1995, A19; NYT, Jan. 29, 1995, sect. 1, p. 1; NYT, Jan. 25, 1995, A1; an article without date, etc., but in sequence; NYT, Feb. 1, 1995, A1; NYT, Feb. 3, 1995, A1; NYT, Feb. 7, 1995, A22.

45. NYT, Feb. 12, 1995, sect. 1, pp. 1, 28; NYT, March 6, 1995, A1; NYT, March 8, 1995, A18; NYT, March 24, 1995, A23; NYT, April 16, 1995, sect. 1, pp. 1, 16; NYT, April 24, 1995, A1; NYT, May 21, 1995, sect. 1, p. 1; NYT, May 9, 1995, A18; TM, June 5, 1995; NYT, June 8, 1995, A1; NYT, June 14, 1995, A18; NYT, June 15, 1995, A22; NYT, June 24, 1995, p. 48; NYT, June 29, 1995, A1–; NYT, July 5, 1995, A11; NYT, July 13, 1995, A1, B10; NYT, Aug. 5, 1995, A9; NYT, Aug. 9, 1995, A1; NYT, Aug. 10, 1995, A7; NYT, Sept. 10, 1995, sect. 1, p. 28; NYT, Sept. 16, 1995, A1; NYT, Sept. 17, 1995, A1–; NYT, Sept. 24, 1995, sect. 1, p. 3; NYT, Oct. 29, 1995, sect. 1, pp. 1, 30; NYT, Nov. 14, 1995, A24; NYT, Nov. 14, 1995, A1, B9; NYT, Dec. 17, 1995, A1; NYT, Dec. 17, 1995, sect. 1, p. 1; NYT, Dec. 19, 1995, A1; NYT, Dec. 23, 1995, A1; NYT, Dec. 29, 1995, A26.

46. NYT, May 21, 1995, sect. 1, p. 8; NYT, Oct. 6, 1995, A10; NYT, June 23, 1995, A6; NYT, June 30, 1995, A1; NYT, July 19, 1995, A6; NYT, June 8, 1995, A10; NYT, Nov. 28, 1995, A1.

47. NYT, Jan. 24, 1996, A1–; TM, Feb. 5, 1996, p. 28; NYT, March 31, 1996, sect. 4, p. 3; NYT, June 23, 1996, sect. 1, p. 23; NYT, July 28, 1996, sect. 1, p. 1; NYT, Aug. 1, 1996, A1; NYT, Aug. 2, 1996, A18; CSM, Aug. 23, 1996, p. 5; CSM, Aug. 27, 1996, p. 7.

48. NYT, Nov. 7, 1996, A33; CSM, Nov. 7, 1996, p. 1; TM, Nov. 18, 1996, p. 53; NYT, Dec. 12, 1996, B22.

49. NYT, March 21, 1996, D24; NYT, April 12, 1996, A1; NYT, April 11, 1996, B10; NYT, Dec. 14, 1996, pp. 1, 28; CSM, April 4, 1996, p. 19; NYT, April 25, 1996, A1, B12; NYT, April 14, 1996, sect. 1, p. 21; NYT, July 26, 1996, A1, B4; NYT, Nov. 6, 1996, A1.

50. NYT, Jan. 21, 1997, A1; USNWR, Jan. 27, 1997, p. 31; NYT, Feb. 5, 1997, A1; NYT, Feb. 7, 1997, A1; NYT, Feb. 15, 1997, A1; NYT, March 9, 1997, sect. 1, p. 1; NYT, Aug. 12, 1997, A1; NYT, Aug. 14, 1997, A31; NYT, Oct. 7, 1997, A1, A23; NYT, Oct. 22, 1997, A1; TM, Oct. 27, 1997; NYT, Oct. 26, 1997, sect. 1, p. 18; TM, Aug. 11, 1997, p. 27.

51. NYT, Dec. 7, 1997, sect. 1, pp. 1, 26; NYT, Dec. 8, 1997, A1, A21; CSM, Dec. 16, 1997, p. 1.

52. CSM, May 12, 1997, p. 19; NYT, May 28, 1997, A11; NYT, May 28, 1997, A11; NYT, Nov. 11, 1997, A1; CSM, Dec. 29, 1997, p. 1; NYT, Dec. 9, 1997, A3; CSM, Dec. 16, 1997, p. 19.

53. NYT, Jan. 12, 1997, sect. 1, p. 16; NYT, Jan. 14, 1997, A15; USNWR, Feb. 10, 1997, p. 26; CSM, Feb. 27, 1997, p. 1; NYT, March 2, 1997, sect. 1, p. 20; NYT, March 4, 1997, A1; NYT, March 5, 1997, A18; NYT, March 16, 1997, sect. 4, p. 15; NYT, April 23, 1997, A1; NYT, May 3, 1997, A10; NYT, May 28, 1997, A20; NYT, Oct. 4, 1997, A1; NYT, Sept. 23, 1997, A1, A24; USNWR, Oct. 6, 1997, p. 84; NYT, Dec. 29, 1997, A19.

54. NYT, Jan. 22, 1998, A1, A24; NYT, Jan. 23, 1998, A16; NYT, Jan. 25, 1998, sect. 4, p. 15; NYT, Jan. 20, 1998, A12; NYT, Jan. 27, 1998, A13; NYT, Jan. 28, 1998, A1; TM, Feb. 9, 1998, cover story; USNWR, Feb. 9, 1998, p. 20; NYT, Feb. 5, 1998, A23; NYT, Jan. 6, 1998, A12; NYT, Feb. 3, 1998, A16.

55. NYT, Feb. 25, 1998, A1; NYT, March 2, 1998, A12; NYT, March 14, 1998, A1, A9; NYT, March 17, 1998, A1; NYT, March 21, 1998, A1; NYT, March 17, 1998, A25; NYT, March 23, 1998, A17; USNWR, March 30, 1998, p. 18; TM, late March or early April 1998, p. 21; NYT, April 2, 1998, A1; NYT, April 5, 1998, A22.

56. TM, Aug. 10, 1998, p. 56; NYT, Aug. 3, 1998, A19.

57. NYT, April 8, 1998, A14; USNWR, April 13, 1998, pp. 20–21; NYT, May 6, 1998, A1; NYT, May 23, 1998, A1; NYT, June 2, 1998, A1; NYT, June 5, 1998, A1, A14; NYT, June 26, 1998, A19; NYT, July 2, 1998, A18; NYT, July 17, 1998, A14; NYT, July 30, 1998, A1; NYT, Aug. 3, 1998, A1; NYT, Aug. 10, 1998, A13.

58. NYT, Aug. 8, 1998, A1, A10; NYT, Aug. 11, 1998, A1; NYT, Aug. 17, 1998, A1, A10; NYT, Aug. 18, 1998, A1; NYT, Sept. 11, 1998, A1, A18; NYT, Sept. 11, 1998, A1; NYT, Sept. 12, 1998, A1; NYT, Sept. 12, 1998, A7; NYT, Sept. 13, 1998, A1; NYT, Sept. 14, 1998, A26; USNWR, Sept. 21, 1998, p. 28; TM, Sept. 21, 1998, p. 43.

59. NYT, Sept. 25, 1998, A1, A22; NYT, Sept. 16, 1998, A22; NYT, Nov. 10, 1998, A26; NYT, Nov. 19, 1998, A1; NYT, Nov. 28, 1998, A1, A12; NYT, Dec. 14, 1998, A26; USNWR, Dec. 21, 1998, p. 21; TM, Dec. 21, 1998, cover story; NYT, Dec. 18, 1998, A1.

60. CSM, July 24, 1998, p. 3; NYT, June 23, 1998, A1; NYT, July 7, 1998, A1; NYT, Dec. 27, 1998, sect. 1, p. 26; NYT, month and day not recorded, 1998, p. 29; CSM, July 10, 1998, p. 3; NYT, June 26, 1998, A1; NYT, month and day not recorded, 1998, A9; NYT, July 17, 1998, A15; NYT, Aug. 21, 1998, A1.

61. Based on general observations over a period of time.

62. USNWR, Jan. 11, 1999, p. 20; USNWR, Jan. 18, 1999, p. 16; NYT, Jan. 20, 1999, A1; TM, Feb. 1, 1999, pp. 22–23; USNWR, Feb. 1, 1999, p. 23; NYT, June 30, 1999, A5.

63. NYT, Jan. 3, 1999, sect. 1, p. 19; USNWR, Jan. 18, 1999, p. 14.

64. USNWR, Feb. 15, 1999, p. 14; CSM, March 22, 1999, p. 2; NYT, April 18, 1999, sect. 1, p. 1; WSJ, Sept. 14, 1999.

65. NYT, Feb. 2, 1999, A1, A21; CSM, Feb. 1, 1999, p. 4; NYT, May 4, 1999, sect. 1, p. 26; NYT, May 16, 1999, sect. 1, p. 30; NYT, May 19, 1999, B10; NYT, July 8, 1999, A22; NYT, June 28, 1999, A1; NYT, June 29, 1999, A1, A16; NYT, July 8, 1999, C1; NYT, July 9, 1999, A12; NYT, July 14, 1999, A16; NYT, July 14, 1999, A22; NYT, July 22, 1999, A16; NYT, Sept. 16, 1999, C1; NYT, Sept. 17, 1999, A1; NYT, Sept. 17, 1999, C1; NYT, Oct. 3, 1999, sect. 1, p. 42; NYT, Oct. 13, 1999, A16; NYT, Oct. 17, 1999, sect. 1, p. 34; NYT, Oct. 19, 1999, F9; NYT, Oct. 20, 1999, A22; NYT, Oct. 25, 1999, A1; NYT, Oct. 30, 1999, A10; CSM, Nov. 9, 1999, p. 4; NYT, Nov. 30, 1999, A20; NYT, Dec. 1, 1999, A19; NYT, Dec. 1, 1999, A21; NYT, Dec. 7, 1999, A1; NYT, Dec. 8, 1999, Rush Limbaugh's radio show, WABC, FM, Dec. 9, 1999; NYT, Dec. 17, 1999, A8; NYT, Dec. 21, 1999, A29; NYT, Dec. 22, 1999, A24; CSM, Dec. 29, 1999, p. 2; NYT, Dec. 20, 1999, A8.

66. NYT, Oct. 16, 1999, A1; NYT, Dec. 4, 1999, A13; CSM, Feb. 17, 1999, p. 5; CSM, July 26, 1999, p. 1; NYT, May 22, 1999, A6; NYT, May 23, 1999, sect. 4, p. 17; CSM, June 7, 1999, p. 2.

67. NYT, Jan. 12, 2000, A12; NYT, Jan. 18, 2000, A18; NYT, Feb. 13, 2000, sect. 1, pp. 1, 24; NYT, Feb. 22, 2000, A1; NYT, March 30, 2000, A26; NYT, May 3, 2000, A6; NYT, May 10, 2000, A14; NYT, May 22, 2000, A8; USNWR, June 26, 2000, p. 26; NYT, July 5, 2000, A13; NYT, Aug. 5, 2000, sect. 1, p. 1; NYT, Sept. 1, 2000, A1, A24; NYT, Oct. 9, 2000, A12; NYT, Oct. 14, 2000, A1; NYT, Nov. 12, 2000, sect. 1, p. 21; NYT, Nov. 20, 2000, A20; NYT, Dec. 25, 2000, A1.

68. NYT, Jan. 27, 2000, A8; CSM, Jan. 25, 2000, p. 27; NYT, Jan. 28, 2000, A1, A14; NYT, Jan. 29, 2000, A8; CSM, Jan. 28, 2000, p. 2; WPNWE, May 8, 2000, p. 11; WPNWE, July 10, 2000, p. 18.

69. WPNWE, March 26, 2000, p. 22; NYT, Oct. 14, 2000, A3; NYT, Oct. 26, 2000, A7; NYT, March 20, 2000, Op-Ed; NYT, April 14, 2000, A20; NYT, May 23, 2000, A1–; NYT, Sept. 21, 2000, A1; CSM, Nov. 7, 2000, p. 4.

70. WPNWE, June 11–17, 2001, p. 6; WPNWE, June 18–24, 2001, p. 22; NYT, Dec. 14, 2001, A33; NYT, Oct. 17, 2002, A1; NYT, Oct. 30, 2002, A22.

71. NYT, March 9, 2001, A12.

72. NYT, Nov. 12, 2000, sect. 1, p. 1; NYT, Nov. 10, 2000, A1; NYT, Jan. 7, 2000, sect. 1, p. 15; USNWR, June 22, 2001, cover story; NYT, Jan. 28, 2001, sect. 1, pp. 1, 14; NYT, Feb. 1, 2001, no page no. avail.; NYT, Feb. 4, 2001, sect. 4, p. 16.

73. NYT, Jan. 14, 2001, sect. 1, p. 1; NYTM, Jan. 14, 2001, p. 22; NYT, Jan. 23, 2001, A16; NYT, Jan. 23, 2001, A14; NYT, March 7, 2001, A15; NYT, March 8, 2001, A19; CSM, March 8, 2001, p. 1; NYT, March 12, 2001, A12; NYT, March 21, 2001, A15; WPNWE, June 18–24, 2001, p. 12.

73a. USNWR, June 29, 2001, p. 16; WPNWE, Jan. 29–Feb. 4, 2001, p. 9; WPNWE, May 14–20, 2001, p. 12; TM, Feb. 26, 2001, cover story.

74. USNWR, Jan. 29, 2001, p. 21; CSM, March 7, 2001, p. 37; NYT, Feb. 20, 2001, A1; NYT, March 11, 2001, sect. 1, p. 34; NYT, July 8, 2001, sect. 4, p. 1–; WPNWE, Jan. 8–14, 2001, p. 6; NYT, March 14, 2001, A14; NYT, May 13, 2001, sect. 1, p. 20.

75. NYT, Jan. 24, 2001, A14; NYT, Feb. 9, 2001, A20; NYT, Feb. 28, 2001, A1; NYT, April 10, 2001, A1; NYT, May 2, 2001, A17; NYT, May 2, 2001, A1–; NYT, June 8, 2001, A22; NYT, July 16, 2001, A1.

76. NYT, May 11, 2001, A9; NYT, May 18, 2001, A1, A15; NYT, July 7, 2001, A9; NYT, Aug. 14, 2001, A1.

77. NYT, Oct. 26, 2001, A1; NYT, Nov. 25, 2001, A1, B4–5; NYT, Nov. 28, 2001, A25; NYT, Nov. 30, 2001, A1–; TM, Dec. 3, 2001, p. 62; NYT, Dec. 2, 2001, sect. 4, p. 14; NYT, Dec. 14, 2001, A26.

78. Above articles appear sequentially in WPNWE, Dec. 3–9, 2001, with lead caption on front cover.

79. NYT, Jan. 1, 2002, A1; NYT, Jan. 6, 2002, sect. 4, p. 1; NYT, Jan. 30, 2002, A1.

80. NYT, Feb. 5, 2002, A1–; NYT, Aug. 30, 2002, A1; NYT, Sept. 5, 2002, A1; WPNWE, Sept. 2–8, 20002, p. 10; NYT, Oct. 2, 2002, A17; NYT, Oct. 3, 2002, A1; NYT, Oct. 12, 2002, A1; NYT, Nov. 8, 2002, A24; NYT, June 25, 2002, A10.

81. TM, April 21, 2003, p. 86; NYT, May 10, 2003, A12; NYT, Sept. 11, 2003, A1; NYT, Oct. 6, 2003, A1; NYT, Sept. 8, 2003, A1; NYT, June 2, 2003, sect. 4, p. 1; NYT, Oct. 19, 2003, sect. 4, p. 11; NYT, July 10, 2003, A16; NYT, May (11?), 2003, sect. 1, p. 12.

82. NYT, Jan. 13, 2004, A22; NYT, March 31, 2004, A1, A21; NYT, April 11, 2004, p. 5; NYT, April 14, 2004, A1; NYT, April 16, 2004, A1; NYT, April 18, 2004, sect. 4; NYT, April 21, 2004, A22; NYT, April 30, 2004, A1.

83. NYT, April 23, 2004, A1, A10; transcript obtained from White House of item dated May 15, 2004; another transcript obtained from White House service; NYT, June 2, 2004, A9; CSM, June 1, 2004, p. 2.

84. NYT, June 29, 2004, A1, A7, A14, A26, two articles and editorial in same issue; NYT, May 7, 2004, A31, earlier editorial; WPNWE, July 12–18, 2004, p. 23, commentary.

85. NYT, Feb. 12, 2002, A1; NYT, Feb. 26, 2002, A23; NYT, March 1, 2002, A17; NYT, March 1, 2002, A17; NYT, March 5, 2002, A18; NYT, March 8, 2002, C6; WPNWE, March 25–31, 2002, p. 11; NYT, April 6, 2002, A12; NYT, April 11, 2002, A26; NYT, May 9, 2002, A26; NYT, May 10, 2002, A30; NYT, May 24, 2002, no page no. avail.; NYT, June 9, 2002, sect. 1, p. 26; NYT, June 14, 2002, A1–; NYT, June 20, 2002, A16; NYT, June 21, 2002, A12; NYT, June 24, 2002, A1; NYT, July 11, 2002, A1; NYT, July 10, 2002, C4; NYT, Aug. 10, 2002, A1; NYT, Aug. 22, 2002, A1; NYT, Oct. 20, 2002, A21.

86. NYT, Nov. 7, 2002, A1, B5.

87. NYT, Nov. 11, 2002, A12; NYT, Dec. 20, 2002, sect. 1, p. 40; NYT, Dec. 20, 2002, sect. 1, p. 40; NYT, Dec. 20, 2002, A34.

88. NYT, Jan. 9, 2003, A23; NYT, Jan. 17, 2003, A1, A24; TM, Jan. 27, 2003, p. 47; WPNWE, Jan. 20–26, 2003, p. 21; NYTM, Jan. 26, 2003, cover story; NYT, Jan. 27, 2003, A21; WPNWE, Feb. 10–16, 2003, p. 29; NYT, March 4, 2003, A20; NYT, Feb. 24, 2003, A1; NYT, Feb. 28, 2003, A22; CSM, March 5, 2003, p. 1; NYT, March 28, 2003, no page no. avail.; NYT, no date avail. yet in sequence; NYT, June 18, 2003, A1; NYT, Sept. 11, 2003, A17; NYT, Nov. 6, 2003, A18; final item has no publication data avail. yet is in sequence.

89. CSM, Jan. 8, 2004, p. 3; NYT, Jan. 17, 2004, A1; NYT, Aug. 7, 2004, A16; NYT, Aug. 14, 2004, A10; WPNWE, Aug. 23–29, 2004, p. 1; NYT, Nov. 4, 2004, A1; NYT, Nov. 5, 2004, A1; NYT, Nov. 8, 2004, A1; WPNWE, Nov. 8–14, 2004, p. 22; TM, Dec. 27, 2004, cover story; NYT, Dec. 23, 2004, p. 22.

90. NYT, June 21, 2005, A1; WPNWE, Jan. 17–23, 2005, p. 12; WPNWE, Jan. 24, 2005, p. 6; NYTBR, Feb. 27, 2005, p. 21; NYT, Feb. 3, 2005, A21; NYT, April 17, 2005, sect. 1, p. 22; WPNWE, June 6–12, 2005, p. 21; NYT, 2005, no date avail. yet in sequence.

91. TM, May 23, 2005, p. 2; WPNWE, May 9–15, 2005, p. 13; NYT, May 15, 2005, sect. 4, p. 3; WPNWE, June 8–12, 2005, p. 12; NYT, June 17, 2005, A1; NYT, Sept. 1, 2005, A21; NYT, Sept. 16, 2005, A27; NYT, Sept. 16, 2005, A1; WPNWE, Oct. 10–16, 2005, p. 21; NYT, Oct. 20, 2005, no page no. avail.

92. NYT, Oct. 29, 2005, A1; NYT, Oct. 30, 2005, sect. 1, p. 1; NYT, Dec. 21, 2005, A36; NYT, Dec. 23, 2005, A20; NYT, Dec. 20, 2005, sect. A, no page no. avail.; NYT, Dec. 23, 2005, A26.

93. NYT, Oct. 31, 2005, sect. 4, no page no. avail.; NYT, Dec. 19, 2005, A1–; TM, Dec. 29, 2005, p. 190.

Notes to Chapter III
The U.S. Congress

1. NYT, Aug. 2, 1987, sect. 1, p. 5.

2. CSM, April 27, 1987, p. 1.

3. CSM, Oct. 7, 1987, p. 1.

4. TM, Oct. 23, 1989, cover story.

5. NYT, Aug. 14, 1987, A14; NYT, Oct. 9, 1989, A10; NYT, Oct. 5, 1989, A1–.

6. NYT, Oct. 15, 1989, sect. 1, p. 28; NYT, Oct. 22, 1989, sect. ?, p. 3; NYT, Dec. 7, 1989, A28; NYT, Nov. 3, 1989, A17; NYT, Nov. 24, 1989, B22; NYT, Oct. 20, 1989, A15; NYT, Oct. 27, 1989, A9.

7. NYT, Oct. 20, 1989, A15; NYT, Oct. 27, 1989, A9.

8. BWM, April 16, 1990, cover story; NYT, Jan. 23, 1990, A22; WP, Feb. 25, 1990, B7; NYT, March 20, 1990, A1, A15; NYT, July 30, 1990, A12; NYT, Aug. 2, 1990, A21; NYT, Aug. 5, 1990, sect. 1, p. 20.

9. NYT, May 15, 1990, A21; NYT, May 25, 1990, sect. A; NYT, May 19, 1990, no page number; WP, May 20, 1990, H1; NYT, Aug. 8, 1990, A14; NYT, Sept. 25, 1990, A1; *ibid.* for 2nd article in same issue; NYT, Sept. 5, 1990, A20; NYT, Sept. 26, 1990, A16.

10. NYT, Oct. 5, 1990, A24; NYT, Oct. 7, 1990, A1, A30; WP, Oct. 7, 1990, A1, A20; NYT, Oct. 8, 1990, A1, A14; NYT, Oct. 9, 1990, A1, A20; NYT, Oct. 12, 1990, A1.

11. NYT, Oct. 22, 1990, A16.

12. TM, Oct. 29, 1990, p. 38; NYT, Oct. 29, 1990, A1; NYT, Oct. 28, 1990, sect. 4, p. 1; TM, Nov. 5, 1990, p. 28–.

13. NYT, Nov. 13, 1990, A1, D19; NYT, Nov. 17, 1990, A1, A11; NYT, Nov. 15, 1990, no page no. avail.; NYT, Nov. 30, 1990, no page no. avail.; NYT, Dec. 1, 1990, A10; NYT, Dec. 16, 1990, E6; NYT, Dec. 9, 1990, B7; NYT, Dec. 17, 1990, B10; NYT, Dec. 26, 1990, D6; NYT, Dec. 23, 1990, E11; NYT, Dec. 5, 1990, B12.

14. NYT, Jan. 25, 1990, A1, A6; NYT, Jan. 31, 1990, A5; NYT, Jan. 28, 1990, p. 3; TM, Feb. 5, 1990, p. 16.

15. NYT, March 31, 1991, sect. 1, pp. 1, 18.

16. TM, April 22, 1991, p. 30; NYT, Aug. 4, 1991, A15; TM, Oct. 14, 1991, p. 18–; NYT, Nov. 10, 1991, sect. 1, p. 23; WP, Nov. 11, 1991, A8; WP, Nov. 10, 1991, A9.

17. NYT, Aug. 4, 1991, sect. 4, p. 5; NYT, Nov. 28, 1991, D22; NYT, Nov. 28, 1991, A27; NYT, Nov. 27, 1991, A20; NYT, Dec. 17, 1991, D20; NYT, Jan. 11, 1991, A16.

18. NYT, Jan. 29, 1991, A10; NYT, Feb. 17, 1991, sect. 1, pp. 1, 54; WP, March 31, 1991, H12; NYT, June 6, 1991, D2; BWM, July 15, 1991, p. 122; WP, Sept. 8, 1991, H1; NYT, Sept. 30, 1991, sect. D, no page no. avail.; NYT, Oct. 5, 1991, A9; NYT, Oct. 26, 1991, A19; NYT, Oct. 31, 1991, A26; NYT, Nov. 5, 1991, A1; NYT, Nov. 8, 1991, D5; NYT, Nov. 6, 1991, D6; NYT, Nov. 13, 1991, D10; NYT, Nov. 15, 1991, D5; NYT, Nov. 24, 1991, sect. 1, p. 24.

19. NYT, March 29, 1991, A11; NYT, May 24, 1991, A18; NYT, Nov. 26, 1991, A17.

20. TM, May 27, 1991, p. 20; NYT, May 2, 1991, B12; NYT, July 8, 1991, A6; NYT, April 9, 1991, A16; NYT, April 18, 1991, B12.

21. NYT, Sept. 8, 1992, A14; NYT, March 22, 1992, sect. 4, p. 3; NYT, Aug. 18, 1992, A19; NYT, April 12, 1992, sect. 1, no page no. avail.; NYT, Oct. 11, 1992, sect. 1, no page no. avail.; *Princeton Alumni Weekly*, Oct. 28, 1992, p. 48.

22. *American Caucus*, June 8–21, 1992; TM, April 6, 1992, p. 20; NYT, March 25, 1992, A14; NYT, April 5, 1992, sect. 1, p. 1; TM, June 8, 1992, p. 64; *Extensions: A Journal of the Carl Albert Congressional Research and Studies Center*, Summer, 1992, p. 15.

23. NYT, Sept. 20, 1992, sect. 1, p. 26; NYT, Jan. 31, 1993, sect. 1, p. 16; NYT, June 6, 1992, A8; NYT, June 8, 1992, B1.

24. NYT, March 12, 1992, A16; NYT, March 14, 1992, A1, A8; NYT, March 15, 1992, sect. 1, p. 1; NYT, March 18, 1992, A16; USNWR, no date avail. but in sequence, p. 36; NYT, April 17, 1992, A1.

25. NYT, Jan. 3, 1992, A14; NYT, March 1, 1992, sect. 4, no page no. avail.; NYT, March 4, 1992, A19; NYT, March 21, 1992, A9; TM, April 20, 1992, p. 48.

26. NYT, May 7, 1992, B12; NYT, June 12, 1992, A1; NYT, July 10, 1992, A12; NYT, July 3, 1992, A1; *State Legislatures*, Jan., 1992, p. 15–.

27. NYT, Sept. 25, 1992, A16; NYT, Jan. 6, 1992, A16; NYT, July 2, 1992, A16; WP, July 12, 1992, C6.

28. NYT, June, 1992, A1; NYT, Jan. 28, 1991, C2; WP, Oct. 11, 1992, A33.

29. TM, Jan. 18, 1993, p. 29; NYT, Jan. 28, 1993, A21; NYT, April 4, 1993, sect. 1, p. 1; NYT, April 2, 1993, A20; NYT, April 5, 1993, A14; NYT, April 22, 1993, A1.

30. NYT, March 26, 1993, A16; NYT, April 30, 1993, A14; NYT, May 14, 1993, A18; NYT, May 20, 1993, A1; NYT, May 28, 1993, A1, A12; NYT, June 17, 1993, A1; NYT, June 18, 1993, A20; NYT, June 24, 1993, A1, A18; NYT, June 26, 1993, A1; NYT, July 15, 1993, A1; NYT, July 22, 1993, A15; NYT, Aug. 3, 1993, A14; NYT, Aug. 6, 1993, A1.

31. TM, Dec. 6, 1993, p. 32; NYT, Nov. 24, 1993, A1.

32. NYT, Nov. 18, 1993, A1; TM, Oct. 11, 1993, p. 31; TM, Oct. 11, 1993, p. 26; NYT, 1993, sect. 1, p. 1, no month or day recorded, but in sequence.

33. NYT, Sept. 2, 1993, A23; NYT, Sept. 7, 1993, A1, A16; NYT, Aug. 8, 1993, sect. 4, p. 15; NYT, July 23, 1993, A23; TM, Aug. 2, 1993, p. 28; NYT, Feb. 23, 1993, A1.

34. NYT, Feb. 27, 1994, sect. 1, p. 20; NYT, March 13, 1994, sect. 1, p. 1; TM, April 4, 1994, p. 28; NYT, May 1, 1994, sect. 1, p. 24; NYT, May 8, 1994, sect. 1, p. 1.

35. NYT, May 19, 1994, A22; NYT, June 10, 1994, A18; NYT, June 16, 1994, A24; NYT, June 17, 1994, A14; NYT, June 20, 1994, A14; NYT, June 24, 1994, A1; NYT, June 26, 1994, sect. 1, p. 1; NYT, June 29, 1994, A16; NYT, June 30, 1994, B10; NYT, July 5, 1994, B13.

36. NYT, July 12, 1994, A16; NYT, July 25, 1994, A12; NYT, Aug. 4, 1994, A15; NYT, Aug. 10, 1994, A16; NYT, Aug. 11, 1996, A20; NYT, Aug. 16, 1994, A1.

37. NYT, Aug. 24, 1994, A1, B7; NYT, Aug. 27, 1994, A1; NYT, Aug. 28, 1994, sect. 1, p. 22; NYT, Aug. 29, 1994, A1, A12.

38. TM, Sept. 19, 1994, p. 40; NYT, Sept. 18, 1994, sect. 1, p. 36.

39. NYT, Nov. 12, 1994, A11; WP, Nov. 12, 1994, A1, A10; NYT, Nov. 14, 1994, B8; NYT, Dec. 18, 1994, sect. 1, p. 34.

40. TM, June 18, 1994, p. 50–; NYT, June 23, 1994, A23; NYT, Sept. 30, 1994, A24; NYT, Oct. 1, 1994, A8; TM, Oct. 10, 1994, p. 28; NYT, Oct. 9, 1994, p. 28; NYT, April 28, 1994, B9; NYT, May 16, 1994, A16; *Princeton Alumni Weekly*, March 9, 1994, p. 19; NYT, Dec. 15, 1994, A24; NYT, Dec. 25, 1994, sect. 1, pp. 1, 27.

41. NYT, Jan. 3, 1995, A16; NYT, Jan. 4, 1995, A14; NYT, Jan. 6, 1995, sect. A, no page no.; NYT, Jan. 5, 1995, A1, A22; NYT, Jan. 5, 1995, A5; NYT, Jan. 5, 1995, B6; NYT, Jan. 6, 1995, A20; TM, Jan. 9, 1995, cover story; TM, Jan. 16, 1995, p. 23; NYT, Jan. 15, 1995, sect. 1, p. 18; NYT, Jan. 15, 1995, sect. 1, p. 1; T.V. show "Washington Week," Channel 13, PBS, Jan. 6, 1995; T.V. show "McNeil–Lehrer Newshour," Channel 13, PBS, Jan. 6, 1995.

42. NYT, Jan. 9, 1995, A1; NYT, Jan. 14, 1995, A10; NYT, Jan. 27, 1995, A16; NYT, Jan. 26, 1995, A1; NYT, Jan. 28, 1995, A8; NYT, Jan. 19, 1995, A1; TM, Jan. 23, 1995, p. 34.

43. NYT, Feb. 13, 1995, A16; NYT, Feb. 10, 1995, A22; NYT, Feb. 7, 1995, A22; NYT, Feb. 14, 1995, sect. B, no page no. avail.; NYT, Feb. 15, 1995, A14; NYT, Feb. 16, 1995, A1; NYT, Feb. 10, 1995, A1; NYT, Feb. 17, 1995,

A1; NYT, Feb. 22, 1995, A14; NYT, Feb. 23, 1995, A1; NYT, Feb. 25, 1995, A7; NYT, Feb. 23, 1995, A1; TM, Feb. 27, 1995, pp. 58–59; NYT, Feb. 28, 1995, A18; NYT, Feb. 28, 1995, A21; NYT, Feb. 12, 1995, sect. 1, p. 22.

44. NYT, March 1, 1995, A1; NYT, March 3, 1995, A10; NYT, March 4, 1995, A8; TM, March 13, 1995, p. 53; NYT, March 17, 1995, A18; NYT, March 23, 1995, A23; NYT, March 25, 1995, A1; NYT, March 29, 1995, A1; NYT, March 30, 1995, A1, A20; TM, April 3, 1995, pp. 43–44; NYT, April 6, 1995, A1, B10; NYT, April 7, 1995, A35; TM, April 10, 1995, p. 28.

45. NYT, April 8, 1995, A1, A8; NYT, April 8, 1995, A1; NYT, April 9, 1995, sect. 1, p. 1; NYT, April 9, 1995, sect. 1, p. 22; NYT, April 9, 1995, sect. 1, p. 14.

46. NYT, April 24, 1995, A12; NYT, April 11, 1995, A1, A22.

47. NYT, April 16, 1995, sect. 1, p. 8; NYT, May 3, 1995, A18; TM, May 15, 1995, p. 37; NYT, May 11, 1995, A1, B12; NYT, May 12, 1995, A22; NYT, May 14, 1995, sect. 1, p. 22; NYT, May 20, 1995, A8; TM, May 22, 1995, special report, cover story.

48. NYT, July 11, 1995, A15; WSJ, July 13, 1995, A8; TM, July 17, 1995, p. 18; NYT, Aug. 22, 1995, A12; NYT, Aug. 6, 1995, sect. 4, p. 6; NYT, Nov. 10, 1995, A32.

49. NYT, Nov. 15, 1995, B8; TM, Dec. 11, 1995, p. 46; TM, Dec. 18, 1995, p. 39; TM, Jan. 1, 1996, cover story; NYT, Jan. 21, 1996, p. 14; NYT, March 29, 1996, B11; NYT, March 30, 1996, A9; NYT, April 23, 1996, A17; NYT, April 25, 1996, A1; NYT, April 26, 1996, A22; USNWR, June, no day avail., 1996, p. 32.

50. NYT, June 7, 1996, A26; NYT, May 29, 1996, A10; NYT, July 18, 1996, B2; NYT, July 24, 1996, A1; USNWR, Aug. 12, 1996, p. 25; NYT, Sept. 27, 1996, A24; NYT, Sept. 28, 1996, A9.

51. NYT, Sept. 30, 1996, sect. A, no page no.; NYT, Oct. 2, 1996, A20; USNWR, Oct. 28, 1996, p. 24; NYT, Oct. 27, 1996, sect. 4, p. 5; NYT, Nov. 15, 1996, A33; NYT, Dec. 4, 1996, A23; NYT, Nov. 16, 1996, A14; NYT, Dec. 22, 1996, sect. 1, p. 16; NYT, Jan. 8, 1997, A1; NYT, March 3, 1996, sect. 4, p. 3.

52. CSM, Jan. 8, 1997, p. 9; NYT, Jan. 18, 1997, A1; NYT, Jan. 22, 1997, A1; NYT, Feb. 12, 1997, A1; CSM, Feb. 27, 1997, p. 9; NYT, Feb. 27, 1997, A1; NYT, Feb. 13, 1997, B10; CSM, March 4, 1997, p. 1; NYT, March 9, 1997, sect. 1, p. 1; TM, April 7, 1997, p. 50; NYT, April 9, 1997, A21; the same for another item; NYT, April 6, 1997, sect. 1, p. 24.

53. NYT, May 3, 1997, A1; CSM, May 2, 1997, p. 8; TM, May 12, 1997, p. 55; USNWR, 1997, p. 26, no further data avail., yet in sequence; NYT, June 26, 1997, D27; NYT, July 29, 1997, A1.

54. CSM, July 14, 1997, p. 1; CSM, May 23, 1997, p. 4; NYT, July 27, 1997, sect. 4, p. 6; USNWR, May 26, 1997, p. 23; TM, May 26, 1997, p. 37.

55. CSM, March 27, 1998, p. 3; NYT, April 4, 1998, A9; USNWR, May 18, 1997 (= 1998), p. 29; WSJ, May 1, 1998, A14; NYT, May 17, 1998, sect. 1, p. 23; NYT, May 21, 1998, A12; NYT, May 23, 1998, A11; CSM, June 4, 1998, p. 3; NYT, June 24, 1998, A17; NYT, Aug. 29, 1998, A5; USNWR, Aug. 17, 1998, p. 23; CSM, July 13, 1998, p. 1; NYT, June 18, 1998, A32.

56. NYT, Sept. 10, 1998, A1; USNWR, Oct. 5, 1998, pp. 20–21; TM, Oct. 12, 1998, p. 30; NYT, Oct. 9, 1998, A1; NYT, Oct. 13, 1998, A18.

57. CSM, Oct. 8, 1998, p. 3; NYT, Oct. 15, 1998, A28; NYT, Oct. 16, 1998, A1; NYT, Oct. 21, 1998, A20; NYT, Oct. 22, 1998, A24; CSM, Oct. 19, 1998, p. 3; NYT, Oct. 18, 1998, sect. 1, p. 22; *ibid.*, p. 22.

58. NYT, Nov. 7, 1998, A1, A8; NYT, Nov. 8, 1998, sect. 1, p. 22; TM, Nov. 16, 1998, p. 39; Lehrer News Hour, Channel 13, PBS, Nov. 10, 1998.

59. CSM, Nov. 13, 1998, p. 16.

60. CSM, Dec. 4, 1998, p. 11; CSM, Nov. 18, 1998, p. 3; TM, Nov. 30, 1998, pp. 38–39; NYT, Nov. 26, 1998, A1.

61. NYT, Dec. 12, 1998, A1; NYT, Dec. 18, 1998, A1; NYT, Dec. 19, 1998, A1; NYT, Dec. 20, 1998, sect. 1, pp. 1, 31; NYT, Jan. 3, 1999, sect. 4, p. 9.

62. NYT, Jan. 7, 1999, A1; NYT, Jan. 8, 1999, A1; NYT, Jan. 9, 1999, A1, A10; NYT, Jan. 15, 1999, A14; NYT, Jan. 23, 1999, A10; NYT, Jan. 24, 1999, sect. 1, p. 25; NYT, Feb. 5, 1999, A1, A22; NYT, Feb., no day avail., yet in sequence, 1999, A1.

63. NYT, Feb. 9, 1999, A1; NYT, Feb. 10, 1999, A22; NYT, Feb. 11, 1999, A1; NYT, Feb. 12, 1999, A25; NYT, Feb. 13, 1999, A1 (the Feb. 12 acquittal as reported the next day, Feb. 13).

64. NYT, Feb. 13, 1999, A10; NYT, Feb. 13, 1999, A18, "Constitutional Justice"; NYT, Feb. 9, 1999, A23.

65. NYT, Feb. 15, 1999, A15.

66. CSM, Feb. 19, 1999, p. 1l; NYTM, Feb. 28, 1999, p. 38; NYT, March 12, 1999, A18; NYT, Sept. 6, 1999, A12; CSM, Jan. 26, 2000, p. 2; WP, June 5, 2000, p. 24; CSM, Oct. 2, 2000, p. 2; WPNWE, Oct. 30, 2000, p. 25; NYT, Nov. 1, 2000, A34; NYT, Dec. 17, 2000, sect. 1, p. 48.

67. NYT, March 26, 1999, A1; NYT, May 24, 1999, A26; NYT, July 31, 1999, A1; NYT, Aug. 6, 1999, A17; NYT, Oct. 20, 1999, A20; an item with no data avail., yet in sequence; CSM, Nov. 17, 1999, p. 3; NYT, Nov. 20, 1999, A1; NYT, Nov. 21, 1999, sect. 1, p. 1; NYT, Jan. 26, 2000, A1; WPNWE, Oct. 30, 2000, p. 30; NYT, Dec. 16, 2000, A1–.

68. NYT, April 29, 1999, A1; NYT, May 2, 1999, sect. 4, p. 6; NYT, Oct. 14, 1999, A14; *ibid.*, pp. A1, A14; NYT, Oct. 15, 1999, A1; TM or USNWR, mid-Oct. 1999, p. 50, no other data avail., yet in sequence.

69. NYT, March 20, 2000, A16; USNWR, Feb. 21, 2000, p. 26; TM, May 15, 2000, p. 63; NYT, June 9, 2000, A1.

70. WPNWE, Jan. 8–14, 2001, p. 14.

71. WPNWE, Jan. 8–14, 2001, p. 13; NYT, March 2001, A22; NYT, March 28, 2001, A1; NYT, March 31, 2001, A10; NYT, April 3, 2001, A1; NYT, June 25, 2001, A12; NYT, July 9, 2001, A8; TM, July 16, 2004, p. 35; NYT, July 13, 2001, A1, A16.

72. NYT, May 24, 2001, A1, A26; NYT, May 26, 2001, A9; TM, June 4, 2001, cover story; WPNWE, June 4–9, 2001, p. 13; WPNWE, June 11–17, 2001, p. 14; WPNWE, July 30–Aug. 12, 2001, p. 13; CSM, June 28, 2001, p. 2; NYT, Dec. 21, 2001, A36; *ibid.*, p. A36.

73. NYT, April 7, 2001, A1; NYT, May 11, 2001, A17; CSM, May 17, 2001, p. 2; NYT, May 23, 2001, A24; *ibid.*, p. A24; NYT, May 27, 2001, sect. 1, p. 1;

NYT, Oct. 24, 2001, A12; NYT, data incomplete yet somewhere between Sept. and Dec., 2001, B9.

74. WPNWE, June 4–10, 2001, p. 22; CSM, March 9, 2001, p. 10; NYT, April 12, 2001, A29; editorial by William Safire.

75. NYT, Feb. 13, 2002, A30; WPNWE, Feb. 14, 2002, no page no. avail.; NYT, Jan. 22, 2002, A18; NYT, Jan. 22, 2002, A16; NYT, Feb. 10, 2002, sect. 1, p. 14; NYT, Feb. 14, 2002, A30, A34; NYT, Feb. 15, 2002, A1; NYT, March 21, 2002, A1, A36; TM, Feb. 25, 2002, p. 42.

76. NYT, Nov. 10, 2002, sect. 1, p. 28; NYT, Nov. 21, 2002, A34; CSM, Nov. 28–29, 2002, no page no. avail.; CSM, Dec. 26, 2002, p. 4; NYT, Jan. 5, 2003, sect. 1, p. 20; NYT, Jan. 19, 2003, sect. 4, p. 1.

77. NYT, Feb. 23, 2003, sect. 1, p. 31; CSM, May 21, 2003, p. 1; CSM, Aug. 1, 2003, p. 2; CSM, Aug. 4, 2003, p. 2; NYT, June 28, 2003, A8; CSM, Sept. 2, 2003, p. 2; NYT, Oct. 26, 2003, sect. 1, p. 20; NYT, May 3, 2004, A1; WPNWE, May 24–30, 2004, p. 12; CSM, Nov. 19, 2004, p. 1.

78. NYT, April 19, 2002, A18; NYT, April 7, 2003, A19; NYT, May 22, 2003, A1; NYT, May 29, 2003, A18; NYT, Sept. 24, 2004, A17.

79. NYT, Sept. 27, 2002, A18; NYT, Oct. 4, 2002, A1, A14; NYT, Oct. 11, 2002, A1, A15; NYT, Oct. 12, 2002, A12; NYT, Sept. 2, 2003, A1, A20; NYT, Oct. 18, 2003, A1; NYT, April 23, 2004, A1, A10; CSM, May 11, 2004, p. 2; NYT, July 22, 2004, A1; NYT, Sept. 7, 2004, A1; NYT, Sept. 8, 2004, A21; NYT, Dec. 7, 2004, A24. Applicable esp. to last sentence of paragraph are: NYT, Dec. 8, 2004, A1; NYT, Dec. 9, 2004, A36; NYT, Dec. 18, 2004, A15; NYT, Dec. 21, 2004, A20.

80. CSM, Jan. 20, 2005, p. 17; USNWR, March 28, 2005, p. 46; WPNWE, Nov. 28–Dec. 4, 2005, p. 27; WPNWE, Dec. 5–11, 2005, p. 13; CSM, June 1, 2005, p. 10; CSM, Feb. 10, 2005, no page no. avail.; NYT, Dec. 25, 2005, A24; NYT, Dec. 24, 2005, A13.

81. WPNWE, June 16–22, 2006, p. 14; WPNWE, Oct. 10–16, 2005, p. 11; NYT, Jan. 9, 2006, A1.

82. NYT, May 19, 2006, A1; NYT, May 20, 2005, A16; WPNWE, May 16–22, 2005, p. 22; NYT, May 22, 2005, sect. 1, p. 24; NYT, May 22, 2005, sect. 4, p. 1; NYT, May 24, 2005, A1; *ibid.*, pp. A1, A19; NYT, June 8, 2005, A1.

83. NYT, Nov. 15, 2005, A1; CSM, Nov. 17, 2005, p. 1; NYT, Nov. 18, 2005, A1; CSM, Feb. 1, 2006, p. 1; CSM, March 24, 2006, p. 1.

84. NYT, May 27, 2005, A17; NYT, July 21, 2005, A20; NYT, July 30, 2005, A11; NYT, Nov. 11, 2005, A1; NYT, Dec. 9, 2005, A20; NYT, Dec. 17, 2005, A1, A20; NYT, Jan. 7, 2006, A1; NYT, March 3, 2006, A14.

85. CSM, Jan. 20, 2005, pp. 1, 4.

Needless to say, source materials for a more formal study of recent legislative history and issues at the federal level are far more massive and diverse than is our purpose even to outline here. A few miscellaneous examples will be suggestive of the vastness of materials available for exploring public records and formal histories in order to document the great all-importance of American public law and legislation for sovereignty and state at the federal level, although such a quest would take one far beyond the present realm of "current news history."

Among the mammoth basic source materials that could be utilized for those purposes are the following select examples: *Federal Legislative Histories: An Annotated Bibliography and Index to Officially Published Sources*, compiled by Bernard D. Reams, Jr. (Westport, 1994), esp. "Introduction: The Use of Legislative History in Statutory Interpretation," "Bibliography," "Congressional Session Index," and "Public Law Number Index"; *United States Statutes at Large: Containing the Laws and Concurrent Resolutions Enacted During the . . . Congress of the United States of America*, produced by United States Government Printing Office, Wash., D.C., multi-volumes (by now well over 100 to date for each Congress since the mid-1800s, Vol. I having been published in 1845, Boston); *United States Code, Containing The General And Permanent Laws Of the United States, In Force . . .* [yearly edns., etc.]; and *Code of Federal Regulations*, e.g., #49, *Transportation*, as of 2003, "A Special Edition of the Federal Register," published by the Office of the Federal Register.

On a different front, there is *How to Find the Law*, by Morris L. Cohen *et al.*, St. Paul, 1989, e.g., Chs. 5–7, "Statutes," "Constitutional Law," and "Legislative History." Also, *The Legislative Process: Lawmaking in the United States* (New York, 1948), broadly informative and still useful, with chs. on, e.g., "The Legislator and His Functions" (8), "Legislative Procedure: Enactment of Bills" (14), and "Lawmaking by the Executive Branch" (20).

Notes to Chapter IV
The U.S. Supreme Court and
Federal Courts

1. NYT, May 18, 1987, B10.

2. CSM, May 19, 1987, p. 3; NYT, May 19, 1987, A30; NYT, June 20, 1987, A1.

3. CSM, March 9, 1987, p. 19; CSM, Feb. 26, 1987, p. 14.

4. NYT, June 23, 1989, A8; NYT, May 2, 1989, A17; NYT, May 22, 1990, A24; NYT, June 28, 1990, A1, B8; NYT, June 22, 1990, A17; WP, April 21, 1991, A4, A6; NYT, May 24, 1991, A1, A19; NYT, Feb. 21, 1991, A1; NYT, April 1, 1992, A1, B8; NYT, March 26, 1992, B13; NYT, April 28, 1992, A1; NYT, May 27, 1992, A17; NYT, June 20, 1992, A1.

5. NYT, May 12, 1989, B11; NYT, Feb. 23, 1990, A10; NYT, Aug. 26, 1990, A31; NYT, July 26, 1991, A1; NYT, Sept. 19, 1992, A5.

6. See *passim* the earlier 2004 book of this series designated as Vol. VI, Bk. I, for discussions of the U.S. Constitution and Bill of Rights.

7. See "Excerpts From Senate Hearings on the Thomas Nomination" in NYT, e.g., Sept. 11, 1991, A22–; Sept. 13, 1991, A18–; Sept. 14, 1991, A6–; Oct. 9, 1991, A18– (above quotation is on A1); Oct. 16, 1991, A18– (on A19 it is reported "Thomas Survives Accusations and Wins Narrow Court Confirmation," while on A1 it is reported "Senate Confirms Thomas, . . . Ending . . . Bitter Battle . . ."). Also, "Trashing Natural Law" ("An Unfair At-

tack on Clarence Thomas") in NYT, Aug. 16, 1991, A23. The stormy Thomas hearings offer a sharp contrast to the bland Souter hearings a year earlier, as in "Supreme Confidence" ("Souter takes the stand, but declines to state his views on abortion rights as foes search in vain for reasons to reject his high court nomination") in TM, Sept. 24, 1996, p. 46.

8. NYT, Feb. 6, 1990, A1–; NYT, Feb. 8, 1990, no page no. avail.; NYT, Feb. 14, 1990, A10; NYT, Feb. 15, 1990, B14; NYT, Feb. 16, 1990, A8; NYT, Feb. 17, 1990, A1; NYT, March 3, 1990, A10; NYT, April 8, 1990, sect. 1, pp. 1–24 (see also WP, April 8, 1990, A22).

9. NYT, Jan. 9, 1990, A1, A10; NYT, Feb. 22, 1990, A1, B8; NYT, March 31, 1990, A1, A8; NYT, Dec. 27, 1991, A20; NYT, July 30, 1992, A9; NYT, Oct. 6, 1992, A20; NYT, April 28, 1991, A24.

10. NYT, July 21, 1990, A1; NYT, Sept. 13, 1991, A25; NYT, Oct. 23, 1991, A23.

11. NYT, Aug. 29, 1990, A21; NYT, May 26, 1991, sect. 4, p. 1; NYT, May 7, 1992, A27; article in *State Legislatures*, April, 1992, pp. 24–25; NYT, June 27, 1991, A28; TM, Jan. 22, 1979, p. 91.

12. NYT, June 30, 1992, A15, A18; NYT, July 1, 1992, A12; NYT, July 1, 1992, A13; TM or NWM, date etc. not avail., but one heading seems to suggest TM, June 3, 1991; NYT, Dec. 1, 1992, A1; NYT, June 26, 1991, A20.

13. NYT, April 25, 1989, A22; NYT, April 19, 1990, A1, A22; NYT, April 20, 1990, A32; NYT, June 19, 1992, A23.

14. NYT, March 6, 1990, A20; NYT, June 22, 1991, A1; NYT, May 10, 1992, A14; NYT, June 22, 1991, A9; NYT, March 27, 1990, A1; NYT, June 22, 1989, A1; NYT, March 5, 1991, A1, A19.

15. NYT, Feb. 2, 1992, sect. 1, pp. 1, 12 (see also NYT, Dec. 20, 1991, sect. A, no page no. avail.); NYT, June 16, 1992, A1, A18; NYT, June 17, 1992, A8; NYT, June 21, 1992, sect. 4, p. 3; NYT, Sept. 17, 1991, A12; NYT, April 10, 1992, A1–; NYT, Sept. 17, 1991, A1.

16. NYT, July 24, 1990, A1; TM, July 30, 1990, p. 16; TM, July 1, 1991, p. 20–.

17. NYT, June 28, 1991, A1–; WP, June 30, 1991, A18; WP, June 30, 1991, C1, C5; NYT, Oct. 7, 1991, A14.

18. TM, July 13, 1991, pp. 18 ff.; NYT, Oct. 12, 1991, A29; NYT, Oct. 18, 1991, A12; NYT, Oct. 12, 1991, A6; NYP, Oct. 15, 1991, pp. 1, 4.

19. NYT, Aug. 3, 1991, A19; TM, Aug. 12, 1991, p. 68; NYT, Sept. 12, 1991, A22; NWM, Sept. 22, 1991, p. 20; WP, Sept. 8, 1991, C4; NYT, July 15, 1991, A15.

20. NYT, July 8, 1992, A19; NYT, Oct. 3, 1992, A19; NYT, Oct. 1, 1992, A16.

21. WP, Dec. 21, 1991, C7; NYT, Oct. 3, 1991, sect. A, no page no. avail.; NYT, Feb. 2, 1992, sect. 4, p. 16.

22. NYT, Dec. 11, 1991, A1, B8 (see also NYT, Dec. 12, 1991, A30); NYT, May 28, 1992, A18; NYT, June 10, 1992, A1, C17; NYT, June 23, 1992, A1–; NYT, April 6, 1991, A20; NYT, Jan. 28, 1992, A1, A14; NYT, Jan. 24, 1992, A12; NYT, May 21, 1990, B13.

23. NYT, Feb. 20, 1992, A1, A7; NYT, Sept. 21, 1991, A8; NYT, Jan. 27, 1992, A1, D12; NYT, April 14, 1992, A1, C7.

24. *Princeton Alumni Weekly*, April 5, 1995, p. 7; NYT, July 5, 1998, sect. 4, p. 1; NYT, July 2, 2000, sect. 4, p. 5; NYT, May 23, 2000, A22; CSM, April 19, 2000, p. 1; NBC TV, March 8, 2000.

25. WPNWE, Jan. 17, 2000, p. 23.

26. CSM, Nov. 9, 1994, A20; NYT, April 19, 1995, A21; NYT, April 29, 1995, A22; CSM, Nov. 15, 1996, p. 4; NYT, Jan. 1, 1997, A14; NYT, Jan. 1, 1998, A1, A14; CSM, Nov. 30, 1998, p. 2; USNWR, May 29, 2000, p. 10.

27. NYT, Aug. 23, 1993, A10; NYT, July 4, 1993, sect. 4, pp. 1, 5; NYT, July 7, 1993, A12; NYT, July 22, 1993, A1, A21.

28. NYT, April 20, 1993, A14; NYT, June 12, 1993, A9; NYT, Sept. 25, 1993, A1; NYT, April 27, 1994, A1; NYT, May 23, 1995, A1, B9; NYT, May 24, 1995, A1; NYT, June 30, 1995, A1, A26; NYT, June 13, 1996, A1, B10; NYT, Sept. 25, 1996, A19; NYT, April 19, 1999, A1–; USNWR, May 3, 1999, p. 50 (see also CSM, April 28, 1999, p. 1); NYT, June 22, 1999, A22; NYT, April 4, 2000, A1–; NYT, May 16, 2000, A1, A20; NYT, June 27, 2000, A1–; NYT, Oct. 12, 2000, A14; NYT, no date etc. avail.

29. Compare the Judiciary's "super-legislative" tendencies explored in this chapter with those of the Executive in Ch. II.

30. NYT, March 8, 1993, A1–; NYT, April 6, 1994, A1; NYTM, May 14, 1994, A1, A10.

31. NYT, May 11, 1994, A18; NYT, June 1, 1994, A18; NYT, March 31, 1995, A1; NYT, April 29, 1995, A12; NYT, June 13, 1995, A1–; NYT, July 21, 1995, sect. 4, p. 1; TM, July 10, 1995, p. 46–; NYT, June 13, 1996, A8; USNWR, Feb. 12, 1996, p. 40; NYT, March 27, 1996, B8; NYT, April 10, 1996, A1; TM, July 8, 1996, p. 48; NYT, April 11, 1997, A1; NYT, April 24, 1997, B7; NYT, May 13, 1997, A16.

32. NYT, May 28, 1997, A1–; NYT, June 24, 1997, A1, B11; NYT, Dec. 19, 1997, A37; NYTM, Oct. 5, 1997, cover story; NYT, Dec. 27, 1997, A1–.

33. NYT, Aug. 3, 1998, A19, editorial by Arthur Schlesinger, Jr.; CSM, Feb. 9, 1998, p. 1; NYT, April 28, 1998, A17.

34. NYT, Jan. 8, 1999, A19; NYT, March 11, 1999, A31; NYT, April 13, 1999, A1–; NYT, June 27, 1999, sect. 4, p. 1–; NYT, June 29, 1999, A19, editorial; NYT, May 14, 2000 (1999?), sect. 1, p. 28; CSM, July 3, 2000, pp. 1, 4; WPNWE, July 10, 2000, p. 30; NYT, Aug. 30, 2000, A1–; NYT, Sept. 14, 2000, A1, A25; NWM, July 10, 2000, cover story.

35. NYT, July 1, 1997, A1, A18; NYT, June 28, 1997, A20; USNWR, June 12, 2000, p. 29.

36. NYT, Dec. 19, 1994, A29; NYT, April 28, 1995, A1–; CSM, April 17, 1996, p. 1–; NYT, Oct. 7, 1996, A1–; NYT, March 28, 1999, sect. 1, p. 30; NYT, April 1, 1999, A25; NYT, June 25, 1999, A20; WPNWE, Jan. 17, 2000, p. 30; NYT, May 17, 2000, A18; WPNWE, Oct. 9, 2000, p. 29; NYT, Nov. 1, 2000, A20.

37. NYT, March 9, 1993, A13; NYT, June 29, 1993, A1–; NYT, Feb. 21, 1994, A16; NYT, May 17, 1994, no page no. avail.; NYT, June 1, 1994, A19;

NYT, June 21, 1994, A1, A13; NYT, July 1, 1994, A16; NYT, Nov. 8, 1994, A15; NYT, Feb. 22, 1995, A17; TM, May 8, 1995, p. 85; NYT, April 20, 1995, A20; NYT, March 28, 1996, B9; NYT, April 3, 1996, A1; NYT, April 11, 1996, A1, B4; CSM, Oct. 11, 1996, p. 19.

38. CSM, May 13, 1997, p. 3; NYT, June 28, 1997, A1; NYT, June 16, 1998, A18; CSM, March 30, 1999, pp. 1, 10; NYT, April 21, 1999, A20; NYT, Oct. 14, 1999, A25; NYT, Nov. 11, 1999, A20; NYT, Dec. 8, 1999, A18; NYT, Nov. 30, 1999, A20; CSM, Jan. 6, 2000, pp. 11–12; NYT, Jan. 13, 2000, A29; NYT, Jan. 22, 2000, A12; NYT, March 7, 2000, A14; NYT, March 23, 2000, A20; CSM, Oct. 31, 2000, pp. 1, 4; NYT, Nov. 4, 2000, A20; NYT, Jan. 17, 2000, sect. A, no page no. avail.

39. Some additional examples from 1997 to 2000 on issues of federalism *vs*. states' rights in relation to the Judicial branch can be found in the following news sources: NYT, Jan. 22, 1997, A16; NYT, May 28, 1997, B4; NYT, May 18, 1999, A1–; NYT, June 8, 1999, A23; NYT, June 11, 1999, A1–; NYT, Jan. 12, 2000, no page no. avail.; NYT, March 29, 2000, A22; NYT, June 5, 2000, A1–; WPNWE, July 3, 2000, p. 12.

40. NYT, June 25, 1994, A10; NYT, April 6, 1996, A1–; NYT, Sept. 2, 1996, A9.

41. NYT, Jan. 9, 1997, A1–; TM, Jan. 13, 1997, p. 60; CSM, Feb. 18, 1997, p. 1; CSM, Feb. 20, 1997, p. 3; NYT, June 24, 1997, A1, B9; NYT, June 26, 1997, A1; CSM, June 24, 1997, p. 1; CSM, June 26, 1997, p. 1; NYT, June 27, 1997, A1; NYT, June 27, 1997, A22; CSM, June 27, 1997, p. 1; NYT, Dec. 13, 1997, A13.

42. NYT, Nov. 4, 1998, A18; NYT, Dec. 2, 1998, A11; NYT, Sept. 19, 1999, sect. 1, no page no. avail.; NYT, Oct. 6, 1999, A21; NYT, Nov. 14, 1999, sect. 4, p. 11; NYT, Dec. 1, 1999, A19; NYT, Dec. 21, 1999, A1–; CSM, Dec. 22, 1999, p. 2; NYT, Jan. 25, 2000, A1–; NYT, April 26, 2000, A1, A19; NYT, June 29, 2000, A1–; NYT, June 30, 2000, A1–; NYT, Aug. 4, 2000, B1–; CSM, Oct. 11, 2000, p. 2.

43. CSM, Nov. 13, 2000, p. 4; WPNWE, Nov. 27, 2000, p. 11; NYT, Nov. 17, 2000, A34, editorial; NYT, Nov. 30, 2000, A34; NYT, Dec. 1, 2000, A36, editorial; NYT, Dec. 2, 2000, A1–; TM, Dec. 4, 2000, p. 42; USNWR, Dec. 4, 2000, p. 45.

44. USNWR, Dec. 4, 2000, cover story; NYT, Dec. 5, 2000, A1; NYT, Dec. 7, 2000, A1; NYT, Dec. 8, 2000, A1; NYT, Dec. 9, 2000, A1; NYT, Dec. 10, 2000, sect. 1, p. 1, reporting on Dec. 9 Sup. Court decision; NYT, Dec. 11, 2000, A1; NYT, Dec. 12, 2000, A1.

45. NYT, Dec. 13, 2000, A1, reporting on Sup. Court decision (also A34, editorial); USAT, Dec. 13, 2000, 1A, 17A; WP, Dec. 13, 2000, A1.

46. NYP, Dec. 13, 2000, p. 1; item for which no info. avail., yet possibly in sequence (NYDN?); USNWR, Dec. 18, 2000, cover story; CSM, Dec. 14, 2000, p. 1; NYT, Dec. 15, 2000, A39.

47. See full text of audio transcript of Bush v. Gore, Supreme Court, Dec. 11, 2000, in *N.Y. Times*.

48. NYT, March 4, 2001, sect. 4, p. 3; NYT, May 11, 2001, A34, editorial; NYT, June 28, 2002, A1.

49. NYT, April 26, 2001, A23; NYT, April 27, 2001, A24; WPNWE, July 9–15, 2001, p. 29; NYT, June 26, 2001, A19; NYT, Nov. 9, 2002, A19; WPNWE, April 4–10, 2005, p. 22; NYT, July 3, 2005, sect. 4, p. 4.

50. NYT, Sept. 5, 2005, A19; TM, July 11, 2005, cover story; NYT, Sept. 13, 2005, A1, A28; WPNWE, Sept. 12–18, 2005, p. 12; WPNWE, Nov. 14–20, 2005, p. 22; NYT, Nov. 7, 2005, A20; NYT, Jan. 10, 2006, A1, A16–17; WPNWE, Jan. 16–22, 2006, p. 6; NYT, July 2, 2006, sect. 1, pp. 1, 22.

51. CSM, Feb. 11, 2002, p. 2; CSM, May 15, 2002, p. 4; NYT, June 8, 2002, A15; NYT, Sept. 1, 2002, sect. 4, p. 3; NYT, Oct. 6, 2002, sect. 4, p. 13.

52. NYT, Sept. 14, 2003, sect. 1, no page no. avail.; NYT, Dec. 19, 2003, A31; NYT, Jan. 27, 2004, A16; USNWR, April 26, 2004, no page no. avail.

53. NYT, April 29, 2004, A22 (transcript = April 28); NYT, probably same issue as one preceding or a day later, no other info. avail.; transcripts of oral arguments before Sup. Court, late April, 2004; NYT, June 29, 2004, A1, A14, A26–27; WPNWE, Aug. 30–Sept. 5, 2004, p. 24.

54. NYT, July 16, 2005, A1; NYT, June 30, 2006, A20–21; NYT, Jan. 17, 2007, A18.

55. NYT, Feb. 22, 2001, A1, A20, A24; CSM, April 19, 2001, p. 4; NYT, April 25, 2001, A14; NYT, Feb. 25, 2001, sect. 4, p. 3; NYT, March 3, 2001, A13; book by William Rehnquist reviewed in WPNWE, Feb. 26–March 4, 2001, p. 32; NYT, May 11, 2001, A26; NYT, Dec. 17, 2001, A13; NYT, June 26, 2001, A15.

56. NYT, Jan. 9, 2002, A1–; NYT, Jan. 10, 2002, A21; NYT, April 17, 2002, A1; NWM, July 8, 2002, p. 64; NYT, Sept. 8, 2002, sect. 4, p. 3; WPNWE, Oct. 7–13, 2002, book review; WPNWE, Dec. 9–15, 2002, book review.

57. NYT, July 27, 2003, A1, A19; Rush Limbaugh on ABC radio, June 26, 2003; Robert Novak on "Capitol Gang" TV show, June 28, 2003; NYT, July 1, 2003, A1, A18–19; NYT, July 20, 2003, sect. 4, p. 7; TM, June 30, 2003, pp. 24–; CSM, July 8, 2003, p. 2.

58. NYT, Jan. 1, 2004, no page no. avail.; NYT, April 18, 2004, sect. 1, p. 20; NYT, June 2, 2004, A13; NYT, May 2, 2004, A14; NYT, June 23, 2004, sect. A, no page no. avail.; NYT, Sept. 30, 2004, A26.

59. NYT, Jan. 1, 2005, no page no. avail.; NYT, Jan. 21, 2005, sect. A, no page no.; NYT, Jan. 13, 2005, A1; TM, Jan. 24, 2005, p. 31; CSM, March 2, 2005, p. 1; NYT, May 6, 2005, A27; NYT, May 17, 2005, sect. 4, p. 13.

60. CBS radio, July 20, 2005; CBS radio, July 20, 2005; NBC TV, July 20, 2005; NBC TV, July 20, 2005; NYT, Sept. 14, 2006, A26; NYT, Sept. 15, 2005, A1; NYT, Sept. 15, 2005, A1; NYT, Aug. 1, 2005, A12.

61. Pres. Bush at news conference announcing Judge Harriet Miers as his nominee to Supreme Court, Oct. 4, 2005; WPNWE, Oct. 10–16, 2005, no page no. avail.; Bush on radio or TV, late Oct. or early Nov., 2006; Frist on CBS TV, Nov. 5, 2006.

62. CSM, June 28, 1999, p. 1; NYT, March 16, 2003, sect. 4, p. 5; NYT, June 7, 2005, A1, A21.

63. NYT, July 14, 2006, A15; NYT, July 13, 2006, A20; NYT, Jan. 18, 2006, A1, A16.

64. CSM, Jan. 20, 2005, pp. 1, 4.

Bibliography concerning the Supreme Court, aside from materials already cited above, includes the following miscellaneous items: Harvey Walker, *The Legislative Process* (cited earlier), Ch. 21, "Lawmaking by the Courts"; Bernard Schwartz, *A History of the Supreme Court* (New York, 1993), Chs. 12, 16 on the Warren and Rehnquist Courts; Robert H. Bork, *The Tempting of America: The Political Seduction of the Law* (New York, 1990), on judicial review, judicial power, etc.; Mark Levin, *Men in Black: How the Supreme Court Has Destroyed America* (Wash., D.C., 2005); and R. Kent Newmeyer, *John Marshall and the Heroic Age of the Supreme Court* (Baton Rouge, 2001).

Notes to Chapter V
U.S. Federal Departments,
Agencies, and Commissions

1. Quotation ("promulgate regulations") is from "Capitol Gang" talk show on CNN TV, Dec. 8, 2001.

2. NYT, June 18, 1991, A19; NYT, Feb. 19, 1992, A18; NYT, Sept. 6, 1991, A1, D5; NYT, March 3, 1992, A17; NYT, April 23, 1992, A1; NYT, April 25, 1992, A1–; NYT, Oct. 1, 1992, A1; NYT, Oct. 14, 1992, A1.

3. WP, Jan. 17, 1993, A4; NYT, Jan. 15, 1993, no page no. avail.; NYT, Jan. 20, 1993, A20; TM, Feb. 15, 1993, p. 28–.

4. TM, July 12, 1998, cover story, pp. 20–21; NYT, March 24, 1993, A1; NYT, Jan. 7, 1994, A1; NYT, Jan. 21, 1994, A1; NYT, May 20, 1994, B20; WSJ, May 23, 1994, A16; TM, Nov. 25, 1996, p. 42.

5. NYT, Dec. 29, 1996, p. 15; NYT, April 28, 1995, D2; NYT, Aug. 20, 1995, A1; NYT, July 26, 1995, A1; NYT, March 23, 1996, A11; NYT, April 29, 1996, D1; NYT, May 19, 1996, sect. 1, p. 12; USNWR, Dec. 16, 1996, p. 80.

6. NYT, June 28, 1995, A1; NYT, Oct. 18, 1995, B8; NYT, Dec. 8, 1995, A24.

7. NYT, June 12, 1997, sect. B, no page no. avail.; NYT, Nov. 6, 1998, A14; NYT, May 20, 1999, A10; NYT, no date avail., but in sequence, A1, B7; NYT, March 31, 2000, sect. A, no page no. avail.; NYT, Jan. 22, 1998, B1.

8. TM, Sept. 29, 1997, pp. 24–25; NYT, Sept. 9, 1998, A1; NYT, Nov. 10, 1998, A1; NYT, Dec. 8, 1998, A26; NYT, June 23, 2000, A18; NYT, Sept. 15, 2000, A1.

9. NYT, Sept. 23, 1999, A1, A22; USNWR, Oct. 4, 1999, p. 29; CSM, Sept. 23, 1999, p. 2.

10. NYT, April 8, 2000, A1; NYT, April 14, 2000, A28; TM, April 24, 2000, p. 33; NYT, no date avail., but in sequence, A1; NYT, April 21, 2000, A19; NYT, April 23, 2000, sect. 1, pp. 1, 16–17; NYT, April 29, 2000, A13; USNWR, May 8, 2000, p. 29.

11. NYT, Dec. 13, 1997, A12; NYT, Dec. 3, 1997, A1; TM, Dec. 14, 1998, p. 36; NYT, Feb. 24, 1999, A14; NYT, Feb. 24, 1999, A21; NYT, Feb. 25, 1999, A24; NYT, March 2, 1999, A16; NYT, March 17, 1999, A1; NYT, April 14, 1999, A1; NYT, June 30, 1999, A1.

12. CSM, Dec. 26, 1997, p. 1; TM, Nov. 3, 1997, pp. 76–77; NYT, Nov. 12, 1997, D2; CSM, Jan. 26, year not recorded, but in sequence, p. 3; NYT, Feb. 9, 1998, D1; NYT, May 19, 1998, A1; NYT, May 20, 1998, A23; TM, May 25, 1998, pp. 58–59; USNWR, July 6, 1998, p. 56; NYT, Aug. 20, 1999, A17; NYT, April 29, 2000, A1; NYT, June 8, 2000, A1–.

13. NYT, March 26, 1998, A18; NYT, June 6, 1998, A1.

14. TM, Jan. 8, 2001, p. 30; NYT, Jan. 14, 2001, sect. 4, p. 5; NYT, Jan. 17, 2001, A1, A19; NYT, Feb. 2, 2001, A1 (and see also NYT, Jan. 22, 2001, cover story).

15. NYT, June 20, 2001, A12; NYT, Aug. 19, 2001, sect. 1, p. 22; NYT, Sept. 7, 2001, C5; NYT, Sept. 9, 2001, sect. 4, p. 3.

16. NYT, Nov. 9, 2001, B1; WP, Nov. 1, 2001, A2; NYT, Nov. 28, 2001, B7; NYT, Nov. 29, 2001, B7; NYT, Dec. 1, 2001, A1; NYT, Dec. 6, 2001, B7; TM, Dec. 10, 2001, no page no. avail.; NYT, April 2, 2002, A13; NYT, April 4, 2002, A19; NYT, Aug. 15, 2002, A21; NYT, Aug. 27, 2002, A17; NYT, Nov. 24, 2002, sect. 1, p. 22; WPNWE, Dec. 9–15, 2000, p. 30; USNWR, Dec. 16, 2002, cover story; WPNWE, Feb. 17–23, 2003, p. 29; NYT, May 21, 2003, A1; NYT, June 6, 2003, A1; NYT, June 13, 2003, A1; NYT, July 15, 2003, A1; NYT, July 21, 2003, A1; NYT, Aug. 19, 2003, A19; WPNWE, Sept. 8–14, 2003, p. 29; CNN TV, Nov. 13, 2004.

17. NYT, Aug. 10, 2002, A10; WPNWE, Sept. 2–8, 2002, p. 22; NYT, Aug. 30, 2003, A12; NYT, June 6, 2003, A18; NYT, Feb. 12, 2004, A1; NYT, Nov. 8, 2001, A14; NYT, March 22, 2002, A16; NYT, May 8, 2002, A29; NYT, Feb. 16, 2003, sect. 4, p. 5; NYT, April 25, 2003, A26; NYT, May 27, 2004, A1.

18. NYT, March 16, 1992, A17; NYT, March 27, 1991, A1; NYT, March 19, 1992, A1.

19. NYT, March 25, 1993, A1; NYT, April 28, 1993, A1; NYT, Sept. 2, 1993, A1, A18; NYT, Sept. 26, 1993, sect. 1, p. 8; NYT, Dec. 23, 1993, A1; TM, June 5, 1995, p. 26; CSM, July 2, 1996, p. 4.

20. NYT, Nov. 10, 1997, A1; NYT, Jan. 28, 1999, A21; NYT, July 22, 1999, A1, A16; NYT, Oct. 8, 1999, sect. A, no page no. avail.; NYT, June 15, 2000, A25.

21. CNN TV, Dec. 8, 2001, "Capitol Gang"; NYT, May 3, 2001, A8; NYT, May 18, 2001, A10; USNWR, May 28, 2001, p. 26; NYT, Aug. 20, 2001, A16.

22. NYT, Jan. 24, 2002, no page no. avail.; NYT, March 30, 2002, A11; NYT, May 9, 2002, A28; NYT, June 17, 2002, A1, A16; WPNWE, Jan. 20–26, 2003, p. 30; NYT, Feb. 12, 2003, A1; NYT, April 23, 2004, A14; NYT, Oct.

26, 2004, A18; NYT, May 11, 2003, A16l; USNWR, Aug. 1, 2005, cover story; NYT, Jan. 19, 2007, A18.

23. WPNWE, Dec. 24–Jan. 6, 2001, p. 6; WPNWE, Jan. 28–Feb. 3, 2002, p. 30.

24. NYT, April 12, 2002, A16; NYT, June 19, 2002, A1; CSM, June 14, 2002, p. 9; NWM, July 8, 2000, pp. 26–27, 34; NYT, July 11, 2002, A20; NYT, Nov. 14, 2002, A32; NYT, Nov. 20, 2002, A1; NYT, Nov. 26, 2002, A17; WPNWE, Nov. 18–24, 2002, p. 30; NYT, Nov. 30, 2002, A12; WPNWE, March 10–16, 2003, p. 29; NYT, Nov. 19, 2003, A25; NYT, March 16, 2004, A1; CSM, June 10, 2005, p. 3.

25. NYT, Jan. 9, 1994, sect. 1, p. 1–; NYT, Dec. 8, 1999, A21; NYT, June 28, 2000, A22.

26. NYT, Jan. 19, 2001, A22; NYT, March 20, 2001, A16; NYT, March 31, 2001, sect. A, no page no. avail.; NYT, April 14, 2001, A7; NYT, June 19, 2001, sect. A, no page no. avail.; NYT, Nov. 14, 2001, C1.

27. NYT, March 28, 2002, sect. A, no page no. avail.; NYT, April 4, 2002, A18; NYT, Aug. 15, 2003, no page no. avail.; NYT, Aug. 19, 2003, B6; NYT, Aug. 20, 2003, A16.

28. CSM, Aug. 19, 2003, p. 1; NYT, Aug. 23, 2003, A10; NYT, Aug. 31, 2003, sect. 1, p. 24; NYT, Aug. 29, 2003, B1; NYT, Oct. 1, 2003, A1; NYT, Sept. 4, 2003, A20; NYT, Oct. 26, 2003, sect. 1, p. 22; NYT, Nov. 26, 2003, A17.

29. NYT, March 10, 2001, A6; NYT, March 10, 2001, A6; NYT, March 23, 2003, A1, A16; NYT, April 26, 2001, A18; NYT, April 27, 2001, A22; NYT, June 19, 2001, A1; NYT, April 25, 2001, C1, C16.

30. NYT, July 26, 1995, A16; NYT, Sept. 20, 1995, B8; TM, April 15, 1996, p. 68; WPNWE, April 23–29, 2001, p. 6; NYT, Oct. 26, 2001, A14; NYT, April 30, 2002, A12; NYT, March 25, 1995, sect. no. not recorded, p. 1; NYT, Nov. 22, 1996, A1; NYT, March 1, 2002, A28; NYT, May 3, 2002, A20.

31. NYT, March 26, 1994, A1; NYT, Nov. 22, 1999, A1; NYT, March 5, 2001, A1; NYT, May 5, 2004, A20; Lehrer News Hour, PBS, Sept. 1, 2003.

32. NYT, July 28, 1993, A13; NYT, April 23, 1996, A23; NYT, March 26, 2004, B5.

33. McNeil-Lehrer News Hour, PBS, July 11, 1995; NYT, March 22, 2001, A1; NYT, Jan. 23, 2003, A1.

34. NYT, date not recorded, but article says it is during the Clinton Admin., A1; NYT, Dec. 21, 2000, A22.

35. NYT, Nov. 22, 2002, A1; NYT, March 7, 2003, A23; NYT, Dec. 3, 2003, A15.

36. NYT, Dec. 20, 2000, A1.

37. NYT, Sept. 3, 1991, A1, D6; NYT, Sept. 5, 1991, D1; NYT, Sept. 12, 1991, D5.

38. NYT, Feb. 27, 1995, A1; NYT, March 2, 1995, sect. A, no page no. avail., editorial.

39. NYT, April 24, 2002, A13; NYT, July 28, 2003, A1.

40. NYT, Sept. 12, 1991, A18; NYT, Feb. 14, 1992, A14; NYT, Feb. 25, 1992, A12; NYT, Feb. 27, 1992, A25, Op-Ed; WP, May 17, 1992, A14; NYT, June 26, 1992, A1; NYT, June 30, 1992, A19.

41. NYT, Aug. 24, 1999, B1; NYT, Oct. 13, 1994, A24; NYT, Dec. 10, 1994, A8; NYT, Dec. 21, 1994, D23; NYT, July 27, 1995, A18; NYT, Aug. 1, 1995, A1; NYT, Aug. 24, 1995, A1; NYT, Sept. 24, 1995, sect. 1, p. 26; NYT, Nov. 19, 1995, sect. 1, p. 21; NYT, Dec. 12, 1995, A1, D23; NYT, month not recorded, but in sequence, 1996, A20.

42. TM, July 17, 1997, p. 32; NYT, Aug. 8, 1997, A1–; NYT, Aug. 12, 1997, B7; NYT, Oct. 11, 1997, A9; NYT, Dec. 17, 1999, A20; NYT, Dec. 29, 1997, A16; NYT, Sept. 25, 1998, A14; NYT, April 18, 1999, sect. 1, p. 16; NYT, July 27, 1999, A1; NYT, Dec. 18, 1999, A1–; NYT, March 4, 2000, A9; NYT, May 17, 2000, A1; NYT, July 12, 2000, A17; NYT, Sept. 29, 2000, B6; CSM, Nov. 7, 2000, pp. 1, 10; ABC radio, mid-July, 2000, Rush Limbaugh Program.

43. NYT, Jan. 18, 2001, A18; NYT, Feb. 15, 2001, p. 5; NYT, Feb. 28, 2001, A16, A18; NYT, March 1, 2001, A19; NYT, March 1, 2001, sect. 1, p. 24; NYT, April 17, 2001, A12; NYT, April 18, 2001, A20; NYT, May 16, 2001, A24; NYT, July 17, 2001, sect. A, no page no. avail.; NYT, Aug. 1, 2001, A1; ABC radio, Aug. 4, 2001, John Gambling Show; WPNWE, July 30–Aug. 12, 2001, p. 29; NYTM, Aug. 19, 2001, p. 40; NYT, Sept. 5, 2001, A12; NYT, Nov. 1, 2001, A18; NYT, Nov. 5, 2001, D1.

44. NYT, March 1, 2002, A19; NYT, April 28, 2002, sect. 1, p. 26; NYT, May 3, 2002, A14; NYT, May 7, 2002, A30, editorial; NYT, Nov. 23, 2002, A1, A16; NYT, Dec. 14, 2002, A17.

45. CBS or NBC TV, evening news, Jan. 1, 2003; NYT, Feb. 21, 2003, A25; NYT, April 22, 2003, A21; NYT, July 14, 2003, A9; NYT, Dec. 4, 2003, A24; CBS radio news, Aug. 22, 2003; CBS radio news, April 18, 2003.

46. NYT, May 11, 2004, A16; WPNWE, May 31–June 6, 2004, p. 14; NYT, May 2, 2004, A14; NYT, Aug. 2, 2006, A13.

47. NYT, Feb. 2, 1992, A12; NYT, March 26, 1992, no page no. avail.; NYT, May 27, 1992, A16.

48. NYT, June 16, 1993, A19; NYT, July 2, 1993, A11; NYT, Feb. 26, 1994, A1; NYT, May 5, 1994, A20; NYT, month not recorded, 1993, sect. 1, p. 28.

49. NYT, Feb. 13, 1995, sect. 1, p. 24; NYT, July 3, 1995, A1; McNeil-Lehrer News Hour, PBS, March 28, 1995.

50. NYT, July 13, 1995, A18; NYT, July 14, 1995, no page no. avail.; NYT, Aug. 10, 1995, A1; NYT, late April, 1997, as per info. at beg. of next article cited here; NYT, May 2, 1997, A1; NYT, July 10, 1997, A20; NYT, Aug. 3, 1997, sect. 1, p. 1; NYT, Aug. 15, 1998, A1, A9; NYT, Dec. 2, 1999, A1; CSM, Nov. 30, 1999, pp. 1, 9; McNeil-Lehrer News Hour, PBS, Dec. 3, 1999 (also cf. March 21, 2000); NYT, March 22, 2000, A1; NYT, March 24, 2000, A19; NYT, March 26, 2000, sect. 1, p. 31.

Here can be added two further examples of other dimensions of the F.D.A. in relation to Congressional legislative actions: "Senate Votes to Streamline F.D.A." and "passed a bill . . . [to] enable the . . . [F.D.A.] to speed the availability of drugs and medical devices [NYT, Sept. 25, 1997, A29] . . ."; and "House Votes to Block F.D.A. on Approval of Abortion Pill," "Attacking a measure to an agriculture bill [that] creates a political dilemma for Clinton [NYT, June 25, 1998, A20]."

51. NYT, April 17, 2001, A19; NYT, June 13, 2003, A28; NYT, Jan. 25, 2004, sect. 1, no page no. avail.; NYT, Dec. 6, 2004, A20; NYT, Aug. 13, 2005, A9; NYT, July 24, 2006, A13.

52. NYT, July 25, 2006, A20; NYT, Dec. 15, 2005, A33; NYT, Sept. 21, 2002, A15.

53. NYT, Oct. 19, 2002, A9; NYT, Dec. 31, 2003, A14.

54. NYT, July 12, 1995, D1; NYT, Dec. 4, 1995, A17; NYT, July 31, 1996, D1; NYT, Aug. 22, 1996, B10; NYT, Dec. 23, 1996, D1; NYT, May 8, 1997, D6; NYT, March 26, 1998, A15; NYT, Nov. 19, 1998, A23; NYT, Aug. 28, 1999, A1; NYT, Oct. 7, 1999, C7; NYT, Jan. 30, 2000, sect. 1, p. 23; NYT, Oct. 12, 2000, A15.

55. NYT, Jan. 17, 2001, A16; NYT, Feb. 7, 2001, C1; NYT, July 28, 2001, A10; NYT, April 3, 2002, C1; NYT, June 3, 2003, A1, C9; NYT, July 23, 2003, A1; NYT, Sept. 4, 2003, A1; NYT, June 25, 2004, A1; NYT, Oct. 4, 2004, A1; NYT, Jan. 22, 2005, A1; NYT, Aug. 6, 2005, C1.

56. NYT, April 18, 1996, B1; NYT, April 25, 1996, D1; NYT, April 5, 1997, A1; NYT, June 9, 1998, A1; NYT, June 12, 2001, C1.

57. NYT, April 25, 1996, D5; NYT, June 4 (14?), 1998, D1; NYT, Nov. 18, 1998, sect. A, no page no. avail.; NYT, May 20, 2000, A1; NSL, July 28, 2000, p. 1.

58. NYT, April 17, 1992, A1; NYT, May 3, 2001, A17; NYT, Jan. 28, 2003, A16; NYT, May 6, 2004, B7; NYT, June 30, 2003, A18; NYT, Sept. 20, 2003, A6.

59. NYT, Sept. 24, 2004, A1; NYT, March 6, 2005, sect. 1, p. 35.

60. NYT, Jan. 2, 2001, A1, A12; NYT, April 10, 2002, A17; NYT, April 25, 2002, A25; NYT, April 26, 2002, A26; NYT, May 23, 2002, A31.

61. NYT, April 9, 1997, A16; NYT, April 15, 1997, A23; NYT, Sept. 28, 1997, sect. 1, p. 30; NYT, Nov. 6, 1997, A1; NYT, Dec. 13, 1997, A1; NYT, March 25, 1998, A18; NYT, April 29, 1998, A16; NYT, May 1, 1998, A20; NYT, May 8, 1998, A1.

62. NYT, Nov. 12, 2001, B1; NYT, April 25, 2003, C1, C4.

63. NYT, June 28, 2000, C1; NYT, June 20, 2001, C1; NYT, Sept. 15, 2001, C1; NYT, May 9, 2002, no page no. avail.; NYT, Oct. 1, 2003, C5; NYT, Jan. 24, 2003, C1; NYT, May 27, 2004, C1; NYT, May 10, 2004, C1; NYT, Jan. 11, 2006, C3; CSM, July 9, 2002, p. 4; WSJ, Oct. 11, 1999, A1.

64. NYT, July 18, 1995, A13; NYT, July 19, 1995, A1; NYT, July 18, 1995, D23; NYT, July 21, 1995, A16; NYT, March 2, 1996, A10; NYT, March 12, 1996, A13; NYT, May 13, 1996, A15; NYT, July 1, 1997, A4; NYT, May 19, 1997, B7; NYT, April 8, 1998, A16; CSM, June 24, 1997, p. 19; NYT, Sept. 14, 1997, sect. 4, p. 4.

65. NYT, Nov. 11, 2000, A1, A16; NYT, Feb. 28, 1999, sect. 1, p. 20; NYT, Oct. 27, 1999, A18; NYT, Dec. 26, 1999, sect. 4, p. 8; NYT, April 8, 2004, A22; NYT, Aug. 17, 2001, A12; NYT, Jan. 22, 2005, A11; NYT, June 5, 2006, A14; NYT, July 7, 2006, A15; NYT, Oct. 18, 2000, A20.

66. NYT, March 2, 2001, A20; NYT, Oct. 11, 2004, A21; WPNWE, Oct. 16–22, 2006, p. 30; NYT, Oct. 12, 2004, A19.

67. NYT, Oct. 13, 2004, E1; TM, Dec. 25, 2000–Jan. 1, 2001, p. 142.

68. WSJ, July 27, 1999, A22; WPNWE, Aug. 15–21, 2005, p. 10; NYT, May 16, 1990, D2; NYT, March 31, 2002, A30; NYT, April 13, 2006, A16; NYT, May 11, 2000, sect. A, no page no. avail.; NYT, Dec. 15, 2005, A24.

69. NYT, Dec. 29, 2005, A26; NYT, Jan. 7, 2006, A1; NYT, Feb. 7, 2006, A1, A18; WPNWE, March 10–16, 2003, no page no. avail.; NYT, Oct. 25, 2005, A16; TM, Oct., day not recorded, 2001, pp. 60–61; NYT, May 31, 2002, A1, A20; NYT, Nov. 5, 1995, sect. 1, p. 20; NYT, June 9, 1996, sect. 1, p. 30; WPNWE, Nov. 6, 2000, p. 29.

70. NYT, Aug. 21, 2007, A17; PCN, March/April 2007, p. 3; PCN, Annual Report, 2006, p. 9; NYT, Jan. 30, 2007, A1, A19; NYT, July 12, 1994, A12.

71. NYT, April 3, 2007, A1, A18; CSM, April 3, 2007, p. 1.

72. USNWR, April 16, 2007, p. 28; NYT, Jan. 5, 2007, A1; CSM, June 16, 2006, p. 3; NYT, March 18, 2006, A1.

Of usefulness for this chapter has been *The 2006–2007 United States Government Manual* (Wash., D.C., 2006). Thanks go to John Hernandez, Social Science Reference Librarian at Princeton University, for information relating to this chapter.

Notes to Chapter VI
States of the American Union

1. NYT, June 4, 1989, sect. 1, p. 26; NYT, Feb. 16, 1989, B7; NYT, Nov. 13, 1989, B6.

2. NYT, May 21, 1990, A1, B14; NYT, June 26, 1990, A17; NYT, Oct. 4, 1990, B18; NYT, Nov. 5, 1990, B10; WP, Nov. 8, 1990, A45; TM, Dec. 31, 1990, p. 15; NYT, Dec. 30, 1990, sect. 1, p. 16.

3. NYT, Jan. 14, 1991, A14; WP, Jan. 6, 1991, C7; NYT, Jan. 31, 1991, A19; NYT, Feb. 9, 1991, A1, A10; NYT, Feb. 10, 1991, sect. 1, p. 2; *State Legislatures*, Feb. 1991, p. 28; WP, March 24, 1991, C7; NYT, March 25, 1991, D6; *Governing*, April 1991, p. 27; WP, July 14, 1991, C3; WP, July 14, 1991, C3; NYT, July 27, 1991, A8; *State Legislatures*, Aug. 1991, p. 14; *State Legislatures*, Sept. 19, 1991, p. 19; NYT, Dec. 4, 1991, A20; NYT, Oct. 30, 1991, A23.

4. NWM, Feb. 17, 1992, p. 40; NYT, Dec. 28, 1992, B10; NYT, April 23, 1992, A14; NYT, May 17, 1992, A9; *State Legislatures*, June 1990, p. 47; NYT, Aug. 2, 1992, sect. 1, p. 34; NYT, Oct. 13, 1992, A1, A20.

5. NYT, Feb. 25, 1993, A16; NYT, April 25, 1993, sect. 1, p. 30; TM, June 28, 1993, p. 30; NYT, Aug. 18, 1993, A19; NYT, Aug. 15, 1993, sect. 1, p. 26; NYT, Aug. 15, 1993, sect. 1, pp. 1, 26; NYT, Nov. 16, 1993, A18; NYT, July 22, 1993, A8.

6. NYT, April 1, 1994, A20; NYT, April 14, 1994, B10; WSJ, early May 1994, A1; NYT, Sept. 29, 1994, B6; NYT, Sept. 6, 1994, A1; TM, Sept. 19, 1994, p. 43.

7. NYT, Jan. 8, 1995, sect. 1, p. 19; NYT, Jan. 3, 1995, A13; NYT, Jan. 13, 1995, A23; NYT, Jan. 18, 1995, A20; TM, Feb. 13, 1995, pp. 30–31; NYT, Feb. 17, 1995, A18; NYT, April 1, 1995, A1; NYT, April 13, 1995, A1; NYT, June 28, 1995, A1; NYT, July 2, 1995, sect. 1, p. 1; NYT, Aug. 1, 1995, A15; NYT, Sept. 19, 1995, A17; NYT, Sept. 24, 1995, sect. 1, p. 24.

8. NYT, March 17, 1996, sect. 1, p. 30; NYT, March 28, 1996, B9; NYT, March 29, 1996, A20; NYT, April 1, 1996, A1; TM, April 8, 1996, p. 45.

9. WP, Aug. 4, 1996, A24; NYT, Sept. 10, 1996, A16; item for which no ref. avail.; NYT, Oct. 1, 1996, A22; NYT, Oct. 15, 1996, A21; NYT, Dec. 20, 1996, sect. 1, p. 1; NYT, Dec. 29, 1996, sect. 1, p. 12.

10. NYT, April 28, 1996, A13; CSM, May 14, 1997, p. 3; NYT, June 30, 1997, A1; NYT, July 12, 1997, A1; NYT, July 31, 1997, A20; TM, Aug. 18, 1997, p. 21.

11. NYT, Jan. 14, 1998, A15; CSM, May 20, 1998, pp. 1, 8; NYT, June 9, 1998, A18; NYTM, July 5, 1998, pp. 26–27; NYT, Sept. 14, 1998, A12; NYT, Oct. 15, 1998, A20; NYT, Nov. 15, 1998, sect. 1, p. 20.

12. NYT, Jan. 13, 1999, A1; NYT, June 27, 1999, sect. 4, p. 17; CSM, June 28, 1999, p. 10; Lehrer News Hour, PBS, June 23, 1999; NYT, July 16, 1999, A1, A13.

13. NYT, July 6, 1999, C6; CSM, Aug. 11, 1999, pp. 1, 4; NYT, Sept. 6, 1999, A12.

14. NYT, Jan. 30, 2000, sect. 1, pp. 1–; NYT, Feb. 14, 2000, A19; USNWR, April 17, 2000, p. 24; USNWR, April 24, 2000, p. 26; NYT, May 20, 2000, A15; NYT, June 12, 2000, A22; CSM, June 19, 2000, p. 2; NYT, Aug. 8, 2000, A1; WPNWE, Aug. 21, 2000, p. 18; NYT, Sept. 15, 2000, C1, C4; NYT, Oct. 4, 2000, A27; WPNWE, Oct. 30, 2000, p. 25.

15. NYT, Jan. 1, 2001, A7; NYT, Jan. 7, 2001, sect. 1, pp. 1, 18; NYT, July 27, 2001, A1.

16. NYT, March 9, 2001, A1; NYT, Nov. 24, 2001, A26; NYT, Dec. 10, 2001, F1; NYT, Jan. 7, 2001, A27.

17. NYT, Jan. 1, 2002, A19; CSM, Jan. 4, 2002, p. 1; NYT, Jan. 13, 2002, sect. 1, p. 23; NYT, Feb. 24, 2002, sect. 1, p. 2; CSM, March 2, 2002, A1; NYT, April 4, 2002, A18; NYT, April 11, 2002, A29; NYT, April 30, 2002, A22; NYT, May 29, 2002, A18; NYT, May 3, 2002, editorial, no page no. avail.; CSM, May 29, 2002, p. 1; NYT, July 4, 2002, B1; NYT, Oct. 16, 2002, A17; NYT, Nov. 6, 2002, A27; NYT, Dec. 2, 2002, A21.

18. NYT, Jan. 1, 2003, A1; NYT, Feb. 14, 2003, sect. A, no page no. avail.; item for which no ref. is avail.; NYT, Aug. 8, 2003, A10; NYT, Nov. 9, 2003, sect. 1, pp. 1, 30; NYT, Nov. 17, 2003, A21, editorial by Eliot Spitzer, as Attorney General of N.Y. State.

19. CSM, Jan. 12, 2004, p. 2; CSM, July 6, 2004, p. 2; NYT, June 7, 2004, A16; NYT, March 25, 2004, A16; NYT, Nov. 22, 2004, A22.

20. NYT, March 23, 2005, A17, OP-ED by Charles Fried, Harvard law professor; CSM, April 13, 2005, p. 3; CSM, April 19, 2005, pp. 1, 10.

21. CSM, June 24, 2005, p. 1; NYT, June 24, 2005, A1; NYT, Feb. 21, 2006, A17; NYT, Aug. 25, 2005, A22; CSM, Dec. 29, 2006, p. 5; NYT, Jan. 1, 2007, A1.

22. NYT, Jan. 4, 1990, B4; NYT, Feb. 6, 1990, no page no. avail.; NYT, April 6, 1990, B1; NYT, March 1, 1991, B1; NYT, May 21, 1991, B1; NYT, May 20, 1991, A1; NYT, May 29, 1991, B4; NYT, June 15, 1991, A1; NYT, Feb. 14, 1992, B9; NYT, May 2, 1994, B6; NYT, June 8, 1994, A1, B4.

23. NYT, April 20, 1992, B4; NYT, Feb. 28, 1992, B1; NYT, March 8, 1992, sect. 1, p. 38; NYT, April 18, 1992, A22; NYT, May 5, 1992, A1, B9.

24. NYT, May 19, 1992, no page no. avail.; NYT, July 17, 1992, B3; NYT, May 7, 1993, B1; NYT, June 21, 1994, A1; NYT, July 4, 1994, A1.

25. NYT, Nov. 21, 1990, B6; quotations from reports sent to constituents by N.Y. State Senator Roy Goodman.

26. NYT, Nov. 10, 1994, B12; NYT, Nov. 14, 1994, A1, B6; NYT, Nov. 16, 1994, B1; NYT, Jan. 2, 1995, A1; NYT, Jan. 31, 1995, B4; NYT, March 4, 1995, A18.

27. NYT, Feb. 16, 1995, A1; NYT, March 8, 1995, A1; NYT, April 5, 1995, A1, NYT, April 15, 1995, A1; NYT, May 21, 1995, sect. 1, p. 1; NYT, June 3, 1995, A1; NYT, June 5, 1995, B4; NYT, June 8, 1995, B1; NYT, Sept. 2, 1995, A25; NYT, Sept. 10, 1995, sect. 1, p. 32; NYT, Dec. 10, 1995, sect. 1, p. 1; NYT, Nov. 2, 1995, A1; NYT, Nov. 28, 1995, A1.

28. NYT, April 29, 1996, B6; NYT, May 23, 1996, A1; NYT, May 25, 1996, A1; NYT, June 4, 1996, B1; NYT, July 3, 1996, B5; NYT, July 13, 1996, A24.

29. NYT, March 29, 1997, A18; NYT, Dec. 26, 1997, B1; NYT, April 15, 1998, B5; NYT, Jan. 2, 1999, B1.

30. NYT, Jan. 18, 2001, A1; NYT, Jan. 19, 2001, A14; NYT, Feb. 28, 2001, B1, B5; NYT, May 8, 2002, B1; NYT, April 16, 2004, A1; NYT, Jan. 13, 2005, B3.

31. NYT, Dec. 23, 1998, A1; NYT, Oct. 15, 1999, B5; NYT, July 11, 2001, B5; NYT, June 7, 2002, B1; NYT, July 8, 2004, B5; NYT, Sept. 25, 2006, A1.

32. NYT, Oct. 20, 2002, sect. 1, p. 38; NYT, Oct. 21, 2002, B7; NYT, April 8, 2003, D5; NYT, May 2, 2005, B7; NYT, May 6, 2003, B6; NYT, April 13, 2006, B7; NYT, April 27, 2006, B4; NYT, Nov. 8, A1, P1, 2006; NYT, Sept. 30, 2006, B2.

33. NYT, Jan. 2, 2007, A1, B1; NYT, Jan. 4, 2007, A1, B4.

34. NYT, March 23, 1989, A1; NYT, April 20, 1989, B6; NYT, April 17, 1989, B1; NYT, April 25, 1989, A1; NYT, May 3, 1989, B1; NYT, May 16, 1989, B1.

35. NYT, May 10, 1990, B6; NYT, June 8, 1990, sect. B, no page no. avail.; NYT, Oct. 18, 1990, B10; NYT, Nov. 17, 1990, p. 1; NYT, Feb. 8, 1991, A1; NYT, Dec. 4, 1992, A1; NYT, June 6, 1989, B4; NYT, July 11, 1991, sect. A, no page no. avail.; NYP, July 23, 1991, no page no. avail.; NYT, Aug. 21, 1993, p. 19.

36. NYT, Jan. 6, 1994, A1; NYT, April 27, 1994, B3; NYT, Aug. 25, 1994, B3; NYT, Oct. 27, 1994, B3; NYT, Nov. 27, 1994, sect. 1, p. 51; NYT, Dec. 1, 1994, A1; NYT, Dec. 3, 1994, A17; NYT, Dec. 24, 1994, A17; NYT, Feb. 15, 1995, A1; NYT, Aug. 25, 1995, A4; NYT, Feb. 13, 1996, B5; NYT, Jan. 7, 1997, A1.

37. NYT, June 5, 1997, B6; NYT, Aug. 29, 1998, B3; NYT, Dec. 18, 1998, B1; NYT, Dec. 29, 1998, B3; NYT, May 23, 1999, sect. 1, no page no. avail.; NYT, Feb. 14, 2000, B5.

38. NYT, Feb. 14, 1996, B5; NYT, March 1, 1996, B3; NYT, Jan. 29, 1999, B10; NYT, June 3, 1999, no page or sect. no. avail.

39. NYT, Oct. 1, 1996, B7; NYT, Nov. 27, 1996, B3; NYT, Dec. 16, 1998, B1.

40. NYT, Jan. 28, 1999, B1; NYT, March 27, 2000, B4; NYT, Aug. 10, 1996, no sect. no. avail., p. 27; NYT, Nov. 21, 1996, sect. 1, p. 42.

41. NYT, March 30, 2002, B2; NYT, April 20, 2002, B1; NYT, April 10, 2003, D1; NYT, April 7, 2003, D7; NYT, April 17, 2003, D7; NYT, Dec. 16, 2003, B1; NYT, May 17, 2004, B1; NYT, Nov. 9, 2004, B3; NYT, June 24, 2003, B1; NYT, Nov. 28, 2002, A1; NYT, Dec. 4, 2005, sect. 1, p. 47; NYT, June 24, 2006, B5.

42. NYT, May 4, 1997, sect. 1, p. 42; NYT, Dec. 16, 1989, A1, A30; NYT, Feb. 10, 1990, no sect. or page no. avail; NYT, Nov. 7, 1990, B7; NYT, Aug. 9, 1993, B6; NYT, Feb. 11, 1992, B1, B4.

43. NYT, Nov. 24, 1991, "Real Estate" sect., no sect. or page no. avail.; NYT, April 2, 1993, no sect. or page no. avail. but probably B1; NYT, Nov. 25, 1993, B6.

44. NYT, April 20, 1994, B7; NYT, June 2, 1994, B6; NYT, June 22, 1994, B5; NYT, June 30, 1994, B7; NYT, July 15, 1994, B1, B4; NYT, Aug. 3, 1994, B4.

45. NYT, Aug. 3, 1996, A22; NYT, Oct. 14, 1999, B5; NYT, Oct. 27, 2000, B5; NYT, Nov. 4, 2000, B6.

46. NYT, Feb. 20, 1997, B1; NYT, April 1, 1998, B5.

47. NYT, Jan. 23, 1990, B6; NYT, March 9, 1990, B1; NYT, April, no day no. avail., 1990, B2; NYT, Sept. 24, 1990, B4; NYT, Sept. 27, 1990, B5; NYT, Nov. 14, 1990, B2; NYT, Nov. 22, 1990, B6; NYT, Dec. 3, 1990, B1.

48. NYT, March 28, 1991, B1; NYT, June 20, 1991, B2; NYT, July 1, 1991, B4; NYT, July 16, 1991, B5; NYT, Oct. 20, 1991, A22; NYT, Dec. 6, 1991, B7; NYT, Nov. 15, 1991, B5; NYT, Dec. 2, 1991, B5; NYT, Dec. 28, 1991, B5; NYT, Jan. 11, 1992, A1.

49. NYT, Feb. 4, 1992, B4; NYT, Feb. 14, 1992, B7; NYT, Feb. 14, 1992, B7; NYT, June 28, 1992, sect. 1, p. 23; NYT, July 21, 1992, B5; NYT, Aug. 4, 1992, A1; NYT, Aug. 5, 1992, B1; NYT, Dec. 1, 1992, B6; NYT, Feb. 26, 1993, A1; NYT, Sept. 28, 1993, B6; NYT, May 25, 1993, B4; NYT, Oct. 18, 1993, B7; NYT, Dec. 5, 1993, sect. 1, p. 56; NYT, Jan. 10, 1994, B3; NYT, Jan. 11, 1994, B4.

50. NYT, Jan. 28, 1994, B1; NYT, Jan. 30, 1994, sect. 1, p. 29; NYT, March 4, 1994, B5; NYT, March 15, 1994, B4; NYT, March 29, 1994, B4; NYT, May 19, 1994, B1; NYT, June 22, 1994, B6; NYT, Aug. 6, 1994, A24; NYT, Aug. 30, 1994, B1.

51. NYT, June 27, 1995, B5; NYT, Oct. 10, 1995, B4; NYT, Dec. 5, 1995, B5; NYT, May 9, 1996, B6; NYT, Feb. 21, 1997, A1; NYT, April 4, 1997, B4; NYT, May 9, 1997, B8; NYT, June 20, 1997, B6; NYT, June 28, 1997, A26; NYT, June 24, 1997, B4; NYT, Aug. 12, 1997, B5; NYT, Nov. 7, 1997, B1; NYT, Dec. 10, 1997, B1; NYT, Dec. 16, 1997, A1.

52. NYT, Jan. 19, 1998, B4; NYT, Jan. 14, 1998, B4; NYT, April 28, 1998, B1; NYT, May 19, 1998, B5; NYT, June 23, 1998, B6; NYT, Sept. 6, 1999,

A12; NYT, April 26, 2000, B6; NYT, April 15, 2000, B5; NYT, June 6, 2000, B6; NYT, July 17, 2000, A1.

53. NYT, Feb. 1, 2000, B5; CBS radio, Jan. 31, 2001.

54. NYT, March 29, 2002, B5; NYT, Feb. 6, 2003, B5; NYT, June 20, 2003, B4; NYT, July 1, 2003, A12; NYT, March 15, 2003, B5; NYT, June 10, 2003, B5; NYT, June 22, 2004, B5; CSM, July 6, 2004, p. 2.

55. CSM, June 21, 2005, no page no. avail.; NYT, Nov. 9, 2005, B11.

56. NYT, Jan. 18, 2006, B1; NYT, March 22, 2005, B6; NYT, March 21, 2006, B5; NYT, July 2, 2006, sect. 1, p. 1; NYT, July 4, 2006, B1; NYT, July 9, 2006, sect. 1, pp. 1, 22; NYT, Nov. 16, 2006, B1; NYT, Dec. 19, 2006, B5; NJN News, Jan. 21, 2007.

57. NYT, Jan. 10, 1991, B1; NYT, Jan. 11, 1991, B2; NYT, Jan. 7, 1991, A36; NYT, May 16, 1991, A1; NYT, May 19, 1991, sect. 4, no page no. avail.; NYT, May 23, 1991, B6; NYT, May 31, 1991, A1; NYT, June 1, 1991, A25; NYT, July 3, 1991, B4; NYT, July 10, 1991, B2.

58. NYT, Aug. 5, 1991, B4; NYT, Aug. 8, 1991, B4; NYT, Aug. 10, 1991, A22; NYT, Aug. 23, 1991, A1; NYT, Aug. 24, 1991, A27; NYT, Dec. 14, 1991, A1.

59. NYT, Feb. 6, 1992, B6; NYT, Feb. 4, 1993, B7; TM, April 13, 1992, p. 16; NYT, Sept. 29, 1994, B6.

60. NYT, Jan. 15, 2004, B7; NYT, June 19, 2004, B1, B7; NYT, June 22, 2004, B8.

61. TM, Sept. 3, 1990, p. 52; NWM, Oct. 22, 1990, p. 60; NYT, Sept. 24, 1990, A16; WP, Oct. 28, 1990, A4; NYT, Oct. 9, 1992, A18; NYT, May 16, 1994, A12; NYT, Sept. 25, 1994, sect. 1, p. 24; NYT, Nov. 11, 1994, sect. B, no page no. avail.; NYT, Feb. 6, 1996, A14; CSM, May 30, 1996, p. 3; NYT, Aug. 4, 1996, sect. 1, p. 17; CSM, Sept. 19, 1996, p. 3; NYT, Oct. 3, 1996, B9; TM, Nov. 4, 1996, p. 72; NYT, Nov. 28, 1996, A1; TM, Dec. 9, 1996, p. 94; NYT, April 9, 1997, A1; NYT, Aug. 29, 1997, A16; CSM, April 14, 1998, p. 4; NYTBR, May 3, 1998, p. 7, a review of *Paradise Lost* by Peter Schrog; CSM, Aug. 25, 1999, p. 1.

62. NYT, Nov. 18, 1990, E1; NYT, April 3, 1991, A12; NYT, Dec. 1, 1995, A22; NYT, Sept. 30, 1990, sect. 1, p. 28; NYT, July 9, 1995, sect. 1, p. 22; *Governing*, Aug. 1991, p. 65; NYT, Feb. 16, 1995, A27, OP-ED; NYT, Nov. 11, 1990, A26; NYT, Feb. 23, 1991, A9; NYT, Oct. 11, 1991, A19.

63. NYT, Feb. 25, 2000, A12; WPNWE, Aug. 18–24, 2003, p. 20; NYT, Sept. 28, 2003, sect. 4, p. 4; NYT, Oct. 24, 2004, sect. 1, p. 20; NYT, June 15, 2003, sect. 4, p. 6.

64. NYT, Aug. 31, 2002, A9; NYT, Sept. 26, 2002, A25; CSM, Aug. 12, 2003, p. 4; CSM, Sept. 19, 2003, p. 2; WPNWE, Oct. 13–19, 2003, p. 12.

65. TM, Dec. 23, 1991, p. 40; NYT, Sept. 3, 1992, B10; Calif. Gov. Pete Wilson's inaugural speech at start of his second term, Jan. 7, 1995; NYT, Dec. 13, 2003, A12; NYT, Jan. 6, 2005, A16; NYT, June 4, 2005, A12.

66. NYT, Dec. 20, 1994, A16; NYT, March 23, 1995, A1; CSM, April 1, 1998, p. 3; CSM, July 12, 1999, p. 3; NYT, July 20, 1999, A13; NYT, Sept. 29, 1999, A1; NYT, Oct. 4, 1999, A18; NYT, Oct. 12, 1999, A1–; NYT, Feb. 2,

2000, A13; WPNWE, Sept. 10–16, 2001, p. 6; NYT, Oct. 27, 2001, A8; NYT, Nov. 4, 2001, A29; NYT, July 2, 2002, A14; WPNWE, July 23–Aug. 4, 2002, p. 29; CSM, Sept. 30, 2002, pp. 1–2; CSM, Sept. 13, 2002, p. 2; NYT, April 29, 2003, A27; NYT, Sept. 26, 2004, A1; NYT, Sept. 7, 2005, A14.

67. NYT, Aug. 11, 1991, sect. 1, p. 16; *State Legislatures*, July 1992, p. 27; NYT, April 4, 1993, p. 1; NYT, April 8, 1999, A22.

68. USNWR, Nov. 22, 1999, p. 31; NYT, Nov. 14, 1999, sect. 4, p. 4; NYT, Aug. 30, 2000, A18.

69. TM, April 29, 1991, p. 32; NYT, May 29, 1991, A17; NYT, July 19, 1991, A10; NYT, Dec. 4, 1992, A26; NYT, Feb. 16, 1993, A12.

70. NYT, Feb. 14, 1995, A16; CSM, Feb. 24, 2000, p. 4; TM, Feb. 21, 2000, pp. 28–33; NYT, April 24, 2001, A14.

71. NYT, Feb. 13, 2005, no sect. or page no. avail.

72. NYT, Nov. 8, 1992, sect. 1, p. 24; NYT, July 17, 2005, sect. 1, p. 14; NYT, July 23, 1996, A10.

73. NYT, Feb. 26, 1990, A17; N.Y. Congressman Bill Green's report to constituents, 1990; NYT, May 17, 1990, A24; WP, July 24, 1990, A14; NYT, Sept. 28, 1990, A14; NYT, Oct. 11, 1990, A1, A18.

74. NYT, Jan. 31, 1991, A17; NYT, Feb. 8, 1991, A18; NYT, Feb. 21, 1991, B7; NYT, Feb. 22, 1991, A18; NYT, Feb. 28, 1991, sect. A, no page no. avail; NYT, July 24, 1993, A26.

75. NYT, Aug. 8, 1993, sect. 4, p. 5; NYT, Nov. 8, 1993, A17; NYT, Nov. 8, 1993, A16; NYT, Nov. 15, 1993, A1, B8.

76. NYT, Jan. 19, 1997, sect. 1, p. 12; NYT, March 6, 1998, A18; NYT, Dec. 14, 1998, A18.

77. NYT, Feb. 12, 1995, sect. 1, pp. 1, 30; TM, April 29, 1996, p. 50; NYT, Jan. 25, 1996, B6; NYT, Dec. 29, 1996, sect. 1, p. 18; NYT, Jan. 15, 1997, A16; NYT, Aug. 18, 1997, A1; NYT, Aug. 21, 1997, A31; NYT, Nov. 27, 1997, A26; NYT, Nov. 11, 1998, A1, A24; NYT, Feb. 22, 1999, A13.

78. WPNWE, May 8, 2000, p. 23; NYT, July 14, 2000, A12; NYT, Sept. 26, 2001, A12; NYT, Sept. 27, 2003, A15; NYT, Feb. 11, 2004, A20.

79. WP, March 25, 1990, A3; NYT, Jan. 16, 1991, A16; *State Legislatures*, March 1992, p. 18; *State Legislatures*, March 1992, p. 15; NYT, Nov. 25, 1992, A15; NYT, June 17, 1993, A26; NYT, Feb. 11, 1996, sect. 4, p. 6; NYT, March 9, 1998, A1; CSM, June 5, 1998, p. 4; CSM, Dec. 2, 1998, p. 2.

80. NYT, Jan. 14, 2000, A16; NYT, Dec. 24, 2000, sect. 1, p. 14; CSM, June 4, 2002, p. 3; Lehrer Newshour, PBS, Sept. 19, 2003.

Notes to Chapter VII
Sectors of American Life
and Society

1. WP, April 21, 1991, A15; NYT, April 22, 1991, no page no. avail.; TM, May 27, 1991, p. 62; NYT, July 9, 1991, D6; NYT, July 29, 1991, A1; NYT, Aug. 18, 1991, sect. 1, no page no. avail.; NYT, Sept. 24, 1991, D1; WP, Dec. 8, 1991, A22; NYT, Dec. 12, 1991, D4; NYT, May 17, 1992, sect. 1, p. 1; NYT, May 22, 1992, A1; NYT, May 23, 1992, sect. 4, p. 6; Malcolm S. Forbes, Jr., on McNeil–Lehrer Newshour, Nov. 20, 1992.

2. NYT, Nov. 28, 1993, sect. 3, p. 4; NYT, Feb. 15, 1994, D1; NYT, March 10, 1994, A1; NYT, April 9, 1995, sect. 1, p. 1; NYT, Sept. 19, 1995, A14; NYT, Jan. 2, 1996, C1; NYT, Feb. 3, 1996, A1; NYT, Sept. 8, 1996, sect. 1, p. 31; NYT, Oct. 2, 1996, D4; NYT, Oct. 15, 1996, A1.

3. NYT, Oct. 1, 1998, C3; NYT, Dec. 13, 1998, sect. 1, p. 38; NYT, Jan. 3, 1999, p. 1; TM, March 22, 1999, p. 58; USNWR, April 19, 1999, p. 55; NYT, May 7, 1999, C1; NYT, July 1, 1999, C1; NYT, Nov. 5, 1999, C5; NYT, Oct. 25, 1999, C1; NYT, Feb. 29, 2000, A1, C10; NYT, April 2, 2000, sect. 1, p. 25; CSM, April 5, 2000, p. 1.

4. WPNWE, Nov. 20, 2000, p. 6; NYT, Feb. 4, 2000, sect. 4, p. 17; NYT, March 11, 2001, sect. 4, p. 15.

5. NYT, Feb. 4, 2001, sect. 4, p. 6; WPNWE, March 12–18, 2001, p. 13; WPNWE, March 19–25, 2001, p. 10; NYT, July 13, 2001, A18; NYT, Nov. 27, 2001, C1; NYT, Sept. 23, 2001, sect. 1, p. 1.

6. NYT, July 14, 2001, C1; NYT, June 8, 2006, C18; NYT, Feb. 10, 2002, sect. 3, p. 1; WPNWE, Nov. 11–17, 2002, p. 20; NYT, July 13, 2006, C1; NYT, July 25, 2002, A1; NYT, March 13, 2007, C1, C8.

7. NYT, Nov. 10, 2001, C1; CSM, Jan. 15, 2002, p. 1; NYT, Jan. 20, 2002, sect. 1, p. 26; NYT, Jan. 23, 2002, A19; CSM, Jan. 22, 2002, p. 41; WPNWE, Jan. 21–27, 2002, p. 19; NYT, Feb. 9, 2002, C5; NYT, Feb. 10, 2002, sect. 1, p. 33; NYT, Feb. 14, 2002, A1; NYT, Feb. 17, 2002, p. 32; NYT, June 10, 2002, A1, A16; NYT, July 31, 2002, C5.

8. NYTM, Sept. 1, 1991, p. 12; TM, April 26, 1993, p. 53; NYT, July 11, 1993, sect. 3, p. 7; NYT, Jan. 9, 1994, sect. 1, p. 1; NYT, May 12, 1994, D2; NYT, Dec. 15, 1994, A1; NYT, Feb. 22, 1995, A1; NYT, Nov. 5, 1995, sect. 4, p. 5; NYT, Nov. 19, 1995, sect. 1, p. 4; NYT, Nov. 26, 1995, sect. 1, p. 16; NYT, Feb. 21, 1996, A11; NYT, Feb. 25, 1996, sect. 1, p. 26; TM, July 29, 1996, p. 42; CSM, Aug. 30, 1996, no page no. avail.; NYT, Oct. 10, 1996, B13; CSM, Dec. 16, 1996, p. 3; NYT, Feb. 14, 1997, A16; TM, March 31, 1997, cover story; NYT, May 19, 1998, A1; USNWR, Sept. 13, 1999, p. 10.

9. NYT, March 9, 2000, B9; NYT, Aug. 25, 2000, A13, OP-ED; NYT, Sept. 4, 2000, A10; NYT, Sept. 9, 2000, C4; NYT, Sept. 26, 2000, A19; NYT, Jan. 24, 2001, A17; NYT, Feb. 18, 2001, sect. 1, no page no. avail.; WPNWE, Oct. 22–28, 2001, p. 11; NYT, Nov. 1, 2001, A27, OP-ED; NYT, Nov. 16, 2001, A1, B9; USNWR, Jan. 12, 2004, p. 24; NYT, Feb. 2, 2005, A18; NYT, Jan. 23, 2005, sect. 3, pp. 1, 4; NYT, May 18, 2005, A14; NYT, Aug. 24, 2005, C1; NYT, Sept. 26, 2006, A14.

10. NYT, May 6, 1991, A9; NYT, Aug. 22, 1993, sect. 3, p. 11; NYT, Aug. 25, 1993, A1; NYT, Oct. 14, 1993, A1, A10; NYT, Dec. 20, 1993, A1; NYT, Jan. 13, 1994, A11; NYT, June 13, 1995, B4; NYT, Aug. 5, 1995, A1; NYT, Aug. 17, 1995, D3; NYT, Dec. 16, 1995, no sect. no. avail., p. 39; NYT, Feb. 2, 1996, A1; NYT, Feb. 8, 1996, A16; TM, Feb. 12, 1996, p. 52; NYT, April 14, 1997, D1; NYT, April 1, 1997, A1; NYT, no other info. but in sequence; NYT, Dec. 18, 1999, C1.

11. CSM, March 20, 2001, editorial; NYT, Oct. 19, 2001, A16; NYT, Sept. 7, 2002, B10; CSM, Sept. 12, 2003, p. 1; NYT, Feb. 1, 2005, C8; NYT, May 14, 2006, sect. 1, p. 20; CSM, June 20, 2006, p. 1.

12. NYT, March 31, 1994, A1; NYT, June 13, 1994, A15, editorial; TM, Aug. 29, 1994, p. 60; NYT, Feb. 22, 2005, D19; TM, June 12, 1995, p. 63; TM, July 3, 1995, cover story; NYT, Dec. 2, 1995, A1; TM, March 4, 1996, cover story and p. 4; NYT, April 6, 1996, sect. 1 (?), p. 23; NYT, March 7, 1997, A35; NYT, March 14, 1997, B2; NYT, March 20, 1998, B1; TM, Nov. 8, 1999, p. 58; TM, Nov. 22, 1999, p. 65.

13. CSM, May 12, 2000, pp. 1, 4; NYT, June 5, 2000, A14; NYT, Feb. 12, 2003, A32; CSM, Feb. 12, 2003, p. 2; USNWR, July 21, 2003, p. 48; NYT, Nov. 23, 2003, sect. 4, p. 3; NYT, Nov. 22, 2003, A12.

14. TM, Aug. 7, 1995, pp. 61–63; TM, Nov. 21, 1994, pp. 102–103; NYT, Feb. 20, 1996, A1.

15. NYT, Jan. 22, 1995, sect. 3, p. 1; NYT, July 7, 1995, A1; NYT, March 17, 2005, D1, D7; NYT, April 28, 2005, D1; TM, March 28, 2005, p. 22.

16. NYT, May 24, 1991, B4; NYT, May 5, 1991, sect. 1, p. 1; NYT, May 27, 1994, B3; TM, July 15, 1991, p. 62.

17. USNWR, April 1, 1996, no page no. avail.; NYT, April 18, 1996, sect. 4, p. 7; NYT, Feb. 6, 1997, sect. B, no page no. avail.; WSJ, April 2, 1991, A14; NYT, Sept. 4, 1997, A18; TM, June 14, 1999, p. 52.

18. NYT, Jan. 18, 1999, A1; CSM, Jan. 21, 1999, p. 9; NYT, Jan. 26, 1999, A10; NYT, March 3, 1999, A15; NYT, March 4, 1999, A18; NYT, March 12, 1999, A1; NYT, Nov. 29, 1998, sect. 1, p. 42.

19. NYT, March 31, 2000, A22; NYT, Aug. 30, 2000, A1–; CSM, April 26, 2001, p. 1.

20. NYT, May 3, 2001, A12; NYT, May 18, 2001, A19, OP-ED; NYT, July 13, 2001, A10; NYT, Dec. 4, 2001, A20; NYT, Dec. 12, 2001, A1; NYT, Dec. 18, 2001, sect. 1 (?), p. 4; NYT, Feb. 16, 2003, p. 33.

21. NYT, Jan. 2, 2004, A1; NYT, Feb. 22, 2004, sect. 1, p. 1; NYT, March 14, 2004, sect. 1, p. 1; NYT, April 21, 2005, A19; NYT, Nov. 7, 2005, A23, OP-ED; NYT, Oct. 20, 2005, no page no. avail.; NYT, March 26, 2006, sect. 1, p. 22; NYT, March 9, 2007, A6.

22. TM, Nov. 11, 1991, cover story and p. 34; WP, May 30, 1993, H4; NYT, April 3, 1993, A21; NYT, Oct. 13, 1994, C2; NYT, Dec. 25, 1994, sect. 4, p. 3; NYT, June 5, 1995, B5.

23. TM, Aug. 25, 1997, p. 28; NYT, Sept. 1998, p. 15, no day or sect. no. avail.; NYTM, April 30, 2000, cover story and p. 46; TM, July 2, 2001, cover story and p. 45; CSM, Aug. 2000, p. 1, no day no. avail.

24. NYT, Oct. 7, 2001, sect. 4, p. 3; WPNWE, March 4–10, 2002, p. 6; WPNWE, June 10–16, 2002, p. 6; CSM, Nov. 21, 2002, p. 1; NYT, Dec. 19, 2002, A18; NYT, Dec. 10, 2002, A24; CSM, June 16, 2003, p. 19; WPNWE, April 18–24, 2005, p. 18; NYT, July 22, 2005, sect. A, no page no. avail.; WPNWE, May 22–28, 2006, p. 23; WPNWE, Jan. 16–22, 2006, p. 29; CSM, June 24, 2005, p. 1.

25. A substantial detailed study of *Intimate Matters: A History of Sexuality in America* by John D'Emilio and Estelle B. Freedman (New York, 1988)—one of many such books once used by this writer in teaching various courses on the history of sexuality in America and Europe—covers from the late-18th through late-20th centuries. Included frequently throughout are informative discussions of significant legislation/regulatory acts on the subject throughout American history.

26. NYT, March 11, 1992, B8; NYT, Nov. 3, 1992, A8; TM, March 16, 1992, p. 48; WP, Nov. 22, 1992, A26; NYT, Nov. 23, 1992, A10; NYT, Dec. 14, 1992, A15; WP, Jan. 3, 1993, A1; NYT, July 28, 1993, B5; NYT, Aug. 8, 1993, sect. 1, p. 30; NYT, Nov. 3, 1993, A1, B13.

27. NYT, June 26, 1995, A13; NYT, July 24, 1995, A9; NYT, March 15, 1997, A8; TM, March 23, 1998, cover story and pp. 48–49; NYT, March 23, 1998, A20; NYT, March 19, 1998, A21; NYT, June 27, 1998, A1, A10; USNWR, July 6, 1998, cover story and pp. 30–31.

28. NYT, Nov. 30, 1991, A36; NYT, Feb. 27, 1992, A1, A6; CSM, May 13, 1997, p. 12; CSM, Sept. 10, 1999, p. 11; NYT, July 2, 2002, A14.

29. NYT, May 27, 1991, A6; NYT, July 31, 1992, B5; NYT, July 25, 1992, A9; NYT, June 11, 1993, A17; NYT, June 11, 1995, sect. 1, p. 6; NYT, July 30, 1995, sect. 1, p. 22; NYT, July 31, 1995, A13; NYT, May 8, 1996, A1; NYT, May 18, 1996, A8; NYT, June 23, 1996, sect. 1, p. 17; CSM, Sept. 5, 1996, p. 4; CSM, Sept. 5, 1996, p. 9; CSM, Sept. 5, 1996, p. 10; NYT, Dec. 11, 1996, p. 24; NYT, Feb. 24, 1998, B6; CSM, Aug. 13, 1998, p. 3; USNWR, March 9, 1998, p. 27; NYT, Oct. 31, 1998, A8; NYT, Jan. 31, 1999, sect. 1, p. 20; NYT, Sept. 25, 1998, B4.

30. NYT, April 22, 2001, sect. 1, p. 22; NYT, April 23, 2002, A20; NYT, May 21, 2002, A14; NYT, March 27, 2003, A18; USNWR, Oct. 13, 2003, p. 45; CSM, March 25, 2004, p. 12.

31. NYTBR, March 29, 1992, p. 1–; NYT, March 15, 1992, sect. 1, p. 16.

32. TM, March 30, 1992, p. 52; NYT, March 26, 1995, sect. 1, p. 34; NYT, Dec. 29, 1995, A1; NYT, Oct. 15, 1995, sect. 4, p. 15.

33. NYT, Feb. 16, 1996, D1; NYT, May 12, 1996, sect. 1, p. 12; NYT, June 29, 1996, A1, A8; NYT, July 30, 1996, A11; CSM, Dec. 6, 1996, p. 10; NYT, March 20, 1997, B10; NYT, June 9, 1997, A25, OP-ED; NYT, Oct. 17, 1997, A35, OP-ED by Robert Bork; TM, Oct. 5, 1998, p. 40; CSM, Dec. 23, 1998, p. 1.

34. This subsection is intended as a bridge between our sectional topics on sexuality and ethnicity.

35. NYT, Aug. 11, 1991, sect. 1, p. 16; NYT, Nov. 2, 1995, A1; NYT, Sept. 20, 1996, A22; NYT, Sept. 24, 1996, A18; NYT, Sept. 27, 1996, A20; NYT, March 10, 1997, B3; NYT, March 21, 1997, A1, A24; NYT, Oct. 2, 1999, A1; NYT, Oct. 22, 1999, A20; NYT, March 11, 2003, A16; NYT, Oct. 2, 2005, sect. 4, p. 14; "Washington Week," PBS, Nov. 4, 2005.

36. NYT, April 26, 1993, A1, B8; NYT, May 21, 1996, A1, A21; NYT, May 23, 1996, A1; CSM, May 21, 1996, p. 3; NYT, no other info. avail., but in sequence; USNWR, June 3, 1996, p. 28; NYT, Sept. 6, 1996, A24; NYT, Sept. 11, 1996, A16; NYT, Sept. 21, 1996, A8; NYT, April 17, 1998, A20; CSM, Oct. 14, 1998, p. 3; NYT, March 23, 1999, B1; NYT, April 27, 2000, A27, OP-ED; NYT, Sept. 14, 2000, A20; NYT, Jan. 26, 2001, A19, OP-ED; CSM, June 27, 2003, p. 1; WPNWE, Feb. 23–29, 2004, p. 21, a commentary; NYT, March 30, 2004, B1; NYT, June 15, 2004, A1; CBS radio news, Feb. 19, 2007.

37. NYT, Nov. 17, 1996, sect. 4, p. 1; NYT, Nov. 17, 1996, sect. 4, p. 13, OP-ED; NYT, July 28, 1998, sect. A, no page no. avail.

38. NYT, Dec. 27, 1995, A1; NYT, Jan. 7, 1996, sect. 1, p. 18; NYT, Oct. 12, 1996, A1, A28.

39. NYT, Jan. 8, 1992, A12; TM, July 8, 1991, p. 12; TM, Feb. 3, 1992, p. 44; NYT, Oct. 16, 1995, A15; NYT, Oct. 25, 1995, A1; TM, June 16, 1997, p. 46; NYT, July 6, 1999, A16; NYT, July 11, 1999, sect. 1, p. 23; NYT, Sept. 10, 2006, sect. 1, p. 1.

40. NYT, Aug. 5, 1991, A13; TM, Feb. 20, 1995, p. 39; NYT, March 1, 1995, A19; NYT, March 15, 1995, A1; NYT, March 16, 1995, A1; USNWR, March 20, 1995, p. 112; NYT, July 6, 1995, A1–; NYT, July 19, 1995, A1; NYT, July 21, 1995, A1; NYT, July 20, 1995, A1.

41. NYT, March 22, 1996, A22, editorial; TM, April 1, 1996, no page no. avail. (and also e.g., NYT, March 31, 1996, sect. 1, p. 30; and NYTBR, April

14, 1996, p. 10, on three books pro and con affirmative action); NYT, Oct. 29, 1996, A1; NYT, June 15, 1997, sect. 1, p. 15, OP-ED; NYT, June 15, 1997, sect. 1, p. 1 (and also TM, June 23, 1997, p. 33); CSM, Dec. 1, 1999, p. 1.

42. NYT, April 15, 2001, A11; NYT, Aug. 28, 2001, A1, A12; NYT, Jan. 26, 2007, A15.

43. NYT, April 10, 1994, sect. 1, p. 1; NYTBR, June 18, 1995, p. 7; NYTBR, Sept. 24, 1995, p. 9; NYT, Sept. 26, 1995, B6; TM, April 29, 1996, cover story and p. 39; NYT, April 2, 2000, p. 5.

44. NYT, May 27, 1995, A8; NYT, Aug. 6, 1995, sect. 1, p. 24; NYT, Sept. 20, 1995, A1, B9; NYT, Sept. 24, 1995, sect. 4, p. 1; NYT, March 10, 1996, sect. 1, p. 20; USNWR, June 3, 1996, p. 32; NYT, Aug. 1, 1996, A22, A25; NYT, Aug. 2, 1996, A1; NYT, Aug. 23, 1996, A22; NYT, Dec. 30, 1997, A1, A16; NYT, April 15, 1998, B4; CSM, Dec. 1, 1998, p. 5; TM, Aug. 16, 1999, p. 24.

45. NYT, Oct. 1, 1994, A8; TM, Nov. 28, 1994, p. 35; NYT, Dec. 4, 1994, sect. 1, p. 1; NYT, Sept. 9, 1995, p. 25, no sect. no. avail.; NYT, Oct. 20, 1995, B5; NYT, Oct. 21, 1995, A1; NYT, Feb. 26, 1996, A9; NYT, March 14, 1996, B12; NYT, March 21, 1996, B25; USNWR, April 29, 1996, p. 28; NYT, May 3, 1996, A1; NYT, May 28, 1996, A1; NYT, Aug. 2, 1996, A12; NYT, Sept. 25, 1996, A1.

46. NYT, Oct. 22, 1996, A20; NYT, Feb. 23, 1997, sect. 1, p. 18; NYT, June 7, 1997, A9; NYT, Oct. 20, 1997, A14; NYT, Nov. 14, 1997, A30; USNWR, Dec. 7, 1998, p. 30; NYT, Dec. 15, 1998, A1; NYT, Dec. 21, 1999, A1; NYT, Sept. 23, 2000, A17; NYT, Feb. 20, 2001, B6.

47. NYT, Oct. 1, 2001, A23, OP-ED; CSM, Oct. 22, 2001, p. 2; NYT, June 25, 2003, A14; NYT, July 12, 2003, A8; NYT, Dec. 23, 2003, A27, OP-ED; NYT, Jan. 7, 2004, A1; USNWR, Jan. 19, 2004, p. 33; NYT, March 28, 2006, A1; NYT, April 7, 2006, A1; WPNWE, Nov. 27–Dec. 3, 2006, p. 12; NYT, Dec. 26, 2006, A1, A29; NYT, May 10, 2006, A19.

48. TM, Nov. 14, 1994, p. 63; TM, Feb. 20, 1995, p. 47; NYT, March 12, 1995, sect. 1, p. 23; TM, March 27, 1995, p. 26; NYT, July 6, 1995, A14; NYT, Dec. 10, 1995, sect. 1, p. 30; NYT, June 15, 1995, B10; NYT, Oct. 3, 1995, A1; NYT, Aug. 13, 1995, sect. 1, p. 1–; NYT, Aug. 10, 1995, A14.

49. TM, June 15, 1996, p. 48; NYT, March 14, 1996, A1; NYT, March 23, 1996, sect. 1, p. 10; CSM, April 8, 1996, p. 1; NYT, April 25, 1996, A18; CSM, March 18, 1996, p. 1; USNWR, April 29, 1996, p. 58; NYT, June 3, 1996, A1; NYT, July 7, 1996, sect. 4, p. 4; NYT, July 29, 1996, B7; NYT, Aug. 2, 1996, A27; NYT, Aug. 2, 1996, A27 (same as previous); NYT, Aug. 11, 1996, sect. 1, p. 23; NYT, Sept. 10, 1996, A1; NYT, Sept. 18, 1996, A14; NYT, Aug. 9, 1996, A1; NYT, Sept. 22, 2006, sect. 1, p. 26; NYT, Aug. 20, 1996, A1; NYT, Dec. 4, 1996, A1–.

50. TM. July 21, 1997, p. 26; CSM, Oct. 31, 1997, p. 3; NYT, April 9, 1997, A14; NYT, Nov. 14, 1998, B6; NYT, Nov. 8, 1998, sect. 1, p. 23; NYT, Oct. 14, 1998, A23; NYT, Oct. 18, 1998, sect. 4, p. 6; CSM, April 9, 1998, p. 12.

51. USNWR, Feb. 8, 1999, p. 26; NYT, March 3, 1999, A10; NYT, April 26, 1999, A17; NYT, May 13, 1999, A28; NYT, May 14, 1999, A1; NYT, May 19, 1999, A18; NYT, May 2, 1999, A1; NYT, May 22, 1999, A10; NYT, June 10, 1999, A29; CSM, June 14, 1999, p. 3; NYT, June 15, 1999, A24; NYT,

June 18, 1999, A1; NYT, June 19, 1999, A11; NYT, Nov. 5, 1999, A28; NYT, Nov. 4, 1999, A29; CSM, Oct. 20, 1999, p. 4; TM, Aug. 9, 1999, p. 28; USNWR, Aug. 30, 1999, p. 30; CSM, Dec. 15, 1999, p. 2.

52. CSM, April 4, 2000, p. 5; NYT, April 11, 2000, A24; CSM, May 22, 2000, p. 3; CSM, May 22, 2000, p. 3 (same as previous).

53. NYT, June 3, 1991, A17; NYT, Nov. 17, 1991, sect. 4, p. 2; NYT, Jan. 10, 1991, A15; NYT, Aug. 21, 1991, A1; NYT, Jan. 12, 1992, sect. 1, p. 18.

54. NYT, Feb. 4, 1992, A21, OP-ED; NYT, Aug. 17, 1993, A17, OP-ED; NYT, April 3, 1994, sect. 1, p. 17; NYT, Aug. 15, 1993, sect. 1, p. 28; NYT, Jan. 13, 1995, B8; NYT, March 10, 1995, A1.

55. NYT, Sept. 15, 1995, A32; NYT, Oct. 11, 1995, A1; NYT, Aug. 4, 1995, A24; NYT, Sept. 22, 1995, A26; NYT, Oct. 12, 1995, A20; NYT, Oct. 20, 1995, A1; NYT, March 29, 1996, B11; NYT, July 30, 1996, B8; NYT, Aug. 29, 1996, sect. A, no page no. avail.; NYT, Sept. 17, 1996, A12; NYT, Dec. 7, 1996, A1; NYT, Dec. 25, 1996, A1.

56. NYT, April 8, 1996, A13; NYT, July 1, 1996, A1; USNWR, Aug. 3, 1996, p. 61; NYT, Aug. 24, 1996, A1; NYT, Oct. 13, 1996, sect. 1, p. 24; NYT, Dec. 23, 1996, A10.

57. NYT, March 10, 1997, A1; NYT, April 2, 1997, A15; NYT, April 20, 1997, sect. 1, p. 1; NYT, May 27, 1997, A1–; USNWR, July 17, 1997, p. 36; NYT, Oct. 10, 1997, A8; NYT, Nov. 20, 1997, A22; NYT, Nov. 24, 1997, A18; NYT, no other info. avail., but in sequence; NYT, Jan. 22, 1998, A18; CSM, March 3, 1998, p. 3; NYT, March 10, 1998, A18, editorial; NYT, March 13, 1998, A17; NYT, June 25, 1998, A20; NYT, July 4, 1998, A9; USNWR, no other info. avail., but in sequence; NYT, Oct. 10, 1998, A1.

58. TM, Feb. 1, 1999, pp. 46–47; NYT, March 12, 1999, sect. A, no page no. avail.; USNWR, March 29, 1999, p. 26; NYT, June 27, 1999, sect. 1, p. 16; CSM, June 30, 1999, A18; TM, July 5, 1999, p. 39; NYT, A1–, no other data avail., but in sequence; NYT, Oct. 8, 1999, A1, A22; CSM, July 9, 1999, p. 11; CSM, Feb. 19 (9?), 2000, p. 2; NYT, July 24, 2000, A12; NYT, Aug. 20, 2000, sect. 1, p. 20; TM, Sept. 18, 2000, p. 29; NYT, Sept. 24, 2000, sect. 4, p. 14.

59. NYT, May 21, 1997, B7; NYT, Oct. 11, 1997, A9; NYT, Jan. 5 (15?), 1997, A10; NYT, Dec. 7, 1997, sect. 1, p. 1; NYT, April 2, 1998, p. 22; USNWR, April 20, 1998, p. 28; NYT, Dec. 10, 1999, A35, OP-ED; WPNWE, Dec. 25–Jan. 1, 2001, p. 34; NYT, July 24, 1998, A21.

60. NYT, Feb. 24, 2001, A18; NYT, June 30, 2001, A1; CSM, June 16, 2003, p. 1; NYT, Sept. 14, 2004, A20; NYT, Sept. 17, 2004, A20; NYT, April 15, 2006, A12, editorial; NYT, Jan. 29, 2006, sect. 1, p. 1; NYT, Jan. 2, 2007, A10.

61. USNWR, Jan. 24, 2001, p. 4 (47?); NYT, Feb. 2001, A1, no other info. on day avail.; NYT, Feb. 27, 2001, A18; NYT, April 19, 2001, A25; NYT, May 11, 2001, A24.

62. NYT, April 6, 2003, A26; WPNWE, June 12–18, 2006, p. 30.

63. WPNWE, July 3, 2001, p. 20; CSM, Aug. 21, 2001, p. 2; NYT, Nov. 13, 2001, F1; NYT, Oct. 24, 2002, A1, A28, A29; NYT, Jan. 23, 2003, A14; CSM, Jan. 13, 2004, p. 2; NYT, April 28, 2005, A22; CSM, May 20, 2005, p. 2; NYT,

Nov. 23, 2005, A22; NYT, Dec. 26, 2006, A26.
  64. NYT, Dec. 19, 1993, sect. 4, p. 5; NYT, Feb. 2, 1994, A1; NYT, Sept. 6, 1994, B5; NYT, March 17, 1995, A20; NYT, April 17, 1995, A12; NYT, May 9, 1995, A23; NYT, May 15, 1995, A12; NYT, May 17, 1995, no page no. avail.; NYT, May 16, 1995, C4; NYT, July 17, 1995, A1; NYT, July 29, 1995, A1; NYT, Feb. 5, 1996, B7; NYT, May 26, 1996, sect. 1, p. 16; NYT, Aug. 7, 1996, A11; NYT, Nov. 28, 1996, A1; NYT, Dec. 1, 1996, sect. 1, pp. 1, 34.
  65. NYT, Dec. 15, 1996, sect. 1, p. 1; NYT, March 16, 1997, sect. 1, p. 28; NYT, May 8, 1997, A19; NYT, May 26, 1997, A22, editorial; CSM, June 12, 1997, p. 1; NYT, June 22, 1997, sect. 1, pp. 1, 16; NYT, June 26, 1997, A1; NYT, March 1, 1998, A1; NYT, March 11, 1999, A20; NYT, May 15, 1999, A11; CSM, May 9, 2000, pp. 1, 5; CSM, Nov. 8, 2000, A20; CSM, Nov. 15, 2000, p. 10.
  66. NYT, Jan. 28, 2001, sect. 1, p. 12; NYT, March 17, 2001, A7; NYT, June 27, 2001, A14; TM, July 10, 2001, p. 26; NYT, Jan. 15, 2002, A16; NYT, Feb. 15, 2002, A6; CSM, Feb. 15, 2002, p. 3; NYT, Sept. 30, 2002, A24; NYT, Oct. 1, 2002, A24; NYT, Feb. 23, 2003, sect. 1, p. 22; NYT, Oct. 29, 2003, A20; NYT, Feb. 6, 2004, sect. A, no page no. avail.; CSM, April 22, 2004, p. 2; NYT, May 2, 2004, A14; NYT, May 14, 2005, A4; WPNWE, Jan. 9, 2006, p. 20; CSM, Dec. 1, 2006, p. 2.
  67. CSM, May 6, 1999, p. 2; USNWR, July 19, 1999, p. 18; NYT, Sept. 6, 1999, A12; NYT, Nov. 17, 1999, A25, OP-ED.
  68. WPNWE, June 19, 2000, p. 21; NYT, Sept. 17, 2000, sect. 1, p. 22; NYT, Nov. 3, 2000, A25.
  69. WPNWE, March 12–18, 2001, no page no. avail.; WPNWE, Nov. 4–10, 2002, p. 6; NYT, Dec. 25, 2002, A18; NYT, Dec. 8, 2002, sect. 4, p. 4; WPNWE, Jan. 20–26, 2003, p. 1; NYT, July 23, 2004, A1, A13; NYT, June 24, 2005, A1; NYT, Sept. 11, 2005, sect. 1, pp. 1, 28; NYT, Sept. 2, 2005, A1; NYT, Dec. 16, 2005, A37; CSM, Dec. 14, 2005, p. 5; NYT, Aug. 18, 2006, A15; NYT, Jan. 6, 2007, A1.
  70. NYT, Dec. 12, 1993, sect. 1, p. 50; NYT, March 8, 1995, A1, A17; NYT, March 11, 1995, A1, A7; NYT, March 20, 1995, p. 38; NYT, May 6, 1995, A18; NYT, May 11, 1995, B10; NYTBR, July 16, 1995, p. 5, by Richard A. Epstein; NYT, Sept. 11, 1995, A1; NYT, Oct. 6, 1995, A18; TM, Jan. 8, 1996, no page no. avail.; NYT, March 7, 1996, A1, B16; NYT, March 21, 1996, A22; NYT, Oct. 16, 1996, A33, OP-ED; NYT, June 22, 1997, sect. 1, p. 14; CSM, June 17, 1997, p. 2; NYT, July 28, 1999, A1; NYT, Aug. 5, 1999, A16.
  71. NYT, March 26, 2000, sect. 4, p. 3; NYT, Aug. 4, 2002, sect. 1, p. 20; NYT, Sept. 21, 2002, A15, OP-ED.
  72. CSM, Aug. 2, 2001, p. 2; NYT, Nov. 13, 2001, B6; USNWR, Jan. 7, 2002, p. 19; NYT, Oct. 26, 2002, A13; NYT, May 9, 2003, A1–; WPNWE, Sept. 20–26, 2004, p. 30; NYT, April 24, 2005, sect. 1, p. 35; WPNWE, Sept. 15–21, 2003, p. 17; NYT, Sept. 28, 2003, pp. 1, 36; NYT, Feb. 6, 2004, A27; NYT, Feb. 11, 2005, A13.
  73. TM, Aug. 25, 1997, p. 46; TM, Sept. 13, 1999, p. 33; CSM, Oct. 31, 2005, p. 2; NYT, Oct. 8, 2006, sect. 1, pp. 1, 26.

74. NYT, May 18, 2001, A20; NYT, May 19, 2007, A11; NYT, May 22, 2007, A1, A19; CSM, May 21, 2007, p. 10; CSM, May 25, 2007, pp. 1, 3; NYT June 3, 2007, sect. 1, p. 1; NYT, June 8, 2007, A1; NYT, June 9, 2007, A12; NYT, June 10, 2007, Sect. 1, p. 35; CSM, June 15, 2007, pp. 1, 4; NYT, June 29, 2007, A1; CSM, June 29, 2007, p. 1; NYT, July 1, 2007, sect. 4, pp. 1, 5.

75. NYT, Sept. 13, 2007, C1; NYT, Sept. 16, 2007, sect. 4, p. 9, editorial.

Notes to Chapter VIII
U.S. Foreign Policy
Under Clinton

1. WP, Oct. 27, 1991, A20; WP, Dec. 8, 1991, A41; NYT, Jan. 1, 1992, A48; NYT, Feb. 7, 1992, A1; NYT, Feb. 5, 1992, A23; NYT, March 8, 1992, sect. 1, p. 14; NYT, March 9, 1992, A17, editorial; NYT, March 11, 1992, A6; TM, March 16, 1992, p. 74; NYT, March 10, 1992, A1.

2. WP, April 12, 1992, C4; NYT, July 23, 1992, A1; NYT, Aug. 2, 1992, sect. 4, p. 11, editorial; TM, July 20, 1992, no page no. avail.; NYT, Aug. 20, 1992, A27, OP-ED; NYT, Dec. 9, 1992, A23, OP-ED.

3. NYT, Dec. 30, 1992, A1, A6; NYT, Jan. 4, 1993, A1, A8, A9.

4. NYT, Feb. 7, 1993, sect. 1, pp. 1, 14; NYT, March 18, 1993, A23; NYT, March 23, 1993, A23, OP-ED; TM, Oct. 11, 1993, p. 41, commentary; NYT, Sept. 22, 1993, A13; NYT, May 28, 1994, A5.

5. NYT, Nov. 10, 1994, A17; NYT, Feb. 13, 1995, A19, OP-ED; NYT, March 5, 1995, sect. 4, p. 15, editorial by Thomas Friedman.

6. NYT, April 30, 1995, sect. 4, p. 4; NYT, March 10, 1995, A5; NYT, March 30, 1995, sect. 4, p. 3; NYT, March 19, 1995, sect. 4, p. 3; NYT, May 25, 1995, A28, editorial; NYT, June 6, 1995, A25, OP-ED by Sen. Bob Dole; NYT, June 11, 1995, sect. 4, p. 15, OP-ED by Arthur Schlesinger.

7. NYT, Sept. 24, 1995, sect. 1, p. 14; NYT, Sept. 20, 1996, B3; NYT, Feb. 16, 1996, A32, editorial; NYT, Jan. 8, 1996, A3.

8. NYT, Jan. 2, 1996, A15, OP-ED; USNWR, Feb. 19, 1996, p. 63; CSM, April 12, 1996, p. 18; NYT, April 14, 1996, sect. 4, p. 19, OP-ED; CSM, April 8, 1996, p. 11; NYT, May 25, 1996, A1.

9. CSM, June 5, 1996, pp. 11, 16; NYT, Aug. 6, 1996, A1; NYT, Sept. 2, 1996, A20; NYT, Sept. 3, 1996, A15, OP-ED; NYT, Sept. 30, 1996, A1; CSM, Dec. 2, 1996, p. 19.

10. CSM, Dec. 11, 1996, p. 19, commentary; CSM, Dec. 13, 1996, p. 18.

11. NYT, Jan. 26, 1997, sect. 4, p. 1; NYT, Feb. 3, 1997, A17; CSM, Aug. 20, 1999, p. 9; NYT, Sept. 23, 1999, A13.

12. NYT, Oct. 1, 1999, A8; CSM, Oct. 7, 1999, p. 1; NYT, Oct. 16, 1999, A19, OP-ED; NYT, Oct. 17, 1999, sect. 1, p. 16; NYT, April 29, 2000, A4; NYT, April 29, 2000, A4.

13. NYT, Jan. 21, 2000, A28, editorial; NYT, Jan. 25, 2000, A3; NYT, Nov. 22, 2000, sect. A, no page no. avail.; CSM, April 7, 2000, pp. 1, 4; NYT, May 20, 2000, A8; NYT, June 7, 2000, A10.

14. NYT, Jan. 22, 2000, A1; NYT, June 24, 2000, A15, OP-ED; NYT, July 1, 2000, A6; NYT, June 30, 2000, A1.

15. CSM, April 2, 1998, p. 3; USNWR, June 15, 1998, p. 30(?); NYT, June 19, 1998, A1; NYT, July 31, 1998, A6; CSM, Feb. 18, 1999, p. 1; NYT, April 26, 1999, A10; CSM, April 3, 2000, pp. 1, 10.

16. NYT, Sept. 28, 1998, A17; WSJ, Jan. 7, 1999, A10.

17. NYT, March 17, 1999, sect. 4, p. 3; NYT, Aug. 5, 1999, A6; NYT, Sept. 22, 1999, A18; NYT, Aug. 26, 1999, A10.

18. CSM, Aug. 24, 1998, p. 1; CSM, June 11, 1999, p. 1; NYT, Jan. 22, 1999, A1, A12.

19. NYT, Nov. 23, 1998, A1; USNWR, Nov. 23, 1998, no page no. avail.; NYT, Dec. 1, 1998, p. 2; NYT, March 18, 1999, A22; NYT, March 19, 1999, A14.

20. NYT, May 21, 1999, A1–; NYT, May 26, 1999, A1, A19; CSM, Dec. 10, 1999, p. 3; NYT, Oct. 13, 2000, A28.

21. NYT, Jan. 13, 1993, A1; NYT, Jan. 14, 1993, A25; NYT, July 20, 1993, A16; NYT, Dec. 19, 1993, sect. 1, p. 1–; NYT, Feb. 10, 1996, A1; NYT, June 27, 1996, B8.

22. CSM, May 27, 1997, p. 3; NYT, June 3, 1997, A12; NYT, June 4, 1997, A14; NYT, June 5, 1997, A1; NYT, June 7, 1997, A9; NYT, Dec. 12, 1999, A1–.

Notes to Chapter IX
U.S. Foreign Policy
Under Bush Jr.

1. WPNWE, Dec. 25, 2000–Jan. 1, 2001, p. 8; WPNWE, April 23–29, 2001, p. 11; WPNWE, Sept. 3–9, 2001, pp. 1–; NYT, May 2, 2001, A1, A10.

2. WPNWE, Feb. 9–15, 2004, p. 6; NYT, March 8, 2004, A19, OP-ED; NYT, March 26, 2004, A10; CSM, July 2, 2004, no page no. avail.

3. NYT, July 4, 2004, sect. 1, p. 6; NYT, Dec. 2, 2004, A39, OP-ED; NYT, Oct. 5, 2004, sect. 1, p. 28; NYT, Dec. 5, 2004, sect. 4, no page no. avail.; WPNWE, Nov. 22–28, 2004, p. 6; WPNWE, Nov. 22–28, 2004, p. 6; CSM, Oct. 2, 2006, p. 1; NYT, May 15, 2004, A7, OP-ED.

4. NYT, Jan. 21, 2005, A1, A12; CSM, Jan. 21, 2005, p. 1; NYT, Jan. 27, 2005, A1; NYT, Feb. 22, 2005, A8; CSM, March 17, 2005, p. 1.

5. CSM, Jan. 30, 2006, p. 1; WPNWE, April 10–16, 2006, p. 24; CSM, April 14, 2006, pp. 1, 10; WPNWE, July 10–16, 2006, p. 16; TM, July 17, 2006, cover story; WPNWE, July 17–23, 2006, p. 5; WPNWE, July 17–23, 2006, p. 12.

6. NYT, Sept. 28, 2006, A20; NYT, Sept. 29, 2006, A1, A20; NYT, Sept. 30, 2006, A1, A11; TM, Oct. 9, 2006, p. 29; NYT, Sept. 28, 2006, A21.

7. The mid-term Congressional elections of 1994 have already been treated in Chs. 2–3 above.

8. NYT, Nov. 12, 2006, p. 30; NYT, March 11, 2006, A1; NYT, Nov. 13, 2006, A1; NYT, no date avail. but in sequence, A1, A18; WPNWE, Dec. 11–17, 2006, p. 10; WPNWE, Dec. 11–17, 2006, p. 10; CSM, Nov. 29, 2006, p. 1.

9. NYT, Dec. 7, 2006, A1, A24; NYT, Dec. 8, 2006, A1, A14; NYT, Dec. 10, 2006, sect. 1, p. 18; WPNWE, Dec. 11–17, 2006, p. 6; NYP, Dec. 7, 2006, p. 1; NYT, Jan. 2, 2007, A1; CSM, Dec. 19, 2006, p. 1.

10. NYT, Jan. 6, 2007, A17; NYT, Jan. 9, 2007, A15; NYT, Jan. 10, 2007, A1; USNWR, Jan. 15, 2007, p. 32.

11. NYT, Jan. 11, 2007, A1, A21; NYT, Jan. 12, 2007, A1, A12; NYT, Jan. 17, 2007, A8; CSM, Jan. 11, 2007, p. 1; CSM, Jan. 19, 2007, p. 1.

12. NYT, Jan. 26, 2007, A1; NYT, Jan. 27, 2007, A8; NYT, Jan. 29, 2007, A16; CSM, Jan. 26, 2007, p. 4; CSM, Jan. 26, 2007, pp. 1, 5.

13. CSM, Feb. 1, 2007, p. 9; NYT, Feb. 11, 2007, sect. 4, p. 14; NYT, Feb. 17, 2007, A1, A6; NYT, Feb. 18, 2007, sect. 1, p. 1.

14. TM, Feb. 12, 2007, cover story and p. 33; NYT, Feb. 11, 2007, sect. 1, pp. 1, 4.

15. NYT, March 4, 2007, sect. 4, pp. 1, 4.

16. NYT, March 9, 2007, A1; NYT, March 14, 2007, A12; USNWR, March 19, 2007, p. 28; NYT, March 16, 2007, A1; CSM, March 14, 2007, pp. 1, 10.

17. NYT, March 24, 2007, A1, A6; NYT, March 28, 2007, A1, A9; NYT, March 29, 2007, A1, A17; NYT, March 30, 2007, A12; CSM, March 26, 2007, p. 2; NYT, March 25, 2007, p. 25.

18. NYT, April 4, 2007, A6; NYT, April 8, 2007, no page no. avail., editorial; NYT, April 4, 2007, A6; NYT, April 7, 2007, no page no. avail.; Lehrer News Hour, PBS, April 10, 2007; NYT, April 11, 2007, A12; WPNWE, April 9–15, 2007, p. 26; CSM, April 9, 2007, p. 1; NYT, April 10, 2007, editorial.

19. NYT, April 27, 2007, A1; NYT, April 28, 2007, A12; NYT, May 2, 2007, A1, A10; NYT, May 4, 2007, A14; NYT, May 25, 2007, A1; NYT, June 20, 2007, A16; NYT, June 29, 2007, A23; CSM, July 3, 2007, p. 2; NYT, July 13, 2007, A1; CSM, July 12, 2007, p. 1.

20. NYT, March 28, 2004, sect. 4, p. 5; NYT, June 8, 2004, A1, A11; NYT, July 22, 2004, A7; NYT, Oct. 24, 2004, sect. 1, p. 12.

21. NYT, Dec. 11, 2005, sect. 4, p. 1; WP, Dec., no day avail., 2005, p. 24, editorial; NYT, Dec. 14, 2005, A1; NYT, March 25, 2007, sect. 1, p. 14; NYT, April 17, 2007, A6.

22. NYT, May 21, 2005, A8.

23. NYT, May 31, 2003, A6; CSM, June 13, 2003, p. 4; NYT, July 12, 2003, A1, A5, A10; NYT, July 13, 2003, sect. 4, p. 1; NYT, July 17, 2003, A1; NYT, Oct. 3, 2004, sect. 1, p. 24; NYT, Oct. 7, 2004, A1, A28; NYT, Oct. 19, 2004, A10.

24. NYT, June 17, 2004, A1; NYT, July 23, 2004, A1; NYT, Dec. 6, 2005, A24 (and see *The Iraq Study Group Report* by James Baker, et al., New York, 2006).

25. TM, Nov. 21, 2005, p. 48; NYT, March 12, 2004, A9; NYT, March 14, 2004, sect. 1, p. 1; NYT, March 7, 2004, A1; NYT, June 19, 2003, A1; NYT, Sept. 12, 2004, sect. 4, p. 12, editorial; NYT, Nov. 17, 2005, A1.

26. NYT, April 25, 2007, A12; NYT, May 2, 2007, A13 (and Lehrer News Hour, PBS, May 2, 2007); TE, May 5–11, 2007, cover story; NYT, May 4, 2007, A3; NYT, May 7, 2007, A12; NYT, Aug. 29, 2007, A12.

27. NYT, July 2, 2007, A7.

Notes to Chapter X
United Mexican States in
Government and Society

1. The following secondary books are useful guides, in present and in next book, to nations around the world: *Nations of the World: A Political, Economic, and Business Handbook* (6th edn., Millerton, N.Y., 2006); *Handbook of the Nations* (15th edn., Wash., D.C., 1995); *Countries of the World and Their Leaders Yearbook* (2 vols., Farmington Hills, 2004); *Statesman's Yearbook* (136th edn., New York, N.Y., 1999, for year 2000); *The Europa World Year Book 2001* (2 vols., London, 2001); *The World Factbook 2004* (Wash., D.C., 2003); *World Government* (New York, N.Y., 1994); and *Nations: A Survey of the Twentieth Century* (Oxford, 1992). Also, *Constitutions Of The Countries Of The World* (20 vols., Dobbs Ferry, N.Y., 2001).

2. TM, Nov. 19, 1990, p. 58; NYT, Dec. 4, 1989, D11; NYT, Aug. 22, 1991, A1; NYT, Aug. 20, 1991, A3; NYT, Aug. 19, 1991, A7; NYT, Aug. 3, 1991, A3; NYT, Sept. 2, 1991, A3.

3. NYT, Nov. 2, 1991, A7; NYT, Dec. 20, 1991, A1.

4. NYT, Jan. 30, 1992, A12; NYT, July 13, 1992, A9; NYT, July 14, 1992, A3; NYT, Oct. 11, 1992, sect. 1, p. 15; NYT, Oct. 10, 1992, A5.

5. NYT, Nov. 2, 1992, A3; NYT, March 31, 1993, A13 (11?); NYT, Sept. 4, 1993, A3; NYT, Sept. 20, 1993, A10; NYT, Dec. 5, 1993, sect. 1, p. 5.

6. NYT, Nov. 29, 1993, A8; NYT, Nov. 30, 1993, A16; NYT, Feb. 29 (?), 1994, A3; NYT, March 1, 1994, A10; NYT, March 21, 1994, A6; NYT, March

24, 1994, A12; NYT, March 25, 1994, A6; NYT, March 27, 1994, sect. 1, p. 3; NYT, March 27, 1994, sect. 4, p. 1; NYT, March 30, 1994, A6.

7. NYT, April 20, 1994, A19; NYT, May 2, 1994, A6; NYT, May 13, 1994, A9; NYT, May 29, 1994, sect. 1, p. 10; NYT, June 12, 1994, sect. 4, p. 3; NYT, July 5, 1994, A17; NYT, July 23, 1994, A3; NYT, July 27, 1994, A3; NYT, Aug. 12, 1994, A8; NYT, Aug. 15, 1994, A3; TM, Aug. 22, 1994, pp. 38–39; NYT, Aug. 18, 1994, A8; NYT, Aug. 19, 1994, A8; NYT, Aug. 21 (2?), 1994, A6; NYT, Aug. 23, 1994, A1; NYT, no date, but in sequence, A10; NYT, Aug. 26, 1994, A10.

8. NYT, Oct. 3, 1994, A9; NYT, Nov. 20, 1994, sect. 1, p. 3; NYT, Nov. 30, 1994, A23.

9. NYT, Jan. 4, 1994, A3; refer. lost, but item is in sequence; NYT, Jan. 7, 1994, A3; NYT, Jan. 9, 1994, sect. 1, p. 1–; TM, Jan. 17, 1994, p. 32; NYT, Jan. 13, 1994, A3; NYT, Jan. 28, 1994, A1; NYT, Feb. 20, 1994, sect. 1, p. 3; NYT, March 3, 1994, A3; NYT, March 14, 1994, A2; NYT, May 11, 1994, A3.

10. NYT, June 1, 1994, A15; NYT, June 13, 1994, A1; NYT, June 15, 1994, A12; NYT, Aug. 6, 1994, A1; NYT, Aug. 8, 1994, A3; NYT, Aug. 28, 1994, sect. 1, p. 14; NYT, Sept. 18, 1994, p. 20.

11. NYT, Aug. 15, 1993, sect. 1, p. 14.

12. NYT, Aug. 16, 1993, A7.

13. WP, April 14, 1991, B3.

14. NYT, Dec. 15, 1991, sect. 1, p. 18; NYT, Nov. 19, 1993, A3; NYT, Sept. 13, 1994, D2.

15. NYT, Feb. 25, 1990, sect. 1, p. 18.

16. NYT, Aug. 7, 1994, sect. 1, p. 16; NYT, Aug. 14, 1994, sect. 4, p. 1.

17. NYT, Dec. 2, 1994, A11; TM, Dec. 5, 1994, p. 84; NYT, Dec. 4, 1994, sect. 4, p. 1; NYT, Dec. 7, 1994, A5; NYT, Dec. 29, 1994, A3; NYT, Jan. 18, 1995, A1, A3.

18. NYT, Dec. 20, 1994, sect. A, no page no. avail.; NYT, Dec. 21, 1994, A3; NYT, Jan. 2, 1995, A7; NYT, Jan. 22, 1995, sect. 1, p. 12; NYT, Jan. 17, 1995, A10; NYT, Feb. 10, 1995, A3; NYT, Feb. 15, 1995, sect. 1, p. 1; NYT, Feb. 18, 1995, A1, A5.

19. NYT, Dec. 25, 1994, sect. 1, p. 14; NYT, Jan. 4, 1995, D1, D4; WP, Jan. 8, 1995, A4; USNWR, Jan. 9, 1995, p. 63; NYT, Jan. 31, 1995, A1; NYT, Feb. 2, 1995, A12; TM, Feb. 13, 1995, p. 34; NYT, Feb. 22, 1995, D6.

20. NYT, Feb. 26, 1995, sect. 1, p. 8; NYT, March 1, 1995, A1; TM, March 13, 1993, pp. 48–49; NYT, March 11, 1995, A3; NYT, Feb. 24, 1995, no page no. avail.

21. NYT, Feb. 14, 1995, A8; NYT, March 14, 1995, A8.

22. NYT, March 26, 1995, sect. 4, p. 3; NYT, Nov. 19, 1995, sect. 1, p. 14; NYT, Oct. 16, 1995, A8; NYT, Oct. 25, 1995, A5; NYT, July 11, 1995, A3; NYT, Aug. 15, 1995, A6.

23. NYT, April 19, 1995, A14; NYT, May 23, 1995, A3; TM, June 19, 1995, p. 33; NYT, June 25, 1995, sect. 1, p. 1; NYT, July 31, 1995, A6; NYT, July 30, 1995, sect. 4, p. 6; NYT, Jan. 25, 1996, no page no. avail.

24. NYT, May 13, 1995, A4; NYT, June 21, 1995, A8; NYT, July 3, 1995, A5; NYT, May 2, 1996, A11; NYT, March 13, 1996, A7.

25. NYT, Oct. 11, 1995, A22, editorial; NYTBR, Dec. 17, 1995, no page no. avail.; NYT, Dec. 9, 1995, A4; NYT, Dec. 28, 1995, A16; NYT, June 13, 1995, A13; NYT, Sept. 3, 1995, sect. 1, p. 13; NYT, July 2, 1995, sect. 1, p. 6; NYT, Feb. 19, 1996, A6; NYT, Dec. 7, 1995, A3.

26. CSM, May 16, 1996, p. 19; NYT, March 21, 1996, A3; NYT, Jan. 6, 1997, A3; NYT, Feb. 23, 1997, sect. 1, p. 8; NYT, Feb. 26, 1997, no page no. avail.; NYT, March 9, 1997, sect. 1, p. 1–.

27. NYT, June 8, 1996, A5; NYT, July 13, 1996, A3; NYT, Aug. 8, 1996, A10; NYT, Dec. 23, 1996, A8; NYT, March 11, 1997, A23.

28. NYT, Oct. 1, 1996, A3; NYT, June 16, 1996, sect. 1, p. 4; NYT, July 27, 1996, A1; NYT, Sept. 23, 1996, A3; NYT, Oct. 1, 1996, A24; NYT, June 27, 1997, A3; NYT, July 2, 1997, A8; CSM, Jan. 10, 1997, p. 6; NYT, March 16, 1996, A3; NYT, Nov. 23, 1996, A4; NYT, July 6, 1997, sect. 1, p. 6; NYT, July 7, 1997, A6; NYT, Aug. 15, 1996, A16.

29. CSM, Aug. 28, 1996, p. 9; NYT, Sept. 25, 1996, A21; an item with no info. avail., but in sequence, probably USNWR; NYT, Feb. 23, 1997, sect. 3, p. 8; NYT, June 13, 1996, A8.

30. NYT, July 2, 1996, A3; NYT, July 17, 1996, A3; NYT, Aug. 30, 1996, A8; NYT, Sept. 2, 1996, A3; CSM, Sept. 3, 1996, p. 6; NYT, Oct. 17, 1996, A11; NYT, Feb. 6, 1997, sect. A, no page no. avail.

31. NYT, July 8, 1997, A1, A6; NYT, July 8, 1997, A16, editorial; CSM, July 8, 1997, p. 1; USNWR, July 21, 1997, p. 44; NYT, Aug. 13, 1997, A3; NYT, Sept. 2, 1997, A3; NYT, Sept. 1, 1997, A2; NYT, Sept. 3, 1997, A6; NYT, Nov. 12, 1997, A5; NYT, Dec. 16, 1997, A6.

32. NYT, Dec. 27, 1997, A11, OP-ED; TM, Jan., day not recorded, 1998, p. 58; NYT, Jan. 17, 1998, A4; CSM, Feb. 5, 1998, p. 6; NYT, Aug. 17, 1998, sect. 1, p. 14; NYT, June 28, 1998, sect. 1, p. 3.

33. NYT, no date recorded, but in sequence, A1, A8; NYT, Feb. 27, 1998, A3; NYT, March 26, 1998, A6; NYT, April 15, 1998, A14; NYT, Dec. 23, 1998, A12; NYT, Jan. 9, 2000, sect. 1, p. 8.

34. CSM, Oct. 6, 1997, p. 6; NYT, April 18, 1998, A3; NYT, June 28, 1998, sect. 4, p. 1.

35. NYT, Feb. 12, 1998, A3; NYT, March 10, 2000, A3; CSM, Aug. 27, 1998, p. 7.

36. NYT, Feb. 9, 1999, A7; NYT, March 4, 1999, A14; NYT, March 5, 1999, A6; NYT, May 23, 1999, sect. 1, p. 17; CSM, May 19, 1999, p. 6.

37. NYT, June 24, 1999, A3; NYT, July 6, 1999, A8; NYT, July 3, 1999, A3; NYT, Aug. 2, 1999, A1, A6.

38. NYT, May 16, 2000, A3; NYT, March 27, 2000, A6; USNWR, July 3, 2000, p. 26; NYT, July 1, 2000, sect. 1, p. 1–.

39. NYT, July 2, 2000, sect. 4, p. 3; refer. lost but in sequence, probably PBS, Lehrer News Hour, or CBS radio; NYT, July 4, 2000, A1, A6; NYT, Sept. 2, 2000, A4.

40. NYT, July 6, 2000, A6; NYT, July 5, 2000, A1; NYT, July 11, 2000, A8; WPR, Sept. 2000, cover story and pp. 6–10; NYT, Nov. 23, 2000, A14; CSM, Nov. 8, 2000, p. 6; NYT, Oct. 29, 2000, sect. 3, no page no. avail.; NYT, Oct. 27, 2000, A3; NYT, Sept. 11, 2000, A6; CSM, Aug. 18, 2000, p. 6; NYT, Dec. 2, 2000, A6.

41. NYT, Feb. 12, 2001, A3; NYT, Feb. 26, 2001, A3; NYT, March 29, 2001, A4; NYT, Oct. 28, 2001, A10; NYT, Nov. 18, 2001, A10; WPNWE, July 15–21, 2002, p. 16; WPNWE, May 28–June 3, 2001, p. 17; WPNWE, June 25–July 1, 2001, p. 15; CSM, Aug. 6, 2001, p. 6; NYT, Sept. 7, 2001, A6; NYT, Jan. 21, 2002, A6.

42. NYT, Jan. 21, 2002, A6.

42a. CSM, April 28, 2005, p. 1; NYT, July 7, 2003, A3; NYT, Nov. 3, 2003, A5; NYT, June 28, 2004, A6; CSM, March 30, 2006, p. 9.

43. CSM, April 6, 2004, p. 6; NYT, Nov. 11, 2004, W1; NYT, Dec. 13, 2005, A3; CSM, June 16, 2003, p. 6.

44. NYT, July 7, 2006, A8; NYT, July 1, 2006, A8; NYT, Sept. 6, 2006, A1, A12; NYT, Sept. 6, 2006, A19, OP-ED.

45. NYT, Dec. 2, 2006, A6; NYT, Dec. 1, 2006, A3; NYT, Dec. 8, 2006, A20; WPNWE, Dec. 11–17, 2006, p. 17.

46. NYT, March 18, 2007, sect. 1, p. 15; NYT, Jan. 7, 2001, sect. 1, p. 8; CSM, May 23, 2007, p. 1; NYT, April 25, 2007, A8.

Notes to Chapter XI
Other Central American
Mainland Nations in
Government and Society

1. NYT, June 28, 1990, A3; NYT, Oct. 21, 1990, sect. 1, p. 10; NYT, Nov. 11, 1990, sect. A?, p. 9; NYT, Jan. 8, 1991, A3; NYT, Aug. 9, 1992, sect. 1, p. 7; WP, Oct. 4, 1992, A35; NYT, May 26, 1993, A3; NYT, May 28, 1993, A6; NYT, June 2, 1993, A8; NYT, June 3, 1993, A3; NYT, June 4, 1993, A5; WP, June 6, 1993, A32; NYT, June 7, 1993, A1; NYT, June 22, 1993, no page no. avail., OP-ED.

2. NYT, Sept. 1, 1993, sect. A, no page no. avail.; NYT, April 5, 1994, A10; NYT, March 11, 1995, A3; NYT, May 28, 1995, sect. 1, p. 14; NYT, Nov. 12, 1995, sect. 1, p. 16; NYT, Jan. 7, 1996, sect. 1, p. 8; NYT, Jan. 9, 1996, no page no. avail.; NYT, Feb. 7, 1996, A11; NYT, March 27, 1996, A6; NYT, May 12, 1996, sect. 4, p. 4; NYT, Aug. 18, 1996, sect. 1, p. 20.

3. NYT, Sept. 20, 1996, A1; CSM, Oct. 3, 1996, p. 1; CSM, Dec. 4, 1996, p. 19 (10?), commentary; NYT, Dec. 19, 1996, A28, editorial.

4. NYT, Dec. 23, 1996, A15; CSM, Dec. 26, 1996, p. 19, commentary; CSM, Dec. 27, 1996, p. 22; NYT, Dec. 29, 1996, sect. 1, p. 8; NYT, Dec. 30, 1996, A8.

5. NYT, March 11, 1997, A3; NYT, April 7, 1997, A8; CSM, April 28, 1997, p. 6; NYT, Feb. 26, 1999, A16; NYT, March 1, 1999, A10; NYT, Nov. 8,

1999, A18; CSM, Dec. 1, 2000, p. 6; NYT, July 26, 2001, A3; NYT, Nov. 10, 2003, A11; CSM, Oct. 26, 2001, p. 5.

6. NYT, Sept. 16, 1990, sect. 1, p. 10; NYT, Feb. 15, 1991, A10; NYT, March 24, 1991, no page no. avail.; NYT, April 5, 1991, A6; NYT, April 25, 1991, A16; NYT, April 30, 1991, A6; NYT, May 5, 1991, sect. 1, p. 9; WP, March 5, 1991, A29; NYT, Sept. 25, 1991, A12; NYT, Sept. 26, 1991, A16; NYT, Jan. 1, 1992, A7; NYT, Jan. 5, 1992, sect. 1, p. 3; NYT, Jan. 7, 1992, A1; NYT, Jan. 17, 1992, A1, A5.

7. NYT, Jan. 19, 1992, sect. 4, p. 1; TM, Jan. 27, 1992, p. 32; NYT, Sept. 7, 1992, A1; NYT, Dec. 15, 1992, A6; NYT, Dec. 25, 1992, A3; NYT, April 29, 1992, A7.

8. NYT, Sept. 11, 1994, sect. 1, p. 12; NYT, March 14, 1993, sect. 1, p. 20; NYT, Dec. 2, 1992, A3; NYT, Jan. 5, 1993, A5; NYT, July 2, 1993, A5; NYT, April 3, 1998, A12; NYT, Dec. 15, 1993, A3; NYT, March 20, 1994, sect. 1, p. 4; NYT, March 22, 1994, A3; NYT, April 20, 1994, A13; NYT, June 2, 1994, A14(?); NYT, July 29, 1996, A6.

9. NYT, Feb. 27, 1990, A1; NYT, March 1, 1990, A20; TM, March 12, 1990, p. 16; NYT, March 6, 1990, A10; NYT, Sept. 18, 1990, A11(?).

10. NYT, Jan. 15, 1991, A3; NYT, April 17, 1991, A3; NYT, April 22, 1991, A3; NYT, June 21, 1991, A3; NYT, June 30, 1991, sect. 4, p. 4; NYT, Sept. 13, 1991, A3; NYT, Dec. 19, 1991, sect. 1, p. 18.

11. NYT, July 10, 1992, A8.

12. WP, May 9, 1993, A29; TM, Sept. 6, 1993, p. 42; NYT, Sept. 6, 1993, A4; NYT, Jan. 26, 1994, A3; NYT, June 5, 1995, A7.

13. CSM, Oct. 22, 1996, no page no. avail.; NYT, Oct. 22, 1996, A16; CSM, Oct. 29, 1996, p. 6; NYT, Feb. 22, 1997, A4; NYT, March 2, 1997, sect. 1, p. 3; NYT, Sept. 10, 2000, sect. 1, p. 14.

14. NYT, July 24, 2004, A12(?), editorial commentary; NYT, Oct. 27, 2006, A8; NYT, Nov. 24, 2006, A14; TM, Nov. 20, 2006, p. 51; CSM, Nov. 8, 2006, p. 6; NYT, Nov. 20, 2005, A5.

15. NYT, Dec. 21, 1989, A18, A21, A24.

16. YT, Dec. 22, 1989, A20; NYT, Oct. 25, 1989, A10; NYT, Dec. 22, 1989, A38; NYT, Dec. 22, 1989, A39; NYT, Dec. 21, 1989, A30, editorial.

17. WP, Dec. 24, 1989; A1, C1; NYT, Dec. 24, 1989, sect. 1, p. 8; NYT, Dec. 24, 1989, p. 8; NYT, Dec. 25, 1989, A8; NYT, Dec. 26, 1989, A10; NYT, Jan. 4, 1990, A12.

18. NYT, Jan. 5, 1996, A10; NYT, Jan. 10, 1990, no page no. avail.; NYT, Feb. 6, 1990, no page no. avail.; NYT, June 9, 1990, A8; NYT, Nov. 3, 1990, A7; WP, Dec. 16, 1990, A51; NYT, Jan. 21, 1991, A3.

19. NYT, Feb. 11, 1991, A1, A15; NYT, June 3, 1991, A11; NYT, Sept. 5, 1991, D22(?); NYT, Nov. 16, 1992, A9; NYT, Nov. 17, 1992, A6.

20. NYT, Feb. 21, 1994, A4; NYT, Sept. 2, 1997, A12; NYT, Nov. 3, 1994, A7; NYT, Dec. 4, 1995, A4; NYT, June 12, 1996, A10; CSM, Jan. 15, 1997, p. 8.

21. NYT, Dec. 15, 1996, sect. 1, p. 16; CSM, April 9, 1997, p. 7; USNWR, Jan. 27, 1997, p. 51; NYT, July 13, 1997, sect. 4, p. 5; CSM, Aug. 20, 1997, p. 7; NYT, Sept. 28, 1997, sect. 1, p. 16; NYT, Oct. 5, 1997, sect. 1, p. 8; TM,

Dec. 15, 1997, p. 56; NYT, Dec. 25, 1997, A1; NYT, April 26, 1998, sect. 1, no page no. avail.; NYT, Sept. 1, 1998, A8; NYT, Sept. 20, 1998, sect. 1, p. 4; NYT, Oct. 14, 1998, A3.

22. NYT, May 2, 1999, sect. 1, p. 22; NYT, May 3, 1999, A8; NYT, Sept. 2, 1999, A12.

23. TM, Sept. 6, 1999, p. 48; USNWR, Aug. 9, 1999, p. 32; NYT, Dec. 12, 1999, sect. 1, p. 6; NYT, Dec. 15, 1999, A14.

24. NYT, Jan. 1, 2000, A16; NYT, Dec. 31, 1999, A10.

25. CSM, Aug. 24, 2000, p. 1; NYT, Oct. 28, 2001, A10; NYT, May 3, 2004, A6.

Notes to Chapter XII
Caribbean Nations in
Government and Society

1. NYT, Feb. 20, 1990, A14; TM, March 15, 1990, pp. 22, 26; WP, April 14, 1991, A1, A20; WP, April 28, 1991, C3; NYT, May 19, 1991, A2; NYT, May 21, 1991, A6.

2. NYT, Sept. 20, 1991, A7; NYT, Dec. 8, 1991, sect. 1, p. 3; NYT, Jan. 14, 1992, A10; NYT, Oct. 12, 1992, A3; NYT, Jan. 13, 1993, A10; NYT, April 23, 1994, A4; NYT, Aug. 6, 1994, A3.

3. TM, Dec. 6, 1993, p. 42; NYT, Jan. 13, 1993, A1; NYT, Jan. 12, 1993, A6; TM, June 21, 1993, no page no. avail.; WP, July 25, 1993, A1; NYT, Sept. 18, 1994, sect. 1, p. 1; NYT, Sept. 26, 1994, A8; NYT, Oct. 27, 1994, A7; TM, Feb. 20, 1995, cover story and p. 57; NYT, June 8, 1995, A12.

4. CNN, Oct. 22, 28, 1995; NYT, Nov. 25, 1992, A1, A10; NYT, May 10, 1993, A19.

5. NYT, Aug. 20, 1994, A1; NYT, Aug. 22, 1994, A10; NYT, Aug. 24, 1994, A14; TM, April 29, 1994, p. 28; NYT, Aug. 25, 1994, A18; NYT, Aug. 26, 1994, A12; TM, Sept. 5, 1994, cover story; NYT, Sept. 10, 1994, A4.

6. NYT, May 5, 1995, A1; NYT, May 3, 1993, A1, A14; NYT, Aug. 15, 1995, A6; NYT, Sept. 22, 1995, A8.

7. NYT, Nov. 3, 1993, A8; NYT, July 8, 1995, sect. 1, p. 5.

8. NYT, Feb. 27, 1996, A1, A15; NYT, Feb. 29, 1996, A1; NYT, March 2, 1996, A18, editorial; NYT, March 3, 1996, sect. 1, p. 8; TM, March 11, 1996,

pp. 36–37; NYT, April 7, 1996, sect. 1, p. 6; CSM, April 10, 1996, p. 4; TM, June 24, 1996, p. 54; USNWR, June 29, 1996, p. 36; NYT, Nov. 13, 1996, A10; NYT, Dec. 25, 1996, B8; NYT, Jan. 4, 1997, sect. 1, p. 1; NYT, Jan. 11, 1997, sect. 1, p. 5; NYT, Feb. 13, 1997, A10; NYT, April 22, 1997, A21; NYT, Dec. 21, 1997, sect. 1, p. 8; USNWR, Jan. 18, 1999, no page no. avail.

9. CSM, Dec. 19, 1996, p. 18; CSM, Jan. 30, 1997, p. 19; NYT, Oct. 11, 1997, sect. 1, p. 10; NYT, Jan. 21, 1998, A8; NYT, Sept. 1, 1998, sect. 4, p. 3; CSM, Oct. 14, 1998, p. 6; NYT, May 30, 2001, A8.

10. NYT, May 15, 2002, A10; NYT, May 14, 2002, A3; NYT, April 10, 2003, A9; NYT, April 17, 2003, A10; NYT, July 25, 2003, A23; NYT, Nov. 28, 2004, sect. 1, no page no. avail.; CSM, June 10, 2005, p. 6; NYT, Aug. 3, 2006, A8; CSM, April 23, 2007, p. 9.

11. NYT, Jan. 5, 1997, sect. 1, p. 8; TM, Jan. 26, 1998, p. 26; NYT, Jan. 22, 1998, A14; NYT, Jan. 24, 1998, A5; NYT, Jan. 25, 1998, sect. 1, p. 8; NYT, Jan. 25, 1998, sect. 4, p. 3; NYT, Jan. 26, 1998, A8, A9; TM, Feb. 2, 1998, pp. 62–63; CSM, Feb. 17, 1998, p. 6; USNWR, Feb. 21, 1998, p. 42; NYT, Sept. 13, 1998, sect. 1, p. 6.

12. NYT, June 23, 1990, sect. A, no page no. avail.; NYT, March 11, 1990, sect. 1, p. 18; NYT, March 12, 1990, A5; NYT, Dec. 17, 1990, A3; NYT, Dec. 18, 1990, A1; NYT, Dec. 20, 1990, A18; TM, Dec. 31, 1990, p. 29; NYT, Jan. 8, 1991, A1; NYT, Feb. 8, 1991, A3; NYT, Feb. 10, 1991, sect. 1, p. 10.

13. NYT, April 23, 1991, A3; NYT, Sept. 11, 1991, A15; NYT, Oct. 1, 1991, A6; NYT, Oct. 3, 1991, A8; NYT, Oct. 4, 1991, A8; NYT, Oct. 6, 1991, sect. 4, p. 2.

14. NYT, Oct. 8, 1991, A10; TM, Oct. 14, 1991, p. 34; NYT, Feb. 5, 1992, A5; TM, Feb. 10, 1992, p. 32; NYT, Feb. 11, 1992, A12; NYT, Feb. 10, 1992, A8; NYT, Feb. 24, 1992, A3; NYT, Feb. 25, 1992, A9; NYT, March 20, 1992, no page no. avail.; WP, May 10, 1992, A32.

15. NYT, May 18, 1992, A1; NYT, March 17, 1993, A1; NYT, July 4, 1993, sect. 1, p. 12; WP, July 4, 1993, A28.

16. NYT, July 5, 1993, A4; NYT, July 8, 1993, A11; NYT, Sept. 26, 1993, sect. 1, p. 24; NYT, Oct. 5, 1993, A3; NYT, Oct. 8, 1993, A12; NYT, Oct. 10, 1993, sect. 4, p. 14, editorial; NYT, Oct. 15, 1993, A8; NYT, Oct. 1, 1993, A1; NYT, Oct. 18, 1993, A6.

17. NYT, Oct. 3, 1993, sect. 1, p. 12; NYT, April 10, 1994, sect. 4, p. 19, commentary; NYT, April 22, 1994, A1; NYT, May 4, 1994, A10; TM, May 9, 1994, p. 39; NYT, May 7, 1994, A1.

18. NYT, May 12, 1994, A1; NYT, June 3, 1994, A3; NYT, June 8, 1994, A15; NYT, June 13, 1994, A10; NYT, June 28, 1994, A6; NYT, July 27, 1994, A3; NYT, Aug. 1, 1994, A7; NYT, Aug. 2, 1994, A3; NYT, Aug. 3, 1994, A9.

19. NYT, Aug. 14, 1994, sect. 4, p. 3; NYT, Aug. 22, 1994, A3; NYT, Aug. 24, 1994, A10.

20. NYT, Sept. 1, 1994, A10; NYT, Sept. 12, 1994, A6; NYT, Sept. 16, 1994, no page no. avail.; NYT, Sept. 17, 1994, A6; NYT, Sept. 18, 1994, sect. 1, p. 14.

21. NYT, Sept. 19, 1994, A1; NYT, Sept. 20, 1994, A1; McNeill-Lehrer News Hour, Sept. 19, 1994, PBS.

22. NYT, Sept. 21, 1994, A1, A17; NYT, Sept. 22, 1994, A12, A14; NYT, Sept. 23, 1994, A35, OP-ED; NYT, Sept. 23, 1994, A1, A12; NYT, Sept. 25, 1994, sect. 1, p. 16; NYT, Sept. 26, 1994, A1, A10.

23. NYT, Sept. 27, 1994, A1; NYT, Sept. 27, 1994, A17; NYT, Sept. 28, 1994, A8; NYT, Sept. 29, 1994, A16 (and also CBS TV eve. news, Sept. 28, 1994); NYT, Oct. 7, 1994, A14.

24. TM, Oct. 10, 1994, pp. 42–43; NYT, Sept. 30, 1994, A6; NYT, Oct. 2, 1994, sect. 4, p. 16; NYT, no other info. avail., but in sequence (probably Oct. 7, 1994, sect. 1, p. 1); NYT, Oct. 4, 1994, A1, A10.

25. NYT, Oct. 5, 1994, A16, A17; NYT, Oct. 7, 1994, A14; NYT, Oct. 9, 1994, sect. 4, p. 5; NYT, Oct. 11, 1994, A14; NYT, Oct. 12, 1994, A8.

26. NYT, Oct. 15, 1994, A1, A6; NYT, Oct. 16, 1994, sect. 4, p. 15; NYT, Oct. 17, 1994, A3; NYT, Oct. 18, 1994, A8.

27. NYT, Oct. 23, 1994, sect. 1, p. 12; NYT, Oct. 25, 1994, A3; NYT, Oct. 30, 1994, sect. 1, p. 1; NYT, Nov. 1, 1994, A16; NYT, Nov. 9, 1994, A3; NYT, Nov. 18, 1994, A6; NYT, Nov. 4, 1994, A8; NYT, Nov. 4, 1994, A32; NYT, Nov. 5, 1994, A8; NYT, Nov. 13, 1994, sect. 1, p. 3; NYT, Nov. 30, 1994, A5.

28. NYT, Dec. 4, 1994, sect. 1, p. 26; NYT, Jan. 15, 1995, sect. 1, p. 8; TM, Dec. 12, 1994, p. 37.

29. WSJ, April 14, 1995, A8; NYT, June 25, 1995, sect. 1, p. 10; NYT, June 26, 1995, A1; NYT, June 27, 1995, A8; NYT, June 28, 1995, A9; NYT, July 10, 1995, A8; NYT, July 24, 1995, A12.

30. NYT, Jan. 8, 1995, sect. 1, p. 10; NYT, Jan. 29, 1995, sect. 1, p. 1; NYT, Feb. 19, 1995, sect. 1, p. 14; NYT, March 25, 1995, sect. 1, p. 1; NYT, March 29, 1995, A10; NYT, April 2, 1995, sect. 1, p. 14; NYT, April 3, 1995, A8; NYT, May 13, 1995, A4; NYT, Oct. 27, 1998, A4; NYT, Jan. 15, 1999, A3; NYT, Aug. 26, 1999, A1; NYT, Nov. 10, 1999, A1; NYT, Nov. 26, 1999, A26.

31. CSM, Feb. 7, 2000, p. 23; CSM, March 30, 2000, p. 8; CSM, Nov. 30, 2000, p. 7; NYT, July, day not recorded, 2000, A8; NYT, Nov. 24, 2000, A35; NYT, Nov. 30, 2000, A35, OP-ED; NYT, Nov. 28, 2000, A28.

32. NYT, Feb., day not recorded, 2001, A6; NYT, Nov. 5, 2001, A17, OP-ED; NYT, July 30, 2002, A7; NYT, Dec. 13, 2002, A3; NYT, Jan. 30, 2004, A3; NYT, Feb. 10, 2004, A3; NYT, Feb. 13, 2004, A3; NYT, Feb. 15, 2004, sect. 4, p. 5; NYT, Feb. 17, 2004, A3; NYT, Feb. 22, 2004, sect. 1, p. 14; NYT, Feb. 24, 2004, A8; NYT, Feb. 26, 2004, A27 (A2?), OP-ED; Lehrer News Hour, PBS, March 1, 2004.

33. NYT, March 1, 2004, A10; NYT, March 1, 2004, A20; NYT, March 3, 2004, A8; CSM, March 2, 2004, p. 10; NYT, March 7, 2004, sect. 1, p. 18; NYT, March 9, 2004, A6; CSM, March 11, 2004, p. 6; NYT, March 29, 2004, A9.

34. NYT, June 2, 2004, no page no. avail.; NYT, Aug. 2, 2004, no page no. avail.; NYT, Oct. 16, 2004, A5.

35. CSM, Feb. 6, 2006, p. 4; TM, Jan. 9, 2006, p. 38; NYT, Jan. 9, 2006, sect. 1, p. 10; NYT, Feb. 7, 2006, A21; NYT, Feb. 7, 2006, A10; NYT, Feb. 10, 2007, A1.

36. NYT, May 20, 1994, A26; NYT, July 24, 1994, sect. 1 (4?), p. 15.

37. NYT, March 28, 1996, A6; CSM, May 16, 1996, p. 7; NYT, May 17, 1996, A10; NYT, May 19, 1996, sect. 1, p. 1; NYT, July 1, 1996, A3; NYT, July 6, 1996, A18; NYT, Dec. 1, 1996, sect. 1, p. 15; NYT, Nov. 24, 1996, sect. 1, p. 1.

38. NYT, May 10, 1998, sect. 1, p. 6; NYT, July 11, 1999, sect. 1, p. 3; NYT, May 17, 2000, A4.

39. TM, Feb. 26, 1996, p. 46; NYT, July 20, 1996, A2; NYT, Oct. 4, 1998, sect. 1, p. 14; NYT, Jan. 31, 1998, A1; NYT, March 13, 1994, sect. 4, p. 4.

Notes to Chapter XIII
South American Nations in Government and Society

1. NYT, Aug. 8, 1990, A3; NYT, Dec. 14, 1990, A16; WP, March 3, 1991, A18; WP, June 9, 1991, A30; WP, Dec. 6, 1992, A39; NYT, April 18, 1993, sect. 1, p. 12; NYT, June 2, 1994, A14; NYT, Aug. 7, 1994, sect. 1, p. 16; NYT, Dec. 26, 1994, A6; NYT, Feb. 8, 1995, A10; NYT, June 13, 1995, A14; TM, Aug. 14, 1995, p. 48; NYT, Aug. 13, 1995, sect. 4, p. 3.

2. NYT, Feb. 2, 1996, A6; USNWR, Feb. 12, 1996, p. 47; NYT, Feb. 20, 1996, A7; NYT, Feb. 18, 1996, sect. 1, p. 12; NYT, March 2, 1996, A5; TE, May 11, 1996, p. 37; NYT, Sept. 1, 1996, sect. 1, p. 12; NYT, Sept. 2, 1996, sect. 1, p. 3; CSM, Oct. 23, 1996, p. 6; NYT, Nov. 4, 1996, A14; NYT, Nov. 26, 1996, A10; NYT, Dec. 12, 1996, A18; NYT, Aug. 22, 1996, A16; NYT, March 30, 1997, sect. 1, p. 3; NYT, July 24, 1997, A8; NYT, Dec. 18, 1997, A17; USNWR, May 11, 1998, p. 38; CSM, Sept. 22, 1998, p. 6; USNWR, Nov. 23, 1998, p. 37.

3. TM, June 18, 1998, p. 44; NYT, Feb. 6, 1999, A3; NYT, March 7, 1999, sect. 1, p. 19; NYT, July 12, 1999, A3; NYT, July 18, 1999, p. 3; NYT, July 14, 1999, A10; USNWR, July 26, 1999, p. 34; NYT, Oct. 21, 1999, A4; NYT, Nov. 22, 1999, A10.

4. WPNWE, March 13, 2000, p. 23; NYT, April 21, 2000, A12; NYT, May 13, 2000, A3; NYT, June 25, 2000, sect. 1, pp. 1–; NYT, Sept. 10, 2000, sect. 1, p. 1; NYT, Oct. 29, 2000, sect. 1, p. 5; NYT, Oct. 30, 2000, A8(?).

5. NYT, Jan. 27, 2001, A1, A7; NYT, March 4, 2001, sect. 1, no page no. avail.; NYT, May 14, 2001, A8; NYT, July 10, 2001, A18, editorial; NYT, Aug. 19, 2001, sect. 4, p. 3; NYT, Sept. 2, 2001, sect. 1, p. 3.

6. NYT, Feb. 23, 2002, A7; NYT, Feb. 25, 2002, A6; NYT, May 27, 2002, A6; NYT, May 28, 2002, A3; NYT, Nov. 9, 2002, A4.

7. NYT, Nov. 26, 2003, A3; NYT, April 25, 2004, sect. 1, p. 8; NYT, July 29, 2004, A3; NYT, Nov. 10, 2004, A3.

8. NYT, June 23, 2005, A3; NYT, Aug. 1, 2005, A5.

9. Lehrer News Hour, PBS, May 13, 2007; NYT, April 30, 2007, A3; CSM, May 2, 2007, p. 6; NYT, May 22, 2007, A3; NYT, Aug. 26, 2007, A3; CSM, June 8, 2007, p. 6.

10. NYT, Feb. 5, 1992, A10; NYT, Feb. 10, 1992, A3; NYT, Feb. 11, 1992, A6; TM, Feb. 17, 1992, p. 4; NYT, March 6, 1992, A12; NYT, April 3, 1992, sect. 1, p. 14; NYT, Oct. 29, 1992, A3; NYT, Nov. 29, 1992, sect. 1, p. 7; NYT, Dec. 3, 1992, A3.

11. NYT, May 22, 1993, A3; NYT, Sept. 8, 1993, A9; NYT, Dec. 7, 1993, A3; NYT, May 16, 1994, A1; NYT, Sept. 3, 1994, sect. 1, p. 18.

12. NYT, Feb. 12, 1996, A5; NYT, May 13, 1996, A6; NYT, July 13, 1996, sect. 1, p. 3; NYT, Dec. 8, 1996, sect. 1, p. 22.

13. NYT, Dec. 6, 1997, A1; NYT, Dec. 14, 1997, sect. 1, p. 3; NYT, Dec. 7, 1998, A1–; CSM, Oct. 2, 1998, p. 6.

14. NYT, Dec. 9, 1998, A6; CSM, Dec. 9, 1998, p. 7; USNWR, Dec. 21, 1998, no page no. avail.

15. NYT, Feb. 4, 1999, A8; NYT, Feb. 3, 1999, A8; NYT, Jan. 25, 1999, sect. 1, p. 13; NYT, Aug. 13, 1999, A5; NYT, Aug. 27, 1999, A8; NYT, Aug. 29, 1999, sect. 1, p. 4; NYT, Aug. 28, 1999, A5; CSM, Aug. 30, 1999, p. 6; NYT, Sept. 5, 1999, sect. 1, p. 13; CSM, Dec. 15, 1999, p. 6; CSM, Dec. 20, 1999, p. 7.

16. NYT, July 28, 2000, A8; NYT, Sept. 10, 2000, sect. 1, p. 17; NYT, Nov. 5, 2000, sect. 1, p. 22; NYT, April 16, 2001, A4; USNWR, June 11, 2001, p. 38; NYT, Dec. 4, 2001, A10; NYT, Feb. 14, 2002, A13; NYT, April 11, 2002, A6; NYT, April 12, 2002, A3.

17. NYT, April 13, 2002, A9; NYT, April 14, 2002, sect. 1, pp. 1, 10; NYT, April 15, 2002, A8; NYT, April 19, 2002, A8; NYT, April 29, 2002, A10; WPNWE, April 29–May 5, 2002, p. 22.

18. NYT, Oct. 25, 2002, A7; NYT, Nov. 20, 2002, A10; NYT, Nov. 29, 2002, A25; NYT, Dec. 9, 2002, A5; NYT, Dec. 15, 2002, sect. 1, p. 16; NYT, Dec. 20, 2002, A14; NYT, Jan. 23, 2003, A8; NYT, Feb. 3, 2003, A8; CSM, Jan. 22, 2003, p. 11; NYT, June 1, 2003, sect. 1, p. 3; NYT, Sept. 13, 2003, A6; NYT, March 1, 2004, A3; NYT, Aug. 14, 2004, A15, OP-ED; NYT, Dec. 9, 2004, A5; NYT, Jan. 30, 2005, sect. 1, p. 3; NYT, Aug. 27, 2005, A7.

19. NYT, Oct. 30, 2005, sect. 1, p. 3; CSM, April 14, 2006, p. 6; NYT, May 20, 2006, A1, A8; WPNWE, Aug. 14–20, 2006, p. 22; WPNWE, Aug. 14–20, 2006, p. 20.

20. NYT, Dec. 5, 2006, A3; NYT, Jan. 9, 2006, sect. A, no page no. avail.; NYT, Jan. 10, 2007, A1, C5; NYT, Jan. 11, 2007, A16; NYT, Jan. 19, 2007, A12; CSM, Jan. 10, 2007, p. 6.

21. NYT, Feb. 1, 2007, A9; NYT, Feb. 17, 2007, A3; NYT, May 2, 2007, A3; NYT, May 17, 2007, A8; NYT, May 28, 2007, A3; NYT, June 1, 2007, A6.

22. NYT, Jan. 11, 1997, A5; NYT, Feb. 6, 1997, A10; NYT, Feb. 7, 1997, A5; NYT, Feb. 10, 1997, A6; NYT, Feb. 11, 1997, A20, editorial; NYT, Feb. 11, 1997, A3; NYT, April 3, 1997, A8.

23. NYT, March 10, 1999, A8; NYT, March 16, 1999, A12; NYT, Jan. 23, 2000, sect. 1, p. 13; NYT, Jan. 30, 2000, sect. 1, p. 3.

24. NYT, April 17, 2005, sect. 1, p. 10; NYT, April 21, 2005, A3; NYT, April 15, 2007, sect. 1, no page no. avail.; CSM, April 17, 2007, p. 6.

25. NYT, Aug. 17, 1991, A3; NYT, Dec. 3, 1991, A17; NYT, April 8, 1992, A12; NYT, April 10, 1992, A8; NYT, April 12, 1992, sect. 4, p. 2; USNWR, April 20, 1992, p. 49.

26. NYT, July 29, 1992, A3; NYT, July 23, 1992, A11; NYT, Aug. 24, 1992, A13; NYT, Feb. 23, 1993, A3; NYT, May 2, 1993, sect. 4, p. 6; NYT, April 26, 1993, A11; NYT, Nov. 25, 1993, A4; NYT, May 4, 1993, A3.

27. NYT, April 11, 1995, A13; NYT, May 19, 1996, sect. 1, p. 6; TM, Jan. 6, 1997, p. 98; NYT, Jan. 5, 1997, sect. 4, p. 8; NYT, April 23, 1997, A14.

28. NYT, April 6, 1997, sect. 1, p. 14; NYT, May 17, 1997, A35; NYT, June 10, 1997, A12; NYT, July 21, 1997, A3; NYT, July 29, 1997, A8.

29. NYT, Jan. 14, 1999, A3; NYT, Feb. 4, 1999, A27; CSM, Aug. 9, 1999, p. 7.

30. NYT, Dec. 28, 1999, A5; USNWR, Jan. 31, 2000, p. 34; NYT, March 12, 2000, sect. 1, p. 18; CSM, April 7, 2000, p. 6; NYT, April 9, 2000, sect. 1, p. 8; NYT, April 12, 2000, A6; NYT, May 20, 2000, A6; NYT, May 29, 2000, A6; NYT, May 30, 2000, A10; NYT, May 30, 2000, A10; WPNWE, June 5, 2000, p. 15; USNWR, June 12, 2000, p. 32.

31. NYT, Nov. 14, 2000, A13; NYT, Nov. 16, 2000, A7; NYT, Nov. 22, 2000, A12; WPNWE, Nov. 27, 2000, p. 15; NYT, Nov. 21, 2000, A6; NYT, Nov. 23, 2000, A14.

32. WPNWE, Dec. 4, 2000, p. 15; NYT, Dec. 3, 2000, sect. 1, p. 20; NYT, Feb. 11, 2001, A14; NYT, June 4, 2001, A6.

33. CSM, Sept. 24, 2002, p. 7; NYT, Dec. 20, 2002, sect. 1, p. 3; NYT, June 24, 2003, A3; NYT, Feb. 16, 2004, no page no. avail.; NYT, April 2, 2006, sect. 1, p. 3; NYT, June 5, 2006, A13; NYT, April 3, 2007, p. 6; NYT, March 24, 2002, sect. 1, p. 16.

34. NYT, May 15, 1990, D8; NYT, Sept. 9, 1990, sect. 1, p. 6; NYT, Oct. 4, 1990, A9.

35. NYT, Feb. 1, 1991, A3; NYT, March 14, 1991, A3; NYT, Aug. 4, 1991, sect. 1, p. 17; NYT, May 25, 1992, A3; WP, Aug. 2, 1992, A30.

36. WP, Aug. 16, 1992, A30; NYT, Aug. 30, 1992, sect. 4, p. 5; NYT, Sept. 30, 1992, A1; NYT, Dec. 30, 1992, A1, A8.

37. NYT, March 29, 1993, A6; NYT, April 22, 1993, A9; NYT, July 25, 1993, sect. 1, p. 10; magazine article, info. lost but in sequence; NYT, Aug. 29, 1993, sect. 4, p. 6; NYT, Oct. 5, 1993, A(?)5.

38. NYT, Jan. 2, 1995, A3; NYT, April 20, 1995, D7; NYT, May 19, 1995, A12; NYT, June 8, 1995, A21; NYT, Nov. 13, 1995, A9.

39. CSM, Jan. 20, 1996, p. 6; NYT, Sept. 7, 1996, p. 33; CSM, Sept. 10, 1996, p. 7; NYT, Sept. 14, 1996, p. 32; NYT, May 22, 1996, A3.

40. NYT, Jan. 29, 1998, A8; NYT, Feb. 8, 1998, sect. 1, no page no. avail.; NYT, Sept. 13, 1998, A5; NYT, May 15, 1998, sect. 1, p. 14; NYT, May 1, 1998, D1; NYT, Sept. 24, 1998, A10; NYT, Nov. 16, 1998, A11.

41. NYT, Jan. 21, 1999, no page no. avail.; NYT, Jan. 14, 1999, A1; NYT, Feb. 4, 1999, A9; NYT, May 23, 1999, sect. 4, p. 5; NYT, June 13, 1999, sect. 1, no page no. avail.; NYT, July 8, 1999, A10; NYT, Nov. 22, 1999, A10; NYT, Dec. 8, 1999, A11.

42. NYT, Aug. 30, 2000, A8; NYT, May 23, 2000, C1; CSM, May 3, 2001, p. 8; NYT, Oct. 2, 2001, A3; NYT, Dec. 9, 2001, A9.

43. NYT, Oct. 28, 2002, A6; NYT, Nov. 3, 2002, sect. 1, p. 8; NYT, Nov. 8, 2002, A7; NYT, Dec. 29, 2002, sect. 4, p. 10.

44. NYT, Jan. 2, 2003, A3; CSM, Jan. 27, 2003, p. 7.

45. NYT, April 5, 2003, A5; NYT, Dec. 15, 2003, A8; NYT, Jan. 21, 2004, A3; NYT, Sept. 22, 2005, A8; NYT, Oct. 20, 2005, A3; NYT, Oct. 16, 2005, sect. 1, p. 6.

46. NYT, Jan. 3, 1992, A12; NYT, Sept. 5, 1992, A4; NYT, May 16, 1993, p. 13; NYT, June 27, 1998, A4; NYT, March 14, 1999, sect. 1, p. 3; NYT, April 10, 2000, A3; NYT, Oct. 19, 2003, sect. 1, p. 13; NYT, Oct. 17, 2003, A3; NYT, Oct. 18, 2003, A5; NYT, Jan. 29, 2005, A3; NYT, March 9, 2005, A14; NYT, June 10, 2005, A9; NYT, June 9, 2005, A8; NYT, Dec. 2, 2005, A3; NYT, Dec. 20, 2005, A8; WPNWE, Dec. 26–Jan. 8, 2006, p. 17; NYT, Jan. 22, 2006, sect. 1, p. 10; NYT, May 2, 2006, sect. A, no page no. avail.; NYT, May 3, 2006, A8.

47. NYT, Aug. 8, 1991, A10; NYT, May 9, 1993, sect. 1, p. 3; NYT, May 10, 1993, A3; NYT, May 11, 1993, A9; NYT, Jan. 7, 1995, A2; CSM, May 30, 1996, p. 19; NYT, Dec. 3, 1998, A19; NYT, March 2, 1999, A11; NYT, March 24, 1999, A3; NYT, April 1, 1999, A3; CSM, Sept. 18, 2002, p. 8.

48. NYT, Nov. 29, 1994, A8; NYT, Feb. 19, 1995, sect. 1, p. 14; NYT, May 3, 1998, sect. 3, p. 3; NYT, July 18, 1999, A3; NYT, Nov. 11, 1999, A3; NYT, Nov. 29, 1999, A8; NYT, Nov. 1, 2004, A11; NYT, March 1, 2005, no page no. avail.; NYT, March 2, 2005, A9; NYT, July 31, 2005, sect. 1, p. 4.

49. NYT, Sept. 15, 1991, no page no avail.; NYTBR, Oct. 13, 1991, p. 11.

50. NYT, Nov. 2, 1991, A3; NYT, Sept. 6, 1992, sect. 3, p. 12; NYT, Oct. 3, 1992, A23; NYT, June 15, 1993, D2; NYT, Dec. 14, 1993, A10; NYT, July 17, 1994, sect. 4, p. 6; NYT, Sept. 11, 1994, sect. 1, p. 13; NYT, Nov. 24, 1994, A3; NYT, April 26, 1995, A13; NYT, May 4, 1995, A8.

51. NYT, May 15, 1995, A1; NYT, May 16, 1995, A3; NYT, June 10, 1996, A8; NYT, July 29, 1996, A6; NYT, May 22, 1997, A3; NYT, June 1, 1997, sect. 1, p. 3; NYT, Aug. 19, 1997, A8; NYT, Oct. 28, 1997, A6; NYT, Feb. 6, 1998, A1.

52. NYT, Oct. 25, 1999, A8; NYT, Oct. 31, 1999, sect. 1, p. 20.

53. NYT, Oct. 9, 2000, A4; WPNWE, June 18–24, 2001, p. 17; NYT, July 5, 2001, A3; NYT, July 20, 2001, A8; WPNWE, Aug. 13–19, 2001, p. 16; NYT, Oct. 6, 2001, A25; NYT, Dec. 4, 2001, A10; NYT, Dec. 20, 2001, A3; NYT, Dec. 22, 2001, A1.

54. NYT, Dec. 22, 2001, A10; NYT, Dec. 23, 2001, sect. 4, p. 3; NYT, Dec. 25, 2001, sect. A, no page no. avail.; NYT, Dec. 30, 2001, A12; NYT, Dec. 31, 2001, A6; NYT, Jan. 1, 2002, A3; NYT, Jan. 2, 2002, A6.

55. NYT, Jan. 5, 2002, A3; NYT, Jan. 9, 2002, A3; WPNWE, Jan. 21–27, 2002, p. 22; NYT, Feb. 2, 2002, A4; NYT, Feb. 24, 2002, sect. 1, p. 16.

56. NYT, April 23, 2002, A11; NYT, April 24, 2002, A8; NYT, April 26, 2002, A8; WPNWE, May 20–26, 2002, p. 22; NYT, March 2, 2003, sect. 1, p. 8.

57. NYT, May 26, 2003, A3; NYT, May 25, 2003, sect. 1, p. 14; NYT, Aug. 2, 2003, A3; NYT, Jan. 3, 2006, A1; NYT, April 3, 2006, A3; NYT, Aug. 20, 2006, sect. 1, p. 1; NYT, Jan. 13, 2007, A3.

58. NYT, March 11, 1990, sect. 4, p. 21; WP, March 11, 1990, A3; NYT, March 24, 1991, sect. 1, p. 10; NYT, March 26, 1991, A10; NYT, March 28, 1991, A3; NYT, July 12, 1992, sect. 1, p. 9.

59. NYT, Nov. 10, 1996, sect. 1, p. 16; NYT, April 16, 1997, A8; CSM, Dec. 26, 1997, p. 6; NYT, March 11, 1998, A4.

60. CSM, Dec. 30, 1997, p. 6; NYT, Jan. 8, 1998, A7; NYT, April 18, 1998, A3; NYT, Oct. 18, 1998, sect. 1, p. 1; NYT, Oct. 19, 1998, A8.

61. NYT, Dec. 8, 1999, A3; NYT, Jan. 17, 2000, A10; NYT, Jan. 18, 2000, A3; NYT, Dec. 10, 2001, A3; NYT, Dec. 17, 2001, A5; NYT, April 13, 2002, A9; NYT, Dec. 13, 2002, A7; NYT, Sept. 7, 2003, sect. 1, p. 3; NYT, Sept. 29, 2003, A4; NYT, March 11, 2006, A3; NYT, April 3, 2007, A3.

62. NYT, March 3, 2000, A1–; NYT, Aug. 9, 2000, A3; NYT, Dec. 2, 2000, A1; NYT, June 25, 2001, A3; NYT, July 10, 2001, A1; NYT, Feb. 7, 2005, A7; NYT, Nov. 24, 2005, A8; NYT, Dec. 11, 2006, A8; NYT, Dec. 11, 2006, A1, B6; NYT, Dec. 24, 2006, sect. 1, p. 3.

63. NYT, Feb. 11, 1990, sect. 1, p. 3; NYT, June 9, 1991, sect. 1, p. 2; WP, Sept. 15, 1991, C5; NYT, Nov. 13, 1991, A1; WP, Jan. 19, 1992, A20; NYT, May 30, 1992, A5; WP, Aug. 9, 1990, A28; NYT, Nov. 21, 1993, sect. 4, no page no. avail.; NYT, April 8, 1994, A3; NYT, Sept. 7, 1994, A1; NYT, Nov. 12, 1994, sect. D(?), p. 49; CSM, April 25, 1995, p. 19; NYT, June 6, 1996, A6; NYT, April 19, 1997, A1; NYT, April 17, 1998, A3; NYT, Dec. 8, 1998, "Special Advertising Supplement"; NYT, April 20, 1998, A10; NYT, Aug. 1, 1999, sect. 4, p. 5; CSM, Nov. 10, 1999, p. 7.

64. NYT, Feb. 28, 2004, A24, editorial; NYT, April 4, 2004, sect. 4, p. 6; NYT, June 24, 2004, A1, A8; NYT, Dec. 12, 2004, sect. 1, p. 32; NYT, June 6, 2005, A8; NYT, June 9, 2005, A8; NYT, July 30, 2005, A8; NYT, Dec. 3, 2005, A6; CSM, Dec. 5, 2006, p. 4; NYT, March 2, 2007, A10; CSM, March 8, 2007, p. 3; NYT, May 14, 2007, A10.

65. CH, April 1998; CH, March 1999; CH, Feb. 2002; CH, Feb. 2002; CH, Feb. 2003.

66. Lehrer News Hour, PBS, March 12, 2007; book by William C. Prillaman (Westport, Ct., 2000).

Notes to Annex
Canada and North American Blocs

1. NYT, Sept. 26, 1989, A14; NYT, May 24, 1990, A3; TM, June 4, 1990, p. 63; NYT, June 24, 1990, sect. 1, p. 1; NYT, June 26, 1990, A3; NYT, July 13, 1990, A6; NYT, July 29, 1990, sect. 1, p. 3; NYT, Aug. 28, 1990, A10; NYT, no other info. avail., but in sequence; WP, March 8, 1990, A58.

2. NYT, Jan. 30, 1991, A3; NYT, Feb. 3, 1991, E4; NYT, Feb. 12, 1991, A4; NYT, Aug. 7, 1991, A5; NYT, Sept. 25, 1991, A10; NYT, Dec. 17, 1991, A7.

3. NYT, Jan. 13, 1992, A5; NYT, Feb. 21, 1992, A4; NYT, May 6, 1992, A17; NYT, Aug. 23, 1992, sect. 1, p. 14; NYT, Aug. 30, 1992, sect. 1, p. 6; NYT, Sept. 20, 1992, sect. 1, p. 15; NYT, Oct. 24, 1992, A5; NYT, Oct. 21, 1992, A16; NYT, Nov. 1, 1992, sect. 4, p. 7, commentary; TM, Dec. 21, 1992, p. 48.

4. NYT, Feb. 25, 1993, A12; NYT, June 14, 2003, A7; WP, June 26, 1993, A22; NYT, Sept. 8, 1993, A10; NYT, Sept. 15, 1993, A7; NYT, Oct. 26, 1993, A1; NYT, Oct. 27, 1993, A10.

5. NYT, Feb. 15, 1995, A7; NYT, Oct. 29, 1995, sect. 1, p. 1–; NYT, Oct. 31, 1995, A1; NYT, Nov. 1, 1995, A8; NYT, Nov. 1, 1995, A22, editorial; NYT, Nov. 2, 1995, A27, editorial; NYT, Nov. 4, 1995, A8; NYT, April 8, 1996, A9; CSM, June 3, 1996, p. 5; CSM, Sept. 30, 1996, p. 6.

6. NYT, May 19, 1997, A8; NYT, May 27, 1997, A3; CSM, May 30, 1997, p. 5; TM, June 16, 1997, p. 55.

7. NYT, Aug. 21, 1998, A3; NYT, Nov. 23, 1998, A1; USNWR, Nov. 30, 1998, p. 39; NYT, Dec. 1, 1998, A1; NYT, Dec. 2, 1998, A8; NYT, Aug. 5, 1998, A1; NYT, Jan. 29, 1999, A1-.

8. NYT, Dec. 2, 1998, A27; NYT, Oct. 10, 1999, sect. 1, p. 4; NYT, Oct. 25, 1999, A3; NYT, Sept. 29, 2000, A24; CSM, Oct. 2, 2000, p. 6; NYT, Dec. 3, 2000, sect. 1, p. 24; NYT, Nov. 29, 2000, A8; NYT, April 16, 2003, A8.

9. NYT, Aug. 23, 1991, B18; NYT, Jan. 14, 1992, A10; NYT, Feb. 21, 1992, A18; NYT, Dec. 22, 1992, A11; NYT, Nov. 22, 1994, A6; NYT, May 10, 1996, A11; NYT, Jan. 18, 1996, D6; CSM, Sept. 17, 1996, no page no. avail.; NYT, Dec. 18, 1997, A14; NYT, Aug. 29, 1999, sect. 1, p. 8; CSM, Nov. 3, 1999, p. 7; NYT, Dec. 7, 1999, A9.

10. NYT, Aug. 9, 2001, A3; NYT, June 25, 2002, A3; CSM, Oct. 3, 2002, p. 6; NYT, Oct. 24, 2002, A20; NYT, May 28, 2003, A11; NYT, June 19, 2003, A8; NYT, Aug. 10, 2003, sect. 1, p. 7; NYT, Sept. 17, 2003, A9; NYT, Aug. 3 (31?), 2003, sect. 1, p. 15; NYT, May 17, 2004, A6; CSM, Aug. 10, 2004, pp. 1, 4; NYT, Dec. 10, 2004, A7; NYT, June 10, 2005, A3; NYT, June 29, 2005, A4; NYT, Feb. 28, 2006, A3.

11. WP, May 17, 1992, C7, commentary; TM, Aug. 10, 1992, no page no. avail.; NYT, Aug. 12, 1992, A1; NYT, Aug. 13, 1992, A1, D4; NYT, Sept. 9, 1992, A1; NYT, Dec. 18, 1992, D1; NYT, Dec. 11, 1994, sect. 1, p. 1; NYT, Feb. 24, 1995, A10; NYT, Nov. 19, 1996, D8; NYT, Jan. 6, 1997, A8; NYT, Sept. 9, 1997, A6.

12. WPNWE, Oct. 2, 2000, p. 6; CSM, April 3, 2001, p. 8; NYT, April 19, 2001, A25, editorial; NYT, April 20, 2001, A6; NYT, April 20, 2001, sect. 1, p. 4; NYT, April 23, 2001, no page no. avail.; NYT, Oct. 19, 2003, sect. 1, p. 20; NYT, July 18, 2007, A4.

13. CSM, Aug. 24, 2007, p. 7.